Fiscal Administration

ANALYSIS AND APPLICATIONS FOR THE PUBLIC SECTOR

WADSWORTH
CENGAGE Learning

Australia • Brazil • Japan • Korea • Mexico • Singapore • Spain • United Kingdom • United States

Fiscal Administration

ANALYSIS AND APPLICATIONS FOR THE PUBLIC SECTOR

Ninth Edition

John L. Mikesell
Indiana University

WADSWORTH
CENGAGE Learning·

Australia • Brazil • Japan • Korea • Mexico • Singapore • Spain • United Kingdom • United States

Fiscal Administration: Analysis and Applications for the Public Sector, Ninth Edition
John L. Mikesell

Senior Publisher: Suzanne Jeans

Acquisitions Editor: Anita Devine

Developmental Production Editor: Michael B. Kopf, S4Carlisle Publishing Services

Assistant Editor: Patrick Roach

Editorial Assistant: Eireann Aspell

Media Editor: Laura Hildebrand

Brand Manager: Lydia LeStar

Content Project Manager: Jill Quinn

Art Director: Linda May

Manufacturing Planner: Fola Orekoya

Rights Acquisition Specialist: Jennifer Meyer Dare

Production Service: S4Carlisle Publishing Services

Cover Designer: Jenny Willingham

Cover Image: © Corbis

Compositor: S4Carlisle Publishing Services

For product information and technology assistance, contact us at
Cengage Learning Customer & Sales Support, 1-800-354-9706.

For permission to use material from this text or product, submit all requests online at **www.cengage.com/permissions**
Further permissions questions can be emailed to
permissionrequest@cengage.com

Library of Congress Control Number: 2012941082

ISBN-13: 978-1-133-59480-2

ISBN-10: 1-133-59480-8

Wadsworth
20 Channel Center Street
Boston, MA 02210
USA

Cengage Learning is a leading provider of customized learning solutions with office locations around the globe, including Singapore, the United Kingdom, Australia, Mexico, Brazil, and Japan. Locate your local office at **international.cengage.com/region.**

Cengage Learning products are represented in Canada by Nelson Education, Ltd.

For your course and learning solutions, visit **www.cengage.com**

Purchase any of our products at your local college store or at our preferred online store **www.cengagebrain.com.**

Instructors: Please visit **login.cengage.com** and log in to access instructor-specific resources.

Printed in the United States of America
1 2 3 4 5 6 7 16 15 14 13 12

About the Author

John L. Mikesell is Chancellor's professor of public and environmental affairs at Indiana University–Bloomington. His work on government finance and taxation has appeared in such journals as *National Tax Journal, Public Budgeting & Finance, Public Finance Quarterly, Southern Economic Journal, Public Administration Review, Public Choice, International Journal of Public Administration, Tax Notes, State Tax Notes,* and *Journal of Public Budgeting, Accounting, and Financial Management.* He is co-author with John F. Due of *Sales Taxation, State and Local Structure and Administration* (Urban Institute Press). He has served as chief fiscal economist and chief of party with the USAID Barents Group/KPMG Peat Marwick fiscal reform project with the Government of Ukraine to develop a macroeconomic analysis and budget policy department in the Ministry of Finance (1995) and as Moscow-based director for assistance in intergovernmental fiscal relations with the USAID Georgia State University Consortium Russian fiscal reform project (1998–99). He directed U.S. Department of State–supported public administration partnerships between the School of Public and Environmental Affairs and the Volga Region Academy for Civil Service, Saratov, Russia, and the North West Academy for Public Administration, St. Petersburg, Russia. He has worked on fiscal studies for several states, including New York, Minnesota, Indiana, and Hawaii; has served on the Revenue Forecast Technical Committee of the Indiana State Budget Committee for thirty years; has worked as consultant on World Bank missions to the Kyrgyz Republic, Kazakhstan, Azerbaijan, Tajikistan, and Turkmenistan; and has been visiting scholar at the U.S. Congressional Budget Office and at the Department of Public Administration, Erasmus University Rotterdam. He has been a David Lincoln Fellow in Land Value Taxation with the Lincoln Institute for Land Policy and Senior Research Fellow, Peking University—Lincoln Institute Center for Urban Development and Land Policy, Beijing, People's Republic of China. Professor Mikesell served as editor-in-chief of *Public Budgeting & Finance,* the journal of the American Association for Budget and Program Analysis and the Association for Budgeting and Financial Management, for fifteen years. Professor Mikesell has headed the Association for Budgeting and Financial Management and served on the Board of Directors of the National Tax Association–Tax Institute of America. He holds a BA from Wabash College and an MA and a PhD in economics from the University of Illinois, where he specialized in public finance and taxation. He is a member of Phi Beta Kappa and received the 2002 Wildavsky Award for Lifetime Scholarly Achievement in Public Budgeting and Finance from the Association for Budgeting and Financial Management.

Preface

Policy analysts, public administrators, public officials, and those working in government financial markets need to understand the principles, processes, and practices of public financial administration. This book seeks to provide a perspective on how and why fiscal systems have developed, to build a basis for understanding the principles and structural dynamics that promise to shape the future of fiscal systems, and to start a foundation of techniques necessary to become a practitioner of fiscal administration. It is not a training manual, but it does provide the foundation for becoming a functional public finance practitioner and does develop the skills appropriate for a mid-level public manager. Because of the nature of the topic, the text uses bits of economics, political science, law, accounting, business management, and other stuff as it goes along, but it is not a text for any of these disciplines. It is directly aimed at those studying public administration, public affairs, and public policy, all areas that require an understanding of applied public budgeting and finance.

As this revision is under way, the United States is just emerging from the Great Recession of 2007–2009, and the finances of federal, state, and local governments have not fully recovered from that shock. The institutions and processes of government finances have been stretched to the breaking point. Governments were unprepared for the recession, and many were unwilling to make decisions during the downturn that could have mitigated some of the personal suffering experienced in that era. In large measure, the political class now engages in battles for points rather than taking steps to strengthen government finances and resolve problems that the recession exposed. As has always been the case, lawmakers are relieved that the recession is ended but then act as if there will never be another. Even if economists knew exactly what to do to avoid a recession (which they do not), politicians would certainly refuse to take the necessary actions. Warning to all: There will be another recession in the United States. What we don't know is when and how deep.

Many of the continuing problems are familiar. The federal government does not complete its fiscal work on schedule, and it cannot figure out an acceptable way of reducing the deficit to levels that would appear to be sustainable, let alone agree on a path that would ultimately lead to the surpluses necessary to reduce the federal debt. If increases to the debt could be stabilized, the nation could grow its way out of the unsustainable burden, as it has always done in the past, but federal lawmakers can't even manage that. There is minimal discipline in spending, and the federal tax system is uniformly regarded as an economic joke, but the lawmakers can get a handle on nothing. Along the way, the federal government has managed to lose its triple-A credit rating, meaning that no longer can federal debt be regarded as the beacon of certainty against which all other credit risk could be calibrated. And politicians continue to insist that America is the greatest country in the world.

State and local governments are enjoying their own levels of poor behavior. State governments have joined the federal government in being unable to complete their budgets on a timely basis, but states lack the extensive history of this bad behavior and lack the accommodating measures that the federal government has. As a result, some states have temporarily gone out of business for varying periods until some sort of agreement can be reached. That's not a great advertisement for states seeking to lure globally competitive firms to their borders. Companies with experience in the rest of the developed world expect government services to be delivered regularly and not to encounter periodic "Out of Business" signs on state facilities.

But possibly local governments take the prize for fiscal excitement. Some local governments have filed for bankruptcy protection from the federal courts because they are unable to pay all their bills. The idea of the bankruptcy is to allow the city to stiff somebody—retirees, the current workforce, and, recently, entities that have loaned it money are the typical targets. While bankruptcy may be a shrewd business move, it is a bit of a stain on everybody in the locality, including those residents with an ethic that says your word is your honor and your bills will be paid. (Is this part of the effort to bring business principles into the operation of governments?) Other states have forced localities into receiverships—harsher medicine because the state receiver often fires all local officials and takes over complete governmental authority. That is harsher than bankruptcy because with bankruptcy the officials who contributed to the fiscal mess usually continue in their jobs.

It is clear that the world of government finance is an interesting place. Understanding and practicing the principles covered in this textbook will help with understanding the critical issues of the day, but, more importantly, putting the lessons taught here into practice tracks a path for resolving these problems and for preventing their future occurrence. Nothing that has happened in American government finance was inevitable.

This edition continues to stick with two distinguishing features. First, a public affairs student and practitioner of public finance needs to understand from where the money comes—not just in general, but quite specifically. Quoting an earlier edition: "If armies move on their stomachs, then governments certainly crawl on their purses." Public administrators who do not understand revenue systems, options, and policies and who do not understand that they are spending other people's money become the sinister "public servants" that conservative commentators revile—spend, spend, spend until someone puts a stop to it. Indeed, everyone should revile such public employees because they are the worst enemy of good government. Shame on you if you just want to deliver services and don't care where the money comes from. Furthermore, you won't be much use in the crunch if you don't know who pays. Second, a public affairs student hasn't learned enough if he or she hasn't crunched some numbers (probably a lot of numbers) during a public budgeting and finance class. Most chapters in this text are followed by questions and exercises that require some calculations to come up with an answer. That is how you learn what is going on and that is how you become useful to a prospective employer. You will discover that a number of these exercises are much easier with a spreadsheet program, and if you don't know how to use these, this would be an outstanding time to learn how. For the basics, you can teach yourself, but there are lots of more formal ways of learning the programs. But learning how to plug numbers into a spreadsheet isn't enough—you need to know why you are doing what you are doing and what it means. The use of spreadsheets is something you can learn on your own, outside of class, so this textbook concentrates on developing the what and why behind the problems. If you understand the principles involved, plugging the numbers into your own spreadsheet will be easy. If you start by plugging numbers into a spreadsheet template prepared by someone else, you will not be able to do independent analysis. Of course, every exercise can be done with paper and pencil. It just takes longer.

This edition features complete updating of all statistics of government finance reported in the text and in the tables to the most recent year available. It includes fiscal actions through the official end date of the Great Recession and beyond, and it includes new legal actions that form government fiscal processes. It includes the Budget Control Act of 2011, the act that established new spending constraints and debt ceiling for the federal government; the ratings downgrade of the federal government; the municipal defaults, bankruptcy filings, and state receiverships that have characterized the recent few years; the financial problems with state and local government pension programs; the arguments about the tax that should be paid by the top 1 percent of earners (the people who are not the 99 percent); and the possibly hopeless struggle to repair the federal income tax. There are new and revised cases and sidebars and some new exercises. All text materials have been updated where needed to reflect new literature, new laws, and new data.

I want to thank my colleagues at Indiana University for their comments and suggestions of ways in which the text could be improved. Many generations of students have also been generous with their thoughts about the text, and they are the best force for quality control that I know. Among the many reviewers that have helped shape this book, I would like to give special thanks to Bill Tankersley of the University of West Florida and Daniel Baracskay of Valdosta State University for their useful comments and suggestions. I want to acknowledge the fine help from graduate assistant Neil Broshears in doing the updates of tables and graphs and final proofing from graduate assistant Christina Van Horn. And Diana Worman provided outstanding secretarial assistance when I couldn't figure out how to make tables, graphs, or figures that were clear and presentable.

John L. Mikesell
Indiana University

Supplements for Instructors

Companion Website for Mikesell *Fiscal Administration*, 9e

- ISBN-13: 9781133596523
- This password-protected website for instructors features all of the free student assets plus an instructor's manual. Access your resources by logging into your account at www.cengage.com/login.

CourseReader: Public Administration 0-30 Selections

- IAC ISBN-13: 9781133350378 (Instant Access card)
- PAC ISBN-13: 9781133350385 (Printed Access card)
- CourseReader: Public Administration allows you to create your reader, your way, in just minutes. This affordable, fully customizable online reader provides access to thousands of permissions-cleared readings, articles, primary sources, and audio and video selections from the regularly updated Gale research library database. This easy-to-use solution allows you to search for and select just the material you want for your courses.

Each selection opens with a descriptive introduction to provide context and concludes with critical-thinking and multiple-choice questions to reinforce key points. CourseReader is loaded with convenient tools like highlighting, printing, note-taking, and downloadable MP3 audio files for each reading.

CourseReader is the perfect complement to any Public Administration course. It can be bundled with your current textbook, sold alone, or integrated into your learning management system. CourseReader 0-30 allows access to up to 30 selections in the reader.

Please contact your Cengage sales representative for details or, for a demo, please visit us at www.cengage.com/coursereader. To access CourseReader materials go to **www.cengage.com/sso**, click on "Create a New Faculty Account," and fill out the registration page. Once you are in your new SSO account, search for "CourseReader" from your dashboard and select "CourseReader: Public Administration." Then click "CourseReader 0-30: Public Administration Instant Access Code" and click "Add to my bookshelf." To access the live CourseReader, click on "CourseReader 0-30: Public Administration" under "Additional resources" on the right side of your dashboard.

Contents

To Karen, Elizabeth, Tom, and Daniel

CHAPTER 1

Fundamental Principles of Public Finance

Why do public managers, whether they work for the government or for a not-for-profit organization, need to study public budgeting and finance? Here is your top ten list:

1. They must make choices about how resources are utilized, and working through the finances gives a good start in organizing the options.
2. They operate in the public trust and need to be able to control the use of public resources—they are using other people's money, and those people get mad when the money disappears.
3. They need to make sure they don't run out of money before they run out of need for the service being provided with the money.
4. They need to make a case for the resources appropriate to provide services to their constituents and clients to legislative and executive bodies.
5. They need to understand the case being made by other managers.
6. They don't want to go to jail for misuse of resources that belong to the public or to their organization.
7. The people in any organization who actually understand what the organization is doing are the people who understand the finances of the organization.
8. Not-for-profit organizations frequently have abysmal financial management practices in place.
9. Government crises, regardless of whether the government is national, state, or local, often have financial underpinnings that could have been avoided with better budget systems and mechanisms for finance.
10. It is simply fun to understand what is going on in public organizations, and understanding finance is the most important single step in gaining that understanding.

Unless you have no interest in providing services to people through the public sector, at least one item on this list of reasons will resonate with you. If none does, then you probably need to reconsider your professional goals and objectives. When you have worked through the chapters, cases, and exercises that follow, you will have at least a start at dealing with everything in that list.

Public finance is not the same as business finance, although it is related. One difference is in ultimate objectives. Financial management in business seeks to increase the value of the firm to its owners by judicious allocation and control of its resources.[1] Public financial management uses similar analytic, technical, and managerial tools to allocate and control finances, but governments differ from private businesses in terms of resource constraints, ownership, and objectives. Four important differences exist: governments may tax to enlarge their resources; "ownership" of the government is not clear because many stakeholders share a legitimate interest in government decisions; the value of government services is neither easy to quantify nor reflected in a single measure (like the sales or profits of a business enterprise); and governments are dealing with the public trust and reputations of all the citizenry. While default on obligations and financial bankruptcy may be seen as just interesting and possibly useful financial tools for a private business, they are indelible stains on governments and their citizens.

Businesses operate by generating an income stream from the sale of goods and services on the market. Production requires inputs that must be paid for from that income stream; efficient producers can end up with money left over (profit) after the inputs have been paid for. Governments similarly provide goods and services that are valued by the community, but the nature of these goods and services is such that the government cannot capture that value in a voluntary sales transaction. The value of the government service is collective, for the community as a whole, as opposed to the individual value received by purchases of business services. The fundamental idea that the provider of a valued product can capture a portion of that value—a link between creating value and receiving revenue—is broken for government operations. Government finance, for this reason, is fundamentally different from business finance.

Governments have the unique power to tax, prohibit, and punish. These coercive powers make governments different from proprietary businesses and voluntary organizations (in this respect, not-for-profits are more like proprietary businesses than like government); the reflection of those differences makes public financial administration distinct from business finance. Both sorts of entities are interested in *fiscal sustainability,* that is, the ability to operate over the long term without reducing the standards of life below those currently enjoyed and even to improve that standard. If fiscal actions now reduce the capacity of future generations to live at least as well as we do now, then those actions violate the standard of sustainability.

---

[1]The collapse of financial institutions in 2008 and 2009 (e.g., Merrill Lynch, Northern Trust, AIG) exposed several instances in which the managers and officers of these institutions enriched themselves while the value of the businesses themselves to the shareholders that owned them was declining dramatically, even heading toward bankruptcy or government takeover. This divergence of interest between owners (the shareholders) and managers (executive officers) has plagued the United States since the emergence of the modern form of corporate ownership in the early days of the last century. Nevertheless, business finance does presume maximization of corporate value, not plunder for the benefit of high executives, as its objective. That is a simpler objective to maximize than the overall best interests of those governed–because not everyone has the same set of interests. I like soccer and you like American football, but there is room in the public park for only one size of playing field. Whose "best interests" will win out? Business managers don't have to worry about such questions. They just go for the best profit.

Many different organizations—private businesses, nonprofit organizations, and government agencies—provide the goods and services that we use every day, including both those necessary for life itself and those that make life more enjoyable. Private businesses sell us food and clothing, cars and television sets, and so on: a vast range of commodities that we purchase for survival and enjoyment. The same applies to services: we go to movies run by private companies, travel across the country on privately operated airlines, and hire the neighbor to feed our cats when we go on vacation. All these and many more goods and services are provided under market principles of voluntary exchange: privately owned businesses provide those services to us in exchange for the payment we make to them. No payment, no service. Much the same applies for many nonprofit organizations, like hospitals and social service organizations, that operate on the basis of charges and government contracts. Other services come from voluntary associations or clubs—the services of the county historical museum, the local neighborhood association, or a local youth organization. Their operations are financed by a variety of contributions and fees. Although voluntary organizations may not require payment before service is rendered, they still need to be paid by someone, voluntarily, in order to survive. After all, those who provide the resources that are used in providing services (utilities, rents, supplies, etc.) need to be paid for those resources.

Finally, we receive the services of police departments, school systems, the judicial and regulatory systems, the social safety net, and so on from governments. But these services are financed differently. Rather than operating from finance by voluntary exchange (market sales) or by voluntary contribution, governments provide goods and services paid for by taxes or other revenues raised by law. This revenue comes not from voluntary purchase or contribution, but, even in a democracy, from the operation of a revenue system based on the legal requirement for payment—ultimately backed by threat of force. Why have a public sector? The reason is not that government services are uniquely essential to life: most countries leave the provision of life's necessities—food, clothing, and usually shelter—to the private sector. But when government fails, the private sector cannot function, and citizens are "bereft of even the most basic conditions of a stable existence: law and security, trust in contracts, and a sound medium of exchange."[2]

Functions of Government: Market Failures

Why can't private businesses selling their products in free markets be relied upon to provide all goods and services that ought to be available? The argument for the efficiency of markets is powerful. The President's Council of Economic Advisors explains:

---

[2]International Bank for Reconstruction and Development/The World Bank, *World Development Report 1997: The State in a Changing World* (New York: Oxford University Press, 1997), 19.

If markets are competitive and function smoothly, they will lead to prices at which the amount sellers want to supply equals the amount buyers demand. Moreover, the price in any market will simultaneously equal the benefit that buyers get from the last unit consumed (the marginal benefit) and the cost of producing the last unit supplied (the marginal cost). These two conditions ensure efficiency: when they hold in all markets, the Nation's labor and other resources are allocated to producing a particular good or service if and only if consumers would not be willing to pay more to have those resources employed elsewhere.[3]

Markets cause the productive capacity of the economy to be used to produce what people want most and cause the least possible amount of resources to be used in that production. In a world of limited resources, it is a valuable result. Markets make people better off.

But there remains an important role for government, even if private markets can deliver most goods and services reliably and at low cost. Indeed, there is an important cooperative relationship between healthy government and healthy markets. Markets need government to function efficiently: "Deals must be enforced and fraud discouraged. Without a government legal system to guarantee property rights and enforce contracts, corporate organizations and market exchange would be virtually impossible. Anarchy and the free market are not synonymous."[4] And markets are useful for government. Governments can obtain important information from market data, use markets as efficient mechanisms for implementing public policy, and acquire goods and services in market transactions to provide government services. The market economy needs government to function properly, and governments need the market economy if they are to serve the public interest.[5]

The role of government, however, extends beyond simply allowing markets to operate because a system of markets is not always able "to sustain 'desirable' activities or to stop 'undesirable' activities."[6] What makes some services a government responsibility? Why can't private action be relied upon to provide public safety, primary education, environmental protection, public health, national defense, and so on? Individuals demand these services, and we expect businesses to respond to customer demand in their quest for profit. Why do markets fail, and thereby create an economic need for government? The role for government begins with what are called "public goods."

---

[3]*Economic Report of the President Transmitted to the Congress February 1997* (Washington, D.C.: U.S. Government Printing Office, 1997), 191.

[4]*Ibid.,* 192.

[5]Some detractors doubt the impact of government services on anything useful. They point, for instance, to the fact that areas that receive heavy policing are areas with high crime rates. But are the police there because of the crime, or is the crime there because of the police, and is there any evidence that more police service would reduce crime? Higher terror alert levels after the 9–11 attacks brought higher policing in the District of Columbia for reasons unrelated to indigenous crime in the area (street crime did not bring the police). Did crime levels go down when alert levels (and intensity of policing) were higher? Evidence suggests that an increase of police presence by 50 percent leads to a decrease in the level of crime of around 15 percent—there is a measurable return from the policing. Jonathan Klick and Alexander Tabarrok, "Using Terror Alert Levels to Estimate the Effect of Police on Crime," *Journal of Law and Economics* 48 (April 2005): 266–79.

[6]Francis M. Bator, "The Anatomy of Market Failure," *Quarterly Journal of Economics* 72 (August 1958): 351.

Public Goods[7]

Some goods will not be supplied in the market or, if supplied, will be supplied in insufficient amounts because of their very nature. The problem comes from two properties: (1) *nonexhaustion,* or nonrivalry, occurs when benefits of the service can only be shared, meaning that a given quantity of the service can be enjoyed by additional people with no reduction in benefit to the existing population; and (2) *inability to exclude nonpayers* occurs when benefits cannot be easily limited to those who have paid for the services. The properties reflected in Figure 1–1 distinguish private goods, public goods, and two intermediate kinds of goods—toll goods and common-pool goods.

What do these public-good properties mean? When services are nonrival, use of the service by one person does not preclude concurrent full use by others at no additional cost of providing that service. To give an extreme example, should some extraordinarily rich individual decide to build a bridge across the Mississippi River for his personal use and because he thought it would look pretty, the extra cost of allowing someone else to use the bridge is nothing. Once the service has been provided for one, the cost of providing the service to additional users equals zero (its marginal cost is zero, in microeconomic terms). Economic efficiency requires that the price paid by the buyer (the value of resources given up by the buyer to make the purchase) not exceed the additional cost of producing the purchased good or service. A private business will charge a price higher than zero, the efficient price, because it cannot afford to do otherwise. Therefore, too little of the good or service will be purchased and consumed, and its price will be too high, compared with quantities and prices in a fully functioning market.

Figure 1–1
The Elements of Nonappropriability

	Alternate Use (Exhausting/Rival)	Joint Use (Nonexhausting/ Nonrival)
Exclusion Feasible	Private Good	Toll Good
	Examples: Food, clothing, television sets	Examples: Turnpikes, toll bridges, concerts
Exclusion Not Feasible	Common-Pool Resources	Public Good
	Examples: Aquifers, fishing grounds, petroleum reserves	Examples: national defense, rule of law, vector control

© Cengage Learning

---

[7]Some argue that individuals do not recognize their own best interest and make "wrong" market decisions. Therefore, the market underprovides museums, ballets, and symphonies because people do not understand their true value, and government needs to support such "merit goods." Junk food, Saturday morning kids' television, and country music could be viewed as "merit bads." Identifying what is good and what is bad is certainly not scientific and ends up in special-interest political battles.

Now suppose a private business has no way of keeping people who have not paid for the service from using the service. That's a big problem: if the business can't keep nonpayers away, it will be hard to get anyone to pay (only the suckers), and the business will have no incentive for providing the service. Again, this is a market failure because the seller can't successfully charge a price, and without being able to charge a price, the service won't be available. Within the range of exclusion failure, if someone provides the service, all receive that service. When one structure in an urban area receives fire protection, given the propensity of fires to spread, nearby structures receive protection as well.[8] (The public good is fire protection, not firefighting; when the equipment is putting out the fire at Smith's house, it is not available to put out the fire anywhere else. Extinguishing Smith's fire, however, provides fire protection equally to many neighbors.) Obviously, there are geographic limits to that range of impact: fire protection provided in Bloomington, Indiana, will not extend to the people in Jackson, Mississippi. Within a specific geographic area, however, all receive the service regardless of payment, whether they want it or not. Such is the special monopoly position of governments: not only are alternative providers unavailable, but also residents do not have the option of not paying for the service because public revenue systems operate independently from service delivery. A governor of Kentucky recognized the difference between operating the state and operating his successful business: "Hell, governing Kentucky is easier than running Kentucky Fried Chicken. There's no competition."[9] Payment regardless of preference or consumption is, of course, a unique feature of government provision.

Private goods do not have appropriability problems: one person's use of the good eliminates the possibility of anyone else using it (additional service means

---

[8]This is not to say that market failure always characterizes fire protection. Private firms sell fire protection in some parts of Arizona, and fire protection is provided by volunteer organizations in much of the United States. Historically, fire insurance companies provided fire protection and firefighting services—they fought fires to reduce the loss they had to cover for insured clients. And that principle still lives: in the Castle Rock, Idaho, wildfires of 2007, AIG (yes, the AIG involved in the financial collapse of 2008) sent in its own fire truck with retardant chemicals to protect seven extremely expensive properties that it covered (the homes were valued at around $35 million, so the insurance company had a lot at risk and this was not an exercise in charity). William Yardley, "The Wealthy Get an Extra Shield for Wildfires," *New York Times,* August 28, 2007. The public-good problem is that fires tend to spread, and if your neighbor does not have fire protection, the fire on his property will threaten your property. That protection of property owned by others is the public-good feature. You can be reasonably certain that AIG wasn't there fighting the fire because of these public benefits. And fire protection can be optional in some rural areas. For example, residents of Obion County, Tennessee, have the option of paying a $75 fee for fire protection from the city of South Fulton. In October 2010, the house of a family that had chosen not to pay caught fire, the firefighters did not respond, and the house burned down. They did respond when the neighbor's field caught fire and endangered his house–the neighbor had paid the fee. Amazingly enough, the same thing happened in December 2011. Another house whose owner had not paid caught fire, and the South Fulton firefighters watched as it burned to the ground. Apparently, there are slow learners in the county. Jason Higgs, "Home Burns While Firefighters Watch" [http://www.wpsdlocal6.com/news/local/Home-burns-while-firefighters-watch-again-135069773.html]. The South Fulton mayor notes that the costs of the fire department have to be covered and if the department responded to nonpayers, there would be no reason for anyone to pay. People in the city, of course, get the service automatically because it is financed by city taxes.

[9]The Honorable John Y. Brown, Jr., quoted in *Newsweek* (March 30, 1981). Mr. Brown had, indeed, once run Kentucky Fried Chicken, so he had some evidence behind his claim. However, he did not face a state legislature with dramatically different political philosophies than his.

extra cost, and sellers charge to cover that cost), and exclusion is feasible. Obviously, the full range of ordinary commodities and services (bread, milk, etc.) constitutes private goods. The only way an individual can receive the benefits from a private good is by paying for it; there are no effects on others, and it is possible to separate payers from nonpayers. The market works!

Public goods include national defense, mosquito abatement, pollution control, and disease control, for example. The common characteristics of these services are the previously described nonexclusion and nonexhaustion or nonrivalry. Consider mosquito abatement. When a given level of control is provided, all people in the area receive the same service. Other people could enter the control district and simultaneously receive that same service without any additional abatement cost (marginal cost equals zero). Furthermore, there is no way to deny service to those not paying for it. Individuals in the service area may value the abatement service differently (reaction to mosquito bites varies among individuals—some people swell up in alarming fashion, while others don't), but all receive the same service. Public goods are the domain of public provision and public finance.

Toll goods and common-pool goods have one public-good characteristic, but not both (as shown in Figure 1–1). Toll goods are nonrival: one person can consume the service to its fullest, while not reducing the amount of service someone else may consume. For these goods, however, exclusion is feasible; boundaries can separate payers and nonpayers. Examples include wifi at Starbucks, drive-in movies, and toll roads: up to a congestion point, a larger number of people can consume these services without exhausting the service concurrently available to others. All are, however, subject to exclusion: those not paying for the service may be kept from receiving the service through passwords, walls, and toll booths.

Common-pool goods are goods or services for which exclusion is not feasible, but there are competing and exhaustive uses. Examples include aquifers, oil and gas deposits, and fisheries. There are no normal means of exercising exclusive property rights on the resource, but when used, the resource becomes unavailable for others. Left to private processes, the resource may be rapidly exhausted because it is valuable and is not, in its natural state, subject to normal ownership controls. (First-come-first-served is a normal allocation principle, so getting those resources out of the ground as quickly as possible is advantageous to any private user—and is why governments frequently intervene in markets for natural resources. That is another element of market failure.) However, Eleanor Ostrom, Nobel Prize winner in economics, observes that self-organized local systems can successfully manage many common pool resources without either well-defined property rights or government intervention, so analysis of the problem requires considerable attention to the institutional circumstances. Sidebar 1–1 describes one common-pool resource problem and how government action sought to remedy it.

Externalities

Government also may have a role when market transactions between buyer and seller affect third parties. The consequences may be negative—as with the exhaust fumes from automobiles—or positive—as with the protection provided pregnant

Sidebar 1–1
Government Creates a Market for Fishing Rights

Market failure does not always require direct government provision of a service as a remedy. Sometimes, the government may intervene in ways that create a market where none could exist before. The Council of Economic Advisors provided one example in the *Economic Report of the President* for 1993:

> There is no practical way to establish ownership rights of ocean fish stocks. Traditionally, fish have been free for the taking—a common pool resource. Theory teaches that such underpricing leads to overconsumption. In the halibut fisheries off Alaska, fishing fleets caught so many halibut that the survival of the stock was threatened. No single fishing boat had an incentive to harvest fewer fish since the impact on its own future catch would be minimal and others would only increase their take. This is an example of what is known as "the tragedy of the commons."

> Officials tried limiting the length of the fishing season. But this effort only encouraged new capital investment such as larger and faster boats with more effective (and expensive) fishing equipment. In order to control the number of fish caught, the season was shortened in some areas from 4 months to 2 days by the early 1990s. Most of the halibut caught had to be frozen rather than marketed fresh, and halibut caught out of season had to be discarded.

> In late 1992, the federal government proposed a new approach: assigning each fisherman a permit to catch a certain number of fish. The total number of fish for which permits are issued will reflect scientific estimates of the number of fish that can be caught without endangering the survival of the species. Also, the permits will be transferable—they can be bought and sold. By making the permits transferable, the system in effect creates a market where one did not exist previously. The proposed system will encourage the most profitable and efficient boats to operate at full capacity by buying permits from less successful boats, ensuring a fishing fleet that uses labor and equipment efficiently. Moreover, the transferable permits system establishes a market price for the opportunity to fish—a price that better reflects the true social cost of using this common resource.

The cap-and-trade system for dealing with environmental protection applies a similar approach. Sources of emissions (like sulfur dioxide) are allocated an initial emissions limitation. The entity is permitted to meet the limit by whatever means it chooses (conservation, revised production technology, end-of-pipe controls, etc.), so each will select whatever method is least expensive. But the entity can exceed its limit by purchasing limit caps from other entities—those who have excess cap because of particularly efficient methods for limiting their emissions. By this means, the intended overall emission reduction is achieved at minimal cost to the economy. The market price for emission limits emerges, exactly in the same way as the price for the opportunity to fish was established.

Both are clever ways to employ market-based approaches to deal with problems of initial market failure and achieve an efficient, effective, and low-cost solution.

The permit system provided a control on overfishing for Alaska halibut and has also been applied in New Zealand with considerable success. By 2007, it was being considered for codfish and haddock in the American northeast because of rampant overfishing in the eastern Georges Bank. Establishing a market provides a way of controlling abuses associated with management of a common-pool resource.

SOURCE: Council of Economic Advisors, *Economic Report of the President, 1993* (Washington, D.C.: U.S. Government Printing Office, 1993); and Bret Schulte, "One Fish, Two Fish, No Fish," *U.S. News & World Report,* August 27, 2007.

women when a boy receives a rubella vaccination—but, either way, that value is unlikely to be fully recognized in the market transaction. For these goods and services, the private return from their consumption is substantial, so the market will not fail to provide. It will not, however, provide at a socially reasonable level.

A positive externality causes the good in question to be underproduced. In the case of the rubella vaccination, those people who are vaccinated receive the benefit of reduced probability that they will contract the disease, a direct benefit to them for which they could be expected to pay. But they also provide protection against the disease to others in that they will not infect others if they themselves do not have the disease. That is a third-party, or external, effect of the vaccination. It is unlikely that everyone considering the vaccination will take full account of these benefits when weighing the advantages of vaccination against the disadvantages (minimal discomfort and some small risk of adverse reaction, time spent and inconvenience in receiving the injection, and the out-of-pocket price of the service), and some will decide not to be vaccinated. Fewer people would be vaccinated than would be in the best interests of society because of the external benefits from the personal choice about vaccination. Governments require young boys to get rubella vaccinations not simply to protect them—rubella itself is not much worse than a common cold—but also because we do not want them to give the disease to a pregnant woman and cause birth defects in her child.[10]

An undesirable (or negative) externality—think of it as a "public bad"—has the opposite effect, an overproduction of the good. Automobile operators pay the operating costs of their cars to enjoy the great personal mobility that cars provide, without full attention to the undesirable health and esthetic effects of the exhaust fumes produced by their vehicles or of the congestion delays caused by having many vehicles competing for highway space. Again, this leads to a misallocation of resources: more car miles traveled than would be the case if their operators based their choices on the full social cost (internal plus external) of using the car.

Governments regularly subsidize or tax to try to correct these market failures caused by externalities.[11] For instance, governments may pay producers or consumers of goods with positive externalities to encourage more consumption of the good in

---

[10]Public health officials refer to the concept of "herd immunity": if enough of a population is immunized against an infectious disease, even those without immunization will be protected because any invading germ will not be able to spread. There is no chain of transmission. When the "herd" is sufficiently immunized, those without immunization are able to enjoy free-rider protection. But if overall immunization levels fall below a critical threshold percentage of the population, that protection is gone. Hence, public health officials work to maintain immunization levels even when prevailing incidence of the disease is low because protection of that "herd immunity" provides protection for all. Public health officials are disturbed by state provisions that allow parents to decline required immunizations for their school-age children for philosophical or religious reasons because children suffer needlessly and die—and transmit preventable disease as the herd immunity declines. Here is an illustration of the importance of the cocoon from vaccination: infants under two months old are particularly vulnerable to pertussis with fatal consequences. However, infants this young cannot be vaccinated for that disease because their immune systems are not fully developed. Older children are vaccinated partly to provide protection for younger children—it's the externality that matters. So parents who do not vaccinate are being particularly selfish.

[11]When transaction costs are negligible, bargaining between users of resources can internalize external effects and cause an efficient level of output with no more government action (i.e., no taxes, no subsidies, and no prohibitions) than to establish private rights to the use of resources. Ronald Coase, "The Problem of Social Cost," *Journal of Law and Economics* 3 (October 1960): 1–44.

recognition of benefits to third parties. They may also levy corrective taxes to make purchasers and sellers respond to the external damage done by other products. The idea is to make buyers and sellers respond to the external effects of the product, to bring the third-party effect into their decision making in an economically tangible way.

Incomplete Markets and Imperfect Information[12]

Governments often intervene in markets when customers have incomplete information about products. Governments test (or supervise the testing of) new drugs, guard against the sale of hazardous products, establish certain financial disclosure standards, and so forth. The market may ultimately provide information—but not until after much grief and suffering by the unwary. Problems in the past few years with the safety of peanut butter, spinach, and dog food; the collapse of financial instrument values; and the like remind us of what happens when the safety net is broken—consumers do not have the information on their own to protect themselves against dangers in the global economy, and if the government inspection and assurance system fails, the consequences are considerable.

Several private markets, particularly those in insurance and finance, can present special problems of adverse selection and moral hazard. *Adverse selection* occurs when insurance purchasers impose higher-than-average costs on sellers (in health insurance, for instance, those more likely to purchase insurance are those more likely to need care) or when sellers exclude such potential purchasers (health insurance companies seek to exclude those more likely to require care).[13] The ultimate adverse selection problem in health insurance is that, in a purely unregulated private insurance system, we all would lose our health insurance if we live long enough. The cost of providing modern medical care typically rises as we get older. Insurance companies would thus keep their costs down by dropping coverage of older people, the policyholders systematically having higher medical costs. Medicare, the federal insurance program for the elderly, saves Americans from this adverse selection problem.

Moral hazard is a problem when those with insurance have an incentive to cause the insured event to happen or to be less than diligent in averting the insured event. In other words, people behave in a more risky fashion when someone else stands behind them to pick up the pieces if things do not turn out well. A "heads, I win; tails, you lose" gamble is going to induce you to play the game a lot and take more risks. For example, with health insurance, there is a tendency for people to seek

---

[12]Governments also may get involved when barriers to entry (like extreme economies of scale or trade restraints) allow firms to exercise monopoly power to charge prices higher than justified by market conditions. These government actions normally involve regulations of various types, not fiscal mechanisms.

[13]Medical care markets suffer from a double market failure. First, patients don't have the information necessary to evaluate medical treatments, so there is an imbalance of knowledge problem. Second, people normally purchase insurance to cover the risk of encountering hugely expensive medical treatments, and insurance companies profit not from providing efficient care, but from trying to limit insurance sales to people who won't need much care, the adverse selection problem. In sum, it is unreasonable to expect good solutions coming from this market.

more treatment when the third party, the insurance company, is paying for it.[14] In a case of government failure, federally subsidized flood insurance (premiums for the federal National Flood Insurance Program, established in 1968 to cover property owners in flood-prone areas that private insurers regarded as having too much risk, represent only about 38 percent of what a full premium would be) makes people more willing to build in floodplains and in coastal areas, thus increasing the loss when the inevitable flood occurs, as with Hurricane Katrina in 2005. Indeed, it has been observed that while nature produces floods, it is human actions that create flood damage. Subsidized flood insurance enables flood damage because few people would build in areas prone to flooding (the probability of flooding is reasonably easy to predict) without insurance being sold to them at less than market rates. Residents of the rest of the country, the ones not building in flood-prone areas, pay for the dangerous behavior of others. For example, the 2005 hurricane damage required that the subsidized flood insurance program receive $20 billion in payment from taxpayers. Some properties have been rebuilt time after time in the same location after receiving flood insurance payments. Indeed, a disproportionate share of total program losses annually comes from "repetitive loss properties."[15] That is moral hazard in action.

One argument made against the federal rescue ("bailout") of financial firms in 2008–2009 was that of moral hazard—that the firms and their officers were being compensated for their risky behavior that created the financial crisis and they would get the message that, should the opportunity for taking huge risks arise again, it was a risk worth taking because the consequences of failure would be cushioned by the federal government. But others argued that the rescue was still necessary because of an externality issue: if the financial institutions were not rescued, their problems would infect other institutions, thereby endangering the entire financial system. It is rather like the problem of fighting fires caused by careless behavior (e.g., smoking in bed)—bringing the fire department to put out the fire backstops poor behavior by reducing the personal consequences of a poor choice, but it does protect neighboring properties, whose owners have done nothing wrong. Letting the fire burn teaches the careless person a lesson that likely won't be forgotten (if the person survives)— but it stands a good chance of harming the innocent neighbors. The idea of trying to stop the problem of financial collapse from spreading ultimately won the day in the financial rescue program.

Reasoned government intervention involves securing widespread coverage (to prevent adverse selection) and regulating markets to ensure that decision makers feel the accurate cost implications of those choices (to prevent moral hazard). Adverse selection and moral hazard keep markets from functioning properly and require

---

[14]Another illustration of moral hazard: there is some evidence that making private automobiles safer has encouraged drivers to be less cautious in their driving. Do you imagine that NASCAR drivers would drive with the abandon that they do if they did not have marvelous safety equipment installed in their cars?

[15] For two excellent reviews of the flood insurance program, see Erwann O. Michel-Kerjan, "Castrophe Economics: The National Flood Insurance Program," *Journal of Economic Perspectives* 24 (Fall 2010): 165–86; and J. David Cummins, "Should the Government Provide Insurance for Catastrophes?" *Federal Reserve Bank of St. Louis Review* 88 (July/August 2006): 337–85.

government intervention to fix the problem. Social insurance systems (public pension, health and disability, unemployment, etc.) throughout the world stem from these market problems.[16]

Functions of Government: Economic Stabilization

Governments seek to stabilize the macroeconomy, in other words, prevent high unemployment, control inflation that could erode purchasing power and distort financial markets, and improve the prospects for economic growth and higher quality of life. The private economy experiences cycles of economic activity that translate into episodes of slow improvements in standards of living (slow or no economic growth) and general price increases that erode purchasing power of incomes and assets, distort financial and other markets, and otherwise make life miserable for the citizenry. Modern democracies accept the principle that they should attempt to mitigate the depth of downturns, to prevent high rates of price increase, and to make prospects for growth better. The Great Recession (December 2007–June 2009: those are the official dates from the National Bureau of Economic Research, the group that gauges these things. If you don't agree, complain to them, not to me.) brought public and political attention to the important role that governments can play in mitigating the misery that macroeconomic decline will produce and, more importantly, in reversing that decline. Few responsible leaders now take the view that, because recessions will eventually end on their own, it would be best for government to do nothing.[17] To do nothing seems to be irresponsible. When politicians crow "Jobs! Jobs! Jobs!" they are implicitly agreeing that the private market has failed and accepting the stabilization role of government.

The stabilization policy that is expected to be the first line of defense is monetary policy. In the United States, this policy is normally in the hands of the Federal Reserve System, our central bank. (Other countries have similar institutions with similar functions.) Through various mechanisms, the Federal Reserve manipulates the supply of money available to the public and the terms under which credit is provided. These manipulations influence interest rates, and, in turn, these rates influence business investment. The impact on national aggregate demand—what policy makers are trying to stimulate to boost economic performance and reduce

---

[16]Another moral hazard: pitchers in the American League do not bat, so they do not face direct retaliation in the batter's box and are thus more likely to throw at opposing batters than are their counterparts in the National League, who do have to bat for themselves. J. C. Bradbury and D. J. Drinen, "Crime and Punishment in Major League Baseball: The Case of the Designated Hitter and Hit Batters," *Economic Inquiry* 45 (January 2007): 131–44.

[17]Few now accept the idea of Herbert Hoover's Secretary of the Treasury, who in the early days of the Great Depression stated that a good, solid recession was a great way to purge the rottenness out of the system. Most current opponents of economic stabilization efforts are probably tenured university faculty members or others with great job security–it isn't their rotten choices that they intend to purge. The job to be saved isn't theirs.

unemployment—occurs when businesses and other borrowers increase their investment spending because of those lower rates. Monetary policy is the first line of defense in economic stabilization because it does not have to flow through the delays of the political process that other stabilization tools must surmount. So long as the Federal Reserve is independent of the national government, it can respond to economic forces rather than political advantage.[18] The problem with monetary policy in the Great Recession was that, even when the Federal Reserve got interest rates almost to zero, businesses still did not borrow and invest in productive infrastructure, and individual households did not borrow to build houses. Without that induced capital investment, monetary policy will not stimulate aggregate demand, and the economy continues to lag. That brought a need for fiscal policy.

Fiscal policy involves making changes in government spending and in tax collections to influence aggregate demand in the economy. Government purchases directly increase aggregate demand, while reducing tax collections (a tax cut) operates indirectly by leaving households and businesses more after-tax income that they are free to spend. Government, household, and business spending increases aggregate demand, and that gives other households and businesses income that they will spend in turn, bringing income to others—and so it goes. The stimulation from a given change will be lower for a tax reduction because some of the higher after-tax income that individuals and businesses have will be saved (or will be used to pay off existing debt) and not spent. Only spending gives the hoped-for boost to aggregate demand. And, in terms of inducing a recovery of the economy, it doesn't much matter whether the initial government spending is to buy Buicks to drive off into the Atlantic or to build wind turbines to provide electricity without using fossil fuel—spending is spending and both provide income to suppliers, who will then use that income to do stimulative spending of their own. In severe recession, it is more spending (increased aggregate demand) that is needed for economic stimulation, and how that happens is of secondary concern.

The problem with fiscal policy is its slowness—it takes time to reach consensus that a problem exists, to get legislative approval for the fiscal changes needed to implement the policy, and to get the changes into the economy. Fortunately, there is a short-cut system for fiscal policy—the automatic stabilizers. These stabilizers are integral and permanent elements of the tax and transfer system that tend to mitigate fluctuations in aggregate demand without requiring any actions by lawmakers. When income declines in a recession, tax liabilities fall, giving households more disposable income, and more households become eligible for transfer programs (like food stamps and unemployment compensation). Those programs work to stabilize consumer spending, thus constraining the potential depth of an economic downturn. They work in the opposite way when the economy is expanding so rapidly that great price increases (high inflation) are a danger.[19]

---

[18]Federal Reserve System profits are returned to the federal government, its operations are subject to regular financial audit, and its leadership is approved by Congress (In 2010–2011, Congress refused to approve appointment of a Nobel Prize–winning economist to the Board of Governors because some members doubted that he has strong enough credentials in economics. How dumb is that?). But its policies are not subject to government approvals.

[19]Congressional Budget Office, *The Effects of the Automatic Stabilizers on the Federal Budget* (Washington, D.C.: Congressional Budget Office, 2011) explains the stabilizer impact and how it can be measured.

The federal government has considerably greater flexibility to work for fiscal stabilization than do the states and localities because it has better access to debt markets (increasing spending and reducing taxes will create a higher fiscal deficit that needs to be covered) and, ultimately, because it can even print money to cover the gap. State and local governments, however, usually must cover all spending in a year with revenue collected in the year (in other words, they must balance their budgets), and, as economic activity declines, they have real trouble doing this. Demand for services rises and revenue from taxes falls in a recession. Being fiscally responsible, as they must ultimately be, too often means tax increases and expenditure reductions—exactly the wrong medicine for the ailing economy. State and local fiscal programs can significantly counterbalance federal stabilization efforts, a reason why the federal government has sometimes included grants to these governments as part of its stabilization efforts.

Governments also attempt industrial policy, meaning an effort to direct economic development in particular directions through support of particular sorts of economic activity that has been politically defined to be appropriate for the future. The targeted subsidies and tax advantages (part of the fiscal structure) are designed to stimulate particular industries, in the belief that they can increase economic growth and reduce unemployment by boosting activities destined to be national or even global leaders. Politicians and bureaucrats have a remarkably bad record at identifying industries or firms whose support will be critical for the long-term success of the nation or a region. Johnson and Kwak give us an idea about why: "the openness of the American political system has always made it possible for the current business elite to use its political power to shift the economic playing field in its favor. Any growing and profitable sector can take this route, from railroads, steel, and automobiles to defense and energy. Each of these industries has used the argument that 'what's good for (fill in the blank) is good for America' in order to obtain preferential tariffs, tax breaks, or subsidies."[20] Politicians and bureaucrats are ripe targets for these arguments, even through there is abundant evidence that targeted support is a sucker bet in which a favored group cashes in without much return for the general public. The 2011 bankruptcy of Solyndra, a solar-panel maker that had received more than half a billion dollars in federal loans because it was judged to be a leader in promising clean energy technology, was one recent example.[21]

There is also not much evidence to support the idea that subnational government use of targeted tax and expenditure programs can have much of an effect on overall development of a state or local economy, but that does not stop state and local politicians from trying. The *Economist* succinctly explains why industrial and economic development policy, whether national, state, or local, has such a low success rate: "Neither economists nor emperors can be relied upon to pick winners.

---

[20]Simon Johnson and James Kwak, *13 Bankers: The Wall Street Takeover and the Next Financial Meltdown* (New York: Vantage Books, 2011), 24.
[21]The federal government—representing both political parties—has a dismal record in its support of energy schemes, including such failures as the Clinch River breeder reactor, Synthetic Fuels Corporation, clean coal, and hydrogen-powered automobiles. Steven Mufson, "Before Solyndra, a Long History of Failed Government Energy Projects," *Washington Post,* November 12, 2011.

The best bet is entrepreneurial trial and error."[22] Government money spent to assist particular industries is, sadly, often badly spent because even the well-advised government usually guesses wrong. If lawmakers really knew how to do effective development, would there be poverty anywhere?

Functions of Government: Redistribution

One of the great strengths of a free market system is that individual effort provides the mechanism for distribution of economic rewards. Successful efforts get rewarded and that encourages people to even greater effort and society benefits. No central directorate establishes who gets what based on support for that directorate or whims of those in power. Markets distribute products of the economy to those people having and using resources (talents, properties, etc.), not distinguishing whether those resources were earned by going to medical school, serving an apprenticeship as a plumber, spending many days in the gymnasium perfecting a jump shot, inherited from rich parents, stolen, or whatever. Those who have the most valuable resources and put them to productive use get the goods. People with few resources—property or skills—may be destined to a life of poverty in a pure market economy. Governments may correct injustices in the distribution of affluence in society, seeking to improve the conditions faced by the less well-to-do that the market alone would leave them with. Some argue for a degree of redistribution out of a social conscience and a desire for a safety net for all humanity; others argue for a degree of redistribution out of a fear that the poor will revolt, taking property from the affluent (the less affluent have numbers on their side in any such struggle). The argument for limited redistribution is that generous support programs will blunt individual work effort and that will cause a loss for everyone in the economy—but a general concern about reducing the sting of poverty generally is more powerful. Most politicians believe that the public wants some protection for the very poor and at least some mild redistribution by the government of the result produced by pure operation of the market. The issue is more how much and how rather than whether there should be some programs. Those concerns are reflected both in government spending programs and in systems for financing those programs.

A dilemma of recent years in the United States is that the highest-income households have done extremely well economically relative to the rest of the population. This is shown in Figure 1–2, a chart that shows the percent of total income earned in the nation by the highest 10 percent of families. In 2007, the latest year for which data are available, this fortunate 10 percent received half of all income earned. That is roughly 15 percentage points higher than was the case in the years from the start of World War II until the early 1980s and higher than at any other time in the 1917–2007 period. The people at the highest income level have done remarkably well. Some argue that this is no major problem, but simply reflects rewards to talent, intellect, skill, and

---

[22]"Finding Your Niche," *Economist* 21 (March 2003): 70. There are a few success stories of government support, including commercialization of penicillin (pharmaceutical companies were reluctant to undermine the market for their profitable sulfa drugs) and, possibly, development of the Internet.

Figure 1–2
The Top Decile Income Share in the United States, 1917–2007

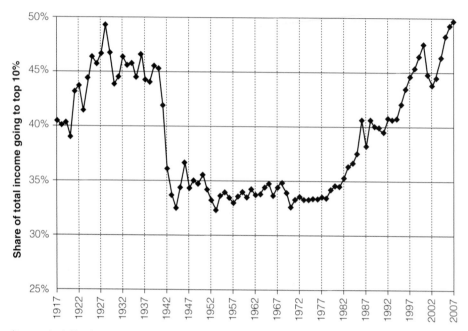

Income is defined as market income, including capital gains. In 2007, top decile includes all families with annual income above $109,630.

SOURCE: Emmanuel Saez, "Striking It Richer: The Evolution of Top Incomes in the United States" (updated with 2007 estimates), August 5, 2009 [http://elsa.berkeley.edu/~saez/saez-UStopincomes-2006prel.pdf].

effort applied to satisfying the demands of the American public.[23] Others argue that the system is rigged and held captive by the fortunate few and that radical reactions are appropriate. For whatever reason, income inequality has risen in recent decades, and American governments do give attention to redistribution, paying particular attention to providing a guaranteed safety net to those at the bottom of the income scale.

Governments employ a variety of different approaches toward redistribution. These include tax structures that levy relatively higher tax burdens on high-affluence households than on low-affluence ones (e.g., income taxes that levy higher effective rates on high-income households), direct income payments to low-affluence families (e.g., the earned income tax credit), programs that provide assistance services for which only low-affluence families qualify (Medicaid), or programs available to all that low-income families use more heavily (unemployment benefit programs). The Social Security system provides income assistance to the disabled and the elderly, although neither program is directed only to low-income families, and Medicare provides guaranteed health insurance to the elderly. Combined, these programs have quite successfully broken the

---

[23] There is evidence that the fortunate few aren't the same people every year and that there is a degree of mobility across the deciles. Gerald Auten and Geoffrey Gee, "Income Mobility in the United States: New Evidence from Income Tax Data," *National Tax Journal* 62 (June 2009): 301–28. However, income class mobility in the United States appears to be somewhat less than found in some European counties.

near-guarantee that growing old would mean income distress and that elderly parents would have to move in with their children out of economic necessity. However, the United States makes less aggressive use of active tax and transfer programs to handle problems of poverty than do other wealthy nations, preferring programs of economic expansion that benefit everyone, trusting that economic expansion will take care of the economic bottom as it benefits the economic top. As a result, the gap between highest and lowest incomes and the level of unrelieved poverty in the United States are considerably greater than in other wealthy nations; upward income mobility from one generation to the next is similarly less here than in many countries in Europe.[24]

Privatization

Modern societies argue about the size of government, that is, where to draw the line between government provision and market provision of goods and services. Many governments have downsized the public sector to achieve efficiency in the belief that market provision may offer more service options to the public, more flexibility in service response, and lower operating costs. Other governments have sold government assets or functions in order to get immediate cash. And others have maintained responsibility for provision of the service, but have arranged for its production by private firms ("outsourced").[25] After considering the appropriate functions of government, as we did in the last section, it is also reasonable to explore the range for which various forms of privatization may be reasonable and to sort out the various meanings of privatization.

Why Privatize?

Several arguments have been offered to support privatization.[26] Here are three of the most frequently used:

1. **Smaller government.** Some argue for a smaller government and fewer public employees largely as a matter of philosophy, a blind faith in the badness of government. Because governments may spend without producing services (e.g., the check writing of the American Social Security system) and may be

---

[24]Another redistribution dilemma emerges because there are considerable interstate differences in affluence: in 2010, per capita personal income in Connecticut was 76 percent higher than per capita personal income in Mississippi, a considerable disparity. However, around those averages, there are poor people in Connecticut and rich people in Mississippi. What is a better federal redistribution approach: assistance to poor places or assistance to poor people? Different program designs emerge, depending on the answer to that question.

[25]An excellent analysis of the economics of privatization is John Vickers and George Yarrow, "Economic Perspectives on Privatization," *Journal of Economic Perspectives* 5 (Spring 1991): 111–32.

[26] A desire to stem corruption was a major influence in nineteenth-century decisions for local government ownership and management of gas, electric, and water utilities and public transport enterprises. Reformers believed that managers of public organizations would have weaker incentives to capture profits for the enterprise from corrupt activities if profits were not received personally. The study also suggests that public ownership is likely to create inefficient operation and excessively high government payrolls. Edward L. Glaeser, "Public Ownership in the American City," *National Bureau of Economic Research Working Paper 8613,* December 2001. The anticorruption argument may have continued applicability in privatization discussions in the developing and transition environment, but it is not a clear call.

deeply involved in the private economy without even spending (e.g., the safety regulations applied to private industry or tax credits to support certain activities), privatization may reduce government production without reducing at all the size of government or state involvement in the economy. This therefore provides a weak basis for privatization. Whatever size of government provides best for the citizenry, not big or small out of a philosophical stand, would seem to be a more appropriate guide for public policy.

2. **Operating efficiency and response to clients.** Governments often consider privatization of public service production as a means for lower-cost or higher-quality services to the public. Governments produce under the political-bureaucratic system of central command and control, often driven from a desire to employ people with minimal attention to the need to at least cover costs of operation. State enterprises frequently lack a hard budget constraint and receive a government subsidy to cover any losses. This situation blunts the incentive for efficient operations and for responsiveness to clients. To survive, private businesses must respond to direct customer demand and must constrain prices out of concern for competition from other businesses. That environment drives private business toward operating efficiency (lower production cost) and improved responsiveness to customers, but only if the new private businesses face a competitive business environment. There is no reason to believe that a private monopolist city water company would be more efficient and responsive than a government monopolist city water company serving the same territory under the same regulatory conditions. The cost reduction associated with improved operating efficiency is a frequent objective of government privatizations in the United States. However, it is not always the case that a private system will outperform a government one.[27] For one example, a number of studies have found the Veterans Health Administration hospital system to be a better performer than the systems available to other Americans.[28] The Internal Revenue Service found that it

---

[27]One example: Kirkpatrick, Parker, and Zhang find no evidence of better performance by private water utilities than by state-owned utilities in Africa, a continent with many nations suffering great loss from an absence of safe and affordable water services. Colin Kirkpatrick, David Parker, and Yin-Fang Zhang, "An Empirical Analysis of State and Private-Sector Provision of Water Services in Africa," *World Bank Economic Review* 20, no. 1 (2006): 143–63.

[28]Steven M. Asch, Elizabeth A. McGlynn, Mary M. Hogan, Rodney A. Hayward, Paul Shekelle, Lisa Rubenstein, Joan Keesey, John Adams, and Eve A. Kerr, "Comparison of Quality of Care for Patients in the Veterans Health Administration and Patients in a National Sample," *Annals of Internal Medicine* 141, no. 12 (December 21, 2004): 938–945. A number of other studies are cited in Phillip Longman, "The Best Care Anywhere," *Washington Monthly,* January/February 2005. Many news stories in 2007 reported poor care provided to those injured in the Iraq war by the Walter Reed Hospital in Washington, D.C. This facility, however, is operated by the Department of Defense, not the Veterans Administration (VA), and the performance of the two systems—both public—should not be confused. The VA has been overwhelmed with the war in Iraq and, arguably, funded at levels lower than appropriate to its assigned tasks, but evidence does indicate that its standard of care is excellent in comparison with those of private providers. The Government Accountability Office in a later study also confirmed the quality of the VA system (U.S. Government Accountability Office, *The Health Care System for Veterans: An Interim Report,* Publication Number 3016 (Washington, D.C.: GAO, December 2007)). In other environments, the public sector compares badly: Jishnu Das and Jeffrey Hammer, "Money for Nothing: The Dire Straits of Medical Practice in Delhi, India," *World Bank Policy Research Working Paper 3669,* Jul. 2005.

could do a better job of collecting revenue from difficult taxpayers than could private contractors forced on it by a Congress determined to prove the private sector is always more efficient. Finally, the Transportation Security Administration, the agency that frustrates all air travelers, found that private air passenger screeners cost around 3 percent more than did federal screeners, although there are problems in making the comparisons.[29] For best results for the citizenry, it is best to take an agnostic attitude when considering private-public supply. Contracting does not assure cost savings, better quality, or better response.

3. **Cash.** Sale of government-operated enterprises may bring government revenue. Operating profits (or losses) in the future would disappear, although the enterprise would then be subject to the tax system (unless the buyer arranged a tax preference as part of the deal). Unfortunately, many government assets produce no revenue or produce revenue that is less than operating cost. That makes their market value extremely low. This is a problem that countries of the former Soviet Union had to face as they tried to move into a market economy. Many state enterprises had high production costs, and, even with private ownership, the product would not sell on national or international markets at a price sufficient to cover those costs. Although the old central plans invested heavily in these plants, their privatized value proved to be low—except in natural resource sectors (oil, gas, etc.). In other environments, the revenues have proved substantial. In some parts of the world, notably Russia, some de-privatizations have occurred, at least in part for political reasons and not because of the economic fundamentals. And a number of localities around the United States have reacquired water supply systems in recent years, often in reaction to higher water rates imposed to finance system upgrades.[30] States and localities have also sold assets (office buildings, parking lots, etc.) that they have then leased back, the asset sale having given them quick cash to close budget gaps. This government resort to pawn shop loans violates fiscal sustainability principles because it uses borrowed funds to support current operations, thus kicking the cost of government to the future. It is just disguised borrowing. If the assets have no public use, then selling them makes perfect sense.[31]

Other motives behind privatization include to provide more appropriate personnel or expertise to perform the service, to permit greater operating flexibility and reduced personnel cost (particularly fringe benefits), to quicken implementation of

---

[29]Government Accountability Office, "Aviation Security: TSA's Revised Cost Comparison Provides a More Reasonable Basis for Comparing the Costs of Private-Sector and TSA Screeners," March 4, 2011.
[30]Jim Carlton, "Calls Rise for Public Control of Water Supply," *Wall Street Journal,* Jul. 17, 2008, A-6. In some instances, the utility had been sold to a private firm in an effort to raise revenue for the municipality.
[31]One fiscal myth is that the federal deficit could be substantially reduced if the federal government were to sell its excess property. While getting properties in better use is a good idea, the revenue potential is modest (a lot of what the federal government owns isn't worth much in alternative use), establishing a disposal process would be complex, and it would be only a single-shot impact. Theresa Gullo, Testimony: Selling Federal Property before the Committee on Oversight and Government Reform, U.S. House of Representatives, Jul. 27, 2011.

new programs, to increase the pace of innovation, and to improve quality of service. Owners of privatized operations also can become important campaign contributors to those officials who have transferred public operations to them, something not possible if the operations stayed in government hands. However, it is important to understand that all government services are not equally susceptible to outsourcing and not all motives will be satisfied in any particular privatization program. And not all motives are clearly in the public interest.

The largest transactions involve formerly nationalized industries under old concepts of the economic role of government or of the need to keep "socially or economically significant" industries under state control: telecommunications, petroleum and petrochemicals, gas distribution, automobile manufacturing, electricity generation and distribution, airlines, steel making, and so on.[32] Government operation of these industries has been notoriously bad because of political influences on service decisions (e.g., a city gets served by the national airline because an important politician lives there) and on operations (e.g., the industry is seen as employer of last resort and the resulting bloated payrolls prevent it from ever producing its product at a competitive cost).[33]

Governments in the United States have historically been less active in privatization in the sense of sale of government assets than those in Western Europe, Latin America, Asia, Japan, New Zealand, and Australia.[34] On a global basis, Western Europe has been preeminent in privatization, largely because countries there had many state-owned enterprises and, accordingly, had lots of property with potential for privatization. Many of the big international privatizations, however, have been in industries never publicly owned in the United States. Privatization of roads, airports, the postal system, schools, and the like raise much more interesting social, political, and economic issues than the state sale of telephone or petrochemical companies, which have produced the largest privatization revenue globally.[35] The services of roads, airports, schools, and so on are different because their services have a degree of publicness and external impact that other publicly owned capital assets may lack.

In recent years, there have been a number of public asset sales or extraordinarily long-term leases in the United States that are huge in the American context.[36] These

---

[32]The largest of all was the sale of Nippon Telegraph and Telephone by the government of Japan. Share offerings in 1987 and 1988 raised almost $80 billion; the $40 billion offering in November 1987 is the largest security offering in history. William L. Megginson, *The Financial Economics of Privatization* (New York: Oxford University Press, 2005), 27–28.

[33]National airlines can face difficult political barriers to efficient operations. Keith Johnson and Luca Di Leo, "Alitalia Can't Stanch Red Ink," *Wall Street Journal,* April 21, 2004, A-16. Staff reductions then being proposed would have brought Alitalia down to about 1,100 passengers per employee, compared with about 9,000 passengers per employee for the competing discount carrier Ryanair.

[34]In the 1977–2000 peak period for privatizations internationally, privatization revenues in Japan and the United Kingdom greatly exceeded those of any other developed country. Bernardo Bortolotti and Domenico Siniscalco, *The Challenges of Privatization, An International Analysis* (Oxford, England: Oxford University Press, 2004), 43.

[35]The pioneer of privatization in the last decades of the twentieth century, Britain, has been unable to fully privatize its coal industry, so apparently technically simple decisions do get muddled by politics and other factors.

[36]Federal tax law regards lease of an asset for a period longer than its useful life to be a sale. Following that reasonable logic, these long-term leases can reasonably be discussed as sales regardless of the packaging of the deal. Edward D. Kleinbard, Testimony at a Hearing of the Subcommittee on Energy, Natural Resources, and Infrastructure of the Committee on Taxation on Tax and Financing Aspects of Highway Public-Private Partnerships, Jul. 24, 2008 [http://finance.senate.gov/hearings/testimony/2008test/ 072408ektest.pdf].

include the 99-year lease of the Chicago Skyway for $1.8 billion, the 75-year lease of the Indiana Toll Road for $3.8 billion, the 99-year lease of Chicago's Midway Airport for $2.5 billion (a deal that seems to have collapsed when the lessors were unable to obtain sufficient financing), the 99-year lease of the Pocahontas Parkway in Virginia for $548 million (plus some additional highway construction), and the 75-year lease of parking meter revenue in Chicago for $1.16 billion. These are toll-supported facilities, and the government is trading the future revenue from the asset for the payment of immediate revenue, a sort of mechanism for "securitizing" (borrowing) that revenue flow. In addition to allowing the move in revenues across time, the new private operators were able to increase charges for use of the facilities, increases that political barriers had prevented the government owners from implementing for years. Because each of these assets is unique, it is extremely difficult to determine whether the sale price was too high or too low. And because all these sales are relatively recent, it is impossible to know whether the public will feel like it is getting good-quality service for the prices being charged by the private operators. The transactions involve changing the timing of revenue rather than the creation of a new revenue source. The public body is collecting the revenue when the lease is made and is losing the revenue that it would have collected from the public asset in future years.

Great care must be used in the selection of government assets for sale and in the use of the proceeds of those sales. Here is the most important point to be made about the sale of public assets: using proceeds from the sale of government assets as revenue to cover operating costs and thinking you have made the public better off is about the same as burning pieces of your house for heat and thinking that you are better off because you haven't had to buy firewood. That is a long-term losing strategy that will make future generations less able to enjoy the standard of life enjoyed now. It uses resources bought by previous generations to subsidize current consumption and leaves a lowered resource endowment for the future. That isn't consistent with fiscal sustainability—although it is always popular with current politicians because it allows them to kick the problem ahead to another set of politicians. Whether sale of public assets for cash will also lead to improved performance for the public is always an open question and should be a point for analysis rather than an operating assumption.

Versions of Privatization: Production/Provision

The American privatization issue frequently concerns the provision-production dichotomy.[37] Goods and services provided by a government because of market failure need not be produced by that government. Provision means government intervention to ensure and control availability or, generally, to finance the service; it does

---

[37]It also encompasses application of user-pay concepts, including sale of service and tax payments based on the benefits received from particular government services. These mechanisms, while bringing some market like principles, do not alter public provision and thus are discussed in the revenue section of this book.

not require production by the government. The production choice should be made according to which entity—a government department, a private entity (profit or nonprofit), or another government—would supply the desired quantity and quality of service at least cost to the citizenry.

The distinction between government and private production and provision can be clarified by examples:

1. *Government provision/government production.* The city street department plows the streets after a heavy snowfall. The job uses department managers, department employees, department equipment, and department supplies.

2. *Government provision/private production.* The county hires a private appraisal firm to estimate values of real estate in the county for use in computing property tax bills. The firm does the work with its managers, employers, equipment, and supplies. Or a library board contracts with Library Systems and Services International for operation of its library branches. At the federal level, the U.S. Department of Defense hires private firms to provide food and other support services to military units in the field. The military has almost always relied on private suppliers for equipment and material rather than trying to produce those resources itself. Outsourcing is almost certainly the most common privatization practiced in the United States.[38] It was a major element in President George W. Bush's management agenda for the federal government, which intended competitive sourcing for federal tasks that are readily available in the commercial marketplace.[39] Many state and local governments similarly seek out opportunities to get services delivered to their citizenry through private operators. Some local governments—for example, Weston, Florida—rely on contract suppliers for all the services they provide.[40]

3. *Private provision/government production.* A racetrack pays a city for extraordinary traffic control services on race days.

4. *Private provision/private production.* A private manufacturer patrols its factory site with its own security employees.[41] Neighboring properties may receive some protection spillover from this security activity.

Production by contract ("outsourcing"), the government provision/private production option, is probably limited more than anything else by the ability to design a contract specifying the service qualities to be delivered. Even parts of the judicial system may be privately produced: California permits litigants to hire private jurists

---

[38]U.S. General Accounting Office, *Privatization: Lessons Learned by State and Local Governments,* GAO/GGD-97-48 (Washington, D.C.: U.S. Government Printing Office, 1997).

[39]The efforts by the George W. Bush administration to outsource government operations are described in John Maggs, "Compete, or Else," *National Journal* (July 12, 2003): 2228–37.

[40]Jonas Prager, "Contract City Redux: Weston, Florida, as the Ultimate New Public Management Model City," *Public Administration Review* 68 (January/February 2008): 155–66. An earlier version of this is the California Lakewood Plan. Robert Bish, *The Public Economy of Metropolitan Areas* (Chicago: Markham, 1971), 85.

[41]Businesses and individuals in the United States spend over twice as much for private security as governments spend on providing public safety. "Welcome to the New World of Private Security," *Economist* (April 19, 1997): 21.

when court congestion or special expertise makes such a procedure attractive to both parties, and private firms have undertaken contractual operation of corrections facilities.[42] School systems have similarly chosen private production through vouchers or charter schools.[43] In these systems, the school district provides financing, but the educational service is actually produced by another entity.

The production choice should be kept open for possible privatization; the idea of government action is to provide services of desired quantity and quality at the least cost to the economy. When might contracting not be an efficient option? One study suggests that in-house production may be warranted when "(1) there are very few potential suppliers, (2) costs of switching from one producer to another are high, (3) information about the production process and supplier performance is expensive to obtain, and (4) the good or service being provided cannot be clearly defined."[44] In other words, the option would be difficult if contracts would be especially difficult to write and the public would end up being confronted with a monopoly supplier. Otherwise, out-of-government production can be an efficient option. A study of the use of private contractors to support military operations in Iraq also noted that security contracts would not need to be renewed if needs declined, whereas military units doing the work would need to remain in the force structure even with the declining need.[45]

The federal government has defined the boundaries for its privatization by contract actions:

> An inherently governmental activity is an activity that is so intimately related to the public interest as to mandate performance by government personnel. These activities require the exercise of substantial discretion in applying government authority and/or in making decisions for the government. Inherently governmental activities normally fall into two categories: the exercise of sovereign government authority or the establishment of procedures and processes related to the oversight of monetary transactions or entitlements.[46]

---

[42]"California Is Allowing Its Wealthy Litigants to Hire Private Jurists," *Wall Street Journal,* August 6, 1980; and U.S. General Accounting Office, *Private and Public Prisons: Studies Comparing Operational Costs and/or Quality of Service,* GAO/GGD-96-158 (Washington, D.C.: U.S. Government Printing Office, 1996). Corrections Corp. of America, the largest private prison operator in the United States, operates sixty-four facilities spread across around twenty states and the District of Columbia. Correction facilities face an interesting incentive problem: it is against their economic interests to rehabilitate criminals in their care because successful rehabilitation reduces demand for their incarceration services, so it is quite important to make sure that their performance contract provides the appropriate incentives and performance metrics. Stephanie Chen, "Growing Inmate Population Is Boon to Private Prisons," *Wall Street Journal,* November 19, 2008, A4.

[43]Gary Putka, "Baltimore Test of Privatization Gets a Bad Start," *Wall Street Journal,* September 23, 1992. Voucher systems provide families an education grant—a subsidy for the purchase of education—which may be spent on services from a variety of producers. Charter schools allow private entities to create schools outside the public system, with financing from public funds. Families pick among schools.

[44]John C. Hilke, *Competition in Government-Financed Services* (New York: Quorum Books, 1992), 8. Why does the federal government run its own printing house, the Government Printing Office? To learn more about mixed motives, see Graeme Browning, "Stop the Presses?" *National Journal* 25 (October 16, 1993): 2483–85.

[45]Congressional Budget Office, *Contractors' Support of U.S. Operations in Iraq* (Washington, D.C.: Congressional Budget Office, 2008).

[46]Executive Office of the President, Office of Management and Budget, Circular No. A-76 (Revised), Subject: Performance of Commercial Activities, May 29, 2003, A–2.

If an activity is "inherently governmental," it should not be carried out by a contractor, but should be undertaken by government employees. Of course, the boundaries of this standard are subject to considerable debate, even though the concept is clear.

Privatization of provision is a more difficult problem. For public goods, the market will not function because the private supplier will not charge an efficient price for the service because of nonrivalry and inability to exclude. Business firms provide goods and services because they intend to make money, not for the sheer enjoyment of providing the goods or services. If it is not possible to charge people for the good or service, a business firm will seldom provide it. Furthermore, the price will exceed the cost of providing service to an additional consumer (recall that the additional cost is zero).

The expectation of government provision of public goods is strong, but occasionally governments will provide private goods as well and often do a very bad job of it. Organizational problems, particularly lack of appropriate production incentives, cause high costs, undesirable production strategies, and a bland product designed by an uneasy consensus. Governments provide toll goods (highways, bridges, etc.), and sometimes they do about as well as the private producer would do. But even some toll goods are provided by private businesses. For instance, in France eight public-private joint ventures and one private company operate the toll highway/tunnel system, the most extensive auto toll system in Europe. Evidence indicates that fewer resources will be wasted if government avoids provision of private goods.

Some observers of public fiscal problems have suggested that privatization would relieve pressures on government finances. That is a realistic response if the service being privatized in fact lacks substantial public-good features; one wonders why, in such a case, the government got involved in its provision. On the other hand, to expect private firms to provide public goods at desirable levels is folly. At best, the private firm may be contracted to produce the public good provided (paid for) by the government.

Building Public Choices from Individual Preferences

The logic of moving from individual choice to choices made by society is built on three fairly simple tenets. First, individuals are the best judges of their own well-being and generally act to improve that well-being as they see it. There is no scientific principle that leads us to reject or accept the judgments made by individuals about their own lives. Second, the welfare of the community depends on the welfare of the individuals in that community. In other words, communities are made up of people, and community welfare increases only if the welfare of those in the community is improved. From that comes the third tenet, judging the impact of a social action on the welfare of the community. The Pareto criterion, named after a nineteenth-century economist, holds that if at least one person is better off from a policy action and no person is worse off, then the community as a whole is unambiguously better off for the policy.[47] Does a social action harming anyone, despite improving the condition of many individuals, improve the welfare of society as a whole? It cannot be indisputably argued that such an action improves the well-being of society, regardless of the numbers made better off, because the relative worth of those harmed cannot scientifically be compared with that of those helped. Such a proposed policy would fail the Pareto criterion for judging social action.[48]

With those standards, we can analyze the implications of nonappropriability for public provision. Suppose that only five people would be influenced by construction of a levee to protect a small area from periodic flooding. The cost of that levee is $20,000. Each individual in this community knows the maximum sacrifice that he or she would be willing to make to have that levee as compared to having no levee at all. Presumably, it would not be larger than the individual damage avoided by having levee protection. The property owners have a pretty good idea of what they would lose in a flood that the levee could protect against. These are the individual benefit numbers in Table 1–1. The levee would be a public good: each individual could use it without diminishing its availability to anyone else in the community (stopping the flooding for one person wouldn't alter the amount of flood averting available to others behind the levee), and exclusion of nonpayers is not feasible (if your property is behind the levee, it will be protected even if you didn't pay the levee charge).

First, would the levee be built without public action, that is, by individual action only? The cost of the levee is $20,000; the most that any single individual (individual D) will pay to get the levee built is $9,000. Thus, the levee would not be produced by any single individual. If the levee only cost $8,500 to construct, however, we suspect individual D would build the levee for his or her benefit, and four other people in the community would receive benefits from the levee without payment. (The four would be *free riders,* and D would still be better off for having built the levee.) Once

Table 1–1
Individual Benefits from the Project: Example 1

Individual	Individual Benefit	
A	$ 8,000	
B	7,000	
C	6,000	*Total cost $20,000*
D	9,000	
E	6,000	
Total benefit	$36,000	

---

[47]Vilfredo Pareto, *Manuel d'Economie Politique,* 2d ed. (Paris: M. Giard, 1927), 617–18.
[48]Benefit-cost analysis, an analytic technique that will be discussed in a later chapter, employs a less restricting and somewhat less appealing rule than the Pareto criterion. This is the Kaldor criterion, which holds that a social action improves community welfare if those benefiting from a social action could hypothetically compensate the losers in full and still have gain left over. Because no compensation need actually occur, losers can remain, and the Pareto criterion would not be met.

the levee is there, it serves all because of its public-good features.[49] The initially presumed construction cost, however, is such that the maximum individual benefit is less than the cost of the project, so the levee will not be built by private action.

Is the levee a good economic choice for the community in the sense that the benefits of the levee are greater than the value of resources going into the construction of the levee? The social cost, the value of the resources being used in the construction of the levee, equals $20,000. The social benefit of the levee, the sum of the improved welfare of the individuals with the levee, equals $36,000. Because social benefits are greater than social costs, it is a desirable project.[50] A responsive government would act to provide the levee and would raise sufficient funds through the revenue structure to finance the project. If the government levied an equal per-capita tax—a payment based on the coercive power of government rather than the voluntary payment of market exchange—on the community to finance the levee ($4,000 each), all individuals would still be better off with the levee and the tax than without the combination.[51] Government can thus provide a desired service that public-good features prevent private action from providing.

A second example yields additional insights. Assume that the community receives benefits from a project as shown in Table 1–2. The project, possibly a levee in another location, is a public good. The cost of the project is $20,000. Because the sum of individual benefits ($19,000) is less than the cost of the project, the project resources would be worth more in uses other than a levee. Suppose, however, that the project decision will be made at a referendum among the people in the community, with a simple majority required for passage. The referendum also includes the method to be used to finance the project: an equal per-capita tax (project cost divided by number of people in the community, or $4,000 per person). If the people in the community vote according to their individual net gain or loss from the project (as computed in Table 1–2), it will be approved (three for, two against). Does voter

Table 1–2
Individual Benefits from the Project: Example 2

Individual	Individual Benefit	Cost Share	Individual Gain
A	$5,000	$4,000	$1,000
B	5,000	4,000	1,000
C	2,000	4,000	− 2,000
D	1,000	4,000	− 3,000
E	6,000	4,000	2,000
Total	$19,000	$20,000	

---

[49]Voluntary associations (clubs) represent an intermediate option between a government with sovereign powers and individual action. Neighborhood associations offer an example popular in some regions.

[50]A small number of people may construct the levee without the full coercion of government. For instance, individuals A, B, and D could form a small property-owners association; the sum of benefits to those three exceeds the cost. These people might privately agree to build the levee for their protection—and benefits would spill over to C and E.

[51]This tax "system" is selected for convenience alone. It is not a "model" or an "ideal" in any sense.

approval make the project desirable for the community? Not at all—because the project misallocates resources: its cost is greater than the amount of benefits that it yields. The majority vote may misallocate resources when used for public decisions, as may any technique that does not involve comparisons of social cost and social return.

A third example further illustrates the problems of public decision making. Table 1–3 presents individual benefits from a project with a total cost of $12,500 and an equal per-capita tax method of distributing project costs. Total benefits do exceed total cost, so the project apparently represents an appropriate way to use scarce resources, and the project would be approved by majority vote if the people voted according to their individual gains or losses. The project, however, does leave one individual worse off. Is the loss to E less important to the community than the gains of A, B, C, and D? That answer requires a value judgment about the worth of the individuals to society, a judgment with which science and Pareto cannot help. One option would be to distribute costs in exactly the same proportion as individual benefits. That is the approach shown in the last column of Table 1–3. Any project for which total benefits exceed total cost has possible cost distributions from which all will be made better off. There is no redistribution of individual cost from which all will be made better off for projects like that demonstrated in Table 1–2, but choices about situations like that shown in Table 1–3 are difficult. Politicians make such decisions regularly, but not with scientific justification.

One voting rule would ensure that only projects that pass the Pareto criterion could be approved. That rule is unanimity, if we assume that people will not vote for policies contrary to their own best interest. This rule is seldom used because reaching decisions often requires substantial costs. James Buchanan and Gordon Tullock identify two elements constituting the full cost of making a community decision.[52] The first element—the cost of reaching the decision, the "time and effort . . . which is required

Table 1–3
Individual Benefits from the Project: Example 3

Individual	Individual Benefit	Cost Share	Individual Gain	Individual Share of Total Benefits	Benefit-Based Cost Share
A	$3,000	$2,500	$500	15%	$1,875
B	5,000	2,500	2,500	25%	3,125
C	8,000	2,500	5,500	40%	5,000
D	3,000	2,500	500	15%	1,875
E	1,000	2,500	−1,500	5%	625
Total	$20,000	$12,500		100%	$12,500

[52]James M. Buchanan and Gordon Tullock, *The Calculus of Consent* (Ann Arbor: University of Michigan Press, 1962), chaps. 6–8.

to secure agreement"[53]—rises as the agreement percentage required for the decision rises. As more of the group must agree on any issue, the effort invested in bargaining, arguing, and discussing normally rises. That investment is a real cost because the effort could have been directed to other uses. The second element—the external costs, or the cost from group "choices contrary to the individual's own interest"[54]—falls as the agreement percentage rises. (These are the costs imposed by a simple majority choice on individuals C and D in Table 1–2. Those costs could have been prevented by requiring a higher vote for approval.) The optimal choice percentage—the lowest combination of the two cost elements—usually would require neither unanimity nor one-person rule because the former has excessive decision costs and the latter has excessive external costs. Certain decisions are more dangerous to minorities (the losers in decisions) than others. For instance, many juries must reach a unanimous verdict because of the very high external costs that juries can place on people. For similar reasons, constitutional revision has high-percentage vote requirements.

Politics, Representation, and Government Finance

Decisions about public spending, revenue raising, borrowing, and so on are intensely political and involve personal interests, interest groups, political parties, and the process of representation. Therefore, irrational choices will be made, resources will get misallocated, and scams will get implemented. Sound governance processes and institutions can improve the odds of reasonable choices, but that's all. Even the clearest preferences of any particular individual are usually filtered through representation, and that one preference becomes part of a vote that may or may not be in the majority whose choice prevails. The many elements that produce a fiscal choice are diverse, but a framework devised by Anthony Downs for exploring the process of representation can help with an understanding of what influences these decisions.[55] He hypothesizes that political parties in a democracy operate to obtain votes to retain the income, power, and prestige that come with being in office. Parties are not units of principle or of ideals, but are primarily seekers of votes. A lack of perfect knowledge, however, permeates the system: parties do not always know what citizens want; citizens do not always know what the government in power or its opposition has done, is doing, or should be doing to try to serve citizen interests. Information that would reduce this ignorance is expensive to acquire. The scarcity of knowledge obscures the path that would lead from citizen preferences to their votes. Neither political parties nor elected representatives know exactly what the voters want, and the voters do not know exactly what the government is up to.

Several consequences for the representative process result. First, some people are politically more important than others because they can influence government action. Democratic government will not treat everyone with equal deference in a world of imperfect knowledge. One person, one vote is the ideal slogan, but it doesn't represent

---

[53]*Ibid.,* 68.
[54]*Ibid.,* 64.
[55]Anthony Downs, *An Economic Theory of Democracy* (New York: Harper & Row, 1956).

political influence particularly well. Second, specialists in influencing people will appear, and some will emerge as representatives of the people. These individuals will try to convince the government that the policies they support, and that directly benefit them, are good for and desired by the electorate. Information provided by these individuals will be filtered to provide only data consistent with the supported cause. A rational government will discount these claims, but it cannot ignore them. Third, imperfect information makes a government party susceptible to bribery simply because the party in power needs resources to persuade voters to keep it in power. Parties out of power are susceptible as well, but they have less to sell. It is no accident that corruption scandals involve more Republicans when the Republicans are in power and more Democrats when the Democrats are in power. Political influence is a necessary result of imperfect information combined with the unequal distribution of income and wealth in society. Parties have to use economic resources to provide and obtain information.

Lobbying is a rational response to the lack of information, but an important imbalance of interests influences the lobbying process. Suppose a direct subsidy to industry is being considered. This subsidy is of great total value to that industry. The total subsidy paid by taxpayers, of course, exactly equals the subsidy received by the industry. However, each taxpayer bears only a small individual share of that total subsidy. Who will undertake the expense of lobbying on the measure? The industry will, not the taxpayer, because the net benefit of lobbying is positive for the industry (comparing the substantial cost of lobbying with the substantial direct benefit to the industry) and negative for any taxpayer (because the substantial lobbying cost overwhelms the small individual share of the subsidy that could be saved).

These efforts to influence fiscal decisions take two general forms. Traditional lobbying is personal: "Affable men in suits would hang around swarming, sweaty legislative chambers, buttonholing lawmakers as they swaggered through lustrous bronzed doors, whispering in ears, slapping backs, winking knowingly."[56] The lobbyists know the elected representatives and have access to them (usually because they can be counted on for contributions and other campaign assistance, often because the lobbyist was once a legislator), know the unelected administrators carrying out public policies, and use these contacts to deliver the message of their clients on issues. Many former legislators and agency administrators—federal and state— develop lucrative careers as lobbyists, using contacts and friendships to help deliver the message of the interests they represent; their value is in their access to the people who remain in government. In one recent example, the member of Congress primarily responsible for the Medicare Prescription Drug Improvement and Modernization Act of 2003 (P.L.108173), an act that provided significant new revenue for the pharmaceutical industry and avoided price constraints on prescription medicines, left Congress for a position as chief lobbyist for brand-name drug companies.[57] Many

---

[56]Ron Faucheux, "The Grassroots Explosion," *Campaigns and Elections* (December 1994–January 1995). Lobbying state legislators can be crass: "It's one of the accepted rules in the unwritten guide to being a lobbyist. The way to get a lawmaker's ear is to get him a drink first." Christi Parsons and Rick Pearson, "Springfield Has a Gift for Grab," *Chicago Tribune,* July 6, 1997.

[57]As Robert L. Livingston, former head of the House Appropriations Committee who became president of a lobbying firm, said about lobbying: "There's an unlimited business out there for us." Jeffrey H. Birnbaum, "The Road to Riches Is Called K Street," *Washington Post,* June 22, 2005, A1. K Street in Washington is where the offices of the major lobbyists are located.

call this easy mobility between legislative or executive positions and interested private entities "a revolving door," and few believe it to be contributory to the public interest. But it is part of the way in which public policies get adopted today.

Grassroots lobbying is the mobilization of constituent action, reflected in letters, phone calls, e-mails, faxes, and other direct contacts to the elected representative. Mass campaigns had great successes in getting civil-rights legislation and in shaping other policies, but communications and information technologies make it much easier to generate what appears to be a groundswell of interest and masses of constituent communications on public policy questions, including those of government expenditure and taxation. Such manufactured communications are called "Astroturf lobbying" because they are only an artificial reflection of public concerns, not the true grassroots.

A final important point in the process of representation deals with the intensity of preference. In ordinary voting, intensity of preference is not registered. Each vote has equal weight. In a legislative body, however, the flow of many issues allows legislators to trade a vote on a minor issue (according to that person's preferences) for a vote on a more important one. Trading votes allows adjustments according to intensity of preference. For example, a member of Congress may be interested in getting a bridge built in her district, another may want a levee in his district, and a third may want work done on a military base in his district. They don't care one way or another about the other projects—the cost of any one isn't big enough to have a discernible impact on tax rates, so they see no obvious impact. In this circumstance, the members of Congress may trade their votes—I'll support your project if you support mine—to get a project approved. This process, called *logrolling,* can produce wasteful spending (an irrigation project yielding benefit to a small area at great national cost, for instance).

How does vote trading create wasteful spending? Let's refer to the example in Table 1–4 for those three projects previously noted. The table indicates the net benefit or cost to voters in five legislative districts of each of the three projects. Let's suppose that the members of Congress vote according to what benefits the people in their districts and that the projects are considered separately (no logrolling here). In this case, four out of five will vote against each project, and the projects, each with

Table 1–4

Logrolling, Project Bundling, and Government Waste

(Net Benefits [+] or Net Costs [–] to Voters in District)

District	Bridge in A	Levee in B	Military Base in C	Bundled Net
A	12	−4	−4	4
B	−8	12	−2	2
C	−2	−4	12	6
D	−2	−4	−6	−12
E	−4	−4	−2	−10
Net for Project	−4	−4	−2	−10

benefits less than project cost, all get defeated. Now suppose that the three members of Congress with project proposals get together and create a bundled proposal with all three projects and an agreement to trade votes. On a bundled basis, district A benefits in total (plus 12 from the bridge, minus 4 from the levee, and minus 4 from the military base), district B benefits in total (minus 8 from the bridge, plus 12 from the levee, and minus 2 from the military base), and district C benefits in total (minus 2 from the bridge, minus 4 from the levee, and plus 12 from the military base). Districts D and E do not gain from the bundled/logrolled package of projects, but their negative votes don't matter because the three members of Congress have a majority in favor of the bundle. Of course, legislative bodies, like Congress, have lots more members, but everybody has pet projects, and by combining the projects and logrolling, lots of money gets wasted. It's as simple as that.[58]

The required majority of those voting (in a referendum) can inflict severe cost on the rest of society with dramatic consequences for the social fabric. The major disadvantage of the referendum process must emerge from the absence of minority power in the direct legislation system. An initiated referendum has no provision for executive veto, creation of political stalemates in the legislative process, or changed negotiating positions in committees, all vital positions of lawmaking that can serve to protect minorities.[59]

The Layers of Government

In the United States, three layers of government with sovereignty of their own (not a single government) provide public services, levy taxes, and borrow money. Indeed, Americans must really love governments because we have so many of them: at last count, we had 89,527 of them—1 federal government, 50 state governments, and 89,476 local governments (of these, 39,044 were general-purpose localities and 50,432 were special-purpose units, including school districts).[60] Or maybe we don't trust governments at all, so we want to keep them small and weak. Whatever the reason, the United States certainly sets the standard for numbers of independent governments.[61]

Not all nations are governed in this fashion. Some governments are unitary, meaning that a single national government has legislative authority over the entire country. There may be local councils with certain powers, but they function only on the approval of the national government. In many unitary states, local revenue and expenditure programs must be approved by the national government, and a single consolidated financial program (or budget) exists for the entire country. Unitary states include Belgium, France, the Netherlands, Norway, Poland, and many countries of

---

[58]Example based on James Gwartney and Richard L. Stroup, *Microeconomics: Private and Public Choice,* 8th ed. (Chicago: Dryden Press, 1997), 503.
[59]John L. Mikesell, "The Season of the Tax Revolt," in *Fiscal Retrenchment and Urban Policy,* ed. John P. Blair and David Nachimaias (Newbury Park, Calif.: Sage, 1979), 128.
[60]U.S. Bureau of Census, Governments Division, 2007 *Census of Governments.*
[61]China has far more local entities, but these units do not have the degree of sovereignty necessary to count them as governments.

the former Soviet Union (but not Russia). The United Kingdom, historically unitary, is devolving some powers to regional parliaments in Scotland and Wales.

Other nations are federal. In the United States, states exist as an independent layer of government with full powers (including independent financial authority) and all residual powers.[62] Other important federal states include Argentina, Australia, Austria, Brazil, Canada, Germany, India, Mexico, and the Russian Federation (although recent changes there to reduce sovereign powers of regional and local governments and move them to the national government have moved the nation closer to being a unitary state—the national administration frets about the "power vertical" from national to subnational governments, a clear indication of less than robust commitment to the federalism concept). In each instance, to understand government finances—spending, taxing, and borrowing—one must understand the intergovernmental structure in the country. In no way are the subnational governments in these countries dependent departments of the central government, as they would be in a unitary state.

In the U.S. federal system, constitutional terms define the elemental financial powers and limits under which the levels function. First, there are powers and limits to national (federal) authority: Article I, Section 8, lists fiscally significant powers. These include the powers

> To lay and collect taxes, duties, imposts and excises, to pay the debts and provide for the common defense and general welfare of the United States; but all duties, imposts and excises shall be uniform throughout the United States.

> To borrow money on the credit of the United States.

> To regulate commerce with foreign nations, and among the several States, and with the Indian tribes.

> To coin money, regulate the value thereof, and of foreign coin, and fix the standard of weights and measures.

> To establish post-offices and post-roads.

> To raise and support armies, but no appropriation of money to that use shall be for a longer term than two years.

> To provide and maintain a navy.

Article I, Section 9, establishes some fiscal constraints on the federal government:

> No capitation, or other direct, tax shall be laid, unless in proportion to the census of enumeration herein before directed to be taken.

> No tax or duty shall be laid on articles exported from any State.

> No money shall be drawn from the Treasury, but in consequence of appropriations made by law; and a regular statement and account of the receipts and expenditures of all public money shall be published from time to time.

---

[62]The national government under the Articles of Confederation, precursor to the Constitution, lacked the power to tax. Payments from the states proved inadequate, so it is no wonder that it resorted to finance by printing money, which proved to be disastrously inflationary.

Of course, legislation and court decisions have, over the years, specifically defined what these powers and constraints mean in practice.

The major constitutional provision for states appears in the tenth amendment of the Constitution: "The powers not delegated to the United States by the Constitution, nor prohibited by it to the States, are reserved to the States respectively, or to the people." The states thus have *residual powers.* The Constitution does not need to provide specific authority for a state government to have a particular power: constitutional silence implies that the state can act in the area in question, thus establishing states as the sovereign "middle layer" in the federal system. Much of what states do in regard to their finances falls within these residual powers.

The Constitution similarly identifies, in Article I, Section 10, what states cannot do. Of fiscal significance is the prohibition against coining money. The Commerce Clause (Article I, Section 8, paragraph 3, listed above) prevents state interference with international commerce and commerce among the states, a particularly significant limit on taxing power and regulatory authority in a global economy. A later amendment (Article XIV, Section 1) requires states to follow due process in their actions and to afford equal protection of the law to all within their jurisdictions. These provisions have had substantial impact on service provision in the states, as courts have reminded state and local governments that fiscal processes must meet federal constitutional tests.[63] The federal equal-protection clause has been often copied in state constitutions. The dramatic change in school finance in California generated by the court case *Serrano* v. *Priest*[64] resulted from state constitutional provisions copied after those in the federal Constitution.

Local governments in the United States typically appear as captive creatures of their states unless state action has specifically altered that relationship. This principle was defined by Judge J. F. Dillon of Iowa:

> It is a general and undisputed proposition of law that a municipal corporation possesses and can exercise the following powers and no others: First, those granted in express words; second, those necessarily or fairly implied in or incident to the powers expressly granted; third, those essential to the declared objects and purposes of the corporation—not simply convenient, but indispensable. Any fair, reasonable, substantive doubt concerning the existence of power is resolved by the courts against the corporation, and the power denied.[65]

Dillon's rule thus holds that if state law is silent about a particular local power, the presumption is that the local level lacks power. In state-local relationships, state government holds all powers. That is a critical limitation on local government fiscal activity.

Several states have altered Dillon's rule by granting home-rule charter powers to particular local governments. Such powers are particularly prevalent in states containing a small group of large metropolitan areas with conditions substantially different

---

[63]Two examples: public schools, as examined in Rosemary O'Leary and Charles R. Wise, "Public Managers, Judges, and Legislators: Redefining the 'New Partnership,'" *Public Administration Review* 51 (July/August 1991): 316–27; and jails, as examined in Jeffrey D. Straussman and Kurt Thurmaier, "Budgeting Rights: The Case of Jail Litigation," *Public Budgeting & Finance* 9 (Summer 1989): 30–42.
[64]Cal. 3d 584, 487 P.2d 1241, 97 Cal. Rptr. 601 (1971).
[65]John F. Dillon, *Commentaries on the Law of Municipal Corporations,* 5th ed. (Boston: Little, Brown, 1911), vol. 1, sec. 237. See *City of Clinton v. Cedar Rapids and Missouri Railroad Company,* 24 Iowa 455 (1868).

from the environment in other areas of the state. The special conditions of such large cities can be handled by providing them home-rule charter power to govern their own affairs. State law can thus proceed without being cluttered by numerous special enactments for the larger units. When charter powers have been provided, local governments can act in all areas unless state law specifically prohibits those actions. Many times, however, fiscal activities are included in the range of areas that are prohibited under charter powers. Thus, it is better to presume limits than to presume local freedom to choose in fiscal affairs. That presumption is accurate if Dillon's rule applies or if charter powers have been constrained in fiscal activities.

Conclusion

An overview of the basis for government action certainly indicates that government choices made in budgeting and raising revenue will not be simple. Government will be unable to sell its services because these services are nonappropriable (neither excludable nor exhaustible). That means that government will not have market tests available to help it with choices and sales revenue will not finance operations.

Governments surely do not want to waste resources—after all, resources are scarce, and most things used by government do have alternative uses—so the benefits to society from government action ought to exceed the cost to society from that action. Determining whether actions really improve the conditions of the community gets complicated, however, when there is no basis for comparing the worth of individuals. The Pareto criterion for the welfare of a community does not require interpersonal judgments, but it leaves many choices open to political decision. Despite sophistication and rigor, science and analysis will not provide definitive answers to many government choices. Votes, either on issues or for representatives, will settle many decisions. Direct votes, however, will guarantee neither no wasteful public decisions nor choices that satisfy the Pareto criterion for improving society. They may well cause the imposition of substantial costs on minorities. Some problems of direct choice are reduced when representatives make decisions, but there will remain imbalances of influence and posturing to continue in office rather than following clearly defined principles. Lobbying—direct or grassroots—is one way in which some interests obtain extra influence.

Finance in a representative democracy is not simple. Governments should be judged on their responsiveness to public preferences and on their refusal to ignore minority positions. Not all governments can meet those simple standards, and not all budget systems used in the United States do much to contribute to those objectives. The U.S. structure delivers and finances services using three tiers of government— federal, state, and local. Although independent in some respects, there are important mutual constraints. The federal level has powers delimited in the Constitution; the states have residual powers. Local governments—under Dillon's rule—have only powers expressly granted by their states. Some states grant local home rule, giving localities all powers save those expressly prohibited. Few home-rule authorizations are complete, however. Thus, budget and finance functions vary widely across the country.

QUESTIONS AND EXERCISES

1. A business improvement district is considering the installation of a new lighting system for the district. If the lighting system is installed, all the businesses in the area will benefit, and there will be no way in which a business that does not pay for a share of the system can be denied full benefits from the system. The system will cost $4,000 and will benefit the five members of the district as follows:

	Individual Benefit	Cost Share
A	$1,500	$800
B	1,500	800
C	700	800
D	600	800
E	600	800

   a. Is the project economically feasible?
   b. Would any individual business be willing to install the lighting system (and pay for it) by itself?
   c. Would the project be approved by a majority of the businesses at a referendum?
   d. Does the project as currently structured meet the Pareto criterion?
   e. If possible, revise the cost shares to allow the project to meet the Pareto criterion and to pass a referendum.

2. Determine for your state the budget and finance constraints that the state places on local government. Does Dillon's rule apply? Do some units have home-rule powers? What is the extent of any such powers?

3. Private businesses have a great interest in quality primary and secondary education because today's students are tomorrow's employees. However, private businesses make limited financial contributions to this sector of education (excluding the taxes they pay to public school systems), even to market-oriented programs like vouchers and charter schools. What do you suppose explains this low contribution level? (*Hint:* Consider what sort of good primary and secondary education might be.)

4. The City of Dobra Kleb has decided to provide all citizens with a loaf of wholesome, nutritious bread every day in order to improve public health. The bread is to be distributed free of charge at city distribution centers located conveniently around the city. Does this program make bread a public good? Explain why or why not.

5. Many local governments in the United States operate public libraries that provide books, reference materials, Internet access, public meeting space, genealogical assistance, and other information/education services at no charge. Are the services of these local libraries pure public goods? What government functions are they seeking to serve? What privatization options might be possible? What services

should be free and what could be subject to a charge? What would be the concerns raised if many services were made available only on a charge basis? Would your reaction be different if charging for services were the only alternative that allowed the library to remain open?

CASE FOR DISCUSSION

CASE 1–1

Market Interplay, Municipal Utilities, and a Common-Pool Resource

Governments often are surprised by private responses to what appear to be relatively straightforward and sensible public decisions. It should be no surprise that businesses respond to higher prices for their purchases by trying to economize on their use of those more expensive resources. What may be surprising is how these reactions themselves create even more complex problems for the government. In the case described here, the normal business response is particularly interesting because it crosses between the operation of a municipal utility and the exploitation of a common-pool resource. Here is a case from the *Wall Street Journal*.

Consider These Questions

1. Identify the various types of goods (private, public, and in between) involved in this case. What was the primary objective being sought, and how was it being financed? Explain the unintended consequences of the financing approach. Is that financing approach appropriate for the type of good involved?

2. What options might governments in the Boston area have?

3. What would you recommend to prevent further damage?

City Dwellers Drill for Precious Fluid

As water rates go up, some Bostonians are going down—about 900 feet to find water. Average water and sewer bills in Boston have more than tripled since 1985 to cover costs of cleaning up Boston harbor. To cut their bills, several Boston businesses have recently drilled their own wells.

"It's a very alarming trend," says Jonathan Kaledin, executive director of the National Water Education Council, a Boston-based group that tracks waterproject funding issues. As customers "leave the system," those who remain must shoulder higher funding burdens.

If such drilling becomes a trend, it could undermine funding in a number of cities for projects to comply with clean-water laws. New York City water projects, for example, are expected to cost more than $10 billion during the 1990s, according to a recent report by Mr. Kaledin's group. Boston officials also worry that buildings in the city's Back Bay area, a fill-in swamp, may sink if wells lower the water table. Structures there rest on immersed wooden pilings that "will rot in two or three years" if exposed to air as the water level drops, warns Boston City Councilman David Scondras. City officials, citing over 400 known hazardous-spill sites in Boston, also fret that wells may tap into polluted water.

But the economic arguments for drilling are overwhelming, says Roger Berkowitz, co-owner of Legal Sea Foods, a Boston restaurant chain that recently drilled a well. Its 15,000 gallon-a-day gusher saves the company $2,500 a month by providing water for laundry and other uses. Though it isn't used for drinking, Mr. Berkowitz says, tests show water from the chain's well surpasses Boston's municipal water in purity.

SOURCE: Reprinted by permission of Dow Jones and Company, Inc., Copyright © 1993 Dow Jones & Company, Inc. All Rights Reserved Worldwide. License number 2912341473491.

CHAPTER 2

The Logic of the Budget Process

The budget process provides the medium for determining what government services will be provided and how they will be financed. It may also help establish how the services will be provided. The basic budgeting problem, simply stated, is the following: "On what basis shall it be decided to allocate X dollars to activity A instead of activity B?"[1] That is a pretty simple-sounding question, but, like many things in life, its application is where the problems lurk. How many dollars should be moved from private businesses and individuals to government, and, once moved to government, how much should go to each government activity? Indeed, the answer is remarkably clear: move money from private to public use and among alternative public uses until it is not possible to move one dollar from one use to another without losing as much from where you took it as you gain from where you put it. It's not a big deal conceptually. There is no lack of theoretical guidance as to how things should work. Markets for private goods do the allocation invisibly, as prices and profits provide the resource allocation signals and private businesses and individuals take it from there. But markets don't work for public goods, the home turf of governments, so here come the lawmakers to do the allocation job that markets can't. They may bungle the job (in a democracy, we elected them, so it is our collective fault), but the budget process is where those choices get made for government operations, not so quietly and we hope not so invisibly, but definitely politically. When governments tax and spend, making decisions within the framework of the budget process, they are doing for the public sector what the private market does for the provision of private goods and services. They are deciding how big government will be relative to the private sector and, within government, the relative sizes of the various-programs and agencies that the government provides. They even make decisions about how programs and agencies will operate. Each government has some method for making these fiscal choices, although the degree of formality varies widely. But we do know

---

[1]V. O. Key, Jr., "The Lack of a Budgetary Theory," *American Political Science Review* 34 (December 1940): 1137. The sentences after this quotation in this text do outline a precise budgetary theory. As it turns out, the title of the article is wrong because there has been no absence of a budget theory for many years. Indeed, there is a cornucopia of theories both of how governments ought to behave (prescriptive) and of how governments actually behave (descriptive).

what the budget process ought to be doing—moving resources to the best advantage of the population.

Except for the limited number of town-meeting processes, referendum decisions, and participatory budget processes, elected representatives make the primary spending and financing decisions. However, in budget preparation and in the delivery of services supported by the budget, nonelected public employees make many crucial decisions. Although these employees enjoy at least some measure of job security and may be less responsive to voters than elected officials, the logic of representative government presumes that such bureaucrats, and certainly the elected executives and legislators who guide their work, will be responsive to the citizenry.[2] And if they aren't, those elected officials deserve to be voted out of office.

Public organizations can operate with a haphazard budget process. Many local governments manage with casual or ad hoc processes, most nonprofit organizations are informal and unstructured with budget documents of limited utility, and a number of observers note that the federal government recently has barely been following its own processes even though they are rather rigidly laid out.[3] However, a system designed with incentives to induce officials to respond to public demands is more likely to produce decisions in the public interest, and thereby provide citizens with the quality and quantity of desired public services at the desired times and locations and at the least cost to society. At a minimum, the process must recognize competing claims on resources and should focus directly on alternatives and options. A major portion of the process involves presentation of accurate and relevant information to individuals making budget decisions on behalf of the citizenry. At its best, the budget process articulates the choices of the citizenry for government services (and how those services will be paid for) and manages efficient delivery and finance of those services. Before considering the logic of the budget, however, it is good to understand some basic facts about government expenditure.

Size and Growth of Government Expenditure[4]

Government spending can be divided into two primary categories: purchases and transfers. Both purchases and transfers need to be financed (as must interest payments on outstanding government debt, another spending category), and both entail a government payment, but their impacts on the economy differ, so the categories

---

[2]This is an example of the "principal/agent problem": bureaucrats and elected officials (the agents) are inclined to pursue their own self-interests, which may well differ from the interests of the citizenry (the principals). "Participatory budgeting," discussed in a later chapter, provides an alternate and direct channel for getting citizen priorities into the deliberations.

[3]Irene Rubin, "The Great Unraveling: Federal Budgeting, 1998–2006," *Public Administration Review* 67 (July/August 2007): 608–17.

[4]One might also measure the size of government by the public-sector share of total employment in the nation. According to recent International Labor Organization data, this is around 16.2 percent in the United States (or 14.5 percent in Germany). However, the governments in the United States (and other nations) do lots of spending without hiring government workers. For example, when the Department of Defense purchases a new aircraft, it buys from a private company and the aircraft was built by employees of that private firm. Looking up government employment data will not give much information about the size of government.

are differentiated in the national economic accounts. Furthermore, transfers and purchases are commonly treated differently by government budget processes, as is discussed in considerable detail in later chapters.[5]

1. **Government purchases** divert productive resources (land, labor, capital, natural resources) from private use by businesses and individuals to government use in the provision of education, national defense, public safety, parks, and all the other services that governments provide. Some of this spending pays wages and benefits to government employees, some pays suppliers of items used by these employees in the production of government services, and some pays private entities who have agreed to produce government services under contract. Most of this spending is for the provision of current services, but part of this spending is government investment—the purchase of long-life capital assets like roads, buildings, and durable equipment.[6] In the national income accounting system, the system that is used to keep track of national economic activity, this direct provision represents the government contribution to gross domestic product (GDP). In other words, when a city outfits its fire department to provide services during the year, pays its firefighters, or purchases a new fire truck, it will be purchasing from *private* suppliers. (In contrast with a socialist system, productive resources in the United States are mostly privately owned.) Some purchases will provide services within the year of purchase (consumption), and others will yield services over the longer useful life of the asset purchased (gross investment). These purchases represent direct acquisition of resources by the government, and these resources purchased will provide public services as they are used by the government. They represent the direct contribution of government to aggregate demand in the national economy.

2. **Transfer payments** constitute the other major element of government spending. These payments provide income to recipients without service being required in return. Such direct payment transfers to individuals include Social Security benefits, unemployment insurance payments, and other cash payments by governments to low-income individuals. These payments amount to almost 40 percent of all current government expenditure in the United States, so they represent an important contributor to the financing requirements of government and an important concern for government operations. While the government is not directly spending the money, it will need to find the money to pay for the transfers, using the revenue resources available to it (taxes most of the time). In contrast to government purchases, the direct impact on GDP is through spending by the transfer recipients, not through spending by the government. The transfers certainly will make things better

---

[5]Two easily available explanations of economic statistics as they relate to analysis of government finances are Congressional Budget Office, *The Treatment of Federal Receipts and Expenditures in the National Income and Product Accounts* (Washington, D.C.: Congressional Budget Office, 2007); and Enrico Giovannini, *Understanding Economic Statistics: An OECD Perspective* (Paris: Organization for Economic Cooperation and Development, 2008).

[6]This gross investment—meaning spending to purchase new assets without taking account of the depreciation (wearing out) of the existing capital stock—amounts to a bit more than 10 percent of total U.S. investment.

for the individual who receives them, but they do not involve direct purchases of anything by the government, nor do they represent direct provision of services by the government.

Table 2–1 shows the path of federal, state, and local government spending in the United States from 1960 to 2010. These data focus on the movement of resources between private and public sectors, that is, the way in which sectors of the economy claim production of the economy. They do not exactly coincide with the fiscal year, cash-outlay data that later chapters use, but they do make important points needed for the understanding of U.S. government finances.[7]

Total spending by all government in the United States—federal, state, and local combined—was 38.1 percent of total economic activity (measured by GDP) in 2010. That is considerably higher than the 26.2 percent fifty years earlier, and even higher than the 30.4 percent in 2000. State and local government spending as a share of the economy increased by about 60 percent over the fifty years, compared with about a 50 percent increase for the federal government. However, the increased total share in the last decade—from 30.4 percent in 2000 to 38.1 percent in 2010—was mostly from the federal government, and that federal increase was primarily driven by the cost of wars in Iraq and Afghanistan and economic stimulation efforts to combat the Great Recession.

Data in the table also highlight two other significant patterns in government expenditure: the importance of transfer payments (spending without making purchases) and of payments to government employees. These transfer payments are payments made to persons without a current work requirement made of them. At the federal level, these are predominantly Social Security payments to the elderly, persons with disabilities, and the surviving dependents of covered individuals; at the state and local levels, the payments are predominantly retirement benefits for former employees and unemployment compensation. These payments have increased substantially as a share of total spending. At the federal level, the increase has been from 21.2 percent of the total in 1960 to 43.7 percent of the total in 2010 and, at the state and local levels, from 9.1 percent to 23.9 percent over the same years. This expansion of share raises considerable concern for fiscal sustainability and is a topic discussed at length in later chapters.

Compensation of current employees, as the table shows, represents an important component of the cost of government services—many services are labor intensive. The share of total spending for state and local governments was

---

[7]The 1995 revision of the national income and product accounts brought significant change in how the accounts treat government expenditure, especially for capital asset purchases. The components in the new structure include the following: gross government investment includes total government expenditures for fixed assets; "government consumption expenditures" replaces "government purchases" and includes the estimated value of the services of general government fixed assets, as measured by consumption of fixed capital (as well as the purchases for use in the year); and government consumption and investment expenditures show the total current-year government contribution to GDP. See Robert P. Parker and Jack E. Triplett, "Preview of the Comprehensive Revision of the National Income and Product Accounts: Recognition of Government Investment and Incorporation of a New Methodology for Calculation Depreciation," *Survey of Current Business* 75 (September 1995): 33–41.

Table 2-1
United States Government Spending in Relation to Gross Domestic Product, 1960–2010

	1960 $ Billion	1960 % Total	1960 % Gross Domestic Product	1970 $ Billion	1970 % Total	1970 % Gross Domestic Product	1980 $ Billion	1980 % Total	1980 % Gross Domestic Product	1990 $ Billion	1990 % Total	1990 % Gross Domestic Product	2000 $ Billion	2000 % Total	2000 % Gross Domestic Product	2010 $ Billion	2010 % Total	2010 % Gross Domestic Product
Federal Government																		
Employee compensation	22.6	24.1%		48.3	23.5%		102.5	16.8%		193.9	14.8%		233	12.3%		466.3	11.9%	
Current transfer payments to persons	19.9	21.2%	3.8%	55.6	27.1%	5.4%	219.6	36.1%	7.9%	445.1	34.0%	7.7%	769.1	40.5%	7.7%	1708.3	43.7%	11.8%
Total expenditures	93.7	100.0%	17.8%	205.3	100.0%	19.8%	608.4	100.0%	21.8%	1307.4	100.0%	22.5%	1900.6	100.0%	19.1%	3906.9	100.0%	26.9%
State and Local Governments																		
Employee compensation	25.5	50.5%		71.1	53.7%		193	53.1%		415.9	51.9%		679	48.3%		1064.2	47.6%	
Government social benefit payments to persons	4.6	9.1%	0.9%	16.1	12.2%	1.6%	51.2	14.1%	1.8%	127.7	15.9%	2.2%	271.4	19.3%	2.7%	534.6	23.9%	3.7%
Total expenditures	50.5	100.0%	9.6%	132.3	100.0%	12.7%	363.3	100.0%	13.0%	801.7	100.0%	13.8%	1404.5	100.0%	14.1%	2237	100.0%	15.4%
All Governments																		
Employee compensation	48.1	34.9%		119.4	38.1%		295.5	33.5%		609.7	30.8%		912	30.2%		1530.5	27.6%	
Government transfer payments to persons	24.4	17.7%	4.6%	71.7	22.9%	6.9%	270.8	30.7%	9.7%	572.7	29.0%	9.9%	1040.6	34.4%	10.5%	2242.9	40.5%	15.4%
Total expenditures	137.7	100.0%	26.2%	313.2	100.0%	30.2%	883.1	100.0%	31.7%	1976.9	100.0%	34.1%	3021.5	100.0%	30.4%	5538.8	100.0%	38.1%

SOURCE: U.S. Department of Commerce, National Income and Product Accounts

NOTE: No adjustment has been made for intergovernmental transfers.

47.6 percent in 2010, about half the total, but not quite as high as in earlier years. This high share reflects the importance of teachers, firefighters, and police officers in the service delivery of these governments. Employee compensation is a much smaller component of federal spending—11.9 percent in 2010, down from 24.1 percent in 1960. The federal government more heavily contracts out work to private firms and also spends more on materials made by private firms (like military equipment and supplies).

Special attention should be given to the difference between price and physical effects on purchases. Government spending increased from $137.7 billion in 1960 to $5,538.8 billion in 2010. That increase resulted from two forces: (1) purchases of more "stuff" (trucks, computers, workers' time, etc.) and (2) payment of higher prices for the items purchased. The total increase encompasses both change in prices and change in physical (real) purchases. Because only the latter represents greater capacity to deliver service, it is important to divide the components of change. Sidebar 2–1 describes the basic mechanics of making price adjustments. The division of total spending into the portion that represents paying higher prices and the

---

Sidebar 2–1
Deflating: Dividing between Real and Price Change

The amount of money spent depends on how many items are purchased and what the price of each item is: 400 gallons of motor fuel at $2.10 per gallon means $840 spent on fuel. More money spent in 2014 than in 2013 does not mean that more things have been purchased if the prices of those things have changed between the two years. It is useful to know whether higher spending is the product of higher prices or more things purchased, since more spending because prices are higher gives no reason to believe that more government services are being provided. So how can analysts compare real purchasing power of money spent across periods when prices are different? The answer lies in the use of price indexes.

Suppose a set of purchases (commodities and services) cost $100 at 2014 prices, but only $75 at 2000 prices. That means that between 2000 and 2014, prices have risen on average by 33 percent ([100 − 75]/75, converted to percentage form), or the ratio of 2014 prices to 2000 prices is 1.33, (i.e., 100/75). This ratio of the value of a group of commodities and services in current dollars (or "then-year" dollars) to the value of that same group in base-year dollars (or constant dollars) is a price index. If 2000 is the base year, its index would be 100 and the index for 2014 would be 133 (or 33 percent higher than the base year). (The index could also be stated in ratio form. In this case, 2000 would be 1.00 and 2014 would be 1.33.) A price index provides a method for identifying to what extent higher expenditure reflects real change (more items purchased) and price changes (higher prices); the index shows how prices, on average, differ from those in a base year.

(continues)

**SIDEBAR 2–1
(continued)**

Here is an example from the budget of the U.S. government. Federal spending for natural resources and the environment increased from $17,055 million in 1990 to $43,662 million in 2010. The deflator for nondefense spending, using 2005 as base year, went from 0.6958 to 1.1256 between those years. That implies a 61.8 percent increase in prices between the years [(1.1256 − 0.6958)/0.6958]. Total spending for natural resources and the environment increased by 156.0 percent, but how much was due to more "stuff" to be used to provide services? In other words, how much of the increase was real? In constant (base year 2005) dollars, natural resource and environment spending in 1990 was $24,511 million [17,058/0.6958], and in 2010, it equaled $38,790 million [43,662/1.1256]. That means that the real increase was 58.3 percent—a big increase, but not as much as the 156 percent for spending without price adjustment.

Analysts use many different price indexes, depending on the expenditure category being analyzed; the *Survey of Current Business* from the U.S. Department of Commerce reports many of these, as do other publications. The data used here came from the federal budget. Prices of all items do not change by the same amount. Some go up a lot, some go up a little, some don't change, and some even decrease. All those changes are captured in a single index by computing a weighted average in which the price change for big purchase items counts for more than the price change for small purchase items. Traditional indices have used fixed weight measures: the base-year spending patterns establish fixed weight values for computing the averages. This practice creates a problem when there is considerable difference in the amount of price change among items: purchasers substitute those items whose price has risen less for those items whose price has risen more. The fixed weights become wrong. Analysts now remedy the problem by using a rolling average, or chain weights, instead of fixed base-year weights. The system sets the weights by taking the average growth of the current year and the preceding year. Price weights are thus constantly updated for changes in relative prices.

Spending calibrated in prices from one year can be easily converted into prices for another. In the previous example, if 1990 were to be the reference year, then the price index for 1990 is 100.0 [= (0.6958/0.6958) × 100], and the price index for 2010 is 161.8 [= (1.1256/0.6958) × 100]. The absolute level of the index and the absolute difference between years in the index differ according to the base year used, but the percentage change remains the same across base years. Price indexes and deflated (constant or real) values have meaning only in a relative sense.

Whenever an analyst is examining spending data over a time span of several years, it is important to make adjustments for changes in prices. In most eras, annual rates of price change in the United States have been relatively modest, but even a small annual rate maintained for a decade will make for a large difference between beginning and end. And price changes in some other countries have been much more dramatic than in the United States. When data from different years are being compared, it is always a good practice to make adjustment for changes in prices. It is never completely wrong to do so, and it can sometimes be catastrophic to fail to do so.

portion that represents purchasing more resources is one of the most basic tools of fiscal analysis because purchasing more resources creates the possibility of providing more services, while paying higher prices creates no such expectation.[8] When adjusted to reflect constant prices (2005 = 100.), the increase was from $939.3 billion to $4,914.6 billion, a big increase, but certainly less than the current dollar comparison would have suggested.

How does the size of the American public sector compare with that of other countries? Table 2–2 reports data for several countries of the Organization for Economic Cooperation and Development (sort of a club for industrialized, market-oriented democracies). Although the conventions used in these measures do not exactly match those of the national income and product accounts just discussed, the basic logic is comparable and can be interpreted in the same way. Measured by final consumption expenditure, the countries ranged from 30.0 percent of GDP in Denmark to 10.7 percent in Mexico; the U.S. value, 17.6, is below the mean of 20.9 percent. As noted previously, purchases do not measure the full extent of public-sector involvement in the economy. Total general government expenditure percentages range from 24.2 percent of GDP in Mexico to 58.5 percent in Denmark. The U.S. percentage, 42.2 percent, is below the mean of 42.7 percent.[9]

The nature of these government expenditures—in other words, the kinds of services governments provide—are examined in the next chapter. But it is now important to learn the general elements of the budget process and the language that applies in fiscal systems.

---

[8]The real and price changes do not add to the total change, but they are mathematically related. If X_{10} = total expenditure in 2010, X_{80} = total expenditure in 1980, and t = the percentage increase in total expenditure between the years; if D_{10}, D_{80}, and g are the similar variables for deflated (real or constant dollar) expenditure; and if F_{10}, F_{80}, and p are similar variables for price levels, then

$$X_{10} = X_{80} + (X_{80} \times t) = X_{90} (1 + 1)$$
$$D_{10} = D_{80} + (D_{80} \times g) = D_{80} (1 + g) \text{ and}$$
$$P_{10} = P_{80} + (P_{80} \times p) = P_{80} (1 + p)$$

In other words, start with the value in 1980 and add to it the increase to 2010 and you will have the value for 2010.
Total expenditure in 2010 equals real expenditure in 2010 times the 2010 price level:

$$X_{10} = D_{10} \times P_{10}$$

Thus, substituting into this equation yields the following:

$$X_{80} (1 + t) = D_{80} (1 + g) \times P_{80} (1 + p)$$

Rearranging terms, we obtain

$$X_{80} (1 + t) = D_{80} \times P_{80} (1 + g) (1 + p)$$

Because $X_{80} = D_{80} \times P_{80}$, then $(1 + t) = (1 + g)(1 + p)$. One plus the rate of price increase times 1 plus the rate of increase of deflated expenditure equals 1 plus the rate of total expenditure increase.
[9]Governments also interact with the private sector through regulations, legal requirements, and mandates. These effects are difficult to measure, but many would place the United States considerably higher in the league table than its ranking according to government-spending share.

Table 2–2
Government Expenditures in Selected Industrialized Countries, 2009

	Total General Government Expenditure (% GDP)	General Government Consumption Expenditure (% GDP) Final
Australia (2008)	35.3	17.6
Austria	52.3	19.9
Belgium	54.2	24.7
Canada	44.1	22.1
Czech Republic	45.9	22.0
Denmark	58.5	30.0
Finland	56.0	25.0
France	56.0	24.7
Germany	47.5	20.0
Greece	53.6	21.2
Hungary	50.5	22.2
Iceland	50.9	26.5
Ireland	48.9	19.5
Italy	51.9	21.5
Japan (2008)	37.1	18.5
Korea (2008)	30.4	15.3
Luxembourg	42.2	16.7
Mexico (2008)	24.2	10.7
Netherlands	51.4	28.4
New Zealand (2008)	41.9	20.1
Norway	46.3	22.9
Poland	44.4	18.4
Portugal	48.3	21.8
Slovak Republic	41.3	20.0
Spain	45.8	21.1
Sweden	54.9	27.8
Switzerland	33.7	11.6
Turkey	n.a.	14.7
United Kingdom	51.6	23.4
United States	42.2	17.6
Mean	46.2	20.9

SOURCE: Organization for Economic Cooperation and Development (OECD).

What Is a Budget?

A budget is a critical document in the operation of any modern public organization. It has an explicit meaning and it has several expected components. In simplest terms, a budget is a financial plan that carries forward the financial implications of carrying out a particular planned response to the anticipated operating conditions in a future period, normally a year. It has been prepared to fit expenditure programs within the constraint of revenues available in that future period. The budget takes a policy plan for provision of physical services and translates it into the cost of providing that plan. It is not a forecast of future spending by the organization, but it represents the intended response of that organization to the conditions that the organization expects to face in the future. It isn't a projection of government spending and revenue collections, and it isn't a target. It isn't a wish list of what the organization would like to do if it had no limits on its resources. And it isn't a shopping list of the things that the organization intends to purchase in a future year. A good budget says, in essence, these are what we believe are likely to be the operating conditions in the budget period (sorts of problems that will emerge, level of prices that the organization will have to pay for what it purchases, resources that we expect to have available within the period, etc.), and here is what we intend to do about the problems and opportunities. The expected operating conditions may not materialize as we have expected, but if they do, here is our operating response. If they don't, we will make adjustments on the fly.

Here are the blunt facts: If a program manager knows what she is doing and intends to do, she will be able to produce a budget. If she doesn't and is just filling a chair, she won't be able to do it. If she believes that producing a budget is keeping her away from the important tasks of running the operation, she should be relieved of duties before she creates any more damage. If you know what you are doing, you can do a budget and can and should use it as an important tool for management and evaluation.

The complete budget will include at least three distinct segments: a financial plan that reflects expenditures intended to carry out the planned response to the operating conditions expected in the budget year, a revenue forecast that reflects how much revenue the government expects to collect in the budget year based on the anticipated state of the economy and the revenue structure that the government intends to have in place, and a plan for managing any difference between the expenditure plan and the revenue forecast. The budget begins with a narrative discussion of what the government expects and how it plans to deal with those expectations; it then moves to a financial section that provides budget numbers. Later chapters of this text will go into considerable detail about the meaning of the sections of the budget, the methods used to prepare each section, and the tools used to analyze the sections. Later chapters will also discuss the revenue side of the budget process, including the development of revenue forecasts. However, budget managers are seldom directly involved in the revenue forecast, and they will be operating within revenue constraints prescribed for them, so our first emphasis will be on the expenditure portion of the budget.

Budget Process and Logic

The market allocates private resources without a need for outside intervention; price movements serve as a signaling device for resource flows. In the public sector, decisions about resource use cannot be made automatically from price and profit signals because of four special features of government decisions. First, public goods, the primary service focus of governments, are difficult, if not impossible, to sell, and, even where sales may be feasible, nonrevenue concerns may be as important as the cash collected. Consequently, profit can neither measure success, nor guide resource allocations, nor serve as an incentive to efficient operations. When markets have failed, it is a mistake to try to use simple market information as a first guide for decisions. Second, public and private resource constraints differ dramatically. Whereas earnings and earnings potential constrain spending of private entities, governments are limited only by the total resources of the society.[10] Resources are privately owned, but governments have the power to tax. There are obviously political limits to tax extractions, but those limits differ dramatically from resource limits on a family or a private firm. Third, governments characteristically operate as perfect monopolies. Consumers of government services cannot purchase from an alternate supplier, and, more important, the consumer must pay whether the good provided is used or not. Again, this makes market-proxy data based on traditional government operations suspect as a guide for resource allocation. Finally, governments operate with mixed motives. They are trying to achieve more goals than the single objective of maximizing value of the firm that characterizes private business decisions. In many instances, not only the service provided, but also the recipients of the service (redistribution) or the mere fact of provision (stabilization) is important. For example, the federal Supplemental Nutrition Assistance Program (SNAP, formerly the food stamp program) seeks to make healthy food available to low-income families by supplementing the money these families have to buy food. But the program is administered by the U.S. Department of Agriculture. In other words, it seeks to help low-income families, but it also aims to increase the income of American food producers (farmers), even though there may be more economical means of achieving either of these objectives by itself. Accordingly, more may hinge on the provision of a public service than simply the direct return from the service compared with its cost. Because these multiple and mixed objectives cannot be weighed scientifically and because achievement of objectives cannot be easily measured across programs, the budget process is political, involving both pure bargaining or political strategies and scientific analysis.

The Parts of the Public Expenditure/Public Revenue Process

Government spending must be financed, but, whereas receiving the benefits of a good or service is linked in the private sector to paying for it (you have to buy it before you can use it), in the public sector what the government provides does not determine how its operations will be financed. When a business makes shirts, it knows exactly from whom the financing will be received: the people to whom it

---

[10]Few have dared suggest natural limits to the ability of governments to extract resources from society since Colin Clark's proposition many years ago: "25 percent of the national income is about the limit for taxation in any nontotalitarian community in times of peace" ("Public Finance and Changes in the Value of Money," *Economic Journal* 55 [December 1945]: 380). That limit was based on zero inflation—so it may not have been truly tested. However, many successful modern democracies exceed that level with minimal general price increases (recall the OECD data in Table 2–2.).

sells those shirts. If people don't buy the shirts, the business is in trouble. But when the federal government decides to increase its provision of national defense, it must make another decision: Who will pay? It isn't going to sell the service; there is no link between who receives the service and how it will be financed. In other words, public expenditure and public revenue involve two separate planning processes. Payment for a government service is not a precondition for benefiting from that service; if the mosquito abatement district has seen to its job, both those who pay taxes to the district and those who don't will be free of mosquito bites.

There are two distinct components of public finance. The *expenditure* side of budgeting should set the size of the public sector, establishing what is provided, how it is provided, and who gets it. The *revenue planning* side, on the other hand, determines whose real income will be reduced to finance the provision of the budgeted services. Although the total resources used must equal the total resources raised (including current revenues, borrowing, and, for national governments, the creation of new money to spend), the profile of government expenditure does not ordinarily indicate how the cost of government should be distributed. In some instances—for example, the Holland Tunnel that connects New York and New Jersey under the Hudson River—it is feasible to identify the direct beneficiaries of the public service and to finance its provision through user charges, thus causing the operators of the facility to be more like a private business than a government, but the range of public services for which such financing would be practical is limited. (Charge financing will be discussed in a later chapter.) More often than not, government services are more like mosquito abatement than the Holland Tunnel, and revenue planning will be distinct from decisions about spending.

Figure 2–1 shows how dollars, resources, and public services logically flow from the revenue system to the procurement process to service delivery. The public procurement process involves exchange transactions (purchase on the open market) and, with few exceptions (eminent domain purchase of property and military draft being two), is economically (but possibly not politically) comparable to procurement by private firms. The unique public-sector features of the flow involve revenue-generation and service-delivery decisions, the concerns of the following chapters. Governments devote much of their attention to the part of the budget process that deals with expenditure and service-delivery processes; the next several chapters examine this part of the budget. Revenue planning is examined in later chapters.

The basic communication device of the process is the budget, a government's plan for operation translated into its financial implications. Governments prepare budgets as a means for (1) elaborating executive-branch intentions, (2) providing legislative-branch review and approval of those plans, (3) providing a control-and-review structure for implementation of approved plans, and (4) providing a template for external review of the legality of what the government has done with funds entrusted to it.[11] As will be discussed in a later chapter, the budget—by explicitly spelling

---

[11]Only appropriation and historical reports of spending and revenue are mentioned in the U.S. Constitution, Article I, Section 9[7]: "No money shall be drawn from the Treasury, but in consequence of appropriations made by law; and a regular statement and account of the receipts and expenditures of all public money shall be published from time to time."

Figure 2–1
Service Delivery and Revenue Systems as Separate Planning Processes`

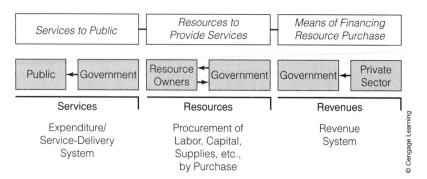

out provisions for spending and identifying responsibility for all money to be spent—provides the first and most critical defense against public corruption. Governments can also use the budget to communicate their program intentions for the future to the public, although not enough governments think of the budget in such terms and the public is not accustomed to looking at budgets at all.[12] At the minimum, the budget includes the expenditure plan, the plan for raising revenue to cover that spending, and the plan for managing any difference between revenue and expenditure. But public budgets are almost always considerably more than that minimum.

Budget Classification, Structure, and Presentation Years

The expenditure side of government budgets deals with plans in terms of spending money to deliver services to the public. Logically, the agency develops plans to provide services and estimates the cost of purchasing the resources necessary to execute those plans. In that respect, government operations are similar to those of private business: resources are acquired and used to deliver a valued output. The public agency's budget is its business plan for the next year, subject to the approval of certain representatives of the people.

The information in that plan can be organized in various ways to facilitate policy formulation, resource allocation, fiscal discipline, and compliance with the law. Three fundamental categorizations are:

1. **Administrative.** An identification of the entity that is responsible for management of the public funds and for provision of public services with those funds. In other words, the budget would be classified according to funds to

---

[12]Recent budgets of the U.S. government have been reformulated so that the main volume is intended as a communication device, with colors, pictures, and charts. It is not clear that the public has paid much attention, however, and not many budget analysts are particularly impressed. Perhaps governments should embed YouTube videos in their presentations to draw more attention. Because budgets of many governments are now posted on websites, such videos would be entirely possible. Mayors could introduce their budgets with a nice song-and-dance routine.

the police department, the fire department, and so on in the city government. This classification is critical for identification of responsibility and for ongoing execution of the budget.

2. **Economic.** An identification of the type of expenditure—compensation of employees, utilities to be purchased, supplies, and so on. This classification is also called line item (the items in a purchase list) or object of expenditure. This represents something like a shopping list for the government.

3. **Functional.** An identification of spending according to the intended purposes and objectives of the government. This classification organizes government operations into their broad purposes (like education or national defense) without regard for the entity responsible for the resources. It is a classification particularly suitable for fundamental resource allocation choices.

The three classifications are independent of each other, and many governments maintain all three in an effort to provide for full transparency of finances.

The most basic (and most traditional) classification is economic or line item, with its focus on inputs to the flow of service provision, that is, on the resources—labor, equipment, supplies, and the like—purchased by the government in the course of responding to the demand for service with organization according to administrative unit for control and responsibility. The budget approved for the fire department of the city of Tempe, Arizona, for 2011–2012 illustrates that classification (Figure 2–2; only a portion of the department budget is shown in the figure) and provides an excellent starting point for understanding how budgets are presented.[13] The 2009/2010 column reports the most recent budget execution, the 2010/2011 budget column represents the budget planned to be executed when the budget for that year was adopted, the 2010/2011 revised column reports how budget execution is proceeding (some categories have had to be increased, either by internal transfers or by more money being approved by the legislative body), and the 2011/2012 column represents the program plan for the upcoming fiscal year. The budget items are for expenditures to be made (purchases) by the department. This format is the basic structure for budget development in that it is the template an agency would use for estimating the cost of carrying out its plan for service.

The budget in Figure 2–2 demonstrates some important features. First, governments develop complete object-classification structures for use across all agencies, but not all agencies will make purchases in all object classes each year. (For instance, this department intends no purchase of landscaping supplies in some years.) The classification systems will not be the same in different governments, but it is important that consistent classification be used within a single government for tests across agencies and for meaningful aggregation of objects. Second, this display is for the fire department. There will be a similar budget component for each administrative agency of the city. Budgets to agencies provide a mechanism for control and responsibility in the process. Administrators of the fire department are responsible

---

[13]Tempe also prepares its budget using other budget classification systems, to facilitate presentation of what the administration intends to do and to make analysis and deliberation about the budget more productive. Presentation of multiple classifications is typical for well-run budget processes.

Figure 2–2

A Portion of the City of Tempe, Arizona, Line-Item Budget for the Fire Department, 2011–2012

	Fire	9/10 Actual	10/11 Budget	10/11 Revised	11/12 Budget
6010	Salaries	12,482,574	13,054,689	12,213,343	13,729,779
6011	Wages	38,789	44,410	76,288	44,581
6012	Overtime	1,511,084	1,520,733	1,544,456	1,621,930
6013	Vacation Pay	759,257	0	808,771	0
6014	Sick Pay	530,400	0	341,157	0
6015	Holiday Pay	686,005	677,351	774,297	815,548
6017	Bilingual Pay	16,911	16,802	15,600	21,812
6020	Event/Reimbursement-Labor	-163,217	0	0	0
	Salary & Wages	15,861,804	15,313,985	15,773,912	16,233,650
6120	Fica Taxes	311,937	404,624	295,803	354,219
6121	Arizona State Retirement	165,487	183,071	162,972	191,420
6123	Employee Health Insurance	2,801,802	2,094,547	2,068,373	2,185,274
6124	Pub. Safety Retirement-Fire	2,460,181	2,585,188	2,413,021	2,900,986
6126	Long-Term Disability	7,529	0	0	0
6127	Mediflex Reimbursed Expense	22,684	37,744	30,812	36,731
6133	Public Safety Cancer Insurance	15,300	15,359	11,300	11,343
6136	IRA Expense- DROP Participants	422,258	420,737	497,646	574,610
6137	Deferred Comp Employer Match	0	2,715	2,600	0
6138	Retiree HRA Contribution	200,445	0	0	0
6141	Vehicle Allowance Pmts	5,000	0	0	0
	Fringe Benefits	6,412,622	5,743,985	5,482,527	6,254,583
6201	General Office Supplies	5,190	8,000	6,000	8,000
6305	Uniform Allowance	205,267	251,422	146,422	146,422
6309	Batteries	11,457	6,000	7,000	7,000
6310	Chemical Supplies	9,353	5,500	5,500	5,500
6315	Landscaping Supplies	-20	0	0	0
6339	Hazardous Material Supplies	19,643	15,000	15,000	15,000
6340	Gasoline + Diesel Fuels	598	500	500	500
6342	Oil + Lubricants	8,948	6,500	7,500	7,900
6344	Propane Gas	232	0	0	0
6350	Hand Tools	3,002	4,038	4,038	4,038
6351	Minor Equipment	8,417	6,000	6,000	5,500
6352	Mechanic Tool Allowance	1,000	1,000	1,000	1,000
6356	Shop Supplies	4,097	3,500	4,500	4,500
6360	Traffic Control Materials	0	750	750	750
6366	Paint, Thinner, Etc.	38	0	101	0
6370	Printing + Copier Supplies	5,202	6,500	6,000	6,000
6401	Building Materials	59	500	500	500
6410	Motor Vehicle Parts	65,404	75,000	65,000	70,000
6415	Communication Equip Part	122	700	700	700
6416	Comm. Parts - Telephone	0	700	700	700
6420	Operating + Maint. Supplies	37,035	42,500	41,000	41,500
6421	SCBA Parts + Supplies	9,555	15,490	17,000	15,490
6422	Fire Hose + Nozzle	15,699	21,755	0	21,755

(continues)

Figure 2–2 (continued)

6423	Emergency Preparedness	-611	1,300	0	1,300
6424	Technical Rescue Team Supplies	10,028	9,000	10,000	9,000
6505	Books + Publications	1,293	6,500	6,500	6,000
6513	First Aid Supplies	97,026	75,000	67,000	75,000
6514	Awards + Recognition	6,433	1,000	1,000	1,000
6552	Other Equipment + Supplies	0	10,500	10,500	9,500
6556	Unrealized Discounts	1	0	0	0
6599	Miscellaneous Supplies	23,003	16,776	16,776	16,776
	Materials & Supplies	547,472	591,431	446,987	481,331
	(other object classes follow)				

SOURCE: City of Tempe, Arizona, 2001–2012 Budget for the Fire Department.

for this appropriated money. Third, the budget display includes information for the upcoming budget year (the plan). But it also includes comparable information for the current year—in this instance, both the initially budgeted amounts and the amounts revised to reflect likely actual execution—and for the most recently completed budget year. This presentation of these years provides a basis for the analyst (or for an inquisitive member of the general public) to get an idea of what changes might be in store for the city in the next year. Multiyear presentations are standard for government budgets. Unfortunately, nonprofit organizations frequently submit only single-year budgets to their boards to get approval of plans. It is not clear what these boards are supposed to do with only a single year. Possibly check the math?

The years appearing in a budget logically are these:

1. **The budget year.** The document focuses on the budget year, 2011/2012 in this example. These numbers reflect what the agency plans for operations, what it has requested for approval by various stages of review, and what resources will be required for the execution of these plans. These columns are the action items for consideration and legislative approval and, once enacted into law, become the template against which the agency will be held responsible. Some executive budgets will report what the agency requested initially, along with the amount recommended by the executive; this one does not.

2. **The progress-report year.** The budget for 2011/2012 will have been considered during the 2010/2011 budget year. The 2010/2011 columns in this budget report what was budgeted for that year and what the actual result is likely to be for the current year. (Frequently, only the likely result for the current year is reported; the figures initially adopted are not reported.) Some budgets, particularly those developed in executive and legislative reviews, also report the amount and percentage of any difference between progress-year and budget-year amounts. This one does not, but you can be certain that those changes were checked by those reviewing the budget.

3. **The final-report year.** This column reports the fiscal figures for the most recently completed fiscal year, 2009/2010 in this illustration. These figures provide a standard for comparison.

4. **Out years.** Some budgets (but not the one in Figure 2–2) also carry figures for out years, or years beyond the budget year in the request cycle. Some governments prepare a multiyear financial framework with budget estimates for from three to five years into the future so that a longer perspective on finances is possible. However, these out years are not part of the basic budget appropriations.

The federal government has recently used a budget year plus four years in executive budget summary presentations.[14] However, the Obama administration's first budget framework, *A New Era of Responsibility, Renewing America's Promise,* returned to a ten-year horizon in its budget summaries, a horizon that was used in presidential budgets from 1997 through 2002. The longer horizon reflects a concern with future implications of fiscal decisions, even though specific actions on those future figures seldom will be taken in that particular cycle. Nor should those fiscal choices be locked in early; priorities, needs, and fiscal circumstances may well change. The earliest multiyear presidential budget presentations date from the Reagan administration. Skeptics suggest that these were developed in order that control over the federal deficit could be shown eventually, although the deficit reductions were only in years at considerable distance from anything actually proposed in the budget. Later Obama budgets provide a five-year horizon.

Budget classification in functional form provides the same budget proposal as an administrative presentation, but it organizes the information to highlight resource allocation choices as opposed to highlighting the entities that are to be responsible for the funds. Table 2–3 illustrates the point with information from the federal budget. Federal outlays are organized according to function in the left side of the table and according to administrative department in the right. Total spending for both sides of the table is the same, just organized differently. The functional classification identifies spending for provision of a particular service or purpose category, without regard for the responsible entity. So spending to provide service for support of natural resources and the environment is considerably different from spending by the Environmental Protection Agency because a number of agencies are involved in supporting services for natural resources and the environment. And so it is with each function and for most agencies—several agencies contribute to the functions and single agencies are contributing toward multiple functions. The functional classification gives a view of fundamental resource allocations to deal with the array of public problems.[15]

Alternative classifications of budgets, including the strengths and weaknesses of each classification, will be discussed in greater detail in later chapters. However, behind any budget classification lurks some "grocery list" of inputs that will be needed for the service plan regardless of the vision or strategy for providing services that has produced

---

[14]In the middle of 1996, the Congressional Budget Office started doing ten-year budget estimates. Nobody but politicians and the media took these seriously, particularly the more distant years of the estimating horizon. It is hard enough to get reasonable estimates for the five years required in laws establishing budget procedures. Rudolph G. Penner, "Dealing with Uncertain Budget Forecasts," *Public Budgeting & Finance* 22 (Spring 2002): 1–18.

[15]The federal budget provides the standard multiple years for both administrative and functional classifications. They are not included in the table because of space limitations.

that plan. Just as a cook has to decide whether to bake cherry pies or angel food cakes before preparing a grocery list (the inputs), a government executive needs to have a service plan before creating the list of inputs to be purchased. And both the cook and the government executive will eventually need a grocery list to carry out the plan. Hence, the input classification is the most basic and durable format of all. In many small governments and nonprofit organizations, it is the only classification structure for the budget.[16]

Functions of the Budget Process

Governments exist to provide services. The budget process provides a time for decisions about the services desired by the public and the options available to the government for providing these services. A traditional expectation is that properly working budget processes act to constrain government and to prevent public officials from stealing. Indeed, public budgeting in the United States developed first at the municipal level to prevent thievery, pure and simple. Budgets should do that, but they should also do more, particularly in regard to seeing that governments fulfill their appropriate role in delivering the services demanded of them by businesses and individuals through choices made in the democratic process and that resources available to government are reasonably used. The process allocates resources among government activities and between government and private use. The great struggle that the budget process contains is between "needs" and "availability." On the one hand, the resources available to the government are limited by economic conditions and the extent to which the government is willing to apply its fiscal authority to draw revenue from the private economy. On the other hand, agencies and departments of government have commitments and opportunities to deliver services to the citizenry. Long-term fiscal sustainability—the ability of the government to maintain its operations on behalf of the public without deterioration of services or dramatic increases in taxation—requires that actual spending be within resource availability. That means continuing tension because opportunities for service always exceed resource availability. The budget process has to work that out as part of the agenda for sustainability.[17] Budget presentations that extend several years into the future, well beyond the term of current budget proposals, are primarily documents for fiscal sustainability and are usually designed to present the fiscal profile that is shown in the presentation.

---

[16]The Tempe budget elsewhere categorizes spending by cost centers within each department, so that it can identify the cost of providing each of its primary services to the public, and it provides substantial performance information. Its classification extends well beyond the traditional budget presented here for an illustration.

[17]Many nations have instituted what are called *medium term expenditure frameworks (MTEFs)* in an effort to provide this balancing of needs and availability over a three- to five-year horizon. The MTEF involves development of a top-down (from the central budget office or Ministry of Finance) resource constraint from a macroeconomic model, a bottom-up (from the agencies) estimation of the medium-term cost of delivering services according to current policies, and a reconciliation against government priorities. The framework feeds into the annual budget process to give better responsiveness to national priorities and some greater predictability of funding to agencies.

Table 2–3

Federal Outlays by Function and by Administrative Organization, Fiscal 2010

Superfunction and Function	$ million	Department or Other Unit	$ million
National Defense	**693,586**	Legislative Branch	5,839
Human Resources	**2,385,731**	Judicial Branch	7,181
Education, Training, Employment, and Social Services	127,710	Department of Agriculture	129, 460
		Department of Commerce	13,236
		Department of Defense–	
Health	369,054	Military Programs	
Medicare	451,636	Department of Education	666, 715
Income Security	622,210	Department of Energy	92,858
Social Security	706,737	Department of Health	30,778
Veterans Benefits and Services	108,384	and Human Services	854,059
		Department of Home	
Physical Resources	**88,753**	and Security	44,457
Energy	11,613	Department of Housing	
Natural Resources		and Urban Development	60,141
and Environment	43,662	Department of the Interior	13,164
Commerce and Housing Credit	−82,298	Department of Justice	29,556
Transportation	91,972	Department of Labor	173,053
Community and Regional Development	23,804	Department of State	23,802
		Department of Transportation	77,750
Net Interest	**196,194**	Department of the Treasury	444,338
Other Functions	**174,065**	Department of Veterans	108,274
International Affairs	45,195	Affairs	
General Science, Space, and Technology	31,047	Corps of Engineers-Civil Works	9,876
		Other Defense Civil Programs	54,032
Agriculture	21,356	Environmental Protection Agency	11,007
Administration of Justice	53,436	Executive Office of the President	582
General Government	23,031	General Services Administration	861
Allowances	....	International Assistance Programs	20,041
Undistributed Offsetting Receipts	**−82,116.0**	National Aeronautics and Space Administration	18,906
Total Federal Outlays	**3, 456,213.0**	National Science Foundation	6,719
		Office of Personnel Management	69,915
		Small Business Administration	6,128

(continues)

**Table 2–3
(continued)**

Superfunction and Function	$ million	Department or Other Unit	$ million
		Social Security Administration (On-Budget)	70,758
		Social Security Administration (Off-Budget)	683,420
		Other Independent Agencies (On-Budget)	−7,507
		Other Independent Agencies (Off-Budget)	4,700
		Allowances	....
		Undistributed Offsetting Receipts	267,886
		Total outlays	3,456,213

SOURCE: Office of Management and Budget, Budget of the Government of the United States, Fiscal 2012 (Washington, D.C.: OMB 2011)

Public financial managers expect budget procedures to (1) provide a framework for fiscal discipline and control, (2) facilitate allocation of government resources toward uses of highest strategic priority, and (3) encourage efficient and effective use of resources by public agencies as they implement public programs.[18] They also expect budget procedures to be the primary mechanisms for creating transparency in the fiscal operations of the government. The procedures work through budget planning and development, budget deliberations, budget execution, and audit. The processes of analysis and management apply equally to government and nonprofit organizations, although they are usually more highly developed and more routine in governments.

1. **Fiscal discipline and control.** The expenditure-control function in budgeting involves restraining expenditures to the limits of available finance, ensuring that enacted budgets are executed and that financial reports are accurate, and preserving the legality of agency expenditures. The control function—making sure that expenditures agree with the legal intent of the legislature—helps develop information for cost estimates used in

---

[18]*Public Expenditure Management Handbook* (Washington, D.C.: The World Bank, 1998), 17.

preparation of future budgets and preserve audit trails after budget years are over.[19] Much of the control comes from within the spending unit, to ensure that funds are being spent within legal intentions because it is better to prevent misuse than to try to punish it after it has occurred. A post-expenditure audit is external to unit administration. Budgeting and appropriating given dollar amounts to purchase given quantities of goods or services simplifies the fundamental external audit question: Do financial statements of the agency tell the truth, is the agency sufficiently protective of public resources, and did the agency use the resources provided it in the intended way? If the appropriation was for the purchase of 10 tons of gravel, was that gravel actually purchased and delivered in a responsible manner, was the gravel adequately protected while it was in the agency's hands, and do the agency's financial reports accurately reflect the gravel transaction?

One of the great challenges of creating a more responsive government may involve restructuring the notion of control away from inputs purchased toward services provided. Unfortunately, the definition of accountability in government has remained relatively constant over the past fifty years: "limit bureaucratic discretion through compliance with tightly drawn rules and regulations."[20] If government is to be flexible, responsive, and innovative, narrow control and accountability to the legislature and within the operating agencies almost certainly must change from internal operations to external results.

2. **Response to strategic priorities.** The budget process should work to deliver financing to the programs and projects that are of greatest current importance to the citizenry. Governments face many fruitful opportunities for providing useful services. Their resources are limited, so they must choose among useful options, recognizing that their choices both influence and must be influenced by community, state, and national environments. They should not have to work around legal or administrative constraints that protect certain activities without regard for their relative importance. All resources controlled by the government should be available to respond to the legitimate demands of the country; the competition for those scarce resources ought to be balanced among the alternatives, with the final decision about how the funds are used driven by the return from the competing uses, not barriers that hinder allocation of those funds. This is difficult for politicians and interest groups—both have an innate tendency to want to tie the hands of future generations with what they believe to be timelessly good ideas. Making sure that fire department horses had access to hay and water was critical in the nineteenth century; it isn't an issue today. Permanent dedication of certain shares

---

[19]An audit trail is a sequence of documents—invoices, receipts, canceled checks, and so forth—that allows an outside observer to trace transactions involving appropriated money: when the money was spent and who received it, when purchases were delivered and what price was paid, and how the purchases were cared for and used.

[20]Paul C. Light, *Monitoring Government: Inspectors General and the Search for Accountability* (Washington, D.C.: Brookings Institution, 1993), 12.

of a tax source to provision of particular services, called tax earmarking, is popular with lawmakers, but represents an effort to tie the hands of future governments, thus inhibiting the prospects of response to strategic priorities.

3. **Efficient implementation of the budget.** Budgets also serve as a tool to increase managerial control of operating units and to improve efficiency in agency operations. This function focuses on government performance and utilization of resources the unit has acquired with funds made available to it. The important concern is the relationship between the resources used and the public services performed by the unit. The public budget—as in a private business plan—serves as the control device for the government and identifies operational efficiency. For this purpose, the agency must consider what measurable activities it performs, an often difficult, but seldom impossible, task. The process should induce agencies to economize in their operations, identify the services of greatest importance to the populations they serve, choose best available technologies and strategies for delivering those services, and respond quickly when service demands or operating conditions change. Simple husbandry of inputs or resources purchased by the agency is important, but is not enough. Not spending funds made available to the agency in its approved budget is not praiseworthy if the agency has also failed to provide desired public services. And it certainly is not praiseworthy if other agencies have pressing service demands that budget limitations have prevented them from meeting.

Delivering Those Budget Process Functions

The budget process should enforce aggregate fiscal discipline, facilitate allocation of government resources to areas of greatest current public priority, and encourage efficient agency operations. Some process features that help to realize those promises are (1) realistic forecasts of receipts and other data useful for development of budgets; (2) comprehensive and complete application of the budget system to all parts of the government; (3) transparency and accountability as the budget is developed, approved, and executed; (4) hard and enforced constraints on resources provided to agencies, but with considerable flexibility in how agencies may use these resources in service delivery; (5) use of objective performance criteria for agency and government accountability; (6) reconciliation between planned and executed budgets; and (7) capable and fairly compensated government officials to prevent susceptibility to corruption.[21] It is expected that the budget will be authoritative, in the sense that spending will occur only according to the budget law, and that records will be accurate with recording of actual transactions and flows.

The budget should also be forward looking, in the sense that, while being prepared and adopted for the short fiscal period of only a single year or two, it sets

---

[21]Ed Campos and Sanjay Pradhan, *The Impact of Budgetary Institutions on Expenditure Outcomes: Binding Governments to Fiscal Performance,* Working Papers Series (Washington, D.C.: The World Bank, Policy Research Department, 1996).

the stage for years in the future. Therefore, the public is best served if the budget is formulated within a medium-term economic framework of four or five years, so that the chances of fiscal sustainability will be improved. That doesn't mean that the budget should be adopted for four or five years at a time.[22] Indeed, the expectations of the budget process are better served if the budget is adopted on an annual basis for better fiscal discipline and responsiveness to changed conditions. It does mean that an effort should be made to track the implications of fiscal decisions made in the current budget process into the medium term as a way to provide better guidance for decisions being made now.

Overarching all the budget process, all budget procedures, and all budget documents is a concern with *fiscal transparency*. This interest is inherent in democratic governance: If the public cannot see what the government has done, is doing, and intends to do, how can it give its informed consent to that government? Fiscal transparency requires that the general public, analysts, and the media have easy access to information about service delivery, financing arrangements, debt management, and the other elements that explain what is going on. Transparency does not mean pictures and pie charts in the budget document, but it does mean provision of accessible information about operations, achievements, and intentions. And it does not mean a data storm of discrete operating details, provided en masse in an arcane data format when inquiries are made by analysts, researchers, or the media. Closing the information door, responding to legitimate information requests in an unhelpful way, and presenting heroic pictures rather than operational information are inconsistent with public transparency and with democratic governance. It is, indeed, appropriate for government officials to believe that someone is watching them closely. After all, it isn't their money that they are spending, and they aren't operating programs according to their own tastes and preferences. It is the public's business, not theirs.

The Budget Cycle

Recurring (and overlapping) events in the budgeting and spending process constitute the budget cycle. Although specific activities differ among governments, any government that separates powers between the executive and legislative branches shows many of the elements outlined here.[23] The four major stages of the cycle—executive preparation, legislative consideration, execution, and audit and evaluation—are considered in turn. The cycles are in fact linked across the years because the audit and evaluation findings provide important data for preparation of future budgets. The four phases recur, so at any time an operating agency is in different executive and

---

[22]In 2008, the Duma of the Russian Federation passed an actual three-year budget covering 2009–2011, an exception to the multiyear budgets that offer only an advisory framework. Apparently, the budget had to be abandoned in 2009 because of political and economic developments.

[23]A parliamentary government would not neatly fit this cycle because there is no separation between executive and legislative branches. The city manager approach to local government does not easily fit the separation either.

legislative roles. But the budget still must be prepared and adopted in phases of different budget years. Suppose an agency is on an October 1 to September 31 fiscal year and it is March 2013. That agency would be in the execution phase of fiscal year 2013 (fiscal years are normally named after their end year). It would likely be in the legislative consideration phase of fiscal year 2014, just at the beginning of the executive preparation phase of fiscal year 2015, and in the audit and evaluation phase of fiscal 2012 and prior years. Thus, the budget cycle is both continuous and overlapping, as Figure 2–3 illustrates.

The federal fiscal year begins in October; many local governments have fiscal years beginning in January; all state governments except Alabama, Michigan, New York, and Texas start fiscal years in July. The fiscal year in Alabama and Michigan starts in October, New York has an April start, and Texas's is in September.

Executive Preparation

Several separate and distinct steps constitute the executive preparation phase. At the start of the preparation phase, the chief executive instructs all departments and units of government to prepare their agency requests. These instructions (sometimes labeled the "call for estimates") include (1) a timetable for budget submissions, (2) instructions for developing requests, (3) indication of what funds are likely to be available (either in the form of an agency ceiling or in terms of a percentage increase), and (4) overall priority directions from the executive. The federal instructions, Circular A-11 revised annually, appear on the Office of Management and Budget website for all to see. Many states also place their instructions on their budget agency's website. The instructions may also, but not necessarily, provide forecasts of certain operating conditions for the fiscal year, including things like input price increases, service

Figure 2–3
Phases of a Budget Cycle

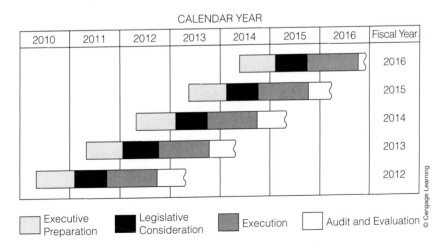

population trends, and so on, with an eye toward making sure that all agencies work with the same basic data. An important element in developing the instructions is a forecast of the economic climate and what it means in terms of revenue and expenditure claims on the government. A forecast of difficult economic conditions and limited revenue growth usually means instructions with limited prospects for the expansion of existing programs or the development of new programs, and possibly instructions to reduce spending.

The agency request builds on an agency plan for service in an upcoming year (the agency response to public demands for service) and an agency forecast of conditions in the upcoming year (the group of conditions influencing the agency, but not subject to agency control). These forecasts ought to be best estimates of conditions in the future. They are not necessarily projections, or simple extensions, of current conditions into the future. And the request is definitely not a forecast or projection of agency spending. For example, a state highway department request for snow-removal funds would involve a forecast of the number of snowy days and a planned response for handling that snow. For any snow forecast, the agency budget request will vary depending on how promptly the agency responds to snowfall (after trace snowfall, after 1 inch, after 3 inches, etc.), which roadways will be cleared (arterial, secondary, residential, etc.), and so on. The forecast does not dictate the request. Some agencies build their plans on inputs (the highway department bought 120 tons of road salt last year, so it will request about that amount for the budget year); this approach makes changes in service-delivery methods and practices difficult and is a pretty good indicator that the agency isn't doing the taxpayers any favors. In sum, the public-service demands and operating conditions will be forecasts, but the amount requested by the agency will reflect its planned response to those forecast conditions. Different response plans will mean different budget requests.

An agency develops not only a cost estimate for providing the services it plans to deliver, but also a narrative justification for the requests. The estimate and its justification reflect the large number of program decisions the agency has made. The chief executive's budget office gathers the requests made by many operating agencies and consolidates these requests. The budget office reviews budget requests for consistency with the policies of the chief executive, for reasonable cost and logical content, and for total consistency with spending directions. Often there are administrative hearings for reconciliation of an agency request and budget office adjustments. Finally, the executive budget document is transmitted to the legislature for its consideration. Law usually establishes the date of transmission to the legislature.

The budget document, or executive budget, incorporates all agency requests into a governmentwide request or plan. The requests by the agencies have been accumulated and aggregated according to the policy plan of the chief executive. Some legislative bodies, including the U.S. Congress, propose their own alternative budgets. Agency requests will almost always be reduced by the chief executive to produce an overall executive plan. And, of course, the expectation is that the vision or priorities of the chief executive will dominate the direction of the final plan. As is discussed later, the substantial changes made in agency requests before proposals are seen by the legislature reflect differences in attitudes and service clienteles of the agencies and the chief executive.

The executive budget is a message of policy; the financial numbers on spending, revenues, and deficits or surpluses are driven by those policies. Dall Forsythe, who once served as New York State budget director, emphasizes the point for governors (and all chief executives): "If you cannot use the budget to state your goals and move state government in the direction you advocate, you are not likely to make much progress towards those goals."[24] For the budget process to meet its expectations, the executive presentation for legislative deliberation should (1) be comprehensive (i.e., cover all government revenues and expenditures), (2) be transparent (i.e., present a clear trail from details to aggregate summaries of revenue and expenditure so that the implications of policy proposals and operating assumptions are clear), (3) establish accountability (i.e., clarify who will be responsible for funds, in what amount, and for what purpose), (4) avoid revenue dedications (earmarks) or other long-term commitments that could hinder response to new priorities or problems, and (5) establish as clearly as possible for what public purpose (i.e., desired result, not administrative input) the funds will be spent.

Legislative Consideration

In a government with distinct legislative and executive branches, the budget document is transmitted to the legislature for debate and consideration. The legislature typically splits that budget into as many parts as appropriation bills will ultimately be passed and submits those parts to legislative subcommittees. This consideration usually begins with the lower house of a bicameral legislature. In subcommittee hearings, agencies defend their budget requests, often calling attention to differences between their initial request and what appears in the executive budget. After the lower house has approved the appropriation, the upper house goes through a similar hearing process. When both houses have approved appropriations, a conference committee from the two houses prepares unified appropriation bills for final passage by both houses. The bills are then submitted to the chief executive. Appropriation acts are the outcome of the legislative process. These laws provide funds for operating agencies to spend in a specified fashion in the budget year. The initial requests by the agency reflect the plans of that agency; appropriation converts these plans (or portions of them) into law.

The chief executive normally must sign the appropriation bill before it becomes law, and thus gives operating agencies financial resources to provide services, but not all executives have the same options. Some executives may sign parts of the bill, while rejecting others (called *item veto power*); others must approve it all or reject it all, thus returning the bill to the legislature. Most state governors have item veto power, but the president does not. Some observers feel the item veto provides a useful screening of projects that political clout, rather than merit, has inserted in the appropriation bill. Others are skeptical about such power because of its possible use for executive vendettas against selected groups, legislators, or agencies.

---

[24]Dall W. Forsythe, *Memos to the Governor, An Introduction to State Budgeting* (Washington, D.C.: Georgetown University Press, 1997), 84–85.

Execution

During execution, agencies carry out their approved budgets. Appropriations are spent, and services are delivered. The approved budget becomes an important device to monitor spending and service delivery. Although there are other important managerial concerns during execution, spending must proceed in a manner consistent with appropriation laws. Law typically forbids (often with criminal sanctions) agencies from spending more money than has been appropriated. The Anti-Deficiency Act of 1906 is the governing federal law; similar laws apply at state and local levels and in other countries with well-developed fiscal systems. Spending less than the appropriation, while a possible sign of efficient operation, may well mean that anticipated services have not been delivered or that agency budget requests were needlessly high. Thus, finance officers must constantly monitor the relationship between actual expenditures and planned/approved expenditures (the appropriation) during the fiscal year. Failure to spend the full appropriation is not necessarily a good achievement. Central budget offices (the Office of Management and Budget for the federal government) normally handle the monitoring and release of funds during execution of the budget. Most governments have some pre-expenditure audit system to determine the validity of expenditures within the appropriation and some controls to keep expenditures within actual resources available. It is normal that funds will be maintained in a single treasury account rather than being distributed among separate agency accounts.

Spending is the direct result of appropriations made to carry out the service envisioned in the agency's initial budget plan.[25] However, because expenditures can involve the purchase of resources for use both in the present and in the future, it would generally be incorrect to expect the expenditure to equal the current cost of providing government services. Some of the current expenditure will provide services in later periods. (In simplest terms, part of the road salt purchased this year may be used next year, but much of the difference between expenditure and service cost will be caused by purchase of capital assets, such as buildings, trucks, computers, etc.) The cost of government would equal the amount of resources used, or consumed, during the current period—some resources coming from expenditure in that period and some from previous expenditures. Focus on expenditure thus renders an inaccurate view of the cost of government. Figure 2–4 outlines the flow of transactions and accompanying management information requirements between budget authority and service cost: (1) *budget authority* provides funding (the appropriation law approves agency Z's plan to publish an information bulletin), (2) *obligation* occurs when an order is placed (agency Z orders paper from business A), (3) *inventory* is recorded when material is delivered (business A delivers the paper to agency Z), (4) *outlay* occurs when the bill is paid (agency Z pays for the paper), and (5) *cost* occurs when the materials are used (agency Z prints an information bulletin on the paper).

Some reference to the federal structure may help clarify. Budget authority—provided through appropriation, borrowing authority, or contract authority—allows agencies to enter into commitments that will result in immediate or future

---

[25]Not all expenditure, however, results from appropriation. This complication is explained later.

Figure 2–4
Financial Information for Management

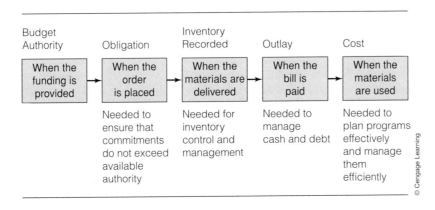

Figure 2–5
Relationship of Budget Authority to Outlays for 2012

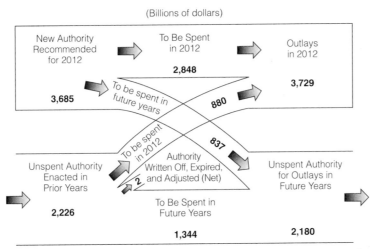

SOURCE: Executive Office of the President, Office of Management and Budget, *Budget of the United States Government, Fiscal Year 2012. Budget Concepts and Budget Process 2012*, p 127 (Washington, D.C.: U.S. Government Printing Office, 2011), 127.

spending.[26] Budget authority defines the upper limit for agency spending without obtaining additional authority. Figure 2–5 illustrates the relationship between budget authority and outlays envisioned in the 2012 federal budget. The budget plans outlays of $3,729 billion. Most of the outlays are based on proposals in this budget ($2,848 billion), but $880 billion (30.9 percent of the total) is based on unspent authority enacted in prior years. Therefore, budget authority in a particular year differs from outlays for the year; outlays may result from either present or previous budget authority.

---

[26]Borrowing authority permits an agency to borrow funds and to spend the proceeds for qualified purposes. Contract authority allows an agency to make obligations before appropriations have been passed.

Operating agencies should have managerial flexibility in the use of funds, allowing them to change the particular mix of inputs they purchase, so long as they can provide the level of service to the public that was envisioned in the adopted budget. Agencies almost certainly know more about new technologies, changes in prices of inputs that could allow cost savings, and emerging problems than does the legislature or the budget agency. Hence, locking agencies to the line-item details of the proposed and adopted budget usually inhibits efficiency and innovation. Ideally, the operating agency should be responsible for budget totals and agency results, not the details of exactly how money was spent (within laws of theft and corruption).

Audit and Evaluation

An audit is an "examination of records, facilities, systems, and other evidence to discover or verify desired information."[27] The audit seeks to discover deviations from accepted standards and instances of illegality, inefficiency, irregularity, and ineffectiveness early enough to take corrective action, to hold violators accountable, and to take steps to prevent further losses. The audit may be internal (in other words, the auditors are subordinate to the heads of the departments being audited) or external (the auditors are outside the structure being audited and, for governments, are ultimately responsible to the citizenry). In general, the auditors verify the assertions made by the audited entity. Information is documented on the basis of a sample of transactions and other activities of the entity—a judgment about purchasing practices, for instance, is made from a review of a sample of transactions, not from an examination of all invoices.

Post-expenditure audits determine compliance with appropriations and report findings to the legislature (or to a judicial body if laws have been violated).[28] At the federal level, the Government Accountability Office (GAO), an agency of Congress, supervises audits of agencies, although the actual auditing is typically done by agency personnel.[29] States frequently have elected auditors or independent agencies that audit state agencies and local governments. Local governments sometimes have audits done by independent accounting firms as well as by government bodies, although some such governments have not frequently had independent audits.[30]

Government audits may be classified according to their objectives into two types: financial and performance. Financial audits include financial statement audits, which "determine (1) whether the financial statements of an audited entity

---

[27]Peter F. Rousmaniere, *Local Government Auditing—A Manual for Public Officials* (New York: Council on Municipal Performance, 1980), 83.

[28]A pre-expenditure audit ascertains the legality or appropriateness of making payment. Such an analysis often occurs, for instance, prior to the delivery of payroll checks.

[29]The international group of audit bodies is the International Organization of Supreme Audit Institutions (INTOSAI). This group establishes international principles of organization and operation for these supreme audit institutions. The GAO is the U.S. member.

[30]Federal general revenue sharing required an audit at least once in three years for general-purpose governments receiving such money. The aid program is long gone, but the tradition of regular audits fortunately continues.

present fairly the financial position, results of operations, and cash flows or changes in financial position in accordance with generally accepted accounting principles, and (2) whether the entity has complied with laws and regulations for those transactions and events that may have a material effect on the financial statements,"[31] and financial-related audits, which "include determining (1) whether financial reports and related items, such as elements, accounts, or funds are fairly presented, (2) whether financial information is presented in accordance with established or stated criteria, and (3) whether the entity has adhered to specific financial compliance requirements."[32] These audits test financial records to determine whether the funds were spent legally, receipts were properly recorded and controlled, and financial records and statements are complete and reliable. They concentrate on establishing compliance with appropriation law and on determining whether financial reports prepared by the operating agency are accurate and reliable. The financial audit still must determine, however, whether there has been theft by government employees or their confederates, although this part of the task should be minor because of protections created by controls within the agency (internal controls).

Performance audits similarly encompass two classes of audits: economy and efficiency audits, which seek to determine "(1) whether the entity is acquiring, protecting, and using its resources (such as personnel, property, and space) economically and efficiently, (2) the causes of inefficiencies or uneconomical practices, and (3) whether the entity has complied with laws and regulations concerning matters of economy and efficiency,"[33] and program audits, which examine "(1) the extent to which the desired results or benefits established by the legislature or other authorizing body are being achieved, (2) the effectiveness of organizations, programs, activities, or functions, and (3) whether the entity has complied with laws and regulations applicable to the program."[34] Economy and efficiency audits might consider questions of procurement, safeguarding of resources, duplication of effort, use of staff, efficiency of operating procedures, management to minimize cost of delivering appropriate quantity and quality of service, compliance with laws governing use of resources, and systems for measuring and reporting performance. Program audits emphasize the extent to which desired results are being achieved, what factors might inhibit satisfactory performance, whether there might be lower-cost alternatives for obtaining the desired results, and whether there may be conflict or overlap with other programs. Some states link performance audits with sunset reviews: "a set schedule for legislative review of programs and agencies and an automatic termination of those programs and agencies unless affirmative legislative action is taken to reauthorize them. Thus, the 'sun sets' on agencies and programs."[35] States with such legislation typically include a performance audit as part of the preparation for action on agencies or programs eligible for termination.

---

[31]U.S. General Accounting Office, *Government Auditing Standards,* 1998 rev. (Washington, D.C.: GPO, 1998), 2–1.
[32]*Ibid.*, 2–2.
[33]*Ibid.*, 2–3.
[34]*Ibid.*
[35]Advisory Commission on Intergovernmental Relations, "Sunset Legislation and Zero-Based Budgeting," *Information Bulletin,* no. 76–5 (December 1976): 1.

A simple example may illustrate the focus of each audit. Consider a state highway department appropriation to purchase road salt for snow and ice removal. A *financial audit* would consider whether the agency had an appropriation for salt purchased, whether salt purchased was actually delivered, whether approved practices were followed in selecting a supplier, and whether agency reports showed the correct expenditure on salt. An *efficiency and economy audit* would consider whether the salt inventory is adequately protected from the environment, whether the inventory is adequate or excessive, and whether other methods of selecting a supplier would lower the cost. A *program audit* would consider whether the prevailing level of winter highway clearing is an appropriate use of community resources and whether approaches other than spreading salt would be less costly to the community.

When all audit work is completed, the budget cycle is complete for that fiscal year. In a complementary fashion, the federal inspector-general system in 18 departments or agencies works within units to identify fraud, waste, or abuse under 1976 and 1978 legislation and reports findings to department or agency heads and, eventually, to Congress. The system has potential as an adjunct to the audits conducted for Congress by the GAO.

Government Accounting and Financial Reporting

Proper accounting and reporting practices make government finances more transparent to constituencies, including public officials, the public, and the investment community. They should improve accountability to the public, including allowing the public to see whether current revenues are sufficient to cover current expenditures; they should make it possible to evaluate the operating results of the government for the year, including determining how financial resources are obtained and how they are spent; and they should help with assessment of the level of services that the government can afford to provide, including supplying information about the financial condition of the government. Important topics in accounting for governments include accounting and reporting standards, use of fund accounting, and the basis of accounting.

Standards

Independent authorities or boards establish the standards (or rules) for accounting and financial reporting; in the United States, the Financial Accounting Standards Board (FASB) sets the standards for the private sector, and the Government Accounting Standards Board (GASB) sets them for the public sector. Similar bodies do the work in other countries. These standards establish the appropriate practices that the accounting system will implement and allow any interested party to understand the finances of the government and to make certain comparisons of finances across governments. However, the accounts, even when prepared according to recognized standards, are not statements of scientific validity, as anyone even slightly familiar with the Enron experience of rigged accounts that showed profitability as the company went bankrupt in 2001 will understand. At best, they seek fair representation, not unassailable truth.

The accounting system allows the manager to assemble, analyze, and report data for the essential work expected of the budget process. The data must be complete, accurate, timely, and understandable for all public constituencies. The focus of the system is on revenues and expenditures, on financial balances, and on financial obligations of the government. The financial reporting system is expected to provide understandability (reports should be sensible to the general public as well as to experts), reliability (reports should be comprehensive, verifiable, and without bias), relevance (information provided should meet the needs of users), timeliness (reports should be issued shortly after the close of the fiscal year), consistency (the basis should be the same for all transactions and across fiscal years), and comparability (it should be possible to compare reports across governments). The accounting system is expected to provide the framework for financial control, but it is also expected to be a ripe source of information for government decision makers and the public.

The full accounting system combines several elements:

1. **Source documents:** These are the receipts, invoices, and other original details of transactions.
2. **Journals:** These are chronological summary lists of all transactions.
3. **Ledgers:** These are reports at varying levels of detail that present the balance in any revenue, expenditure, or other account.
4. **Procedures and controls:** These are the forms and instructions for classifying, recording, and reporting financial transactions in the source documents, journals, and ledgers.

Government accounting focuses on cash flows and improved transparency, control, and accountability to constituencies rather than the profit-and-loss emphasis of private-sector accounting. This difference brings several normal practices in government accounting:

1. Governments use fund accounting to permit compliance with legal restrictions on the use of revenue and to facilitate strong financial administration of multiple government operations.
2. Debt is segregated. Bonds to be repaid from general financial resources of the government are reported as obligations of the entire government; bonds to be repaid from specific funds (bonds issued to build a parking garage being repaid through parking garage revenue, for instance) are reported as such.
3. The budget of a government is at the heart of its system of "checks and balances." Demonstrating compliance with the adopted budget is a critical part of the accounting and reporting process. In the private sector, budgets are more in the order of an initial flexible plan, not an adopted appropriation law. Nonprofit organization budgets are somewhere in between.

Governments have historically made little attempt to account for fixed assets in their financial records. They built an infrastructure for the operations of general government, but did not account for its condition in their financial records. That meant that any balance sheet of the government's assets did not accurately portray the true financial situation of the government. It did not reflect depreciation and deferred maintenance of these critical assets. Accordingly, financial reports could portray a misleading sense of the condition of the government: failure to maintain infrastructure eventually adds to the costs of operation, can lead to more borrowing than would be otherwise necessary, can cause previous capital investment to be wasted if not adequately protected, can cause economic development in the community to be impeded because of low-quality government services, and misleads about the total cost of providing services. A GASB standard—GASB 34—now requires larger governments to account for these infrastructure costs in their accounts, and the standard will eventually extend to all governments.[36] The change is driven by the effort to ensure that governments provide information about the full cost of providing government services, something that the omission of a reflection of cost from the existing infrastructure has prevented in the past. How critical this omission might be is open to dispute: there is little reason to know the "going concern" value of a government because nobody is going to buy or sell it.

Funds

In private-sector accounting, a single set of accounts reports all material transactions and details of financial condition. Government accounting, however, segregates funds or accounts because there are legal restrictions on the use of government revenues and on the purposes of government expenditure. Mixing money prevents a clear demonstration of compliance with restrictions. Therefore, distinct funds ("cookie jar accounts") provide the necessary controls.

Governments prepare financial reports in a number of separate funds or accounting entities that are expected to be self-balancing (equal credits and debits across accounts). Generally accepted accounting principles (GAAP) define funds to be interrelated accounts that record assets (revenues) and liabilities (expenditures/obligations) related to a specific purpose. Municipal accounting divides funds into three basic types: governmental funds, proprietary funds, and fiduciary funds, each with subcategories.

1. Governmental Funds
   a. General fund: general revenues to the government, including taxes, fines, licenses, and fees. Most taxes and expenditures are in this fund. There is only one general fund.

---

[36]A symposium in *Public Budgeting & Finance* analyzes several major implications of the new reporting model produced by Statement 34: Robert S. Kravchuk and William R. Voorhees, "The New Governmental Financial Reporting Model under GSAB Statement No. 34: An Emphasis on Accountability"; Terry K. Patton and David R. Bean, "The Why and How of the New Capital Asset Reporting Requirement"; Earl R. Wilson and Susan C. Kattelus, "The Implications of GASB's New Reporting Model for Municipal Bond Analysts and Managers"; John H. Engstrom and Donald E. Tidrick, "Audit Issues Related to GASB Statement No. 34"; and James L. Chan, "The Implications of GASB Statement No. 34 for Public Budgeting," *Public Budgeting & Finance* 21 (Fall 2001).

   b. Special revenue funds: account for operations of government that are supported by dedicated revenue sources—dedicated taxes, fees, or intergovernmental assistance. Transportation trust funds are one example.
   c. Debt service funds: account for payment of interest and repayment of principal due on long-term debt.
   d. Capital projects funds: include resources used for construction and acquisition of capital facilities or major capital equipment purchases. The fund is dissolved when the project is completed.
   e. Permanent funds: account for resources held in trust, where earnings, but not principal, may be used for public purposes.
2. Proprietary Funds
   a. Enterprise fund: includes the financial records of self-supporting operations, like water or sewer utilities. Accounts for business-type activities of the entity, which are operated for the general benefit of the public, but are expected to support themselves from their own revenue.
   b. Internal service fund: includes the financing of goods or services provided by one agency or department to other agencies or departments of the government on a cost-reimbursement basis, like the operations of a motor vehicle maintenance department.
3. Fiduciary Funds: account for assets held by a government as a trustee for others. Fiduciary funds include (1) pension funds that are used to pay public employees' retirement benefits and (2) trust funds that are used to pay for management of resources, and their use is usually tightly controlled.

In a mature fiscal system, an independent auditor prepares an evaluation of government financial operations at the end of the fiscal year. If the auditor renders a so-called clean opinion, then the way that the government prepared its financial report is considered to have been fair and accurate. Among other things, the auditor's report requires that the agency's statements be prepared according to GAAP. Clean budget processes also bring all government operations together, regardless of the fund structure, in order to preserve the comprehensiveness of public financial decisions.

Accounting Basis: Cash or Accrual

The accounting basis—the method of matching revenues and expenditures over time—may be cash (revenue posted when cash is received, expenditure posted when cash payment is completed), full accrual (revenue posted when earned, expenses posted when good or service is used), or modified accrual (revenues posted in period in which they are measurable and available, expenditure posted when liability is incurred). The traditional standard, cash accounting, records money inflows when received and spending when money is disbursed, generally following the flows of the government checkbook. Those flows can substantially lag changes in the true condition of the government, and capital assets (buildings, highways, etc.) require a cash payment when they are acquired, but no purchase payments over their many years of useful life. GAAP requires a modified accrual basis for governmental accounting, in which inflows are called revenues, not the receipts of cash accounting, and outflows are called expenditures, rather than the disbursements of cash accounting. The revenue measure requires an estimate of taxes owed, but not yet paid; the expenditure measure requires inclusion of purchases for which payment has not yet been made. Expenditure is recorded when liability is recognized, generally meaning when the good or service is delivered to the purchaser and normally well before any check is written to pay for the purchase. GAAP also requires that individual government operations expected to be self-supporting use full accrual accounting, the method of the private sector. In full accrual, outflows, called expenses, are recorded in the period in which benefit is received from the resource.[37]

The accrual basis provides more information for decision makers and for managers, particularly in regard to the distribution of cost over time, and is not susceptible to end-of-year cash manipulations. It has the capacity to place costs properly in the relevant period. Only a handful of national governments around the world prepare financial statements on an accrual basis, although that is the evolving pattern for American state and local governments, and even fewer provide for depreciation of their capital assets in their accounts. The federal government does prepare the *Annual Financial Report of the United States Government* and that is done on an accrual basis, but it is not clear that the report matters much to either the public or government decision makers. The cash basis controls flows of cash and does not distribute cost accurately to periods, but it is less complex than the accrual system and is less subject to fundamental manipulation for impact on financial statements. As *The Economist* summarizes, cash "is far harder to disguise or invent."[38] Either system can be functional, depending on the needs of the entity.[39]

Comprehensive Annual Financial Report (CAFR)

The CAFR is a general-purpose report produced to meet the information needs of public officials, citizens, auditors, and investors. It is expected to be a publicly available document that encompasses all funds and accounts controlled by the government entity. It is comprehensive in depth and breadth, reported in sufficient detail to provide full disclosure, and inclusive of all funds and accounts. The report includes

---

[37]Accrual accounting applies in the preparation of financial reports. Accrual concepts can also be applied in the budget process. Accrual budgeting is used in some countries, including Australia, New Zealand, the Netherlands, Switzerland, and the United Kingdom, and partly used in many more. M. Peter van der Hoek, "From Cash to Accrual Budgeting and Accounting in the Public Sector: The Dutch Experience," *Public Budgeting & Finance* 24 (Spring 2005): 32–45; and Jon R. Blondal, "Issues in Accrual Budgeting," *OECD Journal on Budgeting* 4, no. 1 (2004): 103–19.

[38]"Badly in Need of Repair," *The Economist* 362 (May 4, 2002): 67.

[39]A number of countries that moved to accrual accounting have recently become concerned by some lack of transparency thus created, and others have delayed a move for similar reasons. Andy Wynne, "Accrual Accounting for the Public Sector—A Fad That Has Had Its Day?" *International Journal on Governmental Financial Management* 8 (2008): 117–32. What makes sense for private businesses may not be transferrable to governments.

three sections: an introductory section that seeks to explain the structure of the government, the nature and scope of its activities, and the specific details of its legal environment; a financial section that provides a comprehensive overview of the government's operations and includes an independent auditor's report on the finances; and a statistical section that provides details on government operations and its major financial trends. The CAFR should provide a comprehensive and reliable single source of information about the finances and structure of the government, with financial data presented according to generally accepted accounting principles, so that an external observer can understand the situation of that government without having to do additional research on definitions or context. This report gives a complete overview of finances, prepared according to GAAP, and is critically interesting to those involved in public capital markets. In other words, people who might be loaning money to the government really want to know what the financial condition of the government is, and the CAFR gives them the basic information they want to find out.

Budgets and Political Strategies

Budget decisions, both spending and taxing, are intensely political. They do not spin out of an analytic "black box" programmed by purveyors of information technology and program analysis. Presidents, governors, mayors, and other public executives cannot ignore political forces when they develop their fiscal proposals, and legislators certainly do not ignore these forces as they pass budget laws.[40] Understanding the budget process is vital for shaping public policy, and so is the analysis necessary to innovate and implement programs most likely to be in the public interest. But budget proposals do need to be delivered and defended in a political environment: truth and beauty alone will not save the day. Hence, an understanding of some strategic behavior is important for practitioners of the budget process.

The Incrementalist Insight

The incrementalist concept holds that budgeting is mainly a process of political strategy. It downplays the public-service-delivery attitude of models from public finance economics and the attempts at rationality from policy analysis. As outlined by Aaron Wildavsky and Naomi Caiden,

---

[40]Natural disasters are about as nonpolitical as can be—hurricanes and tornados, for example, are indifferent to the political affiliation of their victims. However, research shows that rates of disaster declarations are higher in states of greater electoral importance, the rate of disaster declaration is higher in election years than in nonelection years, and states with congressional representation on the committees with oversight over the Federal Emergency Management Agency receive larger relief payments than states lacking that voice. Even with natural disasters, spending is driven by politics. Molly D. Castelazo and Thomas A. Garrett, "In the Rubble of Disaster, Politicians Find Economic Incentives," *The Regional Economist* (July 2003): 10–11. This article summarizes several studies of disaster declarations and payments.

The largest determining factor of this year's budget is last year's. Most of each budget is the product of previous decisions. The budget may be conceived of as an iceberg; by far the largest part lies below the surface, outside the control of anyone. Many items are standard, simply reenacted each year unless there is a special reason to challenge them. Long-range commitments have been made, and this year's share is scooped out of the total and included as part of the annual budget.... At any one time, after past commitments are paid for, a rather small percentage—seldom larger than 30 percent, often smaller than 5—is within the realm of anybody's (including congressional and Budget Bureau) discretion as a practical matter.

Budgeting is incremental, not comprehensive. The beginning of wisdom about an agency budget is that it is almost never actively reviewed as a whole every year, in the sense of reconsidering the value of all existing programs as compared to all possible alternatives. Instead, it is based on last year's budget with special attention to a narrow range of increases or decreases. General agreement on past budgetary decisions combined with years of accumulated experience and specialization allow those who make the budget to be concerned with relatively small increments to an existing base. Their attention is focused on a small number of items over which the budgetary battle is fought. Political reality, budget officials say, restricts attention to items they can do something about—a few new programs and possible cuts in old ones.[41]

Dramatic changes in federal expenditure programs, beginning with the end of the Cold War, the Republican Contract with America in the mid-1990s, the beginning of wars in Iraq and Afghanistan, the Katrina hurricane disaster, the Great Recession of 2007–2009, and other political and economic changes in the recent past, have raised some questions about whether the federal budget process is as simple as Wildavsky and Caiden claim. There have been dramatic fiscal changes within extremely short time periods. But the facts remain that some policies—and resulting expenditure and revenue implications—do remain in place over the years; that most spending agencies at all levels of government do begin their new budget development by considering their approved budgets and the changes that should be made to them to adjust to new operating conditions; that budget comparisons in central budget offices, in legislative committees, and in the media are made between the proposed and prior-year budgets; and that the most rational place to get insights about the near future is from the immediate past. Information from looking at incremental change—positive or negative, big or little—ought not to be ignored simply because there have been major shifts in the direction of government spending, especially federal. Looking at change is a tool, not a religion, after all. Indeed, some states and many local governments build budgets from percentage increments to the historical budget base (the prior-year budget) in accord with some notion of fair shares to each agency. In many administrative systems, the base is assumed when the next budget cycle begins.[42] Of course, some local governments are so poorly staffed that they really don't know how to do anything better.

---

[41]Aaron Wildavsky and Naomi Caiden, *The New Politics of the Budgetary Process,* 3rd ed. (New York: Longman, 1997), 45.

[42]What is certainly incremental is tax law. For most major taxes, a tax code is adopted, and it remains in effect until explicitly changed or repealed. Tax changes are made by amending the existing code rather than by adopting a whole new tax. That is completely incremental.

Roles, Visions, and Incentives

Service-delivery choices in the budget process involve several roles, each with different approaches and biases. Participants in the budget process recognize and expect those approaches and are aware of the errors, incentives, and organizational blind spots inherent in each. The major attitude orientations are those of operating agencies, the office of the chief executive, and the legislature. All participants in the budget process seek to provide service to the public without waste. Each, however, works from different perspectives, resulting in different incentives and different practical definitions of that objective. A full understanding of the budget process obviously requires recognition of those roles.

1. **Operating agencies.** Operating agencies (e.g., the Fish and Wildlife Service, the Department of Parks and Recreation, or Immigration and Customs Enforcement) spend money for the delivery of government services. These agencies focus on the clientele they serve. It is unreasonable to expect an agency to be concerned with services provided by other agencies or to be interested in relative priorities among other agency services. The agency probably is not much concerned with comparisons of service cost with service value. The agency recognizes the value of services it provides to its clients and ordinarily tries to increase those services regardless of overall budget conditions of the government. There will be a virtually limitless expanse of service opportunities, many of which go unfunded simply because other uses of public resources are of higher priority to those making fiscal choices. Agencies, however, seldom recognize those competing uses and often complain about their own lack of resources. Large agencies have both operating people who have little direct contact with the budget and budget people who have little direct contact with service delivery. Both groups, however, can be expected to have essentially the same point of view and clientele orientation. Operating agencies usually have identifiable proponents in the legislature—particular people who support the agency in hearings and in committee deliberations—but it is seldom appropriate for the agency to make direct proactive contact with those people in an effort to go around budget decisions made by the chief executive. In most situations, the operating agency is not responsible for raising the revenue that it spends for delivery of services and accordingly can be excused for regarding those resources as free. Service to clientele is the principal focus.

2. **Chief executive.** The office of the chief executive, whether that of president, governor, mayor, or whatever, has budget specialists acting on its behalf. The offices have different names (federal: Office of Management and Budget; state: state budget agencies; etc.), but their function and role are the same regardless of name and level. Analysts in that agency conform to the chief executive's priorities, not their own. The analysts pare down requests from operating agencies until total spending is within available revenue. Reductions are typical for items (1) not adequately justified, (2) not closely related to achieving the agency's objective, and (3) inconsistent with the chief executive's priorities. Whereas agencies have a clientele orientation, the chief executive (selected

by the entire population) must balance the interests of the total population. Thus, priorities for an individual agency should not be expected to coincide with those of the chief executive because specific client-group priorities seldom match those of the general public. The interests of Corn Belt farmers, for instance, are not the same as those of the general population. And the chief executive is going to be responsible for raising revenue, so she is going to be doing some balancing that simply is not part of the operating agency viewpoint.

3. **Legislature.** The priorities of elected representatives can be expected to follow their constituents' priorities. Representatives are concerned with programs and projects serving the people who elect them. It is not reasonable to expect representatives to consistently take an overall view of agencies or agencies' programs. Representatives focus on a specific subset of the population, as is the case for operating agencies. Representatives, however, are oriented to a region rather than a specific client group. Most electoral regions do, of course, contain numerous client groups. And there is a strange lack of cost sensitivity here. Although legislatures will ultimately need to take the unpopular action of paying for government programs with taxes, legislators lose track of cost when arguing for delivering programs to their constituents—the benefits of the program are primarily to people in the legislative district, while the costs are borne by people throughout the state or nation. That diffused cost can make projects that are nationally unattractive extremely popular to the locality.

Forsythe offers another guide for chief executives in understanding the budgetary vision of legislators: "assume that legislators will apply a simple calculus in reviewing your budget proposals: they will want to take credit for spending increases and tax cuts, and they will want to avoid blame for budget cuts and tax increases."[43] The rule may not work all the time in every legislature—sometimes legislators take an ideological stand that all government is bad and happily cut spending—but otherwise it is a reasonable beginning assumption. It is particularly difficult to find legislators in favor of tax increases, especially of broad-based taxes that are not entwined in a complex package. Fiscal responsibility in practice seldom resonates with the general public.

Strategies

Budget proposals must be championed within operating agencies to be included in the agency request, within the administration for inclusion in the executive budget, and within the legislature to receive appropriation. A number of strategies, defined by Wildavsky and Caiden as "links between intentions and perceptions of budget officials and the political system that both imposes restraints and creates opportunities for them,"[44] are regularly used in these processes at every level of government and, indeed, in many different countries. They may also be considered devices for marketing and communicating the agency position.

---

[43]Forsythe, *Memos,* 48.
[44]Wildavsky and Caiden, *New Politics,* 57.

Two strategies are always in use for the support of budget proposals. The first is cultivation of an active *clientele* for help in dealing with both the legislature and the chief executive. The clientele may be those directly served (as with farmers in a particular program provided by the Department of Agriculture) or those selling services to the particular agency (such as highway contractors doing business with a state department of highways). The best idea is to get the client groups to fight for the agency without having the agency instigate the action when the chief executive proposes the reduction; such instigation would look like insubordination, and the agency might ultimately suffer for it. Agencies unable to develop and mobilize such clientele find defending budget proposals difficult. The media can also deliver the support indirectly, but only with some preparations; agencies normally get coverage because they have bungled something.[45] A strategy can help: "Try to stay in the news with interesting stories that do not put the agency in a bad light and that help you maintain good relations with reporters. Then, when you come close to budget time, you can give them press stories that show how well the agency has done with limited resources, and how well its pilot programs are working. Unstated is the premise that with a little more money you could do wonderful things and that if you are cut the public will lose valuable services."[46] The National Aeronautics and Space Administration (NASA) is a master at using the media to deliver its story through the budget process and serves as a model for any agency interested in learning how the strategy is played. With the exception of some reporters for the national papers of record—*The New York Times, Washington Post,* and *Wall Street Journal,* in particular—journalists are remarkably uninformed about government finances and are extremely susceptible to manipulation by interest groups and agencies. Websites, including those offering blogs, are often more specialized, and their writers may have great expertise, but they often have considerable political bias and are subject to no editorial supervision, so they can be both valuable and dangerous.

A second ubiquitous strategy that an agency may use is developing *confidence* in the agency among legislators and other government officials. To avoid being surprised in legislative hearings or by requests for information, agency administrators must show results in the reports they make and must tailor their message's complexity to their audience. All budget materials must clearly describe programs and

---

[45]If I a member of the media is itself involved as the agency, it becomes more interesting for mobilizing clientele. For example, in developing the fiscal 2006 appropriation bill for health, education, and labor programs, the House subcommittee proposed a reduction of about one-quarter of the funds for the Corporation for Public Broadcasting and an end to all funding within two years. Public radio and television stations mobilized their listeners to contact their congressional representatives in a blitz of announcements throughout the nation. The full House voted by a wide margin to restore the funds even as other attractive programs in that bill—like community health care for the uninsured, literacy training for prisoners, maternity group-home funding, and so on—were being eliminated. The fifty-seven programs being terminated did not have the capacity to mobilize clientele like public broadcasting did regardless of their probable value to society. Shailagh Murray and Paul Farhi, "House Vote Spares Public Broadcasting Funds," *Washington Post,* June 24, 2005, A6. A similar saga occurred in 2011 (Elizabeth Jensen, "Public Broadcasting Faces New Threat in Federal Budget," *New York Times,* February 27, 2011), and listeners were mobilized yet again.

[46]Irene S. Rubin, "Strategies for the New Budgeting," in *Handbook of Public Administration,* 2nd ed., ed. James Perry (San Francisco: Jossey Bass, 1996), 286.

intentions. Strategically, budget presenters must develop a small group of "talking points" that concisely portray their program. If results are not directly available, agencies may report internal process activities, such as files managed or surveys taken. Confidence is critical because, in the budget process, many elements of program defense must derive from the judgments of the administrators, not hard evidence. If confidence has been developed, those judgments will be trusted; if not, those judgments will be suspect.

Contingent strategies depend on the budget circumstances, particularly whether the discussion concerns (1) a reduction in agency programs below the present level of expenditures (the budget base), (2) an increase in the scope of agency programs, or (3) an expansion of agency programs to new areas. Some strategies seem strange or even preposterous; they are used, however, and should be recognized because the budget choices involved are vital parts of government action.[47] It cannot be emphasized enough, however, that strategy and clever rhetoric alone are not sufficient; they do not matter at all if the basics of the budget—its logic, justifications, mathematics, and internal consistency—are faulty.

Several strategies are applied as a program administrator responds to proposals for reduction in base (if a program may be terminated or reduced from its existing level of operation). These include the following:

1. **Propose a study.** Agency administrators argue that rash actions (such as cutting their programs) should not be taken until all consequences have been completely considered. A study would delay action, possibly long enough for those proposing cuts to lose interest and certainly long enough for the program administrator to develop other arguments for the program.

2. **Cut the popular programs.** The administrator responds to the proposed reduction by cutting or eliminating programs with strong public support (or at least releasing to the news media plans for such action). By proposing that the school band or athletic programs be eliminated, for instance, the administrator hopes to mobilize sufficient outcry to ensure no budget cuts. The careful reviewer knows of other activities that are particularly ripe for reduction, so that the political horrors painted by the administrator do not dominate discussion.

3. **Dire consequences.** The administrator outlines the tragic events—shattered lives of those served, supplier businesses closed, and so on—that would accompany the reductions. For instance, a zoo in Boston threatened to euthanize its animals if it didn't get more state funding.[48]

4. **All or nothing.** Any reduction would make the program impossible, so it might as well be eliminated.

---

[47]Important sources on strategy are Aaron Wildavsky, *The Politics of the Budgetary Process,* 4th ed. (Boston: Little Brown, 1984), chap. 3; Robert N. Anthony and David W. Young, *Management Control in Nonprofit Organizations,* 4th ed. (Homewood, Ill.: Irwin, 1988), 459–536; and Jerry McCaffery, *Budgetmaster* (privately printed).
[48]"Zoo May Close, Euthanize Animals," WCVB Boston, July 11, 2009 [http://www.thebostonchannel.com/r/20021259/detail.html].

5. **You pick.** The administrator responds that all agency activities are so vital that agency directors are unable to choose which would be reduced or eliminated if agency funds are cut. Therefore, those proposing the cut should identify the targets, thereby clearly tracking the political blame for the cut and hopefully scaring away the reduction. Anyone proposing a reduction for an agency needs a definite package proposal, in case such a strategy unfolds.

6. **We are the experts.** The agency argues that it has expertise that the budget cutter lacks. The reduction is shortsighted, based on ignorance, and thus should not occur.

7. **The Washington Monument.** A time-honored strategy of program administrators, when faced with budget problems like those associated with having no budget approved at the start of a new fiscal year or with running out of money in the midst of the fiscal year, is to respond with a dramatic gesture. In other words, the federal National Park Service says that it will close the Washington Monument, a popular tourist attraction, if the relevant appropriation bill is not passed by Congress (that is how the ploy got its name), or the local police department proclaims that it will no longer respond to vehicle break-ins because its fuel budget is being exhausted.

8. **Spread the bucks.** If the suppliers to a program can be distributed across enough legislative districts, the representatives of those districts can become valuable guardians of the program, should any executive attempt to reduce or eliminate the program. The most striking example of an application of this strategy is the defense of the V-22 Osprey, a tiltrotor aircraft capable of vertical takeoff and landing, as well as short takeoff and landing. It originated in the early 1980s as an aircraft that had some capacities of both a helicopter and a fixed-wing aircraft. The aircraft struggled with difficult development, an embarrassing tendency to crash, failure to meet performance specifications, cost overruns, and a lurking suspicion that it added no actual capability that the Defense Department needed or wanted very much. Administrations sought to terminate the program and defense secretaries tried to kill the program—but it lived on. The prime contractor for the project had made sure that subcontractors for the program were salted around key congressional districts so that people in legislative power would be trusted to make sure that the next piece of acquisition cost would be included in the adopted appropriation.

Other strategies apply when the agency seeks to continue or augment operations of its existing program:

1. **Round up.** Rounding program estimates—workload, prices, costs, and the like—upward to the next highest hundred, thousand, or million creates substantial slack when consistently done.

2. **"If it don't run, chrome it."** The budget presentation sparkles with data, charts, graphs, glittering PowerPoint, and other state-of-the-art management trappings. Much of the material may not relate directly to the decision at hand, and the base data may not be particularly accurate, but the quality of the show aims to overpower weak substance.

3. **Sprinkling.** Budget items are slightly increased, either in hard-to-detect general categories or across the board, after the basic request has been prepared. The layer of excess is spread so thinly that it cannot be clearly identified as padding. If enacted in full, the budget would allow the agency a significant operating cushion. Such a practice may leave no traces; however, surpluses might emerge during budget execution.

4. **Numbers game.** Agency administrators may discuss physical units—for example, facilities operated, grants initiated, or acres maintained—rather than the funds requested and spent. The intent is to divert attention from substantially increased spending for each unit.

5. **Workload and backlog.** Administrators often base their request on greater client demands or a backlog of unfilled requests. The argument is reasonable if the workload measure is germane to the agency's function, if the agency is doing something that needs to be done, and if the backlogs are not simply residuals of poor management of existing resources.

6. **The accounting trap.** Either side in the budget process may argue that a proposed expenditure must be made (or is forbidden) because the accounting system controls such transactions. The argument can be politically important. However, accounting systems exist to help management implement policy and to provide information for policy decisions. Policy choices should not be made difficult by the accounting system.

Programs and agencies develop an institutional momentum. Proposals for a new program entail special challenges because the new program lacks any such momentum. Some budget processes even place new programs in a separate decision structure that considers new programs only after available revenues have covered all requests from existing activities. Other processes cause trouble for proposed programs simply because clients and constituents who could provide political support have not yet developed. Some strategies are characteristic of the new proposal:

1. **Old stuff.** Administrators may disguise new programs as simple extensions or growth of existing operations. When the new operation has developed an institutional foundation (directors, clients, and political allies), it can be spun off into an independent life, having been nurtured through early development by existing agency operations.

2. **Foot-in-the-door financing.** A project starts with a small amount of funding, possibly under the guise of a pilot or demonstration program or as a feasibility study. Modest amounts build each year until the program is operational and has developed a constituency. By the time full costs are identified, it may be more economical to spend more money to finish the task rather than irretrievably abandoning the costs sunk into the project. Here is a classic example: In 1991, the Royal Thai Air Force purchased a squadron of F-16 fighters. The military lacked sufficient money to make the purchase, so the planes were purchased without engines. Delivery was scheduled for 1995, which left plenty of time to gather the extra funds. But a new Thai government took office in 1992. Although it wanted to exert control over military spending, its options were to

approve more money for the engines or to pay for nonflying (probably undeliverable) airplanes. Rather than getting no return from the $560 million spent on airplanes, training, and a new radar system, the purchase was approved—even though the new government sought to constrain military spending and to devote its scarce resources to domestic use.[49]

3. **It pays for itself.** Supporters of new programs sometimes argue that the program will produce more revenue than it will cost. Although many revenue department activities may do just that, the case is made in other areas as well. Examples include arguments made by law enforcement agencies concerning collections of fines and, with growing frequency, by economic development departments concerning induced tax collections from economic activity lured by the project.

4. **Spend to save.** Expenditure on the proposal would cause cost reduction somewhere else in the government. The net budget impact would be nil, or even positive, if spending $1 in agency A would allow spending to be reduced by $1 or more either in that agency or somewhere else in government. Whether that claimed spending reduction actually would occur is another argument.

5. **Crisis.** The proposal may be linked to a catastrophe or overwhelming problem—AIDS, economic underdevelopment, homelessness, homeland security, and so on—even though the link may be tenuous, simply because the agency perceives that such proposals are less likely to be reduced. But an agency must use caution because skeptics will question why it did not deal with the problem before it reached crisis proportions. A substrategy that might merit a category of its own is "Tie it to Terror." For many years (at least since 1966), the National Park Service has sought an underground visitors center at the Washington Monument. When the proposal emerged again in 2003, its name had changed from "Washington Monument Visitors Center Plan" to "Washington Monument Permanent Security Improvements." One critic observes: "As soon as you say that it's for security, any project—however questionable—is able to move forward because everyone is afraid that one of these great monuments might be destroyed on their watches. But in reality, [the underground proposal] has nothing to do with security."[50] At least so far, it hasn't gotten the visitors center and the link between the center and security still is being used as justification.

6. **Mislabeling.** The actual nature of a program may be hidden by mixing it with another, more politically attractive program. Examples abound: military installations may have blast-suppression areas that look strangely like golf courses; university dormitories or office buildings may have roofs that have seats convenient for viewing events on the football field; the rigid upper-surface covers for the new sewers may support vehicular traffic. These

---

[49]Cynthia Owens, "And Now They'll Sneak in Orders for Aviation Fuel and Parachutes," *Wall Street Journal,* January 28, 1993, C-1.
[50]Monte Reel, "Washington Monument Dispute Resurfaces," *Washington Post,* August 4, 2003, A01.

strategies, however, require an essentially supportive environment; all key participants in the budget process must be in agreement on the proposal because budget people remember and make allowances in later years.

7. **What they did makes us do it.** An action taken by another entity may place demands on the agency beyond what could be accommodated by normal management of existing programs. If school libraries were to be closed and teachers continued to assign reference work, local public libraries might argue for new programs to accommodate student requests for assistance. Harsh federal sentencing guidelines for certain classes of drug offenses means that new federal prisons must be built.

8. **Mandates.** Some external entity (a court, a federal agency, the state, etc.) may legally require an agency action that would entail greater expenditure. Rather than rearranging operations to accommodate the new requirement, an agency may use the mandate as an argument for additional funds. The agency may in fact have requested that the external entity issue the mandate as a budget strategy. The approach can be compelling, but analysts need to determine the grounds for and authority of the mandate and the extent to which revised operations can accommodate the mandate before simply accepting the argument for an increased budget. The approach also has applications for base expansion and, if the time frame is sufficient, for defense against cuts.

9. **Matching the competition.** Agencies often compare their programs with those operated by others and use the comparison as a basis for adding new programs. (Seldom does the comparison lead to a proposal that some programs be eliminated because similar agencies do not have them.) The argument is also used to expand existing programs.

10. **It's so small.** Program proponents may argue that a request is not large enough to require full review, that its trivial budgetary consequences do not make the review a reasonable use of time. Those who understand foot-in-the-door financing are naturally wary of such arguments and generally respond that smallness makes activities natural candidates for absorption by the agency without extra funds. Everett Dirksen, a senator from Illinois of many years ago, holds everlasting fame for saying: "A million here, a million there, pretty soon you're talking about real money." Of course, inflation has changed the idea to billions, not millions—and it starts with small stuff.

11. **It's the local economy.** Public projects are often supported on the basis that they will bring local economic development and prosperity. For instance, the development of a local arts program may be supported because of the incomes it will generate and the business activity that spending from those incomes will create. But this impact is not the result of the arts program. It is the result of spending. Building a new city dump would have the same outcome in terms of incomes and business activity. Legitimate arguments for an arts program need to hinge on the services of the arts program, not impacts that are generic to any spending (particularly spending financed by those from outside the locality).

Conclusion

The budget process is where choices about the allocation of public resources get made. The flow of budget decisions from plan to expenditure is accomplished in a four-phase cycle involving executive preparation, legislative consideration, execution, and audit. Although budgets are constructed and approved in a political environment, it is not clear that appropriations are the simple product of adding a small increment to the prior-year appropriation. There is at least some room for attempts at rational choice in budget structures. Later chapters will prepare you to do the tasks required in the budget process and to understand how the process is carried out in practice.

QUESTIONS AND EXERCISES

1. The relative size of government has been a continuing public policy concern. Size and growth questions have been important at the state and local levels, as demonstrated by several state referenda to limit federal, state, or local expenditures. Some evidence for those discussions can be drawn from data on trends of spending activity, using information from the Department of Commerce's National Income and Product Accounts and the Census Bureau's Government and the Bureau of Economic Analysis website (www.bea.gov). From those sources, prepare answers to these questions about the size of government in the United States.

   a. Has the public sector grown relative to the private sector? How does the size of the federal government compare with that of state and local governments? (A benchmark for comparison is the percentage of GDP or personal income accounted for by the appropriate sector.)
   b. Which sectors have grown fastest? Compare growth of the public sector in your state with that of its neighbors and of the nation. Why might a comparison based on expenditure growth differ from one based on employment?
   c. Calculate national defense spending as a percentage of total federal government outlays and as a percentage of GDP. Can you identify the impact of the end of the Cold War and the beginning of the wars in Afghanistan and Iraq on these data?
   d. Which functions account for the greatest share of federal, state, and local government expenditures? Does the pattern differ much among states?
   e. What is the relative significance of local government expenditure compared to state government expenditure in your state? (Make the comparison first counting state aid to local government as state expenditure. Then omit that portion from state expenditure.) How does your state compare with its neighbors and the nation?

2. The following data are from a recent federal budget:

Federal government discretionary outlays ($ billions)

	2000	2010
Defense outlays	294,363	693,586
Non-defense outlays	319.7	658.2
Composite outlay deflators (2005 = 1.00)		
Defense	0.8147	1.1327
Non-defense	0.8900	1.1256

a. Compute the percentage change for federal defense and non-defense outlays in current-year dollars from 2000 to 2010. Divide that change into its real and price components.

b. For non-defense outlays, convert the deflator base to 2000 = 1.0000, and re-calculate the absolute change in these real dollars. Convert the deflator base to 2010 = 1.000, and recalculate the absolute change in real dollars. Why might budget strategists try to use one or the other of these two numbers to argue for more or less spending? Is either of the two base years more correct? Explain. Compute and compare the real percentage increases using the two different base years.

3. Identify the strategy represented in each of the following arguments taken from budget discussions:

a. A bill to increase the number of women eligible for Medicaid-funded prenatal assistance in this state would not only save lives, but also cut state costs for care of low-birth-weight babies and children with disabilities. Studies have shown that every dollar spent on prenatal care reduces long-term health-care expenditures by $3.38.

b. The change in the Board of Health sanitation position from full-time to part-time will demolish the inspection program. Rather than accepting the weak-ened program, we would prefer that the program be terminated.

c. Faculty salaries at Enormous State University rank seventeenth among eigh-teen universities with which it competes. Substantial improvements in pay must come in this budget year if major defections are to be prevented.

d. In March, the second of two school-funding referenda failed (by a 2–1 mar-gin) in the Riverside-Brookfield (Illinois) School District. The school board responded by proposing the elimination of the girls' badminton, swimming, and cross-country teams; the boys' soccer, tennis, and wrestling teams; seven additional coaching programs; the cheerleading program; and the Pup-ettes (a pompom squad). A phase-out of the German language program at the school had been started before the failure of the referendum.

e. The Unipacker II will return its full purchase cost in lower labor and mainte-nance expense within two years of initial operation.

f. An editorial in the *Philadelphia Inquirer* (September 24, 2008) argues for a regional sales tax to support funding for the arts on these grounds: "Making sure attractions thrive is about more than satisfying the need for creative outlet. It's about dollars and good economic sense: The groups surveyed for the study provide 19,000 jobs, generate $657 million in yearly revenue, and raise $526 million in contributions."

g. The AIDS education program I have proposed for the biennial budget carries a price tag of only $200,000. This cost represents an absolutely trivial percentage of the $10 billion the state spends each year and will have no impact on the state fiscal crisis. Furthermore, the medical expense to the state associated with even one AIDS case is more than $100,000, so it is the most misguided, mean-spirited, and shortsighted of economies to deny this proposal.

h. The governor proposes major reductions (80 percent of the $321 million per year program) in state general assistance, a program that provides medical coverage at about $120 per month to its 131,000 recipients (adults with no children or other dependents). This reduction may cost more than the amount it saves if only a fraction of the recipients end up in mental institutions or shelters. For example, keeping one-tenth of the current recipients in the state psychiatric hospital for 90 days would cost more than $200 million, and keeping one-tenth of the recipients in a shelter for 90 days would cost $22 million. The reduction is clearly a false economy.

i. In response to budget reductions driven by a declining tax base, the Detroit school system announced that parents would have to purchase toilet paper for the public schools for the upcoming school year.

j. An internal memo leaked to the media said that cuts to the National Weather Service budget in FY 2005 would have a critical impact on its life-saving mission. For instance, "warning lead times will shorten and tornado detection rates will decrease (as will most other NWS performance standards) leading to the troubling and tragic conclusion that there will be unwarranted loss of life." Its operating budget for FY 2005 had been reduced by 2 percent.

k. Former President George W. Bush left his request for funding to support the wars in Iraq and Afghanistan out of his budget submission for the total government and then submitted a separate request a few months later.

l. In response to a countywide instruction to constrain spending, the Fairfax County, Virginia, fire department announced that it would eliminate "First Team," a program of support to family members of injured firefighters, for an annual saving of $6,000.

m. The police department of the City of Palm Bay, Florida, announced that, in response to a reduced budget and higher fuel costs, it would discontinue responses to burglaries in which the home or car owner had failed to lock his home or car.

n. In response to a state fiscal crisis, the director of the Michigan Department of Human Services proposed cutting money for food banks and homeless shelters and for burials for the dead.

If confronted by such arguments and strategies, what questions would you raise?

4. Determine whether the outlays of your favorite department of the federal government have been increasing, decreasing, or staying the same over the past twenty years. Check the percentage increase in terms of current dollars, constant dollars, and share of total federal outlays.

   Based on your analysis of the budget proposal, what does the most recent presidential budget submission have in mind for the operations of that department in the next five years?

   You will find all the data you need to answer these questions in the current federal budget's historical tables. Check at the website of the Office of Management and Budget for the relevant tables.

5. A city budget transmittal memo to the city council included this statement: "Similar to the 2008 Budget, our 2009 proposed expenditures exceed projected revenues in our levy controlled funds in order to invest cash reserves generated by sound fiscal management back into the community." How would you respond to that approach to budget development?

6. In a period in which motor fuel prices have been increasing at an annual rate of 30 percent, the chief of police submits a budget request to the city council that shows no increase in the budget line for purchases of gasoline, a budget category that constitutes around 15 percent of the department total and is second only to costs associated with personnel in the department budget. Other city departments have increased their fuel budget requests by at least 20 percent and some by even more because, along with higher motor fuel prices, the city has been experiencing considerable population growth. The chief says that the department can hold the line on fuel costs because of smarter management of patrol resources. Should the chief be applauded for his efficient management, or is he using a cynical budget strategy?

7. The data that follow report the damage caused by named hurricanes that caused damages of $500 million or more (nominal or current dollars) in the mainland United States. What is the ranking of the hurricanes in terms of real dollars? You can find various deflators (the implicit gross domestic product deflator would be one option) at the Bureau of Economic Analysis website (www.bea.gov). Hurricane categories gauge the intensity of the storm, with 5 being the highest. What do deflated values tell you that the nominal values do not? Do storms of the same category produce roughly the same damage? Why or why not? Is there a pattern over the years?

Hurricane	Year	Category	Nominal Damages ($ Millions)	Hurricane	Year	Category	Nominal Damages ($ Millions)
Allison	1989	0	500	Agnes	1972	1	2,100
Alberto	1994	0	500	Dennis	2005	3	2,230
Frances	1998	0	500	Frederic	1979	3	2,300
Ernesto	2006	0	500	Opal	1995	3	3,000
Erin	1998	2	700	Fran	1996	3	3,200
Bonnie	1998	2	720	Isabel	2003	2	3,370
Diane	1955	1	832	Floyd	1999	2	4,500

Lili	2002	1	860	Allison	2001	0	5,000
Gloria	1985	3	900	Jeanne	2004	3	6,900
Georges	1998	2	1,155	Hugo	1989	4	7,000
Elena	1985	3	1,250	Frances	2004	2	8,900
Betsy	1965	3	1,421	Rita	2005	3	11,300
Camille	1969	5	1,421	Charley	2004	4	15,000
Juan	1985	1	1,500	Ivan	2004	4	15,000
Bob	1991	2	1,500	Wilma	2005	3	20,600
Alicia	1983	3	2,000	Andrews	1992	5	26,500
				Katrina	2005	3	81,000

CASE FOR DISCUSSION

CASE 2–1

Politics and Budget Strategies in Building the Tenn-Tom Waterway

Consider These Questions

1. What budget strategies do the supporters of the project appear to have employed? Could they have been as effective if the waterway were financed by the states of Mississippi and Alabama instead of being federally financed?

2. Explain how this project might have been part of a logrolling strategy. This project was done in an era in which laws that provided financing (appropriation bills) were adopted without any ceilings or controls. In the 1990s, the system was briefly changed to put rigid ceilings on how much money Congress would allow itself to spend in any single year. How would those controls have changed the ability to logroll projects?

3. Explain how the political power structure built into the legislative process contributed to the success of the project.

4. Would you judge the Tenn-Tom to have been a good use of public funds? Explain your position, whatever it may be. Would your assessment differ, depending on whether you live in the Mississippi-Alabama region through which the waterway flows or in some other part of the country?

Geography

The Mississippi River provides a natural waterway—with significant help from locks and other government assistance along the way—through the central United States to the Gulf of Mexico at New Orleans. But for two hundred years, some have dreamed of a cutoff farther east—a waterway linking the Tennessee River and the Tombigbee River to the Gulf at Mobile, Alabama, a shortcut to the sea for industrial cities of the

North and a remedy for chronic unemployment in the areas through which the waterway would pass. In the French colonial era, the leaders of Mobile proposed a canal and towpath link to the Tennessee, but the King of France thought it extravagant. In the 1870s, the idea surfaced again as a way to allow the year-round shipping on the Tombigbee that sandbars prevented during low-water season. The full waterway would provide a shorter route for cargoes passing through the Ohio River system from the direction of Louisville, Cincinnati, Pittsburgh, and beyond. The trip would be shorter, the nation's economy would be stimulated, and thousands of new jobs would be created. The system is shown in the accompanying figure.

Congress

The U.S. Congress authorized the project in 1946, but construction of the 234-mile waterway did not begin until 1972.[51] It opened for business in 1985, stretching from the Tennessee River immediately above the Yellow Creek port in northern Tishomingo County to the Demopolis lock connecting to the Tombigbee River, which empties into the Gulf at Mobile, Alabama. For any cargo heading to the Gulf of Mexico from the east, the system of ten locks, dams, and ten man-made lakes in the states of Alabama and Mississippi reduced the trip by 235 miles. The project—five times longer than the Panama Canal—was the largest civil works project ever undertaken by the U.S. Army Corps of Engineers, the primary public works agency of the federal government.

The Tenn-Tom Waterway had strong supporters in the U.S. Congress. It was the grand plan of powerful southern politicians who steered the public works project through Congress in the 1970s and 1980s. While the project was under consideration and construction, the chairman of the House Appropriations Committee, the committee that must approve all federal appropriations, was Jamie Whitten of Mississippi, the member of Congress representing the part of northeastern Mississippi through which the waterway would flow. Chairman Whitten said, "Everything is in someone's district. I've got the position in Congress I most want. It doesn't mean you can run [the Appropriations Committee]. It just means you've got the first say."[52] And the chair of the House Appropriations Subcommittee on Energy and Water, the subcommittee through which all waterway development projects must go, was Tom Bevill of Alabama. But even these friends didn't provide complete political insulation. In 1981, when Congress threatened to stop funding, floodlights were installed on the waterway so that digging could continue through the night, getting the project so close to completion that its supporters could argue that to stop the canal would be a horrible waste of public funds.

The Numbers

U.S. Army Corps of Engineers estimates in the late 1970s showed a cost-benefit ratio of 1.2 to 1, based on a construction cost of $1.6 billion and $250 million that would be necessary for maintenance during the 50-year useful life of the

---

[51]In the federal budget process, public infrastructure spending must first be authorized (or approved as a part of government policy) and then appropriated (or provided funds, usually in one-year blocks to the agency responsible for the project). Many more projects get authorized than end up being constructed.

[52]David Rogers, "Rivaling Cleopatra, A Pork-Barrel King Sails the Tenn-Tom," *Wall Street Journal,* May 31, 1985, 1.

waterway. For these estimates, the Corps followed the requirements of the Water Resources Development Act of 1974 and used a discount rate of 3.25 percent, the rate for federal borrowing. A rate estimated for tax funds would have been around 6.625 percent, and the cost-benefit ratio would then have fallen to 0.64 to 1. Construction cost of the waterway finally amounted to $1.992 billion, compared with the initial appropriation estimate of $323 million (and only $117 million when the project was authorized). Its maintenance cost is now around $22 million per year.

Operations

Doubts expressed during development of the waterway about the generosity of other parts of the analysis have proven accurate. The U.S. Army Corps of Engineers estimated that the waterway would move 27.3 million tons of cargo in its first year of operation, eventually expanding to 40 million tons. However, actual traffic has proven to be much less. In 1993, 7.6 million tons of cargo were shipped; in 1988, when a drought made transport on the Mississippi difficult, 10 million tons were shipped. In general, shippers preferred the free-flowing Mississippi to the west, and there have been few new industrial plants springing up along the waterway. The major products shipped on the waterway have been wood products (especially wood chips) and logs (about half the traffic), followed by coal. None of these are high-value, time-sensitive products for which speedier transit is critical. Indeed, transit via the Tenn-Tom appears to be more expensive than using the Mississippi because of the many locks and narrow path of the waterway.[53]

Case 2–1
Map Showing the Tenn-Tom Waterway

SOURCE: S. Chang and P. R. Forbus, "Tenn-Tom Versus the Mississippi River," Transportation Journal 25 (Summer 1986). Copyright © Tennessee-Tombigbee Waterway Development Authority. Reprinted with permission.

---

[53]S. Chang and P. R. Forbus, "Tenn-Tom versus the Mississippi River," *Transportation Journal* 25 (Summer 1986): 47–54.

CHAPTER 3

Federal Budget Structures and Institutions

Budgets perform the same functions for choice making, management, and control regardless of the entity—government, business, nonprofit—that develops them. The particular institutions and structures that an entity uses, however, are subject to much individuality, sometimes because of real differences in the mission, size, opportunities, and so on of the entity, but sometimes only because of institutional history ("That's just the way we do it here because that's the way we always have."). In addition, institutions and practices change as administrations change—if a new president or congressional leadership wants things done differently, processes change. Therefore, details change, but the intentions and expectations of the process will remain. In this chapter, we examine what sort of services the federal government provides with its expenditures and how federal budget structures and institutions operate to plan, execute, and control that spending.

As earlier described, a budget is a financial plan. A government budget, however, reflects choices well beyond those of finance. A congressional agency report makes the point: "Not only is the budget a financial accounting of the receipts and expenditures of the federal government; it also sets forth a plan for allocating resources—between the public and private sectors and within the public sector—to meet national objectives."[1] Even in a market economy, the budget represents the basic national economic plan—the chosen mix of public- and private-sector uses of national resources. It doesn't have sectoral production quotas across industries or assignment of resources to industries that characterized the old and ineffective structure of socialist economic systems, but it does represent a plan, first, for dividing resources between the public and private sectors and, second, for allocating resources across the public operations. While the budget includes a report of recent operations, its reason for existence is to put forward a plan for operations in the near future. The executive plan for federal operations is the president's budget that is delivered early in the calendar

---

[1]Congressional Budget Office, *An Analysis of the Administration's Health Proposal* (Washington, D.C.: U.S. Government Printing Office, 1994), 41.

year for the upcoming fiscal year. The legislative plan for federal operations is the congressional budget resolution that should be delivered a bit later in the calendar year. However, neither of these budgets actually provides resources for delivery of services. That happens only after Congress has passed legislation providing authority to spend that the president has signed into law, and that will be much later.

Federal Spending

The first task is to understand what services federal government expenditure provides. Table 3–1 provides those data for selected years from 1960 through 2011 for the major federal functions. Two-thirds of outlays are for human resources, including income maintenance, health, support for the elderly and persons with disabilities, and education and training. The largest block in the category, more than 20 percent of all outlays, is for Social Security (the income support program for the elderly, for surviving spouses and children, and for persons with disabilities). Much of this human resource expenditure occurs through legal formulas that determine who is eligible and to how much those eligible are entitled. Most elements in this spending category have grown at rates greater than the growth rate for total outlays since 1970, and most are expected (or feared) to continue this rapid growth in the future.

National defense was once the predominant interest of the federal government. This is not to say that defense is no longer a significant interest; however, 1961 was the last year in which defense amounted to half or more of federal outlays; it had been over 70 percent for 1942 through 1946, with a maximum of 89.5 percent in 1945, no surprise in light of the expense (and importance) of fighting World War II. The secular decline in the defense share of federal outlays was interrupted for 1981 through 1987. Many believe that this increase, by forcing a reaction from the Soviet Union that its inefficient socialist economy could not support, caused the collapse of the Soviet Union and an end to the Cold War. That defense buildup essentially won a war without firing a shot, undoubtedly the best way to fight a war, and a record not repeated in the twenty-first century. There is also an increase in the first decade of the twenty-first century, created by the cost of the wars in Iraq and Afghanistan and political pressures.[2] This increased share remains far below its level of the 1960s and 1970s and, with luck, will not approach those levels again. Indeed, the share isn't even up to its level in 1990, let alone the huge share during the WWII years. The lower spending share is more an indicator that we are safer than we were when shares were much higher than a suggestion that we might be dangerously unsafe from inattention to defense. The real question is whether, in the absence of any other military superpower, we might be spending more than would be appropriate.

---

[2]The costs of the Department of Homeland Security are not included as part of national defense in the federal budget. In the spending categorizations in the budget, its spending is categorized as part of transportation, disaster relief and insurance, and law enforcement functions, not national defense. In light of the fact that the Department's own strategic plan states that "the Department was created to secure our country against those who seek to disrupt the American way of life," this may seem a little strange.

Table 3–1
Federal Outlays by Function, 1960–2011 ($ Millions)

	1960	% Total	1970	% Total	1980	% Total	1990	% Total	2000	% Total	2010	% Total	2011	% Total	Growth since 1960
National Defense	48,130	52.2%	81,692	41.75%	133,995	22.7%	299,321	23.9%	294,363	16.5%	693,586	20.1%	705,625	19.6%	5.4%
Human resources	26,184	28.4%	75,349	38.51%	313,374	53.0%	619,297	49.4%	1,115,517	62.4%	2,385,731	69.0%	2,414,738	67.0%	9.3%
Education, Training, Employment, and Social Services	968	1.0%	8,634	4.41%	31,843	5.4%	37,171	3.0%	53,764	3.0%	127,710	3.7%	101,233	2.8%	9.5%
Health	795	0.9%	5,907	3.02%	23,169	3.9%	57,699	4.6%	154,504	8.6%	369,054	10.7%	372,500	10.3%	12.8%
Medicare	.....	.....	6,213	3.18%	32,090	5.4%	98,102	7.8%	197,113	11.0%	451,636	13.1%	485,653	13.5%	11.2%
Income Security	7,378	8.0%	15,655	8.00%	86,557	14.6%	148,668	11.9%	253,724	14.2%	622,210	18.0%	597,352	16.6%	9.0%
Social Security	11,602	12.6%	30,270	15.47%	118,547	20.1%	248,623	19.8%	409,423	22.9%	706,737	20.4%	730,811	20.3%	8.5%
Veterans Benefits and Services	5,441	5.9%	8,669	4.43%	21,169	3.6%	29,034	2.3%	46,989	2.6%	108,384	3.1%	127,189	3.5%	6.4%
Physical resources	7,991	8.7%	15,574	7.96%	65,985	11.2%	126,011	10.1%	84,925	4.7%	88,753	2.6%	161,850	4.5%	6.1%
Energy	464	0.5%	997	0.51%	10,156	1.7%	3,341	0.3%	−761	0.0%	11,613	0.3%	12,174	0.3%	6.6%
Natural Resources and Environment	1,559	1.7%	3,065	1.57%	13,858	2.3%	17,055	1.4%	25,003	1.4%	43,662	1.3%	45,470	1.3%	6.8%
Commerce and Housing Credit	1,618	1.8%	2,112	1.08%	9,390	1.6%	67,599	5.4%	3,207	0.2%	−82,298	−2.4%	−12,575	−0.3%	.....
Transportation	4,126	4.5%	7,008	3.58%	21,329	3.6%	29,485	2.4%	46,853	2.6%	91,972	2.7%	92,965	2.6%	6.3%
Community and Regional Development	224	0.2%	2,392	1.22%	11,252	1.9%	8,531	0.7%	10,623	0.6%	23,804	0.7%	23,816	0.7%	9.6%
Net interest	6,947	7.5%	14,380	7.35%	52,533	8.9%	184,347	14.7%	222,949	12.5%	196,194	5.7%	229,968	6.4%	7.1%
Other functions	7,760	8.4%	17,286	8.84%	44,996	7.6%	60,634	4.8%	113,777	6.4%	174,065	5.0%	177,374	4.9%	6.3%
International Affairs	2,988	3.2%	4,330	2.21%	12,714	2.2%	13,758	1.1%	17,213	1.0%	45,195	1.3%	45,685	1.3%	5.5%
General Science, Space, and Technology	599	0.6%	4,511	2.31%	5,831	1.0%	14,426	1.2%	18,594	1.0%	30,098	0.9%	29,466	0.8%	7.9%
Agriculture	2,623	2.8%	5,166	2.64%	8,774	1.5%	11,804	0.9%	36,458	2.0%	21,356	0.6%	20,661	0.6%	4.1%
Administration of Justice	366	0.4%	959	0.49%	4,702	0.8%	10,185	0.8%	28,499	1.6%	54,385	1.6%	56,055	1.6%	10.4%
General Government	1,184	1.3%	2,320	1.19%	12,975	2.2%	10,460	0.8%	13,013	0.7%	23,031	0.7%	25,507	0.7%	6.2%
Undistributed offsetting receipts	−4,820	−5.2%	−8,632	−4.4%	−19,942	−3.4%	−36,615	−2.9%	−42,581	−2.4%	−82,116	−2.4%	−86,494	−2.4%	5.8%
Total, Federal outlays	92,191		195,649		590,941		1,252,993		1,788,950		3,456,213		3,603,061		7.5%

SOURCE: Office of Management and Budget, Budget of the Government of the United States, Fiscal Year 2013, Historical Tables (Washington, D.C.: U.S. Government Printing Office, 2012).

NOTE: Medicare growth rate since 1970.

Other functional outlays are much smaller parts of the federal total. A particularly high growth rate appears for administration of justice (law enforcement and corrections), but the current share is small. Growth in outlays for health and for Medicare (the federal health program for older people) has been high, and their shares of the total are much larger. Outlays for physical resources, including infrastructure or the federal capital stock, are small in share and not growing as rapidly as totals. Many believe increased public infrastructure investment is critical for improved standards of living, indeed for maintaining the health and safety of the public, but the outlay patterns show physical resource growth to be slow. Spending on other functions is both relatively small and slow growing; the rates of increase often have not kept pace with the combined effects of population increase and inflation.

Changing directions is not impossible, but, as the incrementalists remind us, it is difficult to accomplish. The great counterexample of how spending directions can dramatically change, however, is national defense through the past forty years. Spending shares can change substantially when operating conditions change, no matter what the incremental inertia is. Indeed, we started to reallocate resources away from national defense, enjoying victory in the Cold War, even before the collapse of the Soviet Union at the end of 1991. In no way are spending shares replicated year after year, without regard to what might be happening in the external environment.

Some summarize the federal government by describing it as a heavily indebted, heavily armed insurance company. Here is why: from 2011 outlay data, the federal government spends about 20 percent of its total outlays on national defense, about 20 percent of its total outlays on Social Security, about 20 percent of its total outlays on Medicare (the health insurance program for the elderly) plus Medicaid (a health program for low-income people that is included in the health function), 3.5 percent on military veterans' benefits, 17 percent on income security (federal retirement programs, unemployment compensation, etc.), and 6.4 percent on interest. That doesn't leave much else. As will be described in the next sections, Social Security, Medicare, Medicaid, and net interest are spent according to an automatic formula spending process that is outside the annual budget process. That makes control and discipline over federal spending even more of a challenge.

Fiscal Control and Federal Budget Structures[3]

The first expectation of a budget process is that it will be a tool for fiscal discipline. The experience over the past century does not speak well for the ability of the federal government to maintain a balance between available revenues and expenditures. Expenditure decisions are made through a political process that is governed by a set of laws designed to provide open deliberations about options, attempt to direct

[3]Office of Management and Budget, *Budget System and Concepts, Fiscal Year* (Washington, D.C.: U.S. Government Printing Office)—a document revised each year—explains the system, process, legal requirements, and concepts used to formulate the president's budget each year. It is available through the Office of Management and Budget website [http://www.whitehouse.gov/omb/].

resources to the areas of greatest need, ensure accountability and prevent corruption, and provide a mechanism for fiscal control. The budget process is a critical component of public expenditure management. The federal budget process—its practices, timing, and institutions—is the product of both law and tradition. The federal system emerged over the past century as legislative responses to perceived problems with how the fiscal control structure was performing. More often than not, the problem was that of controlling the deficit, meaning that spending was more, sometimes considerably more, than revenue being taken in, and it was believed that elimination of the deficit—or at least controlling it—was important for the economic prosperity of the country. Figure 3–1, using data from historical tables provided in the *Budget of the United States Government,* shows a pattern of spending more than the amount of revenue received through most of the years since 1900. The deficits never were large enough to threaten the capacity of the government to finance them, but periodically enough to make the trend seem aimed toward an unpleasant conclusion. Bond drives were regularly used during World War II to encourage private purchases of debt for patriotic reasons, not necessarily reflecting sound private portfolio management, but in other times special efforts to sell the bonds have not been needed to support the deficit.[4] You can see that deficits get big during big wars (World Wars I and II) and big economic downturns (the Great Depression and the Great Recession)—and then

Figure 3–1
Deficit/Surplus as a Percentage of Total Federal Outlays, 1901–2011

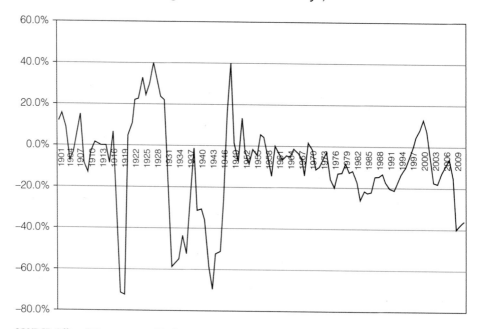

SOURCE: Office of Management and Budget, *Budget of the United States Government, Fiscal Year 2013, Historical Tables* (Washington, D.C.: U.S. Government Printing Office, 2012).

---

[4]Data aggregated for 1789 to 1849 show a 6.4 percent surplus, and data aggregated from 1850 to 1900 show a 6.4 percent deficit. Individual year data are not easily available.

there is that long period from 1970 through the mid-1990s where there is mostly no good reason for the deficits. As you can see, recently around 40 percent of total spending was financed by borrowing, and that is not a pattern that can long be continued. The present budget structures developed through the years largely to provide a process for controlling the deficit—and the figure may have spoiled the story by showing that the structures haven't exactly done their job much of the time.

Fundamental federal law—the United States Constitution—grants the "power of the purse" to Congress, but provides only limited instruction about the fiscal process: "No Money shall be drawn from the Treasury, but in Consequence of Appropriations made by Law; and a regular Statement and Account of the Receipts and Expenditures of all public Money shall be published from time to time." (Article 1, Section 9). That requires Congress to make appropriations before money is to be spent and requires periodic financial reports. But it does not provide any budget framework. In that scheme, agencies would operate by bringing their appropriation proposals to Congress directly, without central executive coordination, and would return for another appropriation when the approved funds were exhausted. Financing of World War I brought large deficits and a concern about establishing a real budgetary process. The first federal debt ceilings were established in the World War I era as Congress became concerned about the great sums of money spent for the war and the resulting borrowing to support the spending. Because there was no budget system to provide a control, the debt ceilings were to provide a substitute. When the budget system came into being, the statutory debt ceilings continued as well, even though their usefulness had ended.[5] The budgetary structure in place today is the result of the major legislative actions outlined here, the first coming shortly after that war.[6] Table 3–2 gives a summary of these laws discussed below.

---

[5]A complete review of the debt limits appears in D. Andrew Austin, *The Debt Limit: History and Recent Increase,* CRS Report for Congress, Order Code RL 31967 (Washington, D.C.: Congressional Research Service, 2008). For decades, the federal government has operated with statutory limits on the amount of debt that could be outstanding, thereby constraining the capacity to run a deficit (i.e., add to the debt) when the ceiling is reached. These laws have historically had little, if any, effect because debt limits have regularly increased. Spending had already been approved in the appropriation bill, and obligations had been made, so the only thing remaining was to have the funds necessary to cover the purchases already made. If necessary, the cash could easily be raised by new borrowing—so long as the ceiling would permit. None doubted the capacity of the federal government to meet its debt obligations, and none doubted the ability of the federal government to borrow. However, in the summer of 2011, a group of members of the House of Representatives chose to delay allowing an increase in the statutory debt ceiling that would permit the federal government to make payments for purchases already made. Although the ceiling increase finally was approved, it was not before there was significant concern about the willingness of the federal government to meet its financial obligations and not before one credit rating agency reduced the credit rating of federal debt below the highest level, a level that the federal government had enjoyed forever.

[6]A more complete listing would include the following: (1) the Federal Credit Reform Act of 1990 (part of the Budget Enforcement Act of 1990), which requires budgetary treatment of direct loans and loan guarantees, not on a purely cash basis, but on estimated present values (see Chapter 7 for an explanation of present values) of the long-term cost of the loans or guarantees to the government; (2) the *Report of the President's Commission on Budget Concepts* (Washington, D.C.: U.S. Government Printing Office, 1967), which, although it has no legal status, remains the only authoritative statement on federal budget accounting; (3) the Chief Financial Officers Act of 1990, which required audited financial statements and increased powers of financial management authorities; and (4) the Government Performance and Results Act of 1993, which required agencies to develop strategic plans, measure performance, and integrate budgeting with performance improvement programs. The rules and procedures for budget execution appear in the Anti-deficiency Act (codified in Chapters 13 and 15 of Title 31, United States Code). Procedures for submission of the president's budget and information to be contained in it are in Chapter 11, Title 31, United States Code.

Table 3–2

Highlights of Major Acts Establishing the Federal Budget Process

Budget and Accounting Act of 1921 (67th Cong., 1st sess., chap. 18, 47 stat. 20).

Established fiscal year from July 1 to June 30
Supplemental appropriation
Bureau of Budget (now Office of Management and Budget [OMB])
General Accounting Office (now Government Accountability Office [GAO])
Required president's budget message (first day of session)
No direct agency submission of appropriation requests

Congressional Budget and Impoundment Control Act of 1974 (Public Law 93–344)

Established fiscal year from October 1 to September 30
Established Congressional Budget Office (CBO)
Established House and Senate Budget Committees
Required Current Services Budget presentation by president (what budget levels would be in the future if no policy changes occur)
Required congressional budget resolutions (first and second)
Established functional classification in president's budget
Required tax expenditure analysis
Established rescission/deferral instead of impoundment

Balanced Budget and Emergency Deficit Control Act of 1985 (Public Law 99–177)

Established deficit targets
Formula sequestration to enforce targets
Required earlier presidential budget message (first Monday after January 3)
No second congressional budget resolution

Budget Enforcement Act of 1990 (Title XIII, Public Law 101–508)

Established mandatory and discretionary spending categories
Pay-as-you-go (PAYGO) requirement for mandatory spending categories and revenue provisions
Established discretionary spending controls
Required presidential adjustment of ceilings for sequester
Supplemental appropriations included in outlay controls, except for wars and dire emergencies

Statutory Pay-As-You-Go Act of 2010 (Public Law 111–139)

New legislation changing taxes, fees, or mandatory expenditures, taken together in a year, must not increase projected deficit
Enforced by sequestration against a select group of mandatory programs (most Medicare payments, farm price supports, vocational rehabilitation state grants, mineral leasing payments to states, social services block grants), but not Social Security, most unemployment benefits, veterans' benefits, debt interest, federal retirement, and low-income entitlements
OMB calculates whether there is a violation at end of congressional session, and president issues any required sequestration order (none required in 2011 report)

(continues)

Table 3–2 (continued)

Budget Control Act of 2011 (Public Law 112–25)

Create discretionary spending caps through 2021
Require congressional vote on balanced budget amendment to Constitution
Create Congressional Joint Committee on Deficit Reduction to propose at least $1.5 trillion in cumulative budget savings over ten years (*Note:* Joint Committee did not meet deadline to report program)
Upon failure of Joint Committee, sequestration program for fiscal 2013 through 2021 to cut $1.5 trillion over ten years, cuts divided equally between defense and non-defense spending (exempt Social Security and low-income programs)
Increase statutory debt ceiling in three tranches

Budget and Accounting Act of 1921 (67th Congress, 1st session, chap. 18, 47 Stat. 20). The 1921 Act established the requirement for a presidential budget (there was no federal budget in the normal sense of the word before this time) and the institutions needed for its implementation. Important elements of that law include the following provisions:

a. The Act required the president to submit a budget message to Congress at the beginning of its legislative session. It would be a regularized and consolidated plan for all operations of the federal establishment, and individual agencies would no longer be permitted to transmit requests directly to Congress. Before the 1921 Act, departments and agencies made individual appropriation requests; their sole submissions were gathered in an uncoordinated "Book of Estimates" for congressional review. The process concentrated on appropriating, the function that is a constitutional requirement before money may be spent.

b. The Act created a Bureau of the Budget (initially in the Department of Treasury, but moved to the Executive Office of the President in 1939 and converted to the Office of Management and Budget, or OMB, in 1970) to assist the president in preparing that budget. The president appoints the OMB's director. Its staff, including both political and professional appointees, is expected to carry out the policies of the president.[7] The OMB develops the executive budget by consolidating agency requests for appropriations within the guidelines provided by the president. The OMB usually reduces initial agency requests; an administrative process within the OMB considers protests of these reductions before transmission of the budget to Congress. After appropriation, the OMB meters the flow of spending to ensure that agencies do not spend more than the amount appropriated.[8]

---

[7]Other countries have central budget agencies as well. John Wanna, Lotte Jensen, and Jouke de Vries, eds., *Controlling Public Expenditure: The Changing Roles of Central Budget Agencies—Better Guardians?* (Northampton, Mass.: Edward Elgar, 2003), provide a cross-national comparative overview of these agencies, including the OMB.

[8]Complete studies of the agency appear in Percival Flack Brundage, *The Bureau of the Budget* (New York: Praeger, 1970); and Larry Berman, *The Office of Management and Budget and the Presidency, 1921–1979* (Princeton, N.J.: Princeton University Press, 1979). Brundage was budget director for President Eisenhower after a career with a national accounting firm.

c. The Act created for Congress and the American people the General Accounting Office (now the Government Accountability Office, or GAO) to ensure that agencies were operating their finances in the manner provided by Congress. The GAO holds accountable the operations of federal departments and agencies and is the primary "watchdog" agency for Congress and the American people.[9] As the external audit agent for the federal government, it supervises the accounting done by the executive agencies, but much of its work emphasizes investigations to improve the effectiveness of government. Much audit detail, in fact, is done by the audit staff of the executive agencies themselves, subject to GAO agreement. The head of the GAO, the comptroller general, is appointed by the president with the consent of the Senate for a single fifteen-year term; the comptroller general is almost unremovable within term.[10] The current emphasis of the GAO's work is the evaluation of government programs, sometimes at the request of a single member of Congress, sometimes at the request of a congressional committee. The GAO's audit and program evaluation is external to the operating agencies of the executive branch, and its reports are to Congress and the American people.

d. The Act established a fiscal year that ran from July 1 to June 30 and provided a process for supplemental appropriations in unexpected instances in which agencies were in danger of exhausting their appropriations before a new fiscal year and new appropriation laws brought new spending authority.

Congressional Budget and Impoundment Control Act of 1974 (Public Law 93–344). The 1921 Act got the nation through the extremes of the Roaring 1920s, the Great Depression, and World War II, and after those episodes, finances seemed calm. However, in the early 1970s, confidence in government began to erode with the Vietnam War, the Watergate break-ins, and the conflict between Congress and President Nixon. Many members of Congress believed that they were not receiving trustworthy fiscal information from the OMB, that the deficit was starting to go out of control, that Congress needed a role in developing its own budget plan and should not simply have the role of appropriating according to the plan proposed by the president, that the president was selectively using his impoundment power (the capacity to not spend all money that had been appropriated that presidents from Washington onward had used for purposes of fiscal management) to punish his enemies, that the budget did not include all data necessary for responsible deliberations, and that Congress needed more time for deliberations between when the president submitted his budget and the start of the fiscal year. The 1974 Act, signed into law

---

[9]The GAO became the Government Accountability Office in the GAO Human Capital Reform Act of 2004 (P.L. 108–271). Along with the name change came greater flexibility for the GAO in staffing matters.
[10]Two major studies provide a detailed view of the GAO. In *The GAO: The Quest for Accountability in American Government* (Boulder, Colo.: Westview Press, 1979), Frederick Mosher traces the development of the GAO to the end of the 1970s; and Erasmus H. Kolman, ed., *Cases in Accountability: The Work of the GAO* (Boulder, Colo.: Westview Press, 1979), collects several cases that illustrate the kinds of audits or evaluations done by the GAO.

by President Nixon only three weeks before his resignation, set about correcting these deficiencies. Provisions of the Act include the following:

a. The Act established a congressional budget process.

b. It required that Congress pass a budget resolution, the product of the House and Senate Budget Committees that the Act created, in April to establish revenue, expenditure, and deficit controls for the budget year and another budget resolution in August to modify those controls (the second resolution was eliminated in 1985). The Congressional Budget Office (CBO), another congressional agency, was established by the 1974 Act to provide Congress generally and the congressional Budget Committees specifically with expertise similar to that of the OMB. Before the CBO, there appeared to be an imbalance: the president had a permanent, professional budget staff with well-honed abilities and continuing knowledge about the mechanics and content of the budget; Congress had appropriations committee staff, none of whom maintained a view of the budget as a whole. The CBO provided a permanent, nonpartisan professional staff to supply Congress three basic services: help in developing a plan for the budget (macroeconomic forecasts, baseline budget projections, deficit-reduction options, analysis of the president's budget), help in staying within its budget (cost estimates for bills, scorekeeping or maintaining frequent tabulations of bills that affect the budget, sequestration reports), and help in considering issues of budget and economic policy.[11] The CBO assists, first, the congressional Budget Committees; second, the other fiscal committees (Appropriations, House Ways and Means, and Senate Finance); and third, other committees and members of Congress.

c. The Act changed the start of the fiscal year to October 1 to provide more time for deliberations and to ensure that the appropriation laws were approved before the fiscal year began.

d. The Act required the President to submit a Current Services Budget that indicated what budget levels would be if no policy changes were made in the future.

e. The Act required the president's budget to present spending in functional classification, in addition to the traditional administrative organization classification, and to provide a tax expenditure analysis, a statement of the fiscal cost of preferences built into the tax structure. (Tax expenditures will be discussed in a later chapter.)

f. The Act eliminated presidential impoundment power, substituting a process whereby the president could defer or rescind appropriated spending, but only with congressional approval. More will be said about this in a later section.

The Congressional Budget and Impoundment Control Act of 1974 was thought to induce greater fiscal responsibility because Congress was required to approve a deficit or surplus appropriate to the existing macroeconomic circumstances and to

---

[11]Philip G. Joyce, *The Congressional Budget Office: Honest Numbers, Power, and Policymaking* (Washington, D.C.: Georgetown University Press, 2010).

adopt revenue and appropriation laws within that standard. That was the idea of the budget resolution (or the congressional budget). No longer would spending increases and tax reductions be free additions; now they would have to be balanced within the ceilings of the resolution. Shortly after the law was passed, deficits soared.

Balanced Budget and Emergency Deficit Control Act of 1985 or The Gramm-Rudman-Hollings Act (Public Law 99–177, revised in 1987). While the 1974 Act undoubtedly made significant procedural improvements to the fiscal system, Figure 3–1 makes it clear that it did not repair the tendency for substantial federal deficits. In contrast to the first two acts, which sought fiscal responsibility and discipline by changing procedures, the 1985 Act took a direct approach. It established firm and declining deficit targets for upcoming fiscal years and established an automatic sequestration (cutting of appropriations) formula if the targets were violated. The amount of the violation would be established, initially by the GAO and later by the OMB because of a constitutional issue, and the amount of sequestration necessary to get back to the target would be divided equally between military and domestic spending (exempting Social Security, Medicare, debt interest, and some antipoverty programs from the calculation). The targets were mandatory, and, if violation was forecast at the start of a fiscal year and legislative changes were not made to correct the violation, a sequestration process at the start of the fiscal year reduced spending by formula to restore the target deficit.[12] Cuts were to be made by the percentage needed to get the deficit back to the legal target, without regard to priorities. The series of deficit targets would have ultimately led to balance in 1993, if actually carried out.[13] Gramm-Rudman-Hollings was, because of its brute force and mindless reductions, intended to be so politically distasteful that Congress would exert extreme caution to prevent a sequester. Instead, Congress chose to kill the process. Three years were sequester-eligible: 1986 (carried out), 1988 (rescinded), and 1990 (replaced by the Budget Enforcement Act of 1990). The 1985 Act quickly was a dead letter in fiscal control significance, although the sequestration concept emerged in later deficit-control discussions.

Budget Enforcement Act of 1990 (Title XIII, Public Law 101–508). The 1990 Act (BEA90), renewed twice and finally expiring in 2002, created an effective deficit-control structure by focusing on controlling spending and taxing rather than deficits. It did not rely on controlling estimated deficit violations, but rather controlled

---

[12]Certain spending categories were exempt; remaining spending was split between domestic and defense, and dollar amounts of needed reduction were equally divided between those categories. Because much spending was exempt, the percentage reduction for the remainder would have been great. Violations were based on expenditure and revenue forecasts. Had the process remained in place longer, it is entirely possible that sequestrations would have been easily avoided by fudging the forecasts.

[13]The 1985 version scheduled balance in 1991, but that date was stretched in the 1987 version. The initial Act assigned the enforcement of sequestration orders to the comptroller general. In *Bowsher, Comptroller General of the United States* v. *Mike Synar, Member of Congress,* 478 U.S. 714 (1986), the Supreme Court held that this assignment of powers by Congress to the comptroller general violated the constitutional command that Congress play no direct role in the execution of laws. The 1987 Act remedied the problem by assigning the task to the OMB, an executive agency.

specific spending actions. Several elements of the Act continue to shape budgetary discussions, even though the Act no longer controls.

a. BEA90 created two federal spending categories: mandatory and discretionary. The difference between the two is that discretionary spending goes through the congressional appropriation process, while mandatory spending occurs automatically, by legislated formula. Roughly speaking, discretionary spending supports operations of federal agencies and mandatory spending supports programs like Social Security, Medicare, and interest on the national debt. The categories continue to be carried in budget documents and discussions.

b. Mandatory spending and revenue provisions are subject to a pay-as-you-go (PAYGO) requirement. A provision to make a mandatory spending formula more lucrative (e.g., to extend the weeks of eligibility for unemployment compensation from 39 to 52) would have to be accompanied by a provision to cover its cost. Revenue lost with tax reductions would similarly need to be recovered. Changes are thus required to be deficit-neutral. The PAYGO requirement meant that revenue reductions or entitlement enhancements must be internally financed by accompanying revenue increases or entitlement reductions.

c. Discretionary spending was subject to rigid annual caps. Outlay levels for spending coming from the appropriation process were controlled for several years into the future (and were extended each time the Act was renewed). Sequesters would apply if any violation occurred.

d. Supplemental appropriations were included in the outlay control structure. The only exception was in the case of war or a "dire emergency." In such cases, outlays could be added without violating the spending caps.

Some observers, reacting to the many adjustments and diffusion of responsibility, have labeled BEA90 as a start toward "no fault budgeting,"[14] but outlay ceilings constrained appropriations until 1998. After that budget year, annual adjustments to original statutory caps allowed considerable expansion of outlays. The Omnibus Budget Reconciliation Act of 1993 (P.L. 103–66) extended new ceilings through fiscal 1998, and the Balanced Budget Act of 1997 (P.L. 105–33, the 1997 budget reconciliation) continued ceilings through fiscal year 2002.[15] The discretionary caps and the PAYGO mechanism expired in September 2002. After its expiration, federal deficits did increase dramatically.

Statutory Pay-As-You-Go Act of 2010 (Public Law 111–139). The deficits that emerged after 2002 brought legislation to partially restore controls of the past. The 2010 Act establishes a control provision that legislation changing taxes, fees, or mandatory spending, taken together in a year, cannot increase the projected deficit. The system requires the OMB to determine whether there has been a violation at the end of the congressional session and, if there has been, the president issues the required sequestration. (No such sequestrations under this law have been required

---

[14]Richard Doyle and Jerry McCaffery, "The Budget Enforcement Act of 1990: The Path to No Fault Budgeting," *Public Budgeting & Finance* 11 (Spring 1991): 25–40.
[15]PAYGO would continue, but without any enforcement mechanism. Other legislation provided caps on highway and mass transit outlays (through 2003) and on conservation outlays (through 2006).

so far.) Sequestration applies to certain mandatory programs (most Medicare payments, farm price supports, vocational rehabilitation state grants, etc.), but not Social Security, most unemployment benefits, veterans' benefits, debt interest, federal retirement, and low-income entitlements.

Budget Control Act of 2011 (Public Law 112–25). The 2011 Act emerged from arguments about increasing the statutory federal debt ceiling in the summer of 2011. The Act established firm discretionary spending caps through fiscal 2021, required Congress to vote on a balanced budget amendment to the Constitution (done, but it did not pass), and created a Congressional Joint Committee on Deficit Reduction to propose at least $1.5 trillion in cumulative budget deficit savings over a ten-year period (the Committee did not meet the deadline for making the proposal, so it has expired). The spending caps do remain in place, so the top line for the budget process has been established for some years to come. The caps are enforced by OMB-initiated across-the-board sequestrations if the cap is exceeded in any year. Cuts are to be divided equally between national defense budget functions and all other budget functions. Non-defense cuts would come from both discretionary and some mandatory programs. However, the caps can be overridden by congressional vote, just as sequesters and caps have been in the past.

Congressional Committees

The budget structure laws establish the budgeting framework, but the fiscal committees of Congress are responsible for the structuring of the laws that actually provide the ability of the federal government to spend. While expenditure and tax laws must be passed by both the Senate and the House of Representatives, the work to create those laws is done in committees of Congress and, indeed, often in subcommittees of those committees. The committees with particularly important roles are the several authorizing committees, the budget committees created by the 1974 Act, the House and Senate Appropriations Committees and their subcommittees (one committee for each appropriation bill), the House Ways and Means Committee, the Senate Finance Committee, and the Joint Committee on Taxation. The Ways and Means and Finance Committees are responsible for legislation that dictates spending for Medicare and Social Security and that creates the tax system, so they have considerable fiscal significance. More about the role played by each of these committees and the procedures that have been established in the process laws will be discussed in the next section.

Phases in the Federal Budget Cycle

The federal budget cycle involves operations by both the executive and the legislative branches of government. Spending cannot occur without the approval of both branches, and the budget cycle involves movement of work between the branches of government.

Executive Preparation and Submission Phase

The executive preparation and submission phase begins about 18 months before the start of the fiscal year.[16] The president establishes general budget and fiscal policy guidelines, and the OMB works with federal agencies to translate them into agency programs and budget requests. Agencies develop requests according to their own procedures, but with OMB coordination.[17] The OMB collects agency estimates of their planned expenditures for the fiscal year and consolidates these requests. Table 3–3 shows the key events and dates in the budget cycle, as outlined in Circular A-11, the primary budget instruction from the OMB. The overall requests are compared with the presidential program objectives, expenditure ceilings set by the president, Department of Treasury revenue forecasts (from the Office of Tax Analysis), and economic forecasts from the Council of Economic Advisers and the Federal Reserve System.[18] The economic estimates—inflation rate, interest rates, level of unemployment, growth rate of GDP, and so on—are especially important for the federal budget because many budget totals are sensitive to the state of the economy. For example, Congress passes laws that provide for spending that depends on the number of unemployed workers who qualify for assistance, and several programs (most notably Social Security) index spending to inflation. Furthermore, federal revenues are particularly sensitive to economic activity, and, given the considerable amount of federal debt outstanding, total outlays change significantly depending on the rate of interest the federal government must pay on its debt. As a result, the forecast of economic activity can substantially affect the budget's spending and revenue plans.

The *budget baseline*—a forecast of the receipts, outlays, and deficits that current law would produce—provides important information to the process by warning of future problems, giving a starting point for formulating the current budget, and offering a "policy-neutral" benchmark against which the president's (and other) budget proposals can be compared[19] without complication from the ways the economy can alter those numbers. The budget baseline becomes the standard against which program proposals are compared. Indeed, when Congress discusses budget cuts for

---

[16]The federal fiscal year begins on October 1. That has not always been the case. The first federal fiscal year began on January 1, 1789. Congress changed the start to July 1 in 1842 and to October 1 for 1977.

[17]The Department of Defense is so large a part of federal government finances that the OMB directly works with the Department as its budget is prepared, so OMB is involved even before the budget is transmitted for OMB review. That is not the case with other government operations.

[18]The Council of Economic Advisers, another part of the Executive Office of the President, provides advice on macroeconomic conditions and overall fiscal policy and on microeconomic issues. *The Economic Report of the President,* which the Council prepares, is an important source document for information and policy discussion. The Federal Reserve System is the American central bank.

[19]The Current Services Budget, one part of the Analytical Perspectives volume of the federal budget, provides a baseline. That volume discusses the baseline concept and its measurement in considerable detail. In general, receipts and mandatory spending (spending that occurs according to a formula, not annual appropriation) are estimated according to current law; funding that must be approved each year is estimated by adjusting the most recently approved appropriation for inflation. The CBO also prepares a budget baseline for its analysis; the CBO baselines have been more widely used in recent years. For an excellent discussion of the problem of defining a baseline, see Timothy J. Muris, "The Uses and Misuses of Budget Baselines," in John F. Cogan, Timothy J. Muris, and Allen Schick, *The Budget Puzzle: Understanding Federal Spending* (Stanford, Calif.: Stanford University Press, 1994), 41–78.

Table 3–3
Major Events in the Federal Budget Process

Major Steps in the Formulation Phase

What Happens?	When?
The OMB issues spring planning guidance to executive branch agencies for the upcoming budget. The OMB director issues a letter to the head of each agency providing policy guidance for the agency's budget request. Absent more specific guidance, the out-year estimates included in the previous budget serve as a starting point for the next budget. This begins the process of formulating the budget the president will submit the following February.	Spring
The OMB and the executive branch agencies discuss budget issues and options. The OMB works with the agencies to: • Identify major issues for the upcoming budget • Develop and analyze options for the upcoming fall review • Plan for the analysis of issues that will need decisions in the future	Spring and Summer
The OMB issues Circular No. A-11 to all federal agencies. This circular provides detailed instructions for submitting budget data and materials.	July
Executive branch agencies (except those not subject to executive branch review) make budget submissions.	Fall
The fiscal year begins. The just-completed budget cycle focused on this fiscal year. It was the "budget year" in that cycle and is the "current year" in this cycle.	October 1
The OMB conducts its fall review. OMB staff analyze agency budget proposals in light of presidential priorities, program performance, and budget constraints. They raise issues and present options to the director and other OMB policy officials for their decisions.	October–November
The OMB briefs the president and senior advisers on proposed budget policies. The OMB director recommends a complete set of budget proposals to the president after OMB has reviewed all agency requests and considered overall budget policies.	Late November
"Passback": The OMB usually informs all executive branch agencies at the same time about the decisions on their budget requests.	Late November
All agencies, including legislative and judicial branch agencies, enter MAX computer data and submit print materials and additional data. This process begins immediately after passback and continues until the OMB must "lock" agencies out of the database in order to meet the printing deadline.	Late November to early January
Executive branch agencies may appeal to the OMB and the president. An agency head may ask the OMB to reverse or modify certain decisions. In most cases, the OMB and the agency head resolve such issues and, if not, work together to present them to the president for a decision.	December
Agencies prepare and the OMB reviews congressional budget justification materials. Agencies prepare the budget justification materials they need to explain their budget requests to the responsible congressional subcommittees.	January
The president transmits the budget to Congress.	First Monday in February

Table 3–3 (continued)

Major Steps in the Congressional Phase

What Happens?	When?
The Congressional Budget Office (CBO) reports to budget committees on the economic and budget outlook.	January
The CBO reestimates the president's budget based on its own economic and technical assumptions	February
Other committees submit "views and estimates" to House and Senate Budget Committees. Committees indicate their preferences regarding budgetary matters for which they are responsible.	Within 6 weeks of transmittal
Congress completes action on the concurrent resolution of the budget. Congress commits itself to broad spending and revenue levels by passing a budget resolution.	April 15
Congress needs to complete action on appropriations bills for the upcoming fiscal year. Congress completes action on regular appropriations bills or provides a "continuing resolution" (a stop-gap appropriation law).	September 30

Major Steps in the Execution Phase

What Happens?	When?
The fiscal year begins.	October 1
The OMB apportions funds made available in the budget process and other available funds. Agencies submit apportionment requests to OMB for each budget account by *August 21* or within *10 calendar days* after the approval of the appropriation, whichever is later. The OMB approves or modifies the apportionment, specifying the amount of funds agencies may use by time period, program, project, or activity.	September 10 (or within 30 days after approval of a spending bill)
Agencies incur obligations and make outlays to carry out the funded programs, projects, and activities. Agencies hire people, enter into contracts, enter into grant agreements, and so on, in order to carry out their programs, projects, and activities.	Throughout fiscal year
The fiscal year ends.	September 30
Expired phase (no-year funds do not have an expired phase): Agencies disburse against obligated balances and adjust obligated balances to reflect actual obligations during the period of availability.	Until September 30, fifth year after period funds expire
Agencies continue to record obligations and outlays pursuant to administrative control of funds procedures, report to Treasury, and prepare financial statements.	

SOURCE: Executive Office of the President, Office of Management and Budget, *Preparation, Submission, and Execution of the Budget,* Circular No. A-11 (Washington, D.C.: Office of Management and Budget, 2011).

out-years, it almost always is considering cuts against some future budget baseline (an extension of present spending under certain projection assumptions, and differing assumptions can create different baselines), not a reduction in comparison with present actual spending levels.

From these discussions between agencies and the OMB during budget preparation, agencies submit requests in the fall for OMB review. Most issues are resolved between the OMB and the agency, but some require a final policy decision by the president. Transmission of the final document—the president's budget message—occurs no later than the first Monday in February (exceptions happen in the transition from one presidential administration to the next because there is too little time between when the president takes office and the February date). This document presents the president's program plans, with requests for funds to carry out those plans, for the upcoming fiscal year. That means for the fiscal year beginning on October 1, 2013 (the 2014 fiscal year), the message would be delivered in early February 2013.[20] The final budget is both printed and posted on the OMB website [http://www.whitehouse.gov/omb/budget] for public disclosure. (Before electronic dissemination, budget release day brought an army of staffers to the Government Printing Office to pick up stacks of paper copies of the budget documents, each set about a foot high, to take back to offices throughout the country. The Internet has completely destroyed that high drama.) The president's budget has no legal impact, but it provides the basis for congressional deliberations about providing budget authority, the result of appropriation legislation. Although the president's budget is sometimes claimed to be "dead on arrival" with no chance of passage, that is never completely true, just as no budget is enacted exactly as presented.

Many months separate the budget message from the end of its fiscal year. Not only can there be economic, international, and social surprises to upset plans, but also Congress may not agree with the presidential agenda. Nevertheless, differences between presidential plans and actual spending have been surprisingly small in relative terms. Total budget outlays seldom differ from the initial executive proposal by more than 2 percent (although that is still a lot of money). In pragmatic terms, this suggests the key role of the executive in aggregate expenditure control. If the president is not willing to make the difficult choices necessary for fiscal discipline and control, it is extremely unlikely that Congress will take on the task. There are, of course, much greater differences in individual programs than appear in these aggregates.

Another product of the long cycle is the phenomenon of lame-duck budgets. A new president faces not only about nine months of appropriations from the previous administration (from inauguration day through October 1), but also a new budget initiated during the term of the prior administration: prior budget instructions, OMB reviews, and so on. The date of the budget message falls just after inauguration day, so not much new perspective can be worked out and any transmission to Congress

---

[20]Unless the transmission date changes—the 1921 Act specified the first day of each regular session; the Budget and Account Procedures Act of 1950 changed the date to within the first fifteen days of the session; Gramm-Rudman-Hollings specified the first Monday after January 3; and BEA90 established the current date. Congress and the president have also changed the date by mutual consent. The Obama administration has characteristically been late in presenting its budget.

might be without much real detail. It isn't entirely clear whether the responsibility lies with the incoming or outgoing president, although outgoing presidents usually submit something (but not the Bush administration in 2009). Presidential transitions have usually involved a more-or-less full presentation from the outgoing president, followed by a short document from the new administration with promise to submit the details in a few months.[21]

Legislative Review and Appropriation Phase

The legislative review and appropriation phase of the federal cycle includes several committee pathways and many political quirks.[22] Appropriations are important because, for general operations of government, agencies are unable to spend (and operate) if they lack an appropriation that provides obligation authority for the fiscal year at hand. There are four different committee paths in the congressional fiscal process, each with different responsibilities, focuses, and interests. Each house has authorization (or substantive) committees, an appropriations committee (with its subcommittees), a budget committee, and a financing committee (Senate Finance and House Ways and Means). In the spending process, the authorization committees set policies and create programs for agencies to carry out. Committees with legislative jurisdiction over subject matter—for example, agriculture—consider (1) enabling, or organic, legislation that creates agencies, establishes programs, or prescribes a function; and (2) appropriation authorization legislation that authorizes appropriation of funds to implement the organic legislation. The latter may be part of the organic legislation, or it may be separate. There is no general requirement that specific authorization precede appropriation committee work, but there are some requirements and operating rules that make this the expected situation. Some programs require annual authorization; others have authorizations for a set number of years or for an indefinite period. Authorizations usually establish funding ceilings for particular programs, but they do not provide money to carry out those programs. Many authorized programs do not receive any appropriation ever. During legislative consideration, the president's view on proposed budgetary legislation is communicated, through the OMB, in Statements of Administration Policy (SAPs). Negotiations over budget policies and programs continue throughout the appropriation

---

[21]President George W. Bush submitted a general document titled *A Blueprint for New Beginnings: A Responsible Budget for America's Priorities* in April 2001, following an initial budget from outgoing President Clinton. This is what President Clinton did in February 1993, when he succeeded the earlier President Bush. President Barack Obama submitted a document titled *A New Era of Responsibility* at the end of February 2009, with a full budget presented in May. Because President George W. Bush presented no budget for that year, all budgets for 2010 had to come from the Obama administration. Karl O'Lessker, "The New President Makes a Budget," *Public Budgeting & Finance* 12 (Fall 1992): 3–18, traces how this revision process has evolved.

[22]The complete details of the legislative consideration phase can be found in Sandy Streeter, *The Congressional Appropriation Process: An Introduction,* CRS Report For Congress, Order Code 97-684 GOV (Washington, D.C.: Congressional Research Service, 2004); and Government Accountability Office, *Principles of Federal Appropriations Law,* 3rd ed., GAO-04-261SP (Washington, D.C.: Government Accountability Office, 2004).

process. However, somewhere there must be authorization from some source in place before agencies can operate.

The appropriations committees, working through their subcommittees, develop the appropriation bills that provide funds for federal agency operations. Appropriation subcommittee and authorization committee jurisdictions do not match up: the agencies falling under the jurisdiction of a particular authorizing committee may have appropriations in several different appropriation subcommittees. Table 3–4 lists the twelve appropriation subcommittees for the House and for the Senate in 2012, each with its own appropriation law to write. Congress can juggle its committees as it wishes. For instance, when the Department of Homeland Security was created in 2003, subcommittee jurisdictions were shifted to create a homeland security subcommittee within a total of thirteen subcommittees. The number was later reduced to twelve. Appropriations can be made in a single, consolidated appropriation act or through a number of separate appropriation acts. However, the last regular (in other words, fully intentional) consolidated appropriation was the General Appropriation Act of 1951 (P.L. 81–759). More recently, Congress has lumped many individual appropriation bills into a consolidated appropriation because it was unable to reach resolution on the individual bills and it had to act because agencies were running out of money. For example, the Consolidated Appropriations Act of 2012 (P.L. 112–74) passed in December 2011, several weeks after the fiscal year had started. It lumped appropriations for much of the federal government together, not because of any policy decision, but because of inability to act on a timely basis on the individual bills.

The financing committees are Senate Finance and House Ways and Means. These committees have jurisdiction over federal tax and revenue measures, an obviously critical part of government finance, but they also have jurisdiction over spending through the Social Security system, the Medicare and Medicaid structures, unemployment compensation, and payment of debt interest, a span that includes

Table 3–4
Senate and House of Representatives Appropriation Subcommittees (2012)

Agriculture, Rural Development, Food and Drug Administration, and Related Agencies
Commerce, Justice, Science, and Related Agencies
Defense
Energy and Water Development
Financial Services and General Government
Homeland Security
Interior, Environment, and Related Agencies
Labor, Health and Human Services, Education, and Related Agencies
Legislative Branch
Military Construction, Veterans Affairs, and Related Agencies
State, Foreign Operations, and Related Programs
Transportation, Housing and Urban Development, and Related Agencies

SOURCE: "United States Senate Committee on Appropriations" [http://appropriations.senate.gov/]; "U.S. House of Representatives Commitee on Appropriations" [http://appropriations.house.gov/].

more than half of all federal expenditure. Hence, these committees are extremely important for the finances of the federal government. More about their spending functions is discussed in a later section on entitlements.

Appropriations normally provide funds through distinct appropriation acts (see Sidebar 3–1), which emerge through the individual appropriations committees. These subcommittees work with pieces of the president's executive budget that reflect the requests from agencies within their jurisdiction. In this stage of legislative deliberation, elements of agency operation are examined, and agencies make the case for their fiscal plans. Committee staff and committee members develop considerable expertise in the subjects of their jurisdiction and watch programs very carefully. However, their focus is exclusively on the operations in their jurisdiction, not on other segments of the federal government. They are not inclined to work toward budgetary balance by cutting programs in their bill so that more can be spent in some other bill.

The appropriation bills are traditionally expected to originate in the House. Each bill is approved by the appropriation subcommittee, then by the full appropriations committee, and then by the House before starting a similar flow through the Senate. In recent years, however, Senate appropriation subcommittees have often started hearings before House action is complete. Both House and Senate must approve the bill before it can be transmitted to the president for signature into law.

Sidebar 3–1
The First General Appropriation Act

Here is the first general appropriation act passed by Congress (1789):

> Be it enacted by the Senate and House of Representatives of the United States of America in Congress assembled. That there be appropriated for the service of the present year, to be paid out of the monies which arise, either from the requisitions heretofore made upon the several states, or from the duties on impost and tonnage, the following sums, viz. A sum not exceeding two hundred and sixteen thousand dollars for defraying the expenses of the civil list, under the late and present government; a sum not exceeding one hundred and thirty-seven thousand dollars for defraying the expenses of the department of war; a sum not exceeding one hundred and ninety thousand dollars for discharging the warrants issued by the late board of treasury, and remaining unsatisfied; and a sum not exceeding ninety-six thousand dollars for paying the pensions to invalids. [1 stat. 95]

That is a total of $639,000: $216,000 for civil or administrative governments, $137,000 for defense, $190,000 to retire short-term debt issued by the prior government, and $96,000 for pensions to the disabled.

Compare this act with any of the recent appropriation acts for a contrast in complexity, length, and money. For instance, the fiscal 2010 appropriation for the Department of Homeland Security alone was for over $42,800,000,000, and the act making the appropriation was forty-nine pages long.

Congress usually passes appropriations in lump sums to accounts that group related activities together, like "Construction, General."[23] The appropriation committees are not supposed to get into policy, just financing. However, the appropriation act may include provisions that designate some funds for particular purposes or particular locations. The provisions may be in committee reports and explanatory statements rather than in the law itself. Agencies generally regard these notes as binding because they do not want to jeopardize their relationship with Congress in future budget cycles. The designation may also be in the appropriation bill itself. Here is an example. In the Omnibus Appropriation Act, 2009, the Army Corps of Engineers received an appropriation for construction of $2,141,677,000. The Act also included the following statement shortly after the appropriated amount: *"Provided further,* That the Chief of Engineers is directed to use $8,000,000 of the funds appropriated herein for planning, engineering, design or construction of the Grundy, Buchanan County, and Dickenson County, Virginia, elements of the Levisa and Tug Forks of the Big Sandy River and Upper Cumberland River Project." Purists might object that such matters are those of policy or substance, thus belonging in the authorization and not in a law providing financing. Purists seldom serve on appropriation committees.

Members of Congress historically coveted membership on the appropriations committee because programs and projects of special constituent interest may be developed, expanded, and protected there. The assignment isn't as attractive as it once was, given the concern about federal deficit control and constraints on federal spending—but it still helps to be among the group that is making the control selections. All members are selected from geographically specific electoral bases, and their constituencies can benefit from location-specific projects—pork-barrel spending or "ZIP code designated expenditure"—that have scant return to the nation, but bring federal money into the home economy.[24] (Of course, programs that do have

[23]Operating agencies are not permitted to move money from one account to another without congressional permission. In 2012, the National Weather Service moved funds from various long-term capital projects to pay employees without asking permission. The NWS believed the account for pay was underfunded and the capital project account was underfunded. Of course, that is a call to be made by Congress, not the agency. The actions did not cause spending that was above appropriation but it violated the appropriation account structure and it appeared that the NWS has been making unapproved reprogramming for some time. After the problem was discovered, it for a time appeared that the NWS would have to furlough 5,000 employees in the summer because of a lack of funds. Finally, Congress acted to make a reallocation to preserve the agency. The NWS's director abruptly retired and other staff were replaced. [Lisa Rein, "Congress to Allow National Westher Service to Reconfigure Budget," *Washington Post,* June 20, 2012.] The appropriation accounts are serious business.

[24]The effectiveness of Robert Byrd as chair of the Senate Appropriations Committee for his home state of West Virginia is legendary, but there are many other successful practitioners as well. For entertaining, but troubling examples, see Brian Kelly, *Adventures in Porkland: How Washington Wastes Your Money and Why They Won't Stop* (New York: Villard, 1992). A more scholarly study of appropriations legislation is Richard Munson, *The Cardinals of Capitol Hill* (New York: Grove Press, 1993). Cardinals are the chairs of the appropriation subcommittees. Ronald Utt notes that the pork projects often do not fit the priorities of the recipient locales. Ronald D. Utt, "How Congressional Earmarks and Pork-Barrel Spending Undermine State and Local Decision-Making," *The Heritage Foundation Backgrounder,* no. 1266, April 2, 1999. More on how it works: Representative John Murtha, chair of the House Defense Appropriations Subcommittee, makes sure that multiple millions of defense and other federal spending gets directed to the Johnstown, Pennsylvania, airport (named after him). The airport has modest activity—three commuter round-trips to Washington per day—and much of the military equipment there is disused; some has never been used. Mr. Murtha argues that upgrades to the airport are important so that it could serve as a backup to Pittsburgh in a crisis. Critics argue that the spending is pure pork, driven solely by the congressman's control over defense appropriations. Carol D. Leonnig, "Murtha Airport Got Military Upgrades," *Washington Post,* April 30, 2009.

national importance have to be situated somewhere, and directing those to the home jurisdiction can be helped by membership on the appropriations committee as well.) Although pork-barrel spending often includes highway projects (the Transportation Equity Act for the 21st Century, H.R. 2400, included 1,850 location-designated projects alone—but that was an authorization bill, so the projects may not have been actually carried out), university institutes and research programs, airports, government office buildings, and the like, no appropriation bill is immune. But what makes a particular project "pork" as opposed to being a program that simply happens to be physically in a particular location? Using standards akin to Supreme Court Justice Potter Stewart's statement about pornography ("I know it when I see it," *Jacobellis* v. *Ohio,* 378 U.S. 184 [1964]), the media can easily identify wasteful government spending, but more careful discussion attempts to hone the concept more precisely. Counting up pork is a slippery task because what an external observer sees as wasteful spending will usually be seen as highly productive by those benefiting from it.

Some common features of identified pork include the following: the project is created as an earmark (a location-specific line item) in the appropriation bill; the project emerges from a member of Congress rather than from the administrative agency review process; and the project is added to the appropriation bill after the regular hearings and deliberations that produced the bill and without any discussions about the particular project. Thwarting such items seems a way to constrain wasteful spending and to constrain the deficit, although some believe that a bit of pork is useful as a means of lubricating the legislative process. They argue that without the pork, deals would be harder to consummate and Congress would do even less than it does already. However, congressional earmarks were one critical element in the lobbyist influence scandals of 2005–2006 that sent people to jail.[25]

The Office of Management and Budget, starting in the later years of the Bush administration, has tracked the amount of earmarks in the appropriation bills, defining earmarks as "funds provided by the Congress for projects, programs, or grants where the purported congressional direction (whether in statutory text, report language, or other communication) circumvents otherwise applicable merit-based or competitive allocation processes, or specifies the location or recipient, or otherwise curtails the ability of the executive branch to manage its statutory and constitutional responsibilities pertaining to the funds allocation process."[26] OMB counts as earmarks (1) add-ons: when the appropriation was more than requested by the administration and had restrictions on how the additional money was to be spent (particularly involving locations); (2) carve-outs: restriction on how some portion of

---

[25]Pork may also be in the eyes of the beholder. Governor Jindal of Louisiana denounced wasteful spending on volcano monitoring in his response to President Obama's message to Congress on the large fiscal stimulus bill. That got a quick eruption from both senators from Alaska, Republican and Democrat, who pointed out the significance of that work for protection of life, limb, and property in areas with volcanos—like Alaska. Shortly after Jindal's speech, Mount Redoubt in Alaska erupted, but damage was not as severe as it could have been because the volcano monitors worked to provide some advance warning. George Bryson, "Alaskans Fume over Jindal Volcano-Monitoring Remark," *Anchorage Daily News,* February 25, 2009.

[26]Office of Management and Budget, "Guidance to Agencies on Definition of Earmarks" [http://earmarks .omb.gov/earmarks-public/earmarks_definition.html].

the appropriation was to be used; and (3) provisions that are so restrictive that only one recipient can qualify for funding. Table 3–5 presents the OMB tally for fiscal years 2005 and 2008 to 2010 for each appropriation bill. The number of earmarks does appear to have fallen over time, possibly the result of improved transparency provided by these tallies, and the number of earmarks varies considerably across the bills. But the largest dollar amount of earmarks always appears in defense appropriations. One suspects that defending the nation from foreign threats was not what was at the top of the agenda in how that money was spent. However, it should be kept in mind that this total amount of earmarks in each year amounts to only a small share of total discretionary spending, never more than 2 percent in any year. Earmarks just do not make much contribution to the overall fiscal position of the U.S. government. Indeed, a number of observers suggest that earmarks do not increase spending, but rather simply direct where money will be spent.[27] If not for the earmarks, the money would still have been spent, just for something else.

It is easy and appropriate to be enraged about earmarks and pork—efficient and effective provision of government services is not served by such interventions into a system that should make decisions based on careful balancing of the returns from various alternatives to spending public money. But there is no simple solution when choices, by their nature, must be political.[28] Rules approved by the Senate and House in early 2011 ban earmarking for the 112th Congress, so members of Congress must use less transparent mechanisms, including convincing federal agencies to roll what would have previously been a congressional earmark into the agency budget request, and whether the ban will continue is unclear. In fact, members of Congress have a pretty good idea into what congressional district money will flow if particular agency operations are funded, even without formal earmarking. And banning earmarks promises little impact on federal spending and presents only a modest impediment to spending to benefit congressional constituencies.

The budget committees develop the congressional budget (the budget resolution). Before the 1974 Act, Congress considered the federal budget only as the several appropriations bills; Congress did not consider the budget as a whole. The budget was fragmented into general administrative department "chunks," and each chunk was considered by a separate appropriations subcommittee. This microlevel budget analysis permitted scrutiny of individual department requests, but it did not permit the overall comparison of revenue, expenditures, and the accompanying surplus or deficit. More important, this practice did not permit consideration of governmentwide priorities—transportation versus defense, national parks versus urban

---

[27]Savage correctly points out that there are significant administrative costs associated with handling the earmarks, over and above the funds directly involved in the earmark. James D. Savage, "The Administrative Costs of Congressional Earmarking: The Case of the Office of Naval Research," *Public Administration Review* 69 (May/June 2009): 448–57.

[28]For many years, the sponsors of earmarks have been anonymous—the member of Congress who inserted an earmark was not identified. In recent years, an OMB database tracks each earmark, identifying the member of Congress who inserted it and what geographic area it would benefit. The idea probably was to shame the transgressors of public efficiency. It didn't work. Members of Congress could now definitively claim credit for bringing back the bucks to their district. In matter of fact, the public likes earmarks when they bring money back home. It is money going elsewhere that the public resents.

Table 3-5
Earmarks by Appropriation Bill, Office of Management and Budget Tabulation

Appropriation Subcommittee/Spending Bill	Number, 2005	$ Thousands, 2005	Number, 2008	$ Thousands, 2008	Number, 2009	$ Thousands, 2009	Number, 2010	$ Thousands, 2010
Agriculture, Rural Development, Food and Drug Administration, and Related Agencies	852	636,880	525	337,204	494	312,830	465	359,859
Commerce, Justice, Science, and Related Agencies	1,277	1,360,918	1,738	932,531	1,556	785,690	1,518	745,389
Defense	2,505	8,386,730	2,087	6,644,746	2,091	5,577,811	1,759	4,592,471
Energy and Water Development	973	1,290,161	1,781	3,686,124	1,839	3,801,893	965	1,185,239
Financial Services and General Government	201	177,329	202	409,240	265	143,204	278	350,766
Homeland Security	7	27,900	122	348,218	131	501,328	177	243,695
Interior and Environment	1,354	965,206	568	436,058	565	447,300	555	371,356
Labor, Health and Human Services, and Education	3,060	1,273,936	2,252	899,278	2,163	882,671	1,786	823,347
Legislative Branch	—	—	—	—	—	—	—	—
Military Construction and Veterans Administration	132	952,686	190	1,177,245	178	1,329,609	184	1,206,086
State, Foreign Operations, and Related Programs	90	307,535	5	23,012	1	5,000	—	—
Transportation, Housing and Urban Development, and Related Agencies	3,041	3,559,376	2,053	1,748,036	1,841	1,495,744	1,505	1,218,913
Total	13,492	18,938,657	11,523	16,641,692	11,124	15,283,080	9,192	11,097,121
Total Discretionary Outlays		968,500,000		1,134,900,000		1,237,500,000		1,347,200,000
Earmarks to Total Discretionary Outlays		1.96%		1.47%		1.23%		0.82%

SOURCE: Office of Management and Budget "Earmarks" [http://earmarks.omb.gov/earmarks-public/]

housing, and so on—that effective budget choices require, and there was nothing in the system that balanced the funds added to one department against the need to finance that increase through either more revenue or less spending somewhere else. Appropriation committees scrutinized appropriations within their individual bill and Congress appropriated to the appropriation bills and that was that.

The revised process, used initially for the 1977 budget, produced an additional flow through Congress: the appropriations committees work as before, but separate budget committees, with staff assistance from the CBO, draft a budget resolution that encompasses budget levels for five years.[29] The resolution presents recommended aggregates for new budget authority, budget outlays, direct loan obligations, primary loan guarantee commitments, revenues, surplus or deficit, and public debt and recommends aggregate revenue change. New budget authority, budget outlays, direct loan obligations, and primary loan guarantees are also divided among twenty functions of government (the major national priorities served by the federal government, such as national defense, transportation, agriculture, and administration of justice). The explanatory statement with the resolution allocates budget authority and outlays in functional categories to committees with jurisdiction over programs in the function. The appropriations committees must allocate budget authority and outlays among their subcommittees. Allocations to each House and Senate committee are called 302(a) allocations, after the section in the 1974 Act that provides for them; their allocations to the twelve subcommittees are called 302(b) allocations. This budget resolution is macro-level; it does not work directly from the detailed agency requests, and it does not provide funds for any agency to spend, although the budget committees (and their staff) are well versed in what agencies have in mind and they do receive budget recommendations from each standing committee of Congress as they develop the resolution. The concurrent budget resolution is approved by both houses of Congress in the spring, before the appropriation consideration begins in earnest.[30] The budget resolution does not go to the president for approval, it is not a law, and it provides no funds for any agency. The deadline for its passage is frequently missed, and Congress has approved no budget resolution in some recent years. (There is some dispute as to whether the 2011 Budget Control Act, with its required ceilings, might have superceded the need for the budget resolution.) The congressional budget provides a template against which the micro-budget actions of appropriations committees can be judged for control and constraint. The timetable that Table 3–3 showed for the congressional budget and appropriation process would have Congress complete all appropriations actions before the start of the fiscal year (it usually doesn't).

There is a final element to the congressional budget process: reconciliation. The 1974 Act created reconciliation as a mechanism for getting the year's tax and expenditure policies to coincide with the targets in the congressional budget. It has come

---

[29]That's the budget year and four out-years. Appropriations continue to be predominantly for only the single budget year.
[30]The formal Clinton fiscal 1994 budget was the first since the 1974 Act received by Congress after it had passed the budget resolution. President Obama presented a budget outline in late February, followed by passage of a congressional budget resolution, followed by a traditional presidential budget. Appropriation subcommittees normally start hearings before the resolution.

to be viewed as the most powerful congressional tool for deficit reduction: rather than minor, one-year adjustments to targets, it now entails five-year instructions to committees for tax or fee increases and for spending cuts. The amounts involved can be large.[31] The reconciliation bill can be powerful, if Congress chooses to use its full clout, because (1) the bill gives binding instructions for changes in taxes and spending by formula or for reductions in spending to all committees except for appropriations committees, which are subject to other ceilings; (2) the bill cannot be filibustered, so it requires only a simple majority to be approved in the face of considerable objection (when majority parties in the Senate lack 60 votes, they like the reconciliation process as a legislative approach); (3) amendments must be germane, and committees cannot add extraneous provisions (both are subject to a sixty-vote test in the Senate); and (4) a committee that fails to meet its reconciliation target is subject to a motion to return its report to committee and return with a proposal that meets the target.[32]

The congressional budget process permits Congress to develop its own spending priorities, particularly with the assistance of the CBO, and to consider the appropriate macroeconomic impact for its fiscal actions. Without the congressional budget, the system would have the president being responsible for budget aggregates and overall policy plans and Congress responding to adjust those priorities by moving funds in the appropriation process. The congressional budget process adds a congressional view on priorities and responsibility for aggregates.[33]

After Congress passes an appropriation bill, it must be signed by the president before it becomes law. The president can veto the bill or sign the bill in its entirety. For almost a century and a half, every president has sought the line-item veto, the power to strike individual parts of spending and taxing bills, while signing the remaining sections into law. The Line-Item Veto Act (P.L. 104–130, April 9, 1996) revised the Congressional Budget and Impoundment Control Act by granting the president additional power to shape federal finances. For calendar years 1997 through 2004, the president was given the power to cancel (1) any dollar amount of discretionary spending authority, (2) any item of new direct spending (roughly, new entitlements), or (3) any limited tax benefit (defined to be a revenue-losing provision with 100 or fewer beneficiaries; the Joint Committee on Taxation was to establish the list of eligible provisions and append the list to the bill sent to the president) within five days of signing into law the act containing the item. The president could cancel whole individual amounts in the appropriation acts or in the reports

---

[31]The reconciliation in 1981 was the medium for implementing President Reagan's economic reconstruction for fiscal 1982 (the 1982 executive budget had originated with President Carter, so this was the best place for President Reagan to revise those plans). The 1993 reconciliation was similarly the medium used by President Clinton.

[32]A complete discussion of the reconciliation process appears in Robert Keith and Bill Heniff, Jr., *The Budget Reconciliation Process: House and Senate Procedures,* CRS Report for Congress, Order Code RL33030 (Washington, D.C.: Congressional Research Service, August 10, 2005).

[33]Not everyone considers this an improvement. Louis Fisher writes, "By looking to Congress for comprehensive action, the unity and leadership that must come from the President have been unwittingly weakened. Creation of multiple budgets opened the door to escapism, confusion, and a loss of political accountability." "Federal Budget Doldrums: The Vacuum of Presidential Leadership," *Public Administration Review* 50 (November/December 1990): 699.

accompanying the acts, but could not reduce the amounts. The cancellation required that the president determine that the action would (1) reduce the federal budget deficit (and special controls ensured that this would occur), (2) not impair any essential government function, and (3) not harm the national interest. Congress had the ability to override the cancellation within a thirty-day review period.[34] In fiscal 1998 appropriation bills, which were the first approved under the item-veto cloud, President Clinton vetoed 77 items, accounting for about 0.10 percent of discretionary budget authority proposed in those bills. Of these, 87 percent were taken from defense and military construction bills, and Congress overrode the veto of the latter. This was the last use of this power because in *William J. Clinton, President of the United States* v. *City of New York,* 524 U.S. 417 (1998), the U.S. Supreme Court ruled that the line-item veto authority departed from the "finely wrought" constitutional procedure for enactment of law. If the president is to have line-item veto power, the Constitution must be amended; the power cannot be provided by simple legislation.

Not all agree that such power would improve government finances or even have much impact. The power can provide the president a tool to prevent pork-barrel and other wasteful spending, but it also gives the president a valuable weapon to punish recalcitrant members of Congress—those who have managed to get on a presidential "enemies list"—by making sure that programs they support receive meager funding. And it cuts the president in on the deal making that builds appropriations and other pieces of legislation: the president can assure a representative's vote on a program by promising not to veto a project dear to the member of Congress. Indeed, the president may be wary of vetoing any pet projects of members of Congress with leadership roles, the people whose support is needed for presidential programs, while other members are not thus protected. Overall, the tool would shift the balance of power toward the president. Many are willing to accept these potential problems for the sake of greater fiscal responsibility and because the president's national constituency might make him less controlled by narrow interests than members of Congress. Others regard it as an inappropriate change in the balance of powers between the legislative and executive branches and believe that it carries the potential for great political evil. For now, only congressional action can rescind an appropriation or tax benefit that the president wishes out of a law.

Execution/Service Delivery

The end dates of the fiscal year set the bounds for the execution phase, the third stage of the process. In this period, appropriated monies are spent and public services are delivered. Fiscal control is critical in budget execution, and budget accounts are used to control funds provided through the appropriations. These accounts are the mechanism Congress employs to control how government services are provided. Appendix 3–1 explains and illustrates the linkage between appropriations (the

---

[34]The first use of the line-item veto: three provisions in the 1997 reconciliation laws. See Jackie Calmes and Greg Hitt, "Clinton Uses Line-Item Veto for First Time," *Wall Street Journal,* August 12, 1997, Z-3.

legal articulation of the financial plan that is the budget) and these budget accounts. The fact that money is appropriated for a purpose, however, does not automatically and immediately lead to public expenditure or even to agencies having money to obligate/spend. To prevent agencies from exhausting funds before the end of the fiscal year and to use expenditure timing for macroeconomic purposes, the OMB divides total agency obligation authority into sums for distribution over the year (apportionments), and agencies obligate those portions as the year progresses.

Historically, appropriations were regarded as the maximum authority available to spend. The president could spend up to the appropriated amount, but not more. Presidents, starting with John Adams, regularly impounded budget authority, acting on their own, to control spending during budget execution. It was regarded as a reasonable device for constraining the pace of spending and for efficient operations. The amounts were modest, and, although it might irritate members of Congress whose pet projects got caught in the trap, the process was accepted as part of executive management of finances. However, President Nixon took the impoundment authority to new heights in the early 1970s, both in size (around 12 percent of appropriations) and targets (members of Congress who were deemed enemies of the president had projects in which they were interested hit by the impoundment axe).[35] Congress responded with provisions in the Congressional Budget and Impoundment Control Act. After the 1974 Act, impoundments became subject to congressional review and were divided into two categories: rescissions of budget authority, or permanent cancellation, and deferrals, or temporary withdrawal, of budget authority in the fiscal year. Rescissions proposed by the president must be approved by Congress within forty-five days of the proposal. (Congress may also initiate rescissions.) If not approved within the deadline, the funds must be released for expenditure. Deferrals require a message to Congress reporting the action; the deferral may not involve a change in policy, but may be justified by a need to provide for contingencies or to achieve savings from changed requirements or operating efficiency. The deferral cannot extend beyond the fiscal year.[36] "Programmatic" delays—when "operational factors unavoidably impede the obligation of budget authority, notwithstanding the agency's reasonable and good faith efforts to implement the program"[37]—do not need to be reported.

Table 3–6 traces the historical record of rescissions since their beginnings. That record clearly shows a number of things. First, compared to total government spending, rescissions—both proposed and enacted—have been modest. Second, rescissions coming from Congress have been larger than those coming from the president. And, third, the success rate of presidential rescission proposals has not been high.

---

[35]The events that caused the change are chronicled in Louis Fisher, *Presidential Spending Power* (Princeton, N.J.: Princeton University Press, 1975), especially Chapters 7 and 8.

[36]Congress may enact legislation disapproving a deferral. Under the initial act, either house could prevent the deferral by passing an impoundment resolution. This was ruled to be an unconstitutional legislative veto in *City of New Haven* v. *United States,* 809 F.2d 900 (D.C. Cir. 1987), and was replaced with the current system.

[37]Office of the General Counsel, General Accounting Office, *Principles of Federal Appropriations Law* (Washington, D.C.: U.S. Government Printing Office, 2004), 21. This is the principal reference on federal budget authority and appropriations for the federal government.

Table 3-6
Summary of Proposed and Enacted Rescissions and Total Outlays, Fiscal Years 1974–2010

Fiscal year	Rescissions Proposed by President Number	Rescissions Proposed by President Dollars (in Millions)	Proposals Accepted by Congress Number	Proposals Accepted by Congress Dollars (in Millions)	Rescissions Initiated by Congress Number	Rescissions Initiated by Congress Dollars (in Millions)	Total Enacted	Total Rescinded ($ Millions)	Total On-Budget Outlays ($ Millions)	President Proposing Rescissions
2010	0	—	0	—	132	10,977.06	132	10,977.06	2,901,531	B. Obama
2009	0	—	0	—	92	12,716.57	92	12,716.57	3,000,661	B. Obama
2008	0	—	0	—	126	12,201.18	126	12,201.18	2,507,793	G.W. Bush/B. Obama
2007	0	—	0	—	56	8,035.71	56	8,035.71	2,275,049	G.W. Bush
2006	0	—	0	—	89	33,361.18	89	33,361.18	2,232,981	G.W. Bush
2005	0	—	0	—	76	6,351.13	76	6,351.13	2,069,746	G.W. Bush
2004	0	—	0	—	49	10,515.46	49	10,515.46	1,913,330	G.W. Bush
2003	0	—	0	—	47	3,123.44	47	3,123.44	1,796,890	G.W. Bush
2002	0	—	0	—	76	4,621.09	76	4,621.09	1,655,232	G.W. Bush
2001	0	—	0	—	67	5,148.14	67	5,148.14	1,516,008	G.W. Bush
2000	3	128.00	0	—	61	3,757.77	61	3,757.77	1,458,185	W. Clinton/G.W. Bush
1999	3	35.04	2	16.80	105	5,081.43	107	5,098.23	1,381,064	W. Clinton
1998	25	25.26	21	17.28	43	4,180.81	64	4,198.09	1,335,854	W. Clinton
1997	10	407.11	6	285.11	96	7,381.25	102	7,666.36	1,290,490	W. Clinton
1996	24	1,425.90	8	963.40	104	4,974.85	112	5,938.25	1,259,580	W. Clinton
1995	29	1,199.82	25	845.39	248	18,868.38	273	19,713.77	1,227,078	W. Clinton
1994	65	3,172.18	45	1,293.48	81	2,374.42	126	3,667.89	1,182,380	W. Clinton
1993	7	356.00	4	206.25	74	2,205.34	78	2,411.59	1,142,799	W. Clinton
1992	128	7,879.47	26	2,067.55	131	22,526.95	157	24,594.50	1,129,191	W. Clinton
1991	30	4,859.25	8	286.42	26	1,420.47	34	1,706.89	1,082,539	G.H.W. Bush/W. Clinton
1990	11	554.26	0	—	71	2,304.99	71	2,304.97	1,027,928	G.H.W. Bush
1989	6	143.10	1	2.05	11	325.91	12	327.97	932,832	G.H.W. Bush
1988	0	—	0	—	61	3,888.66	61	3,888.66	860,012	G.H.W. Bush
1987	73	5,835.80	2	36.00	52	12,359.39	54	12,395.39	809,243	R. Reagan/G.H.W. Bush
1986	83	10,126.90	4	143.21	7	5,409.41	11	5,552.62	806,842	R. Reagan
1985	245	1,856.09	98	173.70	12	5,458.62	110	5,632.32	769,396	R. Reagan
1984	9	636.40	3	55.38	7	2,188.69	10	2,244.06	685,632	R. Reagan
1983	21	1,569.00	0	—	11	310.61	11	310.61	660,934	R. Reagan
1982	32	7,907.40	5	4,365.49	5	48.43	10	4,413.92	594,892	R. Reagan
1981	133	15,361.90	101	10,880.94	43	3,736.49	144	14,617.43	542,956	J. Carter/R. Reagan
1980	59	1,618.10	34	777.70	33	3,238.21	67	4,015.90	477,044	J. Carter
1979	11	908.70	9	723.61	1	47.50	10	771.11	404,941	J. Carter
1978	12	1,290.10	5	518.66	4	67.16	9	585.82	369,585	J. Carter
1977	20	1,926.93	9	813.69	3	172.72	12	986.41	328,675	G. Ford/J. Carter
1976	50	3,582.00	7	148.33	0	—	7	148.33	77,281	G. Ford
1975	87	2,722.00	38	386.30	1	5.00	39	391.30	301,098	G. Ford
1974	2	495.64	0	—	3	1,400.41	3	1,400.41	270,780	G. Ford

SOURCE: Government Accountability Office, *Updated Rescission Statistics, Fiscal Years 1974–2010*, B-321125 (Washington, D.C.: Government Accountability Office, June 23, 2011); and Office of Management and Budget, *Budget of the United States Government, Fiscal Year 2012* (Washington, D.C.: U.S. Government Printing Office, 2011).

President Clinton had the best luck with over 50 percent of the dollar value of his proposals enacted. President Ford fared the worst, with only 16 percent of his proposals enacted. Presidents George W. Bush and Barack Obama did not make any proposals. About one-third of all presidential rescissions have been enacted, both in numbers and in volume.[38] Congress has been more aggressive in rescissions than have the presidents. In contrast to most chief executives, the president does have clearly constrained powers of control in budget execution.

Audit

The audit phase of the federal cycle, supervised by the GAO, formally begins at the end of the fiscal year. Some audit functions, however, do begin during the fiscal year as agencies work to prevent illegal and irregular transactions by various approval stages. In an important sense, the audit phase ensures that everything else in the budget process matters: unless the decisions made elsewhere in the process are carried through, the process is irrelevant. The audit phase determines whether those directions were followed. The GAO reports to the House and Senate Committees on Government Operations, and those reports are accessible at the GAO website [http://www.gao.gov].

Sorts of Budget Authority

Budget authority gives agencies the ability to enter into obligations that will eventually result in outlays (from the Treasury) of federal funds. Agencies receive this authority rather than actual funds to spend. The authority may be one-year, multiyear, or no-year authority; the law providing the authority will define how long the agency will have the authority before it expires. The action may be permanent and amounts may be indefinite. The result of congressional deliberations, including passage of identical statutes by both houses and approval by the president of those statutes, is budget authority. This encompasses several authorities to make commitments (obligations) that result in government outlays (or expenditures), either now or in the future. Important types of authority include the following:

1. **Appropriations authority,** the most common authority, permits "federal agencies to incur obligations and to make payments from Treasury for specified purposes."[39]

---

[38]A much higher percentage of deferrals—99.4 percent of dollars appropriated from 1975 to 1988—has been approved. See Allen Schick, "The Disappearing Impoundment Power," *Tax Foundation's Tax Features* 32 (October 1988): 4.

[39]Accounting and Financial Management Division, Government Accountability Office, *A Glossary of Terms Used in the Federal Budget Process* [http://www.gao.gov/new.items/d057345p.pdf].

2. **Contract authority** provides authority for agencies to enter into binding contracts before the agency has an appropriation to make payments under the contract or in amounts greater than existing appropriations.[40] Eventually, an appropriation must cover the contracts, and, because the contracts legally commit the U.S. government, Congress would have little choice but to provide the appropriation. At one time, contract authority provided a device for "backdoor spending," a way that substantive committees could force the more conservative appropriations committees to accept more aggressive government programs. Now new contract authority can be provided only to the extent appropriations are also provided for that fiscal year.

3. **Borrowing authority** appearing in either a substantive law or an appropriation act allows an agency to incur and liquidate obligations from borrowed funds. That authority may involve some combination of borrowing from the Treasury, borrowing directly from the public (selling agency debt securities), or borrowing from the Federal Financing Bank (selling agency securities to it). Again, this authority now is limited to amounts provided in appropriation acts.

4. **Loan and loan-guarantee authority** consists of statutory authorizations for the government's pledge to pay all or part of principal and interest to a lender if the borrower defaults; no obligation occurs until the contingency (default) occurs. Such commitments, after the Federal Credit Reform Act of 1990, now require specified treatment in appropriation acts of estimated long-term costs (defaults, delinquencies, etc.).

5. **Entitlement authority** provides authority "to make payments (including grants and loans) for which budget authority is not provided in advance by appropriation acts to any person or government if, under the provisions of the law containing such authority, the U.S. government is obligated to make the payments to persons or governments who meet the requirements established by the law."[41] Entitlements provide payments according to formula: Social Security, Medicare, Medicaid, and veterans' benefits (pensions and education) are some important examples. Farm price supports fall in this category as well; they were replaced by a firm appropriation for a time. Entitlement spending results not directly from the appropriation process, but through the extent to which beneficiaries qualify under the formulas erected in substantive law. Entitlements now fall within the scope of the reconciliation process. As noted earlier, much growth in federal spending comes from entitlements. In a later section, we examine the nature of entitlements and "mandatory" expenditure in greater detail.

Regular appropriation is now the checkpoint for most important sources of budget authority, entitlements being the major exception. And controlling the granting of budget authority is the way in which Congress and the President could

---

[40]Most federal highway programs operate with contract authority. U.S. Department of Transportation, Federal Highway Administration, *Financing Federal-Aid Highways,* Publication No. FHWA-PL-92-016 (May 1992), explains this system.

[41]GAO, *Glossary.*

control the growth of government spending, should they be so inclined. There are three types of appropriation measures: regular appropriation bills, continuing resolutions, and supplemental appropriation bills. Regular appropriations come in several durations (periods of legal availability) with different rules attached to each. The traditional appropriation is *annual* (one-year) authority, which provides funds for obligation during a specific fiscal year.[42] Such appropriations usually finance the routine activities of federal agencies; unless specified otherwise, appropriations are annual and may not be carried beyond the current fiscal year for obligation later (funds expire). *No-year* appropriations provide funds for obligations with no restrictions placed on year of use. Most construction funds, some funds for research, and many trust fund appropriations have been handled in this fashion. *Multiple-year* appropriations provide funds for a particular activity for several years. General revenue sharing, a program of federal assistance to state and local governments of the late 1970s and early 1980s, was funded on that basis to provide greater predictability for the recipients. *Advance* appropriations provide agencies with funds for future fiscal years. This structure is seldom used, although it can facilitate agency planning and has been strongly urged for use in defense-system procurement. *Permanent* appropriations provide funds for specified purposes without requiring repeated action by Congress. To add greater certainty to public capital markets, interest on the federal debt is handled with such appropriations. All but annual appropriations reduce the ability of the legislative and executive branches to realign fiscal policy when economic or social conditions change, even though they increase agency ability to develop long-range plans. The trade between control and planning is not an easy one, but responsibility and accountability probably weigh the balance toward annual appropriation, especially in regard to the difficulty of forecasting operating environments many months in advance.

Budget authority not obligated within the time period for which it was appropriated expires. Congress may act to extend the availability of funds, either before or after their scheduled expiration, through re-appropriation. The federal budget structure counts these funds as new budget authority for the fiscal year of re-appropriation.

Two other methods of providing agency funds, in addition to these normal appropriations, should be mentioned. First, a *continuing resolution* allows agencies to function when a new fiscal year begins before agency appropriation laws have been approved for the year. The resolution—an agreement between both legislative houses—authorizes the agency to continue operations.[43] The resolution level may be the same as the prior year, may entail certain increases, or may encompass the appropriation bill as it has emerged from one house of Congress; the resolution may

---

[42]Congress may appropriate for less than a full fiscal year. A fiscal 1980 appropriation to the Community Services Administration for emergency energy-assistance grants specified that awards could not be made after June 30, 1980. Congress wanted to help with heating, not air conditioning (P.L. 96–126), but there was a severe heat wave, and Congress extended the program to include fans; the appropriation was extended to the full fiscal year (P.L. 96–-321).

[43]A good guide to the construction of and experience with continuing resolutions is Thad Juszczak, "Living with Continuing Resolutions," *The Public Manager* 40 (Fall 2011): 40–44.

be for part of the fiscal year or for the entire year. Without some action, however, the agency without appropriations could not spend and would not be able to provide services.[44]

The congressional budget process establishes a timetable for appropriations that would eliminate the need for continuing resolutions, but that deadline often has not been met. How often are continuing resolutions necessary? In the fiscal years from 1948 through 2012, all appropriation acts were signed into law by the first day of the new fiscal year only in 1989, 1995, and 1997—and it was done for 1997 only by rolling six appropriation bills (defense; commerce, justice, state, and the judiciary; foreign operations; interior; labor, health and human services, and education; and treasury) into an omnibus appropriation bill approved on September 30, 1996, just in the nick of time! For fiscal 2012, there were five continuing resolutions before a consolidated appropriation bill got passed, but the extreme was probably fiscal 2001, when twenty-one continuing resolutions were needed. All government operations were rolled into an omnibus continuing resolution for fiscal 1987 and fiscal 1988. In fiscal 2003, 2004, and 2005, several appropriation bills were lumped together in a consolidated appropriation because Congress could not agree on them separately, and they were finally approved well after the start of the new fiscal year. In 2003, the omnibus appropriation included eleven bills (all but defense and military construction); in 2004, it included seven bills (all but defense, energy and water, homeland security, interior, the legislative branch, and military construction); and in 2005, it included nine bills (all but defense, District of Columbia, homeland security, and military construction). Since fiscal 1996, such omnibus appropriation acts have been the rule rather than the exception. Continuing resolutions for major portions of the government went through the full fiscal year in 2007 and 2008. (However, a full eleven bills were passed for 2006.) And various parts of the government were closed for absence of either appropriation or continuing resolution in the early 1980s and, most recently, at the start of the 1996 fiscal year. The timetable for nicely defined appropriations in place with the new fiscal year is not always met.

Continuing resolutions have many trappings of appropriations, but their continued use raises three special issues. First, the continuing resolution in theory would have few, if any, new programs. A steady pattern of such funding could hinder an agency's program development and response to changing service conditions. And, in similar fashion, programs that are scheduled to be terminated, even when there is agreement between the president and Congress on the termination, continue in operation. Second, the omnibus continuing resolution may partly impede the president's veto power. A veto of an omnibus package could harm the flow of services throughout the government, a consequence the president ordinarily would want to avoid, even though there may be some included appropriation bills that might

---

[44]Sometimes an impasse prevents the continuing resolution from being passed in time, and there is an appropriation gap for some days. This has occurred in fiscal years 1977, 1978, 1979, 1980, 1982, 1983, 1984, 1985, 1987, 1988, 1991, and 1996, and "non-essential" portions of the federal government were shut down. The 1996 gap was 21 days. Kevin Kosar, *Shutdown of the Federal Government: Causes, Effects, and Process,* CRS Report for Congress, Order Code 98-844 GOV (Washington, D.C.: Congressional Research Service, September 20, 2004).

individually be vetoed. Third, the omnibus package may tempt members of Congress to add special favors for their constituencies, causing an inordinate number of pet projects to be included, well above the number of those in a smaller appropriation bill, where they are more easily open to scrutiny and rejection. The continuing resolution deserves an uneasy life. Many countries have systems of automatic continuing resolutions to ensure that government does not close. Similar programs have been proposed for the federal government, but as yet there has been no agreement on what formula to use.[45]

A second special form of providing funds is the *supplemental appropriation,* an appropriation of funds to be spent during the current fiscal year. (Requests and appropriations are normally for future budget years.) The supplemental appropriation may be part of a presidential budget submission, or it may be separate. Typical reasons include the need to (1) cover the cost of programs newly enacted by the legislature, (2) provide for higher-than-anticipated prices or workloads, or (3) cope with surprise developments. The request is for appropriation in addition to funds previously approved by the legislature. Forecasts of operating environments are seldom perfect, so most budget seasons include some supplementals. One exceptional example: the terrorist attacks of September 11, 2001, induced an emergency supplemental appropriation for $40 billion—for funds to be spent as required in any fiscal year, pretty much money to be spent anytime, anywhere, for anything. Other examples include supplementals to help deal with the Northridge (Los Angeles) earthquake in 1994, flooding in the Dakotas in 1998, military operations in the 1990s and later, and fiscal 2011 funding for disaster relief for Hurricane Irene. Emergency circumstances produce supplementals outside the normal cycle. The most famous (or infamous) recent supplemental appropriation is the American Recovery and Reinvestment Act of 2009 (P.L. 111–5), more popularly called the "fiscal stimulus bill," that was signed into law on February 17, 2009, shortly before enactment of the omnibus appropriation for 2009 and just as Congress would ordinarily have been starting work on the president's budget proposals for fiscal 2010. Some members of Congress were likely confused by the flurry of appropriation acts coming through at the same time. Certainly, the media and the public were.

The Government Accountability Office has found a great increase in the use of supplemental appropriations in recent years: "Over the 10-year period from fiscal year 1997 through fiscal year 2006, supplemental appropriations provided about $612 billion ... in new gross budget authority, a five-fold increase over the previous 10-year period."[46] Over half went to defense-related emergencies, 28 percent went to natural or economic disasters, and 16 percent went to antiterror, security, and post–9-11 activities.

---

[45]There is a special provision for national defense. The Food and Forage Act (41 U.S.C. § 11), a law passed during the Civil War, allows a Department of Defense contracting office to incur obligations in excess of appropriation to obtain food, fuel, forage, and related items necessary to meet current year needs. In more recent times, it was used during Vietnam, during the first Gulf War, and in 2001 (after September 11). Failure to appropriate won't stop (or cripple) a war.

[46]Government Accountability Office, *Supplemental Appropriations, Opportunities Exist to Increase Transparency and Provide Additional Controls,* GAO-08-314 (Washington, D.C.: Government Accountability Office, January 2008), 3.

The Bush administration chose to finance the wars in Iraq and Afghanistan almost entirely through supplemental appropriations, leaving these costs out of its regular budget message and adding them through the year. This practice is contrary to accepted budget practice because it hinders the capacity to maintain fiscal discipline and to direct limited resources to areas of greatest national priority. It is as if fighting these wars is an afterthought in finance that must automatically be added to the deficit. It is a good way to cripple the national economy. The Obama administration added them into the regular budget. And supplementals that must pass become a great vehicle for special earmarks: the 2005 military supplement had provisions involving oil drilling, the National Park Service, a new baseball stadium in Washington, tsunami relief, aid for Palestinians, and emergency watershed protection in Utah attached to it. A supplemental titled "Kosovo and Other National Security Matters" included funds for a Coast Guard Great Lakes icebreaker. Of course, supplementals are sometimes necessary because someone made a major mistake. For example, the Department of Veterans Affairs needed a supplemental appropriation for fiscal 2005 to cover health services for veterans because it based its budget request on demand in fiscal 2002, before the invasion of Iraq and the resulting significant surge in demand for medical treatment for returning service personnel, even though the request was prepared after the war had started.[47]

Spending by the federal government is divided into spending from federal funds, spending from trust funds, spending that is on-budget, and spending that is off-budget. The budget documents also include reports for a number of government-sponsored enterprises whose finances are not included in the budget totals. Sidebar 3–2 describes the nature of these distinctions and the kinds of operations that fit into the several categories. The distinctions do not help make the process more transparent.

Mandatory and Discretionary Spending

The Budget Enforcement Act of 1990 established the categorization of federal spending into mandatory and discretionary classes, and the helpful division has continued even with the demise of the act. Discretionary spending is spending that flows through the annual appropriation process—the process through which the discussion of the phases has taken you—and shows up in one of the twelve appropriation laws. It is the spending for agency operations involving both defense and non-defense (domestic) services. Mandatory spending includes outlays that are made according to definitions of eligibility and benefit or payment formulas rather than directly through the appropriation process. Table 3–7 shows the major types of mandatory federal spending and divides them into the programs that are *means-tested* (that is, payments are determined by the economic status of the recipient) and those that are *non–means-tested* (transfers are made without regard to economic status, but on the basis of other characteristics of the recipient). Social Security, Medicare, and Medicaid constitute the largest components of mandatory spending. Congress and the president still control the spending, but they exercise control by establishing the definitions and

---

[47]Thomas B. Edsall, "VA Faces $2.6 Billion Shortfall in Medical Care," *Washington Post,* June 29, 2005, A19.

Sidebar 3–2
Some Federal Budget Categories: Federal Funds/Trust Funds, On-Budget/Off-Budget, Government Enterprises

Federal government finance uses a terminology and a categorization of spending all its own. Without some general understanding of some of the principal categories, it is impossible to understand what is going on. Outlined here are a few of the most important special terms, with a short description of what each is and why it is significant.

Federal funds (78.5 percent of federal total gross outlays in fiscal 2011). These include general, special, intragovernmental revolving or management, and public enterprise revolving funds. *General fund* accounts are financed by undesignated receipts and provided for use by appropriation. *Public enterprise revolving funds* receive revenues generated by business-type operations with the public, like Postal Service operations, and are available without appropriation for those operations. *Special fund* receipts are designated for specific uses, deposited into separate accounts, and available for use under statutorily prescribed conditions (the Nuclear Waste Fund receives fees from civilian nuclear power operators; funds can be used only for disposal of high-level nuclear waste). *Intragovernmental revolving funds* collect receipts from government agencies selling services to other government agencies. All federal funds are on-budget (see later in this sidebar for meaning).

Trust funds (42.4 percent of federal total gross outlays in fiscal 2011). These are budget accounts that receive specially designated (or earmarked) receipts and have been designated by law as trust funds. Some of the largest federal trust funds, in terms of receipts, are the Federal Old-Age and Survivors Insurance Trust Fund (X), the Federal Hospital Insurance Trust Fund, the Civil Service Retirement and Disability Fund, the Military Retirement Fund, the Federal Supplementary Medical Insurance Trust Fund, the Unemployment Trust Fund, the Federal Disability Trust Fund (X), the Highway Trust Fund, the Airport and Airway Trust Fund, the Foreign Military Sales Trust Fund, and the Railroad Social Security Equivalent Benefit Account. Most lack the fiduciary relationship present in the normal meaning of trust funds: beneficiaries do not own the funds, and Congress may unilaterally alter tax rates, benefit levels, or other features of the program. The shares of the federal fund and trust fund categories do not add up to 100 percent because of interfund transfers. The trust fund total is typically in surplus (every full fiscal year since 1960).

On-budget and off-budget. The two trust funds marked (X) are legally off-budget. All other trust funds and all federal funds are on-budget (86.2 percent of federal gross outlays in fiscal 2011 were on-budget). Both on- and off-budget operations are in the federal budget. There is currently no particular significance to the distinction. The off-budget portion of the budget is typically in surplus (it has been so since the mid-1980s).

Government-sponsored enterprises. The budget document includes detailed self-reports of financial operations and conditions of several government-sponsored enterprises (GSEs), although these enterprises are neither on-budget nor off-budget, strictly speaking. These enterprises were initiated by the federal government, but are classified as private: the Student Loan Marketing Association, the College Construction Loan Insurance Association, the Federal

(continues)

SIDEBAR 3–2
(continued)

National Mortgage Association (Fannie Mae), the Banks for Cooperatives and Federal Farm Credit Bank, the Federal Agricultural Mortgage Corporation, the Federal Home Loan Mortgage Association (Freddie Mac), the Federal Savings and Loan Insurance Corporation, and the Resolution Funding Corporation. The GSEs are intended to be independent of the federal government, to provide federal support, and not to be subject to any actual federal guarantees. While the legal documents produced by Fannie Mae and Freddie Mac stated that their securities did not have a guarantee by the federal government, the private investors assumed that this was just window dressing and invested in them at low rates because of that implicit backing. It turns out that the private investors guessed right, as the U.S. Treasury bailed both institutions out in 2008 as they suffered the effects of the recession.

The budget document also reports the administrative budget of the Board of Governors of the Federal Reserve System, the independent central bank of the United States. The Fed is neither on-budget nor off-budget, and the system is not a government-sponsored enterprise. However, the federal Treasury does receive profits earned by the Fed. In 2011, that amounted to $76.9 billion, mostly representing interest earned on the Fed's portfolio of Treasury securities and mortgage-backed securities it had purchased to reduce interest rates in order to stimulate economic activity. Before the Great Recession, Fed contributions to the Treasury were much lower (averaging $23 billion per year in the five prior years) because the Fed portfolio was much smaller.

SOURCE: General Accounting Office, *Report to the Chairman, Committee on Government Operations, House of Representatives: Trust Funds and Their Relationship to the Federal Budget,* GAO/AFMD-88–55 (Washington, D.C.: General Accounting Office, September 1988); and Office of Management and Budget, *Budget of the United States Government, Fiscal Year 2013, Historical Tables* (Washington, D.C.: U.S. Government Printing Office, 2012).

rules; when those conditions have been met, however, the government has a legal obligation to pay funds to the eligible person, corporation, or other entity. The government cannot plead lack of funds or more important uses for its funds.[48] Congress and the president cannot increase or decrease the outlays for a given year without changing the law that created the eligibility and the payment rules; these rules, not appropriation actions, determine outlay. Because the spending is outside the annual appropriation process, it frequently is called uncontrollable spending; the annual appropriation checkpoint is gone. And, as we shall see, those expenditures have taken larger shares of all federal outlays. Mandatory spending also includes offsetting receipts—certain fees and charges that are regarded as negative budget authority and outlay. These receipts are collected from other government accounts or from the public in business transactions (like rents and royalties from oil and gas drilling leases on the Outer Continental Shelf). Payment of interest on the federal debt, although not strictly considered a mandatory category, is also outside the annual appropriation process.

---

[48]However, Social Security spending is limited to the amount of money in its trust fund. If that money should be completely exhausted, payments going out would be limited to payments coming in—a total return to a pay-as-you-go system and a violation of the entitlement concept.

Table 3–7
Mandatory and Discretionary Federal Spending, 1975–2010 ($ in billions)

	1975	1980	1985	1990	1995	2000	2005	2010	Annual Growth Rate
Important Means-Tested Programs									
Student Loans	0.1	1.4	3.5	4.4	4.4	1	15	8.9	13.7%
Medicaid	6.8	14	22.7	41.1	89.1	117	182	273	11.1%
Food Stamps	4.6	9.1	12.5	15.9	25.6	18	33	70	8.1%
Child Nutrition	1.5	3.4	3.7	5	7.5	9	13	17	7.2%
Earned Income Tax Credit	1.4	1.3	1.1	4.4	15.2	27	49	77	12.1%
Supplemental Security Income	4.3	5.7	8.7	11.5	24.5	31	38	47	7.1%
Family Support	5.1	7.3	9.2	12.2	18.1	21	24	28	5.0%
State Children's Health Insurance	0	0	0	0	0	2	5	8	–
Veterans' Pensions	2.7	3.6	3.8	3.6	3	3	*	*	–
Important Non-Means-Tested Programs									
Medicare	14.1	34	69.6	107.4	177.1	216	333	520	10.9%
Social Security	63.6	117.1	186.4	246.5	333.3	406	519	701	7.1%
Federal Civilian, Military, Veterans and Other Retirement and Disability	18.3	32.1	45.2	59.9	75.2	88	148	197	7.0%
Unemployment Compensation	12.8	16.9	15.8	17.1	21.3	21	32	159	7.5%
Deposit Insurance	0.5	–0.4	–2.2	57.9	–17.9	–3.1	–1	–32	–
Farm Price and Income Supports	0.6	2.8	17.7	6.5	5.8	30	19	n.a.	–
Social Services	2.9	3.7	3.5	5.1	5.5	4	5	n.a.	–
Veterans' Benefits	10.2	11	12.9	13.4	18.3	24	*	*	–
General Revenue Sharing	6.1	68	4.6	0	0	0	0	0	–
Flood Insurance	n.a.	n.a.	n.a.	n.a.	n.a.	n.a.	1	1.3	–
TRICARE for Life	0	0	0	0	0	0	6	n.a.	–
Universal Service Fund†	0	0	0	0	0	n.a.	6	8.9	–
Offsetting Receipts	–18.3	–29.2	–47.1	–58.7	–79.7	–78.6	–126	–184	6.8%
Total Mandatory and Related Programs	151.1	262	401.1	568.1	738.8	951.2	1320	1912.9	7.5%
Net Interest	23.2	52.5	129.5	184.3	232.1	222.9	184	196.2	6.3%
Total Discretionary	158	276.3	415.8	500.6	544.9	614.8	968	1189.8	5.9%
Defense	87.6	134.6	253.1	300.1	273.6	295	494	608.2	5.7%
Nondefense	70.3	141.7	162.7	200.4	271.3	319.9	474	581.6	6.2%
Total Outlays	332.3	590.9	946.4	1253.2	1515.8	1789.1	2472	3456	6.9%

n.a., Data not available.

*Included with federal civilian, military, veterans, and other retirement and disability

†Partly means-tested

SOURCE: Congressional Budget Office, *The Budget and Economic Outlook* (Washington, D.C.: Congressional Budget Office, various years); Office of Management and Budget, *Budget of the United States Government, Fiscal Year 2012, Historical Tables* (Washington, D.C.: U.S. Government Printing Office, 2011); and U.S. Department of Homeland Security, FEMA, Policy and Claim Statistics for Flood Insurance.

Figure 3–2

Discretionary Federal Outlays as Percentage of Total Outlays, Fiscal 1962–2011

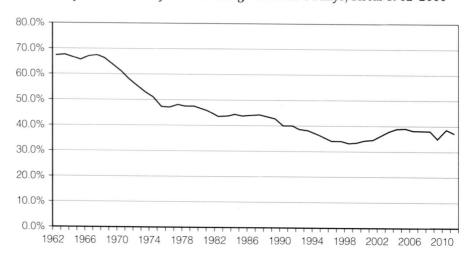

SOURCE: Office of Management and Budget, *Budget of the United States Government, Fiscal Year 2013, Historical Tables* (Washington, D.C.: U.S. Government Printing Office, 2012).

Mandatory spending and discretionary spending have taken dramatically different paths over recent decades. Figure 3–2 shows the trend for discretionary spending. Discretionary spending has fallen from almost 70 percent of total outlays in 1962 to under 40 percent in 2011. The annual growth rate over this long period for mandatory spending (7.5 percent) is more than a percentage point greater than that for total discretionary spending (6.2 percent), and that compounds to a considerable difference in shares over time. The increase since 2000 for discretionary spending is largely caused by defense spending (wars are expensive), although the non-defense discretionary share is also higher.

Two social insurance programs—Social Security and Medicare—are major components of mandatory spending. Social Security, the largest single element of mandatory spending, has been around 20 percent of total outlays since the mid-1970s (in earlier years, it seldom exceeded 15 percent).[49] The aging of the American population guarantees the growth of this outlay. Congress could reduce spending growth by changing the law and increasing retirement age, lowering benefit levels for more affluent retirees, and so on, but without such changes, the spending is predestined. The second largest category is Medicare, the federal health-care program for the elderly, a demographic group that would be unable to purchase private health insurance at reasonable rates because of the adverse selection problem. (Remember that private medical insurance companies make their money by selling insurance to people who

---

[49]The best single source on entitlement spending is "The Green Book": Committee on Ways and Means, U.S. House of Representatives, *Background Material and Data on Programs within the Jurisdiction of the Committee on Ways and Means* (Washington: U.S. Government Printing Office). The book is published periodically and includes major entitlements not strictly in Ways and Means jurisdiction.

don't get sick—a group that generally does not include the elderly.) Spending there has gone from 3.2 percent of outlays in 1970 to 13.5 percent in 2011, a large increase caused by higher prices for medical care in general, but also by enhancements in program coverage and increases in the number of old people. Neither of these programs is means-tested. That is, all those who meet eligibility standards receive assistance according to a payment formula, regardless of their general affluence; changes in either are closely watched by recipient groups. Any changes would be in the domain of the Finance/Ways and Means Committees, not the annual appropriation process. Both are financed through a trust fund arrangement, by which dedicated taxes on payroll, plus interest income received from investment of trust fund balances, are expected to support benefits paid out. More about the financing of these two large entitlements appears in Sidebar 3–3. Other, larger non–means-tested entitlement programs are federal civilian and military retirement programs and unemployment compensation. The long national economic expansion kept unemployment compensation spending low during the 1990s. The Great Recession (December 2007–June 2009) brought increases.

Sidebar 3–3
The Biggest Entitlements: Social Security and Medicare

The two largest federal entitlement programs—59.5 percent of mandatory spending in fiscal year 2011—are Social Security and Medicare, both social insurance programs primarily for the elderly. (Medicaid, the health program for low-income people that is a shared state-federal program, amounts to another 13.6 percent of mandatory spending and is the third largest entitlement, but it is financed through general revenue and is not subject to trust fund issues.) Social Security—more formally the Old-Age, Survivors, and Disability Insurance (OASDI) Program—provides benefits to retired and disabled workers, their dependents, and survivors that replace income lost to a family by retirement, death, or disability of a worker. It originated with the Social Security Act of 1935, although its coverage and role, as well as many structural features, have changed over the years. Medicare is a national health insurance program for the aged and certain disabled people. Part A Medicare covers inpatient hospital services, post-hospital skilled nursing facility care, home health services, and hospice care and is available automatically to almost everyone older than age 65. Part B Medicare covers physicians' services, laboratory services, durable medical equipment, outpatient hospital services, and other medical services; payment is generally limited to 80 percent of an approved Medicare fee schedule after the patient has met an annual $100 deductible amount, and the insurance is provided only to those individuals who purchase it. Part D Medicare provides prescription drug coverage through premiums paid to private insurers and general fund subsidies. Social Security and Part A Medicare are financed by payroll taxes paid by workers covered by their programs (roughly 96 percent of the paid workforce) and their employers and by a tax on the net annual earnings of the self-employed. Part B Medicare is financed by premiums paid by persons in the program and by general federal revenues. Any fund balances are invested in U.S. Treasury securities to earn interest. Benefits are paid as entitlements; the benefit formulas are determined by Congress. The funds do not go through the annual appropriation process.

(continues)

SIDEBAR 3–3
(continued)

Social Security and Medicare are reasonable candidates for "self-financing" (or "actuarial funding") schemes associated with social insurance trust funds because of their focus on the elderly.[1] And we also know that conditions of moral hazard and adverse selection make private medical insurance for the elderly expensive at best and unavailable at worst. With a social insurance system, people must pay into the social insurance fund during their work life and qualify for guaranteed benefits from the fund during that work experience. On retirement, sufficient funds will have accumulated—payments in, plus interest earned—to support pension payments and health insurance coverage for the population cohort. The life cycle of the fund is one of accumulation during work years and disbursement during retirement; the fund will be "fully funded" or "actuarially sound" when the system accumulations are sufficient to cover benefits estimated to be owed to system beneficiaries.

Unfortunately, the American social insurance system for too long operated on a pure "pay-as-you-go" system of finance, wherein people qualified for benefits during their work life, but insufficient money was accumulated to support those benefits on retirement. The scheme worked because it was possible to use revenues collected from the current workforce to support benefits paid to current retirees. But demographic forces create a problem: while there were about five workers for each Social Security recipient in 1960, there are expected to be only about two workers per recipient by 2030—the immediate transfer from worker to recipient cannot be supported anymore. The money accumulated in the Social Security trust funds rapidly disappears. Payments into the system and interest earned on the accumulation are insufficient to finance the system as people live longer, as "baby-boomers" retire, and as labor-force growth slows—all demographic forces now in place. On top of that is the rapid escalation of health-care costs. That hits all sectors of the health system—private insurance, Medicare, and Medicaid. While the social insurance trust funds, both Social Security and Medicare, have been in surplus for a number of years and have provided a partial cushion against the deficits of the general fund, the cruel truth is that those surpluses are not large enough to cover the benefits being earned by workers.

The economic numbers for both programs are chilling. Social Security expenditures exceeded payments into the fund in 2010, the first time that had happened since 1983, roughly the time at which the system was converted from a pay-as-you-go to an actuarial funding logic. A deal at the time of the conversion in the mid-1980s made some adjustments to the formula for taxes in and benefits out and the adjustments were estimated to handle the Social Security funding problem for about 25 years. It was assumed that, before that period had expired, statesman-like law

---

[1]Medicaid is also part of the federal spending problem because of its size and its growth. However, it isn't part of the trust fund discussion because it is not operated from a trust fund. It is supported by general federal finances. While there is a logical cycle associated with Medicare and Social Security—build up money in the fund while the individual is young and working to support payments when the individual is old and retired—there is no such cycle available to logically support a medical program for poor people. People don't go from rich to poor—the cycle needed to set up Medicaid on a trust fund basis. There is no Medicaid trust fund crisis because there is no Medicaid trust fund.

makers would come back for a permanent fix to the system. They were right about the length of the fix; they were wrong about the lawmakers. Surpluses in the Social Security and Medicare trust funds (and other federal trust funds that have accumulations) are invested in federal fund debt, in the same way that private endowment and pension funds invest their annual surpluses in various interest-bearing assets. Because of the desire that these trust fund assets be entirely secure, federal debt is the only asset the trust funds have been permitted to purchase, thus financing the federal funds deficit. (The stock market declines of the recession that began in late 2007 likely have dampened any efforts for more aggressive investment strategies for some years.) However, just as is the case with private investment funds, the debt is owned by the social insurance and other trust fund programs. The problem with the Social Security and Medicare accumulations is that they are not large enough to support the future outflows of benefits without eventual subsidization from other budgetary resources. The Social Security and Medicare (off-budget) surpluses give little reason for satisfaction: the accumulated surpluses are intended to finance benefits for the current workforce when those people retire, and actuarial forecasts show that these accumulations will run out. In other words, the Social Security and Medicare surpluses are too small to cover the benefit obligations that are being accrued by the current workforces.

Fund assets are U.S. government bonds (physical bonds kept in a safe in the Bureau of Public Debt in Parkersburg, West Virginia), so the federal government will have to raise taxes, borrow more (from some lender other than the Social Security system), or cut federal fund spending to repay the debt being liquidated by the Social Security system. If the federal government is unable to repay the debt owned by the Social Security system as it comes due, then the financial problems of the Social Security system will be only one of the fiscal disasters that the country will face.

The trustees of the Social Security system now estimate that, through 2022, annual cash deficits for the system can be made up by reducing trust fund assets, but that interest earnings will be greater than that reduction, so the trust fund balance will continue slow growth. After that year, the fund balance will decline and be completely gone in 2036. Thereafter, the fund would be supported only by annual payments into the fund, and those would allow payment of about three-quarters of promised benefits until 2085.

The trustees find an even worse profile for the portion of Medicare financed through its trust fund. Annual revenue already fails to cover annual cost, and the trust fund will be exhausted in 2024. From that point, either Medicare benefits will need to be dramatically reduced or revenues into the system will need to be significantly increased, either by dedicated Medicare taxes or by transfers from the regular federal revenue system. Medicare costs are estimated to have been reduced because of provisions in the Patient Protection and Affordable Care Act of 2010, but far less than what is necessary to make the program sustainable.

The system trustees give a grim prospect for the future. By 2035, the trustees of the programs estimate that program costs will be 11.8 percent of gross domestic product, leaving little room for any other federal government services unless there are substantial increases in the federal tax burden. There won't be any trust fund balances to cushion the financing burden of promises made to older Americans. It is shaping up to be an unsupportable fiscal problem.

(continues)

SIDEBAR 3–3
(continued)

As with other elements of government finance, the general options are clear: (1) increase current revenues into the system, (2) constrain benefits paid from the system, or (3) increase returns earned while balances are in the system by expanding the investment options available to fund administrators. The rules of the funds provide that, should the fund not have enough money to cover benefits in a year, the benefits will be reduced to no more than the money available— the entitlement promise goes away. Of course, making both programs for the elderly a private responsibility is another option, but returning society to pre-1930 conditions, with individuals being solely responsible for their own old age—an environment in which growing old typically meant being forced to move in with family or to the county poorhouse—is not an attractive prospect for most Americans. What is clear is that neither the Social Security nor the Medicare problem will go away by itself.

SOURCE: Social Security and Medicare Board of Trustees, *Status of the Social Security and Medicare Programs: A Survey of the 2011 Annual Reports* (Washington D.C.: Social Security Administration, 2011); Office of Management and Budget. *A New Era of Responsibility, Renewing America's Promise* (Washington, D.C.: Office of Management and Budget, 2009); and Congressional Budget Office, *Social Security: A Primer* (Washington, D.C.: Congressional Budget Office, 2001).

A second, but smaller, block of mandatory spending is means-tested; only those with limited affluence qualify to receive benefits from the program. Medicaid, a program providing medical assistance for low-income people, persons with disabilities, members of families with eligible dependent children, certain other pregnant women and children, and elderly persons needing nursing home care, is the largest such program, amounting to 7.6 percent of federal outlays in 2011, and outlays have grown rapidly.[50] The two federal medical care entitlement programs—Medicare and Medicaid—combined amount to 23.1 percent of federal outlays, causing many to observe that the key to controlling the federal budget ultimately lies in the ability to constrain the cost of medical care. Other important means-tested programs include (1) Supplemental Nutrition Assistance Program (SNAP, formerly Food Stamps), a program designed to allow low-income households to buy a nutritionally adequate low-cost diet;[51] (2) the Earned Income Tax

---

[50]Medicaid is jointly financed by the federal and state governments. The programs are funded by each of the states within guidelines established by federal legislation. While the poor without Medicaid coverage have access to emergency rooms, charity care, and free clinics, Medicaid program participants have higher health-care utilization, lower out-of-pocket medical care expenses and lower debt, and better physical and mental health. Amy Finkelstein et al., "The Oregon Health Care Experiment: Evidence from the First Year," National Bureau of Economic Research Working Paper 17190, Cambridge, Mass., July 2011.

[51]SNAP also is a powerful force for reducing poverty, particularly childhood poverty, in addition to improving nutrition. Laura Tiehen, Dean Jolliffe, and Craig Gundersen, "Alleviating Poverty in the United States: The Critical Role of SNAP Benefits," Economic Research Report No. 132, U.S. Department of Agriculture Economic Research Service, Washington, D.C., April 2012.

Credit, an income subsidy program for families to encourage work; (3) the Supplemental Security Income program, a cash assistance program for very low-income persons who are elderly, are blind, or have other disabilities; and (4) Temporary Assistance for Needy Families, the former Aid to Families with Dependent Children, which provides family support through federal block appropriations to states rather than on an individual entitlement basis. Such means-tested spending constitutes "safety net spending." The data in Table 3–7 show that, although spending on most means-tested programs has grown more rapidly than has spending on non–means-tested programs, the non–means-tested programs are much larger and create a greater challenge for the budget. In gross budget-control terms, the major financial concern is with the latter programs, especially Medicare and Social Security, the programs for the elderly.

Are Congress and the president powerless to alter the path of mandatory spending? Of course not. They may lack the political will, but they do not lack the political power. Options include (1) capping entitlements (essentially limiting the total amount that can be spent in a program each year, generally causing them to be annual appropriations), (2) making entitlement provisions less generous or at least constraining movements to make them more generous, and (3) making more entitlements means-tested (ensuring that only those classified as needy according to a broader measure of affluence receive benefits). And, for the trust-fund entitlements, another prospect is for increasing revenues into the trust funds by either increasing the taxes dedicated for their support or increasing the income from investment of balances in the funds. The point is that mandatory spending and its impact on the federal deficit can be controlled.[52] The history is, however, that Congress and the president have not been very good at doing the job, particularly when the entitlements being considered are Social Security, Medicare, or Medicaid.

Discretionary spending represents the rest of federal spending, the spending that flows through the annual appropriation process and the appropriation bills. Appropriation acts provide funding, the budget authority discussed earlier, and that funding will be used to make financial commitments or obligations. Outlays (spending) occur when the obligations get paid. This spending is for federal programs and the federal bureaucracy. Operations of agencies—the Department of Defense, the Fish and Wildlife Service, the Internal Revenue Service, and so on—fall in the discretionary category. Being "discretionary" does not mean that the spending is unimportant or that the nation could easily go without the program. It means that the spending goes through the traditional appropriation process and is not automatic. Fees and other charges that are driven by an appropriation action are classified as offsetting collections and offset discretionary spending.

---

[52]Conversion of the Social Security system into a personal retirement savings program is hardly a solution. The federal government currently offers more than a dozen tax-advantaged retirement savings programs, and creating another is not going to do much to provide more retirement security. Diverting some payments into the system to individual accounts serves to reduce the pool available to pay current benefits, thus accelerating the point at which that pool will be insufficient to meet promised payments.

Fighting Federal Deficits

Federal finances are in deficit when outlays exceed receipts and in surplus when receipts exceed outlays. The extent to which outlays have exceeded revenues was shown earlier in this chapter. In terms of economic consequence, it is important to consider how big the deficits are relative to the economy because that gives a gauge of the actual burden that these deficits might become. This federal surplus/deficit record from 1940 to 2011 appears in Table 3–8. The data are presented for a variety of different categorizations: (1) the total (or unified) federal surplus/deficit: all receipts less all outlays of the federal government; (2) the federal funds surplus/deficit, which includes all general operations of the federal government (no trust fund operations); (3) the trust fund surplus/deficit, which includes the dedicated revenue operations of the federal government; and (4) off-budget deficit (Social Security, or the Federal Old-Age and Survivors Insurance and Federal Disability Trust Funds).[53] The total surplus/deficit is also presented as a percentage of GDP to adjust for dramatic differences in the size of the U.S. economy over the years. The off-budget data are in surplus for every year since the mid-1980s; these represent the operations of the social insurance system. Unfortunately, the surpluses are too small to provide for promised benefits in the future. The trust fund data also show surpluses for each year back into the 1960s and, indeed, for almost every year back to 1940. This history is also driven by the social insurance system (and the surpluses are not large enough), but also includes the contribution from some trust funds receiving earmarked excise revenues (like the funds for highways and aviation), which may also be reaching the point of being unable to support demands for the infrastructure they are intended to support. Federal funds were in surplus in fiscal 2000 for the first time since fiscal 1960, but returned to deficit in fiscal 2001 as a result of the 2001 tax reduction and the recession that started in March 2001.

Until around 1960, the pattern with the unified budget (the one bringing all finances of the federal government together) was for mixed years of surplus and years of deficit for the total budget, except during the years of World War II, when huge military expenses relative to the size of the national economy stretched the financing capacity of the country to the limit (and also finally brought the nation out of the economic calamity of the Great Depression). After 1960, the pattern of fluctuation between total surplus and deficit broke down. From 1961 to 1998, federal outlays exceeded receipts

---

[53]There has been considerable concern about the finances of the Pension Benefit Guaranty Corporation (PBGC), an entity created by the Employee Retirement Income Security Act of 1974, to ensure that voluntary private pension plans can meet benefit payments, even if the private sponsor of the plan becomes financially unable to make payments. The PBGC is financed by insurance premiums from employers with insured plans; Congress sets the premiums that employers pay. The exposure of the PBGC is huge, exceeding the accumulated premiums it held in 2004 by an estimated $96 billion. But, despite the fact that the PBGC was created under federal law, there is no direct federal exposure: the PBGC receives no general tax revenues, and the federal government provides no guarantees for its program. But does the federal government have an implicit or moral guarantee of PBGC benefits? If so, then when bankrupt private employers like United Airlines turn their underfunded pension plans over to the PBGC, the federal government faces even more spending pressures.

Table 3–8
Mandatory and Discretionary Federal Spending, 1975–2010 ($ in billions)

Fiscal Year	Total	Off-Budget	Federal Funds	Trust Funds	Total as % of GDP
1940	−2,920	564	−4,045	1,125	−3.0%
1941	−4,941	653	−6,360	1,419	−4.3%
1942	−20,503	830	−22,496	1,992	−14.2%
1943	−54,554	1,041	−57,648	3,094	−30.3%
1944	−47,557	1,178	−51,818	4,261	−22.7%
1945	−47,553	1,167	−52,972	5,419	−21.5%
1946	−15,936	1,028	−19,847	3,910	−7.2%
1947	4,018	1,157	577	3,441	1.7%
1948	11,796	1,248	8,834	2,962	4.6%
1949	580	1,263	−1,838	2,417	0.2%
1950	−3,119	1,583	−3,055	−65	−1.1%
1951	6,102	1,843	2,451	3,651	1.9%
1952	−1,519	1,864	−5,005	3,486	−0.4%
1953	−6,493	1,766	−9,921	3,427	−1.7%
1954	−1,154	1,677	−3,151	1,997	−0.3%
1955	−2,993	1,098	−4,173	1,180	−0.8%
1956	3,947	1,452	1,313	2,634	0.9%
1957	3,412	773	1,657	1,755	0.8%
1958	−2,769	546	−3,017	248	−0.6%
1959	−12,849	−700	−11,271	−1,578	−2.6%
1960	301	−209	791	−490	0.1%
1961	−3,335	431	−4,193	858	−0.6%
1962	−7,146	−1,265	−6,847	−299	−1.3%
1963	−4,756	−789	−6,630	1,874	−0.8%
1964	−5,915	632	−8,588	2,673	−0.9%
1965	−1,411	194	−3,910	2,499	−0.2%
1966	−3,698	−630	−5,165	1,467	−0.5%
1967	−8,643	3,978	−15,709	7,066	−1.1%
1968	−25,161	2,581	−28,373	3,212	−2.9%
1969	3,242	3,749	−4,871	8,112	0.3%
1970	−2,842	5,852	−13,168	10,326	−0.3%
1971	−23,033	3,019	−29,896	6,863	−2.1%
1972	−23,373	2,695	−29,296	5,924	−2.0%
1973	−14,908	338	−25,683	10,774	−1.1%
1974	−6,135	1,063	−20,144	14,009	−0.4%
1975	−53,242	906	−60,664	7,422	−3.4%
1976	−73,732	−4,306	−76,138	2,405	−4.2%
1977	−53,659	−3,726	−63,155	9,495	−2.7%
1978	−59,185	−3,770	−71,876	12,691	−2.7%
1979	−40,726	−1,093	−59,061	18,335	−1.6%
1980	−73,830	−689	−82,632	8,802	−2.7%
1981	−78,968	−5,109	−85,791	6,823	−2.6%
1982	−127,977	−7,384	−134,221	6,244	−4.0%
1983	−207,802	−110	−230,874	23,072	−6.0%

(continues)

Table 3–8 (continued)

Fiscal Year	Total	Off-Budget	Federal Funds	Trust Funds	Total as % of GDP
1984	−185,367	−98	−218,272	32,905	−4.8%
1985	−212,308	9,222	−266,457	54,149	−5.1%
1986	−221,227	16,688	−283,120	61,893	−5.0%
1987	−149,730	18,627	−222,348	72,618	−3.2%
1988	−155,178	37,087	−252,902	97,724	−3.1%
1989	−152,639	52,754	−276,122	123,483	−2.8%
1990	−221,036	56,590	−341,181	120,145	−3.9%
1991	−269,238	52,198	−380,971	111,733	−4.5%
1992	−290,321	50,087	−386,338	96,018	−4.7%
1993	−255,051	45,347	−355,436	100,385	−3.9%
1994	−203,186	55,654	−298,508	95,322	−2.9%
1995	−163,952	62,415	−263,211	99,259	−2.2%
1996	−107,431	66,588	−222,052	114,621	−1.4%
1997	−21,884	81,364	−147,826	125,942	−0.3%
1998	69,270	99,195	−91,927	161,197	0.8%
1999	125,610	123,690	−87,120	212,730	1.4%
2000	236,241	149,819	1,629	234,612	2.4%
2001	128,236	160,681	−100,513	228,749	1.3%
2002	−157,758	159,659	−360,156	202,398	−1.5%
2003	−377,585	160,833	−555,977	178,392	−3.4%
2004	−412,727	155,234	−605,365	192,638	−3.5%
2005	−318,346	175,265	−555,093	236,747	−2.6%
2006	−248,181	186,313	−537,271	289,090	−1.9%
2007	−160,701	181,452	−409,395	248,694	−1.2%
2008	−458,553	183,295	−724,621	266,068	−3.2%
2009	−1,412,688	136,993	−1,539,978	127,290	−10.0%
2010	−1,293,489	77,005	−1,416,821	123,332	−8.9%
2011	−1,299,595	67,182	−1,396,642	97,047	−8.7%

SOURCE: Office of Management and Budget, *Budget of the United States Government, Fiscal Year 2013, Historical Tables* (Washington, D.C.: U.S. Government Printing Office, 2012).

in every year except 1969, when there was a tiny surplus.[54] Within that period, through both economic expansion and economic decline, each year the federal government spent more money than it collected, and hence had to borrow to make up the difference (the federal debt is the result of accumulated deficits through the country's history). There were unified surpluses from 1998 to 2001, and, in 2001, the CBO baseline projection showed a cumulative surplus of $5.6 trillion over the 2002–2011 period.[55] There were fears about the problems that would result when the federal government had paid off all its outstanding debt. This would have been a real shocker: since the beginnings of the United States in 1789, the only time there had been no federal debt was for a short time

[54]Before the late 1990s, the last actual unified surplus (on-budget and off-budget combined) occurred in fiscal 1969 (but the budget message planned a deficit); the last planned unified surplus occurred in fiscal 1971 (but actually ended with a deficit); the last surplus, counting federal funds/on-budget transactions alone, occurred in fiscal 1960 (planned and actual).
[55]Congressional Budget Office, "Changes in CBO's Baseline Projections since January 2001," May 12, 2011 [http://www.cbo.gov/sites/default/files/cbofiles/ftpdocs/121xx/doc12187/changesbaselineprojections.pdf].

in 1835, so having no debt would have been confusing. But the lawmakers rescued us from that problem by getting us back into deficit when the 2001 recession hit, and deficits continued to pile up after the recession because of the revenues lost by tax reductions in 2001, 2003, and 2010; the effects of the wars in Iraq and Afghanistan; additions to Medicare benefits that were not covered by added revenue; and, importantly, the effects of significantly increased domestic discretionary spending. Federal finances were unprepared when the Great Recession hit in late 2007, and deficits jumped with reduced tax revenues, increased spending in automatic stabilizer categories, and added discretionary spending undertaken to boost the economy (the 2009 stimulus package). John Maynard Keynes wrote: "The boom, not the slump, is the right time for austerity at the Treasury."[56] The Clinton administration understood this and used the prosperity of the last portion of the 1990s to repair federal finances. The second Bush administration did not and left the federal government in sad shape for dealing with the Great Recession. As the country moves further away from the Great Recession, it is time to close the budget gap.

To close the deficit when it needs to be closed requires the mathematically simple exercise of some combination of increasing receipts and reducing outlays. (And even the calculation of the deficit can have interesting complications, as Sidebar 3–4 illustrates in regard to the 2008 Troubled Assets Relief Program.) It is the politics that are complex because elected officials, Congress and the president both, expect the public to object to higher taxes, even to want tax reductions, and to object to any proposals to reduce spending by reducing the benefits from public programs. While the people may argue that they want the deficit and spending to be reduced, the evidence suggests that they have in mind reduced spending that benefits somebody else and do not intend that the reduced spending be for the programs that they are interested in. Each tax increase and each expenditure reduction would hit some part of the public, and those interests would object. Running deficits has proven politically much easier than acting to balance budgets or to run surpluses in good economic conditions, and no massive Great Depression or period of hyperinflation has yet occurred, even with the long deficit history. But providing services without taxing to cover their cost gives the public misleading signals, and government services seem cheaper than they actually are. In addition, financing current services with an operating deficit leaves ensuing generations the responsibility of paying for those services (plus interest), along with paying for their own services. That violates the standard of fiscal sustainability—the future generation has a lower standard of living because it is forced to pay for services provided in the past, as well as the cost of services for itself. So does the harm from deficits make it worthwhile to control them? Although the actual economic effects of persistent central government deficits remain a topic of debate among economists,[57] there is no economic argument

---

[56]John Maynard Keynes, *Collected Writings of John Maynard Keynes* (London: Palgrave Macmillan, 1937/1983), vol. 21, p. 390.

[57]Four good introductions to the deficit argument are Michael Dotsey, "Controversy over the Federal Budget Deficit: A Theoretical Perspective," *Federal Reserve Bank of Richmond Economic Review* 71 (September/October 1985): 3–16; John A. Tatom, "Two Views of the Effects of Government Budget Deficits in the 1980's," *Federal Reserve Bank of St. Louis Review* 67 (October 1985): 5–16; K. Alec Chrystal and Daniel L. Thornton, "The Macroeconomic Effects of Deficit Spending: A Review," *Federal Reserve Bank of St. Louis Review* 70 (November/December 1988): 48–60; and Robert Eisner, "Budget Deficits: Rhetoric and Reality," *Journal of Economic Perspectives* 3 (Spring 1989): 73–93.

Sidebar 3–4
TARP and Budget Deficits

The Troubled Assets Relief Program (TARP) was enacted as part of the Emergency Economic Stabilization Act of 2008 (P.L. 110–343) in an effort to combat the recession that began in December 2007. The idea was to use federal funds to help stabilize the American financial system and mitigate the ongoing economic collapse. In sum, the program worked along these lines: the U.S. Treasury borrowed money on the open market, gave the money to banks in exchange for partial ownership in the banks, and would, over time, receive ownership dividends from those banks on a preferred basis. The Treasury was, essentially, in the front of the line of owners when returns from bank operations got distributed. Eventually, the banks would repay the Treasury in full, and they would no longer have the American taxpayers as partial owners. At that point, everyone would let out a great sigh of relief.

All these plans were good for the forces of economic recovery, but a real bother for keeping track of the federal budget deficit. How should the money moving back and forth be accounted for in tallying the budget aggregates?

One approach was adopted by the U.S. Treasury. The approach was to treat TARP spending like all other spending. The TARP funds out would be spending and the bank repayment would be revenue. That meant a bump toward a bigger deficit when the Treasury was giving money to the banks and a bump toward a lower deficit when the banks repaid the money. That certainly would be how the cash would go.

The Congressional Budget Office, however, had a different view from the flow-of-cash view taken by the Treasury:

> CBO believes that the equity investments for TARP should be recorded on a net present value basis adjusted for market risk, rather than on a cash basis as recorded thus far by the Treasury.... The estimated cost accounts for subsidized interest rates and market risk, but also for the likelihood that the government will ultimately get much of its money back.[1]

In sum, the CBO view of the deficit impact takes account of the fact that the payment out is matched by an obligation for payment back in and netting of the flows needs to take place to get the appropriate view of the deficit impact. Some money won't get repaid and the payments will be in the future. The CBO measure makes allowance for those factors in netting against the initial cash paid out. But the CBO view is that the Treasury approach is overestimating the deficit impact now and would give a misleading view of federal finances when repayment occurs.

The first Obama budget message generally accepts the CBO view.[2] (That may not be surprising: the director of the Office of Management and Budget had been the director of the Congressional Budget Office when the CBO view of TARP was developed.) This revised impact showed the net cost to the government to be around 33 cents on the dollar. Had the administration accepted

[1]Congressional Budget Office, *Monthly Budget Review,* December 4, 2008.
[2]Office of Management and Budget, "Significant Presentation and Technical Changes in the Administration's Budget for Fiscal Year 2010," *A New Era of Responsibility: Renewing America's Promise* (Washington, D.C.: Office of Management and Budget, 2009).

the Treasury view, it would have been to its benefit in terms of deficit impact: the majority of TARP outflows occurred in the previous administration, while the flows back into the Treasury would have started in the Obama administration.

The CBO is required to prepare an annual report on TARP transactions. Its report for 2011 estimates that only $428 billion of the $700 billion that was authorized will actually be disbursed. After repayments, it is estimated that the total net subsidy cost of the program will be $34 billion.[3]

[3]Congressional Budget Office, "Report on the Troubled Asset Relief Program—December 2011," December 16, 2011.

and probably even no popular sentiment that deficits are acceptable every year. When pushed to the limits, it comes down to this: If deficits really do not matter, why bother having taxes? Finance everything by borrowing (that's what running a deficit means) and have no tax burdens at all. That is obviously silly.

The effects of continuing large deficits are expected to be largely long-term. First, federal deficits threaten long-term economic growth in the nation. In general, national saving (the difference between what is produced and what is consumed in a period of time) may be used to finance investment (increases in the physical productive capacity of the nation) or to accommodate government deficits. Given the overall saving rate, the deficit absorbs savings that otherwise could have been productively invested. Real interest rates rise as extra government borrowing occurs at the expense of financing private projects. That reduces the capital stock, a limiting factor in the output of the nation, thus constraining standards of living. Current deficits harm the future by reducing the nation's long-term economic potential.

Second, effects on international capital markets from the continuing deficit promise to reduce standards of living in the United States. The Council of Economic Advisers outlines the problem:

> When government borrowing or tax increases reduce the supply of available domestic savings, interest rates in the United States tend to rise. Foreign investors take advantage of the higher yields by investing in U.S. assets, either directly, as when a foreign automobile company builds an assembly plant in the United States, or indirectly, by buying debt issued by the government, or the debt or equity of U.S. firms.
>
> Foreign investment in the United States tends to reduce the effect of the deficit (or a current tax increase) on private domestic investment and the capital stock. Whether the government chooses deficit or tax finance, foreign investment in the United States adds to the domestic capital stock. American workers are more productive and earn higher wages when foreign capital augments domestic saving.
>
> Even with foreign capital inflows, however, future generations are still relatively worse off with deficit than with tax financing if the deficit absorbs more saving than a tax increase would have. With deficit financing, foreigners will own more of the U.S. capital stock than with tax financing, and future generations will have to make larger payments to foreign investors (or, equivalently, will enjoy lower payments from foreign debtors).[58]

[58]Council of Economic Advisers, *Economic Report of the President Transmitted to the Congress* (Washington, D.C.: U.S. Government Printing Office, 1993), 248–49.

Thus, the accumulation of debt held outside the U.S. economy will cause reduced domestic standards of living when that debt is serviced, and a surprisingly large percentage of federal debt is in foreign hands. For much of the last half century, observers were not much concerned about the accumulated federal debt. The debt was mostly internal to the U.S. economy, so debt service payments (paying interest and repaying the amounts borrowed) amounted to a transfer from American taxpayers to American bondholders without leakage from the economy—not much more impact than moving money from one pocket to another in the same pair of pants. As recently as the mid-1970s, more than 90 percent of the federal debt was internal, and it was around 80 percent as late as 1990. But that has changed—from June 1997 to the end of 2010, foreign ownership increased from 35 percent to 53.0 percent. Debt service now means payments outside the U.S. economy, and those will definitely challenge the living standards of future generations. What if international holders threaten to dump all those claims on the bond market and to refuse to purchase new issues? The increase in interest rates would potentially be calamitous, and the impact on the economy would be a shock like never before experienced. Should the United States lose its attractiveness as a safe haven for funds, the foreign dumping of debt holdings would present a great challenge to federal finance and private financial markets.

Third, to the extent the deficit remains a political issue, it constrains the capacity of the federal government to respond to legitimate national concerns. In a deficit-dominated climate, the first reaction to any policy initiative, whether it is national health-care reform, welfare reform, or reaction to a severe recession, is not whether a problem exists that the federal government might try to resolve, but what the deficit impact of the response might be. Hence, the deficit can place difficult hurdles in the path of important policy debate and decisions. The deficit overhang in 2008–2009 certainly restrained the federal government in making a quick response to the recession that started in 2007, once the recession was recognized.

Fourth, deficits could increase the rate of inflation, but that depends on whether the Federal Reserve System (the United States' central bank) "monetizes" the debt. Debt monetization occurs when the Federal Reserve purchases government debt—the product of the deficits—with newly created currency or bank reserves. The increased money supply creates a purchasing force that drives general price levels upward. This is not likely to be a problem in the United States because the Federal Reserve System is politically independent of the federal government and shows no tendency to monetize deficits. That is also true in most other developed countries, but it definitely was not the case in the early days of the newly independent nations that had been part of the Soviet Union, during the 1980s in several Latin American countries, or recently in Zimbabwe. Deficits there were financed by debt monetization (creating new money to purchase the debt), and hyperinflation (price increases at triple-digit or higher annual rates) was the result.

Finally, continuing deficits bring higher future interest obligations. Each succeeding Congress will find a large share of federal resources to be already committed—not to provide services to those paying taxes in that year, but to cover interest on funds spent to provide services in the past. Financing for the current needs of the public gets eaten away by necessity to service the costs of the past. That is not an attractive situation for the public or for the politicians elected to serve the public.[59] Indeed, it threatens the basic principle of fiscal sustainability, that is, that each succeeding generation will be able to enjoy a standard of living at least as good as that of the previous one. If the generation has to pay for its services plus the cost of services in the past, its chances aren't so good.

The difficult problem in deficit reduction is that the gain is long-term and the costs are immediate, including both the previously mentioned politics and the danger that higher taxes or reduced expenditure will throw the national economy into recession. How can a long-term national perspective be reflected against the short-term home-district perspective of Congress? This is not a simple question. Neither is identifying when the national issues are significant enough to make a small deficit more reasonable than raising taxes or constraining spending to prevent the deficit.

Nobel prize–winning economist Joseph Stiglitz outlines the justification for deficit financing: "The three basic rules of deficit financing are still true: Run a deficit when there is insufficient demand; try to get the biggest bang for the buck—the most stimulation for the economy for each dollar of deficit spending; and try to spend the money in ways which enhance long-term growth and address the country's basic social needs."[60] It is difficult to match this to how the federal government has behaved through much of its recent history, so it is reasonable to expect efforts to patch the system.

Will the federal budget—with and without Social Security flows—be in surplus or deficit? A good way to consider the question is by looking at the deficit relative to the national economy and the extra governmental draw that would be required to close the deficit and, ultimately, to service the resulting debts. In the 1950s, the mean deficit relative to GDP was 0.4 percent; in the 1960s, 0.8 percent; in the 1970s, 2.2 percent; in the 1980s, 3.9 percent; in the 1990s, 2.2 percent; in the 2000s, 2.4 percent; and, so far in the 2010s, 8.8 percent. However, in six of the twelve years of the twenty-first century so far, the deficit has exceeded 3 percent of GDP, and the three most recent years have had deficits above 8 percent of gross domestic product. Figure 3–3 puts federal deficits/surpluses and debt into a long-term perspective. The data are actual through fiscal 2011 and then use Office of Management and Budget forecasts beyond. Data from 1940 to 1946 show how the fiscal challenge of fighting WWII brought a huge increase in the deficit and, accordingly, in debt held by the public. With the end of the war, small deficits (even surpluses) and an expansion of the national economy reduced the significance of the federal debt, although the WWII debt was never actually paid back (neither was the debt from the Civil War or from WWI). However, the absence of fiscal discipline in the 1970s, 1980s, and early 1990s, even when the economy was basically strong, brought the debt burden back up. The collapse of discipline in the 2000s created a fundamental imbalance that left no fiscal slack for the recession beginning in 2007. The drastic expenditure

---

[59] A high ratio of debt to GDP (the result of accumulated deficits over the years) can also be an incentive to allow higher rates of inflation. The inflation causes an increase in the denominator, but not the numerator, thus reducing the ratio—but at considerable cost to the economy.

[60] Joseph Stiglitz, "The Parties' Flip-Flops on Deficit Spending: Economics or Politics," *The Economists' Voice* 1, no. 1 (2004): 5. Available online at http://www.bepress.com/ev/vol1/iss1/art2.

Figure 3–3

Federal Debt and Deficit as a Percentage of Gross Domestic Product, 1940–2017

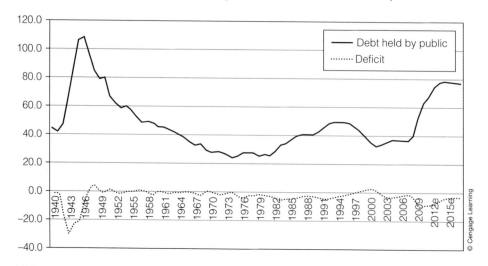

SOURCE: Office of Management and Budget, *Budget of the United States Government, Fiscal Year 2013, Historical Tables* (Washington, D.C.: U.S. Government Printing Office, 2012).

increase/tax reduction measures taken then created great debt expansion.[61] The path during the Great Recession, when the federal government needed to become spender of last resort to prevent an even worse economic collapse, makes the financing challenge greater, but that was the cost of dealing with economic collapse; without the fiscal actions, the prospects would likely have been even bleaker. However, the debt-and-deficit profile does show a clear need for discipline in regard to all elements of federal finances. After beating the recession, the challenge for the federal government will be a return to strict fiscal discipline in regard to the tax system (tax incentives do cause a loss of revenue), to the growth of domestic discretionary spending (control over earmarks and an item veto would have trivial impact in regard to the sort of controls that are necessary), and, most importantly, attention to the Medicare and Social Security trust funds and to the exploding cost of Medicaid.[62] A debt burden as high as 80 percent of total national production would not be as high as the nation experienced at the end of World War II, but it would be a management challenge and would prospectively endanger the living standard that Americans have come to expect.

---

[61]The graph uses actual debt and deficit data from the Office of Management and Budget for years to 2008. Later years are projections from the Congressional Budget Office.

[62]Even in domestic discretionary spending, change is difficult because every program that might get cut impacts some congressional district. For example, President Obama's 2010 budget proposal would terminate a program to provide the president with a new helicopter. It's his helicopter, so why shouldn't he be permitted to say that the old one is good enough? But the helicopter program—$835 million in 2009—supports 800 jobs in the district of Rep. Maurice D. Hinchey (D–NY), and Mr. Hinchey vows to save the program. At the national level, the program is not worth the cost, but it amounts to big money from that district. Lori Montgomery and Amy Goldstein, "Democrats Assail Obama's Hit List," *Washington Post*, May 8, 2009.

Conclusion

The federal government prescribes a precise budget cycle with clearly defined boundaries between the executive and legislative branches and clearly defined dates for steps in the cycle to follow. But the process is in disarray. Administrations have submitted budgets that intentionally omit major expenditures that are transmitted later in supplemental requests. Executive budgets are not transmitted on schedule. Congress regularly fails to pass its own budget (the budget resolution). Fiscal years begin without appropriations in place, and, in some fiscal years, no appropriations are actually made. Two programs that contribute a major share of mandatory expenditure are in severe fiscal distress. The congressional budget process functions with no meaningful controls, the appropriation process faces an unclear future, and prospects are for significant deficits throughout the planning horizon. Federal finances are in deficit in both economic expansion and economic recession. It is not the picture of a government on a sustainable path.

QUESTIONS AND EXERCISES

1. Using the *Historical Tables* available at the budget tab of the website of the U.S. Office of Management and Budget, prepare an analysis of the trends in the following data: total federal outlays, total defense spending, total spending on Medicare and Medicaid, and total ground transportation spending. Do the analysis in both current and constant dollars. Provide your interpretation of what forces are driving the patterns that you observe.

2. Use the following federal agencies for this exercise: Fish and Wildlife Service, Forest Service, Bureau of Land Management, Bureau of Reclamation, National Oceanic and Atmospheric Administration, U.S. Geological Survey, Army Corps of Engineers, Environmental Protection Agency, and U.S. Coast Guard. You will be able to locate the answers in the *Budget of the United States Government,* available through the OMB website, and through the various appropriation acts passed by Congress.

   a. Determine where each agency lies in the administrative structure of the federal government. Is it in an executive department, or is it an independent agency?
   b. Determine which of the appropriation subcommittees has jurisdiction over each agency's budget request.
   c. Determine where each agency's operations fall in the functional classification of the budget.
   d. Pick one agency and, for a recent budget year, determine (1) the budget authority and outlays proposed for the agency and (2) the actual outlays and budget authority for the agency in that year.

3. Identify the congressional committees to which the member of Congress representing your district has been assigned. If the member is on the appropria-

tions committee, identify the subcommittee as well. Try to determine why those committees are interesting to him or her. Thinking about economic interests and major employers in the district is a good start. (Your member of Congress almost certainly has a website that lists his or her committee and subcommittee assignments. Check that first. Another basic source is Congress's own website: http://thomas.loc.gov. It lists all committees and the membership of each. ("Thomas" is for Thomas Jefferson, the spirit behind the Library of Congress.)

4. Pick a federal agency of your choice. Find that agency's appropriation for a recent fiscal year. That may be located in an annual appropriation act or in a consolidated appropriation bill that lumps a number of normal appropriation acts together. Are there provisions of a somewhat substantive nature that are included in the appropriation act?

CASE FOR DISCUSSION

CASE 3–1

Pork and Earmarks: A Variety of Options

Members of Congress have a variety of tools for delivering projects to the voters back home. This selection describes an approach that leaves fewer tracks than the regular earmark.

Consider These Questions

1. Describe the difference between hard and soft earmarks.

2. Which do you believe to be more effective—hard or soft earmarks?

3. Do soft earmarks add to total spending?

4. Do you believe control of earmarks to be an important public issue?

5. Are earmarks necessary to deliver pork?

6. How could soft earmarks be controlled?

Pork Barrel, by a Softer Name, Remains Hidden in the Budget

New York Times, The (NY)—Monday, April 7, 2008
Author: RON NIXON Tom Torok contributed reporting from New York.

Sometimes on Capitol Hill, lawmakers find that it pays to ask nicely instead of just ordering the bureaucrats around.

With great fanfare, Congress adopted strict ethics rules last year requiring members to disclose when they steered federal money to pet projects. But it turns out lawmakers can still secretly direct billions of dollars to favored organizations by making vague requests rather than issuing explicit instructions to government agencies in committee reports and spending bills. That seeming courtesy is the difference between "soft earmarks" and the more insistent "hard earmarks."

How much money is requested for any specific project? It is difficult to say, since price tags are not included with soft earmarks. Who is the sponsor? Unclear, unless the lawmaker later acknowledges it. Purpose of the spending? Usually not provided.

How to spot a soft earmark? Easy. The language is that of a respectful suggestion: A committee "endorses" or notes it "is aware" of deserving programs and "urges" or "recommends" that agencies finance them.

That was how taxpayer money was requested last year for a Christian broadcasting group to build a shortwave radio station in Madagascar, a program to save hawks in Haiti, efforts to fight agriculture pests in Maryland, and an "international fertilizer" center in Alabama that assists farmers overseas.

After hard earmarks figured into several congressional scandals and prompted criticism of wasteful spending from government agencies and watchdog groups, Congress cut back on their number last year and required disclosure of most of them. (There were more than 10,000, costing nearly $20 billion last year, according to the Congressional Research Service.)

But soft earmarks, while not a new phenomenon, have drawn virtually no attention and were not included in the ethics changes—and current ones under consideration—because Congress does not view them as true earmarks.

Their total cost is not known. But the research service found that they amounted to more than $3 billion in one spending bill alone in 2006, out of 13 annual appropriations bills. And the committee that handles the bill, which involves foreign operations, has increasingly converted hard earmarks to soft ones.

"This shows that even though lawmakers now have to disclose their pet projects, we're not getting a full accounting of earmarks," said Ryan Alexander, director of Taxpayers for Common Sense, a group in Washington that tracks earmarks. "We may just be looking at the tip of the iceberg."

Representative Jeff Flake, Republican of Arizona, said he did not believe gentler language changed anything when it came to pork-barrel spending.

"No matter what you want to call it, an earmark is an earmark," said Mr. Flake, a longtime foe of earmarks. "If Congressional leaders don't believe that soft earmarks are earmarks, then I think that makes the case as to why we need tougher reforms in place."

Soft earmarks are included in a number of spending measures, but they tend to occur more frequently in spending bills that give money to the State Department, the United States Agency for International Development, and other foreign aid programs.

Federal agencies are not required to finance soft earmarks. However, officials have traditionally felt obliged to comply with such requests.

"Soft earmarks, while not legally binding, frequently come with an implicit threat: If you don't take our suggestions, we will give you a hard earmark next," said Andrew Natsios, former administrator of A.I.D. in the Bush administration.

In its report, the Congressional Research Service said agencies also could face budget cuts if they did not finance soft earmarks.

Mr. Natsios said two lawmakers once threatened to cut his budget if he did not pay for one of their requests. He declined to identify them.

Congressional leaders say soft earmarks are merely suggestions and not really earmarks. They argue that money is awarded at the discretion of the agency, largely through a competitive process.

"Recognizing organizations with a record of relevant work is part of Congress's budgetary role," Representative Nita M. Lowey, Democrat of New York, said in an e-mail message.

"It broadens the competitive grant process beyond administration priorities and encourages current recipients to maintain high performance standards," said Ms. Lowey, who is the chairwoman of the House appropriations subcommittee on state and foreign operations.

Mr. Natsios agreed that some soft earmarks in the bill could result in a competitive bidding process. But that is not the case if the report names a specific organization, which routinely happens.

In considering lawmakers' spending requests, some committees in recent years have switched hard earmarks to soft ones, saying it gives agencies more flexibility. Critics, including Mr. Flake, suggest it is being done to avoid scrutiny.

"With the efforts to shine more light on the earmarking process," he said, "I am concerned that we might see increasingly creative ways to steer funding to recipients of funding that members of Congress want to see it go to." Financing for the shortwave radio station, called the Madagascar World Voice, for example, began as a hard earmark request by Representative Pete Sessions, Republican of Texas.

Mr. Sessions originally sought $2.5 million for World Christian Broadcasting, a group based in Nashville that broadcasts in several countries and promotes abstinence to prevent AIDS. The House Appropriations Committee converted it to a soft earmark.

A spokesman for World Christian Broadcasting said the organization had been in discussions with A.I.D. about the financing.

Another soft earmark was included for the International Fertilizer Development Center, in Muscle Shoals, Ala. The group has been criticized as wasteful by watchdog groups and Senator John McCain of Arizona, a critic of earmarks who is the presumptive Republican nominee for president.

John H. Allgood, director of finance and administration for the group, which teaches third world farmers about soil fertility management and other agricultural practices, confirmed that his organization received financing from A.I.D. but did not know whether it was through an earmark.

Mr. Allgood would not say how much money the group received, and the aid agency did not respond to requests for the information. The fertilizer center previously received a $4 million hard earmark requested by Senator Richard C. Shelby, Republican of Alabama.

A soft earmark, of course, does not guarantee financing. For example, the Sesame Workshop, home of Big Bird and the rest of the Sesame Street gang, said it did not receive any money despite such a request.

Still, organizations spend millions each year lobbying Congress for them. Lobbyists say getting a client's organization into language in committee reports, which accompany spending bills and contain more detailed instructions to agencies, can have an impact.

"I certainly wouldn't call them earmarks, but it does say to the agency that this is something that Congress is serious about," said Fredrick Baird, known as Tripp, a lobbyist with J. C. Companies, a lobbying firm headed by former Representative J. C. Watts, an Oklahoma Republican.

Other than the amendment that Mr. Flake offered last year to shed more light on the process, no efforts to curb soft earmarks have been proposed.

President Bush signed an executive order in January that directed agencies to ignore all earmarks in committee reports.

But legal opinions by the Congressional Research Service and the Government Accountability Office found that Congress could get around the order by simply inserting them in the text of spending bills or including language in the bills that directed agencies to treat earmarks listed in committee reports as if they were written into the law. That frustrates groups seeking openness in government.

"Soft earmarks are even more insidious than hard earmarks," said Keith Ashdown, vice president of Taxpayers for Common Sense. "With hard earmarks, at least you know something about the amounts and recipients. With soft earmarks, everything is done in secret."

SOURCE: Copyright © 2008 The New York Times Company.

APPENDIX 3–1

Appropriations, Departments, Agencies, and Budget Accounts

Congress appropriates funds for the operation of the federal government. These funds go through the appropriation acts, to departments, and then to agencies within those departments. The funds are controlled within accounts within agencies. Departments do not, no matter how they might wish it to be true, receive funds that they might spend as they see fit. Instead, Congress maintains a reasonably close control over those funds.

The system of control operates through a system of budget accounts. These budget accounts also serve as the basis that program administrators use to build their budget requests that eventually become part of the president's budget request (and, they hope, come back as congressional appropriations). OMB Circular A-11 describes the accounts as follows: "A budget account generally covers an organized set of activities, programs, or services directed toward a common purpose or goal. Budget accounts are the basic building blocks of the President's Budget.... In addition, budget accounts are the basis for congressional action on the budget."[63] The budget accounts receive a defined funding amount available for a prescribed time period to be used by a specific organization in the agency to support the cost of similar programs or activities.

---

[63]Office of Management and Budget, Circular A-11, Section 71-1.

The following example shows how the budget account system functions.[64] Table 3A–1 show the numbers of accounts in the several departments in the U.S. government.

The number of accounts varies widely among departments, and there is no relationship between the amount of money being spent by the department and the number of budget accounts. For instance, spending levels by Interior and State are roughly comparable, but Interior has 81 budget accounts, while State has only 34. How many budget accounts a department has is determined by how Congress chooses to appropriate the funds. Adding accounts provides Congress an additional degree of control over the money it provides a department.

The next step in understanding the process involves looking within a department at its bureaus or main organization units. Table 3A–2 shows the budget accounts within the bureaus of the Department of Interior.

As with the budget accounts within departments, these accounts within bureaus are determined by Congress. More accounts within a bureau usually mean more congressional desire to control, and, again, there is little relationship between amounts to be spent and number of accounts. The funds provided each are part of the congressional appropriation.

Table 3A–1
Budget Accounts and Spending by Department, Fiscal Year 2006

Agency Code	Department	Number of Accounts	Spending ($ Billions)
005	Agriculture	103	102.0
006	Commerce	33	6.6
007	Defense	111	538.8
018	Education	27	90.4
019	Energy	35	25.0
009	Health and Human Services	43	908.9
024	Homeland Security	64	33.1
025	Housing and Urban Development	44	49.4
010	Interior	81	16.4
011	Justice	40	23.1
012	Labor	26	52.1
024	State	34	13.8
021	Transportation	61	65.1
015	Treasury	43	472.7
029	Veterans Affairs	21	74.3

SOURCE: Arthur W. Stigile, Chief, Budget Concepts Branch, Budget Review, U.S. Office of Management and Budget. Reprinted by permission.

---

[64]The accounts described here are from the perspective of the OMB and are from a high-level view. Agencies themselves use an even more detailed account framework in budget execution and reporting to Treasury. Each separate account in the Treasury database has additional codes to identify the fiscal year of the appropriation and whether funding is single-year, multiyear, or indefinite. Treasury, in cooperation with the OMB, establishes and maintains the official set of accounts in its FAST book [http://www.fms .treas.gov/fastbook/index.html]. All of these are crosswalked to an OMB account.

Table 3A–2
Bureau Accounts and Spending by Bureau, Department of Interior, Fiscal Year 2006

Bureau Code	Bureau	Accounts	Spending ($ Millions)
04	Bureau of Land Management	11	2,883
06	Minerals Management Service	7	2,585
08	Office of Surface Mining Reclamation and Enforcement	2	351
10	Bureau of Reclamation	10	1,105
11	Central Utah Project	2	34
12	United States Geological Survey	2	972
18	United States Fish and Wildlife Services	16	2,072
24	National Park Service	9	2,593
76	Bureau of Indian Affairs	7	2,397
84	Departmental Management	3	372
85	Insular Affairs	3	424
86	Office of the Solicitor	1	55
88	Office of the Inspector General	1	39
90	Office of the Special Trustee for American Indians	5	464
91	Natural Resources Damage Assessment and Restoration	1	37
92	National Indian Gaming Commission	1	12
	Department Total	81	16,395

SOURCE: Arthur W. Stigile, Chief, Budget Concepts Branch, Budget Review, U.S. Office of Management and Budget. Reprinted by permission.

Financing within the bureaus is based on the funds within the budget accounts. Table 3A–3 provides the details of the budget accounts in the National Park Service. Its authorizing legislation defines the mission of the Park Service to be to "preserve unimpaired the natural and cultural resources and values of the national park system for the enjoyment, education, and inspiration of this and future generations." Its park system includes 388 units covering 88 million acres in 49 states, the District of Columbia, American Samoa, Guam, Puerto Rico, the Northern Mariana Islands, and the Virgin Islands.[65] It provides these services through the funds provided by these budget accounts.

The account structure is determined by Congress and defines the activities of the National Park Service that it intends to support. This is the level at which Congress does its budget analysis and makes its appropriations. It is also the level at which the National Park Service prepares its budget proposals for inclusion in the president's budget. It should be noted that one large account is for operation of the national park system. This account gives the Service the flexibility to devote its attention to whatever park in that system needs greatest

---

[65]"National Park Service Budget Highlights, Fiscal Year 2006" [http://www.doi.gov/budget/2006/06Hilites/BH71.pdf].

Table 3A–3

Spending by Budget Account for the National Park Service, Fiscal Year 2006

Account ID	Account Title	Spending ($ Millions)
010-24-1036	Operation of the National Park System	1,719
010-24-1039	Construction and Major Maintenance	335
010-24-1042	National Recreation and Preservation	54
010-24-1049	United States Park Police	80
010-24-5035	Land Acquisition and State Assistance	47
010-24-5140	Historic Preservation Fund	72
010-24-9924	Other Permanent Appropriations	100
010-24-9928	Recreation Fee Permanent Appropriations	166
010-24-9972	Miscellaneous Trust Funds	20
	National Park Service—Total	2,593

SOURCE: Arthur W. Stigile, Chief, Budget Concepts Branch, Budget Review, U.S. Office of Management and Budget. Reprinted by permission.

attention, whether that be the result of visitors or repairs after a natural disaster. The accounts do not go down to the level of individual parks. The budget account structure is particularly important for administrators because it is forbidden to move funds from one budgetary account to another, even within a single bureau, without congressional approval. Therefore, the budget accounts are a critical control device for Congress—the broader the account, the greater the flexibility that the organizational unit has in responding to what it sees as the important public demands that it faces.

The last important step to help develop an understanding of how the appropriation and budget account system operates is to look at the text of an appropriation act. An example, the Environment and Related Agencies Appropriations Act of 2006 (P.L. 109–54), is presented in Figure 3A–1.

Within the Act, notice these elements:

1. The Act identifies the funding as going to the Department of Interior and for the 2006 fiscal year and then for the operation of the National Park Service. It also is worth noting that the Act was passed before the beginning of the fiscal year, something of a rarity in this era. Other accounts for the National Park Service are funded in later provisions of the Act.
2. The Act describes the purposes for which the funds may be used and the total amount of money being appropriated.
3. The Act indicates how some portions of the total appropriation are to be used. A purist would object that this is mixing policy with funding and would properly belong in authorization rather than appropriation, but these provisions are a normal element of the modern appropriation process.
4. The Act explicitly limits the extent to which funds in this budget account may be used for the United States Park Police. Recall from Table 3A–3 that there is a separate budget account (010-24-1049) for them, which will be provided for later in the Act.

Figure 3A–1
2006 Appropriation Act Language for National Park Service

Making appropriations for the Department of Interior, Environment, and Related
Agencies
  For the fiscal year ending September 30, 2006, and for other purposes.

NATIONAL PARK SERVICE
OPERATION OF THE NATIONAL PARK SERVICE

For expenses necessary for the management, operation, and maintenance of areas and
facilities administered by the National Park Service (including special road
maintenance service to trucking permittees on a reimbursable basis), and for the
general administration of the National Park Service, $1,744,074,000.

  Of which $9,892,000 is for planning and interagency coordination in support of
Everglades restoration and shall remain available until expended.

  Of which $97,600,000, to remain available until September 30, 2007, is for
maintenance, repair or rehabilitation projects for constructed assets, operation of the
National Park Service automated facility management software system, and
comprehensive facility condition assessments;

And of which $2,000,000 is for the Youth Conservation Corps for high priority
projects.

  Provided, that the only funds in this account which may be made available to
support United States Park Police are those funds approved for emergency law and
order incidents pursuant to established National Park Service procedures, those funds
needed to maintain and repair United States Park Police administrative facilities, and
those funds necessary to reimburse the United States Park Police account for the
unbudgeted overtime and travel costs associated with special events for an amount
not to exceed $10,000 per event subject to the review and concurrence of the
Washington headquarters office.

SOURCE: Department of the Interior, Environment, and Related Agencies Appropriations Act, 2006,
(P. L. 109–54), August 2, 2005.

  In summary, the budget account structure provides the framework for preparation of agency budget requests, the basis for congressional review of those
requests and for congressional appropriation of funds to agencies, the basis for
agency provision of services to the public, and, ultimately, the basis for an external audit of agency spending. It represents the basis for congressional oversight
and control over agency operations.

CHAPTER 4

State and Local Budgets

Budgeting by subnational governments—states and localities in the United States—is different from budgeting at the national level. For one thing, subnational governments operate in open economies, meaning that economic activity and populations served can easily move across jurisdictional boundaries. People living on the outskirts of a city can easily enjoy many public services provided by that city government without paying for them, and people can move from one locality to another in a metropolitan area, picking among the mix of local services and means of providing them, without having to change jobs.[1] The prospect of telecommuting makes flexibility even greater. Efforts by the city to stimulate its local economy will immediately spill over to other areas. And many tax bases are easily mobile: for instance, residents of a city can respond to a sharply increased city sales tax rate by shopping in the suburbs. Easy border crossing makes the service delivery and financing different for subnational governments.

Another fundamental difference between national and subnational governments is that subnational governments lack one powerful fallback tool. The national government, when pushed to it, can actually create spending power out of thin air: it can print money (actually, it can create bank accounts for itself to use). That is something not available to states and localities, and it is a powerful cushion. Of course, it is a power that cannot be heavily employed even by national governments because of concern about rampant inflation, but it is a power that has its uses, and only the central government has it.

Finally, subnational governments operate in a different legal environment than do national governments. National governments frequently establish limits on the fiscal powers of the lower tiers, for instance, in terms of what taxes subnational governments might adopt, what services they are to provide, and what fiscal constraints they must operate under. However, that is not the case in the United States. Subject to a few constitutional fundamentals, state governments in the United States have great freedom in regard to the revenues they use and the government services

---

[1]In many respects, the several localities operating in a metropolitan area operate like firms competing in a marketplace. See Charles Tiebout, "A Pure Theory of Local Public Expenditures," *Journal of Political Economy* 64 (1956): 416–24. Their competition for residents and economic activity leads to efficient provision of government services, much in the way that competition between firms leads to efficient allocation of resources in private markets.

they provide. There are few national standards that must be followed, and, where there are such provisions, they are frequently attached to federal assistance programs that the states may choose not to participate in. In contrast to most of the world, American states are close to being fiscal free agents with lots of discretion in their operations. However, state governments often establish their own fundamental and constitutional limits to their fiscal operations, for instance, in regard to how much debt they can have outstanding, the revenue sources they can draw upon, and so on. And local governments usually must operate under the narrow confines permitted them by their state, including sometimes a requirement that a state agency review the local budget before it can be adopted. Of course, there are 50 states and 89,000 local governments within them, so there is great variety among budget processes. The best this chapter can do is to give some idea of the general nature of state budget structures and processes. The details must remain for individual state research.[2]

State and Local Spending and Services Delivered

Table 4–1 reports expenditures by state and local governments in the United States. Both levels devote most of their attention to services closely related to the general public—education, public safety, welfare, sanitation and health, and so on—not the more global reach of international affairs and disputes that is the province of the national government. Those are the larger spending categories seen in the table. But before commenting on the spending patterns, a couple of reporting conventions need to be noted. States transfer considerable sums to their local governments; this table tallies such spending at the recipient level only (which makes the expenditures "direct"). The table also follows the convention of separating general expenditure from expenditures of government-operated utilities, liquor stores, and insurance trust systems (unemployment compensation, public employee retirement, etc.). Surpluses from the utilities and liquor stores may ultimately support general government operations (or their losses may have to be subsidized); insurance trust operations, especially unemployment compensation, have little direct link to general finances, although general finances of the government do have to maintain employee retirement programs and may need to make up fund shortfalls.[3] Problems associated with state and local government retirement programs are discussed later in this chapter.

---

[2]Several states have provisions that allow the state government to take over the finances of local governments that experience extreme fiscal problems. For instance, in early 2011, New York State took over the finances of Nassau County, and a state-installed manager took over operations of Benton Harbor, Michigan. Michigan has taken over finances of seven localities since a program was established in 1990 (but not yet Detroit). Atlantic City ceded fiscal management to the state of New Jersey in 2010. Various cities in Pennsylvania have fallen into a state recovery program in past years. The federal government would not take over finances of a state (or a locality) in the American system–under the U. S. Constitution, states have residual powers and localities are created by the states and not by the federal government. State take-overs are discussed in greater detail in Chapter 15.

[3]Surpluses in these trust funds, if invested in government debt, normally are invested in federal rather than state-local debt. Hence, merging them with general state-local operations as is done at the federal level would not be appropriate.

Table 4-1
State and Local Government Expenditures, 2008 ($ Thousands)

	State and Local Government Amount	Percent Direct General Expenditure	State Government Amount	Percent Direct General Expenditure	Local Government Amount	Percent Direct General Expenditure
Direct expenditure	2,834,074,613		1,256,776,878		1,577,297,735	
Direct general expenditure	2,400,204,391	100.0%	1,024,665,561	100.0%	1,375,538,830	100.0%
Education	826,063,178	34.4%	232,212,206	22.7%	593,850,972	43.2%
Higher education	223,299,543	9.3%	186,830,495	18.2%	36,463,048	2.7%
Elementary and secondary	565,631,236	23.6%	8,243,312	0.8%	557,387,924	40.5%
Other education	37,138,399	1.5%	37,138,399	3.6%	—	–
Libraries	11,611,470	0.5%	445,608	0.0%	11,165,862	0.8%
Public welfare	404,623,719	16.9%	354,047,572	34.6%	50,576,147	3.7%
Hospitals	128,853,219	5.4%	51,937,541	5.1%	76,915,678	5.6%
Health	79,704,063	3.3%	40,033,167	3.9%	39,670,896	2.9%
Social insurance administration	4,088,785	0.2%	4,071,956	0.4%	16,829	0.0%
Veterans' services	1,083,098	0.0%	1,083,098	0.1%	—	–
Highways	153,514,687	6.4%	90,644,565	8.8%	62,870,122	4.6%
Air transportation (airports)	21,264,242	0.9%	1,757,667	0.2%	19,506,575	1.4%
Parking facilities	1,602,479	0.1%	7,909	0.0%	1,594,570	0.1%
Sea and inland port facilities	4,940,135	0.2%	1,492,064	0.1%	3,448,071	0.3%
Police protection	89,676,481	3.7%	12,034,322	1.2%	77,642,159	5.6%
Fire protection	39,683,287	1.7%	—		39,683,287	2.9%
Correction	72,904,099	3.0%	47,239,040	4.6%	25,665,059	1.9%
Protective inspection and regulation	14,936,798	0.6%	9,297,965	0.9%	5,638,833	0.4%
Natural resources	29,916,526	1.2%	19,942,068	1.9%	9,974,458	0.7%
Parks and recreation	40,645,523	1.7%	5,509,852	0.5%	35,135,671	2.6%
Housing and community development	50,974,243	2.1%	10,856,663	1.1%	40,117,580	2.9%
Sewerage	46,678,848	1.9%	1,272,666	0.1%	45,406,182	3.3%
Solid waste management	23,756,966	1.0%	2,438,631	0.2%	21,318,335	1.5%
Financial administration	40,994,582	1.7%	23,233,998	2.3%	17,760,584	1.3%
Judicial and legal	41,450,902	1.7%	20,442,128	2.0%	21,008,774	1.5%
General public buildings	15,091,402	0.6%	3,565,073	0.3%	11,526,329	0.8%
Other governmental administration	29,460,307	1.2%	4,861,052	0.5%	24,599,255	1.8%
Interest on general debt	100,055,452	4.2%	44,719,371	4.4%	55,336,081	4.0%
Miscellaneous commercial activities	5,656,056	0.2%	1,647,572	0.2%	4,008,484	0.3%
Other and unallocable	120,973,844	5.0%	39,871,807	3.9%	81,102,037	5.9%
Utility expenditure	193,352,869		26,072,981		167,279,888	
Water supply	55,214,708		354,255		54,860,453	
Electric power	76,666,763		15,439,994		61,226,769	
Gas supply	10,527,452		12,107		10,515,345	
Transit	50,943,946		10,266,625		40,677,321	
Liquor store expenditure	5,933,639		4,944,650		988,989	
Insurance trust expenditure	234,583,714		201,093,686		33,490,028	
Unemployment compensation	35,567,964		35,470,883		97,081	
Employee retirement	180,057,751		146,664,804		33,392,947	
Workers' compensation	12,052,535		12,052,535		—	
Other insurance trust	6,905,464		6,905,464		—	

SOURCE: U.S. Bureau of Census. Federal, State, and Local Governments: State and Local Government Finances, 2008.

Local government expenditure is dominated by elementary and secondary education, amounting to 40.5 percent of total spending. Much of this spending is by independent school districts, local governments with a single purpose. However, a number of large cities operate their schools as a municipal department. A considerable portion of school spending is financed by state aid, even though the local unit administers the program. Often the aid comes with requirements about how the money will be spent, usually to the irritation of local authorities who are convinced that they know local needs better than do those people in the state capital. No other category amounts to as much as 10 percent of the total, but welfare (3.7 percent), hospitals (5.6 percent), and police protection (5.6 percent) are the largest remaining categories. Categories that have grown rapidly in recent years include corrections, health, air transportation, solid-waste management, and interest payments.

The largest single category of state government spending is public welfare programs (34.6 percent). The 1996 changes in the federal welfare program—converting Aid to Families with Dependent Children (a federal entitlement to individuals) to Temporary Assistance for Needy Families (a grant program with conditions that assign responsibility to state governments)—place even greater responsibility on states and provide them a great incentive to administer carefully and move people off assistance rolls. Medicaid, the federal-state health-care program for the poor that states operate according to federal guidelines with both federal and state funding, is a major component of this category and a major factor in its expansion. Of the other functions, only higher education (18.2 percent) amounts to as much as 10 percent of the total. Larger shares go to highways (8.8 percent), hospitals (5.1 percent), corrections (4.6 percent), and health (3.9 percent). Although there are major interstate differences, particular problems for state finances emerge from corrections—an area in which both growth of inmate populations and judicial requirements for humane treatment of inmates have increased spending—and from health—especially Medicaid.[4]

The data in the table are the nation as a whole and there are variations from one state to another. States and localities make their own decisions and are not guided by any national standards. Jurisdictions differ dramatically in how they allocate their fiscal resources. The patterns shown here can give a first guess about how any jurisdiction is allocating its budget, but only by looking at the government's finances specifically can you be certain about how it is spending its money. In making comparisons across states and localities, it is particularly important to consider operating environments. For example, two school districts—one serving an affluent, educated, homogeneous suburb and another serving a low-income, poorly educated, distinctly heterogeneous inner city—are likely to have to spend radically different amounts to provide the same level of learning because of the operating conditions, not because one is more efficient than the other.

---

[4]For a good outline of the details of Medicaid, see Jane Sneddon Little, "Medicaid," *New England Economic Review* (January/February 1991): 27–50. The article explains the cost growth concerns that haunted the program in 1991—and those same concerns continue even today. The program has not been repaired.

State and Local Budget Processes

The federal government uses a closely defined (but frequently shifting) budget process with narrowly drawn deadlines (that are often missed), regulations, roles, and authority that specify the flow of resources from the germination of an idea for service through the audit of outcomes. Virtually all states and larger localities use the familiar four-phase budget cycle. However, it should be no surprise, in light of the great diversity of state and local governments, that there is no one process that all such entities use.[5] Therefore, the process must be learned within the context of the government at hand. The way it works in Wichita may not apply in Altoona, and both governments may have budget processes that function perfectly well where they are applied.[6] Hence, the discussion about the state and local government budget process can only be general in nature. Justice Louis Brandeis observed in *New State Ice Co.* v. *Liebman,* 285 U.S. 262 (1932), that "it is one of the happy incidents of the federal system that a single courageous State may, if its citizens choose, serve as a laboratory; and try novel social and economic experiments without risk to the rest of the country." And so it is with the budget process. (Appendix 4–1 at the end of this chapter describes the budget process in Texas as an example of one system.)

State and local budget processes and staffing may be comparable to that of the federal government, except in scope, but many, especially local processes, are remarkably informal, in part because nobody in the process has any training in the systems of government finance. Indeed, there may be no executive budget for the locality. Agency heads may submit their requests directly to a legislative body (e.g., a city or county council), without any executive directive for developing those requests. Those local requests, especially for small governments, may be transmitted according to no regular schedule, but simply as agencies run out of funds or encounter new program options, rather like the federal government did before the 1921 Act. States are more formal and more controlling in their processes: "the days of agencies having the freedom to request budgets in whatever amounts they see fit are gone, and in their stead are various control mechanisms or types of ceilings that must be observed when requesting funds."[7] That guidance may involve (1) rankings of certain priorities; (2) instructions in regard to allowed program improvements, maintenance of current services, or continuance of only minimum services; or (3) specific dollar-level ceilings within which to prepare proposals. State budgets are frequently driven by the baseline (or current services) revenue forecast that gives budget participants a hard budget constraint under which the spending totals must fall if operations are to be sustainable in the long term. Although the state budget

---

[5]Some sense of the range is shown in Edward J. Clynch and Thomas P. Lauth, eds., *Governors, Legislatures, and Budgets: Diversity across the American States* (New York: Greenwood Press, 1991). National Association of State Budget Officers, *Budget Processes in the States* (Washington, D.C.: NASBO, 2008), provides the most complete overview of the structure of each state's budget processes.

[6]The websites of most states and some localities provide descriptions of the jurisdiction's budget process, sometimes also including the most recent set of budget preparation instructions distributed by the chief executive.

[7]Robert D. Lee, "The Use of Executive Guidance in State Budget Preparation," *Public Budgeting & Finance* 12 (Fall 1992): 29–30.

office may be housed in various places (for example, in the governor's office, in a freestanding executive agency, or in a larger department of administration or finance), it provides supervision of the entire process, review of proposals as they are assembled into the budget, and control of the execution of the adopted budget.

Among localities, however, a wider range of practices exists, with and without much budget guidance and control. Some of the more glaring problems emerge in budget preparation and legislative consideration. First, many localities continue *Christmas list budgeting,* in which department heads prepare requests without any executive guidance about budget targets or conditions. This practice leads to unrealistic requests that are usually cut without much attention given to programs and priorities. The proposals from the various departments may be at odds with each other and may have been created without any particular policy guidance. Second, some state and local operating agencies may have elected heads (e.g., a county sheriff); these officials may not feel bound by such directions constraining their proposals. Third, agency requests may not have been reviewed by an executive budget office, often because there is no such staff or because the staff is small and untrained. Therefore, the requests may arrive for legislative review in inconsistent format, following no particular standards in preparation, with no unifying plan for service delivery, and without screening for technical or presentation errors. In essence, the budget message has been prepared with a stapler only, not according to an analytic template or generally consistent executive vision. Such a system (or nonsystem) swamps the legislative body with details. Members of the legislative body must verify arithmetic and often fall into deliberations about each proposed purchase (or line item). Rather than considering policy questions, they plunge into the intimate cost estimates of the particular requests and usually exhaust their deliberative time and energy before they reach higher-order questions of program, performance, efficiency, or missions. Seldom do members of the legislature have any skill in budget analysis, so poor reviews are no surprise. Finally, any guidance may focus entirely on the things that the government purchases and not on what services the government actually provides. A local county government may instruct departments to build their budget request by giving everyone a 4 percent raise and holding all other spending categories constant. That is not a particularly useful way to make sure that the public gets good government services for the money they are paying. But those sorts of inefficiency and ineffectiveness are the result of having limited capacity for budgeting and finance in local government.

Many state and local governments also differ from the federal government in the audit phase of the budget cycle. Although a number of these governments have a public agency serving as external auditor, much in the way that the Government Accountability Office (GAO) serves Congress, a number have privatized the function by allowing audits to be done under contract with qualified private accounting firms. So long as audit procedures, audit standards, and audit questions are prescribed and audit firms are qualified before they may bid, there is no particular reason why states need to establish their own version of GAO.[8] States do, however, usually have legislative audit staff (a legislative service agency or legislative counsel,

---

[8]There is some concern that a private audit firm may be less willing to produce negative audit reports out of fear that the contracting government will replace it with a more flexible competitor.

for example) who perform program audits, program evaluation, and fiscal analysis; this work is kept separate from the financial and compliance audits necessary for control and is less likely to be privatized. In contrast to the recommended model, some states place the audit agency in the executive branch; some states have both executive and legislative audit units.

Executive-Legislative Powers and Functions[9]

The federal budget process has, over the years, created an uneasy and shifting balance of fiscal power between the executive and legislative branches of government. The balance that has emerged there does not immediately transfer to state and local governments.

First, not all state and local governments have an executive budget in the normal sense, although a budget proposal is prepared. Some states have budgets prepared by the legislature, and others have budgets prepared by the governor and the legislature in a joint budget committee. These joint budgets are difficult to categorize without understanding the details of each state; in some instances, they may be truly joint, built by a consensus between the governor and the legislature, but in others, the committees may be arranged in such a way that the governor has sufficient votes to guarantee that the budget is an executive budget regardless of its official title. Some local governments have budgets prepared by professional managers working at the direction of a legislative body. In these governments, there is considerable blurring of the preparation and legislative consideration phases of the budget cycle. Indeed, a council-manager system has, for purposes of the budget, more similarity to parliamentary structure (i.e., a governmental structure with no clear distinction between the legislative and executive branches of government) than to the system of separation of powers between the legislative and executive branches that characterizes our federal and state governments. In many cities, it is common for the council and the mayor to meet before budget deliberations to discuss priorities for the next year. This can be an important contributor to getting a consensus when the budget is actually presented, but what results could hardly be seen as an executive budget.

Second, state and local government executives often possess extraordinary fiscal powers in regard to expenditure during the fiscal year. Many states do not have year-round legislatures; the body meets in the early months of the calendar year, passes the state appropriations (and other laws), and adjourns for the year. More importantly, states and localities have limited capacity to deal with budget deficits (i.e., ability to borrow) that might emerge during budget execution because of unexpected economic or other problems. To deal with interim surprises, the governor

---

[9]Most states and many large cities post a description of their budget process on their websites. In addition, local processes frequently involve some supervision, review, or even approval by state agencies to assure that the budget does not violate state controls. Recall from Chapter 1 that localities are legally creatures of their states, so this involvement is not surprising. When local governments have gotten into great financial difficulty, it is not unusual for states to take over their operations, installing managers with the capacity to override local decisions, replace local officials, and the like.

may have broad impoundment powers—the ability to postpone or cancel expenditures in approved appropriations. The governor may also be able to spend for certain emergencies without appropriation, although almost always with agreement of some interim legislative committee.[10] These accommodations give governors considerable ability to manage finances during budget execution. They do not face a rescission process like the one that the president must deal with. They can simply adjust the approved budget to match fiscal resources.[11] Most state and local governments have allotment processes to control spending through the budget year, with funds parceled out quarterly or, when times are tight, monthly. Unfortunately, some governments have sought to recapture balances not obligated in that control period, thereby eliminating any incentive for agencies to economize—spend the money quickly before the governor takes it away.

Third, state and local governments differ in the accommodating mechanisms that provide funds for operations when the legislative and executive branches cannot agree and fiscal years end without new appropriations in place. Some operate with near-automatic continuing resolutions, whereas others provide governors with considerable discretion. Others have no stop-gap option clearly available and are required to shut down if the budget has not been passed by the start of the new fiscal year. Minnesota state government shut down for about two weeks in 2011 because of a legislative impasse between the governor and the legislature. (A shorter shutdown occurred there in 2006.) California regularly has experienced the sort of budget impasse one would expect in a comic republic, in large part because state budgets there required a two-thirds majority for passage, a unique feature among the states, and a requirement that was reduced to a simple majority in 2011. In the previous system, a small minority of disgruntled legislators could prevent adoption of the budget, even as the fiscal year was ending and authority for state spending was expiring. As a result, the state regularly experienced fiscal crises in which it could not pay its bills—rather bizarre for a state whose economy, if it were a nation, would be in the top ten in the world. Sometimes, as in 2009, the state managed through the impasse by making payments by issuing scrip (interest-bearing registered warrants) instead of checks to employees and suppliers as an interim solution; the scrip could be redeemed for state checks when the appropriation passed.[12]

States with part-time legislatures often require that special legislative sessions be called when the constitutionally designated regular session ends without a new set of appropriations in place. (Local governments are more likely to have year-round legislative meetings, so the process may become continuous and without year-end

---

[10]The executive may also have substantial contingency funds provided for various emergencies or surprises.

[11]The authority of the mayor to make unilateral budget adjustments was an issue of serious contention in San Diego in 2007. The city switched from a city manager system in which the mayor was primarily the chair of the city legislative body to a system in which the mayor was chief executive in 2006. The mayor made budget adjustments and the council objected on the grounds that such changes required their approval. The city has experienced great financial problems in the past half-decade for reasons that may or may not be related to the change in systems.

[12]California hopes to accelerate the process through a state constitutional amendment that prevents legislators from getting paid if the budget is not approved on time—and prevents them from ever getting back pay for the delayed period when the budget is passed.

crises.) The specific accommodation depends on the institutions and laws of the particular state. When state legislatures are close to the time that their session must end and are also close to passing a state budget, it is not uncommon for them to agree to stop the hands of the official clock to keep the legislative day from ending until the job is done. (Too bad Cinderella did not have this option—the fairy tale might have had its happy ending without forcing the prince to bear the cost of travel around the countryside looking for her.)

Finally, most governors have long-established line-item veto power.[13] Indeed, only five—the governors of Indiana, Maine, Nevada, New Hampshire, and Rhode Island—may veto only an entire appropriations bill, giving them only the same all-or-nothing basis as the president of the United States. Of those governors with line-item veto power, forty may delete funding for a particular line item, and thirty-two may even veto funding for an entire program or agency. Eleven may reduce an appropriation line without full veto. Although specifics of these line-item vetoes vary, all allow the governor to alter the bill approved by the legislature and sign the remainder into law, with the legislature having the power to override that partial veto.[14] These, along with impoundment authority, are powers presidents can only dream about having.

Budget Features

State and local government budgets show great basic variety. First, budgets may be annual or biennial (Table 4–2 gives a recent tally). At one time, state legislatures usually met only every other year. That meant making appropriations for two years in one legislative session. Even as legislative sessions became more frequent, several states continued the biennial budgets, so that annual sessions became distinguished between the budget session and the policy session (or, in less-dignified terminology, the correction session). States have generally moved toward annual sessions and toward single-year budgets; local governments have no biennial tradition, probably because they tend to meet throughout each year. In cities, administrators commonly rebudget and adjust the approved appropriations in midyear.[15] Some local governments are in rebudgeting-and-appropriating mode almost all the time, at every meeting of the council or governing board, even though a budget has been passed before the start of the fiscal year. Because of the difficulty of foreseeing

---

[13]Louis Fisher, "Line Item Veto Act of 1996: Heads Up from the States," *Public Budgeting & Finance* 17 (Summer 1997): 3–17, reviews state experiences with the line-item veto, including legislative strategies for avoiding the executive control that it might bring.

[14]The Wisconsin governor has the most sweeping line-item veto powers, including the ability to strike words and numbers without much limit, even to the extent of reversing the meaning of the bill (try striking the "not" from "thou shalt not commit adultery" to see what the power could do). Until recently, the governor could veto letters in words, thus permitting a game of legislative anagrams. Governor Tommy Thompson had 457 vetoes in the single 1991–1993 biennial budget bill. Dennis Farney, "When Wisconsin Governor Wields Partial Veto, the Legislature Might as Well Go Play Scrabble," *Wall Street Journal,* July 1, 1993, A-16.

[15]John P. Forrester and Daniel R. Mullins, "Rebudgeting: The Serial Nature of Public Budgeting Processes," *Public Administration Review* 52 (September/October 1992): 467–73.

Table 4–2
State Budget Cycles

Annual Budget (31 states)	Biennial Budget (19 states)
Alabama	Connecticut
Alaska	Hawaii
Arizona†	Indiana
Arkansas	Kentucky
California	Maine
Colorado	Minnesota
Delaware	Montana
Florida	Nebraska
Georgia	Nevada
Idaho	New Hampshire
Illinois	North Carolina
Iowa	North Dakota*
Kansas†	Ohio
Louisiana	Oregon
Maryland	Texas
Massachusetts	Virginia
Michigan	Washington
Mississippi	Wisconsin
Missouri	Wyoming*
New Jersey	
New Mexico	
New York	
Oklahoma	
Pennsylvania	
Rhode Island	
South Carolina	
South Dakota	
Tennessee	
Utah	
Vermont	
West Virginia	

SOURCE: Ronald K. Snell, "State Experiences with Annual and Biennial Budgeting," National Conference of State Legislatures. Available online at http://www.ncsl.org/default.aspx?tabid=12658

*Biennial budget states that enact a consolidated two-year budget. Other biennial budget states enact two annual budgets at one time.

†Annual budget states where smaller agencies receive biennial budgets.

what problems may face the state beyond a single fiscal year, states are inclined to regard the single-year budget as best suited to responding to public problems and to maintaining fiscal discipline.[16]

[16]Converting the federal government to a biennial budget is a perennial reform idea brought forth by members of Congress who have state government experience. Only if the president and Congress absolutely foreswear any reopening of the budget in off-years, an almost impossible temptation, would there be any time saved, and there would be guaranteed inability to respond quickly to new issues. General Accounting Office, *Biennial Budgeting: Three States' Experiences,* GAO-01-132 (Washington, D.C.: General Accounting Office, October 2000).

Second, state and local governments may have a single appropriation law covering all expenditures, or they may have many appropriation laws. In other words, the legislature may actually pass a complete budget in a sense not traditionally practiced by Congress, or there may really be no budget as ordinarily considered. The range is vast—about one-third of the states typically pass a single appropriation bill, but, at the other extreme, Arkansas passes around 500 appropriation bills. When there is a single appropriation bill, however, line-item veto power is probably more important for the executive. With a large number of appropriation bills, it is difficult to have any sort of unified plan for services being delivered by the state.

Third, in contrast to the unified federal budget process, many state and local governments use a dual budget system in which recurring operating expenses are controlled in one budget and acquisition of capital infrastructure is managed in a separate capital budget. Capital budgeting will be discussed in a later chapter. For now, suffice it to say that regularization of infrastructure purchases can be particularly important in maintaining fiscal stability in smaller budget processes. But some governments go beyond dual budgets. Cities are likely to establish multiple appropriation ordinances, one for each fund that the government has established, with something like a separate budget process for each fund. And, violating the budgetary principle of comprehensiveness, many of these governments do not move monies between funds, despite the appropriateness of directing public resources to the highest priority and greatest public need. (Capital and operating budgets are reasonably kept separate, however.)

Fourth, state and local governments historically have passed firm appropriations. They have not passed formula legislation (entitlements), which allow spending to occur at whatever level results from qualifying activities during the year. An exception is the Medicaid program, the federal-state program for providing medical care for certain low-income families. State assistance to local schools, a program for aiding primary and secondary education, distributes aid according to formula, but state funds ordinarily enter the distribution by appropriation, not vice versa, and the formula may well be underfunded in a particular year. States also do not separate authorizing and appropriating in their legislative processes.

Fifth, state and local governments have historically been unable to accommodate deficits with the easy access to borrowing that the federal government enjoys, and, furthermore, the vast majority faces statutory or constitutional restrictions against deficit operations. This has induced many to develop rainy-day or budget stabilization funds to stabilize their finances in an economic downturn, when revenues are likely to decline. Forty-eight states plus the District of Columbia now operate such a fund to deal with the problem.[17] Some funds are financed by periodic legislative appropriation, but others are automatic. For instance, when year-to-year real total personal-income growth exceeds a particular threshold, the formula directs a deposit to the fund (so long as the fund is below a critical limit, usually defined in terms

---

[17]National Association of State Budget Officers, *Budget Processes in the States* (Washington, D.C.: NASBO, 2008). Similar budget stabilization funds, although aimed at stabilization over the long term rather than in a business cycle, have been established in a number of resource-rich countries, like Kazakhstan, Kuwait, Russia, Norway, and Kiribati, to ease the transition when the resource has been depleted.

of general fund revenue); when that growth falls below another threshold, funds may be withdrawn. Along with providing a degree of stability in finances, properly designed budget stabilization funds—by reducing perceived default risk on state debt—can reduce the borrowing cost of state debt.[18] There is evidence that such state funds played a significant role in propping up state spending in the recession that began in 2001, although there remained some significant budget shortfalls in the first years of the twenty-first century.[19] The funds certainly provided a cushion for some states in the Great Recession, but no states had enough money in their funds to insulate them from the fiscal shock. Lawmakers forget how severe the problems are in a recession as the years pass by after the recession and become reluctant to let the fund continue to accumulate. The funds just don't get big enough to cover the problems of a severe recession. Local governments are less likely than states to have such stabilization funds, although some do. They tend to rely on real property taxes for revenue, and this source is less sensitive to changes in ambient economic activity than are the taxes upon which states rely. Local government revenues tend to be much more stable than those of either state or federal governments. However, localities that rely heavily on local sales taxes do face considerable revenue instability.[20]

Sixth, because local governments are closest to the people of any tier of government, they are most able to get ordinary citizen input into the fiscal choice processes. It is quite common for cities to integrate citizen hearings and citizen comments into both executive preparation and legislative consideration phases of the budget process. (A later chapter will discuss participatory budgeting, a formalized system for introducing this input into the process for portions of the budget. But citizens participate in local budget processes without that system.) This is input from ordinary citizens, not lobbyists representing interest groups. Such broad opportunity to include individual concerns in budget deliberations would not be feasible at state or federal levels. Even without formal integration of citizens into the process, citizen input is easier at the local level—the general public runs into their city council members, mayors, and the like on a regular basis at school events, the grocery, the hardware store, and so on, and they feel free to let their elected representatives know how they feel about public policy. Of course, in parts of New England, the fiscal business of small local governments gets transacted in town hall meetings in which everybody gets their say and their opportunity to vote on what the government will do. Such a

---

[18]There is evidence that the rainy-day funds are something of an illusion. One study indicates that rainy-day funds simply substitute for general fund savings that would have occurred without the rainy-day funds. The evidence is that every dollar deposited into a rainy-day fund increases total savings (rainy-day plus general fund balance) by between $0.44 and $0.49. Gary A. Wagner, "Are State Budget Stabilization Funds Only the Illusion of Savings? Evidence from Stationary Panel Data," *Quarterly Review of Economics and Finance,* 43 (Summer 2003): 213–18.

[19]Elaine Maag and David F. Merriman, "Understanding States' Fiscal Health during and after the 2001 Recession," *State Tax Notes,* August 6, 2007, 359–77.

[20]Members of Congress periodically call for the federal government to establish a federal rainy-day fund, following in the successful footsteps of state governments. Possibly a useful idea, but it would first require the federal government to get into surplus. Otherwise, the federal government would effectively be establishing the rainy-day fund with borrowed funds. That being the case, it might as well wait until the rainy day to do the borrowing and avoid the interest cost between the establishment of the fund and the date of its use.

system of direct citizen input can work with such governments, although transaction costs would become an issue if the system were to be tried for a larger city or state.

Seventh, state and local budgets and appropriations will frequently include details about what the money is to be spent for; that is, the details of the grocery list of supplies (the line items) that the agency will be expected to purchase. This is in marked contrast to the budget account appropriations that characterize the control structures of the federal government. Such object-level appropriations hamper the flexibility of response by these agencies and represent a throwback to the narrow control orientation that was a driving force for the earliest public budgets.

Finally, state and local governments often earmark or dedicate portions of some broad revenue sources, like personal income or general sales taxes, to particular narrow uses.[21] For example, a state may earmark a percentage of the state sales tax to primary and secondary education. That would mean that proceeds from that portion of the tax would be tracked to that purpose regardless of any other needs that the state might have. Around ten states earmark more than one-third of their tax collections to some purpose or another, thereby reducing the ability of the fiscal system to respond to changing public priorities. The average for states is around 20 percent; it is probably somewhat higher for general-purpose local governments. Although there is some possible logic to directing tax and charge revenue directly associated with a public function to that function, in the way that motor-fuel tax collections are frequently dedicated to operation and maintenance of highways, there is no economic sense to locking in general revenue to a specific use; that is a choice that priority balancing in the budget process should make. Not only does it hinder the capacity to respond, but also it adds an extra degree of complexity to the fiscal system. Furthermore, revenue is fungible (or easily mixed) in a general-purpose government, allowing easy substitution between uses, while keeping a clear accounting trail to satisfy the requirement for dedication.

Legal Constraints

State and local governments may face extraordinary legal constraints when they make appropriations and other fiscal decisions. Many have legal limitations, statutory or constitutional, on their capacity to tax or to spend, as Table 4–3 shows. Both limits, taxing and spending, may constrain the size of government and change the manner of finance (strong local limits may, for instance, induce a larger state contribution to joint responsibilities). Some fiscal decisions, like increasing a tax or borrowing to build a new school, may be made only after referendum approval, and that vote may require a supermajority. Many state and local governments operate under limitations, or caps, on spending (or revenues to be collected) in the fiscal year; the limit may be linked to personal income, population growth, or inflation.

---

[21]The federal government earmarks payroll taxes to support the social insurance system and earmarks some selective excises (e.g., aviation fuel, childhood vaccines) for certain other trust fund uses. The broad-based corporate and individual income taxes, are, however, not earmarked at all.

Table 4–3
Appropriation Limits States Have Placed on Themselves

Alabama	–
Alaska	Appropriation limited to growth of population and inflation since 7/1/81
Arizona	Appropriations limited to 7.41 percent of personal income
Arkansas	Extraordinary vote required
California	Appropriation limited to personal income growth and population
Colorado	General Fund appropriation growth limited to 6 percent of prior year's appropriation
	General & Cash Fund revenues limited to growth of population and inflation
Connecticut	Appropriations limited to greater of personal income growth or inflation
Delaware	Appropriations limited to 98 percent of estimated revenue
Florida	Revenue limited to 5-year average of personal income growth
Georgia	–
Hawaii	Appropriation limited to 3-year average of personal income growth
Idaho	Ongoing appropriations limited to 5.33 percent of personal income
Illinois	Appropriations limited to estimated available funds
Indiana	State spending cap
Iowa	Appropriations limited to 99 percent of adjusted General Fund receipts
Kansas	–
Kentucky	–
Louisiana	Appropriation limited to 3-year average of state personal income growth
	Revenue limited to a ratio of personal income in 1979
Maine	Base year appropriation multiplied by one plus average real personal income growth, but no more than 2.75 percent, plus average population growth, or multiplied by average real personal income growth plus forecasted inflation plus average population growth, depending on state ranking of state and local tax burdens compared to other states.
Maryland	Legislature sets a spending affordability limit each year
Massachusetts	Revenue limited to growth in wages and salaries
Michigan	Revenue limited to 9.49 percent of prior year's personal income
	Expenditures in any fiscal year limited to state revenue limit, federal aid, and previous fiscal year surplus
Minnesota	–
Mississippi	Appropriations limited to 98 percent of projected revenue
Missouri	Revenue limited to 5.64 percent of prior year's personal income
Montana	None—current statute 17-8-106 has been deemed invalid by state Attorney General
Nebraska	–
Nevada	Expenditures limited to growth of population and inflation
New Hampshire	–
New Jersey	Appropriations for direct state services limited to personal income growth
New Mexico	–
New York	–
North Carolina	Appropriations limited to 7 percent of state personal income
North Dakota	–
Ohio	Appropriations growth limited to 3.5 percent or inflation plus population growth
Oklahoma	Appropriations limited to 95 percent of certified revenue
Oregon	Appropriations limited to personal income growth
Pennsylvania	–

(continues)

Table 4–3 (continued)

Rhode Island	Appropriations limited to 97.8 percent of projected revenue
South Carolina	Appropriations limited to personal income growth
South Dakota	–
Tennessee	Appropriations limited to personal income growth
Texas	Appropriations limited to personal income growth
Utah	Appropriations limited to growth in population, inflation, and personal income
Vermont	–
Virginia	–
Washington	State General Fund/related fund expenditures limited to 10-year average growth of personal income
West Virginia	–
Wisconsin	Noneducation spending limited to growth in personal income
Wyoming	–

SOURCE: National Association of State Budget Officers, *Budget Processes of the States* (Washington: NASBO, 2008): 46.

For instance, overall appropriations are limited to the state personal-income growth rate in Oregon and to the combined growth of population and inflation in Alaska.[22] Sometimes, the state may be required to refund excess revenues to taxpayers (Colorado, Florida, Indiana, Louisiana, Massachusetts, Michigan, and Missouri), and, sometimes, appropriations may be limited to anticipated revenues.[23] Limits, caps, referenda requirements, and supermajorities are common features of state and local fiscal processes; they are not characteristic of the federal government.

State and local governments usually have balanced budget requirements, a fact often noted when comparisons are made between them and the federal government. Indeed, Indiana and Vermont are the only two state governments that do not face a balanced budget requirement. That requirement, however, has various meanings across the states, including (1) the governor's proposed budget must be balanced when presented, (2) the enacted budget must be balanced, and (3) the budget must be balanced when the year is over. Some states may, within the requirement, carry a deficit into the next year, making the standard much easier to achieve. In addition, the language of the requirements can be interesting. For instance, the Massachusetts constitutional requirement for balance reads as follows: "The governor shall submit a budget which shall contain a statement of all proposed expenditures of the commonwealth for the fiscal year, including those already authorized by law, and of all taxes, revenues, loans, and other means by which expenditures shall be defrayed" (Massachusetts Constitution, Article LXIII, paragraph 2). By that standard, federal budgets have always been balanced because deficits have been successfully covered by loans! Although requirements usually extend well beyond the state or local general

---

[22]National Association of State Budget Officers, *Budget Processes,* 46.

[23]Mandy Rafool, "State Tax and Expenditure Limits," *The Fiscal Letter* 18, no. 5 (1996): 4–7; Philip G. Joyce and Daniel R. Mullins, "The Changing Fiscal Structure of the State and Local Public Sector: The Impact of Tax and Expenditure Limitations," *Public Administration Review* 51 (May–June 1991): 240–53.

fund to include trust funds, special funds, and funds set up to operate federal programs, they typically do not include capital budgets set up to fund capital improvements (highways, buildings, etc.) and financed by bonded indebtedness (borrowing). One study of state balanced budget provisions observes that "it is the tradition of balancing budgets, the mindset this tradition creates, and the importance placed on balanced budgets that result in states complying with their requirements."[24] The same probably applies for local governments. Both state and local governments must remain concerned about access to capital markets; profligate behavior will eventually restrict their ability to borrow, and they lack the ultimate backstop of finance by money creation that the federal government has. These requirements by themselves are not sufficient to ensure the long-term fiscal health of state or local governments because if there is political will, there will always be a way to get around the limits.[25] It is that will, not the legal limits, that provides the constraint.

State and local governments also typically face limits on their capacity to issue debt, either to finance capital construction (building highways, schools, prisons, etc.) or to cover operating deficits. These limits may involve a requirement that the voters specifically approve the borrowing or dollar limits on debt that can be outstanding, either in absolute terms or in some relationship to the tax base (e.g., constrained to 5 percent of a county's total property tax base). As is described in the chapter on public debt, governments have devised many legal mechanisms to surmount these legal obstacles without much difficulty.

State and Local Deficits

Individual state and local governments characteristically do not run large surpluses or deficits. Whether this results from law, tradition, concern about eventually being denied access to capital markets, or concern about eventually being unable to service accumulated debt (these governments cannot print money, after all, through either printing presses or access to loans from the national central bank) is not clear, but regardless of reason, it remains true even in difficult economic and social times.[26] That does not mean that every state and local government spends no more than it takes in every year or that all state and local governments in total will run a surplus. Figure 4–1 shows the pattern of state and local government net lending (total receipts greater than total expenditures) and net borrowing (total expenditures above total receipts) as a percentage of gross domestic product (GDP), as reflected in the

---

[24]National Association of State Budget Offices, "State Balanced Budget Requirements: Provisions and Practice," *State Tax Notes* 3 (July 27, 1992): 117.

[25]By implication, those who believe that a balanced budget amendment to the U.S. Constitution is the solution to the federal deficit problem do not understand the lessons of state experience. The limits are easily circumvented unless there is political will to maintain balance. Political will trumps legal barriers (plus the barriers themselves aren't very rigid). Rule of thumb: if a government's finance officers cannot find a way around whatever balance requirement the lawmakers have erected, they are not very good.

[26]It may also reflect the limited effectiveness of state and local expansionary fiscal policy. Any stimulus from a tax reduction or an expenditure increase would quickly leak outside the political (and electoral) boundaries of the government. The beneficiaries of the new deficit would be outside the local citizenry.

national income and product accounts reported by the Bureau of Economic Analysis, from 1959 through 2010.[27] Although there are considerable fluctuations over the years, the difference from zero is usually modest, certainly in comparison with the federal experience. However, since the late 1970s, there has been a general trend toward greater net borrowing, particularly for state governments. State borrowing has been at record levels as share of GDP in recent years, although there was some recovery as the 2001 recession effects diminished. The impact of the Great Recession starting in 2007 is also apparent, with significant increases in net borrowing by both state and local governments. State and local deficits are considerably lower in total (and in individual units of government) than the federal deficits. There is, within state and local governments, a fervent understanding that continuing deficits are not sustainable, and there is an expectation that finances will be roughly in balance over time, although there are more years in a net borrowing situation than there are years in a net lending situation. Recessions (like those in 1973, 1980–1981, 1991, 2001, and 2007–2009) dramatically increase net borrowing, and recent recoveries have not returned the governments to net lending positions. The trend is troubling, particularly when the additional problem of financing retiree and other post employment benefits is considered.

Figure 4–1
State and Local Net Lending (Borrowing) as a Percentage of GDP, 1959–2010

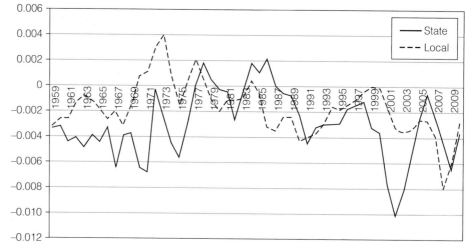

SOURCE: U.S. Department of Commerce, Bureau of Economic Analysis, *National Income and Product Accounts* [www.bea.gov]

---

[27]Total expenditures equal consumption expenditures, social benefits payments, interest payments, and gross investment less capital consumption allowances plus net purchases of nonproduced assets. Total receipts includes tax revenue, federal grants, income receipts (dividends, interest, etc.), contributions for social insurance, current surplus or deficit of government enterprises, and federal grants for capital expenditures.

State and Local Retiree and Other Post-Employment Benefits

A normal element of the traditional employment relationship in the United States is the promise of a pension upon retirement operated through the employer. That is true for both public and private employers. The financing of these pensions (and other post-employment benefits) has become a significant issue for state and local governments.[28] When a government has to compensate both current employees and past employees at the same time, the total cost can become unmanageable. That is the problem that many state and local governments now face. They made promises of post-employment benefits (pensions, health insurance, etc.) to past employees as a part of their compensation packages while they were working, but did not make financial allowances for these promises while the employees were delivering services to the government. As governments face the cost of paying both current employees and past employees, the financial crunch hits. While various benefits may be involved, the area of greatest recent concern has involved pensions. These pension programs may be state employee pension systems, state-operated local pension systems, or pension systems operated by individual local governments. The programs may be for all employees of the particular government, but there are frequently different systems for public school teachers, for police officers, and for firefighters. They all face similar concerns.

To understand the nature of the problem, it is important to distinguish between two different sorts of pension arrangements. One style of pension is a *defined contribution* pension.[29] In this system, the employer is obligated to make a regular payment into a pension account for the individual employee. Payment amounts are usually driven by the salary of the employee; that is, the payments equal some defined percentage of the employee's salary. The employee may also be required to make a payment. This account is then invested with the idea that the payments into the fund plus the return earned on the fund will provide the pension for the employee when the employee retires. The amount that has accumulated in the fund will determine what level of pension payment the retiree will receive. The retiree is not guaranteed a particular pension level, but the employee is promised that a set amount will regularly be put into the retirement account. Thus, the contribution is defined, and what it ultimately accumulates to—total payments plus returns from their investment—will define what the retiree will receive. Defined contribution plans, by their nature, require that the government bear the cost of future retirement benefits at the time the employee earns them.

---

[28]The retirement payments include pensions and other benefits. The most critical other benefit involves promises of health insurance for the retiree. Because many public employees, particularly police and firefighters, have arranged full retirement well before the age at which Americans qualify for Medicare, these retirees fall into the costly-to-insure group that private insurers are not excited about selling insurance to at reasonable rates. Unless the early retirees become employed again, they need health insurance, so negotiated post-retirement health insurance is vital for the quick retirement scheme these people have negotiated. These benefits have historically been handled on a pay-as-you-go basis rather than from a fund program, and that is expensive.

[29]These programs are similar to the private-sector 401(k) pension plans.

The other style of pension is a *defined benefit* pension. In this system, the level of benefits upon retirement is determined according to a benefit formula driven by such factors as the number of years the retiree worked for the employer, the final salary earned by the employee, cost of living adjustments, the age of the employee upon retirement, and possibly other factors. The employer maintains a fund that is intended to cover benefit payments, but there are no individual employee accounts. Employees may be required to contribute payments into the fund with each paycheck, but the employer is obligated for the defined benefit payments and not for particular payments into the fund. It is expected that the employer will be making payments into the fund so that, in total, those payments plus fund earnings will be sufficient to cover the promised benefits when employees retire. If the fund does not have sufficient resources to meet the contracted payments, then the employer is expected to come up with the payment from other resources. Payments are guaranteed by state statute, constitution, or contract law. The vast majority of public employee pension programs are defined benefit programs.[30]

State and local governments traditionally have operated defined benefit pension programs, and that is an important source of the current fiscal dilemma. The problem is that government administrations, when facing difficult fiscal choices, have given their employees improved pension benefits (earlier full retirement, higher benefits, lower individual contributions into the system, more generous calculation of salaries upon which pension payments are based, or some combination of all) rather than giving them higher wages and salaries. The wages and salaries would come from current resources, while the pensions will need to be paid at some point in the future. It was a sort of deal between governments (mayors, governors, legislators, administrators) and employee groups (unions): the government offered an attractive benefit package to the employees, financed in a politically attractive but fiscally unsustainable way, and the employee groups, seeing a fine deal presented, took the offers. Taxpayers also were in on the scam: they got artificially reduced taxes and maybe the burden could be kicked down the road indefinitely. Of course, a responsible government would accumulate funds to meet those future payments as the pension promise is earned. The problem is that it can be convenient to delay those payments (the payment is called the annual required contribution) in difficult fiscal times (or even in good times), on the assumption that later administrations will make up for the missed contributions at a later date. Except each administration does the same thing, kicking the date of fiscal reckoning further into the future. When employees do retire, the jurisdiction faces a fiscal squeeze because prior administrations have not been making the required contribution. Employee groups are not particularly inclined to protest these failures by the government to put aside enough to meet future promises because the pension promise is the future benefits and it is the problem for the government to find the money to do it. The employees are not directly impacted by the failure to make the necessary payments; the impact

---

[30]Exceptions to the rule that government employees are in defined benefit programs: faculty at many state universities are in the TIAA/CREF defined contribution program and federal employees in the Federal Employee Retirement System Thrift Savings Plan. In 1996, Michigan established a defined contribution plan for all new employees. In 1991, West Virginia school employees were put in such a plan.

is on the taxpayers and citizenry in the future. If accumulations are insufficient to meet the promised pensions, the government will need to significantly reduce current services or to dramatically increase revenues to meet the pension promises that have been made to employees of the past. The politics are that it is better to boot the cost of government to the future than it is to pay the costs now because, by the time those deferred costs actually come due, those administrators and lawmakers who have deferred the costs will have moved on to other things and it won't be their problem.

That is not the end to the dilemma. The defined benefit pension requires the accumulation of a pension fund from which promised pensions will be paid. There are two particular problems with these funds. First, there are questions about how much money needs to be accumulated in these funds to make them actuarially sound. That amount depends on how long payments will be made into the fund, what the benefits paid out will be, how long retirees will be drawing benefits, and, crucially, what rate of return will be earned on the money in the fund. The higher the rate of return that will be earned on the money in the fund, the less the employer will need to place into the fund. A set of benefit obligations in the future can be supported with a lower fund accumulation the higher the rate of return is and any gap between money that needs to be in the fund and actual funds accumulated (the unfunded liability) will be lower when the rate is higher. Of course, nobody knows what that actual future rate of return will be so the fund liability will be based on an estimated rate. In recent years, there has been a heated debate about what rate should be used. It has been common practice (approved by the Government Accounting Standards Board) to use a rate of 8 percent for these investments, but critics have pointed out that this is considerably higher than the returns that have been recently earned (a fair market approach). In 2012, the Government Accounting Standards Board revised its rules for pension accounting and reporting of financial condition in annual financial reports. Pension systems that are adequately funded may continue using their historical average returns in estimating liability (8 percent is a general standard). Systems lacking that funding must use a return equal to the yield on a tax-exempt 20-year AA-or-higher rated municipal bond, a much lower rate.[31] When lower rates are used, the unfunded liability of state and local pension funds becomes shockingly large.[32] The gap is large enough to raise questions about the financial viability of some governments, although the new gap is only from reporting rules and not from any change in the substance of the condition of the funds. Fortunately, the unfunded liability does not come due immediately, but the governments do need to reform their programs and initiate efforts to build their pension fund balances.

---

[31]In light of the fact that state and local government employee retirement funds hold such a small share (0.1 percent in 2010, according to Federal Reserve fund accounts data) of their assets in such low-yield bonds, this is a somewhat strange basic rate to employ. These bonds are attractive to entities subject to high federal marginal tax rates and these retirement funds are not subject to federal income tax.

[32]Novy-Marx and Rauh are particularly critical of the return assumption and, when using what they believe to be a more realistic rate, find unfunded liabilities on the order of 24 percent higher than gross domestic product. Robert Novy-Marx and Joshua D. Rauh, "The Liabilities and Risks of State Sponsored Pension Plans," *Journal of Economic Perspectives* 23 (Fall 2009): 191–210.

Second, even though state and local pension funds fall far below levels necessary for actuarial soundness, they still amount to a large pool of money.[33] Of the 50 largest employee pension funds by amount of assets, 33 are public employee funds. That makes the funds attractive to those with interests contrary to maintaining the security of pension promises. Investment advisors and other participants in the financial services industry seek business from the funds for the commissions that can result, and, because of the considerable sums of money involved, shadowy financial arrangements involving bribes, campaign contributions, hiring of relatives, and so on may emerge. Business may not be directed in a way that best serves the public interest. In similar fashion, the pension funds may be seen as a pot of money to be used to stimulate the local economy (providing low-cost financing for economic development, using local investment advisors rather than national professionals, etc.), practices that are contrary to the best interests of the funds. Even inadequate funds create the temptation for misuse, a temptation that is particularly great when benefit payments are a number of years in the future and the beneficiaries are not directly depending on amounts in the fund. It will be the taxpayers in those future years who will face the implications of misuse now, so they are not paying much attention.

In 2011, public pension funds had almost $3 trillion of assets invested. Almost 60 percent of payments to beneficiaries came from investment income.[34] Although the Great Recession had a substantial impact on the value of assets invested in stocks, values are recovering, and a 2012 GAO report concluded that the funds have sufficient assets to cover all benefits for a decade or more, even as the funds are making changes to improve long-term sustainability.[35] State and local governments are paying more attention to the finances of their pension funds and to the need to maintain required payments into the funds. Some jurisdictions are working to negotiate benefit levels downward, and some are increasing payments into their funds, including getting increased employee contributions. Some have explored converting their pension programs to defined contribution systems, a switch that is expensive because the jurisdiction has to continue payments to their traditional program beneficiaries at the same time as it makes contributions under the new program.[36] Some states (Alaska, 2008; Connecticut, 2007; Illinois, 2009) have issued bonds to cover some portion of the funding gap, thereby making the long-term obligation explicit as it provides resources for the pension funds to invest. Some jurisdictions have explored bankruptcy as an option to get court protection for unilateral change in pension contract provisions for both current and retired workers. While pension

---

[33]Nineteen of the twenty-five largest defined benefit pension programs in terms of assets owned are state or local employee plans. In 2012, these nineteen plans had total assets exceeding $1.5 trillion, and that counts as a large pool of money (*Pensions & Investments* database).

[34]National Association of State Retirement Administrators, "NASRA Issue Brief: Public Pension Plan Investment Returns," October 2011.

[35]Government Accountability Office, *State and Local Government Pension Plans: Economic Downturn Spurs Efforts to Address Costs and Sustainability,* GAO-12-322 (Washington, D.C.: Government Accountability Office, March 2012).

[36]Defined contribution programs do, however, deal directly with the early retirement issue. Employees will have funds accumulated in their personal retirement accounts and it is financially immaterial to the employer when the employee retires.

contributions are typically a relatively small part of the total operating budget—roughly 3.8 percent in 2010, but promising to grow significantly if funding levels do not increase[37]—state and local governments have become more concerned about appropriate management of their cost and more focused on the impact of making promises that require significant future financial obligations.

Conclusion

State and local governments provide services close to property and persons: education, public safety, public welfare, highways, and so on. Each state establishes its own budgeting system and procedures and makes service choices largely according to the preferences of its citizens, without standards or requirements from the federal level. Local governments largely work within systems and expectations established by their state. States put more constraints and limits on their spending than the federal government puts on its spending. States and local governments are more constrained in their capacity to run deficits, although in aggregate deficits are rather common, particularly in recessions.

QUESTIONS AND EXERCISES

1. Look at the budget preparation instructions issued by a state budget agency on the state's website. What is the timetable for submission, what is the basic format for preparation of the submission, and are certain displays explicitly required? Do the instructions give suggestions about important areas that the governor wants to emphasize or indications about limits to increases in funding?

2. Identify these key elements of your state budget process:
   a. Does your state have an annual or a biennial budget? Does it appear to have a separate budget for acquisition of capital assets (buildings, roads, bridges, etc.)?
   b. What units direct the preparation of the executive budget? (Not all states have an executive budget.)
   c. How many appropriation bills are usually passed?
   d. How much object-of-expenditure detail appears in these bills?
   e. What item veto power, if any, does the governor have?
   f. Is the budget process described on a state website? Does the website have the budget instruction issued to state agencies?
   g. Is the state budget easily accessible on the state website?

---

[37]A. Munnell, J. Aubry, and L. Quinby, "The Impact of Public Pensions on State and Local Budgets," State and Local Issue Brief, Center for Retirement Research, Boston College, October 2010.

h. Does the website provide information on the agency requests, in addition to the executive proposal and adopted appropriations?
The National Association of State Budget Officers provides much of this information in its publication *Budget Processes in the States,* which may be accessed at its website [http://www.nasbo.org].

3. Go to the website of a city or county of your choosing and look for documents relating to that unit's budget and finances. Look for the following:

a. Find the chief executive's budget message. What is the tone of that message? What are the major priorities?
b. Find the budget timetable and budget instructions if they are available on the website.
c. Locate the budget presentation, including any agency narrative and the budget data. Look for budget year, progress year, and report year. Are any out-years provided? Does the budget give other information (e.g., agency request versus council recommendation)? Does the presentation for each agency explain what the agency does, does it provide an organization chart for the agency, and does it explain what its primary objectives for the budget year are? What is the distribution of revenue by source and of expenditure by agency and function?
d. Does the budget give you enough information to allow you to understand what the tasks of the agencies are?
e. What is your overall evaluation of the budget presentation? Does it meet your transparency standard? What information did you not find that you would have found useful?

APPENDIX 4–1

An Illustrative State Budget Process: Texas[38]

State and local governments apply the standard four-phase budget cycle involving the executive and legislative branches of government, but there are many individual characteristics in each application. The differences reflect the particular characteristics of government in the various entities and the differing attitudes of the citizenry regarding the appropriate powers of the executive and legislative branches of government. The state of Texas offers an interesting illustration because there are a number of features that operate somewhat differently from those seen in the federal process.

The general flow of the preparation and legislative consideration/adoption phases of the biennial Texas budget cycle is shown in Figure 4A–1. (Execution and audit are not shown in the figure; those phases are generally comparable to the federal scheme.) In general, agencies prepare appropriation requests in one

---

[38]Based on House Research Organization, *Writing the State Budget,* State Finance Report No. 79-1 (Austin, Tex.: Texas House of Representatives, February 4, 2005); and Senate Research Center, *Budget 101: A Guide to the Budget Process in Texas* (Austin, Tex.: Texas Senate, 2005).

Figure 4A–1
Preparation and Legislative Consideration/Approval Phases of Texas Biennial Budget Cycle

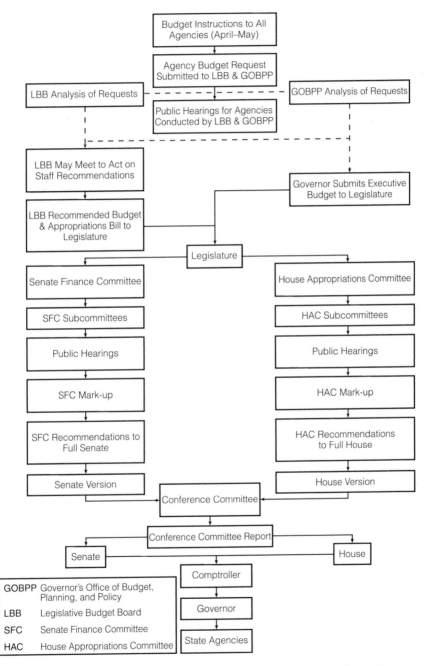

SOURCE: Senate Research Center, Budget 101. *A Guide to the Budget Process in Texas* (Austin, Texas Senate, 2011).

year, the legislature passes a General Appropriations Act in the next, and the budget is executed over the next two years. And, of course, the cycle continues and overlaps. Notable differences from the federal system are seen in terms of legislative power, item veto, role of a second elective executive agent (the Comptroller), a single appropriations bill, and constitutional restraints.

Budget Preparation

The process begins with cooperation between the governor and the Legislative Budget Board (LBB), an entity not seen in the federal system. The LBB consists of the lieutenant governor; the speaker of the House; the chairs of the Senate Committee on Finance, Senate Committee on State Affairs, House Committee on Ways and Means, and House Committee on Appropriations; two members of the Senate appointed by the lieutenant governor; and two members of the House appointed by the speaker. The LBB has a permanent staff and is responsible for adopting a spending limit; preparing the general appropriations bill (the budget); preparing agency performance reports; guiding, reviewing, and finalizing agency strategic plans; identifying the probable cost of proposed legislation (these are called fiscal notes); and managing transfers among purposes within agencies or among agencies. The LBB provides staff support for the appropriation process during the legislative session: tracking committee decisions, answering committee member inquiries, performing analyses, and providing testimony.

The executive branch is involved through the Governor's Office of Budget, Planning, and Policy (GOBPP) (reflecting the governor's policies) and, of course, the agencies that develop their requests for funds according to instructions issued to them. The governor and the LBB develop goals for each state agency to use in developing strategic plans and develop the instructions (Legislative Appropriation Request or LAR instructions) the agencies must use in preparing their appropriation requests. The LARs are submitted to the governor, and hearings are held on those requests in conjunction with the LBB. The governor submits a budget within the first six days of the legislative session and delivers a general appropriations bill within thirty days after the start of the session. The governor's budget is often seen as the statement of policy, and the LBB bill is used as the appropriations bill.

The budget is biennial, and both legislative and executive branches are involved in preparation of the budget and the strategies upon which it is based.

Legislative Consideration and Adoption

The legislature receives the budget and general appropriations bill. It also receives from the comptroller of public accounts (comptroller), an elected state official, a *Biennial Revenue Estimate* of funds expected to be received during the budget period. This is important because the Texas Constitution prohibits the legislature from appropriating an amount greater than estimated revenue collections.

The two houses of the legislature take turns acting as the originating chamber for the general appropriations bill and chairing the conference committee that works out differences between the bills ultimately passed by each house. The House bill goes through the House Appropriations Committee; the Senate bill goes through the Senate Finance Committee. The general appropriations bill has the following articles: general government, health and human services, education, judiciary, public safety and criminal justice, natural resources, business and economic development, regulatory, general provisions, legislature, savings clause, and emergency clause.

After approval of the appropriations bill, the comptroller must certify that the state will have sufficient revenue to cover the money approved. In case of an "emergency and imperative public necessity" (Article 3, section 49a of the state's constitution), appropriations may exceed revenue on approval of four-fifths of the membership of each house. Normally, the comptroller can certify; appropriations bills are not passed if they violate the revenue provision. If the comptroller does not certify the bill, it returns to the house of origin.

The governor has the power to veto specific items in the appropriations bill. Some agencies have received "lump sum" appropriations, in which case the governor can only veto the entire agency appropriation, not individual components of the agency's appropriation.

Supplemental appropriations are possible when agencies are in danger of running out of funds before the end of a budget period. The legislature may also reduce appropriations during the budget period.

The growth of spending is constitutionally forbidden (Article 8, section 22) to exceed the LBB's official estimate of growth of the state economy. However, spending from dedicated tax revenue is outside the limit. The state constitution also prohibits deficit spending (Article 3, section 49a) and requires that any unanticipated deficit at the end of a biennium be eliminated in the subsequent budget.

Execution

Execution is by state agencies within the biennium that begins on September 1 of odd-numbered years, subject to monitoring by the LBB and the State Auditor's Office (SAO). The SAO operates under the direction of the Legislative Audit Committee, which consists of the lieutenant governor, the speaker of the House, the chairs of the Senate Finance Committee and the House Appropriations and Ways and Means Committees, and a member of the Senate appointed by the lieutenant governor. The LBB is heavily concerned with agency performance objectives.

The governor and the LBB have joint authority to transfer funds within or between agencies.

Audit

The SAO, a legislative agency, is the external auditor of state agencies. It conducts financial, compliance, and performance audits of agencies and reports its findings to the legislature.

CHAPTER 5

Budget Methods and Practices

Many tasks in the budget cycle can be learned only by dealing nose-to-nose against, and elbow-to-elbow with, other participants. However, understanding some methods and perspectives before that first crunch is important. This chapter introduces some methods and activities in each phase of the budget cycle. In particular, it deals with (1) preparation of agency budget requests, (2) review of agency requests, (3) construction of the final executive budget, (4) management of budget execution, and (5) audit.

The first weapon in the arsenal of those responsible for the preparation and analysis of budgets is the calculation of annual growth rates. They are useful for the development of budget proposals, the analysis of what has been proposed, and the examination of what actual spending has occurred. This is a basic tool for fiscal analysis and for development of budget cost estimates.

Growth Rates and Simple Forecasts

Budgets are prepared for future years, and that means that somebody is going to have to be forecasting what the future will bring in terms of the operating conditions for government. The forecast is not of spending for those future years, but rather of the conditions in which the government providing services will operate in the future. What will the demands for government services be in the budget year? What will prices for the things that governments need to buy to produce those services be in the budget year? What revenue will the government collect in the budget year? One of the most fundamental tasks that those who prepare and analyze budgets have is that of preparing forecasts. In much of this work, the methods used in actual practice are relatively simple. Simplicity in these forecasts is appropriate because seldom will there be time, resources, or data to do much else. In addition, simplicity is a virtue for process transparency. Fortunately, the accuracy of simple techniques can be quite good.

Annual growth rates can be extremely useful in analyzing budgets and fiscal results, as well as in providing a useful grounding for the forecasts upon which budgets are prepared. Here is an example of their applicability and the technique.

At what annual rate has the population—those expecting to receive government services—grown over the years? Suppose the state population increased from 1.8 million in 1990 to 4.5 million in 2005. The compound rate of growth is computed according to the formula

$$R = (Y/X)^{(1/N)} - 1$$

where

R = the growth rate,
Y = the end value,
X = the beginning value, and
N = the number of periods of growth.

In this case, the population growth rate would equal the following:

$$R = (4.5/1.8)^{(1/15)} - 1$$

That isn't as imposing as it looks, so long as you have an inexpensive calculator in your pocket or an Excel (or other) spreadsheet program on your computer. For using a spreadsheet, think of the calculation like this:

$$R = [(4.5/1.8) \wedge (1/15)] - 1 = 6.3\%$$

For calculator users, look for the y^x key to do the work.

Annual growth rates are useful for comparing changes in data series when the numbers of years of observation are different and, as a result, comparing overall percentage changes won't help. For instance, suppose you have population levels for 1985 and for 2005 and total income levels for 1983 and 2007. Has income increased more or less rapidly than population? You can't tell by comparing percentage change between beginning and ending years because they are different for the two sets of data and because the data cover different spans of time. But you can compare annual growth rates, calculated as above, to learn which was growing faster, and that is useful for analysis.

So why not just calculate the total percentage change over several years and divide by the number of years? Mostly because it will give you the wrong answer. Back to the original data: the calculation would look like this:

$$\text{Wrong } R = [(4.5 - 1.8)/1.8]/15 = 0.10 \text{ or } 10\%$$

To see whether this is the right answer, start with 1.8 and increase it by 10 percent, then increase that result by 10 percent, then increase that by 10 percent, and so on until you have gone out fifteen years. If 10 percent is the right annual growth rate, you should have reached 4.5. But running the numbers shows a result of 7.5. So that calculation does, indeed, produce the Wrong R!

What happens if you use the right growth rate—the one calculated to be 6.3 percent? Go through the same process of starting with 1.8 and increase it by 6.3 percent for fifteen years. You get 4.5, which is what you would expect from doing it right.

It is useful to know the annual growth rate for analysis, but you can also use that growth rate to do a simple and easy forecast. In other words, you are assuming that growth into the future will be roughly the same as has been experienced in the recent past. That might not be right, but it is likely to be the best you can do, and most of the time such a forecast will produce a usable result. Suppose you wanted to forecast the number of clients your agency would need to serve in the next year. The amount is probably more than in recent years, but how many more? Assuming growth comparable to the recent past is at least a good first approximation. You might want to revise a little from your personal knowledge about what is going on, but you might not want to change at all. Suppose your agency served 14,450 clients in 2008 and 17,680 in 2012. You don't have complete data for 2013 because the year is not completed, and you need a forecast for preparation of the 2014 budget. Compute the growth rate between 2008 and 2012:

$$R = (17{,}680/14{,}450) \wedge (1/4) - 1 = 5.2\%$$

And use that rate to forecast 2014 client workload:

Clients in 2013 = [17,680 × 1.052] = 18,600
Clients in 2014 = [18,600 × 1.052] = 19,567

You could get to the forecast number without the two calculations by using this simple equation:

$C = A (1 + R)^N$ or $C = A (1 + R) \wedge N$ on your calculator or computer spreadsheet.

where

C = the future value you want to forecast,
A = the base year from which your growth forecast will be made,
R = the growth rate used for the forecast, and
N = the number of periods between the base year and the future year.

In our case, $C = (17{,}680) \times (1.052) \wedge 2 = 19{,}567$.

That's your forecast and it is pretty simple. But, as it turns out, this sort of forecast is used very often in the construction of annual budgets for forecasting likely workloads, the prices that might be paid by the agency for the things that it purchases, and so on. Figure out how to calculate annual growth rates and to use them for simple forecasts. You will do these calculations all the time when you are preparing budgets. You will also discover that such growth rates, not some complex forecasting model, are regularly used in the preparation of long-term fiscal scenarios. The ability to create credible forecasts for periods many years in the future is extremely limited, so complexity provides minimal improvement over the simple growth rates. You will learn more complex forecasting methods in a later chapter about revenue forecasting, but you will use simple forecasts like these most often when you are developing and analyzing the expenditure sections of an annual budget. Just don't use growth rates to create your expenditure requests directly (i.e., spending has grown at a rate of 3 percent over the past five years, so I will just add 3 percent to spending this year to get the spending request). That means that you haven't a clue about developing an action plan for your agency, but are simply willing to go with the flow and aren't actually doing your job. Forecast the operating conditions; then develop your spending proposal around your planned response to those conditions.[1] This approach puts you in command of building your planned response, rather than projecting on the basis of a history that mixes changes in plan and changes in operating conditions in some unknown mix.

Preparation of Agency Budget Requests

Operating agencies work from the budget instruction transmitted by the central budget office to develop their operating plans for the year and the budget requests that will accommodate those plans. Ideally, the instructions provide (1) the chief executive's main goals for the people, (2) forecasts of critical operating conditions for the budget year (inflation, service populations, etc.), (3) a format for the budget proposal (usually including prescribed forms that tell you what expenditure categories to use in your request), (4) a time schedule to be followed in developing the budget, and (5) some indication of the amount of money that the agency ought to build its budget around (either a ceiling control total or an estimated maximum increase from prior years).

How do the chief executive and central budget office know whether the instructions to agencies should emphasize extreme fiscal constraint, allow modest expansion of existing programs, or permit consideration of sound new programs? Many governments prepare, as a starting point, a preliminary baseline forecast of the surplus or deficit. The baseline provides the projected budget conditions if policies embedded in existing law are maintained.[2] In this analysis, the budget office forecasts revenue for the budget year and compares that forecast with the cost of continuing existing programs at their current level of operations under the conditions expected

---

[1] Many economic and fiscal variables are subject to regular variation across the months of the year, influenced by the calendar (holidays), weather, and other regular patterns. For instance, construction work in the northern United States tends to decline in winter months, and retail sales throughout the country tend to rise before Christmas, both regardless of the underlying economic strength. Therefore, economic variables for quarters or months are often reported on the basis of their implied annual levels. In other words, recognizing patterns of economic activity through the year, personal income for the fourth quarter would be reported at what personal income would be for the year if income were to be generated through the full year at the rate experienced for the fourth quarter. The logic is this: if the historical pattern is for 30 percent of annual personal income to be earned in the fourth quarter and if unadjusted personal income reported in the fourth quarter was $ 3,500,000, then the annual rate, based on the fourth quarter, would be $ 11,666,667 (calculated as 3,500,000 divided by 0.30). That is the nature of quarterly data normally presented in the Bureau of Economic Analysis reports, for example. The data aren't quarterly totals but are annual rates based on activity in the quarter.

[2] Establishing exactly what the baseline should entail is not without controversy. See Timothy J. Muris, "The Uses and Abuses of Budget Baselines," in *The Budget Puzzle: Understanding Federal Spending,* ed. John F. Cogan, Timothy J. Muris, and Allen Schick (Stanford, Calif.: Stanford University Press, 1994): 41–78. The argument concerns what exactly current policy should mean.

for the next year (prices, workloads, etc.). In many instances, the simple projection approaches presented earlier in this chapter are used, although sometimes more complex forecasting models may be applied. The gap, either positive or negative, between revenue and expenditure under current law gives a first guidance for the budget instruction: Will agencies be allowed to propose new programs? Will they work under hiring freezes? Will they be constrained in their capacity to request new equipment or to make capital outlays? What sort of ceilings will they face in making their requests? How the chief executive feels about deficits and surpluses and whether that executive is willing to propose revenue increases (tax or charge increases) also shape the instruction.

A good place for the agency administrator to start her budget development, along with making sure she understands what the chief executive wants, is to reflect on where the agency's operations have been in the recent past and to consider where she would like the agency to head in the near future—three to five years, with more attention to the near years than to the distant years. This reflection provides, along with the instruction, the basis for creating the service policy that will shape her budget proposal. After she gets into the numbers, it will be too late to do much policy reflection and revision, so she should start by thinking.

Within that instruction and service intention, the agency develops the three important pieces of its budget proposal: (1) a *narrative*, which describes the agency (mostly the same from year to year), indicates its managerial objectives for the budget year and beyond (probably changing from year to year), and is keyed to the agency mission statement; (2) *detail schedules*, which translate the managerial objectives into requests for new agency appropriations; and (3) *cumulative schedules*, which aggregate the new initiatives into existing activities to form the complete request. The presentation also probably includes *workload, productivity,* and *performance measures* for the agency. The workload identifies measurable activities of the agency with historical trends and projections for the future. Productivity relates these workload measures to numbers of personnel, and performance measures identify quantity and quality of service delivered to the public, sometimes including the results of citizen satisfaction surveys (a later chapter will discuss the use of performance indicators in the budget in some detail).

The most important lesson for the neophyte to learn about budget preparation, and possibly the most surprising, is that narrative dominates the numbers. The request narrative must describe and justify the plan; the numbers follow from that. Budgeting is logic, planning, justification, and politics, not mathematics or accounting. The narrative, detail schedules, and cumulative schedules are all critical because they provide governments the "how much" and "what it does" information needed for successful public decisions. The whole process begins with the agency's explanation of what it intends for the budget year. The narrative explains the policy response that the agency has decided to make in response to the operating conditions it believes it will face in the budget year. The basic rule: "The words come before the numbers." When the words (the narrative) are clearly provided, the numbers fall easily out. An agency administrator who builds his or her budget request by projection of historical patterns of expenditure categories is not serving the public well and really does not understand the job.

Agency budget documents are likely to include details not just on how money has been and is intended to be spent, but also on agency performance and accomplishments. It is a reasonable expectation that an agency be able to explain what it has done with the money—besides spend it!—and to explain what the public can expect to receive from the planned operations of the agency in the upcoming budget year. This performance information and these plans may be embedded as an important element of the budget narrative, but, increasingly, the budget proposal has a distinct and identifiable section that deals with performance. Central administrations, legislatures, and the citizenry all seek performance information as they consider budget requests and operating plans of public agencies.

Budget Justification

Program status reports, requests for supplemental funding, supporting explanations for increased staff, budget increases, and so on require justification for any planned agency action. Well-developed justifications are the key to successful agency budget requests.[3] The standard rules of English prose apply, but there are also several general and specific guidelines for effective budget justifications.

1. The justification must avoid jargon and uncommon and unexplained abbreviations because its audience includes individuals less familiar with the details of the proposed activity than the operating agency's personnel. Neither budget-agency examiners nor legislators are likely to approve poorly described projects. Never create your own acronyms. The justification should follow the basic standards of expository writing: short sentences, short words, active voice, no footnotes, and no unnecessary words.[4]

2. The justifications must be factual, provide documented sources, and go through ordinary review and revision to produce a polished presentation. Some of the justification may be technical; however, the technical parts cannot overwhelm the rest or be left unexplained. The justification has to focus on the small number of points that the reader should pay attention to and remember.

3. The justification structure must address the current situation, additional needs, and expected results from honoring the request. One section of the justification should describe the current program in terms of measurable workloads, staffing, funding, or productivity trends. It should briefly and specifically inform the budget examiner of existing conditions, without extraneous detail that might misdirect the examiner's attention. Another section of the justification should describe the additional needs. It must specifically identify additional funds, personnel, and materials needed for the budget activity at issue. The reason for the need must be explicitly developed. The examiner must not have to guess what and why.

---

[3]They are also critical for grant proposal writing for public and nonprofit organizations.
[4]Be a Hemingway, not a Faulkner. Check with an English-major friend if you don't understand.

4. The request must indicate what beneficial results will come from granting the request. It must make clear that something important will be made better if the requested activity is carried out and that the agency has the capacity to carry it out.

The details of what belongs in the justification are ordinarily covered in the instructions. Hence comes the basic rule for doing budget justifications: *read the instructions and follow them.* If the instructions leave you with any uncertainty about what the justification should include, you won't go wrong by explaining (1) what resources the agency wants for the budget year, (2) what it intends to do with those resources, and (3) what good will result from that intention.

Common reasons for requesting funds include the following:

1. **Higher (or lower) prices.** Prices of supplies and services needed to maintain agency operations at their existing level may be increasing (or decreasing). For instance, the local electric utility may have received approval for a rate increase during the next year. That could elicit a request for a budget increase to accommodate the increased cost of the service.

2. **Increased demand for service (workload).** The clientele served by the agency may increase. To maintain service levels, the agency's budget may need to increase. An agency providing education to children of the homeless, for instance, could argue for a larger budget if the population of such children is expected to increase.

3. **Methods improvement.** Administrative changes or innovations can alter the budgets of agencies. An operating unit can become more productive and generate fewer errors if it has more space, if it has more modern equipment, or if it has better information technology. That would require a budget request. Methods improvement can also allow savings, in which case the budget change would be negative. Some improvements may have been mandated or required by the courts, the legislature, or a higher level of government.

4. **Full financing.** Agencies frequently start new operations at some point other than the start of a fiscal year. Initial appropriations for new operations are thus partial; to cover full operations would require larger appropriations, a change that needs to be described in the agency request.

5. **New services.** New services, enlarged services, improved services, or services to an expanded clientele should be identified and justified. Because new services would not have been previously considered in legislative deliberations, they do require separation in the budget. New services are likely to be closely linked to initiatives in the basic narrative. As with method improvements, some new services may have been mandated.

There may be other categories of justification that would be applied to allow agencies to identify the underlying case for their request. For instance, some federal agencies recognize a judicial restraining order as a separate category. Those noted here, however, are among the most common.

The narrative should describe expected results from the proposal and try to convince the budget office and the legislature of the need for the proposed activity. The narrative should describe the consequences if the requested resources are or are not provided. Because the reviewer will want to know whether partial funding will help, whether critical program objectives will be endangered without funding, whether workload can be backlogged to get around the problem, and what the implications of the request will be for future requests, answers to those questions should be available and defensible. The justification should make a solid case for a realistic increase. There is no reason to spread a justification thin to defend a large increase when a solid case for a smaller increase is possible. Table 5–1 presents a brief checklist for elements to include in a sound justification. An agency should never assume that its request for additional resources, no matter how reasonable it may appear to agency staff, will automatically bring more funds. When an agency does not receive its full budget request, the agency cannot complain that it has not been "fully funded." Its legislative masters, the representatives of the citizenry, have not agreed to the plan proposed by the agency, but it has fully funded the plan that it has accepted. The agency is expected to execute the plan that has been accepted.

Elements of Cost Estimation

Estimates of what the cost would be of fulfilling the agency service plan for the budget year may be developed and organized through one or more of the following classification structures. First, the cost may be grouped by the *organization*

Table 5–1
Checklist for Budget Justification

Completeness	Are the major elements (objective of program, magnitude of need, benefits, or results) covered?
Explicitness	Are program benefits and related funding increases clearly stated?
Consistency	Are the statements or data appearing in several places the same or easily reconcilable?
Balance	Are the most important programs and issues given the most prominence? Do the programs' objectives adequately support the budget level requested?
Quantitative data	Are quantitative data used appropriately and effectively?
Organization	Is the material well organized to bring out only the significant matters? Are appropriate headings or titles used? Is introductory or summary material used appropriately?
Relevance	Is the material in the justification relevant to the proposal?

SOURCE: U.S. Office of Personnel Management, *Budget Presentation and Justification* (Washington, D.C.: Office of Personnel Management, 1982) with additions.

(branch, section, division, etc.) incurring the cost. The estimates originate in the offices where the costs occur. The costs thus follow the organizational chart. For example, if a city has six organizational units (police, fire, parks, public works, streets, and mayor and council), a cost estimate would be prepared for each unit. The estimates would entail each unit's planned responses to forecast operating conditions. Some plans and forecasts would ideally be common; that is, everybody has integrated into their plans the closing of a military establishment on the edge of town. But some plans would impact almost exclusively one department; for example, the street resurfacing program matters for the streets budget, but not for the others. Second, costs may be grouped by *task, purpose, function,* or *program cost center* or by program outcome group. For instance, program cost centers for a police department might include central administration, the jail, criminal investigations, crime prevention, traffic, training, communication, and records. Each represents an identifiable task for which operating plans and budget cost can be identified. Alternatively, cost may be divided by outcome program: transportation, public safety, environmental protection, and so on. Sometimes, the organizational breakdown coincides with these task or program breakdowns, but often organizational costs are attributable to several different tasks or programs. Third, the costs may be broken down by *object* (or economic) class, that is, by the nature of goods and services to be purchased (personnel, utilities, motor fuel, etc.). This amounts to the agency's planned shopping list. Agencies organize their cost estimates according to the uniform object classification required and provided by the budget office of that particular government.

The beginning of any budget cost estimation, regardless of eventual focus on department, task cost center, or program outcome, is the object class. This is the basis for estimating resource requirements regardless of how costs will eventually be organized. Ideally, the agency would determine what it intends to do, determine what resources it needs to do it, estimate the price of those resources, and multiply the price by the number of input units to get a cost total. In routine budget preparation, some of the estimates for smaller input categories are based on what the agency has experienced in the recent past ("last year plus 5 percent," for instance, implicitly says we aren't changing our operating plan and costs of inputs associated with that plan haven't changed very much). Such an incremental estimation for significant budget categories is not appropriate or acceptable—it does not distinguish the reason for the change. Is it because service demand is higher, because prices of inputs have changed, because policy for responding to public service demands has changed, because of some combination of reasons, or because of something else? The public and the legislative body need to know the reason, as must the program administrator. Budget costs occur as agencies acquire resources (personnel, materials, and facilities) to provide public services. Somewhat different estimating techniques apply to each class, with a particular distinction between personnel and non-personnel costs. The agency is always working toward estimating the cost of carrying out the plan described in the narrative.

Personnel Costs: Paying the Staff

Agencies need workers if they are to produce government services or, even if production is contracted out to private firms, to monitor this production by others. Indeed, payments to employees—wages and salaries plus other agreed benefits (pensions, insurance, etc.)—usually represent the largest single component in government agency budget requests and a major element in the total cost of government. For instance, compensation of employees amounts to more than 70 percent of state and local government consumption expenditures, with some agencies even much more labor intensive. A considerable portion of the total cost of modern government is determined by compensation paid to employees, even though the wage-and-salary component of spending has declined through the years as governments provide more services by contract with private firms and by transfer payments and as they substitute technology for personnel to improve service quality and constrain cost.

WAGES AND SALARIES

The task is to estimate personnel cost for a budget request: to determine the kind and amount of personnel services needed (established by the agency's planned response to forecast operating conditions)—the time to be spent by employees at work—and then apply prevailing wage and salary rates to compute the total cost. In other words, total personnel cost equals the number of workers in each pay category multiplied by the payment per worker in that category. A standard procedure uses personnel data on individuals in each pay category, adjusted for anticipated movements to the next pay step in the budget year. Thus, if there are fifty people in the Tax Auditor I category with five years' experience this year, there will likely be fifty people in the Tax Auditor I category with six years' experience next year, assuming the tax department plans about the same operating pace as in the prior year. The budget estimate for them would be 50 times the annual pay of a Tax Auditor I with six years' experience. Governments normally maintain a position management system that charts authorized positions by pay class, which positions are filled and which are vacant, and the pay rate in each class. The system both provides a control over employment and its costs and offers an excellent tool for cost estimation.

The request for payment of staff must be supplemented by lapses that reduce total cost: turnover (retirements, quits, and terminations) with replacement at lower pay grades or nonreplacement, delays in filling vacant positions, and so on. Such lapses may be estimated from experience with the agency workforce. Requests for new personnel ordinarily are based on greater expected workload, on a desire to improve the quality of service, or on new programs. At least at the agency request level, staffing decisions have moved away from regarding government as the employer of last resort, where those unable to find jobs elsewhere can turn, and toward staffing to ensure the agency delivers planned services and achieves its objectives.

But how much should each employee be paid? This question is critical for sound government finances and for the delicate political balance between, on the one hand, the interests of public employees and the groups that represent them and, on the other, the concerns of taxpayers/service recipients who both receive what governments provide and pay the bill for that provision. A reasonable objective in determining pay rates for government finances might be to ensure delivery of government services at least cost to the taxpayer. If employees are overpaid, the taxpayer pays too much for services provided; if employees are underpaid, the taxpayer receives subsidization at the expense of those employees. In practice, pay rates may come (1) from law or tradition, as with the salaries of elected officials; (2) from pay rates established in a civil service classification structure that attempts wage comparability across position factors; or (3) from collective-bargaining agreements.[5] Most governments establish some salaries in each of these ways. For example, a city could well have the salaries of the mayor and the members of the council established by state statute, the wages and salaries in most city department employees established in a personnel classification system, and the wages of police officers, firefighters, and sanitation workers established in a collective-bargaining agreement.

NON-WAGE-AND-SALARY PERSONNEL COSTS

The total cost of workers includes both direct compensation (wages and salaries) and fringe benefits associated with employment, including the cost of post-employment benefits promised the employees. At least some fringe-benefit payments are included in object classes separate from wage and salary payments, but they must be considered when estimating total compensation and when developing budget estimates. These payments may include payments into public employee pension systems, health and/or life insurance premiums, clothing or uniform allowances, employer Social Security or other payroll tax payments, and so on. Most such benefits are computed by applying formulas, which are established by law, labor contract, or (less frequently now) prevailing practices. Cost is normally driven either by the number of employees (hospital insurance premiums, for example) or by the amount paid to employees (e.g., payments into a public employee pension fund based on a certain percentage of wages). Calculation is thus relatively straightforward (although the formulas can sometimes be quite complicated). Some costs associated with employing workers may be in budgetary accounts other than those of the agency in which the person works. For example, the government may put employee benefits (pensions, vacation pay, etc.) in the budget of a Department of Personnel. That complicates the work of analysts who are trying to discern how much a government is spending to provide a particular service—looking at the spending in the police department will not provide the whole answer if some police officer benefits are being covered in the personnel department budget.

---

[5]See Charles A. Pounian and Jeffrey J. Fuller, "Compensating Public Employees," in *Handbook of Public Administration,* 2nd ed., ed. James Perry (San Francisco: Jossey-Bass, 1996), for more discussion of pay systems.

Non-Personnel Costs

Other object costs may be more difficult to estimate than personnel costs.[6] Non-personnel costs are often computed using estimating ratios, as adjusted by recent experience. Much information for the request can be located in prior-year budget materials. Five estimation techniques are frequently used in these computations:

1. **Volume × unit price.** This method is attractive when an identifiable quantity and a single average price are applicable to a relatively high-ticket object class. Candidates for this approach include requests for items such as automobiles or personal computers. These items represent fairly homogeneous categories that can constitute a large share of cost in an object class. If the police department plans to purchase ten new vehicles, each of which would likely cost $35,000, the estimated cost of the plan is $350,000.

2. **Workload × average unit cost.** This approach uses recent cost experience with adjustments for changed plans, inflation, or productivity changes. For instance, food expenses for a training class could be estimated by such a method (300 trainee days at $20 per trainee day, for a request of $6,000).

3. **Workforce ratios.** Some categories of cost, particularly small categories of miscellaneous costs, can be estimated by relating them to the workforce. For example, office supply expenses for a revenue department district office could be related to the size of the staff stationed there. A proposal to hire new police officers may bring with it the need to purchase new police vehicles. (Similar estimates can be made by linking the expense category to the clientele being served by the local office.)

4. **Ratios to another object.** When there is some relationship between certain categories and other resources used in the production process, that expense group can be estimated by use of ratios to the non-personnel object class. As an example, a parts inventory for motor vehicles can be linked to the number of vehicles in the motor fleet. Purchase of ten new police vehicles would require some additional costs for operation and repair.[7]

5. **Adjustment to prior-year cost.** Small, heterogeneous cost categories can be estimated by adjusting prior-year lump sums, using whatever adjustment percentage seems right. This method may be necessary when other means are not feasible or economical, but it lacks the attempted precision of other techniques and should not be used for any substantial cost category.

No formula or ratio can be automatically applied without hazard. Cost ratios and other relationships may change if operating methods are altered, prices of inputs

---

[6]See Susan A. MacManus, "Designing and Managing the Procurement Process," in *Handbook of Public Administration,* 2nd ed., ed. James Perry (San Francisco: Jossey-Bass, 1996), for an excellent analysis of the procurement of goods and services.

[7]Sometimes things do not work out well. For instance, a federal judge ordered LaPorte County, Indiana, to remedy chronic jail overcrowding, and the county spent $23 million on a jail renovation and expansion, completed in 2004. Unfortunately, the county did not have enough money to hire additional jailers, so a new wing with space for 200 inmates had to remain empty. Too bad the judge did not order jailers to accompany the jail space.

change, or production technologies change. All of these change in a dynamic economy, often with great impact on operating cost. Sidebar 5–1 describes break-even analysis, an estimating device often used by managers in public, private, and non-profit agencies as they develop fiscal plans.

Sidebar 5–1
Break-Even Analysis

Break-even analysis is a helpful tool for certain managerial problems, including budget estimation, subsidy determination, scaling, and the like. Agencies that have sales revenue can make more frequent direct use of the technique, but most managers will find some applications. The technique plots cost against revenues as the quantity of service (output) provided varies. That allows the manager to identify the service level at which service revenue equals service cost (the break-even point) and the required subsidy or contribution (profit) at other operation levels. With the costing model developed here, a budget administrator can easily see how changing demand for a service (or work loads) will influence the agency's spending pace, and that can be useful in both developing a budget request and monitoring spending within budget execution.

The logic of the method is illustrated with this example. Suppose the Smithville Solid-Waste Management Authority has a trash collection fee of $2 per 40-gallon container; that means its revenue in a particular time period will equal the number of containers of trash collected multiplied by $2. Algebraically,

$$TR = P \times Q$$

where TR equals the total revenue, P equals the price per unit, and Q equals the number of units or service level. Thus,

$$TR = 2Q$$

The Authority faces two types of cost, some that are fixed (they do not change with the quantity of service provided, at least within normal service ranges) and some that are variable (the cost increases with the level of service). Authority estimates show the following costs:

Fixed (Annual)	
Administration (staff, utilities, etc.)	$35,000
Equipment lease	85,000
Total	$120,000

Variable (Per Container)	
Landfill tipping charge	$1.00
Equipment operation on collection routes (fuel, maintenance, etc.)	0.15
Collection crew payment	0.25
Total	$1.40

Sidebar 5–1

An algebraic statement of total cost would be

$$TC = FC + (VC \times Q)$$

where TC equals the total cost, FC equals the fixed cost, and VC equals the unit variable cost. Thus,

$$TC = 120{,}000 + 1.40Q$$

The Authority can now estimate the level of collections at which the operation will break even and, probably more important, the necessary subsidy at actual levels of operation. The break-even service level is the one at which TR equals TC:

$$2Q = 120{,}000 + 1.40Q$$

The break-even Q is 200,000; collection levels above that will provide a surplus (or contribution) for use elsewhere, and collection levels below that will require a contribution from elsewhere (maybe a tax) to cover the cost. By substituting the manager's best guess for actual service level into the equation, the actual contribution or subsidy requirement may be estimated. The analysis can also help the manager identify the relative impact of controlling fixed or variable costs in reducing the overall subsidy requirements.

Managers need to recognize the limitations of the analysis, even as they use it. Costs may be difficult to estimate and may not be easily divided into fixed and variable categories. There may also be cost discontinuities. In other words, certain costs may be fixed up to some production level, but need to increase to support further service production. Service levels almost certainly vary with the price charged, especially with larger price changes. The assumption of linearity can only be seen as a working approximation. The technique, however, remains one of great applicability. Managers often develop break-even charts to visualize the costs and revenues of their operations as level of operations changes. The charts plot total cost and total revenue against service (or output) levels, as shown here.

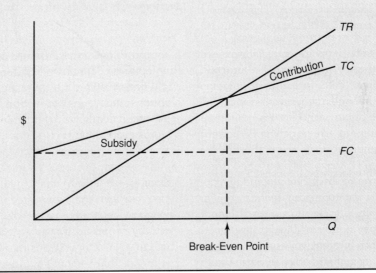

Screening for Errors

Budget estimates must be carefully prepared because the quality of the presentation shapes the impressions that budget analysts (and others) develop about agencies. Analysts are less likely to trust judgments of budget officers who prepare sloppy budget requests. Several simple errors are particularly frequent, although they should never occur. The budget should not be transmitted outside the agency until a check has been made for the following errors because these errors will be the first things that the central budget examiner will look for:

1. **Instructions not followed.** Budgets may not coincide with current budget instructions, budget guidelines, and forms. A budget may be developed using the prior-year budget as a guide, but the submission itself must coincide with current regulations. Failure to follow instructions produces needless embarrassment and may put the request at extra risk.

2. **Missing documentation.** Budget submissions may lack required supplemental documents, or the documentation may not be properly identified. Budget examiners are not inclined to give the benefit of the doubt to budgets with missing materials.

3. **Internal inconsistency.** Cost-estimate detail columns may not add to totals carried forward in the presentation. One must continuously cross-check to preserve the internal consistency of the budget request.

4. **Math.** The math may not be right. Failure to check all calculations can lead not just to professional embarrassment, but also to rejected budget requests and to terminated employment. Even spreadsheet calculations need to be verified to ensure that formulas do what is expected and that the formulas are right. The computer does exactly what it is told to do, even when you tell it to do the wrong thing.

Review of Budgets

Agency requests are reviewed by a central budget office before proposals are included in the executive budget (and by legislative committees after inclusion in the proposal). The central budget office is working under a total resource constraint—revenue forecast to be available in the budget year, funds to be borrowed during the budget year, and any balances forecast to be available from prior years—and the sum of all executive budget requests must be within that constraint. In almost every circumstance, the sum of requests is more than the money available to spend—so the central budget agency is going to have to reduce some requests. But the budget agency is also concerned that the budget and operating plan finally approved can actually be executed. That means that it may need to add omitted items from some requests if the examiner finds that a program supported by the chief executive cannot be executed with the resources initially proposed by the agency. Furthermore, the budget examiner is less informed about agency operations than are those in the agency who prepared the budget. That means that the budget must clearly communicate and explain what is in the budget proposal.

How do budget examiners review budgets? In many respects, the budget examiner will "reverse engineer" the budget proposal to get behind the gross numbers to see what is driving them, to see what policies are being implemented, to see what environmental forecasts are involved, and to see what the internal logic of the proposal actually is. The examiner will have the budget narrative as a road map, but will deconstruct the numbers to make sure that she understands how the service delivery plan works and how that matches the narrative. The examiner will be less knowledgeable about details of the program under review than those who run the program, but will not be uninformed and powerless to review. Some of the work is background, and Appendix 5–1, instructions to Oregon budget analysts, gives a good overview of what work must be done and how a budget examiner would proceed with the review task.

Agency budget requests will often be analyzed twice within the executive branch. First, an analyst within an agency is looking to bring forward a request that best reflects the program of that agency and stands the best chance of ultimately being approved and executed. The objective is to produce the best case for the agency's proposals against those from other agencies. Second, an analyst within a central budget office is reviewing a request to ensure that it best reflects the program interests of the chief executive and, if approved, can be executed as intended. Both examiners ultimately have the interests of the public as their objective, but their particular twists on the analysis will be slightly different, as you can appreciate.

Reviewing a Budget Request

A budget reviewer will go through several steps in the analysis of a department or division budget. The materials used in the review will include (1) the budget instruction under which the budget proposal has been prepared (chief executive priorities, ceilings, standard price increases for categories like motor fuel that are purchased by many departments, etc.), (2) the narrative for that agency, (3) the budget request numbers for that agency, (4) prior-year budgets and appropriations to that agency, and (5) a report of execution of that budget for the current year (budgets are always being reviewed in the midst of budget execution, and those reports give useful information about the budget proposal because the execution gives the freshest fiscal information about the agency—a first review step is to determine whether the current pace of spending will use up the appropriation and whether what is found is consistent with the budget request).[8] With those information sources, the analyst considers these questions:

1. **Policy.** The reviewer must consider what the policy rationale is for the agency's proposal. Among the questions to be considered are these: Is the problem real? Is the problem something that this government should be doing something about? Is the strategy that the agency is proposing likely to be

---

[8]In other words, if the budget request is being analyzed with three months left in the fiscal year, divide actual spending by the agency to date by 9 and multiply by 12 to see whether the resulting number is considerably above or below the appropriation. If it is considerably below, is the budget request for the next year reduced, and, if not, why not? At least ask questions about the request on the basis of the comparison.

successful? Will the program make any difference? What is the chief executive's view on the policy under consideration? Does the narrative reflect the chief executive's expressed priorities? If not, it is unlikely that the chief executive will want the budget transmitted for legislative approval to be heavy on that sort of proposal. The analyst would normally check with the agency to see whether or not it might want to try again, no matter what the submission timetable was.

2. **Arithmetic.** The math gets checked again. The reviewer must verify the arithmetic used to produce program requests. Errors and overambitious rounding seem to increase requests more often than they reduce them.

3. **Linkages.** Reviewers should check linkages between justifications and dollar requests. Is there reason to believe that the request will have the expected result, or will things stay about the same regardless of the money requested? Requests in the latter category are good candidates for elimination. Does the budget narrative get reflected in the budget request? Suppose the police department narrative emphasizes a new program that moves the police out of cars and onto bicycles as a program of heavier engagement in the community and of environmental sensitivity. If that is there, the analyst would look for bicycles in the budget and maybe for less motor fuel. The words need to be reflected in the numbers because the words establish the intended policy response to the expected service environment.

4. **Agency competence.** Does the budget request suggest that the agency understands what is going on? If the request appears to have been prepared by an extrapolation or projection of expenditure categories in prior years, then the agency administrator is either lazy or inept or has no understanding of the process of providing the assigned service. This person is officially a wiener, and it is the job of the budget examiner to roast him or her. Projections of prior growth do not make a legitimate budget request—no policy, no expectations about operating conditions, no idea how the agency fits together.

5. **Spending drivers.** Figure out what drives the budget and make sure that relationships are reasonable. For instance, many city police department budgets are driven by cops and cars—those two inputs, and inputs closely associated with them (e.g., motor fuel and fringe benefits), create much of the budget and changes from one year to the next. The budget analyst needs to ensure that changes in these critical inputs are consistent with the narrative and that internal relationships between these inputs are reasonable. For instance, is the police budget request being manipulated by a change in the established replacement cycle for police cars? If so, is this a reasonable and conscious policy, or is it simply an attempt to kick the problem down to later years? Agencies will differ in terms of what the drive inputs are—a city water utility is likely to have different critical inputs than the city police department, and the U.S. Department of Defense will be completely different. Part of the reverse engineering that the budget examiner does will involve identifying the major spending drivers.

6. **Omissions.** The reviewer must seek omissions from the budget requests. Some years ago a major university constructed a large center for performing

and creative arts, but neglected to request money to cover electricity and other utilities needed for its operation. That created significant budget problems during the first year because major reductions had to be imposed on other university activities (but not football) to cover that utility bill. The reviewer should also consider whether the agency is planning to mix capital funds with operating funds.

7. **Ratios, shares, execution, and trends.** The reviewer must use all resources available for analysis, particularly the prior-year budget and actual expenditure, the current-year budget and reported expenditure to date, and the proposed budget. A comparison of these documents can be made without undue trouble, especially since the analyst has been keeping track of the agency through the operating year. The analyst should establish the cause of any deviations from trends apparent in those comparisons. The analyst often computes ratios and shares of cost elements over time and across agencies to identify variances and to raise questions for the agency (Sidebar 5–2 discusses ratios and shares in greater detail). Ratios, shares, and trends seldom answer questions by themselves, but they do frequently open up matters for further inquiry. Compare the budget request with the requests and appropriations for previous years and, crucially, with the execution report for the current year. Are there significant changes in trends and relationships between inputs and programs, and are any changes explained in the narrative? Are changes based on different service policies or on changing prices for

---

Sidebar 5–2
Ratios and Shares

Management guru Peter F. Drucker writes, "A database, no matter how copious, is not information. It is information ore. For raw material to become information, it must be organized for a task, directed toward specific performance, applied to a decision. Raw material cannot do that itself."[1]

Budget documents provide a rich lode of data about agencies, but those data are raw. Budget analysts regularly calculate ratios and shares from that data to convert it into information that might help make a decision. For example, it may be interesting to know that East Liverpool spends $400,000 on police salaries, but real insight requires the number to be related to something, often through a ratio or a share. What ratio or share might help, given the considerable array of possible computations that could be made? Here are some fundamental data questions:

1. What period-to-period increase or decrease appears in the categories being examined? What reasons induce the changes, and are they likely to continue in the future?
2. What are the growth rates of elements in the budget totals? Which categories are driving the overall growth, what appears to be causing those patterns, and what are the prospects for the future?

[1]Peter F. Drucker, "Be Data Literate—Know What to Know," *Wall Street Journal,* December 1, 1992, A-16.

inputs? Are certain input categories likely to be underspent or overspent this year, based on the execution reports, and is there a reasonable adjustment in the budget request?

8. **Choices within limits.** The reviewer must understand that resources are finite and choices must be made among worthwhile programs. Government programs to improve adult literacy and to reduce fatalities at rural intersections both yield a return that is important for society. But if government resource constraints prevent both programs from being included in the executive budget at the full amount requested by the operating agencies proposing them, a choice has to be made between the two—and there is no common denominator (a social value "converter" between more literate adults and fewer deaths in the country) between the two programs. The choice will be fuzzy, imprecise, and somewhat discomforting. But it is a choice (one of many) that has to be made. Also, if the request involves moving some activities to outside contractors or moving some previously contracted activities back into the agency, the reviewer needs to question the reason and the justification to see whether performance improvement or cost reduction has been sufficiently demonstrated (movements in and out are costly, so they should not be done on whim).

9. **Performance.** The reviewer considers the performance documentation provided by the agency, the extent to which the measures provided are consistent with the mission and goals of the agency, the extent to which accomplishment is appropriate to the budgetary resources available to the agency, and how the performance plan relates to the budget request of the agency. It is important to consider the extent to which measures are germane to the mission of the agency and extend beyond just measuring things that are easily measured. Poor performance may, if the work of the agency is sufficiently important to the citizenry, provide a reason for increasing the budget of the agency rather than for cutting its budget. It is expected that there will be a link between achievement of the performance measures and the implementation of the budget.

The reviewer is examining the budget request as representative of the chief executive and of the taxpaying/service-receiving public. The objective is not to irritate the person who prepared the request, although that may happen along the way, but to make sure that planned services get provided as effectively, efficiently, and economically as possible.

The Budget Presentation

Although the budget has been presented in written form, agency administrators usually will need to make a formal, oral presentation of the budget to a budget policy committee, a legislative group, or others. There are varying degrees of formality to the presentation and of tension associated with the event. In many instances, the group to which the budget is being presented, while well meaning and serious, has no idea what is going on and what the budget issues actually are. It is wrong, however, for the administrator to do anything other than take the presentation as completely serious. The administrator should prepare as if the survival of the agency vitally depends on the outcome of the meeting, even if it is likely to be entirely pro forma. There will be some people at the meeting who care only about a tiny portion of the total budget and are willing to tie up the entire budget process until they get satisfaction about their concern. That is how democracy works.

The presentation should provide an overview of what the budget is about and, in particular, how each segment contributes to the fundamental objectives of the organization. It should direct special attention to the larger elements of the budget, even though nonexperts will feel more comfortable in discussing smaller items. The administrator's objective in the presentation is to bring the committee into support of the agency budget, and that includes support for the large elements, even though their understanding may be somewhat imperfect. In many respects, the administrator seeks to teach the committee about the agency, its reason for existence, the things it intends to achieve, and how the budget works to reach those objectives.

Some administrators take a hide-and-seek approach with their budget presentations. In other words, there are problem areas in the budget request, but the review committee will have to find them on their own if they can. An alternate approach is entirely opposed to this. The administrator directs the attention of the committee to the problem areas and then takes the offensive in terms of building the agency view (or spin) on the topic. In this approach, the agency position sets the standard, establishes the environment, and draws the boundaries for the committee discussion. Many administrators are more comfortable with this approach and find it to be extremely useful. It also has the advantage of better following the governance principle of transparency than does the hide-and-seek approach.

Budget committee processes are ultimately uncontrollable by the agency administrator making the budget presentation, and a committee member can raise an entirely unpredictable question of fact, one that even the best administrator would not be able to answer without doing considerable background research. In this eventuality, the administrator has a choice: (1) admit that he or she does not know the answer, but will provide the answer soon after doing some checking, or (2) give a ballpark answer from out of thin air with great confidence and great precision, knowing full well that nobody will be able to verify whether the answer is right or not and that the answer has no real bearing on the operations of the agency. Both approaches are regularly used, but the former is much to be preferred for the sake of good governance. When that approach is taken, the follow-through must be quick and complete.

The Executive Budget: The Plan and the Balancing

The executive budget document delivers the financial plan for the government, provides a clear statement of the policy vision that shaped that plan, tells the legislature and the public what enactment of the plan would bring, and provides an archive of information about the government and its agencies. It also includes information about the operating performance of the government and about the performance plan that is inherent in the financial support that is requested. In all these areas, the message needs to be communicated clearly, but concisely; many participants in the process immediately conclude malicious intent for everything that is vague. In other words, the budget should be (1) a policy document, (2) a financial plan, (3) an operations guide, and (4) a device for communicating to the legislature and the public. Many governments post their budget, in detail ranging from summary to complete, on the government's website for easy access by all. Some governments also post the budget requests transmitted by the agencies to the central budget office.

The budget, like that delivered to Congress by the president or presented by other executives to their legislative bodies, typically contains four basic elements:

1. **The budget message** is an introduction, from the chief executive, that highlights the major conditions surrounding the budget's preparation (economic conditions, perceived social problems, service priorities, etc.) and the primary changes proposed in the budget. The message sets the tone for the budget ("hard times," "new beginnings and new challenges," "change," "emerging from severe fiscal crisis," "new hope," "new era of responsibility," etc.); in simple budgets, this may be the only narrative in the entire document.[9] The message is where the executive (president, governor, mayor, etc.) makes a statement about which goals matter to him or her.

2. **Several summary schedules,** the type and number of which vary by budget, gather the major aggregates planned in the full document. These schedules include both revenue and expenditure categories, each organized by classification schemes seen as important by the government (revenue by source, expenditure by object class, expenditure by organizational unit, expenditure by function, etc.). Schedules ordinarily include the budget-year amounts and comparable figures for the current and most recently completed years.

3. **Detail schedules,** the heart of the budget, explain why the administrative departments seek the money they hope to spend. Estimates may also be presented for several out-years to provide information about long-term trends and impacts on budgets of decisions now and of external developments (e.g., economic or demographic change). The details are presented in at least one and usually more of the following organizational structures: by administrative unit (the department, division, etc., responsible for spending and delivering services), by program or function (the type of service delivered), or by object of expenditure (the input classes to be purchased). Most governments also include a performance plan and report for each agency. These schedules state the actual results in terms of measured indices for the closed fiscal year and planned accomplishments for the budget year.

4. **Supplemental data** may also be included in the budget document, depending on the information requirements placed on the executive by the legislative body and on the special problems or opportunities encountered by the

---

[9]For more about the strategy of that message, see Henry W. Maier, *Challenge to the Cities: An Approach to a Theory of Urban Leadership* (New York: Random House, 1966). Maier was the longtime mayor of Milwaukee.

subject government. Most budgets, including the federal budget, include supplemental tables and displays that are useful and interesting, but have no direct bearing on the key tasks of the budget. Other examples of displays that governments use include detailed historical tables on tax rates, analysis of grant revenue, debt schedules, and special detail on pension and other trust funds.

Building the executive budget from the agency plans requires a serious struggle to get program plans to fit within resources available to the government. Using executive priorities as a guide, the central budget office crafts the budget on behalf of the chief executive by cutting some plans, scaling back other plans, stretching out the pace of programs, and even proposing revenue options to enhance available resources. Controls on filling vacant positions, cuts in supply and equipment purchase proposals, and reduction of inflation adjustments are reasonably uncomplicated mechanisms for dealing with minor imbalances; such adjustments, along with the savings resulting from normal review of agency proposals within the template offered by the chief executive's vision for the future, provide orderly accommodations to resources that "meat-ax" approaches (such as reducing all proposals by a flat percentage, denying all plans for new services, or cutting any proposed increases that exceed a prescribed rate) do not afford. The responsible budget office makes a spending program proposal that can be executed within the funds that the government has for the year. This is the place where the avalanche of good ideas for service to the public gets adjusted to fit within the resources available to the government for that year, where fiscal sustainability ultimately gets enforced (or not).

Phantom Balance and Deficit Reduction

Governments may find it politically convenient or legally necessary to produce a balanced operating budget or to reduce the size of the estimated deficit without changing intended policy or its implementation.[10] Governments have developed a number of devices to "cook" budget numbers; many are widely and regularly used to avoid the difficult tasks of actual deficit reduction (increasing actual revenue or reducing actual expenditure). None of these approaches represents sound financial management.

1. Rosy scenarios. Any budget must be constructed with revenue forecasts for the upcoming fiscal year. Phantom budget balances can therefore be developed by using artificially high revenue estimates for that year. Such forecasts can be produced by assuming unrealistically high economic activity (state and federal

---

[10]Richard Briffault, *Balancing Acts, The Reality behind State Balanced Budget Requirements* (New York: Twentieth Century Fund, 1996), explains that state-balanced budget requirements are not nearly so binding as a casual observer might assume. An operating budget would include the expenditures to be made for services delivered within the year; the resources purchased from the operating budget would largely be used within that year.

taxes as well as many local non-property taxes are sensitive to the level of economic activity),[11] by positing impossibly diligent administration of the tax, or by presuming that the link between revenue collections and economic activity has improved. Local property taxes ordinarily could not be overestimated because rates are set on the basis of assessed value on a prior valuation date (more about this in a later chapter). The estimated revenue can be manipulated, however, by assuming unrealistically low delinquency (or noncollection) levels: if 90 percent of the levy has historically been collected, a budget boost is possible by assuming 95 percent collection. During its fiscal troubles of the late 1970s, New York City apparently got such boosts toward balancing the budget by presuming 100 percent collection, a completely unrealistic basis for budgeting. Similar effects may result from overly optimistic assumptions about intergovernmental assistance from either federal or state sources or about the possibility that some other government or a private organization will assume responsibility for a service previously provided through this budget. New York State has, for a few years, included around $150 million in revenue from collection of cigarette taxes on Indian reservations in its budget—in spite of doubts that such taxes can actually be enforced—but they do help with the budget gap. Rosy scenarios also can reduce planned expenditures—a healthy (forecasted) economy reduces social program needs and entitlement flows.

2. One-shots. An unrepeatable revenue boost can be produced by the sale of property or other assets held by the government, a "one-shot." As long as that revenue is not viewed as a long-term boost to the fiscal base and the asset is truly no longer needed for government service, the sale may be perfectly reasonable. But this is not always the case. One example was the fiscal 1991 sale by New York State of the Attica Correctional Facility to the state Urban Development Corporation for $200 million (the Corporation borrowed $240 million—the difference being administrative costs—with debt service being met by leasing the prison back to the state), a high-cost and transparent scheme to fill a budget hole.[12] The "green sale-leaseback" is a recent reincarnation. Providence, Rhode Island transferred three city buildings, including City Hall, to the city's Public Building Authority. The building authority borrowed $35 million, using the buildings as collateral. The city will lease the buildings back for 15 years and those rental payments will cover debt payments. Of the bond issue, about

---

[11]There is some evidence that, at the federal level, neither the administration (through the Council of Economic Advisers) nor Congress (through the Congressional Budget Office) exercised as much bias as has been alleged. See Michael T. Belongia, "Are Economic Forecasts by Government Agencies Biased? Accurate?" *Federal Reserve Bank of St. Louis Review* 70 (November/December 1998): 15–23. One study of the Office of Management and Budget (OMB) alone concludes, "Contrary to popular belief, the OMB under both political parties has consistently produced unbiased forecasts of the major macroeconomic variables, and unbiased estimates of total receipts. The traditional OMB ethic of neutral competence appears to be alive in its economic forecasts and revenue estimates." Paul R. Blackley and Larry DeBoer, "Bias in OMB's Economic Forecasts and Budget Proposals," *Public Choice* 76 (July 1993): 229.
[12]Elizabeth Kolbert, "Albany's Budget—Balancing One-Shots Will Reverberate for Years to Come," *New York Times*, April 21, 1991, sec. 4, 18.

$5 million will go for building energy-efficiency upgrades and $30 million will cover the city's budget deficit.[13] Other examples include privatization proceeds, the more profitable of which may bring in substantial revenue in the sale year, but mean the loss of profit flows in later years.[14] An eastern state took the one-shot to its ridiculous extreme. A state hospital was declared surplus, was appraised at a handsome value, and was advertised for sale, and the anticipated revenue from that sale was included in the state revenue estimate. It helped balance a tight budget. But the facility did not sell, so the anticipated sales revenue was included as part of revenue expected for the next budget year! As long as the property remained for sale, the state felt justified in including appraised proceeds as anticipated revenue. Recent presidential budgets have included revenue from the sale of AMTRAK, oil leases in the Arctic National Wildlife Refuge, the Naval Petroleum Reserves, the telecommunications spectrum, and so on.[15] The sales have not taken place as planned in the budget presentation; whether gimmick or plan is for others to decide. But Congress is skeptical; revenues from asset sales do not count against official deficit targets. Nor should they. Sale of an asset reduces the financial resources of the government by an amount equivalent to the amount of the sale and should not be treated the same as sustainable operating revenue (like taxes or charges).[16] As noted in Chapter 1, in recent years a number of states and localities have sold various infrastructure assets—bridges, highways, and the like—for a quick jolt of revenue, sometimes wisely used and sometimes not. Such proceeds are capital revenue, not current revenue, inasmuch as they are not repeatable. They do not reduce the cost of government, do not improve the revenue prospects of the government, and do not repair a fundamental fiscal gap. Another favorite one-shot during the Great Recession was the state tax amnesty, programs whereby tax cheats would be forgiven consequences of their cheating (penalties and interest) if they would pay previously evaded taxes in a brief amnesty period—a quick revenue boost, no matter the questions about rewarding dishonest taxpayers and potentially losing future revenue from the demonstrated success of cheating.

3. Interbudget manipulation. State and local governments often have capital budgets in addition to and separate from operating budgets. Capital budgets finance purchases of assets with long, useful lives (as will be discussed in Chapter 7) and often have no requirement for balance because such long-life assets may logically be financed on a pay-as-you-use basis through the issuance of debt. Some governments have shifted activities that would ordinarily be included in the operating budget to the capital budget to produce the desired

---

[13]Michael Corkery, "Cities Deep in Red Turn to Green Deals," *Wall Street Journal*, September 9, 2011, C1.
[14]Privatization is best defended to improve operating efficiency and delivery of service, not as a one-shot revenue enhancer.
[15]Portions of the spectrum have, in fact, actually been auctioned—but not as soon as the revenue started appearing in budgets.
[16]International standards hold that sales of government-owned assets should be treated as means of financing the deficit, not revenue, because they are asset conversions only, not continuing sources of revenue. For instance, this is the required treatment for privatization receipts from sales of state-owned properties in countries of the former Soviet Union.

balance in the operating budget. For instance, in its fiscal 1992 budget, New York City included an $80 million bond issue to finance the four-year job of painting 872 city bridges "Yankee Blue," clearly a basic and continuing maintenance expenditure, but not included in the operating budget.[17] The shift can destroy the logic of the capital budget and, more important, can endanger the capability to finance the government's capital infrastructure.

The federal government currently has no separate capital budget, but simply rolls all spending together. Some argue against creating dual federal budgets to prevent such play between documents. Even without dual budgets, there is room to manipulate: the first President Bush's fiscal 1990 budget proposed that a company, the Resolution Financing Corporation, be established to borrow funds to finance assistance for insolvent savings and loan associations. The Corporation, similar in structure to government-sponsored, privately owned enterprises like the Federal National Mortgage Association, would be outside the federal budget (but guaranteed by the federal government for repayment). The money borrowed would be turned over to the federal government to permit the savings and loan bailout, but the money would—by budget accounting convention—be a receipt, thus reducing the estimated deficit.[18]

4. Bubbles and timing. Deficits may be managed by accelerated collection of revenue to create a cash "bubble" in the year of acceleration.[19] The advantage accrues only in the acceleration year without influencing the fundamental revenue base. The bubble can be duplicated in forthcoming fiscal years only by further accelerating collections, an unlikely possibility. Here is how acceleration can work: Suppose a state requires that vendor collections of sales-and-use taxes in one month (say, May 2014) be paid to the state by the end of the next month (June 2014). The payment from the vendor then will actually be received by the state early in the next month (July 2014). If the state changes the due date from the end of the month to the 20th, however, the checks will almost certainly be received by the state in that month, that is, in late June rather than early July. But for a July 1 fiscal-year state, June is in the 2014 fiscal year, and July is in the 2015 fiscal year; fiscal 2014 thus receives 13 months of sales-and-use tax collections. Because a similar schedule applies for 2015 and beyond, each year continues to receive 12 months of collections. (Acceleration gets more complicated when payments are electronic rather than by checks in the mail, but it still can be done. Most of the accelerations were done in the era of mailing checks.) Only a return to a slower schedule would leave a fiscal year a month short of revenue. States started the speed-up approach in the 1970s and extended it with early payment and prepayment requirements in later years. Well over half of the states require either early payment of collections within the month (e.g., partial payment of May collections in May) or prepayment of estimated

[17]John J. Doran, "New York City Comptroller Kills Bonding Plans for Bridge Painting; Cites Mistakes of 1970s," *Bond Buyer,* July 16, 1991, 2.

[18]Alan Murray, "Bush S&L Bailout Creates Illusion of Deficit Cut That Congress Questions But Wants to Believe," *Wall Street Journal,* February 22, 1989, A-16.

[19]In New York State, these accelerations are called "spin-ups."

collections with reconciliation against actual collections later (estimated May collections paid in May with adjustment against actual collections later) for some major taxes remitted by businesses. Virginia is a recent participant: in fiscal 2010, retailers with annual sales of at least $1 million were required to make advance payment of sales tax owed, bringing 13 months of tax revenue into that fiscal year. These manipulations are politically less difficult than raising statutory tax rates and can provide added revenue for a problem.[20]

The balance problem may also be concealed by manipulating the timing of expenditure.[21] One approach loads the cost of multiyear programs in later fiscal years rather than in a sequence consistent with normal project-development flow. The low current budget-year request may help achieve balance in that year; the result, however, may well be greater problems in achieving balance in future budget years. A somewhat different method of expenditure manipulation, particularly within a fiscal year, delays payment for purchases made toward the end of a fiscal year until the next fiscal year (and the next year's appropriations). For instance, the federal government temporarily stopped payments to Medicare providers for the last six business days of fiscal 2006—moving the spending from one year to the next. The technique artificially reduces the operating deficit in the first year and amounts to short-term borrowing from suppliers across the two fiscal years. In general, the technique kicks the deficit down the road and reduces funds available for the next year. Unless the imbalance is corrected, similar problems will result in following years, and the operating deficit carryover will expand with time.[22]

The federal system creates a somewhat different version of the timing game. Budget presentations work with an out-year window of five or ten years. In order to conceal the long-term impact of fiscal policies being proposed, legislation may be proposed that has its largest impact on the deficit just outside the budget window. That can involve when provisions expire, when tax rates change, or when other changes will have a significant impact on the deficit. If the change were within the presentation window, the impact would stir controversy. By being just beyond, it can slide through with a minimum of attention.

---

[20]Similar shifts may substitute for ordinary borrowing. For instance, the city of Philadelphia used a property tax provision: businesses willing to pay estimated 1978 taxes along with their 1977 taxes were given a special discount on their 1978 tax bill. See "Early Taxpayers Can Get a Break in Philadelphia," *Louisville Courier-Journal,* April 3, 1977. This shift, however, does reduce aggregate collections, whereas acceleration does not.

[21]For example, in 1980 the city of Chicago, to avoid bank loans in a cash crisis, delayed payments to vendors who regularly did business with the city. The problem emerged because property tax bills were not mailed as scheduled because of a judicial challenge of a homestead exemption program. The city had short-term borrowing authority, but feared it was insufficient to cover the shortage. "City May Delay Payment to Suppliers," *Chicago Tribune,* August 19, 1980. Because the taxes were actually levied, there was no borrowing across fiscal years in this instance; the strategy was simply one of cash-flow management.

[22]In 1992, New York City required 2,104 police recruits to begin training at 11:59 P.M. on June 30, the last minute of the fiscal year. These orders met a state requirement for starting the new class in the 1991–1992 fiscal year, but deferred required city pension contributions for them ($20 million) until the 1993–1994 fiscal year. Kevin Sack, "Fiscal Footwork Is Fancy in Plan for Police Recruits," *New York Times,* June 30, 1992, B-3.

5. Ducking the decision. A balanced executive budget may omit some activities that political pressures would prevent the legislature from excluding. The executive may thus claim a balanced budget (or a smaller deficit), though the hard choices have not been made; appropriations actually made will likely produce a deficit, or proposals will be radically realigned before appropriation. An illustration: Texas requires that its Legislative Budget Board (LBB), the body responsible for preparing the budget document for appropriations, submit a balanced budget. In the fall of 1984, after substantial work had been done on the document for presentation to the 1985 session, the state comptroller substantially reduced the official estimate of oil and natural gas tax revenue (a major source of Texas state revenue). The revision occurred just before the LBB reviewed higher education requests, the last item on its schedule. Rather than altering recommendations for all state agencies, the LBB opted to balance the budget entirely through reductions in higher education and recommended a 26 percent appropriation decrease. Possibly the LBB intended to stimulate efficiency in higher education, but it is probably more likely that it was practicing phantom balance. In any case, the legislature made substantial readjustments; virtually all reductions were restored, and some institutions received increases.[23] Another example: the Bush administration omitted any funding to support the wars in Iraq and Afghanistan from its 2006 budget presentation, preferring to use supplemental appropriations (a request for $81.9 billion for those purposes was transmitted on February 14, 2005, just a few days after the budget was presented, with more requested after the start of fiscal 2006).[24] This was in a budget presented as one aimed at reducing the deficit.

An artificially balanced budget may even be passed, with the legislature relying on supplemental appropriation in the next year to provide required funds. Such proceedings may go largely unnoticed by the media and the citizenry because emphasis traditionally focuses on the budget presentation and consideration, not on what actually happens during the budget year. In a similar fashion, the imbalance may be handled by shifting expenditures normally planned for the early part of the coming budget year into a supplemental request for the current budget year. Unfunded public employee pension promises, as discussed in Chapter 4, are probably the largest American example in gross dollar terms of ducking the decision.

6. Playing the intergovernmental system. States regularly manage their budget problems by changing the fiscal relationship with their local governments. First, states can assign local governments responsibility for services that have previously been state-financed. For instance, highway maintenance is usually a shared state-local responsibility, with certain roads being state and

---

[23]Lawrence Biemiller, "How the University of Texas, Flexing Its Political Muscle, Foiled Budget Cutters," *Chronicle of Higher Education* 30 (June 19, 1985): 12–15.
[24]David Stout, "Bush Proposes an Ambitious Budget Aimed at Cutting Deficit," *Washington Post,* February 7, 2005.

others local. By moving more of the statewide network to the local system, the state can reduce its expenditure requirement. Second, states can reduce the amount of aid they provide local governments. For example, state aid to school districts represents a considerable share of total state spending (the national average is around 15 percent of state spending). By reducing the amount distributed to schools, the state can reduce its budget problem. Cutting aid to local governments, actually presented as loans to the state, was one approach that the state of California used in its budget-balancing fiasco in the summer of 2009. Third, states can delay appropriated aid payments to local governments, moving expenditure from one state fiscal year to another. When the dates of local fiscal years do not match those of the state year, the change may not even alter the total funds to the localities in their fiscal year, just the timing within their year. Suppose the state is on a July 1 fiscal year and its school districts are on January 1 fiscal year, a common situation in the United States. The state owes school districts 12 monthly aid payments during a year. Suppose that the June payment is made in July rather than June. This saves the state one payment during the first fiscal year, although it still pays the school districts the same amount through their calendar fiscal year. But all these strategies do have considerable potential for moving state fiscal problems to their localities. Indeed, states sometimes simply skip a payment to local governments, kicking the problem down to them.

7. Magic asterisk. David Stockman, President Reagan's first director of the Office of Management and Budget, coined the phrase "magic asterisk" to mean budget savings to be identified later, or "whatever it took to get a balanced budget ... after we totaled up all the individual budget cuts we'd actually approved."[25] Because so much media and public attention is focused on proposed deficits, the fact that the budget provides no clear funding plan gets overlooked. Many times the asterisk will be linked to "administrative savings," which no one has the foggiest idea about how to achieve. The same kind of unspecified savings appears in many gubernatorial budgets, especially during the first year of office when there is little time between election and budget presentation. The new governor may have almost no idea about how to get some outcome promised in the campaign, but the public still remembers the promise. A magic asterisk permits the desired bottom line and gives the administration some time to figure out how to do it.

If you have been paying attention, you should realize that balanced budgets and balanced budget requirements are largely a myth. If there is no political will to maintain fiscal sustainability, legal requirements will be no barrier.[26]

---

[25]David A. Stockman, *The Triumph of Politics* (New York: Harper & Row, 1986), 124.
[26]One good review of state balanced-budget requirements and how they are avoided is Institute for Truth in Accounting, "The Truth about Balanced Budgets: A Fifty State Study," February 2009 [http://www.truthinaccounting.org/news/listing_article.asp?section=451&section2=451&CatID=3&ArticleSource=572].

Actually Making Budget Reductions

When the crunch hits and service programs have to be reduced for the government as a whole, there is no easy approach. It is assumed that the poorly justified and unjustifiable programs have been purged from the proposal and that options for increasing revenues have been rejected—and that the jurisdiction has rejected the policy of deliberately not paying its bills or of delaying their payment into future budget years. So how does a budget executive proceed with making the reductions among good public programs? There is no standard "best practice" for this task. Here are some approaches that administrators have regularly used to make the reductions:

1. **Make across-the-board reductions.** If proposed spending exceeds anticipated revenue by 5 percent, then reduce all budget proposals by that flat amount. It punts the hard choices to the program administrators who then have to decide how to manage the reduction. But at least the program administrators make the detailed adjustments; because they understand program operations better than the central administration, the odds of preserving the most significant elements of programs are improved. It is certainly a better approach than alternatives like the next one.

2. **Make centrally determined reductions in certain expense categories.** In this alternative, the central executive directs what changes will be made in expense categories. For instance, the directive may be to cut personnel expenses by no more than 1 percent, utilities by no more than 3 percent, contracted services by no more than 5 percent, and so on, until a given expense saving is produced. The problem is that opportunities for economization are not the same in all departments and the administrator of the program is far more likely to know what those alternatives are than is the central executive. The cutback program needs to utilize the knowledge and skills of program administrators to the greatest degree possible, and these category constraints stand in the way of that.

3. **Postpone all new programs.** This approach protects existing programs and those who benefit from them. As a result, it can help politically because the new programs have not developed a constituency yet. It may not be a good result for the public, however, because some of the new programs may be far more valuable than the existing ones.

4. **Stop or slow capital spending.** The purchase of new capital infrastructure usually involves large-ticket items. One such delay can have a far greater fiscal impact in the year than lots of decisions about operating expense categories. Some capital equipment, like police cars or computers, may be on a standard replacement cycle, and money can be saved by stretching out that cycle (so that cars are kept four years rather than three). But that piece of new capital equipment may provide lots of service for the public and may reduce the cost of operating old equipment. Therefore, the cost saving may come at considerable expense to the public. Deferred maintenance is also a regular strategy, at least until the bridges start collapsing.

5. **Fire people/furlough people/leave vacant positions vacant/pay people less/cut benefits.** Government programs tend to be labor intensive, so a considerable share of total spending for operations each year is for personnel. If the administrator looks for cuts in places where there is money, the personnel line item will pop up. This is a tough choice politically. But it also is tough for efficiency: losing people hurts the productivity of those remaining, requires readjustment in how services are delivered, and creates gaps that will be hard to fill when government operations expand in the future. In addition, some governments operate under terms of union contracts, and this can significantly complicate the process. Some governments have reduced spending by contracting out provision of certain services to a surrounding or overlapping government, as when Pontiac, Michigan, disbanded its police department in 2010, replacing the service with a contract with the Oakland County sheriff's department.[27] Cost may be reduced—and probably also the level of service.

6. **Draw down supply inventories.** Service production requires some inventories of materials and supplies (fuel, road salt, paper and forms, etc.). Agency operations over time will have developed a particular supply system that automatically orders more when the inventory falls below a set level. Moving that level lower will reduce the ordering pace and the amount spent in a particular year. Similarly, agencies may stretch out the replacement cycle for some operating equipment, for instance, delaying the cycle for replacement of police vehicles for a year. Operating and maintenance costs will increase, but probably by less than postponed vehicle cost.

7. **Suck it up and make the hard choice.** Somebody got elected to make the tough choices on behalf of the people. That person or group of people has to decide what services are most important to the public as a whole and what services are less important and, on that basis, make the appropriate shifts in resources. Cut where the return to the public is less and protect where the return is greatest. That's what executives are supposed to do. You wanted the job, so do it. The choices can't be contracted out.[28] Once the choices about what services are most important and what services can be reduced have been made, it is reasonable to leave the detailed management choices to the program administrators. Within their range of competence (fire protection, parks and recreation, etc.), they know more about operations than do the central executives and are better positioned to deal with the spending reductions.

---

[27]Mike Martindale, "Pontiac Disbanding Police Department," *Detroit News*, October 13, 2010.
[28]In a classic dereliction of responsibility, Alexandria, Virginia, city officials hired a professional ethicist to guide their budget priorities in 2008. What did those people think their job was when they assumed their positions? Only to make choices when the choices meant more for everybody? Michael Laris, "A City Looks to Its Moral Compass in Lean Times," *Washington Post*, December 14, 2008.

Managing Budget Execution

The appropriations approved by the legislature, not the budget proposed by the executive, determine the amount of funds available for delivery of services during the budget year. This approved budget becomes the standard against which actual operations are controlled, and thus the critical managerial tool in execution, both guiding agency operations and ensuring that spending does not exceed appropriations. Appropriation is the tool that legislatures use to keep check on the actions of the executive. The approved budget establishes the control standard; other elements of the execution process measure actual performance against that standard and implement control systems to correct the variance.[29] In practice, systems institute several budget controls:

1. **Preventive controls** are established to block actions that would violate standards. To prevent such violations, some governments establish extraordinary procedures for reviewing planned purchases with price tags that exceed a set limit; the limits tend to be lower when funds are tight. Even more governments apply special pre-audits to establish the appropriateness of payment before checks are written, often requiring approval by multiple independent authorities before spending occurs. (Some of these approvals may represent needless red tape.)

2. **Feed-forward controls** perform diagnostic or therapeutic actions in the spending process. Variance reports may automatically place stop orders on certain accounts when differences between actual expenditures and budgeted expenditures exceed certain levels.

3. **Feedback controls** start corrections into the budget cycle for the future. The comparison between budgeted expenditures and actual expenditures within the fiscal year is important information for those preparing, reviewing, and directing budgets for the next year.

Ordinarily, budgets are approved for an entire fiscal year, but execution of the budget occurs on a day-to-day, week-to-week basis. How can the annual budget establish a control standard for this execution? Well-functioning fiscal systems divide the total budget appropriation to operating units for the year into quarterly (or monthly) allotments by agreement with the central budget office. Suppose the department of streets and storm sewers has an appropriation of $4 million for the fiscal year from January 1 to December 31 and relatively constant expenditure rates

---

[29]In developing and transition countries, problems have arisen with "arrears," or payment obligations that the government has been unable to discharge in an acceptable time period. That stresses the economy as workers, pensioners, and suppliers who have not been paid cannot, in turn, pay their bills, and the people they owe cannot pay their bills, and so on. The problem may emerge from unrealistic budgets built on unrealistic revenue forecasts, inadequate monitoring of budget execution, or poor controls on budget administrators. The remedy, along with correcting the problems previously mentioned, is a system of commitment controls that requires clearance from a treasury or similar central entity before an operating agency can order goods or services to assure that funds/appropriations are available for paying the resulting obligation.

are anticipated during the year. An allotment plan adopted by the department and the city budget office could then be as follows:

	Allotment to Quarter	Cumulative Allotments
January 1	$1,000,000	$1,000,000
April 1	1,000,000	2,000,000
July 1	1,000,000	3,000,000
October 1	1,000,000	4,000,000
Total	4,000,000	4,000,000

A comparison of actual expenditure at each quarter's end with the allotment provides an early warning for controlling department activity and preventing overspending or unnecessary underprovision of service. If reports of spending plus commitments to spend (encumbrances) through the end of June exceed $2 million, the pace of operations would need to be reduced to keep within appropriations. The comparison between expenditure plan and spending activity must include both payments made and contractual commitments made that will involve payment later. These latter totals have different titles in different fiscal systems (encumbrances and obligations are two), but, regardless of title, they reduce the available spending authority and must be included in the comparison against the plan. Although the accounting system (correctly) would not regard the money as having been spent, the manager must recognize that the budget resource is gone as soon as the commitment occurs.

Service delivery, and hence spending profiles, for many agencies is not spread equally through the year. A typical outdoor swimming pool in the northern United States will be in service during the summer months only, so its operating expenditures concentrate in these months; equal quarterly allotments would not be useful for control and management. Activities that produce uneven expenditure flows during the year (seasonal needs, major capital equipment acquisitions, opening or closing new facilities, etc.) require uneven allotments. The allotment schedule must be consistent with both the approved budget and the activity-flow expectations if it is to be useful for control and management.

Comparisons of the allotments and expenditures to date (variances) can suggest (1) areas in which expenditure may have to be curtailed, (2) areas in which surpluses may be available for use against deficits in other areas, (3) patterns that may be helpful in the preparation of future budgets, and (4) the possible need to request a supplemental appropriation (funds beyond those initially appropriated for the fiscal year). Some faster-than-allotment spending may simply be accelerated acquisition (e.g., transfer between quarters to take advantage of low prices not anticipated when the budget was prepared). Other spending may imply spending above the approved appropriation. These latter overruns require spending-unit action to control the flow, generally according to budget office direction. Both agencies and finance officers can thus maintain better control of budget execution with these periodic allotment-to-expenditure comparisons. Although the objective of execution is delivery of services to the public, funds must not be spent in a fashion contrary to the appropriation.

Some government units find that there is no special seasonal pattern to their major expenditure categories. Those units may use simple budget-status reports, which compare the percentage of total budget used (spent and obligated) at a particular date with the percentage of the fiscal year expired. If the percentage of budget used exceeds the percentage of year expired, a problem may exist in that portion of the agency operations. Such a budget-status (or budget-variance) report for a town appears as Figure 5–1. This report is for the midpoint in the fiscal year and works to focus attention on spending categories in which the rate of spending appears to vary from the full plan. Notice the explanation of some variances at the bottom of the report. The managerial consequences of this report style are the same as for allotment-expenditure reports. There are dangers, however, in being lulled into inattention by percentages: a small percentage variance in a large budget line can be more disastrous than a large percentage variance in a small line. The analysis of variances should distinguish between those caused by price surprise, unanticipated variance in demand for services, efficiencies, or supply problems and those caused by alternative use of resources. There should not be a variance because the agency changed its basic service provision plan, however.

Figure 5–1
A Budget Variance Report

TOWN OF CROMWELL
2010–2011 QUARTERLY BUDGET VARIANCE REPORT

MILRATE: 26.84

Expenditures	Budget	Pro-Rated Budget	2nd Quarter Ytd Actual	Difference From Pro-Rated Budget
1. First Selectman	$ 255,521	$ 127,761	$ 122,432	$ 5,329
2. Town Clerk	205,537	$ 102,769	89,495	$ 3,274
3. Registrar Of Voters	58,426	$ 29,213	34,042	$ (4,829)
4. Planning & Zoning	2,140	$ 1,070	728	$ 342
5. Economic Development	40,200	$ 20,100	5,784	$ 4,316
6. Board Of Finance	29,080	$ 14,540	22,356	$ (7,816)
7. Capital Expend. Comm.	90	$ 45	-	$ 45
8. Charter Revis. Comm.	571	$ 286	519	$ (234)
9. Board Of Asses. Appeals	1,300	$ 650	156	$ 494
10. Zoning Board Of Appeals	1,100	$ 550	341	$ 209
11. Inland Wetlands	1,685	$ 843	527	$ 315
12. Handicapped Comm.	525	$ 263	195	$ 68
13. Donations And Dues	37,863	$ 18,932	31,851	$ (12,919)
14. Board Of Selectmen	9,384	$ 4,692	3,491	$ 1,201
15. Legal Expense	166,636	$ 83,318	38,312	$ 5,006
16. Central Services	97,700	$ 48,850	51,397	$ (2,547)
17. Insurance Expense	436,158	$ 218,079	335,832	$ (117,753)
18. General Expense	86,650	$ 43,325	433,446	$ (390,121)
19. Developer/Planner	85,288	$ 42,644	42,367	$ 277
20. Development Compliance	69,048	$ 34,524	33,851	$ 673
21. Conservation Comm.	1,250	$ 625	450	$ 175
22. Finance Dept.	323,719	$ 161,860	159,246	$ 2,614
23. Tax Collector	177,652	$ 88,826	88,218	$ 608
24. Assessor's Office	186,628	$ 93,314	94,916	$ (1,602)

Figure 5–1 (Continued)

25. Treasurer's Office	300	$ 150	114	$ 36
26. Public Works Admin.	174,806	$ 87,403	78,212	$ 9,191
27. Engineering	335,698	$ 167,849	142,607	$ 5,242
28. Sol. Waste/Recyc. Cntr.	687,860	$ 343,930	289,611	$ 4,319
29. Building Inspection	153,066	$ 76,533	74,564	$ 1,969
30. Highway Dept.	1,148,772	$ 574,386	465,998	$ 108,388
30. A Vehicle Maintenance	267,427	$ 133,714	121,854	$ 1,860
31. Building Maintenance	504,663	$ 252,332	284,171	$ (31,840)
32. Parks & Grounds	278,094	$ 139,047	138,752	$ 295
33. Public Wks/Gen. Exp.	438,125	$ 219,063	187,151	$ 1,911
34. Civil Preparedness	9,700	$ 4,850	3,723	$ 1,127
35. Police Dept.	2,721,469	$ 1,360,735	1,325,224	$ 5,510
36. Animal Control	80,441	$ 40,221	46,453	$ (6,233)
37. Health Dept.	149,255	$ 74,628	67,582	$ 7,046
38. Human Service Admin.	95,975	$ 47,988	47,705	$ 283
39. Senior Services	77,648	$ 38,824	34,115	$ 4,709
40. Transportation Svc.	95,464	$ 47,732	45,860	$ 1,872
41. Youth Services	101,392	$ 50,696	44,887	$ 5,809
42. Recreation Dept.	366,188	$ 183,094	180,082	$ 3,012
43. Library	525,309	$ 262,655	263,287	$ (632)
44. Employee Benefits	2,832,707	$ 1,416,354	1,160,946	$ 255,407
Total General Government	$ 13,318,510	$ 6,659,255.00	$ 6,592,848	6,407
45. Bonded Debt	4,135,977	2,067,989	701,470	1,366,519
46. Board Of Education	24,834,587	12,417,294	8,706,018	3,711,275
Total General Government	$ 42,289,074	$ 21,144,537	$ 16,000,336	$ 5,144,201

Expenditures:
Most budget areas are at, or near, targeted levels with exceptions due to the timing of actual expenditures. For example, the Highway Department and the Public Works-Other budgets experience heavier expenditures during the winter months. Donations and Dues are generally paid at the outset of the fiscal year. The Recreation Department's budget has slightly greater outflow early in the fiscal year due to its summer programs. There are no budget areas of significant concern at this time and budgets are anticipated to be expended as approved.The Board of Education budget lags slightlybehind since teacher salaries are paid on a school-year cycle, with balloon payments made in June.Interest payments on bonds have a

Governments establish special rules within which their agencies may move funds around in response to conditions not foreseen when appropriations were made. At the federal level, *reprogramming* is the use of funds within an appropriation account for purposes other than those contemplated at the time of appropriation. Consultation between the agency and the appropriate substantive and appropriation committees of Congress usually precedes the action, which may involve formal notification and an opportunity for disapproval by the committees. *Transfers* move all or part of budget authority in an account to another account or subdivision of an account (e.g., moving funds from Operation and Maintenance to Personnel). Such changes require statutory authority, although some agencies have transfer authority within an established percentage or absolute limits.[30] State and local governments have similar, although often less formal, procedures. Often states establish interim committees to provide needed flexibility during periods of legislative recess, a vital adjustment feature where the legislature meets only periodically.

---

[30]General Accounting Office, *Budget Reprogramming, Department of Defense Process for Reprogramming Funds,* GAO/NSIAD-86-164BR (Washington, D.C.: General Accounting Office, July 1986).

Internal Controls

Program managers are obviously concerned with delivery of services according to plan. Financial managers are simultaneously concerned with maintaining internal control, defined as the methods and procedures within the agency established to safeguard assets, check the accuracy and reliability of financial and other data, promote operational efficiency, and encourage adherence to the prescribed policies and procedures of the agency.[31] Internal controls represent the first line of defense against fraud.

Some basic steps in establishing internal control include the following:

1. **Provide qualified personnel, rotate duties, and enforce annual leaves/vacations.** This policy ensures capable handling of tasks and ensures that irregularities can be found when new staff take over tasks on rotation or on temporary assignment. Personnel who are required to work beyond the limits of their capabilities are dangerous because they hold employment more tenuously and are thus more susceptible to requests for inappropriate actions.

2. **Segregate responsibility.** Dividing related duties and operating responsibilities among two or more qualified people reduces the chance of error or fraud by providing checks and balances on work performed.

3. **Separate operations and accounting.** Divide the responsibilities for operational transactions (purchasing, receiving, collecting, etc.) from maintenance of accounting records to reduce chances for error or theft. Maintain a separate reconciliation of transaction records.

4. **Assign responsibility.** This ensures that tasks are performed and that the appropriate party in questioned transactions can be identified.

5. **Maintain controlled proofs and security.** Maintain segregated bank accounts and closely control cash and negotiable documents. Issue sequentially numbered receipts for collections, and avoid cash payments as much as is feasible. Make orders only from numbered and controlled standard purchase orders. Make payments only according to standard separate authorizations, and require bonding for any employees with access to significant amounts of organization funds. Require dual signatures on checks so that no single person in the organization can write a check. Regularly review and test internal-control systems.

6. **Record transactions and safeguard assets.** Promptly record and accurately classify events and transactions. Limit access to source records and government assets to authorized individuals.[32] Deposit revenue collections quickly.

These steps can help implement the internal-control standards of the International Organization of Supreme Audit Institutions, of which the Government

---

[31]Paul E. Heeschen and Lawrence B. Sawyer, *Internal Auditors Handbook* (Altamonte Springs, Fla.: Institute of Internal Auditors, 1984), 36.

[32]The federal standards for internal controls appear in OMB Circular A-123, available on the OMB website.

Accountability Office is a part: documentation, prompt and proper recording of transactions and events, authorization and execution of transactions and events, separation of duties, supervision, and access to and accountability for resources and records.[33] These control devices can reduce the chances of theft, error, and fraud. Although they offer no protection against poor public choices, they can help ensure that choices get executed as they have been made, for better or worse.

An Intra-Year Cash Budget

A cash budget is a detailed translation of the enacted budget into revenue and expenditure flows through the operating year. It yields a forecast of disbursements, receipts, cash balances, and needs for financing over the budget period, taken at regular points through the year. It is based on likely (or known and controllable) patterns.

1. The pay cycle for employees is known, as are the wage and salary commitments in the enacted budget. From that information, the payment amounts can be forecast through the year—employees will be paid agreed amounts on certain days of the month through the year.
2. The pattern of payments to suppliers (contractors, utilities, etc.) is established, along with the budgeted amounts of those payments.
3. Large payments—payments of principal and interest of debt or purchases of large equipment—are in the adopted budget and are known in advance. Purchases of some large-ticket items may even be controlled within the budget year, so that payment is made shortly after large revenue inflows, not shortly before, to ensure that sufficient cash is on hand without any need for short-term borrowing.
4. Tax and charge revenues are usually driven by regular seasonal patterns. Collections are high in some months and low in others because of the fluctuations of economic activity within the year (high season and low season for some industries, due dates for quarterly payments, etc.). For instance, analysis of data from several recent years might show that sales tax payments received in January are typically 8.5 percent of the annual total. With these patterns known, the revenue forecast for the budget year can easily be translated into its likely monthly flow. Multiply the total sales tax forecast for the entire year by 8.5 percent to get the expected collections in January and so on through the rest of the months.

The cash budget is helpful to execution of the annual budget because it shows when the government might not have sufficient funds to cover the bills coming due at particular points during the year. That warns when the government might need to arrange a very short-term loan from local banks to tide it over the cash shortage and may allow the government to adjust some flows in or out to avoid the need for

---

[33]Internal Control Standards Committee, International Organization of Supreme Audit Institutions, *Guidelines for Internal Control Standards* (June 1992), 9.

such a loan. That would save the interest that otherwise would need to be paid on the loan. Preparing such an estimated cash budget is a helpful practice for government fiscal officers. Furthermore, careful estimation of the payment outflows can be helpful in establishing allotment patterns for dividing the annual appropriation for individual agencies.

Audit and Evaluation

When the budget year is over, several questions should be asked. One basic question is whether the budget was executed as it was passed. The adopted budget should reflect priorities for government expenditures and the intentions for funding that spending. If the budget was responsibly developed and became, by legislative action, the legal fiscal plan, then it should be executed intact, subject to emergency changes beyond accommodation within the enacted budget.

A first key check is to establish that the executed budget and the adopted budget do coincide. Did spending occur according to plan or did it have to be reduced because of revenue shortfalls? Do the plans reflected in the budget match actual expenditure patterns at the close of the year? If they do not, have appropriate procedures been followed during execution to make the changes? In other words, the budget law must be followed if the budget process is to be meaningful in terms of legally adopted plans to be executed. This highlights the need to make sure that, during execution of the budget, expenditures get accounted for properly. For instance, an agency likely has more than one budget account to administer—for example, an account for central office administration and another one for field delivery of services. As the agency works through the year, it will spend from both accounts. It is important that, when payments get made, the accounting system takes payment from the proper account—the telephone bills for the field get paid from the field account and not the central account, for instance. A correct accounting is necessary to keep operations in line with the adopted plan reflected in the budget, prevents illegal movement of funds from one account to another, and provides a sound information base for development of future budgets.

Other questions are asked through the external audit process. Many audits are conducted using a prescribed checklist of steps to establish uniformity in how several different auditors perform a class of audits. Much of the audit focuses on controls built into the systems of the agency. If the internal control/internal audit system operates satisfactorily, the external audit agency need not be concerned with tracing the body of individual transactions because the system produces substantial compliance. The audit does, however, test that system. Accounting controls prevent fraud and waste, ensure the accuracy of operations, ensure compliance with applicable laws, and promote adherence to stated policies (including legislation). The audit determines whether those control systems work. In their audit, examiners look for errors and abuses such as those listed in Table 5–2. Much of the audit employs statistical sampling to permit probabilistic inferences about the extent of error in the total record population. There is seldom reason to scrutinize all records.

Table 5–2
Some Errors, Abuses, and Manipulations Sought by Auditors

Year-end accounting manipulations that push revenues and expenditures from one year to the next to increase or decrease totals in the year

Unrecorded liabilities: commitments to vendors that are suppressed by withholding written agreements and purchase orders from the paperwork system

Overforecasting of revenues, to keep tax rates down or spending up

Failure to reserve adequately for nonpayment of taxes

Miscalculation of utility, hospital, and other service bills

Unauthorized transfer of funds between appropriation accounts

Recording of grant receipts in the wrong funds

Use of a commingled cash account to disguise use of restricted funds for unauthorized purposes

Failure to observe legal requirements for review and approval of budgets

Failure to compile and submit financial reports to state and federal agencies punctually

Improper computation of state aid claims

SOURCE: Peter F. Rousmaniere, *Local Government Auditing—A Manual For Public Officials* (New York: Council on Municipal Performance, 1980), 10 with revisions.

What Audits Need to Prevent: Some Methods of Stealing from Government

Stealing from government is normally rare in the twenty-first century. A robust budget process, including strong internal controls, clear appropriations and fiscal responsibilities, and capable external audit, usually keeps theft in check. (Waste is another matter.) Nevertheless, thefts from government do still happen and receive extensive publicity when they are discovered. It is worthwhile to review some of the methods that have historically been used to steal from government.

GHOSTING

Theft through phantom resources—receiving payment for resources not actually delivered—can take several forms. One method, the ghost employee, involves placing on an agency payroll an individual who does not work for that agency. The person receives pay, but provides no service. A second method is payment for supplies or services that are not actually delivered. Invoices sent by the firm show delivery, but the agency never receives the supplies or services. A third method is double payment for supplies or services. The services are performed once, but invoices show delivery of two shipments. Each method causes the government to pay for resources not delivered, and each artificially increases the cost of public service.

BID RIGGING

The procurement fix involves rigging bids on supply contracts. Suppose a section of highway is to be repaved. Potential suppliers would establish beforehand the bid winner and the winning price; other firms would submit noncompetitive bids. Firms would cooperate in the collusion because their turn to win would come on another project. The collusion increases the profits of the firms and increases the cost of government. Government employees may or may not profit from the procurement fix, depending on the arrangements of the scheme.

HONEST GRAFT

"Honest" graft uses advance information or information known only to a small number of government officials to produce private profit for the individual employee. The reminiscences of George Washington Plunkitt, Tammany Hall leader of early twentieth-century New York City, describe the process:

> There's an honest graft, and I'm an example of how it works. I might sum up the whole thing by sayin': I seen my opportunities and I took' em.

> Just let me explain by example. My party's in power in the city, and it's goin' to undertake a lot of public improvements. Well I'm tipped off, say, that they're going to lay out a new park at a certain place.

> I see my opportunity and I take it. I go to that place and I buy up all the land I can in the neighborhood. Then the board of this or that makes its plan public, and there is a rush to get my land, which nobody cared particular for before.

> Ain't it perfectly honest to charge a good price and make a profit on my investment and foresight? [34]

That profit measures the extent to which the honest grafter, through use of inside information, steals from the public by forcing excess payments for a resource. Honest graft may similarly involve acquisition or establishment of companies to do business with a government. Bid specifications may be written so that a company would be the only one qualified. Requirements for the commodity or service would be artificially increased for the enrichment of the government employee.

DIVERSION[35]

Public assets or the service of employees may be stolen for private use. Office supplies, equipment, gasoline, and so on are as usable for private purposes as for government activities. Public employees may be diverted to private uses, including construction or maintenance projects on property owned by government officials. Employees are sometimes used as workers in political campaigns while on government time—a special illegal advantage of incumbency. These activities involve straightforward stealing because individuals use assets owned by the government

---

[34] William L. Riordon, *Plunkitt of Tammany Hall* (New York: E. P. Dutton, 1963), 3.
[35] For good illustrations of how diversion and shoddy material approaches to corruption work, watch *Catch 22*, a 1970 movie based on Joseph Heller's novel of the same name and pay particular attention to the work of First Lieutenant Milo Minderbinder.

without payment. But there are other approaches: poor controls over the use of government credit cards can provide modern thieves a highly effective tool for diverting public assets far beyond the dreams of corrupt public employees of earlier years.[36]

SHODDY MATERIAL

Because low-quality supplies and materials can generally be delivered at lower cost than can higher-quality supplies and materials, government contract specifications require delivery of quality material. A contractor who provides lower-than-specified quality (shoddy material) can thus profit at public expense.

KICKBACKS

Public officials who have power to select who receives contracts to do business with governments, what banks receive public deposits, and who works for government agencies may profit by arranging for artificially high contract awards or artificial wage payments with a portion of that payment kicked back to the government official. The favored individual or firm receives higher than the appropriate price for the contracted service and thus is able to profit even after making the payment to the contracting agent. Also, legislators have opportunities to shape appropriation bills to include the goods or services sold by a particular vendor. Sometimes, the payment goes to the public official or a relative, or the business purchases something from the official or the legislator at an inflated and highly profitable price. Sometimes, the payment is in the form of giving a job to a relative of the official or the legislator. Sometimes, the payment assists the finances of the election campaign of that official or of that official's political party; in the language of the politics of the 2000s, the former is "hard money" and the latter is "soft money." Unfortunately, kickbacks and special deals seem to have become an important influence in American politics and policy making.

Corrupt businesses in less developed countries and countries in transition to market economies use political power to steal in slightly different ways from those found in developed democracies. Johnson and Kwak summarize some standard approaches: "An emerging market oligarchy uses its political power and connections to make money through such means as buying national assets at below-market prices, getting cheap loans from state-controlled banks, or selling products to the government at inflated prices."[37] Transparency, regularized fiscal processes, and internal controls normally prevent such easy pickings in other nations, although they do remain a problem in subnational governments of the United States where unskilled government officials and inadequate systems make public resources ripe for picking.

The twenty-first century provides interesting new twists for corrupt behavior. For example, the finance director of the Los Angeles Memorial Coliseum put the purchase of new sound equipment for the government-owned facility on his personal credit

---

[36]In a recent example, the long-time comptroller of Dixon, Illinois, apparently used $30 million in city funds to support her champion quarter horse breeding operation. Amazingly enough, the town's annual budget was only in the $9 million range. Her efforts were discovered when she took 4 months off for horse business and the employee filling in discovered suspicious bank activity. [Andy Grimm and Melissa Jenco, "Small Town Rocked by $30 million Theft Case," *Chicago Tribune*, April 18, 2012]

[37]Simon Johnson and James Kwak, *13 Bankers* (New York: Vantage Books, 2011), 133.

card, earning a fabulous number of reward points.[38] Not only did the action violate procurement policy that forbade use of personal cards for major acquisitions, but also it raised questions about conflict of interest in choices made by the director, evaded financial controls for the jurisdiction, and probably caused the warranty on the equipment to be voided. Major purchases are done by check, not credit card, because such payments are more readily controlled against unauthorized use of public funds.

Conclusion

Budget skills combine techniques that can be taught with a cunning that comes only with experience. The start for all budgets must be a sound understanding of what the agency request intends to accomplish. Without that foundation, no amount of tricks can help much. As in many government operations, the great problem is information—those who have that information and are able to communicate it have greater-than-average success. Beyond that, there are few general truths.

QUESTIONS AND EXERCISES

1. The data in the following table present revenues and expenditures by categorized type for the School of Public Affairs at Enormous State University. As with most elite programs at state universities, the school has accepted missions of teaching, research, and service to the university, state, and nation. The data include budgeted and actual data for three years and the proposed budget for fiscal 2014–15. Your task as a budget analyst is to learn as much as possible about the operations of the school and its plans for the budget year just from these data. In particular, you should look for trends, changes in shares and ratios, and the categories that are particularly important in driving the finances of the school. A few notes about the reported data: First, the state appropriates money to the university and then the central administration distributes that money to the various operations on campus. That is the source of the state appropriation number—it has been assigned to the school, so this number for 2014–15 is an actual. All others are part of the request. Second, the central administration charges the school for the services that it provides (central library, computer networks, etc.). This charge is the assessment number in the table. It is based on school operations during the year, so it is an estimate and it counts as a negative component in school revenue. Your answer to this exercise should include both your conclusions from your analysis and a list of questions that your analysis has led you to have for the person who prepared the 2014–15 budget. Suppose the central administration has asked for each school to reduce its spending by 5 percent. Where would you suggest that the school turn to make that reduction?

---

[38]Paul Pringle and Rong-Gong Lin II, "Coliseum Finance Director Earned Visa Points on Stadium Upgrade," *Los Angeles Times,* December 10, 2011 [http://articles.latimes.com/2011/dec/10/local/la-me-coliseum-20111211].

	FY 2011–12		FY 2012–13		FY 2013–14		FY 2014–15
	Budget	Actual	Budget	Actual	Budget	Estimated	Budget
Student Fees	14,691,883	14,617,508	14,852,883	15,505,988	16,290,202	14,648,218	17,356,000
State Appropriation	5,391,233	5,391,233	5,155,353	5,155,353	5,100,703	5,100,703	5,150,000
Indirect Cost Income	850,000	1,048,415	900,000	943,279	900,000	1,256,485	900,000
Other Revenue	130,622	136,561	97,750	111,031	104,450	121,263	120,000
(Assessments)	(7,297,873)	(7,079,459)	(7,497,632)	(7,356,908)	(8,072,512)	(8,249,461)	(8,100,000)
TOTAL REVENUE	13,765,865	14,114,258	13,508,354	14,358,743	14,322,843	12,877,208	15,426,000
UG Financial Aid	28,000	22,500	28,000	29,075	32,000	27,000	36,000
Grad Financial Aid	1,184,510	1,181,212	1,100,510	1,147,754	1,200,442	1,358,033	1,400,000
Total Financial Aid	1,212,510	1,203,712	1,128,510	1,176,829	1,232,442	1,385,033	1,436,000
Compensation	1,1616,746	1,1202,082	1,1674,484	1,0979,134	1,1563,133	1,1253,420	1,204,1159
General Expenses	974,359	732,636	937,150	801,710	949,267	886,242	950,125
Travel	286,400	232,158	254,700	193,637	265,250	231,331	265,755
Capital Outlay	11,667	0	0	0	0	14,231	0
Transfers for Indirect Cost	286,848	412,080	326,304	1,164,942	439,491	688,102	458,650
TOTAL EXPENDITURES	14,388,530	13,782,668	14,321,148	14,316,252	14,449,583	14,458,359	15,151,689

2. The Department of Revenue wants to add more people to the unit that attempts to collect unpaid taxes through telephone contact. What questions would you, as a budget analyst, have after you receive the following request justification memorandum?

   Date: June 19, 2013

   Subject Collection Telephone Pursuit

   Currently, there are 19 employees working on telephone pursuits on a full-time basis. Each employee can make an average of 25 to 40 phone calls per day. The amount collected by the 19 employees for the past year is $17,858,623. If we could add an automated phone system and increase our staff by 10 full-time employees, we could double the number of phone calls made and increase our collections by 59 percent, or $8,900,000.

3. This table shows the staffing and pay rates of the Marshall City Fire Department:

Employee Grade	Number in Grade	Salary
Chief	1	$105,000
Shift commander	3	70,000
Firefighter 1	12	39,000
Firefighter 2	26	30,000
Clerical (part-time)	3	15,000

   The city is part of the federal Social Security system. The city and the employee each pay Social Security payroll taxes of 6.2 percent of all salary paid up to $90,000 per employee to finance federal retirement and disability insurance and 1.45 percent of all salary paid to finance Medicare. The city pays a portion of the cost of health insurance for each full-time employee, an amount equal to $180 per month. Employees are part of a pension system financed by a city payment of 20 percent of the employee's salary and an employee payment of 5 percent of the employee's salary. Full-time employees receive an allowance for uniforms of $750 per year.

   Estimate the city's full cost of fire department labor during the fiscal year, assuming no change in staffing. Separate that cost into salary and fringe-benefit components.

4. Write budget requests and justifications for each of the following program conditions. Start your request by categorizing each request as (1) new service, (2) other continuing, (3) workload change, (4) change in service level, (5) price change, (6) full financing, or (7) methods improvement. The program conditions are as follows:

   a. The agency sends about 275,000 pieces of mail each year. The postal rate has increased by 2 cents per ounce.
   b. The division travel appropriation has been $15,000 per year short of actual expenditure for the last three years, after internal transfers of funds.

c. Fifteen account examiners process 115,000 assistance files per year. Client growth estimates indicate that, in the next budget biennium, files will increase to 125,000 in the first year and 130,000 in the second year. (Account examiners' salaries are $3,775 per month plus fringe benefits of 25 percent.)

d. The city council appropriated $18,000 for a program to track down those not paying traffic fines. The program began in the second quarter of the fiscal year and has produced fine revenue far greater than its cost. The legal affairs division wants to continue the program throughout the entire new fiscal year.

e. The division wants to replace the computer workstations for five administrative assistants. Each workstation includes a personal computer, laser printer, and standard office workstation software.

5. The local water utility has maintained records over several years of its monthly purchases of raw water from the state water authority. The monthly averages are shown in the following table.

   Assume that the city pays a flat rate per thousand gallons of water purchased and that the fiscal year begins on July 1. Payment is made in the month after use. Prepare quarterly allotments for $8 million appropriated for water purchase.

Gallons (000s)		Gallons (000s)	
January	35,000	July	125,000
February	35,000	August	125,000
March	50,000	September	90,000
April	65,000	October	60,000
May	68,000	November	50,000
June	100,000	December	40,000

6. A progress report for the division of tourism promotion prepared for transactions through March 31 of the fiscal year, which runs from July 1 to June 30, shows that the travel account, with a total appropriation of $9,000, has expenditures to that date of $2,500 and encumbrances of $3,500. Because of an important trade fair in May, the allotment distribution for the division had 40 percent of the division budget planned for expenditure in the last quarter of the fiscal year. What is the status of the division's travel account? What managerial actions are appropriate?

7. Analyze this budget justification:

   Workload Change—Biennial Cost: $84,300

   Because of the recognition of new social procedures, our psychometricians are now able to obtain valid test results and scores, enabling our valuators to make sociological recommendations that are realistic and not stereotyped views of battering. Our evaluation professionals, plus specialty counselors with special training, in conjunction with their statewide supervisors, have made great strides in bringing together battered spouses throughout the state. To achieve maximum effectiveness, an additional four counselor teams to be strategically located are essential. This success factor that we have experienced has also brought about an increase in the referral of abused children, which will also require additional case service funds.

a. List the questions you would raise about the justification if you were a budget analyst.

b. Rewrite the justification according to your understanding of what the request intends.

8. A 9-1-1 emergency telephone line provides a single telephone number to be called when help is needed. An operator receives the call and directs police and/or firefighter assistance as needed. The address of the call is displayed on a computer screen, along with other information appropriate to guiding a response. Calls are also recorded, providing full information about the nature of the conversation. In a major metropolitan county, the cost is around $ 3.6 million per year, after an installation cost of $4.5 million. The system would be financed by a tax of 1.5 percent of the monthly line charge paid to the local telephone company.

   Prepare a narrative justification for initiation of such a system.

9. The Public Budgeting and Finance Association is planning its annual conference. The conference hotel has quoted the following prices for services:

Thursday afternoon	Conference facilities rental: $425
	Coffee-break service: $10 per person
	Audiovisual equipment rental: $55
	Evening reception: $25 per person
Friday	Conference facilities rental: $750
	Coffee-break service, morning
	and afternoon: $15 per person
	Continental breakfast: $15 per person
	Luncheon: $20 per person
	Audiovisual equipment rental: $150
Saturday morning	Conference facilities rental: $375
	Continental breakfast: $15 per person
	Coffee-break service: $10 per person
	Audiovisual rental: $75

   Program materials and marketing would cost about $550. The association charged $130 for each participant last year and would like to use the same price this year.

   a. Prepare a break-even chart for the conference and determine the break-even attendance level.

   b. Suppose the association wanted to encourage student participation by charging a rate that would cover only the costs directly caused by their attendance. What price would you charge?

   c. Prepare a budget for the event if you expect 110 people to attend.

10. Suppose you work for the city budget office. The chief budget officer for the city reports to the staff that revenues are 7.3 percent below the forecast level of $6.8 million for the first five months of the budget year. She asks for ideas on what, if anything, should be done to deal with the problem. The city is legally forbidden to borrow to cover operating deficits.

11. The manager of a municipal ice rink is concerned that the flow of patrons will not be sufficient to maintain the long-standing policy of keeping the rink on a self-supporting basis. Revenues come mainly from the hourly rental of ice time (the city has set that at $2.50 per hour per person) and skate rental ($1.50 per pair). The average ice time per patron over the last three years has been about 1.5 hours. Approximately half the patrons rent skates. Salaries, scheduled maintenance, and other overhead expenditures amount to $94,500 per year; these costs do not vary with the number of patrons. Costs that vary with the number of patrons (direct maintenance and supplies) are estimated to be $1.80 per patron hour. The number of patrons has been averaging 85,000 per year for the last three years. Is the manager right to be concerned?

12. Grantsville is a medium-sized midwestern town, not quite rural, not quite urban, and not quite a willing participant in the twenty-first century. As the new clerk-treasurer, you are eager to bring new aggressiveness to the city administration, so long as none of the "Old Guard" gets mad. You suspect that a non-irritating first step would be the development of a cash plan and short-term investment strategy for the city. You further believe that an appropriate start would be with the four largest funds in the city financial structure: general, parks and recreation, motor vehicle, and cumulative capital. The following data emerge from your search.

    Fund Balances for January 1:

General fund	$ 620,860
Parks and recreation	$ 62,968
Motor vehicle	$ 102,015
Cumulative capital	$ 639,611

    Revenue Estimates:

    Property tax: Collections are received by the city on May 1 and November 1.
    Because of a discount for early payment, five-eighths of the collections come in the first installment. Delinquency has historically been about 2 percent of the levy.

    Levy:

General fund	$ 2,985,200
Parks and recreation	$ 718,300
Cumulative capital	$ 385,400

    Parking meters (general fund): Revenues run about $6,000 per month, except in September and October (football season), when they run about 5 percent higher; December, when they are about 10 percent higher; and July, when they are about 15 percent lower.

    Building permits, inspection fees (general fund): Estimated at $400,000 for the year. The engineer's office transmits collections to you at the end of each quarter. You estimate the seasonal collections as QI, 85,000; QII, 105,000; QIII, 125,000; QIV, 85,000.

    Traffic fines (half to general fund, half to motor vehicles): Estimated at $6,500 per month. The court remits at the end of each month.

Swimming pool admissions (parks and recreation): Estimates are based on prior years.

May	$ 800.00
June	$ 950.00
July	$ 1,750.00
August	$ 2,500.00
September	$ 750.00

Community auditorium rental (parks and recreation): Estimates are based on prior year.

July 4 Freedom Celebration	$ 800.00
Labor Day Customs Show	$ 1,500.00
Casual rentals (square dances, Rotary, etc.)	$ 150.00/month

State shared tax (motor vehicles): The state department of revenue provides data.

March 31	$ 114,000
June 30	$ 125,000
September 30	$ 115,000
December 31	$ 113,000

Expenditures, as Appropriated by City Council:

Payrolls: Paydays are every other week. The first payday is January 7.

General fund	$ 95,000 biweekly
Parks and recreation	$ 15,000

Also, the following temporary expenses are paid biweekly from May 15 to September 10:

Summer lifeguards, playground supervisors	$ 20,000 biweekly
Motor vehicle fund	$ 10,200 biweekly

Other regular expenditures: Checks to suppliers and other nonemployees are issued only on alternate Thursdays. The first such date is January 13.

General fund	$ 25,000/disbursement
Parks and recreation	$ 4,000/disbursement
Additional summer payments	
(May 10–September 15)	$ 3,000/disbursement
Motor vehicle	$ 7,000/disbursement

Cumulative capital:

Bond service due May 15 ($150,000) and November 15 ($125,000)

Special expenditures:

General fund: Two police cars at $14,500 to be paid for October 1

Motor vehicle fund: Dump truck with sand-salt distributor and snowplow at $34,000 to be paid for October 1

From these data, prepare a complete cash budget for the year and include end-of-year balances. Estimate what amounts are available for investment and what fund shortages will occur. Identify any management strategies to prevent the fund shortages, if possible.

13. When state finances get tough, many governors have special impoundment authority available to them. Indiana's governor is one of those. A section of the budget law states that the state may "withhold allotments of any or all appropriations ... if it is considered necessary to do so in order to prevent a deficit financial situation." In the middle of fiscal year 2009, the Indiana governor informed the public radio station that is associated with Indiana University that it would not receive its fourth-quarter allotment. The payment was not delayed; it was gone forever. This took away revenue upon which the station had built its budget. That revenue distribution was the following: support from Indiana University, 36 percent; individual gifts, 22 percent; corporate underwriting, 17 percent; miscellaneous, 12 percent; federal support, 10 percent; and state support, 3 percent. The station reports that it has frozen hiring, cut down on travel, and postponed equipment purchases to deal with the unexpected shortfall. It also initiated a number of announcements over the air, outside of its regular fund-raising events, in which it asked current donors to increase their donations and for new donors to step up. What is your assessment of this situation? What is your view of this power to suspend appropriations?

14. Federal outlays for water resources increased from $5,723 million in 2005 to $11,618 million in 2011. The deflator for non-defense federal expenditures increased from 1.0000 in 2005 to 1.1524 in 2011. Answer these questions:

    a. What is the real rate of change in spending for water resources over this period?
    b. Suppose the rate of change of prices continued through 2015 at the same rate as from 2005 to 2011. What outlay level in 2015 would provide the same real level as in 2011?

15. Governments and not-for-profit organizations need systems for providing fiscal discipline and control, for directing resources to uses with the highest priority of the entity, and for encouraging technical efficiency in the use of resources. However, not all such organizations have developed these budget and finance systems to the same degree, and those with systems do not have them structured in the same way. Select a local government or not-for-profit organization in your area and analyze the budget and finance processes that it employs. This entity may be a local government (a city, a county, a township, a school district, a solid-waste district, a library district, etc.) or a not-for-profit organization located in this area. The entity should be chosen because you are interested in the service it provides and because the entity will cooperate with your review and assessment.

    a. Investigate the budget, revenue, and financial management processes and practices of that entity. The topics that should be investigated include, but are not limited to, the following: (i) *budget process*—how the budget is developed, what the cycle is, how decisions are made in developing the budget, what the review procedure is, who adopts the budget, how the process was established, what the style/nomenclature of the budget is, whether processes are transparent, whether there is a separate capital budget and budget process, whether there are extrabudgetary funds or earmarked revenues, whether appropriate internal controls are in place, what the external audit arrangement is, and so on; and (ii) *budget analysis*—explore expenditure patterns and trends to the extent possible, analyze inputs and performance results, and examine the extent to which the entity operates with fiscal discipline and control.

b. On the basis of your investigation, what do you conclude about the fiscal situation, processes, and procedures of the entity? Be specific. Link your conclusions to the information developed in your analysis. Outline and defend your proposals for reform or restructuring of the entity you have examined.

For the entity you select, you will need to talk with the administrators responsible for the entity's finances; to analyze budget preparation materials, budgets, and annual financial reports; and to examine laws or other documents establishing and governing the entity's framework. You may locate other source materials on some entities (debt rating reports, newspaper stories, etc.).

16. The Midwest Reptile Society, a nonprofit organization housed at the University of Illinois, sends a newsletter to its members three times per year. The objective of the newsletter is to provide information on the care and feeding of reptiles, to communicate information about reptile seminars and workshops, and to facilitate reptile exchange among Society members. Provision of this information to the membership is a primary goal of the Society. The newsletter is not particularly time sensitive (reptiles are slow moving), and Society members tend to be well educated and have higher-than-average family incomes. There is no expense for preparation of the substance of the newsletter because all materials are submitted by Society members in electronic form, ready to put into the newsletter, and the University donates the technological equipment appropriate for preparation of the newsletter. Physically, the newsletter has four printed pages on a single, folded sheet of paper. The newsletter is mailed at the standard first class rate.

The Society executive director is preparing her budget for the year, and the newsletter is an important service to the membership. However, newsletter costs are constraining the ability of the Society to provide other important member benefits. Here are some data she has available:

	2012	2013	2014	2015 est.
Society Members, Average for Year (#)	5,570	5,800	5,550	5,700
Postage Expense ($)	6,786	7,139	7,400	7,540
Printing Expense ($)	13,050	14,160	14,280	15,660

The director expects that the postage rate will increase by 2 cents per newsletter in May 2016; it increased from 46 to 48 cents in May 2014. Prepare the newsletter budget for 2016 under at least two different plans for providing this service to the membership. Explain and justify your budget, along with providing the dollar request.

17. The state budget director has asked you to create a medical care cost inflation index to use in evaluating certain items in the state budget. You are to use 2013 as the base year (2013 = 100.0) for your index. If costs have risen at an average annual rate of 4.35 percent in recent years and the budget director believes that this rate will continue, what is the value of your index in 2017?

18. Many city governments post their full budgets on a public website. Go to one of these websites, pick a department of that city government (e.g., police, fire, parks and recreation), and analyze the budget of that department. Questions that you should explore include the following:

    a. What inputs to the production process are the primary drivers of the budget? In other words, what expenditure categories are most important in the total spending by the department?
    b. Compare the planned expenditure for the budget year with the actual expenditures in prior years. Where are there significant changes? Is there a narrative that accompanies the budget that could help explain the differences?

19. Absurdistan must develop a medium-term budget condition baseline in order to qualify for credits from the International Monetary Fund. In the current year (2013), it expects revenues of A\$ 135,000 million, discretionary spending of A\$ 98,000, and formula assistance spending for the dependent population of A\$ 50,000. In the medium term, the government expects revenue to grow at the same rate as gross domestic product, discretionary spending to grow at the same rate as inflation, and formula assistance to increase with population and inflation (in other words, for real per capita formula assistance to remain the same as in 2008). Gross domestic product increased from A\$ 180,000 to A\$ 270,000 from 2005 to 2011, population increased from 35,780,000 to 68,550,000 over the period from 2000 to 2010, and the GDP deflator rose from 98 to 107 from 2008 to 2012. Calculate the following for the period 2014 through 2016: revenue baseline, discretionary spending, formula assistance spending, and budget surplus or deficit.

CASE FOR DISCUSSION

CASE 5–1

Green Felt-Tip Pens, a Tape Recorder, and Embezzlement: Where Did the Budget Process Fail?[1]

The New Hope/Solebury School District serves students in part of Bucks County, Pennsylvania. The county, just north of Philadelphia, has been a peaceful refuge since its colonial beginnings as a stopover on the road between New York and Philadelphia.

---

[1]References for this case include Thomas Moore, "A New Scam: Tele-blackmail," *U.S. News & World Report* 108 (June 11, 1990): 51; "An Alert Reader Lends a Hand to the FBI," *U.S. News & World Report* 108 (June 25, 1990): 8; and Joseph A. Slobodzian, "Telemarketer Sentenced in New Hope Scam," *Philadelphia Inquirer,* January 31, 1991, B-1.

But modern telemarketing reaches even the quietest parts of the county and can expose even the most straightforward budget-execution tasks to million-dollar fraud.

Consider These Questions

1. What standards of internal control were violated here?

2. How would you revise financial practices in the District to prevent similar fraud in the future?

3. Compare the roles of internal control and post-audit in the war against waste, fraud, and abuse.

The scam involved the business manager of the District, Kathryn Hock, and American Corporate Supplies, an office-supplies distributor operated as a telemarketer by Marc and Teresa Suckman. The District serves about 825 students, with an annual budget of $6.6 million. Hock, business manager since 1978, had worked her way up from school secretary. Some school board members had questioned her ability to deal with more sophisticated accounting systems and methods and had expressed doubt about her qualifications. She had managed to keep her job, although uneasily.

American Corporate Supplies, located in California, made phone calls to prospective purchasers (public, private, nonprofit—it mattered not) around the country, offering products at discount. Often the discounts were from artificially inflated prices. Their business was to induce customers to purchase felt-tip pens from them; the scam was that the pens often had not been ordered at all or, if ordered, were never delivered. Their business was good: along with the school district, victims included an Idaho priest ($66,000), a St. Louis businessman ($40,000), and a Pennsylvania man ($155,000). But the $2 million from the school district apparently was their best.

Hock received a long-distance call from American Corporate Supplies in 1983, offering green felt-tipped pens. Because district teachers had requested the color, she placed an order. The shipment arrived as promised, and she paid the bill.

Through the year, the business manager made more pen orders. Eventually, her contact, William Chester of American Corporate (possibly Suckman), informed her that her good-customer status entitled her to receive a pocket tape recorder, a gift that she accepted. That put Hock in jeopardy, although she did not realize it.

After a few weeks, Chester called in regard to filling her back order. There actually was none, but he convinced her that such an order did exist and that she had a legal obligation to complete the order. Mr. Chester then proceeded to call one or two times each month to obtain a new order from her.

By April 1984, the District definitely needed no more markers. They had arrived in regular batches, and there was room for little else in the storage closet. Hock tried to stop the flow, but Chester told her that the District had an outstanding balance of $3,547.14 and that she should send a check to close the account. The claim was excessive, Hock objected, but Chester threatened to tell the school board about the gift she had accepted for placing the orders. That would cause her to be fired, so she settled the account and stopped the orders.

Or so she thought. A month later Chester called again, this time with an outstanding balance of $4,229.53. She again objected, but Chester threatened to inform both the school board and the police about the unauthorized payment for goods not received. The stakes for her were higher.

Hock felt in even greater jeopardy and, because of this vulnerability, was going to be called on to provide even greater sums of money. *U.S. News & World Report* describes her response:

> Hock knew then she was in deep water. "I was panic-stricken," she says. "I had never come up against anything like this and didn't know how to handle it." She paid that bill, and then another the following month, and dozens more, sometimes three in a month. "Each time he said it would be the final order, but it never was," she says. When the amounts Chester demanded escalated as high as $30,000, she started breaking up the payments with several different checks so they would be easier to hide in the books. She had authority to sign checks and stamp them with the signatures of two board officials. When the canceled checks came back from the bank, she would white out American Corporate Supplies and type in the name of the local fuel oil company and other regular suppliers, inflating their costs. Then she would alter the computerized accounts accordingly.[2]

This process continued until 1988, when the accumulated overspending had grown so large that Hock could no longer conceal it. She quit in June, just as the District superintendent who had supported her against the skeptical board retired. The new superintendent and business manager soon found discrepancies and performed a special audit. The FBI and the U.S. Attorney received the results, and Hock confessed.

In July 1989, Hock pled guilty to embezzling $2,043,903 from the District; evidence indicated that she kept none of the money, but sent it all to Suckman. She was sentenced to 16 months in prison and ordered to pay back the money she had stolen. She cooperated in further investigations to help find the Suckmans. The District had to borrow $1 million to replace the missing funds.

In April 1990, a federal grand jury indicted the Suckmans on 38 counts of transporting stolen securities obtained by fraud, 20 counts of engaging in monetary transactions in criminally derived property, and single counts of conspiracy to commit interstate transportation of stolen money and securities. Marc Suckman was also indicted on three counts of blackmail. The Suckmans were arrested in Costa Rica and transported to Philadelphia for trial. They pled guilty shortly before jury selection; Marc Suckman faced up to six years in prison and Teresa Suckman up to four years and three months. They agreed to help in further investigations of telemarketing scams. U.S. District Court Judge James McGirr Kelly ordered restitution (the Suckmans claimed all proceeds had been "dissipated" by high living) and forbade them from working in telemarketing again.

APPENDIX 5–1

Budget Preparation, or How to Be a Budget Analyst

A new budget analyst may well be overwhelmed by the scope and complexity of the task at hand. Nothing can completely prepare one for that first attempt, but most bright, inquisitive, energetic people survive. Here is a memo outlining

---

[2]Moore, "A New Scam," 51.

methods and procedures for analysts in Oregon. Except for references to the particular budget system used there, it could have been written for guidance in any government, and the advice is as fitting today as it was when it was written.

State of Oregon   Interoffice Memo
To: Budget Analysts   Date: June 30, 1982
From: Jon Yunker, Administrator
Budget and Management Division
Subject: Budget Preparation—or—How to Be a Budget Analyst

The Role of the Analyst

Budget analysts are key persons in the development of the governor's biennial budget. While others are responsible for development of the broad program and fiscal policies for the state as a whole, it is the individual analysts who must convert these broad policies to balanced, properly financed programs for assigned agencies. In this regard, several points should be emphasized.

1. You must function as an equal with agency heads or other top agency administrative staff. You are expected to have the maturity necessary to avoid being intimidated by imposing titles, higher-salaried officials, or executives your senior in age. You have a professional assignment and must carry it out with the confidence of a professional.

2. You work primarily for your budget supervisor and the budget and management administrator. Direct relationships with the director, other administrators and staff within the executive department, and governor's assistants are frequently necessary and desirable. However, you should inform the budget and management administrator, in writing, in cases where these contacts will significantly influence your recommendations. All reports submitted to other individuals should be routed through your budget supervisor and the budget and management administrator to ensure that they are fully informed about activities of the division. They are responsible for your actions; make sure you are responsible to them.

3. You must be flexible. Don't busy yourself in work related only to your assigned agencies. State government is too dynamic and interrelated and the central staff too small to allow the luxury of specialists within the division. The analyst must be reasonably conversant with the governor's total program and should be constantly aware of the role a particular assignment plays within it.

During the executive budget preparation season, you will be in an essentially negative posture as far as an agency is concerned. During the legislative session, however, you will be intimately allied with the agency in "selling" approved budget recommendations to the legislature. In some cases, you may be expected to effectively support a program that you originally recommended against.

Responsibilities Prior to Budget Season

The work performed during the budget season represents the culmination of many months of preparation and field work. Prior to receipt of the agencies' request documents, the analyst should be concerned with the following:

1. Budget field work. This phrase simply describes the process whereby an analyst develops a sufficient knowledge of assigned agencies' programs to enable him or her to make informed budget decisions when the time comes. Budget field work may be accomplished in a variety of ways:
   a. Review of items submitted for consideration by the state emergency board.
   b. Execution of special management of fiscal studies affecting your assigned agencies.
   c. Completion of a formal field work program during which you personally visit individual agency activities and discuss them with the person directly responsible for their administration.
   d. Preview of agency budget requests for format and content.
2. Development of the Biennial Budget Preparation Manual. This activity enables the analyst to foresee special problems in format or budget organization, which some of his assigned agencies might encounter in meeting executive department requirements. Your knowledge of your assigned agencies enables you to assist in developing budget preparation instructions to be followed by all state agencies. Each analyst must completely understand all instructions included in the manual and supporting documents.
3. An analyst frequently assists agencies in the preparation of their biennial budget requests. It is imperative that the analyst express no opinion about the content or amount, or the ranking of decision packages, to be included in the request. Your role is that of technical advisor on format and compliance with specific budget instructions. You have neither the authority nor the responsibility to advise the agency on what should be requested; you will only assist in ensuring that it is properly presented.
4. As budget season approaches, the analyst should become familiar with the internal procedures to be used by the budget and management division during the biennial budget preparation process. You must learn and understand all significant internal procedures performed by the technical staff to enable you to "track" the budget request and related documents through the entire budget season.
5. Based on your field work and knowledge of the internal procedures, specific deadlines for review of each of your assigned agencies should be established. You cannot spend a disproportionate amount of time on one agency and hope to do an adequate job on the entire assignment. You must assess your assignment and plan your own individual work schedule for that assignment. Keep in mind that time must be spent where the money is—minor, stable, low-cost agencies may be fascinating, but should not take time away from those agencies competing for scarce resources.

When the Budget Request Is Submitted

Don't panic! DON'T PANIC! DON'T PANIC!!!

There will be a few surprises, but generally the request will reflect the same programs you saw during your budget field work. It will look bigger and more complicated than you expected, but bear in mind that it represents all activities of that agency for a two-year period. Several steps are critical at the time of initial receipt of the budget request.

1. Make sure that the budget is given immediately to the coordinating secretary so that internal processing is properly performed. Know where it is at all times.

2. Read the entire budget request. Skim the summary reports and other detailed forms. Read all narrative for content. Study the performance measurement forms. Review previous biennia's performance claims and compare them with what was actually accomplished during that biennium. Finish the job. You will have plenty of opportunities to go back and review various sections, so plow right through the entire request before taking any steps toward detailed analysis.

3. After reading the request, skim the status related to the agency. This will provide you a context in which to assess the programs the agency is proposing to fulfill its legal responsibilities.

4. The analyst should carefully review the objectives and levels of accomplishment upon which the agency has predicated its budget request to make certain they correspond with the agency's statutory responsibilities and executive priorities. These objectives and levels of accomplishment may be modified or augmented by the analysts in the governor's budget to more accurately reflect the executive department recommendations regarding the agency's mission.

5. Identify the major policy issues in the request. A policy issue is a proposed new program or revision in an existing program (either expansion or retrenchment), which represents a significant change in the agency's scope or level of activity.

    The budget analyst must determine which decision packages are major policy issues and if any significant changes are contained in the base budget. In addition, you must determine if the numerical ranking of decision packages represents a major policy shift.

    You should summarize these policy issues (including costs by fund source), develop alternatives, and prepare your recommended course of action. This report, or policy memo, should be submitted through your budget supervisor to the budget and management administrator. This memo will be further distributed to other appropriate members of the executive department.

6. You may also prepare a memo to the budget and management administrator outlining the need for an analysis of a particular portion of a budget request which you will not have time to perform yourself during budget season. In some cases, these analyses can be performed by the management section or by other divisions of the department in time to be considered by you in

developing budget recommendations. Their special expertise in the areas of data processing, management analysis, local government relations, personnel administration, or economic analysis can be most helpful to you in arriving at your final recommendations. Bear in mind that they are advising you; the budget recommendations are yours.

In other cases, the needed analysis will be beyond the capability of the executive department staff to perform during the executive budget season. In these cases, the proposed analysis will be considered as an "item for future study" and held until staff time becomes available. A special form for these memos will be available on which the budget analyst will be expected to enter his or her recommendations as to whether the study should be performed during budget season or deferred as an "item for future study."

7. Review the request for any proposed programs and interagency transfers of funds which affect other state agencies. These proposals should be described and submitted, in writing, to the analyst assigned to the affected agency or agencies. The governor's budget must be internally consistent among agencies.

8. Develop a list of questions about the request you want the agency personnel to answer....You will have many unanswered questions in your mind at this stage (since you are an insatiably curious person), and the easiest way to get answers is to reduce the questions to writing and submit them to the agency. Don't be afraid to ask agency personnel to work for you in this way. You have to do the analysis, but agency personnel can produce needed data for you.

Detailed Analysis

Only after you have read the document and identified the items listed above are you ready to review the request in detail. Once again, don't spend too much time on one agency. Know where all of your assigned budgets are at all times. Detailed analysis should include the following steps:

1. Always contact the agency head first. He or she is responsible for all items in the budget and has the best understanding of how the components interrelate. You should discuss several items during this first meeting:
   a. What approach does the administrator prefer—are you free to meet individually with subordinates on matters in their areas, or does the administrator want to participate in all budget discussions?
   b. What about the role of governing boards or commissions—are they to be involved in the budget review process?
   c. Solicit the administrator's description of the program achievements proposed in the budget request. He or she may have goals or accomplishments proposed in the budget that you missed in your preliminary review.
   d. Explain your personal schedule for review of the request. You may find conflicts which will require revisions in your internal deadlines.

2. Review past approved budgets and Joint Committee on Ways and Means reports and, if possible, talk to analysts previously assigned to the budget.

This will acquaint you with past analytical approaches and will highlight executive and legislative decisions of the past few years.

3. Divide the budget into manageable segments. The request may be divided by program or organizational lines—or both. Choose one segment for detailed analysis. Remember that no individual segment should be considered complete until all of your recommendations are prepared.

4. Approach the request with skepticism, not cynicism. Your job is not to justify the request, nor is it to eliminate the agency (usually). All activities of the agency are subject to question, even those most politically popular or well established. It is important to remember that you must not interject your personal philosophy or biases in your review. You deal with facts or clearly understood gubernatorial policy, not emotion.

5. Approach the request with an open mind. You are not responsible for interpreting the governor's political statements or public positions on issues. Don't let the agency tell you that "confidentially, the governor is keenly interested in this program." If he is, you'll find out through normal budget procedures.

6. Don't analyze dollars—analyze programs and decision packages. Dollars are an important item in budgeting. However, it is the program achievements that are budgeted; and the dollars merely provide a common denominator in expressing the resources necessary to provide these programs. Understand the programs and decision packages first, and the dollar levels will follow.

7. When comparing proposed program levels, your base for comparison is the latest legislatively approved level. It is not the agency request. The legislatively approved level will be expressed in both dollar and program terms in the latest Joint Committee on Ways and Means report. Review the performance of the agency during the first year of the biennium and compare it with the levels approved by the previous legislature. You may find areas where we are actually spending more and accomplishing less.

8. In reviewing the budget, use a zero-based conceptual attitude and consider the following questions:
   a. Is the base budget consistent with the existing approved level?
   b. Does the base budget include expenditures which were originally approved on a "one-shot" or nonrecurring basis?
   c. Are there activities in the base budget which are of lower priority than some proposed expansions, new programs, or decision packages? In an austere budget season, program expansions may have to be financed by offsetting program retrenchment.
   d. Are there activities in the budget request which, for various reasons, should be stopped or could better be performed by a different agency? In these cases, prepare a policy memo outlining the issue. Minor reorganizations can be recommended within the governor's budget.

9. In reviewing decision packages based upon increased workload, consider the following questions:
   a. Is the projected workload self-generated? That is, does it represent activity levels controllable by the agency, or does it truly reflect increased demands for service by the public or other beneficiaries?

b. Is the proposed volume of increased workload consistent with workload patterns of the past few years and supported by adequate justification?

c. Are the requested levels of staff, support costs, and facilities properly related to the volume of increased workload? Ratios, economies of scale, seasonal peaks and valleys of activities, and the existing capacity to absorb increased workload should be considered.

d. What is the true program impact of not providing the requested increased volume of service in a particular program?

10. In reviewing program adjustments which have taken place in the interim, consider the following questions:

a. Was the adjustment approved in the manner and at the level described? (Review emergency board minutes and other relevant documents.)

b. Was the adjustment intended for continuation into future biennia?

c. Does the adjustment retain sufficient priority for continuation or was it provided to meet an emergency need which is no longer critical to the agency's program?

11. In reviewing requests for operation of new facilities, consider the following questions:

a. Has the capital project already been approved, or is it contingent on future executive or legislative action?

b. What is the latest estimate for the building to come on-line and require operational support?

c. What standards or other empirical justification are available to support the estimated costs to operate the new facilities?

d. What offsetting savings, such as vacation of rental space, are available, and have they been reflected in the request?

e. What effect will the new facilities have on basic programs? Is the agency using the new facility as a smoke screen to go into new programs not fully analyzed? What are the future costs and benefits of these new programs?

12. In reviewing decision packages which constitute program improvements, consider the following questions:

a. What is the true effect or product of the improvement?

b. What are the bases of the request for the improvement—who originated the demand for expanded or improved services?

c. What is the impact of the improvement on existing programs?

d. What criteria were used to develop the staff and support costs of the improvement? Are they valid?

e. Has the improvement been previously requested and denied? If so, on what grounds?

f. Is the improvement consistent with agency objectives?

g. Is the improvement of a higher priority than an existing program or activity?

h. What are the future costs and benefits of the requested improvement?

13. In reviewing requests for new programs, all items listed for program improvements should be considered. In addition, ask the following:
    a. Is this the appropriate agency to perform this service? Is the service now being provided by another state agency, other governmental units, or private industry?
    b. Are there any revenue sources, such as special fees, available to offset the cost of implementing this program?

14. A note of caution—don't ignore programs simply because no program improvements or new programs are being proposed. The thorough analyst will examine ongoing programs for continued relevance and necessity. This is one of the most lucrative areas of investigation for an economy-minded analyst.

15. Another note of caution—don't get trapped by counting desks—either literally or figuratively. After some frustration in considering the solutions to major social problems, you will be tempted to revert to considering the minor details of bureaucratic operation. Don't yield to the temptation—you'll learn to accept the frustration and maybe even be instrumental in really solving a social problem.

    Conversely, do not become so awed by the social issues that you lose sight of your basic purpose—to produce a responsible budget. Don't get lost in the clouds.

16. Still another note of caution—GET ORGANIZED AND STAY ORGANIZED. Know where you've been and know where you are, and where you have to get at all times during the season. If you realize you are becoming disorganized—STOP—get reorganized and then start again.

17. In the course of detailed analysis, you will prepare a variety of memos, worksheets, and other written material. General suggestions:
    a. Keep them neat. Most likely the analyst preparing the budget recommendations will not be responsible for executing that budget. Give your successor a break—and some useful budget files.
    b. Identify your worksheets. Columns of numbers with no headings or other identification are useless to everyone, including the analyst. Each worksheet should be readily identifiable as to content. Date them! Date them! Date them!
    c. Keep your files in an organized manner. Make sure your assistant knows where you keep certain work papers (such as memos from governor's assistants or other executive department staff). She may need to find something in your absence—and in a hurry.

18. You will never have the time to perform as detailed an analysis as you think is necessary. If you encounter a problem or issue too complex to review in the time available, it may be necessary to prepare a memo recommending an item for future study and move on. This is not a cop-out, but a realistic appraisal of the volume of work which can be done in a limited period of time. Meet your deadlines! Meet your deadlines! Meet your deadlines!

19. Analyze the agency's revenues as well as the expenditures. They matter.

20. After you've completed the detailed analysis of a budget request—step back and "look at the forest." Review the sum of your detailed work to see if the total makes sense and is reasonable.

Preparing the Recommendation

You earn your salary when you tie all of the analytical efforts, alternatives, and mass of data together into one proposed course of action. Remember that you are only recommending. You don't allow or deny. Use these words around an agency and you'll feel rather silly when items are restored at the appeal hearing.

Remember that, even though you are to recommend one course of action, you are also to consider and be prepared to implement various alternatives. Presentation of alternatives is required when forwarding a policy memo, and alternatives can be included in the analyst report....

Although you don't have the authority to include or exclude items in a budget, don't expect your boss to make your decisions for you. You are responsible for your recommendations; and you must be in a position to defend them with hard, objective data. You are telling your superiors what you think they should do—they must also consider other factors in arriving at their decisions.

In developing your specific recommendations, consider the following:

1. Recommendations are transmitted through the analyst report. This document must be a concise, complete summary of your findings. Keep it understandable; don't try to show off your knowledge of agency jargon. Slang and obscure abbreviations have no place in the analyst report.
2. You are displaying a piece of specific analysis, not presenting a discourse on the theory of the agency. All narrative should directly relate to specific recommendations.
3. Don't devote more than a minimum of discussion to items which you have not recommended. If they are significant in size or content, mention them briefly. Otherwise, concentrate your efforts on what you are recommending.
4. The analyst report is an internal document. However, it will be the basic vehicle for transmitting the executive department's recommendations to the agency. Keep it objective. If you have special comments of a confidential nature, attach them as a special memo which can accompany the analyst report through its internal review, or transmit your ideas orally.
5. In developing final recommendations, remember that an unreasonable budget is useless to everyone. You're not paid on a commission of dollars cut from the request. Unrealistically low recommendations place a burden on your superiors to restore the funds. If an agency has erred in preparing its request, you may find yourself in a position where you'll be adding money in a particular area. Don't be alarmed—remember, the goal is a realistic budget.
6. Conversely, your job is to recommend the least amount of money and the least number of positions necessary to support the agency at the recommended program level. Let your superiors make most of the generous gestures to agencies.
7. After you have developed your preliminary recommendations, try them out on the agency administrator. (Even though you may have a big ego, you also are an honestly humble person who realizes you don't know everything. Besides, the agency may be able to correct some bad work you've done before someone else uncovers it.)

Agency Appeals

We cannot predict accurately how the various levels of appeal will be handled. There is no question but that agencies generally will appeal the decisions and recommendations of the analyst. These appeals will probably take several forms:

1. The pro forma appeals: These include those agencies which have never accepted the legitimacy of the budget staff and are satisfied only after discussing the budget with the director of the department or the governor.
2. Appeals to correct errors: During the course of a budget season, other analysts (not you) will make some arithmetic or reasoning errors. When the agency discovers these, it has every right to request correction.
3. Emotional appeals: These occur most frequently when the analyst has failed to establish good personal rapport and the agency head is convinced that "he just doesn't understand our problems." Stick to the facts and don't get drawn into personal conflicts. When you lose your objectivity, you lose your usefulness.
4. Objective or "legitimate" appeals: These represent judgments by the agency that your recommendations do not adequately support the programs during the coming biennium. Sometimes the agency will produce supplemental data not made available to you during the course of budget review. The technical word for this is "dirty trick." Most items in this type of appeal, however, deal simply with judgments made by the analyst and questioned by the agency. Be equally objective in analyzing them for your superiors.

In all types of appeals, the analyst is responsible for several actions:

1. Review of the appeal letter and development of specific recommendations with reasons for each item included.
2. Detailed minutes of the proceedings of the appeal hearing.
3. An immediate update of all appropriate documents as soon as the final decisions are made. Draft a letter summarizing the results of the hearing for distribution to the agency and your superiors.
4. Informing the coordinating secretary and technical support section of the results of the hearing so they can update their master summaries.

When the Numbers Are Firm

Don't relax! There is still a lot of work to do. First priority is the final preparation of reproduction copy. Reproduction copy is the narrative and supporting schedules that will be printed in the governor's budget released December 1. Careful editing must be done to ensure that the narrative and fiscal data accurately describe the final budget decisions.

The governor's budget is written primarily for the legislature. It is not the prime working document for the Joint Committee on Ways and Means—that honor belongs to the updated agency request document. The printed budget must be meaningful to the freshman legislator, who has never seen a state budget, and the most experienced member of Ways and Means.

After repro copy has been prepared and all master summaries have been updated, the analyst still has several responsibilities:

1. Edit your working papers. You'll be using them throughout the legislative hearings, so make sure you're not cluttered with excess baggage. Organized, orderly, neat working papers are essential during hearings.

2. Prepare material explaining the budget for your agencies. Additional analyses can be performed and presented in narrative, graphic, or tabular presentations that can be used in orienting the Legislature, selling the budgets to Ways and Means, and informing the public about the proposals.

   The emphasis in these analyses should be on program and decision packages, not dollars. While you should be able to speak very precisely about proposed expenditure levels if asked, don't plan to explain your budgets by accounting for dollars. It's boring—and meaningless.

3. Keep in close communication with your assigned agencies to ensure that they are on schedule in updating their request documents to reflect the governor's recommendations.

4. There are many things not described in this report. A budget season must be experienced before any level of understanding is possible. Hopefully, these comments will provide some help to those analysts about to participate in their first. Good luck!

CHAPTER 6

Budget Classifications, Systems, and Reform: Trying to Make Better Choices

The budget process discussion in previous chapters has focused primarily on fiscal discipline and control, important concerns if government operations are to be fiscally sustainable. Making sure that government resources are not stolen and that governments do not spend more money than they actually have are important roles for the budget process, but we ought to expect more than that from government. Surely we can consider how government spending and the resulting services provided might actually be useful. We now move to considering how the budget process can serve in facilitating choices among government programs and in inducing efficient use of resources within programs.

Governments may provide many different valuable services, but they do not have sufficient resources to do everything. At some point, they have to make choices among good ideas. To make those choices, government decision makers need good financial information and effective systems to help guide those choices. The next two chapters deal with structures and processes that can inform those choices, sometimes through entire systems for budget development and sometimes through smaller changes in what sort of information is provided and how it is organized.

Budget processes can help governments allocate public resources, control agency operations, and manage service delivery. Budgets can be clear statements of plans, priorities, performance, and costs, as well as the basic template for administrative control. Unfortunately, prevailing practices often impede the full use of budgeting for planning and analysis to guide public choices. Too often our systems and decision processes cause budget participants to bounce between Oscar Wilde's cynics and sentimentalists, as defined in the exchange between Cecil Graham and Lord Darlington in *Lady Windermere's Fan:*

Cecil Graham: What is a cynic?

Lord Darlington: A man who knows the price of everything and the value of nothing.

Cecil Graham: And a sentimentalist, my dear Darlington, is a man who sees an absurd value in everything, and doesn't know the market price of any single thing.[1]

The budget process isn't helped by the fact that it often does not even give information on what the price actually is, let alone provide a usable assessment of what the value is. Knowing neither the value of a service nor its cost of provision leaves the decision maker rather uncertain about making a decision.

The task of the fiscal process must be to avoid the seductions of both cynic and sentimentalist, to understand that reasonable choice entails both value and price, and to recognize that, although good ideas are limitless, resources to finance those good ideas are not.

The basic concerns of a budget process are to create an executable annual budget using economic (line-item) classification, with effective controls on budget execution, reliable financial reporting, and control over payments from the treasury. The first concern is spending control, not resource allocation. In the United States, this emphasis was critical because public budgeting processes emerged in the first decades of the twentieth century when theft of public resources was rampant, especially at the municipal level, and budget procedures sought to put a stop to this. Hence, early budgets focused on control of resources (or inputs) and little else. Modern governments have moved beyond that stage, but too much of budgeting retains that old preoccupation (although these first principles remain relevant because of their absence in developing and transition countries around the world). Governments provide valued services, so budget processes must serve as more than devices for restraining thieves, for stopping spending, and for limiting the extent to which political hacks provide employment for inept friends and relatives. Narrow controls designed almost exclusively to provide fiscal constraint almost certainly thwart innovation, constrain capacity to respond to citizen clients, and increase the unit cost of services. Decision makers must control waste and make allocation choices among actual government services desired by the public; budget structures need to facilitate this work, not just tie the hands of managers. The discussion in this chapter focuses on efforts to reformulate the budget process, often by reconfiguring information, so that it can do more than simply prevent theft.

Logically, the task of budget allocation is simple: allocate funds among government programs until an additional dollar moved to any program yields an additional return to society equal to the return lost from the program from which that dollar was taken.[2]

---

[1]Oscar Wilde, *Lady Windermere's Fan* (London: Methuen, 1908), 134.
[2]This rule also applies for a perfectly altruistic nonprofit organization. However, most nonprofit organizations are narrow interest groups, aiming to protect the environment, to ease the plight of the homeless, to care for the indigent sick, and so on. Hence, the budgetary allocation rule for a nonprofit organization is more related to that of a private, proprietary business than to that of a general-purpose government—allocations among its operations should work toward the particular purpose of the organization, just as the business aims for the highest profit, not the multiple competing objectives of society that governments have to balance. Otherwise, all tools of public budgeting—budget development, review, adoption, execution, audit, and so on—apply to these entities just as they apply to governments.

That is the public-sector equivalent of the familiar resource allocation rule for profitability in business operations. But the private decision maker maximizes a clear and measurable objective—profit—and measuring profitable return from several lines of operation is feasible because the standard is clearly calibrated and uniform. Public-sector operations usually (1) have multiple objectives (e.g., subsidized school lunches both feed children and support the income of farmers), (2) have conflicting objectives (e.g., the reservoir needs to be nearly empty to provide flood control and to be nearly full to allow water skiing), and (3) have no standard measure or common yardstick to compare the return from various programs (e.g., the gains from cleaner streams and lakes are not measured in the same units as are reduced traffic fatalities). Furthermore, the beneficiaries of the various programs are not often the same people, so choices among programs cause there to be winners and losers, in violation of the Pareto criterion. And the taxpayers paying for the programs may well not be the people benefiting from the public services being provided, complicating the decision process even more, as does the fact that program beneficiaries are not evenly distributed among the electoral districts of the lawmakers deciding what programs will receive appropriations. Hence, the simple public-program allocation rule, so easy to define, may only be a glimmer in the politics of budget policy. Lawmakers working in the public interest face tough choices, well beyond the complexities a business executive will confront. One of the stickiest problems is that different lawmakers define what is in the public interest in different ways—what a member of Congress from New York City sees as the public interest may well diverge from the view of a member from South Dakota. The budget process is where choices are made among program alternatives. It will be far from perfect, but some budget classifications and structures may make the allocation choices more likely to improve conditions of society. Thinking about format is important because, as Fenno says it, "the form of the budget determines what the conversation will be about."[3]

Considering the Flow of Provision of Government Services: The Logic of the Service System and Budget Classifications

Government agencies may be thought of as operating entities that buy resources, use those resources in the performance of certain tasks, and, as a result of performing those tasks, achieve certain results that are valued by society. Budget classification schemes may organize and control government expenditure—the total sum paid by agencies for purchases of inputs; for contractual services to be delivered by others; for transfer payments made to individuals, businesses, or other governments; for

---

[3]Richard F. Fenno, "The Impact of PPBS on the Congressional Appropriation Process," in *Information Support, Program Budgeting, and the Congress,* ed. Richard L. Charhand, Kenneth Janda, and Michael Hugo (New York: Spartan, 1968), 183.

interest paid on debt outstanding; for post-employment benefits paid to retirees; and so on—in a variety of ways. Figure 6–1 provides a simple outline of service provision. The following explains the terms in that outline:

1. **Inputs.** Inputs are the resources an agency purchases to use in its service-delivery operations and are what the agency's budget purchases. A city's street department buys resources (asphalt, crushed stone, fuel to operate its equipment, the services of its employees, etc.). The funds in the budget are not inputs; the funds are what the agency uses to purchase the inputs. The inputs are the items on the shopping list of the government.

2. **Outputs.** Outputs are direct products or services produced by the agency. With the resources it has purchased, the department undertakes certain tasks or activities (fills chuckholes, resurfaces roadways, teaches students, audits taxpayers, etc.). However, these are the steps taken toward the end objective, not the end itself. Outputs are important for measuring internal operations of the agency, but do not indicate the extent to which the agency's purpose is being achieved. For example, if dangerous childhood diseases could be prevented without giving children vaccinations, the world could be a better place: we want an absence of sick children, not lots of children vaccinated.

3. **Results or Outcomes.** Because of the activities undertaken, desirable outcomes result (e.g., people and property can move through the city more quickly and safely, with less damage done to vehicles, or fewer children suffer from whooping cough, measles, etc.). The measured result or outcome indicates progress by the agency toward achievement of its purposes of

Figure 6–1
The Flow of Public-Service Provision

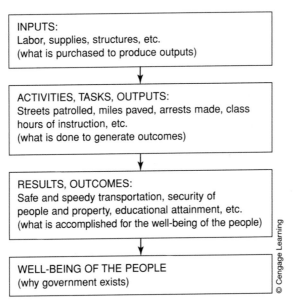

improving the economic or social condition of the citizenry. The measures can reflect successful events, occurrences, or conditions and may also indicate the quality of the service being rendered. Citizen satisfaction surveys may play a role in the measurement of outcome performance, particularly in regard to service quality, and they may be the basis for evaluating public goods that cannot be sold and are equally available to all.[4] The practice of budgeting regularly confuses outputs and outcomes. Here is a guideline for determining whether a particular measure is outcome or output: we would be happy to reduce the outputs if doing so would not reduce the outcome; we are not happy about reducing the outcome.

4. **Consequences for Society.** The outcome improves the standard of life for residents of the city. This is why the agency exists—to improve life for the citizenry. Something about why the agency matters to the standard of living should appear in the agency's mission statement, and that should be helpful in specifying the results produced by the agency and the outputs that help with accomplishing those results.

Government expenditures can be classified for the purposes of planning, analysis, reporting, and control according to frameworks that generally follow the previously outlined flow of public-service provision. Classifications found in public budgets include the following:

1. **Items purchased** (line item or object of expenditure). This is the grocery list classification that we have seen in Chapter 2. The focus is on what the government buys, either directly from its suppliers or indirectly through transfer, subsidy, and loan programs. The input format is basic and traditional—and has been around as long as governments have been constructing budgets. It is the building block for budget cost estimates and provides the focus for the control structures of government operation. This classification emphasizes purchase type: personnel, supplies and equipment, utilities, contractual services, and so on. The spending on inputs is categorized according to the administrative unit (the department or agency) responsible for use and control over the items that are purchased. This classification is critical for assigning organizational *responsibility* for delivery of services and *accountability* for public resources.

2. **Activities or tasks.** This format classifies according to the direct output of government, the intermediate product, the activities the government engages in, or the tasks it performs. The classification emphasizes measurable tasks: lane miles paved, pupil class hours taught, prisoners incarcerated, arrests made, tons of solid waste managed, number of border inspections, and so on.

3. **Function, purpose, or program.** This format classifies expenditure according to broad public purpose. The orientation is toward the final customer, the people served by the government. Classification focuses on the reasons

---

[4]Uwe Deichmann and Somik V. Lall, "Are You Satisfied? Citizen Feedback and Delivery of Urban Services," World Bank Policy Research Working Paper 3070, Washington, D.C., June 2003, reviews the return from citizen feedback surveys.

that the government exists: for example, protecting persons and property or maintaining a healthy citizenry.[5] The agency administration should have a pretty good idea of the linkages that go from inputs to activities to programs—because that is how management would be effective.

Budgets for governments and public organizations mix these classifications in several ways as they attempt to provide information useful for planning the utilization of resources, for devising efficient operations of agencies, and for controlling use of resources. Most actual budgets are hybrids, but Table 6–1 provides information on some fundamental features of traditional budgets, traditional performance budgets, program budgets, and new performance budgets. The elements in the table will become clearer in the discussion that follows.

Budget presentations increasingly provide performance measures for each agency, and increasingly these measures attempt to gauge outcomes or results of agency operations, not just the activities that the agency is engaged in. Executive agencies, legislators, and the general public are not satisfied with

Table 6–1
Features of Alternative Budget Formats

Format	Characteristics	Primary Organization Feature	Budgetary Focus
Traditional	Economic or object of expenditure classification to administrative units	Inputs purchased	Fiscal responsibility and control
Traditional Performance	Spending by unit of workload	Tasks/activities/outputs	Managerial control and technical efficiency
Program or Functional	Spending according to common public goals or purposes	Outcomes, final products, results	Resource allocation
New Performance or Results-Oriented	Performance measures by administrative unit	Outcomes (outputs)	Resource allocation

---

[5]Budget systems do not use a consistent language in distinguishing between concepts of performance (activity or task) and program (function or purpose). In some budgets, "program" means a service area (like street maintenance), for which a cost center is established; in other budgets, "program" means an outcome group (like safe and speedy transport of persons and property), which can be balanced against other purposes of government. In the discussion here, "what governments do" means task, activity, direct output, or intermediate product, and "why governments exist" means achievement, consumer output, final product, or outcome. "Program" refers to the latter. The distinction is particularly important in examination of municipal budget processes. The two uses of "program" might be considered "service area programs" and "outcome programs."

compilations of money to be spent or even the tallies of activities that have characterized such documents in the past. Simply spending appropriations without stealing too much is no longer an acceptable indicator of accomplishment. Agencies are expected to provide services for the common good and are held accountable for serving the public.

Budget classifications focus on different stages of the expenditure-delivery system, from resources purchased (*line item*) through activities performed (*traditional performance*) to services delivered (*program*). Line-item and performance systems maintain traditional department structures in the organization of expenditure plans; program budgets classify government outputs (or services provided) without regard for the administrative unit charged with service provision. All seek to improve the job done by the government and to keep government operations consistent with the wishes of the citizenry, but their fundamental concerns differ. Line-item budgets have as their foremost concern expenditure control and accountability. Performance budgets seek to improve internal management and cost of services provided. Program budgets emphasize arranging details in a manner to improve decision capacity for rational choice. (See the budget illustration in Chapter 2 for a reminder of how the line-item format looks.)

This chapter will examine several alternative budget formats and budget systems, including traditional budgets, traditional performance budgets, program budgets, zero-based budgets, new performance budgets, and participatory budget systems. Each format has reform of particular parts of the public-expenditure/ service-delivery process as its primary focus, and each has weaknesses in application. A review of each provides good insights into the practice of government finance in many different environments. But the place to start is with the most frequently utilized structure, the budget organized by administrative departments and purchases intended to be made by those departments.

Traditional Budgets: A Flawed Tool for Decision Making (But Pretty Good for Control and Accountability)

Traditional budgeting spends a lot of energy on figuring out what to buy and not enough energy on what results to achieve. Traditional budget procedures embody several impediments to efficient and effective public management and planning. These include (1) the administrative department basis for budget requests and appropriation; (2) the short-period concept for costs in budget considerations; (3) the focus on agency inputs rather than services provided, outputs, or outcomes; and (4) the failure to compare project costs with project benefits. Budget details often take on such bulk that they intimidate inexperienced users and discourage those with limited time from extracting the budget's policy plans. Unfortunately, legislators— the people who are supposed to review and approve the plans inherent in the budget document—may be just as inexperienced and short of time as the general public. Traditional budgets do not present information in a way that is well organized for making decisions.

ADMINISTRATIVE DEPARTMENT BASIS

Public decisions require meaningful measurement of the cost of achieving a desired objective. Traditional budget processes, although driven by cost estimates, do not provide that information in a usable format. Budgets are proposed and appropriations are made on an administrative department basis, not on the basis of what departments actually intend to achieve.

Such categorizations blur the allocation process and impede consideration of alternatives, the essence of resource allocation. Categories of administration—departments of defense, transportation, or justice at the federal level; departments of public works, economic development, public safety, or social services at the state-local levels—are too broad for judgments about the appropriate amounts of resources to be allocated to each. Some activities of a particular department may be of extreme importance for social goals, whereas others could be of considerably lower consequence and less significant than activities proposed by other departments. But the traditional budget approach tends to focus on departments, treating all work within them as being of equal contribution to public well-being. An important consequence of traditional budgets is that *where you are establishes what you get.* Departments and even agencies within them include activity conglomerations; some of those activities are related more to the work of other agencies than to that of the rest of their own agency. The Army Corps of Engineers' work in U.S. rivers and the services of security officers in city park departments offer two examples of work not matching larger titles or primary operations of the larger department. Budgets and appropriations that go through organizational charts complicate identification of the cost of achieving a particular objective because most agencies have multiple outputs. Edmond Weiss notes the "fallacy of appellation...the rhetorical act of obscuring the distinction between the name of a budget category and the actual phenomenon generally associated with that name."[6] In short, intelligent resource-allocation decisions are unlikely to emerge from budget considerations based on administrative departments. (Case 6–1 gives a famous illustration of how administrative department classification enters into budget results.)

ADMINISTRATIVE CONVENTIONS

Budgets and appropriations to administrative units can conceal the full cost of delivery of government services. For example, cities frequently have departments of public works that are responsible for maintenance of all infrastructure and even for some new construction and that may provide employee fringe benefits (pensions, vacation pay, etc.) through the human resources department budget. That makes management of related activities easier and allows for specialization in performing and supervising tasks, but it doesn't help with fiscal decision making. In this circumstance, identifying the amount the city spends for provision of a city service—like parks and recreation or police protection—would require analysis of the operations

---

[6]Edmond H. Weiss, "The Fallacy of Appellation in Government Budgeting," *Public Administration Review* 34 (July/August 1974): 377.

of the primary department. but also analysis of some spending of these other departments that have no immediately visible link to that agency's role. This violates the transparency standard for government operations and lessens the utility of the budget document in making public choices.

SINGLE-YEAR BASIS

Traditional budgets are developed and considered on a single-year basis without developing cost profiles over time. Appropriation decisions usually cover a single year of agency operation[7]—an appropriate period for fiscal control—even though many activities proposed by an agency have significant future cost implications. The single-year cost is often little more than a program down payment with many installments ahead. Reasonable decision making requires that the total cost of a project be examined, not just the single-year cost. Because data with so full a scope are seldom a part of the budget process, budget choices must be made without appropriate information. The federal budget now displays the budget year plus nine out-years; because few appropriation decisions lock in choices for full program life, the impact on decision processes is not clear, but those numbers can give an early warning of unsustainable fiscal conditions for the future. (The detailed department-by-department presentations from which the appropriation committees work include only the single budget year.) The out-years can contain much mischief when governments try to prove their fiscal conservatism by showing how they will control deficits—in the future. Nevertheless, good-faith attempts to identify future (out-year) cost implications of choices made now are necessary for reasonable budgetary deliberations.[8]

INPUT ORIENTATION

Reasoned choice requires a comparison among alternative methods of reaching a desired objective. The input orientation of traditional line-item budgets blocks operational vision and traps agencies into conventional operations.[9] The input orientation blocks consideration of the objectives of the spending and of alternatives to the present mode of operations. Agencies traditionally build budgets from existing input combinations. The agencies lock themselves into "normal" operating techniques and overlook alternative methods, and legislatures appropriate into definite line items. Public agencies and legislatures focus on what they buy (inputs) to the near exclusion of what they provide (services or outputs). Ordinary reviews emphasize changes in the objects of expenditure—that is, the personnel to be hired (or fired) and their pay grades, changes in the pay of current staff, and the supplies and equipment to be purchased. An input orientation produces the following logic: If the price of gasoline increases by 25 percent, agency operation requires a 25 percent increase in the appropriation for those purchases. Otherwise, the agency must cut back its services.

---

[7]Some governments have biennial budgets, but these are essentially single-year budgets times two. Only by accident will the complete cost of a project be captured in a biennial budget.

[8]A medium-term fiscal framework is an expected feature of good fiscal governance in international assistance programs.

[9]David Osborne, "Escaping from the Line-Item Trap," *Governing* 5 (September 1992): 69.

This logic implies that the objective of the agency is the purchase of given amounts of specific inputs. A budget process should induce consideration of alternative production strategies to economize on the use of resources that have become more expensive; are there ways of accomplishing the agency mission that do not use as much gasoline? Seldom is there but a single way to provide a service, and budget processes need to consider alternatives, especially when the price of some inputs has increased dramatically. A simple analog to traditional budgeting would be a baker who purchases flour, milk, and sugar without considering either the number of cakes, cookies, breads, and so on to be sold or alternative recipes for their production. That would be a silly way to run a business, and it is a silly way to run a government. How is it possible to make reasonable choices between programs that offer different services to the population when the budget presentations and discussions focus on what the government agencies will be buying? It isn't a responsible way to make decisions across government agencies, and it isn't a responsible way for agencies to make decisions about their internal operations. Unfortunately, that is the emphasis of traditional budget classification systems, and change from that emphasis has been agonizingly slow.

These physical input requirements are selected before any cost estimation and without reference either to alternative production methods or to the programs sacrificed if a particular choice is made.[10] Indeed, some governments treat final appropriations to input class so rigidly that agencies, faced with a burdensome series of approvals should they adjust to changed operating conditions during the budget year, choose to do nothing. The language of the appropriation law defends them against the need to respond to the legitimate service demands of the public.

THE QUESTION OF VALUE

The toughest, but most fundamental problem of all is that public decisions must weigh the cost of public programs against their worth to society. The line-item costs in traditional budgets are financial, out-of-pocket costs. They exclude social costs not directly paid; they reflect financial transactions, not the value of opportunities not chosen; and they do not distinguish between sunk and incremental costs of actions. Thus, the cost data presented may not be quite right for making decisions. A number of governments have experimented with activity-based costing (ABC) as a way to improve their decisions. Sidebar 6–1 discusses this approach. Yet budget costs are often all decision makers consider. The needed comparison between cost and program value, vital to intelligent resource allocation, is not a regular component of budget processes because the value of programs delivered is seldom reported or formally considered. Without such regular comparison, poor public decisions are

---

[10]William Niskanen, Gordon Tullock, and others point out that agency administrators have individual incentives to spend as much as possible (conduct any project at the highest feasible cost). See Gordon Tullock, *The Politics of Bureaucracy* (Washington, D.C.: Public Affairs Press, 1965); and William A. Niskanen, Jr., *Bureaucracy and Representative Government* (Chicago: Aldine, 1971). Whether the budget-maximizing bureaucrat is an accurate reflection of reality has been empirically argued many times over the years. One recent answer ("no") appears in Julie Dolan, "The Budget-Minimizing Bureaucrat? Empirical Evidence from the Senior Executive Service," *Public Administration Review* 62 (January/February 2002): 42–50.

Sidebar 6–1
Activity-Based Costing and Government Budgeting

Many government decision makers need information about the cost of services provided. Activity-based costing (ABC), initiated in the late 1980s in the private sector and extended to public and nonprofit agencies about a decade later, offers a system for organizing input cost data to help with program and operational choices.

ABC assigns cost to products or processes according to the resources they consume. It seeks to move accounting data from its traditional input organization (personnel, supplies, contractual services, etc.) to organization according to output, service provided, or project. The idea became popular initially as a way to allocate indirect (overhead) costs to manufacturing and then was applied to services sold by businesses. Finally, the approach has been extended to government operations, not with an eye to the private-sector concerns about pricing or gauging profitability of a product line, but rather with the intent of improving operational efficiency by cost control and identifying opportunities for economical contracting out of public-service production. It seeks clear assignment of cost to each government activity without cross-subsidization of one activity by another.

Traditional cost accounting focuses on the product as the consumer of resources. Cost is measured according to the number of direct labor or machine hours in production or material dollars consumed. It is a "volume-based" cost system. Overhead is added according to some allocation factor or factors linked to direct use of resources in production. ABC, on the other hand, traces costs to activities (entering data, processing reports, maintaining equipment, etc.) and then to products (or services) according to the product's use of the activities in its production process. In skeletal form, ABC has three steps:

1. Define cost categories (salaries, materials, travel, utilities, etc.).
2. Identify key processes and principal activities associated with each, and estimate activity costs for each. First-stage cost allocations assign costs from resource categories to activity centers.
3. Assign costs by activity to appropriate categories, that is, services or products produced. Second-stage cost allocations assign costs from activity centers to products or services.

In the language of ABC, resources used are linked to activities by "resource drivers," and activities are linked to costs by "cost drivers." In application, some costs are calculated by detailed record keeping, and some are calculated by an allocation cost driver, that is, distributed or allocated according to some reasonable basis. The degree of precision required depends on how material the cost, how significant the service, and the extent to which the costing might distort incentives for efficient operations.

There are limits to the utility of full-blown ABC to government decision making. First, cost recovery is not an important concern for most government services. Accurate cost estimates may be interesting as an intellectual and philosophical exercise, but may not mean much for actual public choice. Second, precise allocation of overhead cost, the primary advantage promised for ABC, matters for decisions only if those costs can be avoided. Marginal or incremental

---

**Sidebar 6–1
(continued)**

costs—those costs that can be avoided by making a particular choice—are critical for decisions about what services will be provided and what services will not. These costs change as a result of the decision made but much of government overhead is independent of service choice. Effort toward the precise allocation of such costs therefore yields little extra value to the decision process because the service is not being sold and the extent of cost recovery is not relevant. The allocated share of administrative or overhead costs will not be recovered if the activity to which they have been allocated gets terminated, and it won't get reduced if some of the resources directed to the activity get shifted somewhere else. So ABC doesn't give much information that will be useful for most government decisions.

If services are being financed on a charge basis, however, ABC may be useful for guiding choices about service provision. Better identification and measurement of avoidable cost can be an important aid to improved decision making in all aspects of government.

---

likely. Public decisions based only on program cost—because costs are either remarkably high or affordably low—will not consistently lead to a wise use of scarce resources; neither will consideration based solely on project worth to the exclusion of cost. A society with scarcity must require consideration of worth against cost, if only in the sense of considering how society would be poorer in the absence of the service. Regardless of whether worth is easily measurable, no choices are possible solely on a cost basis. Budget people must avoid the blind spots of both cynic and sentimentalist. Unfortunately, the traditional budget does not provide important information for choice. In addition, too many budget deliberations focus on the purchase of agency inputs with little regard for services being provided to the public.

Traditional Performance Budgets

One of the oldest budget reform inclinations is to put agency performance information together with agency spending. The principal idea behind performance budgets of all varieties, both the traditional format to be discussed here and a newer format to be discussed later in the chapter, is that putting performance information alongside budget numbers will improve public decisions and will keep agencies focused on productive use of funds provided them. Traditional performance budgets emphasize agency-activity performance objectives and accomplishments, not the purchase of resources. The traditional performance budget presents the cost of performing measurable accomplishment units during the budget year, so the budget process has the dual role of providing funds and establishing performance objectives.

The idea of performance budgets is not new. Performance budgeting dates to the mid-1910s in New York City; similar efforts continue in state and local governments to the present.[11] The primary impact of performance budgeting on the service-delivery process, however, dates from the first Hoover Commission (Commission on Organization of the Executive Branch of the Government) report of 1949.[12]

The performance budget concept entails certain shifts in thinking from that of the traditional line-item budget.

1. Budget information should be organized in terms of activities (repairing roads, planting trees, treating patients, teaching students, making arrests, etc.) rather than in terms of individual line items only.
2. Activities should be measured, costs should be identified for these activities, and efficiency in performance of these activities should be evaluated.
3. Performance should be monitored by comparing actual cost and accomplishment against the planned levels for each agency.
4. Although the performance measures would ordinarily not be "end products" of government, the activities ideally should be associated with these beneficial results or outcomes. In modern terminology, these performance measures are on the order of "means to an end" rather than being the end themselves.

The performance classification promises better services at lower cost from more accountable officials; improved legislative review as attention and debate shift away from issues of personnel, salaries, supplier contracts, and the like toward activity issues more related to how resources are used; and decentralized decision making, allowing top management to concentrate its attention on policy matters. Classification of requests follows the activities of the agency, not the inputs it purchases. Performance budgets link costs with activities. This linkage permits unit-cost comparisons across agencies and over time within agencies to emphasize improvements in operating efficiency.

Figure 6–2 further illustrates the performance classification. It includes performance-budget material for snow removal from the 1981–1982 Salt Lake City budget, a historical document noted for its faithfulness to the performance concept. Note the following elements:

1. **The demand section** defines the expected operating environment for the budget year, with prior- and current-year levels for comparison.
2. **The workload section** establishes how the operating unit intends to respond to expected demand by allocation of staff time.
3. **The productivity section** presents the cost per activity unit that emerges from the budgeted costs. This is the special identifying feature of full performance budgets. Most budget documents will not, for instance, allow easy

---

[11]General Accounting Office, *Performance Budgeting: State Experiences and Implications for the Federal Government,* GAO/AFMD-93-41 (Washington, D.C.: General Accounting Office, 1993), surveys these experiences.
[12]Commission on Organization of the Executive Branch of the Government, *Budgeting and Accounting* (Washington, D.C.: U.S. Government Printing Office, 1949).

Figure 6-2
The Salt Lake City Performance Budget

Program: Snow Removal Department: Public Works
Program Description: To remove snow and ice from city streets for safe travel during inclement weather conditions.

Resource Requirements	Program Operating Expense			
	1979–1980 Actual	1980–1981 Budget	1980–1981 Estimated	1981–1982 Recommended
Personnel/personal services	19.5/$279,318	16.9/$325,358	11.25/$190,618	4.7/$111,975
Operating and maintenance supplies	39,081	48,300	29,763	47,720
Charges and services	61,774	193,169	111,864	199,379
Capital outlay	0	17,596	12,570	0
Work order credits	(212)	0	0	0
Total	$379,961	$584,423	$344,815	$359,074
Program Resources				
General fund	$379,961	$584,423	$344,815	$359,074
Total	$379,961	$584,423	$344,815	$359,074

Program Budget Highlights
The 1980–1981 budget indicators had an overallocation of man hours in the snow and ice program which has been rectified by mid-year adjustments and is now correctly reflected in the 1980–1982 request. During 1980–1981, a study was conducted analyzing the past five winters. It was obvious as a result of this study that our projections for the 1980–1981 budget year were unrealistic, so we reassigned employees' time to other programs causing other program expenditure levels and personnel allocations to rise.

Performance Objectives
1. To review "scale" of snow fighter program.
2. To develop an expanded U.D.O.T. and S.L.C. responsibilities exchange where practical.
3. To evaluate an "exceptional storm" emergency backup system.

Performance Review	1979–1980 Actual	1980–1981 Budget	1980–1981 Estimated	1981–1982 Recommended
Demand				
1. Lane miles of priority snow routes	400	400	460	460
2. Inches of snowfall	63	68	45	68
3. Storms requiring crew mobilization	15	19	16	19
4. Storms requiring salt only	7	10	10	10
5. Storms requiring snow plowing	8	9	6	9
Workload				
1. Man hours salting streets	n.a.*	12,640	1,000	2,060
2. Man hours plowing streets	n.a.	18,960	1,400	3,090
3. Tons of salt applied	7.410	8.000	4.900	8.000

(continues)

**Figure 6–2
(continued)**

Performance Review	1979–1980 Actual	1980–1981 Budget	1980–1981 Estimated	1981–1982 Recommended
Productivity				
1. Cost/priority lane mile	962	1,418	874	765
2. Average cost/storm	25,663	29,864	25,138	18,513
Effectiveness				
1. Vehicle accidents in which snow				
and ice are a contributing factor	253	250	135	250
2. Complaints received	49	50	35	50

*n.a. = Not available.

identification of either historical or proposed costs of dealing with snow removal after a snowstorm; the performance classification does because it links costs to measured units of activities. Even budgets with cost centers identified within departments will not provide answers to those sorts of questions.

4. **The effectiveness section** shows the unit's performance against criteria that indicate whether the unit is accomplishing its intended objectives. This is important because one avenue to lower cost is lower quality of service—one pickle slice fewer per hamburger will reduce the cost of producing hamburgers by millions of dollars in a national restaurant chain, and the same goes for government services.

The performance structure has some special implications. First, the budget should become a powerful tool for management responsibility and accountability. In that structure, budgeting must be a central management responsibility because activity levels and their costs are specifically presented in a document that guides agency operation. Operating supervisors can no longer permit separate budget personnel to prepare budget requests (it is bad practice to do this, in any case, of course) because they become detailed operating plans for the budget year.[13] Many agency managers do not like the performance-budgeting concept because it exposes the agency operating details (demand estimates, workload trend, etc.) to the scrutiny of external observers—like taxpayers and legislators. Second, legislatures must change their review and appropriations procedures from traditional line-item reviews to agency-activity reviews. The legislature may feel uncomfortable considering something other than objects of expenditures, particularly where there is no apparent linkage to revenue and budget balancing and when the activities may be difficult to measure or relate to what the citizenry really wants. Third, a performance budget

---

[13]Traditional budgets are operating plans as well, except they do not contain identifiable operating objectives. That addition provides the new constraint on the agency.

can make a management-by-objectives program easier to operate. The objectives would be the performance measures (activities) appearing in the budget. Performance and budget attainment can thus be monitored through the fiscal year.

The performance budget hinges on the quality of its performance measures and a legislative-executive consensus that those measures are the proper ones for agency attention. Some performance measures may be misleading or irrelevant, despite the fact that they can be measured and reported. Audit quality, for instance, may be more important than simply the number of audits conducted. The number of audits could well be the performance measure, however, simply because it is more easily quantified. If the Department of Parks and Recreation is going to be responsible for maintaining flower beds, then it will need to define a standard flower bed to calculate unit costs. Furthermore, the performance budget does not ask whether the performance being measured is the service the public actually wants. Of course, there is no necessary consideration of alternate ways to do a particular task. The drive to lower a government's unit cost of performance should induce development of improved methods, not sacrifice the unit's quality—but the technique is not geared to handle that problem.

Curiously enough, advocates of performance budgeting come from two ends of the political spectrum. Some public officials see performance budgets as a way to justify their contributions to the community and possibly to expand their budgets. Others see performance budgets as a tool to expose waste and, hence, a guide for expenditure reduction that would permit tax cuts.

The performance budget structure does not question whether objectives are appropriate or a service is worth its cost of production. Performance budgets consider whether the activity is being done at low cost; they do not consider whether the activity is worth doing. And that brings up the Achilles heel of performance budgets: they are extremely expensive to develop. Unless the government really will use them as an integral part of public management and decision making, they are not likely to be a worthy use of government resources.

Program Budgets

The program-budget format organizes proposed expenditure according to consumer output/outcome or contribution to public objectives.[14] Program budgets focus on the right question for public decisions: What are governments doing that is valued by the public? They don't focus on what governments buy or the tasks that agencies perform. They get to the heart of the matter: What of value are you intending to do? Programs are constructed on the basis of their contributions to those objectives without regard to administrative organizations responsible for delivery of the particular service. In essence, the program format requires the government—and agencies

---

[14]These programs are linked to fundamental missions. In recent years, some jurisdictions have started to identify service areas (like street cleaning) of government agencies as programs. That obviously creates some confusion in discussion of budget structures.

in the government—to identify what products or services it provides and then to organize its budget requests and budget execution along those product or service lines. The format redirects focus from the expenditure objects or economic classifications (the things that the government purchases) or from those doing the spending (the administrative departments) to the subjects of that expenditure (the services to society that the government provides), and it breaks down the administrative boundaries between government agencies. A complete program budget combines services that contribute to a similar objective so that competition for funds occurs among real alternatives, contrary to the style of an ordinary budget, in which agencies or departments compete for funds, as do service units within agencies or departments. Similar service units may receive different treatment simply because different agencies house them. In a program budget, similar service units compete with each other, not with dissimilar programs housed in an administrative agency, and budget decision makers can see proposed spending organized according to services to be provided, in addition to what agencies might be involved in doing the spending.

Program budgeting defines the goals of the government and classifies organizational expenditure contributing to achievement of each goal. To focus competition for resources on objectives and alternative programs for achieving objectives, items are grouped by end product. The program structure identifies agency products; it does not focus on the inputs used by the agency or on the agencies. Table 6–2 illustrates the program-budget classifications used by the commonwealth of Pennsylvania. Notice that the format classifies by service provided to the public rather than by individual department (several services would in fact be provided by more than one department), input purchased, or department activity. The structure seeks a final product orientation. For example, you will see that several agencies are providing services in the Protection of Persons and Property program. To look at only one of these—the State Police, for instance—would provide a misleading view of the significance of the program in the budget. The Direction and Supportive Services classification is normal in program budgets; those functions provide inputs unallocable to the provision of the other services. The Pennsylvania display shows that many agencies contribute to several programs and that most programs include operations of more than one agency (Transportation is the exception).

Program budgeting requires careful definition of programs, an exercise in taxonomy that is the essence of such budgets. Although a good understanding of government operations is vital for program classification, the logical criteria for program design provided by Arthur Smithies are generally helpful:

1. **Facilitate comparisons.** Design programs so they "permit comparison of alternative methods of pursuing an imperfectly defined policy objective."[15] If there are competing ways of reducing some social problem, make certain they end up in the same program. That breakdown can clarify issues for analysis.

---

[15]Arthur Smithies, "Conceptual Framework for the Program Budget," in *Program Budgeting*, 2nd ed., ed. David Novick (New York: Holt, Rinehart & Winston, 1969), 42.

Table 6–2
Program Budget Structure Illustration: Commonwealth of Pennsylvania, 2007–2008 to 2013–2014

EDUCATION (23.4% of 2008 total): The goal of this program is to ensure that funds for education are spent on proven practices that will boost student achievement. This program includes funding for pre-kindergarten, full-day kindergarten and class size reduction. In addition, this program funds basic education and special education programs and educational support such as tutoring, improving teacher practice and curricula and technology upgrades. This program also ensures high quality career and technical education and higher education experiences...

Subcategories: Educational Support Services, Basic Education, Higher Education.

Some Agencies involved: Departments of Education, Revenue, Public Welfare, and Labor; Higher Education Assistance Agency; Tax Equalization Board.

PROTECTION OF PERSONS AND PROPERTY (13.2% of 2008 total): The goal of this commonwealth program is to provide an environment and a social system in which the lives of individuals and the property of individuals and organizations are protected from natural and man-made disasters and from illegal and unfair actions...

Subcategories: General Administration and Support, Public Protection and Law Enforcement, Control and Reduction of Crime, Juvenile Crime Prevention, Adjudication of Defendants, Public Order and Community Safety, Protection from Natural Hazards and Disasters, Consumer Protection.

Some Agencies involved: State Police; Departments of Banking, Corrections, Attorney General, Liquor Control Board, Military Affairs, State, Environmental Protection, Agriculture; Emergency Management Agency; Milk Marketing Board; Insurance Commission; Homeland Security; etc.

HEALTH AND HUMAN SERVICES: (43.4% of 2008 total): The goals of this program are to ensure access to quality medical care for all citizens; to support people seeking self-sufficiency; to provide military readiness and assistance to veterans and maximize opportunities for individuals and families to participate in society...

Subcategories: Human Services Support, Social Development of Individuals, Support of Older Pennsylvanians, Income Maintenance, Physical Health Treatment, Mental Health.

Some Agencies involved: Departments of Aging and Long Term Living, Health, Public Welfare, Agriculture, Labor and Industry, Military and Veterans Affairs, Revenue, Transportation, etc.

TRANSPORTATION (9.7% of 2008 total): The goal of this program is to provide a system for the fast, convenient, efficient and safe movement of individuals and cargo within the commonwealth that is interfaced with a national and international system of transportation.

Agency involved: Department of Transportation.

RECREATIONAL AND CULTURAL ENRICHMENT (1.3% of 2008 total): The goal of this program is to improve the quality of life in Pennsylvania's urban, suburban, and rural communities. This program focuses resources on our recreational and cultural amenities ensuring that Pennsylvanians can fully enjoy the natural beauty of the commonwealth. This program also ensures that residents and visitors can explore the diversity of cultural traditions, the creativity of our artistic community and the bountiful history of our state and its prominence in forming the heritage of our nation...

Subcategories: Recreation, Cultural Enrichment.

Some Agencies involved: Departments of Conservation and Natural Resources and of Education; Historical and Museum Commission; Fish and Boat Commission; Game Commission, Public Television Network; Council on the Arts; etc.

(continues)

Table 6–2 (continued)
Program Budget Structure Illustration: Commonwealth of Pennsylvania, 2007–2008 to 2013–2014

ECONOMIC DEVELOPMENT (4.5% of 2008 total): The goal of this program is to create jobs for Pennsylvanians. To do so, this program offers a variety of grants, loans, and loan guarantees designed to stimulate economic investment, growth and expanded employment…

<u>Subcategories</u>: Economic Development Support Services, Commonwealth Economic Development, Workforce Development, Community Development

Some Agencies involved: Department of Community and Economic Development; the Pennsylvania Economic Development Financing Authority; the Infrastructure Investment Authority; Auditor General; and Departments of Education, Labor and Industry, and Revenue.

DEBT SERVICE (1.6% of 2008 total): The goal of this Commonwealth program is to provide sufficient financial resources necessary to meet the timely payment of Commonwealth debt obligations. Debt financing is used by the commonwealth to finance its capital programs and voter-approved bond referenda and to fund certain disaster relief programs…

Agency involved: Treasury.

DIRECTION AND SUPPORTIVE SERVICES (3.0% of 2008 total): The goal of this Commonwealth program is to provide an efficient and effective administrative support system through which the goals and objectives of the Commonwealth programs can be attained.

<u>Subcategories</u>: Administration and Support Services, Fiscal Management, Physical Facilities and Commodities Management, Interstate Relations.

Some Agencies involved: Governor's Office; Executive Offices; Lieutenant Governor; Auditor General; Legislature; Treasury; Civil Service Commission; Departments of Revenue and General Services; State Employees' Retirement System; etc.

NOTE: Some agencies have activities that are included in more than one program. Not all programs have subcategories.
SOURCE: Governor's Office of the Budget, 2009–2010 Executive Budget, Commonwealth of Pennsylvania (Harrisburg, Pa.: Commonwealth of Pennsylvania, 2009).

2. **Include complementary resources.** Programs must include complementary components that cannot function separately. Thus, health programs require physicians, nurses, physical facilities, and the like in appropriate proportions, and those elements must all be in the program. In addition, public infrastructure used to provide a service requires upkeep and maintenance, and those costs should be associated with the program.

3. **Recognize the unallocable.** When one part of a government serves several other parts of that government, separate supporting service programs may be needed. Thus, centralized electronic data processing, personnel administration, and so forth may permit operating economies that would not be possible if each agency handled them separately. These activities can be handled as programs, even though their outputs are not government objectives (e.g., the Direction and Supportive Services program in Pennsylvania). It isn't reasonable to try to allocate the time of the mayor or governor to the specific programs. In addition, eliminating a particular program element to

which part of the mayor's office has been allocated is not going to cause a change in mayor's office cost, so any such allocated costs are not relevant to the program decision. Joint costs are just that, joint, and trying to divide them up is folly, as well as adding no useful information to the decision-making process.

4. **Multiple structures.** Governments may need overlapping program structures to achieve their objectives. Many revenue departments, for instance, have structures arranged both functionally and geographically. That approach appears when both national and regional (or statewide) objectives are important. Unless the government chooses to reorganize along pure program lines, appropriations will be made to agencies and departments in order to maintain fiscal control, so there will be an organization-chart financial structure on top of the program budget.

5. **Recognize long-term activities.** Some activities involving research, development, or long-term investment may be considered separate subprograms because of the long time span over which the expenditures take effect. Uncertainties preclude reasonably reliable estimates of resource requirements beyond short portions of their lives.

It can be assumed that all government activities seek to improve the general welfare. Program budgeting's goal is to identify the components of that broad objective so that choices can be made among those components and among alternative approaches to achievement of that objective.

Program construction is the identifying feature, but program budgets often include other elements. First, budget time horizons expand beyond an annual appropriation to the program's lifetime. Although appropriation remains annual, decision makers are presented the total program cost, not simply a down payment. Second, steps in preparation induce agencies to consider alternate operating methods and to propose only those that require the least cost to achieve the desired results. Because agency administrators traditionally have incentives toward larger budgets for prestige or advancement, such steps are difficult to enforce. Third, program budgets often include some cost-benefit analysis of the resource use of proposed programs (a technique discussed in the next chapter). Programming combines costs for achieving particular objectives, so an important piece of the data needed for cost-benefit analysis is provided.

All these elements appeared in the federal planning-programming-budgeting system (PPBS) experiment, applied initially to the Department of Defense in 1961, expanded to other federal agencies in 1965, and officially terminated in 1971. The Department of Defense continues with a formal system renamed in 2003 the Planning Programming Budgeting and Execution System (PPBES).[16] The system provides a link between the missions or programs of the Department of Defense and the departments within Defense (Army, Navy, Air Force, etc.) charged with delivery of

---

[16]An excellent description and analysis of the budget and other financial management systems in the Department of Defense, including PPBES, is L. R. Jones and Jerry L. McCaffery, *Budgeting, Financial Management, and Acquisition Reform in the U.S. Department of Defense* (Charlotte, N.C.: Information Age Publishing, 2008).

those missions and, through the secretary of defense, provides an important element in the principle of civilian control of the military force.

The logical steps of the PPBES system are these.

1. **Planning.** Define, identify, and examine alternative strategies for dealing with the environment of the future. In Defense terms, the planning involves analysis of trends, adversary capability, threats, strategies, technologies, and long-term implications of current choices. The process determines service requirements. The plans are long-term and multiyear.
2. **Programming.** Balance resources among the various program options. The programming process considers alternatives for meeting the previously established service requirements. It will derive what are believed to be the best programs for meeting those requirements.
3. **Budgeting.** Formulate, justify, execute, and control the budget that embodies those selected programs. The programs previously established are rolled into a budget request for approval by department leadership, the president, and Congress. Resources will be controlled according to the relevant appropriation law.

Elements of the old PPBS system remain in budget frameworks of many federal agencies. In addition, the PPBES process has recently been expanding, as it has now been adopted by the National Oceanic and Atmospheric Administration (NOAA), the Department of Homeland Security, the Library of Congress, and the National Aeronautics and Space Administration (NASA). It continues in various versions among several states and localities.[17] The advantages: it provides a long-term connection to objectives and strategic plans, it ends a process in which budgets were constructed on an annual increment basis, and it focuses on distributing available resources reasonably among competing programs in the agency. Its process is ideal when the department has separate units that are performing similar or interrelated tasks. It does move fundamental decision making higher in the department.[18]

The functional classification required by the 1974 Congressional Budget and Impoundment Control Act provides a program format for federal expenditures that appears in the congressional budget resolution and in the president's budget, alongside the administrative classification. The functions frequently include more than a single department (the national defense function, for instance, encompasses activities of the Defense and Energy Departments), and departments may have activities in more than a single function. The complete federal functional classifications are described in Appendix 6–1. Appendix 6–2 presents the United Nations classification of functions of government (COFOG), a functional classification that applies

---

[17]See Allen Schick, *Budget Innovation in the States* (Washington, D.C.: Brookings Institution, 1971), for a review of state use of program and performance structures. About thirty-five states have implemented modified PPBS at one time or another.

[18]West and colleagues identify complaints and resistance in the recent introduction of PPBES to NOAA. William F. West, Eric Lindquist, and Katrina N. Mosher-Howe, "NOAA's Resurrection of Program Budgeting: Déjà vu All over Again?" *Public Administration Review* 69 (May/June 2009): 435–47. Agencies never like change in how they do things. People cherish the power that comes from understanding a process, and changing any process erodes that power.

to services provided by all levels of government, not just the national functions of Appendix 6–1. This classification, because of its breadth, provides a good thinking template for any government—national, regional, or local—that is developing a functional classification for its operations, and it serves as the basic template for making comparisons of government operations across countries.

As is characteristic of program budgets, the federal functional classification cuts across agencies so that decision makers may think about use of public resources to the advantage of the citizenry without regard for organizational boundaries. Figure 6–3 shows the extent to which functions are distributed to agencies and the extent to which agencies support multiple functions in the U.S. government. A Government Accountability Office (GAO) report describes the situation for fiscal 2003:

> Sometimes there is a "match" between a function and a department—for example, the Department of Transportation is associated almost exclusively with the Transportation function (400) and over 80 percent of spending within the Transportation function (400) is by the Department of Transportation. Sometimes, however, there is an imbalance between the importance of an agency in a mission area and the importance of the mission area within the department. For example, while almost all obligations in the Agriculture function (350) are by USDA [U.S. Department of Agriculture], that function represents only about 41 percent of the spending by the department. Over 40 percent of USDA's obligations are for the Income Security function (600).[19]

One classification focuses on resource allocation choices for the federal government; the other focuses on establishing responsibility and accountability. Barring a reorganization to make functions (or programs) and agencies match, the sort of dual classification with a crosswalk between the two is critical for getting all that is expected from the budget process. Without an easy, quick, and understandable crosswalk, the function or program format yields numbers that are not usable by budget decision makers, and choices continue to be made in the familiar setting of the traditional budget. That problem contributed heavily to the demise of the earlier federal PPBS. Computer spreadsheet and database programs make translation between classifications—from function or program to administrative agency accounts, for instance—almost instantly possible. That was not the case in the 1960s, when the Johnson administration tried it.

Three operational problems with program budgets require special attention. First, many public services contribute to more than one public objective, and the best programmatic classification for them is not always apparent. Whatever choice is made will emphasize one set of policy choices at the expense of another. For example, federal expenditures on military academies might be attributed to higher education or to defense objectives. The placement of that expenditure establishes which analysis it faces, so placement must depend on the most important current issues raised by the expenditure. It should be apparent that any long-maintained program structure produces the bureaucratic blindness associated with continued examination of the same issues from the same approach. Furthermore, difficult

---

[19]Government Accountability Office, *Federal Budget: Agency Obligations by Budget Function and Object Classification for Fiscal Year 2003,* GAO-04-834 (Washington, D.C.: Government Accountability Office, 2004). The numbers in parentheses refer to function numbers in the classification system.

Figure 6-3
Federal Spending by Agency and Function: Multiple Agencies for Functions and Multiple Functions for Agencies

Budget Function →	National Defense (050)	International Affairs (150)	General Science, Space, and Technology (250)	Energy (270)	Natural Resources and Environment (300)	Agriculture (350)	Commerce and Housing Credit (370)	Transportation (400)	Community and Regional Development (450)	Education, Training, Employment, and Social Services (500)	Health (550)	Medicare (570)	Income Security (600)	Social Security (650)	Veterans Benefits and Services (700)	Administration of Justice (750)	General Government (800)	Net Interest (900)	Number of functions charged by agency
Executive Branch																			
Department of Agriculture		●			●	●	●		●	●	●		●				●		9
Department of Commerce					●		●		●	●									4
Department of Defense	●	●			●						●		●		●		●		7
Department of Education										●						●			2
Department of Energy	●		●	●													●		4
Department of Health and Human Services										●	●	●	●				●		5
Department of Homeland Security	●				●		●		●		●		●			●	●		8
Department of Housing and Urban Development							●		●				●			●			4
Department of Justice	●	●														●			3
Department of Labor	●									●	●		●		●		●		6
Department of State		●			●								●						3
Department of Transportation	●							●											2
Department of Veterans Affairs															●				1
Department of the Interior				●	●			●	●	●									5
Department of the Treasury		●			●		●	●	●		●		●			●	●	●	10
Environmental Protection Agency					●														1
Executive Office of the President		●											●				●		3
General Services Administration							●										●		2
Independent Agencies	●	●		●	●	●	●	●	●	●	●		●		●	●	●		14
National Aeronautics and Space Administration			●					●			●								3
National Science Foundation	●		●																2
Nuclear Regulatory Commission				●															1
Office of Personnel Management											●		●				●		3
Postal Service							●												1
Small Business Administration							●		●										2
Social Security Administration														●	●		●		3
Number of Executive Agencies Charging this Function	8	7	3	4	9	2	9	5	8	7	9	1	11	1	5	6	12	1	
Judicial Branch													●			●			2
Legislative Branch		●					●			●		●	●			●	●		7
Number of Agencies Charging this Function		1					1			1		1	2			2	1		
All	8	8	3	4	9	2	10	5	8	8	9	2	13	1	5	8	13	1	

SOURCE: Government Accountability Office, *Federal Budget: Agency Obligations by Budget Function and Object Classification for Fiscal Year 2003*, GAO-04-834 (Washington, D.C.: Government Accountability Office, 2004).

interrelationships among public programs remain. Thus, highway transportation activities may influence urban redevelopment or complicate environmental protection. These interrelationships can baffle any budget navigator.

Second, cost estimates for programs may be less meaningful for public decisions than imagined. There is no scientifically defensible method for allocating substantial joint agency costs or administrative overhead costs. Because most agencies work with several programs, many resources used by an agency are shared and are not clearly attributable to a single program. Furthermore, public decisions require concern for social implications—not simply money out of pocket—but program budgets still focus on agency cost alone. Thus, the program-cost data are unlikely to be directly usable for decision making.

Third, programs cannot entirely displace departments to deliver all expectations from the budget process. This is because responsibility and accountability for performance and for funds must be assigned to an organizational unit. Programs cannot be accountable; departments (and the people in them) can. Hence, fiscal discipline, in the final analysis, requires a budget and appropriation structure beyond that provided by a program format.

Finally, program budgets may have little impact on appropriations. Legislatures, lobbyists, and government departments have experience with the traditional budget format. Participants know where their allies are located, and the location is in a department. All are familiar with that construction and have developed general guidelines for its analysis. New presentations require new guidelines and extra effort by all. Unless the major participants in the budget process actually want the improved presentation, it will be ignored in favor of the format to which they are accustomed. But, ultimately, that may not matter.[20] The program budget and a process like PPBES are initially for development of an executive budget. As a tool for developing that budget, the executive branch can find it extremely useful in developing its policy responses, in choosing among options, and in creating its proposal to the legislative branch. Therefore, even if the legislature insists on looking at the traditional budget, what is in that traditional budget will have been created according to the PPBES principles. If the executive believes the format to be useful for making fiscal choices and a crosswalk can be created at little cost, there is no reason not to use the system. As with all higher-order budget processes (in other words, those that try to go beyond line items and organization charts), there are costs associated with program budgets, so they should be created only if they are going to be used. As we know, the current federal budget comfortably crosswalks from agency appropriations and functional categories without problems, surely creating more transparency, if nothing else.

An Illustration of an Expenditure in Alternative Classifications

The budget system reforms discussed so far involve recategorization of spending to provide information in alternative formats. How this would impact information may be shown with a simple illustration. This is demonstrated in Figure 6–4. How might the salary of a teacher employed in a state correctional facility appear in traditional-, performance-, and program-budget formats? With a traditional budget,

---

[20]And confusing the lobbyists, even for a legislative session or two, might even be a good thing. Never fear; they will figure things out soon enough.

Figure 6–4
Salary Classification in Traditional, Performance, and Program Budgets

Morris Hall is employed by the Green Valley Correctional Facility as a teacher in the basic literacy program. His salary is $25,000 per year. Where would Mr. Hall's salary appear in different budget classifications? Follow the asterisk (*).

Traditional Departmental	Performance	Program
Department of Corrections 　Green Valley Correctional Facility 　　Personnel 　　　Director 　　　Clerical 　　　Guards 　　　Instructors* 　　Supplies and equipment 　　Contractual services 　Jackson State Correctional Facility Department of Highways Department of Education	Department of Corrections 　Activity: Adult literacy 　　Personnel* 　Supplies 　　Cost per student 　　instructional hour 　Activity: Incarceration Department of Highways	Human Resource Development 　Service: Adult literacy 　　Local 　　State facilities* 　Service: Vocational education Protection of Persons and Property Provision of Safe and Speedy Transportation

that salary would appear as a part of the personnel (wage-and-salary) line of the state Department of Corrections budget. It would thus compete for funds, in the first instance, within that department. Money received could well depend on how the governor and legislature viewed the overall prison system. More money appropriated to the corrections system could end up being directed to the educational systems in the institutions.

If that budget was classified according to performance, that expenditure would appear as part of the cost of achieving a target number of departmental instruction hours. Again, competition for resources would be with other activities of that department. It would be distinguished, however, from activities not related to instruction. There would be a distinction between money for the education program and money devoted to stronger security and detention apparatus.

A program structure might classify that expenditure as a part of a human development program, separating the expenditure from its link to incarceration and causing it to be considered with training and education activities. It would be considered with primary and secondary education, job training, and other education activities, and not with money associated with improving and maintaining public safety.

The salary expenditure is the same dollar amount, but the different budget classifications require different treatment to accommodate different budget purposes. The budget classification undoubtedly would influence the questions asked about the expenditure and, possibly, the size of its appropriation. In creating a budget classification system other than one following the traditional administrative unit system, it will be necessary to reclassify funds away from their accounting location to provide information groups more appropriate for the public decisions being made. The funds need to be associated with an administrative unit for fiscal control and responsibility, but other classifications will be more useful for other budgetary purposes.

The Zero-Based Budget System

Many local budget officers proclaim that their budgets are zero-based. The implication is that the budget was developed without reference to the previous year's budget, that there are no foundation presumptions about what will be proposed for the budget year, and, very definitely, that there is no assumption agencies are assured of an appropriation at least as great as their current level. Everything starts with a clean slate, and all options for service and how the services are to be delivered are on an even competitive basis. Of course, that is both fundamentally preposterous and the right way to prepare a budget proposal. Any city starts the year with lots of carryovers from years past—it has four fire stations, three city parks, a police station in a particular location, probably a collective-bargaining agreement with city employees that sets compensation rates and possibly staffing levels, and a whole history of decisions that previous administrations and city councils have reached over the years about city responsibilities and limits. The budget is going to be built from those foundations because many choices are not going to change (indeed, they may be legally binding), and, even with any instruction to ignore the recent past, capable administrators are going to pay attention to the information from that experience in building service programs, policies, and budget requests. What one does hope is that the agency administrators will build their budget proposals with an open mind in regard to serving the public and in regard to ways in which services might be provided and that nobody—not agencies, budget agencies, or lawmakers—assumes that current levels of funding are guaranteed, that increments only go up, and that adding two percent to last year's budget is how to create a budget. That is a far more effective approach than to make the unrealistic claim that budgets are being prepared entirely from scratch every year.[21]

That is, however, considerably removed from the experience with a full-scale zero-based budgeting system that was briefly in place for the U.S. federal government and in some states. When Jimmy Carter became president in 1976, he instituted what was called a zero-based budgeting system, one based on what he had used as

---

[21]The House Appropriations Committee instructed that the appropriation proposal for the legislative branch for fiscal 2013 be constructed on a zero base. "The Committee believes that there are considerable opportunities to realize meaningful savings by carefully reviewing each agency's budget requirements from a zero base, rather than by reviewing only incremental changes to the base. Such a review would not only assist the Committee in its appropriating and oversight responsibilities, but would also require agencies to systematically examine all of their budgetary requirements as they relate to the individual mission. Therefore, the Committee directs each and every agency of the Legislative Branch to develop and present their budget requirements from a zero base. The individual reviews should examine and justify each and every program, project, and activity (PPA) as if the PPA were nonexistent." Committee Reports, 112th Congress, House Report 112-148, Legislative Branch Appropriations Bill, 2012.

governor of Georgia some years earlier. His idea was to implement a rational program to reallocate public resources to areas of greatest public need and to break the limitations ingrained in an incrementalist budgetary system (recall the incrementalist insight discussed in Chapter 2). In theory, the zero-based budget (ZBB) annually would require each agency to defend its entire budget, with no presumption that the agency would receive at least its prior-year appropriation.[22] Deliberations in both executive preparation and legislative approval would be about the full budget, not just the proposed increase, and the assumed incremental lock on fiscal decision making would be broken. The system would make government more flexible, eliminate low-return programs, allocate resources to the highest-return programs, improve government effectiveness by forcing programs to be justified in their entirety every year, and simplify reallocations of government spending in response to changed program demands—all good objectives. Choices about programs and funding would be made based on a system of internal rankings of those options, and the whole budget would be put together on that totally rational basis. The federal government and a number of states did implement such systems in the later years of the 1970s.

ZBB systems in implementation had individual peculiarities, but many included the elements diagrammed in Figure 6–5.[23] In the first stage, unit managers prepare *decision packages,* which are alternatives for performing a particular function with differing amounts of money. Each package includes funding levels and increments, a description of the activity, and a statement of the activity's impact on major objectives of the agency. The decision package also describes the implications of not providing funds for the package.[24]

Unit managers submit their ranked decision packages to agency heads. Agency heads consolidate the packages received from the several unit managers, rank the packages, and transmit the packages forward in the government hierarchy. The packages flow through successive consolidations and rankings to the department level. The final consolidation and ranking produces the budget request transmitted to the central budget office for eventual inclusion in the president's budget.[25] Each program element will have survived a number of rankings if it ends up in the budget. As many packages as can be afforded within available revenue will be in the budget, all priority-ranked.

The process has several potential strengths. It will produce much operating data—workloads, performance indicators, and so on—for use in management and should induce consideration of alternative delivery approaches. Furthermore, it will require formal consideration of priorities throughout the organization, something not done when the process takes previous operations as a given as the

---

[22]The federal PPBS process just discussed was intended to start budget development from a zero base as well.

[23]Executive Office of the President, Office of Management and Budget, "Zero Base Budgeting" (Bulletin No. 79-9), April 19, 1977, provides a full description of the federal version of ZBB.

[24]The ZBB system in Georgia and at the federal level actually didn't start with zero; agencies were to start with 80 percent of the previous year's appropriation. But 80 percent–based budgeting doesn't sound so impressive. Robert N. Anthony, "Zero-Base Budgeting Is a Fraud," *Wall Street Journal*, April 27, 1977.

[25]President Carter claimed that, as governor of Georgia, he actually did the final ranking of the thousands of decision packages flowing up through the state government. Had he done so, he would have had time for little else during the year.

Figure 6-5
Decision Package Flow in the Federal ZBB System, Late 1970s

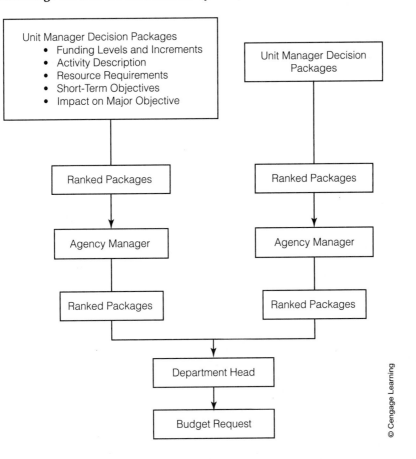

budget is prepared. Budget construction builds from the bottom of the organization, where the best operating information resides, not from the top down, as is characteristic of most budget processes. Finally, ZBB requires considerable thought about the objectives of the agency. However, there are considerable problems. First, package development generates many package options that have absolutely no chance of serious consideration. Some programs cannot realistically be considered candidates for zeroing out, some packages will never be seriously considered for funding, and some production alternatives will not be meaningful contenders. Many capable administrators, recognizing all that, will not take ZBB seriously. Second, performance information may be contrived and not especially germane to the operation of the agency. Measures may be accurate, but not meaningful to the ultimate purposes of the agency—and they may not be accurately reported. Third, many spending activities will not be amenable to zero-based treatment. Several such categories include mandates at the state and local levels, activities controlled by earmarks, contractual payments (debt service and pensions), and formula entitlements. These constitute a considerable share of many budgets. Finally, the rankings of those in the program delivery flow may not reflect the rankings of society. One suspects that these administrators will have protection of their programs shaping their rankings. It is not unreasonable to expect people to rank their programs high and to rank those of others low—and that inclination is unlikely to lead to the best fiscal choices for the public as a whole. The idea that federal programs could be objectively ranked from highest to lowest priority missed the basic fact that most programs cannot be evaluated on numerical terms and, even where programs can produce numbers, the numbers are not comparable from one program to another. The numbers from veterans' benefits are not the same as numbers from farm price supports.

Most observers doubt that federal ZBB had much impact on federal spending. The Reagan administration put an end to it as soon as it took office. Allen Shick says that zero-based budgeting "changed the terminology of budgeting, but little more."[26] Zero-based budgeting probably directs too much attention to the routine of the budget process and away from the tough questions of that process—the questions of program objectives and social values. Some pieces continue in federal, state, and local budget systems, including elements of target-based budgeting processes in which budget units develop alternative budget proposals based on different levels of potential funding.[27]

Results-Based/New Performance Budgeting

The last two decades have brought a heightened concern with government account-ability and a renewed interest in integrating performance into the budget cycle. As David Osborne and Ted Gaebler write, "Cynicism about government runs deep within the American soul."[28] Nothing will dislodge this cynicism—popular discus-sions refer to the public as "taxpayers," not "service recipients," after all. Giving the public a clearer view of what the results or outcomes of government expenditures are and providing some assurance that government agencies are focused on per-formance and are being held accountable fit into that doubting attitude. There is nothing wrong about expecting a decent return from money spent. It should be no surprise that there is a demand for performance reports and performance targets for the budget year—and that this information would logically be attached to the policy proposals for spending public money. As the only annual event that considers all operations of a government, the budget process is the best place to involve a look at government performance, and being able to link it to decisions about government

[26]Allen Shick, "The Road from ZBB," *Public Administration Review* 38 (March/April 1978): 178.
[27]Robert K. Goertz, "Target-Based Budgeting and Adaptations to Fiscal Uncertainty," *Public Productivity and Management Review* 16 (Summer 1993): 425–29.
[28]David Osborne and Ted Gaebler, *Reinventing Government, How the Entrepreneurial Spirit Is Transforming the Public Sector* (Reading, Mass.: Addison-Wesley, 1992), xv.

resources should make it even better. A budget that looks for results is certainly more reasonable than one that has as its primary focus money being spent and inputs being purchased.

A discussion of performance budgeting directed toward the achievement of measured public results is somewhat complicated by the fact that there "never has been an agreed-on definition of performance budgeting."[29] The systems proposed and implemented have varied features, they operate at different points in the fiscal structure, and their intentions are not always the same (some seek efficiency, some seek to cut the size of government, some seek improved transparency and information flow, and some have more complicated objectives). It is difficult to generalize, but the basic elements of new performance budgeting include information about objectives and results of government expenditures (key indicators and program evaluation) and a budget process that facilitates use of this information in appropriation decisions, including presentation of performance measures directly in budget documents. It is the aspiration of performance budgeting that performance measures (outcome measures) will be transparently available and will be integral to each phase of the budget cycle. In one way or another, the ultimate expectation is that funding will be directly linked to measured agency results. These elements may help improve allocation of fiscal resources among alternatives and may encourage agencies to spend more efficiently and effectively.[30]

That identifying results may be difficult and time consuming, and even embarrassing, for administrators does not mean that the inquiry is inappropriate. Every agency administrator should have answers available, even if they are not in the detail required by the budget process. A quick perusal of budgets presented on government websites will show that, one way or another, performance measurement has gotten tied into many budget presentations and deliberations. One difference from the traditional performance budgets discussed earlier is that, while the traditional examples tended to link costs to the outputs or activities of government agencies and to calculate unit costs of these activities, the new performance budgets are more likely to simply present performance results and targets associated with departmental operations and to make at least some effort, often not very successfully, to provide outcome or result measures in addition to activity statistics. They do not provide unit costing, and they seldom provide evaluation evidence that the results are actually the product of government programs, not just a happy accident.

The idea of such results-driven budgeting is that the societal goal, the outcome or result, is what matters for government performance, not the direct output or activity of the agency. That is the same logic that drove program budgeting, but this new approach does not cross agency lines to put operations with similar societal objectives in the same category. It emphasizes that the concern for fiscal decisions should be not what the government purchases (its inputs), but rather what it produces. This

---

[29]William C. Rivenbark, "Defining Performance Budgeting for Local Government," *Popular Government* 69 (Winter 2004): 2. A good summation of the ideal of performance budgeting is Marc Robinson and Duncan Last, *A Basic Model of Performance-Based Budgeting* (Washington, D.C.: International Monetary Fund, 2009).

[30]The effort to link performance is not limited to the United States: Organization for Economic Cooperation and Development, *Performance Budgeting in OECD Countries* (Paris: OECD, 2007).

focus on results is comparable to that of the private sector—auto companies manufacture cars to make a profit, not to buy materials (the focal point for traditional government budgets) or even simply to sell cars. While governments won't be expected to yield profits, they can be expected to produce beneficial results for society. The performance budget looks toward the *result,* or *outcome,* of agency operations and accordingly tests agencies on results, not on how results are attained (i.e., not on input use or operational management). Its performance, result, or outcome orientation flips the input control focus of traditional budgets on its head.

The ideal results-oriented performance budget would have sparse details on what the agency would purchase—the line items would not be controlled in plan or execution—because control would be on what services the agency would provide. Agencies might have some focus on operational outputs or tasks (for example, caseloads or miles of highway patrolled), but that would be for internal management, not for indicating agency performance success. Agencies would identify the outputs and outcomes to be produced by their programs, set performance targets and make budget requests based on that performance, and be accountable for those results without micromanagement of inputs or operations. By focusing on results, governments could become more responsive to the interests of the citizenry; by allowing greater flexibility, governments could become more entrepreneurial and efficient in service delivery.

New performance budgeting integrates information on government outcome performance into the budget process and involves these principles:

1. **Objectives/strategic plan.** The agency should state what it is trying to accomplish that matters for the citizenry. In part, the agency develops a strategic plan (Sidebar 6–2, an outline of the Government Performance and Results Act of 1993 [GPRA], shows the requirements for federal agency strategic plans), but it must also consider why it exists in the first place. Annual performance plans and annual budgets are to be linked to the strategic plan, but the thinking about existence (and its justification) comes first.[31] The strategic plan should show how the agency intends to achieve results.

2. **Performance measures.** From that strategic plan must be developed measures that will gauge progress toward meeting these objectives. Performance measurement should provide the connection between the strategic plan and the results. The measures, however, are to focus not on agency activities, but on the agency's broader societal consequences. Budget processes focus on inputs (the resources purchased by the agency) or direct outputs (the agency's activities or tasks); the performance budget measures outcomes (the results or the extent to which agency activities have their intended effect). Executive budgets would include these planned performance standards, as would the approved appropriations. Table 6–3 illustrates the activity (direct output) to outcome shift for several basic government functions. Some performance measures can be observed from existing social, economic, demographic, or health status data,

---

[31]The National Aeronautics and Space Administration states that the goal of the Space Science Program is to "chart the evolution of the universe from origin to destiny." Performance measures would likely not be easy to spin from this goal.

Sidebar 6–2
The Basic Elements of the Government Performance and Results Act of 1993,
Public Law 103–62

The Government Performance and Results Act (GPRA) seeks to reduce inefficiency and ineffectiveness in government programs by directing attention to agency performance and results. The Act has three important elements:

A. Multiyear (three- to five-year) strategic plans that identify the fundamental mission of the agency, the general goals that will be used to accomplish the mission, and resource requirements consistent with the mission. Strategic plans are to be updated at least every three years. The Act provides for the following required parts of the strategic plan:

(1) a comprehensive mission statement covering the major functions and operations of the agency;
(2) general goals and objectives, including outcome-related goals and objectives, for the major functions and operations of the agency;
(3) a description of how the goals and objectives are to be achieved, including a description of the operational processes, skills and technology, and the human, capital, information, and other resources required to meet those goals and objectives;
(4) a description of how the performance goals included in the plan required by section 1115(a) of title 31 shall be related to the general goals and objectives in the strategic plan;
(5) an identification of those key factors external to the agency and beyond its control that could significantly affect the achievement of the general goals and objectives; and
(6) a description of the program evaluations used in establishing or revising general goals and objectives, with a schedule for future program evaluations. (5 U.S.C. § 306)

B. Annual performance plans that drive day-to-day operations. The plans include objective, quantitative, and measurable performance goals: measurable indicators to determine whether programs are meeting goals: and a summary of funding and staffing resources being used to achieve the goals. The plans are expected to link to the strategic plan.

C. Annual performance reports to be made six months after the end of the fiscal year to relevant committees and subcommittees for evaluating the agency record. The report is based on achievement of planned measurable performance indicators.

The intent was that these performance activities would link into a performance budget process and that federal appropriations would be made on a more rational basis. As a federal law, GPRA has had considerably greater staying power than budget systems established by presidents for development of their executive budgets. However, the president is free to develop the executive budget without paying any attention to GPRA.

---

but some may require new tests or surveys to gauge performance. The three principles that the Health Care Financing Administration uses to guide its national performance measurement strategy give good standards for any agency: (a) measures should be consumer driven, (b) measures and the collection tools used to obtain them should be in the public domain to assure broad access and validation, and (3) content and collection of measures should be standardized. Agencies face greater pressure in the budget process to show improvement in

Table 6–3
Outputs (Activities or Tasks) versus Outcomes (Results)

One of the most difficult tasks in measuring government performance is that of identifying what performance to measure. The concept of inputs is easy to understand, and their measurement does not differ much from one program or department to another. Inputs are the resources, such as labor, building materials, utilities, and so on, that go into the production of government services. They are measured the same whether they are purchases by the fire department or by the department of environmental protection. There are more problems with regard to outputs and outcomes.

Outputs are the tasks that agencies perform as they go about their business. They are not ends in themselves, but are intermediate measures leading toward achieving the objectives of the organization. Indicators of output focus on the amount of measured work accomplished or on the quality of the processes used to accomplish that work. It is expected that the outputs are working toward the agency's intended purpose.

Outcomes are the final desirable results that the agency hopes to accomplish. They are results that directly contribute to the objectives of the agency and represent measures of the agency's reason for existence.

The following material gives some examples of outputs and outcomes (or results) for a number of government functions.

Fire Department

Outputs: inspections performed, fire calls answered, arson investigations performed, hours of educational programs offered, property value protected in service area

Outcomes: ISO fire insurance rating, dollars of fire loss (negative), number of fire-related injuries and fatalities (negative), number of traffic accidents during fire runs, number of reported and unreported fires

Police Department

Outputs: hours on patrol, responses to calls for assistance, crimes investigated by category, number of arrests, police officer presentations to school children

Outcomes: deaths, injuries, and property losses from crime in service area, crime clearance rate, citizen complaints about officer abuse

Elementary and Secondary Education

Outputs: instructional days, students promoted or graduated

Outcomes: test score results, parent/student satisfaction ratings, percent of graduates employed

Public Health

Outputs: number of persons served, number of vaccinations given, number of restaurant inspections, training program days

Outcomes: mortality rates, morbidity rates, cases of infectious diseases by category

Table 6–3
(continued)

Public Welfare

Outputs: number of clients, number of clients by type of assistance category

Outcomes: former clients leaving the welfare system

Solid-Waste Management

Outputs: waste collected and processed, residences served, miles of road cleaned

Outcomes: proportion of streets rated as clean, incidence of vector-borne disease, citizen satisfaction ratings, achievement of environmental standard

Tax Department

Outputs: returns processed, processing time, delinquency rates

Outcomes: overall compliance rate, taxpayer complaint rates, measured uniformity of treatment of taxpayers

Environmental Protection and Management

Outputs: permits granted, inspections performed

Outcomes: percent of state residents living where air quality meets state or federal standard, percent of groundwater that meets drinking water standard, release and generation of solid waste as percent of baseline year

Juvenile Justice

Outputs: number of children in the system, worker caseload

Outcomes: juvenile justice recidivism rate, juvenile justice system clients leaving system for school or employment

Employment Training Program

Outputs: number of trainees in class, number of hours taught

Outcomes: number of placements in improved employment

their performance results. The focus is intended to be on performance outcomes, not performance outputs—not the number of passengers subjected to search by the Transportation Safety Administration, silver-haired grandmothers, infants, and all, but whether flying is safer from terrorist threats. If you can't find real terrorists to test the performance, the success at finding weapons brought in by testers from the GAO would be a good proxy.

There are six critical principles in selecting outcome performance measures:

a. *External focus.* The measure should relate to the client or customer, not to internal procedures of the agency.

b. *Truly measurable.* It should be possible to gauge success or failure and whether performance is improving, deteriorating, or staying the same.

c. *Outcome based.* It should measure service delivery to the citizenry rather than impact within the entity.

d. *Significant.* The measure should encompass the full scope of agency work so that a complete idea of success is portrayed.

e. *Manageable.* The number of measures should be no greater than necessary to cover the scope of agency operations. There should be no danger of user overload. For the integration of performance measurement and budgets, cost must be tied to performance, and the capacity for good costing is not limitless.

f. *Verified.* Measures should be independently verifiable if not produced by a third party. If the measure matters in the allocation of funds, there will be a temptation to cheat.

Getting the measures right is extremely important for the functioning of a results-driven budget system, as Campbell's Law makes clear: "The more any quantitative social indicator is used for social decision-making, the more subject it will be to corruption and the more apt it will be to distort and corrupt the social processes it is intended to monitor."[32] Choosing the wrong measures is worse than having no measures at all, and choosing measured targets that are easy to achieve does little to further agency efficiency.

3. **Flexible execution.** Agencies, after appropriations are received, are responsible for service delivery. They should not be constrained by the narrow control of how resources get used during budget execution (the details of spending) that is the hallmark of traditional accountability. Accountability should focus on outcomes, not expenditures. Both executive and legislative branches would need to agree on places and measures (points 1 and 2) for this flexibility. Agencies might also be allowed to retain at least some portion of unexpended funds for use in upcoming fiscal years, rather than following the traditional practice of having unspent funds returned to the general treasury, so that agencies would not face the "use it or lose it" choice.[33]

4. **Reporting.** At the end of the year, agency reports emphasize service outcomes with their financial reports. Audit and evaluation emphasize outcomes and deemphasize details of how money was spent. Ideally, agencies would have received lump-sum appropriations, without any itemization about how the money is to be spent, so the resource utilization plan against which actual use would be tested would be largely aggregate in any case. The federal Chief Financial Officers Act of 1990 requires financial officers to develop and report *systematic measures of performance* for their agencies. At the state and local levels, the Government Accounting Standard Board (GASB) seeks to have annual financial statements include a *service efforts and*

---

[32]Donald T. Campbell, "Assessing the Impact of Planned Social Change," in *Social Research and Public Policies,* ed. G. M. Lyons (Hanover, N.H.: The Public Affairs Center, Dartmouth College, 1976), 54.
[33]A strong internal-control structure is necessary if agencies are to have greater flexibility regarding their finances. A strong control structure frees auditors to focus on performance rather than financial issues.

accomplishments (SEA) report. Both emphasize performance measurement in terms of outcomes. Performance measures for individual agencies appear in the budget documents of well over half the states and many cities, although the extent to which responsibility and control focus on these measures, as opposed to the input categories, is generally limited.[34] Systems often continue to measure direct outputs (or activities), not outcomes.

Figure 6–6 illustrates the integration of performance measures into a budget presentation with a display for the Iowa Department of Public Safety in the 2013

Figure 6-6
Performance Measures in the Iowa State Budget, Department of Public Safety, Fiscal 2013

Measure	FY 2011 Actuals Achieved	FY 2012 Current Year Budget Estimate Target	FY 2013 Total Department Request Target	FY 2013 Total Governor's Recommended Target
Number of ISP Narcotics Arrests	1,561	1,100	1,100	1,100
Percent of Sex Offender Registry Records Validated w/in 3 Mo	100	100	100	100
Number of Narcotics Awareness & Education Programs Delivered	16	20	20	20
% of Sex Offender Registry Records Revalidated w/in 12 mo.	100	100	100	100
Drug Trafficking Orgs Disrupted	79	80	80	80
Pharmaceutical Diversion Investigations	21	30	30	30
Interdiction Investigations	35	30	30	30
SOR Email Notification	4,522	3,100	3,100	3,100
Number of Motorists Assisted	22,306	20,000	20,000	20,000
Rate Alcohol-related Fatals per 100 Million Miles Traveled	0.23	0.34	0.34	0.34
Rate Serious Injury Crashes per 100 Million Miles Traveled	4.16	6.3	6.3	6.3
Number of Responses to Clan Labs	34	35	35	35

(continues)

[34]Melkers and Willoughby find that all but three states require strategic planning regarding agency mission, goals, and objectives and a process that requires measurable data on program outcomes. See "The State of the States: Performance-Based Budgeting Requirements in 47 out of 50," *Public Administration Review* 58 (January/February 1998): 66–79.

Figure 6–6

Performance Measures in Iowa State Budget, Department of Public Safety, Fiscal 2013 (continued)

Financial Summary

Object Category	FY 2011 Actuals	FY 2012 Current Year Budget Estimate	FY 2013 Total Department Request	FY 2013 Total Governor's Recommended
Resources				
State Appropriations	86,967,527	90,924,963	95,924,963	95,924,963
Receipts from Other Entities	29,644,243	41,233,959	40,674,702	40,674,702
Interest, Dividends, Bonds & Loans	14,283,184	5,289,575	5,291,475	5,291,475
Fees, Licenses & Permits	19,033,736	5,593,296	5,730,756	5,730,756
Refunds & Reimbursements	17,011,211	14,243,225	13,143,225	13,143,225
Sales, Rents & Services	9,575	6,000	6,000	6,000
Miscellaneous	177,152	390,500	390,500	390,500
Beginning Balance and Adjustments	248,156,524	256,958,991	244,961,586	246,908,914
Total Resources	415,283,153	414,640,509	406,123,207	408,070,535
Expenditures				
Personal Services	85,890,257	90,899,011	90,844,180	90,840,989
Travel & Subsistence	9,251,350	7,524,162	7,470,162	7,470,162
Supplies & Materials	2,091,400	1,933,505	1,923,763	1,923,763
Contractual Services and Transfers	22,102,255	26,248,033	31,518,895	31,321,834
Equipment & Repairs	4,561,088	6,109,395	5,464,232	5,464,232
Claims & Miscellaneous	3,882,025	3,559,542	3,347,942	3,347,942
Licenses, Permits, Refunds & Other	35,659	49,770	48,270	48,270
State Aid & Credits	20,366,878	21,022,468	20,000,520	20,000,520
Plant Improvements & Additions	50,000	50,000	50,000	50,000
Budget Adjustments	0	0	0	(1,370,551)
Appropriations	9,793,589	10,335,709	10,335,709	10,335,709
Reversions	299,664	0	0	0
Balance Carry Forward	256,958,989	246,908,914	235,119,534	238,637,665
Total Expenditures	415,283,153	414,640,509	406,123,207	408,070,535
Full-Time Equivalents	941	946	953	953

Figure 6-6
(continued)

Appropriations from General Fund

Appropriations	FY 2011 Actuals	FY 2012 Current Year Budget Estimate	FY 2013 Total Department Request	FY 2013 Total Governor's Recommended
Public Safety Administration	4,007,075	4,007,075	4,007,075	4,007,075
Public Safety DCI	12,533,931	12,533,931	12,533,931	12,533,931
DCI - Crime Lab Equipment/Training	302,345	302,345	302,345	302,345
Public Safety Undercover Funds	109,042	109,042	109,042	109,042
Narcotics Enforcement	6,429,884	6,429,884	6,429,884	6,429,884
DPS Fire Marshal	4,298,707	4,298,707	4,298,707	4,298,707
Iowa State Patrol	48,505,765	51,903,233	51,903,233	51,903,233
DPS/SPOC Sick Leave Payout	279,517	279,517	279,517	279,517
Fire Fighter Training	612,255	725,520	725,520	725,520
DPS-POR Unfunded Liabilities Until 85 Percent	0	0	5,000,000	5,000,000
DPS-POR Permissive Service Credit Purchase	95,417	0	0	0
Total Public Safety, Department of	77,173,938	80,589,254	85,589,254	85,589,254

Appropriations from General Fund

Appropriations	FY 2011 Actuals	FY 2012 Current Year Budget Estimate	FY 2013 Total Department Request	FY 2013 Total Governor's Recommended
DPS Gaming Enforcement - 0030	9,793,589	10,335,709	10,335,709	10,335,709
Total Public Safety, Department of	9,793,589	10,335,709	10,335,709	10,335,709

SOURCE: Iowa State Budget for Fiscal Year, 2013.

state budget. The presentation includes the department mission statement and a short description of the department and its divisions. It then provides performance measures—mostly outcomes, but some activities—with performance targets and comparisons with prior years. The second part of the presentation is a standard object-of-expenditure presentation. These are standard features for a performance budget of the current style and represent a good example in terms of bringing all information together and providing outcome-oriented performance measures. Appropriation acts in Texas include performance indicators, both output and outcome varieties, directly in the law; the result is too large to summarize with an illustration here, but can be seen on the state website.

Although some states, localities, and national governments in countries such as Australia, New Zealand, the United Kingdom, and Canada, and even the United Nations, have been more aggressive than the U.S. federal government in their use of results-oriented budgeting, there have been efforts under way for some time. The Chief Financial Officers Act of 1990 requires financial officers of federal agencies to develop and report systematic measures of performance for their agencies, and, even stronger, GPRA (P.L. 103–62) directs agencies to develop strategic plans, to measure their performance, and, at least tentatively, to work toward performance budgets. In this context, performance budgeting means the process of linking results to budget levels, not the cost of activities in the traditional performance budgets.[35] GPRA documents, easily accessible on the Internet, give excellent illustrations of materials developed for outcome performance measurement.

Some Challenges for New Performance Budgeting

Moving the budgetary focus away from an input orientation seems to be getting it right for making public decisions. Nevertheless, there are some crucial concerns in this important transition:

1. **The need for agreement on what is to be accomplished.** The mission statement of the agency is the place to start when defining measures for the performance budget. What agencies are supposed to do is not always clear. Managers have to respond to elected executives, legislative bodies, and the general public. Programs often have multiple and conflicting objectives and disagreements about the relative importance of the objectives. Without strong consensus about agency objectives, establishing performance measurement and budget systems based on those measures will be difficult, and legislatures will continue to insist on riders to constrain agency operations. Furthermore, there has to be agreement on the need to spend the money necessary to measure performance. Measurement is a nagging problem.

   In addition, focused measures can be a problem. As a pilot agency under GPRA, the Internal Revenue Service (IRS) developed strategic goals and performance measures to guide its operations. The IRS sought to increase its

---

[35]General Accounting Office, *Performance Budgeting, Past Initiatives Offer Insights for GPRA Implementation,* GAO/AIMD-97-46 (Washington, D.C.: General Accounting Office, 1997).

collection performance to at least 90 percent of total taxes due through a mix of increased voluntary compliance and enforcement. It also sought public satisfaction with the conduct of the IRS in terms of ethical behavior, fairness, and uniformity of application of tax laws. The agency proceeded with aggressive pursuit of these objectives, and soon congressional hearings showed dissatisfaction with zealous efforts to improve compliance and media accounts of taxpayer harassment. The IRS abandoned its performance measures.[36] Now it works with "balanced measures" to guide its work: customer satisfaction (provide accurate and professional services to internal and external customers in a courteous, timely manner), employee satisfaction (create an enabling environment for employees by providing quality leadership, adequate training, and effective support services), and business results (generate a productive quantity of work in a quality manner and provide meaningful outreach to all customers). With these measures, it is hard to know that the IRS is actually a tax collection enterprise! So much for the value of precision in defining missions, goals, and performance, at least for tax collectors.

Experience with new performance budgeting has taught that all stakeholders—the executive branch, the legislature, the citizenry, and community leaders—should agree on the performance measures if the system is to have the most impact on spending outcomes. However, even without that agreement, the executive branch can very effectively use its own performance system for creating its budget, which may or may not be seen as helpful by the legislature.

2. **Performance budgets do not cross agencies.** Outcome measures give minimal guidance in comparisons among agencies, in other words, in answering the traditional budget allocation question: "How much to agency A, and how much to agency B?" There is no standard performance measure or yardstick that makes sense for all agencies, the causal link between agency effort and performance outcome differs dramatically among agencies, and the ease of measuring outcomes varies widely among agencies. The results orientation can give guidance within each department, but government budgets have to allocate between departments, not just within. For example, results orientation in Transportation and results orientation in Natural Resources do not help with resource allocation choices between Transportation and Natural Resources—and failure to achieve results in Transportation is as likely to signal a need for better management of existing resources in Transportation as it is to signal a need for a reduction in those resources. Simply taking funds from agencies that fail to meet performance targets and giving the funds to those that do makes no sense. Suppose, for instance, that the Department of Homeland Security did not meet its targets, while the National Endowment for the Arts (NEA) did. Would Congress move funds between agencies on that basis? Or would it be reasonable to continue to pay attention to basic national priorities, which likely still rank homeland security above the programs of the

---

[36]Brian Friel, "IRS Learns Results Act Lesson," *GovExec.com Daily Briefing,* September 16, 1998 [http://www.gov-exec.com/dailyfed/0998/091698b1.htm].

NEA? Should funds for homeland security decrease, or should they increase, based on the missed performance target?

3. **Cost must be tracked.** Government accounting systems need to provide cost information that can be linked to outputs or activities that generate particular outcomes. Decisions need appropriate measures of outcomes that can be linked to outputs that track to appropriate measures of input (or resource cost). Even with better tracking, including the use of ABC, a fair amount of the cost of government—policy formation, information technology, and general administration, for instance—is not associated with any particular activity and cannot fairly be assigned.[37] In addition, some costs are fixed and will not be reduced if a program is reduced or eliminated. Will the cost of having the mayor around be reduced if the curbside recycling program, toward which the mayor devoted some time, is eliminated?

4. **Responsibility without control.** Agencies find results-oriented goals to be difficult to accept because they correctly understand that many measured performance outcomes may be outside their control. They do not want to be held responsible for objectives that they can only influence. They prefer to focus on activities or outputs because these can be controlled. Until agencies, budget offices, legislatures, and the public can come to an understanding on what results agencies can really be responsible for, the movement toward results orientation will be slow. For example, diligent effort by a local job-development agency can control the number of trainees run through its seminars, but many environmental conditions—especially overall economic conditions—determine how many of those graduates end up in lasting employment from any annual crop of graduates. Great effort by local schools may produce dismal educational results if parents and the community do not cooperate in the learning process. Agencies are reluctant to be responsible for objectives that they cannot fully control. In addition, no participants in the process are likely to pay much real attention to measured performance unless they have an incentive to do so, that is, unless budget decisions are actually made on the basis of the performance outcome measures.

5. **Trust and no micromanagement.** New performance budgeting requires a different relationship between operating agencies and legislatures. If the agency is to be flexible in its service delivery and to be responsible for results instead of input use, then the legislature must leave it alone. For example, Congress should not dictate which installations it is to close (the Defense Department and Congress, for instance, do not agree on which military bases—inputs to the provision of national security—are redundant to national security) and should not place other restrictions on how the agency uses its resources. Those are input-oriented requirements, the antithesis of a results orientation. Some financial controls need to be relaxed, and agencies need the flexibility to reallocate funds freely. It is sometimes suggested that, because elected officials find micromanagement hard to resist, they ought not to be provided line-item expenditure information at all. It is not at all

---

[37]Retirement, health insurance, capital expenditure, and similar costs can and should be tracked to their source agency programs. But this involves better tracking, not allocation of the unallocable.

clear that the advantages of flexibility can accrue unless there is considerable trust between branches of government.

6. **Refocused audit.** Audit can no longer focus on financial detail. Agencies would be responsible for the sum appropriated, but the detailed use of those appropriations, within the normal laws of financial propriety, would no longer be an oversight concern. Attention would be directed to performance measurement, achievement of outcome expectations, and audit of the performance measurement and reporting process, not to the details of how money was spent. However, the need for accountability means that the appropriation must be made to the agency—ideally, agencies would be accountable for appropriated sums of money and for agreed-upon performance measures, but for no other expenditure details.

7. **Information overload.** When performance measurement becomes an element in the budget process, large quantities of information will be produced. More measures will get introduced and measurement will become more important in actually making decisions. Everyone wants his or her own favorite included when measures start to matter. Experience in the states shows that decision makers become overloaded with the details and find it difficult to locate what would be useful to them. This potential overload means that it is critical to have a distillation process to outline and summarize the most important elements for the decision makers. An effort must be made to limit the measures that are collected and reported to a manageable and useful number. One or two good measures are far more useful than a laundry list of ones that are not so good. Just because the agency has a particular measure does not mean that it should report it.

8. **Outcome measurement.** In practice, outcome measurement is not easy for all government agencies, and many units eventually resort to output, not outcome, indicators. Frequently, client satisfaction surveys are part of the measurement process to gauge the quality of service provided.[38] In general, an outcome orientation increases the administrative expense because some outcome measures are unlikely to emerge from the normal flow of agency operations. Every agency dreads the prospect of more data collection, and there are questions of interpretation. For instance, if tax audits find few mistakes, should that be taken as evidence of poor performance by the tax auditors or evidence of success in the tax authority's efforts to induce taxpayers to pay voluntarily without being audited? Are low arrest rates evidence of little crime or poor police work? Perhaps the most basic concern is with honest measurement. When appropriations are at stake and measures are self-reported, mischief is a concern. In Texas, the State Auditor's Office does periodic reviews to determine whether agencies have adequate systems for

---

[38]Some governments, both in the United States and internationally, conduct citizen "report card" surveys of satisfaction with particular public services. Along with being an element in performance budget processes, they also contribute to campaigns for more open governance, accountability, and control of corruption. The International City/County Management Association conducts "citizen surveys" on contract for local jurisdictions to assist with such evaluation measurement.

[39]Government Accountability Office, *Performance Budgeting: States' Experience Can Inform Federal Efforts,* GAO-05-215 (Washington, D.C.: Government Accountability Office 2005).

collecting performance measures and whether measures are reported accurately.[39] Not all reports are accurate. For example, high-stakes testing in Atlanta public schools with fiscal consequences from the results appears to have caused rampant cheating, and some follow-up analysis suggests that the problem is actually national in scope.[40] In addition, exaggerated performance indicators when money is involved are not just an American problem: countries being paid by the Global Alliance for Vaccines and Immunizations for improved immunization rates in children appear to have received twice as much as they should have in recent decades because actual rates were exaggerated.[41] Unaudited, self-reported information is the worst option of all for high-stakes performance measurement.

There is much optimism about what can be gained from the new performance budgeting and the focusing of budget decisions on results. But experience indicates a need for some wariness. The PPBS experiment in the 1960s and the ZBB system of the 1970s were results-oriented systems, as were various efforts at establishing Management by Objective (MBO) systems in government.[42] None brought lasting, systematic reform in how governments budget, although each experiment left some positive residual. The new results-oriented budget focus has brought revisions in how all levels of government develop and present their budgets; vastly greater attention to measurement, testing, and citizen satisfaction surveys; and, most important, greater focus on outcomes or results. As with any other system for budgeting, a performance budgeting system may not remain in place for the long term. For instance, a number of states that have instituted performance-driven budgeting and funding for higher education (significant because of the importance of this service in overall state finances) have ended such systems after only a few years for various reasons, including loss of political support and support from the institutions, lack of interest from the business community, and declines in education funding.[43] Seldom do systems do either as much as their advocates claim or as little as their opponents argue. Whether much will change in terms of real government performance and allocation of budget resources remains an open question. As Hilton and Joyce observe, "the development of better performance and cost information can itself spur greater attention to performance, even in places where an input focus has been ascendant. Transparency concerning the relationship between funding and results can shine a light on practices that result in failing to allocate resources toward desired societal ends."[44]

---

[40]Heather Vogell, "Investigation into APS Cheating Finds Unethical Behavior across Every Level," *Atlanta Journal Constitution,* July 6, 2011; and Heather Vogell, John Perry, Alan Judd, and M. B. Pell, "Cheating Our Children: Suspicious Test Scores across the Nation," *Atlanta Journal Constitution,* March 25, 2012.

[41]David Brown, "Number of Children Immunized Has Been Inflated for Years," *Washington Post,* December 12, 2008, A-3.

[42]General Accounting Office, *Performance Budgeting, Past Initiatives Offer Insights for GPRA Implementation,* GAO/AIMD-97-46 (Washington, D.C.: General Accounting Office, 1997).

[43]Kevin J. Dougherty and Rebecca S. Natow, "The Demise of Higher Education Performance Funding Systems in Three States," Community College Research Center CCRC Brief No. 41, May 2009.

[44]Rita M. Hilton and Philip G. Joyce, "Performance Information and Budgeting in Historical and Comparative Perspective," in *Handbook of Public Administration,* ed. B. Guy Peters and Jon Pierre (London: Sage Publications, 2003), 411. So does it work? For an international assessment, see Marc Robinson and Jim Brumby, "Does Performance Budgeting Work? An Analytical Review of the Empirical Literature," International Monetary Fund Working Paper WP/05/210, Washington, D.C., 2005.

Federal Integration of Performance and Budgeting: The Budget and Performance Integration Initiative and the Program Assessment Rating Tool

The most complete implementation of performance budgeting in the development of an executive budget was the use of the Program Assessment Rating Tool (PART) system by the administration of President George W. Bush.[45] The PART process, an effort to integrate performance measurement and budgeting, was an integral part of federal budget development from the fiscal 2003 budget until the fiscal 2009 budget. (President Bush did not submit a fiscal 2010 budget, and President Obama did not use the PART system in his eventual 2010 submission or in later years.) Even though the system is no longer used in the federal government, it is worth considering because, first, it is the most complete formal linkage between program performance and funding proposals in a budget presentation and, second, some performance measurement elements of the system remain in agency budget development systems. The first federal budget developed using PART explained that the process "asks not merely 'How much?'; it endeavors to explain 'How well?'"[46] Overall, the initiative had a results orientation and a zero-based philosophy, and it expected federal programs to bear the burden of proof in demonstrating that they were achieving results in the most effective and efficient way. The specific objectives were, as outlined in the fiscal 2006 budget, (a) "increasing accountability, effectiveness, and efficiency—implementing plans designed to improve the management and performance of programs"; (b) "investing in high pay-off or high priority activities—focusing on programs that can achieve demonstrably greater results for the same or less cost"; and (c) "improving program design—developing, enacting, and implementing legislative or other proposals to fix flaws identified through the Program Assessment Rating Tool (PART) that impede performance."[47] The system sought to link requested resources to strategic and programmatic outcomes, to shift focus from expense items to resource allocation based on program goals and measured results, to identify full costs of program activities to link them to goals, and, overall, to move beyond inputs and outputs to outcomes.

The PART process involved the systematic application of a series of questions about each program of the federal government (there were scores for more than 1,000 programs). These are some of the questions that each program review asked:

Does the program address a specific and existing problem, interest, or need?

Is the program designed so that it is not redundant or duplicative of any other federal, state, local, or private effort?

---

[45]Federal budget process innovations tend to get copied by a number of states and localities. That was the case for both PPBS (the forerunner of PPBES) and ZBB. PART had less spread. Indiana has used the PROBE (Program Results: an Outcome-Based Evaluation) system for budget development (the governor was OMB director when PART was implemented), and Illinois has developed the SMART (Strategic Management Assessment Rating Tool) for assistance in budget development. The PART structure appears not to have spread to other jurisdictions.

[46]Office of Management and Budget, *Budget of the United States Government, Fiscal 2003* (Washington, D.C.: U.S. Government Printing Office, 2002), 5.

[47]Office of Management and Budget, *Budget of the United States Government, Fiscal Year 2006, Analytical Perspectives* (Washington, D.C.: U.S. Government Printing Office, 2005), 2.

Does the program have a limited number of specific long-term performance measures that focus on outcomes and meaningfully reflect the purpose of the program?

Does the program have ambitious targets and time frames for its long-term measures?

Does the program (including program partners) achieve its annual performance goals?

Are independent evaluations of sufficient scope and quality conducted on a regular basis or as needed to support program improvements and evaluate effectiveness and relevance to the problem, interest, or need?

Are budget requests explicitly tied to accomplishment of the annual and long-term performance goals, and are the resource needs presented in a complete and transparent manner in the program's budget?

Does the program use strong financial management practices?

Has the program demonstrated adequate progress in achieving its long-term performance goals?

Does the program demonstrate improved efficiencies or cost-effectiveness in achieving program goals each year?[48]

Each question produced a yes or no answer and was accompanied by a brief explanation of the answer and a short presentation of the evidence upon which the answer was based. Overall, the questions focused on four general sections: (1) whether the program had a clear purpose and was well designed to meet its objectives; (2) whether the program had a strategic plan with valid annual and long-term goals; (3) rating the management of the program, including its financial oversight and program improvement efforts; and (4) the results that the program could report with accuracy and consistency. Answers to the questions in each section were scored from 1 to 100 and led to a program rating of effective, moderately effective, adequate, ineffective, or results not demonstrated (the last for programs lacking agreed-upon performance measures or having inadequate baseline or performance data). Scores for each section were weighted in the final evaluation with these weights: program purpose and design, 20 percent; strategic planning, 10 percent; program management, 20 percent; and results/accountability, 50 percent. This system focused on *summary performance* measures, not the direct measures discussed earlier (e.g., percent of days with clean air), although the focus is on evaluated performance.

The process was intended as an exercise in developing a results orientation, in linking performance and budgets, and in providing transparency in the evaluation system (all scores were available through the OMB website).

Figure 6–7 illustrates the PART system with the Cultural Resource Stewardship program of the National Park Service of the Department of Interior. This program seeks to protect and preserve historic structures, archaeological sites, museum objects, and other cultural resources in the national parks. The figure identifies the performance measures for the program (the presentation identifies them according to whether they are outcomes, outputs, or efficiency improvements); the full display

---

[48]Sample questions from ExpectMore.gov, an Office of Management and Budget website [http://www.whitehouse.gov/omb/expectmore/partquestions.html].

Figure 6–7
Program Performance Measures in the PART Process: Cultural Resources Stewardship Program of National Park Service, 2008 Report

Type of Measure	Measure
Outcome	Percent of historic and prehistoric structures in good condition
Outcome	Percent of preservation and protection standards met at park museum facilities
Outcome	Percent of recorded archeological sites in good condition
Outcome	Percent of cultural landscapes in good condition
Output	Percent of historic and prehistoric structures that have complete and accurate inventory information
Output	Percent of museum objects catalogued and submitted to the National Catalog
Efficiency	Average cost to catalog a museum object
Outcome	Condition of all NPS historic buildings as measured by a Facility Condition Index.

SOURCE: Office of Management and Budget, Detailed Information in the National Park Service – Cultural Resource Stewardship Assessment [http://georgewbush-whitehouse.archives.gov/omb/expectmore/detail/10002356.2004.html]

provides the questions and answers to the PART questions for the program. This program received PART scores in the four rating sections of 100 percent, 75 percent, 57 percent, and 53 percent for an evaluation of adequate.[49] Scores were reported for each program of each agency, and they became one factor in developing the president's budget proposal. They were intended to give insights into how the federal government could improve what it does for the citizenry and to generate program improvements through recommendations made in the PART process.

The process was internal to the executive branch, although its results were transparent to all. It did move the focus of budget development aggressively toward agency performance in ways never done before. And the years in which the PART process was in place did show an improvement in program performance, at least as measured by that process. Figure 6–8 shows considerable decline in the "results not demonstrated" category and considerable increase in the "effective" category. Whether these ratings improvements were the product of improved performance, gamesmanship on the part of program administrators, the work of consulting firms hired to boost the

---

[49]PART scores were once posted on an Office of Management and Budget website, along with funding levels for each program, in the interest of transparency, but the end to PART has brought an end to this easy access.

Figure 6-8
Improvements in PART Ratings over Time

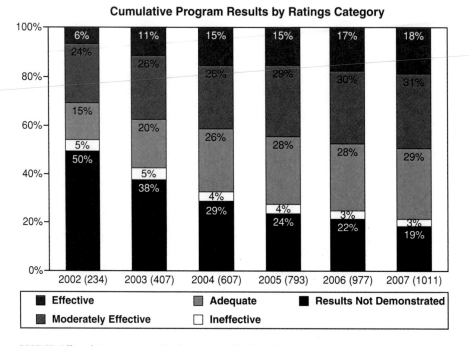

Cumulative Program Results by Ratings Category

	Effective		Adequate		Results Not Demonstrated
	Moderately Effective		Ineffective		

SOURCE: Office of Management and Budget, *Budget of the United States Government, Fiscal Year 2009, Analytical Perspectives* (Washington, D.C.: U.S. Government Printing Office, 2008).

scores, or grade inflation is beyond the scope of the present discussion. However, it is clear that program administrators paid close attention to the PART process.

What about its impact on the fiscal system, in other words, on presidential budgets and on Congress and appropriations? There have been evaluations from both inside and outside the federal government. The GAO has considered the PART impact more than once. In an assessment of its use in building the fiscal 2004 budget, very early in the life of PART, the GAO found that the tool highlighted recommended changes in program management and design, helped structure the use of performance information for OMB analysis, made the process more transparent, and focused agency attention on integration of performance and budgets. The GAO also noted that PART was not well integrated with GPRA, the statutory framework for strategic planning and reporting, and substituted its process for GPRA goals and measures, leaving a wide range of stakeholders out.[50] Later GAO work noted the focus that PART brought to performance measurement and program review in

---

[50]Government Accountability Office, *Performance Budgeting: Observations on the Use of OMB's Program Assessment Rating Tool for Fiscal Year 2004 Budget,* GAO-04-174 (Washington, D.C.: Government Accountability Office, 2004).

agencies and expressed a concern about getting Congress more involved in defining programs, goals and measures, and methodology.[51] A final GAO report found that the review process got agencies to increase their evaluation capacity to meet the needs of their programs, but not necessarily evaluation for broader objectives, and that a requirement for frequent evaluation may create superficial reviews of minimal use that overwhelm agency evaluation capacity.[52]

Evaluations from outside government also give useful insights into what PART was doing, although empirical analysis of impact is rare. A study by Gilmour and Lewis of the fiscal 2004 budget found that there was a modest connection between performance as measured by PART scores and OMB budget decisions and that the limited influence that appeared was on programs traditionally linked to Democrats. Merit seemed to matter only in regard to programs traditionally supported by the other party.[53] Frisco and Stalebrink found that Congress made only limited use of PART in its appropriation deliberations, although members were fully exposed to the scores and conceptually supported budgeting based on performance.[54] But the impact on federal appropriations is certainly unknown, just as its longer-term impact on the executive budget is unknown. What we know something about are the impacts on process.

So what happened to PART? Just as PPBS was a system for President Johnson and ZBB was a system for President Carter, PART was a system for President Bush. President Obama's first budget message said that his administration would reconfigure PART to open the process to the public, Congress, and outside experts: "The Administration will eliminate ideological performance goals and replace them with goals Americans care about and that are based on congressional intent and feedback from the people served by Government programs. Programs will not be measured in isolation, but assessed in the context of other programs that are serving the same population or meeting the same goals."[55] Through the 2013 budget, there has been no apparent replacement or refinement for PART. The budgetary wrinkle eventually introduced by the Obama administration is discussed in Sidebar 6–3.

Participatory Budgeting

Local, and sometimes state, budget processes include an opportunity for ordinary citizens to speak their mind about proposed expenditures before the legislative body votes to approve the budget. By that time, virtually all fiscal decisions will have been made,

---

[51]Government Accountability Office, *Performance Budgeting: PART Focuses Attention on Program Performance, but More Can Be Done to Engage Congress,* GAO-06-28 (Washington, D.C.: Government Accountability Office, 2005).

[52]Government Accountability Office, *Program Evaluation: OMB's PART Reviews Increased Agencies' Attention to Evidence of Program Results,* GAO-06-67 (Washington, D.C.: Government Accountability Office, 2005).

[53]John B. Gilmour and David E. Lewis, "Does Performance Budgeting Work? An Examination of the Office of Management and Budget's PART Scores," *Public Administration Review* 66 (September/October 2006): 742–51.

[54]Velda Frisco and Odd J. Stalebrink, "Congressional Use of the Program Assessment Rating Tool," *Public Budgeting & Finance* 28 (Summer 2008): 1–19.

[55]Office of Management and Budget, *Fiscal Year 2010 President's Budget—Overview: A New Era of Responsibility: Renewing America's Promise* (Washington, D.C.: Office of Management and Budget, 2009), 39.

Sidebar 6-3
Evidence-Based Budgeting

The Office of Management and Budget directed federal agencies to prepare their requests for fiscal year 2014 using an "evidence based" structure. The idea was to require more attention to program evaluation in budget development. An OMB memorandum instructed that submissions should "include a separate section on agencies' most innovative uses of evidence and evaluation."[1] By evidence, the memo meant that agencies should employ program performance evaluations, rigorously conducted, as part of their budget development process. The direction was in conjunction with a directive to prepare discretionary budget requests that were 5 percent below totals for fiscal 2013.[2]

The directive invited agencies to develop new program evaluations that capitalized on administrative data or new technologies, linked to program waivers and performance partnerships, expanded evaluation efforts in existing programs, and provided systematic measurement of costs and cost per unit of outcome. The OMB sought to encourage agencies to use evidence to compare the cost-effectiveness of how they spent their money, including both funding across and within agencies.[3] Agencies were expected to employ such performance evidence in their grant programs of all types. Examples include Departments of Justice and Labor programs that provide payments only after successes have been shown ("Pay for Success"). Evidence was expected to be the basis for enforcement of criminal, environment, and workplace safety laws, with agency allocation and reallocation of resources based on what program evidence shows. Finally, agencies were expected to improve their capacity to conduct evaluation research.

While this instruction brings new emphasis, the effort to bring program effectiveness evidence into budget development (and, with luck, budget adoption) is certainly not new or particularly innovative. It was a part of program-planning-budgeting systems of the 1960s, zero-base budgeting in the 1970s, and President Bush's PART system of the 2000s. What may be notable in the instruction is that it encourages agencies to devote resources to evaluation (developing evidence) even as the agencies face diminished total funds. That direction of scarce resources may not be popular, given the normal agency interest in delivery of services to clientele, and using constrained budgets for evaluation must mean some sacrifice of service capacity.

The effort continues several elements of budget reform and restructuring: focus on outcomes, attention to performance, willingness to reallocate budgetary resources, and attention to effective allocation of scarce resources. The continuing problem is that the evidence about programs is fundamentally internal. That is, the effectiveness of a program is directed toward the achievement of its outcomes; for example, the program does or does not reduce infant mortality, and it does or does not achieve a reduction that is or is not better than an alternative way of reducing infant mortality. This information is critical in regard to establishing which programs might well be worth terminating or expanding in regard to approaches to reducing infant mortality. However, the information doesn't help cut across programs with different objectives—say, infant mortality versus adult literacy (and all the other valuable services provided by government). There is no common measure; the valuable outcomes come in different measures, and the outcomes accrue to different persons in society. Even with excellent program outcome information— that such and such program effectively achieves these desirable outcomes—the best that the evidence can do is inform the actual lawmakers. One hopes that chief executives will employ

---

**Sidebar 6–3
(continued)**

---

the information in crafting budgets, and one hopes that legislatures will employ the information in making appropriations, but the evidence itself will not make the determination. Hard political choices, not collection of useful information, continue to be the heart of effective budgeting.

[1]"Use of Evidence and Evaluation in the 2014 Budget," Memorandum to the Heads of Executive Departments and Agencies, M-12-14, May 18, 2012.

[2]"Fiscal Year 2004 Budget Guidance," Memorandum to the Heads of Executive Departments and Agencies, M-12-14, May 18, 2012.

[3]The attention toward identifying least-cost approaches focused on results within the budget development process has been an important element in some state systems. The state of Washington is regarded as a leader in this budget program-evaluation effort.

---

so it amounts to just telling the public what the decisions have been. It leaves minimal opportunity for meaningful citizen input. It means that choices are made by unelected government administrators and by elected representatives of the people, but that direct citizen impact on those choices will necessarily be felt only at the margins. With the state of communication technology, it should be possible to get the interests of the population more directly into the decision process.[56] The systems of participatory budgeting go beyond citizen hearings, access to budget documents on websites, or televising budget deliberations. They attempt to actually alter the fabric of the budget process to actively involve the citizenry early and often in each stage of the budget cycle. It doesn't work by plastering some new openness on the traditional systems.

Participatory budgeting systems integrate citizen input more fundamentally into the budget cycle, not just at the end of the legislative consideration phase. Participatory budgeting is a budget process in which many different stakeholders debate, prioritize, and monitor choices made about public expenditure so that ultimate choices are more transparently made, so that the process is more inclusive, and so that the results are more equitable. The system is characterized by direct citizen involvement early in the development of the budget, direct citizen involvement in the monitoring of budget execution, and formal engagement of civil society organizations in the budget process. Citizens and their local governments, in a process of prioritization and joint decision, together establish the final allocation of public expenditures. The stakeholders are broadly determined to include the general public, poor and vulnerable groups including women, private businesses, organized citizen groups, representative bodies, and, in developing and transition countries, donor groups. The process seeks a wide spectrum of views. The executive still presents the budget proposal to

---

[56]New England town hall meetings in which all the citizenry gather to make fiscal decisions might be seen as the ideal for public participation. However, the cost of assembly and the cost of reaching decisions make that model impractical and inefficient for larger governments.

a legislative body, and the legislative body still makes the final choice about putting the budget into law, but the public participates quite formally in the process. It seeks transparency, responsiveness, and broad representation in the budget process.

The participatory influence can be integrated into three stages of the budget process:

1. **Budget preparation**. Citizens participate in budget allocation according to priorities they have identified in meetings and workshops.
2. **Expenditure monitoring**. Citizens track whether spending is consistent with allocations made in the adopted budget and track the flow of funds to agencies responsible for the delivery of public services.
3. **Service-delivery**. Citizens monitor the quality and quantity of government services relative to the expenditures made for the services.

The main features of the process are the following:

1. Clearly defined regional boundaries within the territory of the government practicing participatory budgeting. In one of the most famous applications, the town of Porto Alegre, Brazil (population 1.4 million), is divided into sixteen regions for citizen meetings. These geographical structures are crucial for decision making and service monitoring.
2. Open meetings to discuss thematic issues (Porto Alegre has five areas: transportation; education, leisure, and culture; health and social welfare; economic development and taxation; and city organization and urban development), to decide strategic priorities, to develop action plans, and to monitor current results. Meetings occur both within the regions and according to the thematic issue areas. Priorities from these meetings complement the representative democratic structures. Tens of thousands of people are reported to participate in the Porto Alegre process, vastly more people than ever are directly involved in any local budget process in the United States (or most other places). Participants in these meetings receive information directly from operating departments and transmit their views directly to the agencies as budgets get developed. Budget discussions are live long before any formal budget hearings would be.
3. An annual cycle of participation, planning, and meeting to regularly involve the citizenry.
4. A budget decision process that brings the priorities in the regions directly into the development and approval of the budget. The Porto Alegre process is particularly focused on the public works section of the budget (or the investment budget).

The process can lead to more responsive and effective government, more equitable distribution of government services, greater consensus among the citizenry regarding government programs, stronger nongovernmental organizations, and improved support for government reforms and restructuring. It is particularly aimed at providing a voice for the traditionally underrepresented sections of the population and at controlling government corruption through openness and monitoring. It is a tool for good governance and effective decentralization of government.

However, even in the Porto Alegre case, noted as a considerable success, only about 1.5 percent of the population regularly participates in the process. How does this modest, self-selected group of people making fiscal decisions represent an improvement over a system in which freely and openly elected representatives make those decisions? Is it likely to get responsible fiscal decisions in a process that establishes spending programs without an equivalent discussion about how the programs will be paid for?

Countries in which some localities practice participatory budgeting include Albania, Brazil, Bolivia, the Czech Republic, Canada, Ireland, India, Uganda, the United Kingdom, Romania, and South Africa.[57] Some U.S. cities have brought direct citizen participation into parts of budget development and allocation. New York City provides one example. During the development of its 2013 budget, discretionary capital budget funds were set aside in some council districts for citizen allocation. Budget delegates selected in district assemblies prepared budget proposals for those funds, and district residents voted to select the specific proposals to include in the budget. A similar alderman district allocation process has been employed in some Chicago wards. In both these cases, the funds have been from allocations assigned council members for discretionary use in their districts, so getting greater direct citizen involvement both is feasible and likely represents improved allocation in the public interest. But these are not a process for developing and adopting a full city budget.[58] They do get the public more directly involved in public spending (one wonders if the budget delegates would be as enthusiastic about the spending if they were also being required to raise the money to finance the spending) than do traditional systems and make portions of the system more transparent than does posting city budget documents on a website.[59] To be explicit, the New York City and Chicago experiments involve citizen decisions about dividing the budgetary spoils distributed to local council districts, something like deciding the distribution of a political kickback in the fiscal process. Citizen decisions about this part of the budget are likely better than having distributions to political cronies, but the geographic split of city funds is itself questionable. These programs should not be confused with the full integration of public participation into the city budget process.

---

[57]Case studies of participatory budgeting experiences from around the world are discussed in Anwar Shah, ed., *Participatory Budgeting* (Washington, D.C.: World Bank, 2007).

[58]For more information about the application and outcomes of participatory budgeting, see Aimee L. Franklin and Carol Ebdon, "Are We All Touching the Same Camel? Exploring a Model of Participatory Budgeting," *American Review of Public Administration* 35 (June 2005): 168–85; and Yves Cabannes, "Participatory Budgeting: A Significant Contribution to Participatory Democracy," *Environment and Urbanization* 16 (April 2004): 27–46.

[59]Another approach to bringing service choice down to the community level is the business improvement district, a nonprofit organization of entities in an area that have privately organized to finance the provision of extra services to the area (policing, sanitation, beautification, etc.) without calling on existing local governments. The district members decide on what services are to be provided and how their cost will be divided among district members. They are spending their own money, not revenues raised by a larger government, as it the case in the participatory budget model.

Conclusion

Budget classifications away from the traditional try to improve the rationality of budget choices. None provides the complete solution to the budget problem—it is wrong to expect any system to provide judgments that must be made by people. These systems, however, try to organize information so that decision makers can make choices in a reasonable fashion. They arrange information in more usable ways than do traditional budgets and, in varying degrees, seek to increase the decision makers' flexibility. People will continue to make budget decisions, and that is appropriate; the useful organization of information and the erection of reasonable organizational incentives are the roles of budget systems.[60] Each of the structures described here can represent significant improvements over the traditional, line-item, administrative-unit structure—if executive, bureaucratic, and legislative branches choose to use them. Reluctance to participate on the part of any group can doom any structure. In addition, there is no magic bullet that will replace budget judgment and budget politics with science. Furthermore, government officials are not likely to find for agency evaluation a public-sector equivalent to the easily definable, measurable, and widely accepted indicators of performance that private-sector profitability comparisons afford. What budget classification reform can do is provide performance data and other information when political decisions are made and provide information that might contribute to discussions more likely to lead to better results for the general public. Any system that moves attention toward outcomes and toward achievement of those outcomes has a better chance of working in the public interest than does the traditional system.

QUESTIONS AND EXERCISES

1. Refer to question 1 from Chapter 5. What alternate budget-classification systems are possible for the School of Public Affairs at Enormous State University? Identify (a) the measurable performance activities, programs, and outcomes for which the School might be responsible, (b) the budget classifications you would prescribe for each, and (c) the problems you would encounter in assigning spending to the categories.

2. The new mayor of a midwestern city has developed a list of administration goals and objectives for the city: (a) establish effective government by incorpo-

---

[60]Embedded in most efforts to reclassify and reform government budgeting is the assumption that there is a clear understanding of the link between government spending and results or outcomes. This confidence is misplaced if it is cast too broadly. In the government-service area subjected to the greatest amount and intensity of study, primary and secondary education, Eric Hanushek's extensive and intensive review of 147 separately published studies leads him to the conclusion that "there is a consistency to the results: there appears to be no strong or systematic relationship between school expenditures and student performance. This is the case when expenditures are decomposed into underlying determinants and when expenditures are considered in the aggregate." Eric A. Hanushek, "The Economics of Schooling: Production and Efficiency in Public Schools," *Journal of Economic Literature* 24 (September 1986): 1162.

rating improved information systems and management practices; (b) improve intergovernmental cooperation for more effective, cost-effective service delivery; (c) build public support for administration priorities through two-way communication; (d) make timely investments in roads, utilities, sewers, parks and alternative transportation systems to encourage responsible growth and sustain a healthy economy; (e) maintain and improve the city as a place where people can live and work without fear; (f) protect the community's natural assets and enhance environmental quality; (g) work to improve the economic health of the city in an equitable manner for all citizens; (h) support and facilitate access to basic social services for all citizens; (i) establish a customer-driven city workplace; and (j) maintain and improve park services and facilities. Use this statement to structure both a program budget format and a new performance budget format for the city. For the latter, identify measurable performance indicators.

3. The U.S. Coast Guard has five central missions: search and rescue, preservation of national marine resources, enforcement of federal laws at sea, ship safety in American waters, and national defense. The first of these is recognized as its main job, but dealing with pollution and preserving marine resources takes the largest share of its budget.

   An article in *The Economist,* commenting on a 1999 budget request presentation by Admiral Robert Kramek (the request was for $2.77 billion), proclaimed:

   > He dwelt on something rare in the armed services: results. In the past four years, he proudly informed the legislators, the Coast Guard has saved 20,000 lives and $9.3 billion in property, seized 370,000 pounds of illicit drugs, interdicted (or assisted) 75,000 foreigners trying to enter America, reported 64,000 cases of marine pollution and checked 59,000 fishing boats for possible catch violations. "We're a model of better government at least cost," said the Admiral. ("The Coast Guard: Keeping All Channels Open," *The Economist* 12 [September 1998]: 28–29.)

   Discuss and answer the following questions:
   a. Did Admiral Kramek provide outcomes as envisioned by mission- or results-oriented performance budgeting? Explain your answer.
   b. From what you understand to be the Coast Guard mission, what sort of performance measures would you propose for use by the agency?
   c. How could we test whether Admiral Kramek is right when he asserts that the Coast Guard is delivering "better government at least cost"?
   d. What budgetary strategy is the admiral using, and what questions would you prepare for Admiral Kramek if you were on the staff of the appropriation subcommittee considering his request?

4. Select a government agency or a nonprofit organization. From documents available to you (budgets, financial reports, mission statements, legislation, media reporting, etc.) and your general knowledge about that entity, do the following: (a) identify the inputs used by the entity (personnel, contractual services, etc.), (b) identify the activities or outputs produced by the entity, and (c) identify the measurable performance outcomes of that entity. What new data systems (testing, sampling, surveying, etc.) might be necessary to produce the outcome measures? What environmental influences outside the easy control of the entity are

important in shaping those measured outcomes? What budget classification system or systems does the entity currently use in its budget processes?

5. Look for a city that has posted its traditional budget on its website. Using the information there, including descriptions of the work of its departments, identify the reclassifications that you believe to be necessary to create these two program budget categories: protection of persons, property, and the public order and provision of recreation and cultural opportunities.

6. The local historical society museum is hoping to receive a municipal operating subsidy to help it with its finances and keep from having to increase its modest admission charge. However, your municipality expects each budget entity to include outcome-oriented performance measures with every budget request. What measures would you propose for the museum, using the standards previously identified in this chapter? You should consider the purpose of the museum, the outputs or activities conducted by the museum, and the measurable outcomes that would result from successful museum operations.

7. A state wants to use measured outcomes to decide budget amounts to provide to its public universities. Here are a few outcomes: students in class, total graduates in the year, total graduates with undergraduate degrees, total graduates with advanced degrees, state resident students in class, graduates with employment within six months of graduation, graduates from underserved populations, and graduates in critical academic fields. Discuss the advantages, disadvantages, relevance, and measurability of each outcome. If you were developing a performance budget for this state, what measures would you use?

CASE FOR DISCUSSION

CASE 6–1

Following Departmental Lines (and Scores?)

This selection illustrates the budgetary impact of being in the right department at the right time when traditional budget structures are being used. It requires no additional comment, except to note that there continue to be many military bands. The U.S. Army bands website identifies more than 100 for the Army alone in 2011, and nobody knows how many the Navy and Air Force have.

Spending for B1s and MXs Is Rising, So the Tubas Got an Increase, Too

By Richard L. Hudson

Washington—Military spending is going up. So spending for military bands is going up. What could be more natural?

It isn't fair, say outraged partisans of the arts, to spend more money on Sousa oompahs when spending for genuine classical music is being cut. They note balefully that the National Endowment for the Arts has been targeted by the administration for a 50 percent budget cut this year, to $77 million, while the Army, Navy, Air Force and Marine bands are in line for a 2 percent increase, to $89.7 million.

The discrepancy has arts hawks in Congress seething. "There are three full (military) bands in the Washington area, and each of them has a larger budget than the National Symphony Orchestra," says Rep. Fred Richmond, a New York Democrat and a leading congressional Medici. "I don't think it's fair," he says, that civilian arts should suffer while military music prospers.

Noncombat Troops

Such cries draw a sympathetic audience among legislators worried about Pentagon "waste." One is Republican Sen. Mark Hatfield of Oregon, whose Appropriations Committee scrutinizes defense spending. He recently lambasted the military brass for budgeting bands, historians, museum curators, and 1,605 "recreation specialists and sports technicians," all of whom "contribute little or nothing to our military strength."

Democratic Rep. Dan Glickman of Oklahoma calls the band budget "a sacred cow that has waded" through prior spending debates with insufficient scrutiny.

Preserving Morale

"It looks like everybody's trying to chop our heads off," complains an Army band official, Sgt. Major Donald Young. The bands "wave the flag" and "stir patriotism," he says. A Pentagon spokesman says the 5,355 military-band members are needed to help lure recruits, preserve morale at foreign bases, and burnish the military image.

It remains to be seen if critics of the military band buildup can torpedo Mr. Reagan's plans to raise funding. But arts lobbyists say the sniping has at least helped protect the arts endowment from the full 50 percent cut pushed by the White House. The Senate last Tuesday backed a 25 percent cut, and the House approved a token 1 percent reduction.

The critics aren't denying that a good military band plays a rousing tune. It does, says Representative Richmond. But "it's sure as heck not the National Symphony."

APPENDIX 6–1

Functional Categories of the Federal Budget

The functional classification arranges budget resources so that budget authority and outlays, loan cap guarantees, and tax expenditures can be related to the national needs they address. The congressional budget resolutions establish budget targets for each function, and the president's budget presents the functional classification along with the classification by administrative unit.

According to the Budget of the U.S. Government, Fiscal Year 1986, these criteria are used in assigning activities to functions:

A function must have a common end or ultimate purpose addressed to an important national need. (The emphasis is on what the federal government seeks to accomplish rather than the means of accomplishment, what is purchased, or the clientele or geographic area served.)

A function must be of continuing national importance and the amounts attributable to it must be significant.

Each basic unit of classification (generally the appropriation or fund account) is classified into the single best or predominant purpose and assigned to only one subfunction. However, when an account is large and serves more than one major purpose, it may be subdivided into two or more subfunctions.

Activities and programs are normally classified according to their primary purpose (or function) regardless of which agencies conduct the activities.

The functional classification of federal spending, as outlined in the federal budget, follows:

Function and Subfunction*

050 National defense:	051 Department of Defense—Military
	051 Subtotal, Department of Defense—Military
	053 Atomic energy defense activities
	054 Defense-related activities
150 International affairs:	151 International development and humanitarian assistance
	152 International security assistance
	153 Conduct of foreign affairs
	154 Foreign information and exchange activities
	155 International financial programs
250 General science, space and technology:	251 General science and basic research
	252 Space flight, research, and supporting activities
270 Energy:	271 Energy supply
	272 Energy conservation
	274 Emergency energy preparedness
	276 Energy information, policy, and regulation
300 Natural resources and environment:	301 Water resources
	302 Conservation and land management
	303 Recreational resources
	304 Pollution control and abatement
	306 Other natural resources
350 Agriculture:	351 Farm income stabilization
	352 Agricultural research and services

*The functional classification is discussed in detail in the GAO report *Budget Function Classifications: Origins, Trends, and Implications for Current Uses,* GAO/AIMD-98–67 (Washington, D.C.: General Accounting Office, February 1998).

370 Commerce and
housing credit: 371 Mortgage credit
                          372 Postal service
                          373 Deposit insurance
                          376 Other advancement of commerce
400 Transportation: 401 Ground transportation
                          402 Air transportation
                          403 Water transportation
                          407 Other transportation
450 Community and
regional development: 451 Community development
                          452 Area and regional development
                          453 Disaster relief and insurance
500 Education, training,
employment, and
social services: 501 Elementary, secondary, and vocational education
                          502 Higher education
                          503 Research and general education aids
                          504 Training and employment
                          505 Other labor services
                          506 Social services
550 Health: 551 Health care services
                          552 Health research and training
                          554 Consumer and occupational health and safety
570 Medicare: 571 Medicare
600 Income security: 601 General retirement and disability insurance (excluding
                             Social Security)
                          602 Federal employee retirement and disability
                          603 Unemployment compensation
                          604 Housing assistance
                          605 Food and nutrition assistance
                          609 Other income security
650 Social Security: 651 Social Security
700 Veterans benefits
and services: 701 Income security for veterans
                          702 Veterans education, training, and rehabilitation
                          703 Hospital and medical care for veterans
                          704 Veterans housing
                          705 Other veterans benefits and services
750 Administration
of justice: 751 Federal law enforcement activities
                          752 Federal litigative and judicial activities
                          753 Federal correctional activities
                          754 Criminal justice assistance
800 General government: 801 Legislative functions
                          802 Executive direction and management
                          803 Central fiscal operations
                          804 General property and records management
                          805 Central personnel management
                          806 General purpose fiscal assistance
                          808 Other general government
                          809 Deductions for offsetting receipts

900 Net interest:
901 Interest on Treasury debt securities (gross)
902 Interest received by on-budget trust funds
903 Interest received by off-budget trust funds
908 Other interest
909 Other investment income

920 Allowances:
923 Legislative Branch Allowance
925 Debt collection initiatives

950 Undistributed
   offsetting receipts:
951 Employer share, employee retirement (on-budget)
952 Employer share, employee retirement (off-budget)
953 Rents and royalties on the Outer Continental Shelf
954 Sale of major assets
959 Other undistributed offsetting receipts

APPENDIX 6–2

United Nations Classification of Functions of Government

The United Nations classification of functions of government (COFOG) divides the major service commitments accepted by governments as follows:

- General Public Service (legislative, executive, fiscal management, public debt service, etc.)
- Defense
- Public Order and Safety (police services; fire protection; courts; prisons)
- Economic Affairs (general economic, commercial, and labor affairs; agriculture, forestry, fishing, and hunting; fuel and energy; mining, manufacturing, and construction; transport; communications)
- Environmental Protection (waste management; waste water management; pollution abatement; protection of biodiversity and landscape)
- Housing and Community Amenities (housing development; community development; water supply; street lighting)
- Health (medical products, appliances, and equipment; outpatient services; hospital services; public health)
- Recreation, Culture, and Religion
- Education
- Social Protection (sickness and disability; old age; survivors; family and children; unemployment; housing)

Data in these programs or functional categories provide a good basis for making international comparisons and a good start for developing the framework for a program budget.

SOURCE: United Nations [http://unstats.un.org/unsd/cr/registry/regcst.asp?Cl=4&Lg=1].

CHAPTER 7

Capital Budgeting, Time Value of Money, and Cost-Benefit Analysis: Process, Structure, and Basic Tools

Capital expenditures purchase physical assets that are expected to provide services for several years; the outlay will yield benefits in the future without having to repeat the purchase.[1] Capital spending also includes capital improvements or rehabilitation of physical assets that extends or enhances the useful life of these assets (as distinct from the operating expenditures for repair or maintenance expenditures, which assure functionality during the expected life of the asset).

Public capital assets, also called infrastructure, become inputs into production of both private and public goods and services. The Congressional Budget Office (CBO) writes, "The production and distribution of private economic output depends on public transportation and environmental facilities including highways, mass transit, railways, airports and airways, water resources, and water supply and wastewater treatment plants."[2] All these fit directly into production processes yielding *private* goods and services. Roads, sewers, and transportation systems have become part of the competition between states and localities for new industrial and commercial development, so a sound system of infrastructure finance represents a crucial factor for regional economic growth. But public infrastructure also enters into production processes that deliver *public* services: elementary and secondary school buildings, park and recreation areas, state hospitals, administrative complexes, jails and police facilities, fire stations, the defense establishment, and so on, and these are critical for society

---

[1]The work of teachers also lasts for many years. But compensation for teachers does not belong in the capital investment category because, if you want the services of the teacher next year, you are going to have to pay again. Public buildings are not so demanding—pay to build them once and they continue delivering services for many years without paying again. The buildings will require maintenance, but this is a recurring operating cost, not a capital expenditure.
[2]Congressional Budget Office, *How Federal Spending for Infrastructure and Other Public Investments Affects the Economy* (Washington, D.C.: Congressional Budget Office, July 1991), x.

as well. Therefore, the public capital stock matters for the production of both private and public goods and services. Infrastructure failure can be catastrophic, as when the Mississippi River bridge in Minneapolis–St. Paul collapsed in 2007 or when the levees broke in New Orleans in 2005—but the costs of deficient or deteriorated public infrastructure are great even without catastrophe, as with traffic delays and extra fuel use when slowed by congestion or by potholes on highways, delays and crowding on elderly public transit systems, time spent waiting to take off from airports, loss of drinking water through leaking pipes, pollution with poorly treated sewage, and so on. Public capital stock acquired through the capital budgeting process is an important contributor to the quality of life enjoyed by the public.[3] In the United States, spending for public infrastructure—roads, bridges, school buildings, water supply, airports, and the like—is primarily a state and local government responsibility: in 2011, 89.3 percent of gross government investment in structures was by states and localities.[4]

Capital expenditures can be combined with operating expenditures in a unified budget, or the government may employ a dual budget process with one budget for operating expenditures and a second one for capital expenditures. Regardless of approach, capital spending is different from spending for current operations and does merit special attention. Three obvious differences are (1) that capital asset decisions can have future impact and thus merit extraordinary care (long life), (2) that capital assets usually have high price tags and their purchase may destabilize the finances of a government (high price), and (3) that capital asset purchases tend to occur at irregular intervals and may need special attention in regard to scheduling (nonrecurring). Therefore, capital spending, whether done through a separate process or not, merits special attention.

Why Have a Separate Capital Budget Process?

A budget process helps decision makers select between individual projects for funding, while keeping expenditures within a total resource constraint. Identifying capital projects for special attention, possibly even creating a separate budget for them, complicates an already complex process. For special treatment of capital acquisition to be defensible, it must make a substantial contribution to improved fiscal choice. These are the arguments. First, separate consideration can improve

---

[3] Human capital and research and development spending also contribute to long-term economic growth, so this attribute is not unique to capital spending. See General Accounting Office, *Choosing Public Investments,* GAO/AIMD-93-25 (Washington, D.C.: General Accounting Office, July 1993). But teachers and researchers expect to be paid year after year, as noted previously, so spending to pay them is considerably different from spending to build a bridge.

[4] Bureau of Economic Analysis, *National Income and Product Accounts of the United States* [http://www.bea.gov]. The state and local share of all government investments, including equipment and software with structures, is lower, only 66.7 percent of the total, primarily because of federal national defense purchases. Two-thirds of federal investment spending is for national defense.

both the efficiency and the equity of providing and financing nonrecurrent projects with long-term service flows. These projects serve the citizenry, for good or bad, for many years beyond the year of purchase. Considering them in a process that might allow financing by borrowing, not the annual balance expected of current operating expenditures, provides important opportunities to improve equity between generations and among local citizenry pools. In other words, the spending program in a capital budget can be covered either by revenue raised currently (current taxes, charges, grants, etc.—a "pay-as-you-go" system) or by borrowing on the promise to repay from future revenues (a "pay-as-you-use" system). Incurring debt for such projects is consistent with the "golden rule" of government finance and fiscal sustainability because the borrowing is to cover the acquisition of long-life capital assets. Future generations face the debt, but they also have the infrastructure financed by that debt. The spending in the capital budget must be covered (the money is raised from current revenue or debt sources), but the budget need not necessarily be balanced (total expenditure equals current revenue). The general standard is that operating budgets typically must be balanced; capital budgets, financed. The inequity of the "pay-as-you-go" approach is apparent: If a local government project with a thirty-year service life is constructed and paid for this year, no construction cost will be incurred during the remaining life of the project. Anyone entering the area tax-paying pool after the construction year (by moving into the area or by growing up) may receive project service without appropriate contribution. This inequity does not occur if the project is paid for over its useful life. Handling high-price, long-life projects through a debt-financed capital budget has strong equity advantages. Furthermore, the use of capital budgets can improve decision efficiency. In a combined budget, big-ticket investment looks expensive relative to consumption (operating expenditures), even though the true cost of that investment (its depreciation or its "wearing out") occurs over many years. Separate consideration can avoid that bias and improve the chances for more reasonable responses to service demand.[5] Special treatment of capital, including dual budgets with a balanced operating budget and a financed capital budget, can thus make important improvements in the equity and efficiency of providing projects and producing long-term service flow.

Second, special treatment of capital expenditure can stabilize tax rates when individual capital projects are large relative to the tax base of the host government. If a city with a tax base of $1.5 billion decided to construct a $150 million water reservoir, it would undoubtedly be dissuaded if it were required to collect sufficient revenue for construction in one year. The cost would be 10 percent of the total city tax base, hardly leaving enough tax capacity for police and fire protection, street operation, and so on. However, the reservoir may have a service life of fifty years or more. It is reasonable, then, to divide the construction cost over the service life,

---

[5]Lennox Moak and Albert Hillhouse suggest that governments having financial trouble may find that identifiable capital projects are more easily postponable than are expenditures for operating agencies. A separate capital budget can improve the chances for preserving capital projects when the operating budget is under great pressure. See Moak and Hillhouse, *Concepts and Practices in Local Government Finance* (Chicago: Municipal Finance Officers Association, 1975), 98. Cities regularly use capital spending reductions as a means of dealing with difficult fiscal conditions. See Michael A. Pagano, "Balancing Cities' Books in 1992: An Assessment of City Fiscal Conditions," *Public Budgeting & Finance* 13 (Spring 1993): 28.

thus reducing the burden on the tax base each year and, accordingly, preventing the dramatic fluctuation in tax rates that would result from financing the project in the construction year. The case for a regular capital budget process is strong whenever projects are large enough to significantly influence tax rates. However, the entire capital budget need not be debt-financed to maintain stable tax rates; recurring capital outlays should be financed from current revenue.

Third, special reviews of capital budgeting are appropriate because capital projects are permanent—mistakes will be around for many years. Kenneth Howard describes the problem:

> If a new state office building is built today, it will stay there for a long time. Everybody may know by next year that it is in the wrong place, but not much can be done about moving it then. Perhaps it is disrupting the development of a downtown business district; perhaps it is affecting traffic flows and parking facilities in a most undesirable way; or perhaps its location makes it psychologically, if not geographically, far removed from certain segments of the population. Whatever these effects may be, they are real, and they will endure awhile. They should be anticipated to the fullest extent possible before the project is undertaken.[6]

The special reviews for capital expenditure will not prevent all mistakes, but they can reduce costly errors. Those reviews and associated planning processes can produce the orderly provision of public capital facilities to accommodate economic development. Thus, the capital budget process serves to reduce errors of both commission and omission in public infrastructure construction.

Finally, special reviews of capital expenditure provide valuable tools for managing limited fiscal resources, particularly in light of the special care required to plan activities that necessitate long-term drains on those resources. Items in this budget tend to be "lumpy." The process provides a mechanism to smooth out peaks and valleys, regularize construction activity in an effort to avoid local bottlenecks that can delay projects and inflate their costs, avoid excessive drains on the tax base when projects must be paid for, and balance spending with the resources available within political, economic, and legal tax and debt limits.

American governments are mixed in regard to their utilization of dual budgets. The states are almost evenly divided between those legislatures receiving executive capital budget requests in a separate budget document and those receiving requests with the operating budget. There is no separate capital budget or capital budgeting process at the federal level. Capital and operating expenditures are mixed together throughout the budget process, and appropriations for big capital projects are made on an annual basis to provide Congress greater control over spending.

The reasons supporting a separate capital budget are stronger for local and state governments than for the federal level. First, critics of a federal capital budget fear that a separate capital budget would create a bias toward deficit spending or, more accurately, add to the existing bias that is apparent in the historical record. The danger is that all items potentially definable as investment (and politicians love to refer to every dollar spent for anything as "investment"), whether the addition contributes

---

[6]S. Kenneth Howard, *Changing State Budgeting* (Lexington, Ky.: Council of State Governments, 1973), 241.

to physical or human capital, would be inserted into a debt-financed capital budget, even if the spending were recurring. It has been politically much easier for the federal government to borrow than to tax, so this extra incentive is dangerous.

Second, the federal government is so large that no single infrastructure project is likely to influence tax rates. Although a careful physical inventory and planning for estimated demand conditions are helpful, scheduling of projects to control tax rates is of little practical consequence. Large projects may, however, create "spikes" in budget authority to individual agencies—but that does not make a case for the smoothing that a capital budget process might create for the federal government as a whole.

Third, the federal government does not need the careful project planning inherent in capital budgeting to preserve its debt rating. The federal government has, after all, the ultimate power of printing money to cover deficits, and capital project financing is not a factor in the federal credit rating. Its debt rating is endangered primarily by arguments among politicians, not basic financial capacity, not by finances directly.

Finally, skeptics say that another budget would simply provide federal bureaucrats and lawmakers with another way to conceal fiscal conditions. Adding operating capital to the existing on-budget/off-budget, federal fund/trust fund complications doesn't contribute to fiscal transparency and would likely muddle citizen understanding even more, even as it satisfies fiscal purists. Thus, the gains from capital budgeting at lower government levels, particularly local, may not be translated to a similar federal case.

Even without a distinct capital budget process, the federal budget has included outlays and budget authority for federal investment—outlays that yield long-term benefits—in a special section on federal investment expenditure for more than half a century. The coverage is included in the *Analytical Perspectives* volume of the budget.[7] Outlays are divided into (1) physical investment (construction and rehabilitation, purchase of major equipment, and purchase or sale of land and structures), (2) conduct of research and development, and (3) conduct of education and training. The information about federal investment outlays is greater than is found in quite a few state and local capital budgets, despite the absence of a federal capital budget. (Note the inclusion of both recurring and nonrecurring expenditures in the listing of investments, further highlighting the danger of allowing the federal authorities to employ dual budgets.)

Outlays are further categorized by broad functional classes within those divisions. Major acquisition proposals are specifically identified by agency. Agency proposals for capital asset investment are expected to demonstrate a projected return on the investment that is clearly equal to or better than alternative uses of available public resources. Return may include improved mission performance in accordance with measures developed pursuant to the Government Performance and Results Act; reduced cost; increased quality, speed, or flexibility; and increased customer and employee satisfaction.[8]

---

[7]Office of Management and Budget, *Budget of the United States Government, Fiscal Year 2010, Analytical Perspectives* (Washington, D.C.: U.S. Government Printing Office, 2009), 33–41. However, the investment program is not extended beyond the budget year.
[8]Office of Management and Budget, *Planning, Budgeting and Acquisition of Fixed Assets*, Circular A-11, part 7 (Washington, D.C.: Office of Management and Budget, 2009).

The federal budget and budget process, however, remain unified, in that there is no other separation between capital and operating spending. Agencies develop operating and capital projects in the same budget cycle, Congress reviews proposals and makes appropriations without distinguishing between the two sorts of spending,[9] and there are no separate rules for the finance of capital as opposed to operating programs. Agency appropriations include budget authority for both operations and capital projects on the same basis. The budget process attempts to achieve full appropriation for long-term, large-ticket capital projects (e.g., the International Space Station) by a combination of current and advance appropriations. Up-front funding for the full cost allows Congress to control spending at the time of commitment. However, it requires agencies to bear that cost in the annual budget, even though returns will accrue over the long life of the project and the cost may absorb a considerable portion of discretionary spending.[10] Critics of the current system argue that this full cost/up-front funding discriminates against and discourages capital spending because it goes up against the small price tag of operating expenditures without distinguishing the fundamental difference in flow of returns.

The scope of the presentation in *Analytical Perspectives* includes many recurrent, noncapital asset purchases, and it does not establish separation and protection of capital asset decisions in the process. Sidebar 7–1 describes one way in which the federal government might move toward capital budgeting through the use of special accounts, one for capital, one for operating, and one that would consolidate the two accounts.[11]

A Process for Managing Capital Expenditure

The capital budget process, whether separate from the process for operating expenditures or whether part of a unified budget, seeks to constrain the financial impact of capital asset acquisition on the overall budget, while delivering the infrastructure needed to satisfy the citizenry's public-service demands. Formal capital budget processes operate in many different ways, using various terms, steps, and the

---

[9]A General Accounting Office study reports that federal capital project requests provided to the appropriate House and Senate committees do not always identify the total cost of proposed projects (funding has been sought in increments, not total), have not always identified funds already spent on the project, and have often provided scant descriptions of the nature of the project. General Accounting Office, *Budget Issues: Agency Data Supporting Capital Funding Requests Could Be Improved,* GAO-01-770 (Washington, D.C.: General Accounting Office, June 2001).

[10]General Accounting Office, *Budget Issues: Budgeting for Federal Capital,* GAO/AIMD-97-5 (Washington, D.C.: General Accounting Office, November 1996), offers a good review of capital investment practices of the federal government and the problems that they create.

[11]Private capital budgeting is quite concerned with proper allowances for depreciation. This is important for defining profitability and for establishing the value of the business as a going concern. These are critical concerns for owners of the business. Owners of government—that is, us—are concerned about the services provided and the taxes we pay in their support and are not focused on either profitability or the value of the government if sold. Government depreciation charges might be useful for some internal management questions, but are not so important for the owners.

Sidebar 7–1
An Approach to Federal Capital Budgeting with CBO Comments

This description of how the federal government might handle capital expenditure is from the Congressional Budget Office. It is an approach particularly aimed at getting costs measured properly, while maintaining proper fiscal controls.

Capital Accounts in a Unified Budget

One approach to capital budgeting would create a series of federal accounts.[1]

- A capital budget that would contain all investment outlays;
- An operating budget that would include depreciation as a cost; and
- A consolidated account that would combine the operating and capital accounts into a unified view.

The capital account would report how the government is investing for the future. The operating account would reveal how much of the nation's resources the government is actually consuming. The consolidated account would report the total budget deficit or surplus just as the unified budget currently does, which distinguishes this approach from the private-sector financial accounting approach. Depreciation would be an internal charge—an expense to the operating budget and income of the same amount to the capital budget—leaving the unified budget unchanged.[2] With this budgeting system, policy makers would have both cash and accrual numbers on capital spending, but only the cash flows on capital spending would affect the unified deficit or surplus.

This approach still faces the implementation issues that would affect the financial accounting model of a capital budget, including decisions on how to define capital and how to define depreciation. However, policy makers could have clearer budgetary information for decision making, which might affect how much they are willing to spend on capital projects. As long as up-front budget authority is required for capital spending, control over spending should not be adversely affected. Moreover, agencies would be charged with the cost of using their capital, so their incentives to manage assets efficiently could improve. However, given the presence of three different budget concepts, the system could be more complex than the current system. Interest among lawmakers in developing a federal capital budget waxes and wanes, never completely disappearing, but never (so far) becoming intense enough to actually cause the systems to change.

[1]Statement of Robert Eisner, Northwestern University, *A Capital Budget for Truth in Packaging,* before the President's Commission to Study Capital Budgeting, April 24, 1998, available at http://clinton2.nara.gov/pcscb/wt_cisner.html.
[2]For an illustration of what the accounts would show, see Office of Management and Budget, *Budget of the United States Government, Fiscal Year 2004, Analytical Perspectives* (Washington, D.C.: U.S. Government Printing Office, 2003), 159, Table 7-9.

SOURCE: Congressional Budget Office, *Capital Budgeting* (Washington, D.C.: Congressional Budget Office, 2008).

---

sequencing of those steps, and function separately from the process producing the annual (operating) budget. The process outlined here is based on those from several different state and local governments. The processes are concerned with selecting capital projects from the multitude of possible alternatives, timing expenditure on the projects selected, and fitting capital projects into the overall financial program of the government. The politics of capital projects can be complicated because each project is at a known and specific location and will likely have specific impacts on the area surrounding it, some desirable (a new park) and possibly some not (a new incinerator). NIMBY ("not in my back yard") deals with capital projects, after all. This focuses citizen interests in ways far beyond concerns about, for instance, social programs or police protection, which have general impact.[12] In that environment, it can be difficult to limit discussion of capital asset programs to capital assets only.

The capital budget typically becomes an element of the annual budget, either as a section of the overall budget or as a separate capital budget document.[13] The capital budget should have cost estimates (requests) for all infrastructure projects that are proposed, including both the proposed investment cost and the implications for the operating budget. The budget usually goes through the normal legislative review and enactment requirements that any expenditure program would face, and, once approved, spending follows the same control mechanisms as faced by any public expenditures. The future years of the capital budget may or may not be appropriated when the facility proposal is first considered, and the government may or may not honor future capital expenditure requirements as later components of the plan are proposed. Executives and their priorities change, as do legislatures. One would hope that an approved capital budget does not include facilities so repugnant as to bring their cancellation when legislatures and chief executives change, but later governments do not always feel bound by decisions made by their predecessors.

A fully developed capital budget process functions in some respects separately from the process for the annual budget, although they obviously intersect in the final states of the cycle. The four elements in the capital budget process—planning, budgeting, implementation/execution, and audit—are specific applications of the standard budget cycle, although with some variations in the tasks undertaken in each. Table 7–1 provides a general outline of a capital budget process, one that can apply regardless of whether the government uses a unitary budget that includes both capital and operating expenditures in a single budget or whether it uses a dual budget system. The steps are those that are appropriate for implementation of a capital asset management program.

Planning

Governments need to start their infrastructure development programs with a good assessment of the existing situation. The necessary information base would include an inventory of the capital facilities owned by the government with these data for each facility: (1) its age, (2) an assessment of its condition, (3) its degree of use, (4) its

---

[12]Participatory budget processes often focus exclusively on capital infrastructure because of that high citizen interest.

[13]The federal system records the full cost of a capital asset as an obligation when resources are committed, and resulting cash expenditures are counted as outlays as payments are made. Budgetary control is on obligations. Many agencies would like to spread costs over several years, rather than facing a full up-front obligation, so they do not take such a large budget hit in the year that projects begin.

Table 7–1
Logical Flow of Capital Budget Process

Phase	Step	Result
Planning		
	Update inventory and assess asset condition	Inventory of infrastructure, analyze condition and adequacy of maintenance spending
	Identify projects	Project list with cost estimates (capital improvement plan), multiyear horizon
	Project evaluation	Detailed costing, estimation of any revenues, compare with strategic plans, cost-benefit analysis for most promising
	Project ranking	Establish ranking of projects, re-rank each year
Budgeting		
	Financing	Financing arrangements for projects to be included in the budget (borrowing, intergovernmental transfers, current revenues)
	Budget	Include expenditures in budget proposals of appropriate departments, placement in resource envelope available to government, inclusion of project operating costs in budget
Implementation/Execution		
	Procurement	Process for selection of contractors for projects
	Monitoring	Review of physical and financial progress of project, coordinate spending with revenue flow
Audit		
	External audit	Ex-post review of financial records, project completion

capacity, and (5) its replacement cost. Such an inventory can help the government estimate needs for renewal, replacement, expansion, and retirement of its existing capital stock. It can also contribute information for the repair and maintenance portion of the operating budget. The level of detail for the inventory and the degree of accompanying analysis vary by the significance of the facility to the operations of the government. Errors in inventorying capital assets and in doing something about identified infrastructure issues can be fatal.

After the inventory, a catalogue of possible infrastructure projects can be developed, along with general estimates of their cost. The government may have a capital improvement program (CIP), with a list of projects coming from government agencies and, sometimes, private organizations; each project proposal includes a justifying narrative and cost data. These project proposals may be screened by a governmentwide planning department or a similar body to evaluate costs, locate interrelationships, and establish initial priorities. Some decisions can be guided by established service goals of the community. For instance, if a local government has certain fire protection standards it wants to achieve for all properties in its jurisdiction and it cannot achieve that goal because of infrastructure limitations, then this unmet standard can shape an element of the investment plan.[14]

A number of priority systems are possible. These include priorities based on (1) functional areas, such as natural resources, higher education, transportation, or assistance for local government projects; (2) problem severity, such as the health and safety of the population, critical maintenance of facilities, facility improvements, and new construction; (3) status of support, such as the governor's priorities, agency priorities, legal or federal mandate, and passage of referenda; or (4) a formal scoring system according to ranked criteria.[15] Realistically, the priorities of the chief executive (governor or mayor) have to play an important role in making the choices, and the interests of the legislature cannot be ignored. Many states provide no clear ranking, but there does continue to be some preference for maintaining existing facilities against new construction. In addition, concern for public health and safety is usually important—as are court orders. Other projects may be evaluated with cost-benefit analysis, as described later in this chapter.

Evaluating projects for the capital budget is not a simple task because the decisions intertwine economic, political, and social forces. An Urban Institute study identified a number of criteria that were important in evaluations done by local governments:

1. Fiscal impacts, including capital, operating, and maintenance costs; revenue effects; energy requirements; and legal liability
2. Health and safety effects on both the citizenry and government employees
3. Community economic effects on the tax base, employment, incomes of people and businesses, and neighborhoods
4. Environmental, esthetic, and social effects on the quality of life in the community
5. Disruptions and inconvenience created during the work on the project
6. Distributional effects across age and income groups, neighborhoods, business and individuals, people with and without automobiles, and people with and without disabilities
7. Feasibility in terms of public support, interest-group opposition, special federal or state permitting procedures, consistency with comprehensive plans, and legal questions
8. Implications of deferring the project to a later year
9. Amount of uncertainty and risk with regard to cost and other estimates, technology, and the like
10. Effects on relationships with other governments or quasi-governmental agencies that serve the area
11. Effects on the cost or impacts of other capital projects[16]

---

[14]A good guide for developing facilities plans is Alan Walter Steiss, *Strategic Facilities Planning, Capital Budgeting and Debt Administration* (Lanham, Md.: Lexington Books, 2005).
[15]National Association of State Budget Officers, *Capital Budgeting in the States*, preliminary draft (Washington, D.C.: National Association of State Budget Officers, April 1997). The participatory budgeting process outlined in the previous chapter provides one approach to making these decisions.

The extent to which these concerns matter differs across types of projects—a new jail raises different questions than a sewage-treatment plant, for instance. Furthermore, evaluation signals may conflict for particular projects. But these are the kinds of questions that apply when evaluating such choices. Table 7–2 identifies several standard questions that budget examiners raise. Because capital projects are place-specific, political pressures can be intense. Some projects are desirable and can become parts of pork-barrel trading and rewards; others may be unattractive and subject to considerable protest from residents of the host locality. For example, controversy surrounds proposals for both a new community college and a nuclear waste storage facility.

This screening is particularly concerned with scheduling: projects should be timed to avoid waste (the new sewers should be put in before the streets are resurfaced), predetermined program emphases should be implemented, and projects that can be postponed should be identified.[17] Part of this priority review may be linked to a community (or state) master plan—a long-term (ten- to twenty-five-year), broadgauge estimate of community growth encompassing estimated needs for public improvements and controls on private use of property. Because long-term forecasts

Table 7–2
Selected Questions for a Capital Budget Request

What evidence is given of the need for the project, and what happens if the project is not funded?

What benefits are claimed for the project, and how convincing are the claims?

What plans have been developed for the project?

What happens if the project is delayed another year?

How sensitive is the justification to changed circumstances: population growth or decline, major technological change, decline or increase in service demand, change in government structure, actions of other governments or businesses, and so on?

Is the capital cost comparable with experience on similar projects here and elsewhere?

Are all costs—land acquisition, planning, insurance, and the like—included in the request?

What are the operating costs for the life of the project? Are they reasonable and affordable? Could project design changes allow savings?

Can the project more properly be financed by someone else? By a private business, by another government, or through some partnership arrangement?

Are there other options? Renovating or retrofitting existing infrastructure? Leasing?

What financing options are appropriate: current budget, general obligation bonds, revenue bonds, lease-purchase agreement?

---

[16]Harry P. Hatry, "Guide to Setting Priorities for Capital Investment," *Guides to Managing Urban Capital* (Washington, D.C.: Urban Institute, 1984), 5: 716.
[17]Moak and Hillhouse, *Concepts and Practices in Local Government Finance,* 104–5.

of social, demographic, and economic behavior are so inaccurate, that plan should not be taken too seriously as a guide to actions if the government intends to base its operations on what people want as opposed to the schemes of politicians and bureaucrats.

The capital program ordinarily is developed in agencies, but with central instruction, oversight, and coordination. Governments are becoming especially concerned that CIP outcomes contribute to overall government goals. The final capital improvement program has a segment scheduled for each year of its multiyear span. The capital budget proposal for the year includes current-year expenditures from the capital improvement program.

An analysis of project costs and time schedules in the CIP ordinarily shows a need for reprioritization of projects. Because priorities change across the years, the plan should be revised annually to create a rolling, multiyear investment plan. (Unfortunately, some governments develop a master plan with the intention that it will be permanent for years into the future and try to stick with it, even as conditions change.) The plan should include the time schedule and estimated costs for all projects in the plan. Such a multiyear plan should help the government manage its limited financial resources, induce the government to manage toward more cost-effective approaches to infrastructure development, and assist with prudence in the financial management of infrastructure acquisition.

Budgeting

The government must keep its infrastructure development program within its financial capacity. The limit to its capacity depends on several factors, including the government's operating expenditure level, the fundamental revenue capacity of the government, any revenues produced by the infrastructure facility itself, the extent to which other governments or private entities will share the cost of the infrastructure facilities or of their operation, and the debt structures and instruments available to the government. Any impact of the facility on recurring expenditures of the government must be part of the financial analysis; facilities can either reduce or increase the operating expenditures of a government.

This part of the process coordinates a financial analysis of the government with the facility additions envisioned in the capital improvement program. This interrelationship is vital because of the long-term fiscal commitments that such facilities involve. Just as a poorly conceived physical structure can disrupt a city for many years, a poorly conceived financing approach can disrupt that city's fiscal condition. Finance officers must examine the present and anticipated revenue-and-expenditure profile to determine the financial cushion available for new projects. Particularly important are the status of existing debt issues (Will any debt issues be retired soon? Will funds be available to meet contractual debt service—principal and interest—payments? Are there needs for extra funds for early bond retirement?), estimated growth profile of the tax base, and potential for new revenue sources. This fiscal profile, year by year, may then be related to the priority list of projects, again scheduled by years. In this analysis, fiscal officers usually consider the financing alternatives available for specific projects (special assessments for sidewalks, user charges for water utilities, state or federal aid for highways, etc.), and further reports will have financing sources attached to projects. Choices also need to be made about whether to finance by borrowing (general or limited obligation bonds), by use of capital reserve funds (special funds accumulated over time for future capital spending), or from current sources (pay-as-you-go financing). Some projects may involve a public-private partnership, in other words, a joint ownership and financing arrangement between a government and a private business. From those considerations, the project list is revised in preparation for its insertion into the annual budget process.

The capital component for the annual budget—infrastructure investment—must be prepared to be transmitted either in a capital budget or as an element of a unified budget. Cost estimates for projects need to be prepared with greater precision than was sufficient for the capital plan, and justifications must be developed in the format prescribed for that budget cycle. The financial analysis may indicate that the full project schedule can remain intact for the year, but more often fiscal conditions require choices to fit a proposal to the scarce available resources.

The projects surviving agency and executive cuts become the capital section of the annual budget. The document usually provides a distribution of projects by function and agency, shows prior and estimated future costs of the project (initial appropriations may well have been annual—each year's construction plan requires a new appropriation), and summarizes sources of financing (type of debt, aid, etc.). The capital improvement program thus feeds the capital budget proposal for the next year, subject to revisions produced by the environmental conditions and the legislative process. The projects are reviewed by the legislature and sometimes are substantially modified. When projects are approved, provision must also be made in the operating budget for operation and maintenance of the completed facility. A new civic arena will not be usable if the operating budget has no money for its interior lighting, and the new convention center will not meet its expectations if no money is available for marketing.

Total government expenditure includes both operating expenditures from the operating budget and capital purchases from the capital budget. Operating expenditures are normally financed by current revenue (taxes, grants, charges, etc., collected in the current year). If operating expenditures are financed by borrowing instead of by current revenue, the current-period expenditures must be paid in the future, along with necessary interest. Thus, that future period will bear the costs of both current and past operating expenditures; the overhang from previous years can severely restrict the capacity to provide necessary services. That is why the operating portion of the budget needs to be balanced as a requirement for long-term fiscal sustainability.

In terms of the comprehensive budget, the revenue that must be generated in any budget year equals the operating budget plus a capital project component. The latter equals capital items purchased without debt plus the *debt-service* requirements (interest and repayment of principal) on borrowing for capital items purchased in prior years. Those debt costs would ideally approximate a depreciation charge for capital assets acquired in the past; serial bonds (bonds in a single project issue that are to be paid off at various dates through the life of the project) can provide a rough approximation of that cost distribution. Debt financing is discussed in detail in Chapter 15.

Implementation/Execution

The third step in the capital budget process is execution of projects for which funds have been appropriated. Special attention must be given to (1) the rules (bidding, procurement, etc.) under which contracts can be issued; (2) controls to keep project work on schedule, so that facilities will be completed as planned; and (3) monitoring to keep project cost within budget. A full capital asset management program also requires a scheme for financing routine maintenance and upgrading of capital assets (not as politically attractive as building new facilities) and a system for keeping a current inventory of capital assets, thus feeding back into the beginning of the process.

Audit

External audit for capital projects typically follows the same cycle and procedures as does external audit for the rest of the budget. It can become more critical with capital spending because of the sums of money involved and the accompanying attractiveness of cheating for personal advantage.

Problems in Capital Budgeting

As is always the case with mechanisms to help make public decisions, there are problems in applying capital budgeting. First, the capital improvement/capital budget process assumes a continuous cycle of reappraisal and revaluation of project proposals. The cycle is necessary because the world changes, causing substantial changes in the value of public projects. For instance, decisions between mass transit and highways may differ, depending on whether the price of motor fuel is expected to be $3 per gallon or $6 per gallon. Unfortunately, many processes assume established priorities to be unchangeable, even in the face of different project costs and different project demands. As Howard points out, "Too often cost fluctuations do not generate a reassessment of priority rankings; original rankings are retained despite the fluctuations."[18] In a related manner, the time a project has spent in the priority queue sometimes establishes its priority rank; all old project proposals have higher rankings than any new ones. That approach makes no sense because time alone does not improve the viability of a marginal project. Indeed, items entering the priority queue some years before may, by the time they reach the funding point, have outlived their usefulness or may have been superseded by adjustments made by people and markets. The project may have gone unfunded for many years because sensible people in the administration understood that the project would be a bad use of money. The passage of time has not made it any better. Again, the problem can be resolved by maintaining reviews of projects in the capital improvement program.

Second, availability of funds can alter decisions. The appropriate approach in establishing final priorities should involve a general comparison of the cost of the project with the project's return to the community—the money's source doesn't matter in this comparison. Some projects can get favored treatment, however, because earmarked funds are available (a special tax creates a fund pool that can be spent only on one class of project), because they produce revenue that can be pledged to repayment of revenue bonds without identifiable tax burden or the need to satisfy restrictions placed on general debt, because federal or state assistance is available for particular projects, or because a private partner is contributing something to the project. If somebody else (a donor or a different level of government) is paying for a large share of the cost of the project, that cannot be ignored when making project choices. The project becomes cheaper and should be evaluated on that basis.

Third, capital budgeting can unduly and uneconomically favor the use of debt finance. Borrowing to purchase capital assets may not always be desirable. For instance, items that are purchased regularly and in considerable numbers—vehicles used by a larger city government, for instance, or buses for a large school district—may be more economically purchased on a regular-flow basis, even though the purchase of individual vehicles would appear to be a good candidate for debt finance. Furthermore, debt-financed capital budgets can add to inflationary pressures during strong economic expansion, when government finances are robust and legislatures feel good enough about fiscal prospects to respond to pent-up demand for infrastructure. To put long-life assets in a capital budget can create a strong temptation to debt finance, even when sound economic management would suggest that their purchase should be made with current revenues.

Finally, there is a standard problem in all public decisions: establishing priorities. How do items get into the capital budget? Cost-benefit analysis, examined in a later section, gives some assistance, but as with operating programs, there are no unambiguous answers. Projects that the elected chief executive is interested in always have a good shot at being included.

---

[18]Howard, *Changing State Budgeting*, 256.

Accounting for Time: Discounting and Compounding

The principles of discounting and compounding are the building blocks of most financial analysis. Not only are they used in capital budgeting but also, as is seen in later sections, they are critical for cost-benefit analysis, debt administration, fund investment, and tax policy. An understanding of the time-value concept is essential to becoming fully functional in government finance. Its application is vital in infrastructure finance. The costs and benefits of most public projects, particularly those long-life, high-price capital infrastructure projects, seldom occur in any single year. More often than not, an initial capital expenditure is made at the beginning—for instance, when a fire station is constructed—and both operating cost and program returns accrue over a long project life. In that event, special attention must be given to the timing of the flows, recognizing that a return available only at some point in the future has less value than an equal return available now.

The approach for comparing such impacts on personal, business, and public finance is discounting, a process of converting a stream of returns or costs incurred at different points in time to a single present value. The present value accounts for both the absolute size and the timing of impacts of a proposed action. It applies the concept of *time value of money*.

Why is a payment of $100 received one year from now not equivalent to $100 received now? If inflation's erosion of purchasing power and the uncertainty of the future seem to make the answer obvious, assume that the $100 is certain to be received and has been adjusted for price-level changes: the reason for discounting is related neither to inflation nor to uncertainty. The reason is simply that the $100 available now can yield a flow of valuable services (or interest) throughout the year. Or, even more to the point, the private market tells us that people must be compensated if they sacrifice current use of resources for future use. At the end of the year, the holder could have $100 plus the flow received from use of the $100 during the year. Therefore, $100 now has greater value than does $100 received at the end of the year. As the date of receipt is more distant, the present value of a given dollar amount is lower: the flow of services between now and then would be greater.

Compounding

Although the principle of time value applies to any resource or service, the mechanics are most often done using market-exchange equivalents (dollar values) of those returns, and the analysis uses investment for interest as the earned service flow. Thus, $X available now (the principal) becomes $X plus $X times the rate of interest (the principal plus interest earned on that principal) at the end of one year. Suppose the appropriate rate of interest is 5 percent; if $1,000 is invested today, it will accumulate to $1,050 by the end of the year. In other words,

$$\$1,050 = \$1,000 + (\$1,000 \times 0.05)$$

or

Amount at end of year = Original principal + Interest earned

Algebraically, if r = the rate of interest, PV = the present amount, and FV_1 = the amount at the end of a year, then

$$FV_1 = PV + PV \times r \quad \text{or} \quad FV_1 = PV(1+r)$$

that is, FV_1 equals the original principal (PV) plus accumulated interest ($PV \times r$).

Many policy and management questions involve multiple-year decisions in which the returns are permitted to compound over several years. In other words, the principal plus accumulated interest is reinvested and allowed to accumulate. An example is calculation of the amount to which $1,000 would have accumulated at the end of five years with 5 percent annual interest. Figure 7–1 shows annual account balances. There is an easier way, however, to compute compound interest. Using the symbols previously introduced for values now and values at the end of a year, the calculations look like this:

$$FV_1 = PV(1+0.05) = PV(1.05)$$

Figure 7–1
Compounding

Initial Deposit, $1,000	Interest Earned (interest rate × previous balance)	Account Balance
End of year:		
1	$50.00	$1,050.00
2	52.50	1,102.50
3	55.13	1,157.63
4	57.88	1,215.51
5	60.78	1,276.29

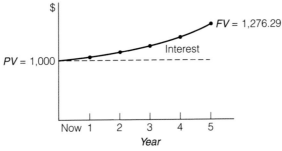

At the end of the second year, the account balance would increase from interest earned:

$$FV_2 = FV_1(1.05) = PV(1.05)(1.05) = PV(1.05)^2$$

The same increase from interest earned occurs at the end of the third year:

$$FV_3 = FV_2(1.05) = \{[PV(1.05)](1.05)\}(1.05) = PV(1.05)^3$$

For the fourth year,

$$FV_4 = FV_3(1.05) = \{[PV(1.05)](1.05)\}(1.05)(1.05) = PV(1.05)^4$$

The same process applies regardless of the number of years. In general, if PV = the present amount, r = the appropriate interest rate, n = the number of periods of compounding, and FV_n = the account balance at the end of the periods, then

$$FV_n = PV(1+r)^n$$

From the previous example,

$$FV_5 = 1,000(1.05)^5 = 1,276.29$$

With each passing year, the annual increase in value gets higher. That is because the interest compounds, which means that interest is earned on interest received in prior years. Private financial advisors talk about the "magic of compounding" and earn their living by encouraging people to invest and leave their money invested to get that magic. It isn't magic, but it does work.

Financial contracts often provide for compounding more frequently than once a year. The compounding formula can easily be adjusted to allow for semiannual, quarterly, or any other regular frequency-of-interest payment. For example, suppose interest is paid twice a year. With an annual rate of 10 percent, that system would mean 5 percent interest is paid for the first half of the year and 5 percent is paid for the second half of the year. Thus, principal plus interest amounts at the end of the half-years would be:

$$FV_1 = PV(1.05) \quad \text{(balance at end of one half-year)}$$
$$FV_2 = PV(1.05)^2 \quad \text{(balance at end of two half-years)}$$
$$FV_3 = PV(1.05)^3 \quad \text{(balance at end of three half-years)}$$

and so on. Thus, at the end of n years,

$$FV_n = PV(1.05)^{2n}$$

In general, if interest is added x times per year and other definitions are as before,

$$FV_n = PV\,[1+(r/x)]^{xn}$$

Discounting

Discounting adjusts sums to be received in the future to their present-value equivalent, the amount that will accumulate to that future sum if invested at prevailing interest rates. It amounts to going in the other direction from compounding. Recall that FV_1, the accumulated balance at the end of one year, equals $PV(1 + r)$, the balance at the start of the year multiplied by 1 plus the rate of interest. That formula can be algebraically rearranged to become

$$PV = FV_1 / (1+r)$$

This means that amount PV invested at interest rate r will grow to FV_1 by the end of the year. Suppose $1,000 will be received at the end of one year ($FV = 1,000$). If the interest rate that could be earned is 5 percent, what sum today (PV) would accumulate to $1,000 by the end of the year? Calculate the amount by use of the present-value formula:

$$PV = \$1,000 / (1+0.05) = \$952.38$$

That means that $952.38 now, plus 5 percent interest earned in one year ($952.38 $\times$ 0.05 = 47.62) equals $1,000: the present-value equivalent of $1,000 received at the end of one year when the available prevailing interest rate is 5 percent is $952.38. That prevailing rate is called the discount rate.

What happens if the return is received more than one year into the future? The same logic of adjusting for interest that could have been earned still applies, but the computations look messier because the interest earned would compound. In other words, interest earned during the first year would earn interest in the second year, and so on through the years. The general formula for compounding, $FV_n = PV (1 + r)^n$, can be rearranged in the same way that the single-year compounding formula was rearranged to produce the general present-value formula:

$$PV = FV_n / (1+r)^n$$

where

PV = the present-value equivalent,
FV_n = a value received in the future,
r = the discount rate, and
n = the number of years into the future that the sum is received.

For example, $800 received ten years in the future, assuming a 10 percent discount rate, would have a present value of $800/(1 + 0.10)^{10}$, or $308.43.

Projects yielding dramatically different returns over time can and must be compared using this technique. Suppose an agency has two projects under consideration. Each costs $1,900 (all occurring at the present), but the profile of returns from the projects differs substantially across the five years of the project:

Received at End of Year	Project A	Project B
1	1,000	480
2	300	480
3	1,000	480
4	0	480
5	0	480

Neither project lasts beyond the fifth year. Which project yields greater net benefits? Recognize that simple addition of returns—$2,300 for project A and $2,400 for project B—is wrong because the timing of those returns is not the same.

An accurate comparison requires that both streams be converted to their present value equivalents. Suppose that prevailing interest rate conditions indicate that resources should earn a 10 percent return. Ten percent is then a reasonable discount rate to use, with the following results:

Received at End of Year	Discount Factor	Project A Return ($)	Discounted ($)	Project B Return ($)	Discounted ($)
1	$1/(1.1) = 0.909$	1,000	909	480	436
2	$1/(1.1)^2 = 0.826$	300	248	480	396
3	$1/(1.1)^3 = 0.751$	1,000	751	480	360
4	$1/(1.1)^4 = 0.683$	0	0	480	328
5	$1/(1.1)^5 = 0.621$	0	0	480	298
Total			1,908		1,818

Under those conditions, the present value of project A is $1,908 and that of project B is $1,818. Of the two projects, only A has a value exceeding its cost.

What would happen if 3 percent was the appropriate discount rate? As the following table shows, the present value of both would be above the cost of the projects.

Received at End of Year	Discount Factor	Project A Return ($)	Discounted ($)	Project B Return ($)	Discounted ($)
1	$1/(1.03) = 0.971$	1,000	971	480	466
2	$1/(1.03)^2 = 0.943$	300	283	480	453
3	$1/(1.03)^3 = 0.915$	1,000	915	480	439
4	$1/(1.03)^4 = 0.888$	0	0	480	426
5	$1/(1.03)^5 = 0.863$	0	0	480	414
Total			2,169		2,198

In fact, project B now has a present value greater than that of project A because returns in the future make greater contributions to present value when the discount rate is lower. Choice of the appropriate discount rate clearly matters for public decisions—an artificially high or low rate can lead to wasteful choices.

Analysts sometimes compare alternatives by determining what discount rate would cause the present value of projects under consideration to be equal. Thus, the present value of projects A and B would be the same at a rate around 4 percent. If the rate is above that level, A is better; if below, B is better. The discount rate that would equate the two streams is called the *internal rate of return.*

The Annuity Formula—A Special Case

In some situations, the income stream to be discounted may be constant for several years. For instance, a new maintenance garage might reduce costs by $20,000 per year for 25 years, and that cost savings is to be compared with the construction cost of the garage. The flow in each year could be discounted back to the present as discussed above; a quicker approach entails use of an annuity formula to compute the present value of the income stream in a single computation. This formula does the same discounting, but it has been mathematically simplified. If S equals the amount of the annual flow and other variables are as previously defined,

$$PV = (S/r)[1 - (1/(1 + r))^n]$$

All rules about more frequent compounding (quarterly, semiannually, monthly) apply in this formula as well. In the example here, the present value of those maintenance garage cost savings if $r = 10$ percent would equal

$$PV = (20,000 / 0.10) [1 - (1 / 1.1)^{25}] = \$181,541$$

This formula is used later in bond pricing (Chapter 15) and in converting a capital cost into an annualized cost equivalent.[19]

Organizing Information for Choices: Cost-Benefit Analysis

Because society cannot afford to waste its scarce resources, judging whether a particular program is worth its cost is a constant problem in public-program choice. Cost-benefit analysis provides a way of organizing information about a program under consideration so that priorities may be reasonably established.[20] A private

---

[19]This formula can also be used to determine the mortgage payment (principal and interest) needed to pay off a loan and is often used by engineers to convert a capital cost into an annual cost equivalent (annualization). In the formula, change PV (present value of the flow) to P (amount of the loan) and solve for S (the periodic payment):

$$S = (P/r) [1 - (1/(1 + r^n))]$$

For example, the monthly principal and interest payment for a $80,000 mortgage taken for 20 years at a 7 percent interest rate would be computed as follows:

$$S = (80,000/(0.07/12))[1 - (1/(1 + (0.07/12))^{20})] = \$620$$

[20]One source for more complete coverage of cost-benefit analysis is Edward M. Gramlich, *Benefit-Cost Analysis of Government Programs,* 2nd ed. (Englewood Cliffs, N.J.: Prentice Hall, 1990).

firm considers a major project (say, the purchase of a new delivery truck to replace an older, smaller one) and compares the anticipated increase in revenue from the new truck with the anticipated increase in costs. If the revenue exceeds cost, the purchase of the truck is a wise use of the firm's scarce resources; if not, the purchase is unwise. There is no sense using resources badly, whether the use is by a private firm or by a government.

Cost-benefit analysis is the government analog to that process of private capital budgeting. Governments can use the tool for assistance in making decisions as diverse as purchasing information technology systems, modernizing vehicle fleets, developing water-resource projects, developing communicable disease control programs, and building new highways and bridges. It has also been used to evaluate the worth of numerous government regulations.[21] For capital budget purposes, however, cost-benefit analysis is similar to decision-making processes used by private firms: the analysis estimates whether the gain to society (benefit) from the project is greater than the social sacrifice (cost) required to produce the project. If so, the project is worthwhile; if not, the project is not worthwhile. Worthwhile projects improve economic conditions in that worthwhile projects direct resources where their use provides a greater return than would alternative uses.

Skeptics point out that what characterizes the public decision process is political bargaining, not an exercise in rational consideration by nonpolitical administrators.[22] So what service can cost-benefit analysis provide? First, the analysis augments the political influence of underrepresented potential beneficiaries and identifies the position of cost bearers. A display of costs and benefits makes it more difficult for the unrepresented to be ignored in political bargaining. In some instances, it can be a valuable weapon (for either side) in the "it pays for itself" budget strategy. Second, economic efficiency—the guiding force of cost-benefit analysis—is but one of several public goals. Even though a decision may not be based primarily on those grounds, the potential gain sacrificed in the selection of a particular public policy is important information. Third, cost-benefit analysis forces public decision making to focus on the value of competing alternatives. Valuation and the accompanying process of competing priorities are the keys to sound decision making, so cost-benefit analysis directs attention to vital questions.

The cost-benefit logic is not limited to complex projects; it can be particularly useful in more narrow public management decisions about alternative methods of accomplishing a particular task. Among the applications are repair-replace and lease-purchase decisions, fuel conversion, modernization choices, and data processing equipment acquisitions. In these decisions, the objective is simply to perform a task at least cost, often when one option involves a capital expenditure and others do not.

---

[21]"Best practices" for preparing economic analyses of regulatory actions are presented in Executive Office of the President, Office of Management and Budget, *Economic Analysis of Federal Regulations under Executive Order 12866* (Washington, D.C.: Office of Management and Budget, 1996).

[22]Federal water resource projects have one of the longest histories of cost-benefit applications. Even here, Eric Schenker and Michael Bunamo indicate that these projects are strongly influenced by purely political factors when examined across regions in the United States. See "A Study of the Corps of Engineers' Regional Pattern of Investments," *Southern Economic Journal* 39 (April 1973): 548–58.

Elements in Cost-Benefit Analysis

Five steps make up formal cost-benefit analysis: (1) categorizing project objectives, (2) estimating the project's impact on objectives, (3) estimating project costs, (4) discounting cost and benefit flows at an appropriate discount rate, and (5) summarizing findings in a fashion suitable for decision making.[23] The content of the analysis varies according to the project considered; the following discussion focuses on common elements and their application in selected situations.

PROJECT OBJECTIVES

The project analysis should identify the project's benefits. What desirable results will happen because of the project?[24] The relationship between the project and the objective must be traceable to establish a sound foundation for the analysis. The following are some examples: a rapid transit system could increase travel speed (saving time for travelers), reduce accident costs, and reduce private-vehicle operation costs; a water project might reduce flood damage, provide water for residential and other use, and improve effluent dilution for water-quality management; a new fire station might reduce operating costs of an older facility and reduce prospective fire loss in a service area; and a word processing system might reduce labor costs, material costs, and filing expenses. The analysis must focus on the factors that are different in the options under consideration. Nothing can be gained by examination of factors that are not changed by the decision. The principle seems too simple to matter, except that much policy argument takes place about elements that will not change regardless of the choice selected.

This simple example illustrates some elements of the necessary incremental logic. Suppose a town is contemplating a newspaper-recycling project; its garbage truck will be fitted with a rack to collect bundles of newspapers along the collection route. Cost and revenue estimates prepared by the town clerk appear in the following list:

	Annual Cost
Labor (one extra worker to gather and process papers)	$14,000
Purchase and installation of rack (one-year useful life)	400
Apportioned share of truck operation and maintenance	1,500
Apportioned share of Public Works Department administrative expense	2,000
Total	$17,900

---

[23]The Office of Management and Budget provides in Circular A-94 an instruction guide to preparing cost-benefit analyses for the federal government: Executive Office of the President, Office of Management and Budget, Circular A-94 Revised (Transmittal Memo No. 64), October 29, 1992.

[24]This is benefit-cost analysis, not economic impact analysis, so spending effects are not included in the analysis. People employed in the project are a cost, not a benefit, and expenditures net out. A new football stadium might result in increased spending at local bars and restaurants, a positive impact for those firms, but that spending comes from the pockets of their patrons and that is a negative for them. For the economy as a whole and for benefit-cost analysis, the impacts cancel out.

	Annual Revenue
980 tons of paper at $15 per ton	$14,700
Annual Loss (or Required Subsidy)	($3,200)

Although the estimates are consistent with accounting principles that require each activity to bear its share of entity-operation cost, the conflict is with the incremental principle: only costs or revenue that change with a decision should be considered in making the decision. In the preceding example, there is nothing logically wrong with estimates of revenue, labor cost, or rack cost: none of those would exist without the recycling, so they are incremental to the decision. There are problems, however, with the administrative, operational, and maintenance cost figures: Will any of these costs be different because of the recycling program? If not (which is probably the case), they should be excluded in making the decision. When the adjustment to incremental reasoning is made, the program actually will subsidize the general government ($300 incremental revenue over incremental cost) rather than requiring subsidization. In addition, there may be further gains if costs of the traditional waste-management operation are reduced because newspapers are no longer in the stream going to the landfill.

BENEFIT ESTIMATION AND VALUATION

A Senate guide to water-project evaluation defines benefits as "increase or gains, net of associated or induced costs, in the value of goods and services which result from conditions with the project, as compared with conditions without the project."[25] The same logic applies to any project. Thus, the analyst must estimate for the life of the project both physical changes from the project and the value of these changes. No single method applies for all projects: specific techniques used to estimate benefits of a personnel-training project would not be the same as those used in water projects. Regardless of the project, however, the decision must be made from estimates, not facts. Facts in economic or social relationships can be only historical. Present decisions cannot change what has already happened, and what will happen can only be estimated. The analysis must proceed with best estimates; it cannot be paralyzed by lack of complete information because complete information is available only when it is too late to decide.

An initial step estimates the physical size of the project's expected change. Sometimes a controlled experiment on a sample can estimate probable effects before resources are committed to the entire program. For instance, the state of Virginia estimated the likely benefits of reflectorized motor vehicle plates by comparing accident frequency among a random sample of cars equipped with these plates with frequency in the remainder of the population.[26] The controlled experiment results could be used to estimate accident reduction from reflectorized plates for the entire state.

[25]U.S. Senate, *Politics, Standards and Procedures in the Formulation, Evaluation and Review of Plans for Use in Development of Water and Related Land Resources,* 87th Cong., 2nd sess., S. Doc. No. 87-97 (May 1962).
[26]Charles B. Stoke, *Reflectorized License Plates: Do They Reduce Nighttime Rear-End Collision?* (Charlottesville: Virginia Highway Research Council, 1974). Drivers were not told and could not control the type of plates they received. The plates did not make a difference in the incidence of such collisions.

Controlled experiments, however, are seldom possible. More often, models developed from the social, physical, or engineering sciences are used to estimate that change. For water-resource projects, hydrological models can yield estimates of the influence of reservoirs, canals, and channelization on water flows and levels. From that information, the effects on navigation, probability of flooding, water supply, and so on can be derived. Gravity models from economic analysis and marketing can indicate likely drawing power of various public facilities. Trip-generation models can suggest traffic flows from transportation facility changes. Any model allows the analyst to apply evidence from other environments to predict the results of projects under consideration so that these changes can be valued: analytical models are the key to linking government inputs to government outputs. Harold Hovey describes the importance of models:

> To analyze any program … requires a model, which describes the relationship between what we put into the activity (inputs) and what we expect to get out of it (outputs). Good models explain what exact relationships are, not just that a relationship exists…. To require that the model be made explicit is one of the greatest potential contributions of systematic analysis to government. An explicit model can be studied, criticized, evaluated, and improved. Too often, decisions are made without explicit models. The result can never be better than if the model is explicit, it can frequently be worse.[27]

When the project's impact has been estimated, the worth of its benefits must then be gauged. Such valuation permits comparison of project cost to project returns and helps establish whether the undertaking increases the net well-being of the region. Money values are used, not to glorify money, but to provide a common yardstick to compare how individuals value the project with how they value the resources used by that project. For example, 1 million tons of concrete applied to highway construction may prolong by one year the useful life of 5,000 automobiles; resources of one type are used to save resources of another type. Will the community be better off with that use of its scarce resources? A direct comparison is impossible because units being measured (cars and concrete) are not the same. Our only meaningful alternative is to estimate the relative value individuals place on cars and concrete: How much general purchasing power are individuals willing to give up to acquire each? Those purchasing-power units provide the measuring standard.

The particular valuation approach depends on the project, but the task is always easiest when values can be connected to a private market, that is, when the public good being considered is an intermediate good. For instance, river-navigation projects may reduce shipper costs: the estimated difference between costs of river shipment and costs of the cheapest available alternative can indicate the value of an increased volume of shipping. (Recall the Tenn-Tom Waterway case several chapters ago.) The value of employment-training projects can best be estimated from differences in anticipated pre- and post-project incomes of trainees. Many capital

---

[27]Harold A. Hovey, *The Planning-Programming-Budgeting Approach to Government Decision-Making* (New York: Praeger, 1968), 23.

expenditure items purchased by governments may reduce operating costs, in which case those savings are the primary benefit from the project.[28]

For some projects, however, outputs are not linked to goods or services sold in private markets: the output is desired for its own sake (relaxation in a city park), not because it contributes to another production process. In other words, these outputs are final products as opposed to the intermediate products that contribute to the production of a private good.[29] When the government product or service is a final product or when prices of marketed commodities change as a result of the project, a different approach is used. That approach is the estimation of *consumers' surplus*—the difference between the maximum price consumers would willingly pay for given amounts of a commodity and the price that the market demands for the commodity (which would be zero for public services provided at no direct charge). The underlying logic of consumer surplus is relatively simple, although its application is anything but simple: Points along an individual's demand curve for a product or service represent the value the person places on particular amounts of the product in question. The individual would voluntarily pay a price up to the level on the demand curve rather than not have the product. He or she would not pay more, so the price on the curve represents the individual's valuation of the product.

Figure 7–2 is a representation of an individual's demand for visits to a park; for 10 visits to the park, the maximum that individual would pay is $5. If the price actually charged is above $5, the individual would visit fewer times (if at all); if the price is below $5, the individual receives a consumer surplus—the consumer receives the service at less than the price he or she would have willingly paid. Consumer surplus then equals the difference between the maximum price the individual would have paid and the price he or she actually pays multiplied by the number of units

Figure 7–2
Individual Demand for a Park

[28]The public value of a National Football League (NFL) franchise has been estimated by real property rents in NFL cities compared to cities without a franchise. Gerald Carlino and N. Edward Coulson, "Compensating Differentials and Social Benefits of the NFL," *Journal of Urban Economics* 56 (June 2004): 25–50. A cost-benefit analysis of government subsidies to NFL franchises (mostly stadium subsidies) working from this benefit calculation suggests that they may be a good investment for cities.
[29]Richard A. Musgrave, "Cost-Benefit Analysis and the Theory of Public Finance," *Journal of Economic Literature* 7 (September 1969): 797–806.

purchased. If the price were zero (the park has no admission charge), the total consumer surplus here would be

$$(\$10 \times 5) + (\$5 \times 5) + (\$2 \times 5) + (\$1 \times 5) = \$90$$

That is the entire area under the demand curve for the service.

Public services are seldom sold, so how is it possible to consider quantities demanded as a function of price? The demand curves are constructed by recognizing that implicit prices must be paid to use even free services. Individuals must bear the cost of getting from where they live to the free facility; this cost is the implicit price. User-pattern analysis allows estimation of a demand curve. Use (quantity demanded) usually is greater by those who are closest to the facility (travel cost, or implicit price, is lower), following the configuration of a conventional demand curve.[30] Estimating consumer surplus is not without problems, but it really is the only reasonable technique for that class of public services. Contingent valuation, as described in Sidebar 7–2, provides another approach to estimating the demand for a pure public good.

ESTIMATING PROJECT COSTS[31]

A project's resource cost estimate includes construction cost and operating cost for the life of the project. Obviously, the preparation of these estimates requires the close cooperation of engineers and accountants skilled in costing, particularly if heavy public-work facilities are involved. The analyst must recognize, however, that the important cost for society is the opportunity cost of the resources used in the project: "By the opportunity cost of a decision is meant the sacrifice of alternatives required by that decision…[O]pportunity costs require the measurement of sacrifices. If a decision involves no sacrifices, it is cost free."[32] The cost that matters for decisions is the value of paths not taken, the true cost of any decision. That complication can produce three types of cost estimate adjustments based initially on resource purchase prices. First, ordinary project cost estimates include only private or internal costs. Many public projects, however, can create undesirable effects on others, or negative externalities. Examples include the damage done to surrounding properties by pollutants produced by a municipal incinerator and the traffic delays

---

[30]An often-cited example of estimating a demand curve from travel costs is Frank Lupi et al., "The Michigan Recreational Angling Demand Model," Agricultural Economics Staff Paper 97-58, Department of Agricultural Economics, Michigan State University, January 1998, which estimates the demand for recreational fishing in the state.

[31]A close relative of cost-benefit analysis is cost-effectiveness analysis. This technique compares the relative costs of achieving a given objective, but does not attempt to estimate benefits of reaching that objective. For instance, a cost-effectiveness analysis of stopping aircraft hijacking found that the cost of saving one life by putting federal air marshals on aircraft would be $180 million per life saved, while the cost per life saved of hardening cockpit doors would be $800,000 per life saved. M. G. Stewart and J. Mueller, "Assessing the Risks, Costs and Benefits of United States Aviation Security Measures," Center for Infrastructure Performance and Reliability, University of Newcastle (Australia) Research Report No. 267.04.08, 2008. Within a fixed budget, hardening cockpit doors makes much more sense than putting marshals on planes.

[32]William Warren Haynes, *Managerial Economics* (Plano, Tex.: Business Publications, 1969), 32.

Sidebar 7–2
Measuring the Value of Nonmarket Goods

The nonappropriability feature of a public good prevents direct measurement of the market value of that good. Market value emerges from the independent decisions of buyers and sellers in exchange transactions. Nonappropriability means that sellers cannot charge an appropriate price to cover the cost of resources needed for service provisions and buyers will not pay a price sufficient to reflect the full social value of the service. Where transactions do occur, they cannot be expected to reflect the social value of the service.

So is there a way in which market-type valuation information can be obtained for a pure public good? The Council of Economic Advisers in its 1993 *Economic Report of the President* describes one approach that has been used.

> Since a public good is not traded on a competitive market, the market cannot assign it a price based on its value. Measuring the benefits public goods provide is problematic. One method is to infer the value of public goods from actual markets or observable economic behavior. For example, to estimate the value people put on scenic beauty, economists may measure the effect of scenic beauty on actual real estate prices. The value that people put on a park may be reflected in the amount of time and money that they spend to visit and use it.
>
> The contingent-valuation method (CVM) uses public opinion surveys. A polltaker asks people to estimate the amount they would be willing to pay to maintain or create a certain public good or the amount they would require to compensate for its loss. Advocates of the CVM argue that it can generate reliable estimates of value in cases where it is impossible to make inferences from actual markets or behavior, and in principle, it takes into account the fact that some people value a good more highly than others do.
>
> However, the CVM also has generated considerable criticism. For example, those surveyed do not actually have to pay the amount they report, a factor that can lead to overstatements. Responses are sensitive to the way questions are posed. (In one case, the estimated value of protection from oil spills changed by a factor of 300 when polltakers asked additional questions before eliciting this value.) CVM results can be inconsistent. (For example, one CVM study showed that people were willing to pay more money to clean up small oil spills than to clean up both small and large spills.) In many cases, CVM results cannot be verified except by another CVM study.
>
> These problems are exacerbated when the CVM is used to estimate the value of goods that are abstract, symbolic, or difficult to comprehend. One study showed that if the CVM were used to estimate the value of saving whooping cranes from extinction, resulting estimates might be as high as $37 billion per year (more than the Federal Government spends each year on education and Head Start programs). Finally, even if all the problems of the CVM could be resolved, care must be taken to ensure that it is not used to analyze policy in a one-sided way. For example, a proposed program to protect whooping cranes might put people out of work. The $37 billion figure could be cited by those who claim that the benefits of the program exceed its costs. But opponents of that view could undertake a CVM study of their own asking people how much they would be willing to pay to protect these jobs.

A valuation by CVM will not be perfect, but it certainly is preferable to ignoring these nonmarket impacts—which generally amounts to assuming that they have no value.

SOURCE: Executive Office of the President, Council of Economic Advisers, *Economic Report of the President Transmitted to the Congress January 1993* (Washington, D.C.: U.S. Government Printing Office, 1993), 209.

created when streets are blocked by construction of a government office building. These are costs inflicted on parties outside the market transaction, but the costs are just as real to society as wages or payment for construction materials. These adjustments are made using the same indirect methods applied in benefit estimation—these impacts are, logically, negative social benefits.

Second, adjustments are appropriate if the project uses completely unemployed resources or resources for which there is no alternative use. If such is the case, there is nothing sacrificed in consuming those resources in the project being considered. Thus, the actual social opportunity cost of the resource to the project is zero, not the financial cost involved in paying the resource's owner. For that reason, it may be sensible to undertake programs in areas with massive unemployment when that program ordinarily would not be economically justifiable: putting the idle resources to work adds a desired product without economic loss.

Third, many public projects use property already owned by the government. Property acquisition brings no out-of-pocket cost; when sites for a new highway, incinerator, and so forth are being compared, the site using public property has the lowest financial cost. The real social cost of that site for the proposed project is the site's value in its existing (or other possible) use. What does the community lose if the site is selected for the new use? There is no justification for valuing already owned properties at zero. Furthermore, the amount paid for the resource (its historical cost) may not be a usable guide. For example, if a municipality invests $1.5 million in a new incinerator plant that will not burn the refuse mix generated by the city, the value of the plant clearly is less than $1.5 million and, unless there is some salvage value for the facility, approximates zero.

Decisions have to be based on alternatives sacrificed and opportunities forgone. Amounts paid in the past (historical costs) have no necessary bearing on cost in present decisions. Options now establish the cost that matters for current choices.

Selecting a Discount Rate

Public projects usually create a flow of costs and returns that spans several years. Therefore, both streams must be converted to present value for comparison; discounting is necessary. There is, however, no single discount rate that is immediately obvious as the appropriate rate for analysis.[33] Market imperfections and differences in risk cause a broad spectrum of interest rates in the economy. Two important alternatives for discounting are the cost of borrowed funds to the government (the interest rate the government must pay) and the opportunity cost of displaced private activity (the return that private resources could earn). There are conditions under which either may be appropriate.

The cost of borrowed money provides the closest analog to private-project analysis—it is an interest rate that presumably must be paid by a borrower. Because

---

[33]The Federal Reserve discount rate is the interest rate at which the Federal Reserve will make loans to banks that are members of the Federal Reserve System. Although this rate is published as the discount rate, it is not appropriate for discounting or compounding in financial management.

most public programs are ultimately financed by tax revenues, use of the rate at which a government can borrow would not necessarily direct resources to their best-yield uses. Absence of default risk on (federal) government debt makes that rate abnormally low. Allocation using that rate would pull resources away from higher-yielding private activities to prospectively lower-yielding public use. Sidebar 7–3 describes the different philosophies and rules in the federal government. For state and local governments, the borrowing rate could be particularly misleading because the exclusion of interest on most state and local debt from federal income tax allows these governments to borrow at well below the market rate.[34]

Sidebar 7–3
What Discount Rate to Use?

The big three of federal government finance—Office of Management and Budget (OMB), Government Accountability Office (GAO), and CBO—all do discounting in consideration of capital expenditure programs, lease-purchase decisions, regulatory reviews, valuation of assets for sale, and so on. But the discount rates they use are not the same. Here is a quick summary of their rates.

OMB establishes the discount policy for almost all executive agencies in its Circular No. A-94. The current base case analysis prescribes a real discount rate of 7 percent, a rate to approximate the marginal pre-tax rate of return on average private-sector investment in recent years. There are exceptions to that base policy. Water-project analysis uses a rate based on the average yield during the previous fiscal year on interest-bearing marketable securities of the United States, which have terms of fifteen years or longer to maturity. Cost-effectiveness analysis with constant-dollar costs should use the real Treasury borrowing rate on marketable securities of comparable maturity to the period of analysis. In addition, lease-purchase analysis of nominal lease payments should use the nominal Treasury borrowing rate on marketable securities of comparable maturity to the period of analysis. Internal federal investments that either increase federal revenue or decrease federal cost should generally use the comparable maturity Treasury rate.

The GAO uses a discount rate based on the average nominal yield of marketable Treasury debt with maturity between one year and the life of the project, with benefits and costs in nominal terms. The same rate applies for all evaluation uses; the GAO endorses sensitivity analysis.

The CBO uses the real yield of Treasury debt and estimates that rate to be 2 percent with a sensitivity analysis of 2 percentage points to test variability. Asset valuation uses comparable private-sector interest rates.

SOURCES: Randolph M. Lyon, "Federal Discount Rate Policy, the Shadow Price of Capital, and Challenges for Reform," *Journal of Environmental Economics and Management* 18 (March 1990), Part 2; and Office of Management and Budget, Circular A-94 Revised (Transmittal Memo No. 64), October 29, 1992.

---

[34]An individual in the 35 percent federal tax bracket would receive the same after-tax rate of return on a taxed corporate bond yielding 15 percent as on an untaxed municipal bond yielding 9.75 percent, calculated by subtracting the tax that would be owed on that 15 percent rate to get the net after-tax rate, that is, $(15 - (.35 \times 15)) = 9.75$.

Public authorities that generate revenue from sales of products or services might use that rate because it estimates the market attitude toward the prospects of the enterprise. Even here, however, the interest excluded from income taxes complicates the analysis.

The return that could have been achieved in displaced private spending is generally more appropriate for the logic of cost-benefit analysis (an analysis aimed at discovering actions that increase the welfare of the community). It is a rate the analyst must estimate—there is no defined interest rate. William Baumol lucidly expresses the essential argument:

> If the resources in question produce a rate of return in the private sector which society evaluates at *r* percent, then the resources should be transferred to the public project if that project yields a return greater than *r* percent. They should be left in private hands if their potential earnings in the proposed government investment are less than *r* percent.[35]

The problem is to estimate what the rate of return would have been on these displaced resources because that is the opportunity cost a public project must exceed if it is not to misallocate community resources. In general, this rate can be estimated according to the formula

$$r_p = k_1 r_1 + k_2 r_2 + \ldots + k_n r_n$$

where

r_p = rate of return on displaced resources (the project discount rate),

k = fraction of project cost extracted from a particular sector (usually the percentage of total taxes collected from it),

r = return on investment in a particular sector, and

n = the number of private sectors with displaced resources.

This weighted average provides a workable estimate of the private opportunity cost of the displaced resources, and the resulting discount rate is applied to the estimated benefit and cost flows.[36]

Decision Criteria

The final stage in project analysis applies a decision criterion to the discounted cost and return flows to summarize the economic case for the project. The summarization can either identify whether a project is economically justifiable or establish rankings

[35]William J. Baumol, "On the Discount Rate for Public Projects," in *Public Expenditures and Policy Analysis,* ed. Robert H. Haveman and Julius Margolis (Chicago: Markham, 1970), 274.
[36]When the time span for the consequences is very long—hundreds of years, as would be the case for certain environmental policies—it is extremely difficult to identify an appropriate discount rate. The long-term ramifications may be huge, but disappear at any normal discount rate. Some options are proposed in Paul R. Portney and John P. Weyant, eds., *Discounting and Intergenerational Equity* (Washington, D.C.: Resources for the Future, 1999).

among projects to be fitted into a limited budget. Two criteria often used are the benefit-cost ratio (BCR; the present value of benefits divided by the present value of costs) and the net present value (NPV; the present value of benefits less the present value of costs). If B = project benefit, C = project cost, r = the appropriate discount rate, t = the year in the life of the project, and T = the life of the project, then

$$NPV = \sum_{t=1}^{T} \frac{(B_t - C_t)}{(1+r)^t}$$

and

$$BCR = \sum_{t=1}^{T} \frac{B_t}{(1+r)^t} \Bigg/ \sum_{t=1}^{T} \frac{C_t}{(1+r)_t}$$

The test of economic efficiency requires an NPV greater than 0 or a BCR greater than 1. If the test is met, resource use for the project will increase economic well-being because alternative use of those resources would produce a lower return for the community. Application of these criteria ignores politics, desires for wealth redistribution, regional problems, and other important concerns, but both NPV and BCR capture the economics of the project. Sidebar 7–4 illustrates how capital projects can be evaluated with the cost-benefit analysis tool.

Two additional measures sometimes proposed should be mentioned briefly. These are the payback period and the internal rate of return. The payback-period method divides the estimated net annual flow of project returns into the capital cost of the project to obtain the number of years it would take to fully recover (pay back) the capital cost. Thus, if $2,000 is the net annual return from a project with a capital cost of $8,000, the payback period is four years. The shorter the period, the more attractive the project. This measure is defective in that it ignores both the time profile of returns (proceeds available only late in project life are valued as if equal to earlier returns) and proceeds received after the payback point. For example, consider the projects in Table 7–3. By payback-period reasoning, the project ranking (best to worst) would be A, B, C. If a discount rate of 10 percent were appropriate, the NPV of A = 2,909, of B = 909, and of C = 1,292. Crude payback periods are simply not generally reliable as a project guide.[37]

The internal-rate-of-return method seeks the interest rate that would equate the present value of benefits with the present value of costs. That return is compared with the discount rate: the project passes the economic efficiency test if its rate of return is higher than the discount rate. Computation of an internal rate of return may

---

[37]However, a recent study of Canadian municipalities found a distinct preference for the payback approach in doing capital budgets, in spite of its clear deficiencies. Yee-Ching Lillian Chang, "Use of Capital Budgeting Techniques and an Analytic Approach to Capital Investment Decisions in Canadian Municipal Governments," *Public Budgeting & Finance* 24 (Summer 2004): 40–58.

Sidebar 7–4
An Application of Net Present Value to Evaluate a Capital Project

A major university hosted a nationally televised football game toward the end of its unsuccessful season, and the field was in such poor condition that alumni from around the country called to complain about the poor image it gave their alma mater. The university must replace the field in any case. It has two alternatives: a conventional sod field or a synthetic turf called Astro Play. The Astro Play would cost $446,000 to install, requires no annual maintenance, and can be used for eleven seasons. The sod field would cost $110,000 to replace, will last three seasons, and requires an annual maintenance cost of $20,000 in each nonreplacement year. Suppose that 5 percent is a reasonable discount rate. What is the NPV of installing the Astro Play?

The NPV of installing Astro Play is computed by comparing the NPVs of the costs for the two field options over the eleven-year period. The NPV of the cost of the sod field would equal the benefit from installing the synthetic surface because it is these costs that would be avoided with the Astro Play. The cost of Astro Play simply equals its installation cost because there are no other costs through its useful life.

The flow of costs from the alternatives, the appropriate discount factor [$(1.05)^n$ where n = years since initial installation], and the discounted costs of the alternative are as follows:

	Cost of Sod Field ($)	Discount Factor	Present Value of Sod Field Cost ($)
Beginning	110,000	1.000	110,000.00
End of Year 1	20,000	1.050	19,047.62
Year 2	20,000	1.103	18,132.37
Year 3	110,000	1.158	94,991.36
Year 4	20,000	1.216	16,447.37
Year 5	20,000	1.276	15,673.98
Year 6	110,000	1.340	82,089.55
Year 7	20,000	1.407	14,214.64
Year 8	20,000	1.477	13,540.96
Year 9	110,000	1.551	70,921.99
Year 10	20,000	1.629	12,277.47
Year 11	20,000	1.710	11,695.91
Total			479,033.22

The NPV of installing Astro Play equals the difference between discounted benefits and discounted costs. Discounted benefits equal $479,033.22; discounted costs equal $446,000. The NPV equals $33,033.22 and the benefit-cost ratio equals 1.07. The internal rate of return (IRR) may also be calculated: the first term in the stream of benefits would equal negative 336,000 (the extra initial cost from choosing Astro Play), and the remaining stream would be the benefits from choosing Astro Play (the costs from grass that are saved). The IRR equals 6.788 percent.

The football team may still lose, but the cost-benefit analysis indicates that it should be playing on the synthetic turf to save the university some money. If nothing else, it will look good while losing!

Table 7–3
Payback Analysis

		Annual Net Benefits (End of Year)			
Project	Capital Cost ($)	Year 1 ($)	Year 2 ($)	Year 3 ($)	Payback Period
A	10,000	10,000	0	0	1 year
B	10,000	9,000	1,100	0	1+ years
C	10,000	3,000	4,000	7,000	3+ years

be illustrated using the data for project C in Table 7–3. The internal rate of return (r) is the rate that causes the stream of net benefits in the future to exactly equal the present capital cost:

$$10,000 = (3,000/(1+r)) + (4,000/(1+r)^2) + (7,000/(1+r)^4)$$

r may be computed only by successively trying values of r until the value for the right side equals that for the left side. The computations are relatively simple in this instance (the solution is $r = 16.23$ percent), but iterations involving flows over many years are tedious. Fortunately, computers can be programmed to do the work, and internal-rate-of-return calculations are standard features of good personal computer spreadsheet programs and many electronic calculators.[38]

However, the present-value methods are "simpler, safer, easier, and more direct"[39] because they can be adapted to use multiple discount rates during investment life, they avoid the problem of multiple internal rates of return that can emerge in computing internal rates, and they do not require additional tests to determine the validity of a computed rate of return. Project analysis may require not just an evaluation of the economics of a number of projects, but also selection of particular projects from several alternatives. Two ranking indexes are available: the benefit-cost ratio (BCR) and net present value (NPV).[40] Project rankings are often the same with either criterion, but sometimes—especially when project sizes are substantially different—the ranks are different. Which ranking should apply: that produced by NPVs or by the BCR?

Table 7–4 presents the discounted cost and benefit data for two capital projects. If $500 is to be budgeted, should project A or project B be undertaken? Project B has the higher NPV, whereas project A has the higher BCR. Each criterion supposes particular facts about the projects. Ranking by BCR assumes that either project can be increased in any proportion without changing the return relationships. In the present comparison, ranking by BCR presumes that project A can be expanded to

[38]In an Excel spreadsheet, the internal rate of return may be calculated using the following: @irr(values, guess), where "values" is the range of cells containing the flow for which you want to calculate the internal rate of return (the first value is going to be negative) and "guess" is your guess about what the internal rate of return is. Usually, you don't need to insert a guess because the spreadsheet will use 10 percent and that will work.

[39]Harold Bierman, Jr., and Seymour Smidt, *The Capital Budgeting Decision* (New York: Macmillan, 1975), 57.

[40]The ratio of excess benefit to cost (benefit minus cost, divided by cost) provides no additional information because project ranks are the same as with the BCR: $B/C = [(B - C)/C] + 1$.

Table 7–4
Projects with Ranking Criteria Conflict

Project	Cost ($)	Benefit ($)	NPV ($)	BCR
A	150	200	50	1.33
B	500	600	100	1.20

3⅓ times its present size at the same benefit rate ($667), yielding a NPV of $167. That expansion must be technically and economically possible if ratios are to guide the decision. Ranking by NPV presumes that the alternative investment streams are the size indicated, without the possibility of changing project size at the same BCR.

In many situations, of course, neither presumption is met entirely. When such is the case, the decision must rely on a comparison of present value of benefits from the use of available funds in feasible combinations of all project sizes. If the analysis attempts to determine economically feasible projects, not allocation within a fixed budget, either method will be satisfactory: if NPV is positive, the BCR will be greater than 1. Conflict emerges only with rankings. In public-project analysis, the difficult questions involve estimating benefits, costs, and discount rates; conflict between criteria seldom is the concern. More often than not, knowing how a project stands according to either criterion is enough because the choice is whether or not to proceed with a project, not how to rank a group of projects.

Some Special Problems of Cost-Benefit Analysis

MULTIPLE OBJECTIVES

Cost-benefit analysis provides information about the economic impact of projects. Overall economic impacts, however, may not be the sole or even the most important objective of some programs, particularly those concerned with redistributing income. If redistribution is important, benefits received by some groups in society will be more important than benefits received by others. Market values do not measure this objective, so benefit values would need explicit adjustment to encompass redistribution concerns.

Normal cost-benefit analysis accepts all portions of the economy as equal; who gains and who loses does not matter. It accepts the hypothetical compensation criterion of theoretical welfare economics: a public decision will be regarded as sound if those gaining from a public action receive sufficient benefits to compensate any losses, with some surplus gain remaining.[41] The principle ignores distribution of gains and losses across society and can be defended by these arguments: (1) changes affecting income distributions can be viewed as negligible;[42] (2) public investment is neither a proper nor an effective tool for redistribution, and other fiscal policies

---

[41]J. G. Head, "The Welfare Foundations of Public Finance Theory," *Rivista di Diritto Finanziaro e Scienza-Della Finanze* 24 (September 1965): 379–428.
[42]Otto Eckstein, *Water Resource Development* (Cambridge, Mass.: Harvard University Press, 1958), 36–37.

can easily correct for any investment-related maldistribution; and (3) many projects over time will have benefits randomly distributed, causing the overall effect to average out at no redistributional change. On these grounds, distribution effects can be ignored with some theoretical justification. The view has been growing, however, that such treatment assumes way too much and that some groups in society seem always to be the loser in public choices.

Two general techniques have emerged to deal with this distributional concern. Some analysts have allowed for distribution effects by weighting benefits according to a measure of the societal importance of the recipient. Benefits received by meritorious groups (those society wants to help) count more than benefits received by others. Selection of weights is obviously a problem. Burton Weisbrod has applied weights derived from past public-project decisions that have not followed strict cost-benefit rankings.[43] This approach does not, however, attack the problem of how the distribution should be changed, but rather weighs analysis in the historical pattern. Besides, this pattern may simply reflect the clout of congressional delegations, not the relative importance of certain groups in society. John Krutilla and Otto Eckstein approach the problem by using marginal rates of federal taxation as weights, assuming that these rates roughly measure the importance of redistribution to society.[44] The technique does focus directly on the income distribution, but it, too, has political pressure problems. Furthermore, it ignores the difference between statutory rates (those quoted in the tax law) and effective rates (those applicable after loopholes). And whenever the tax structure changes, the evaluation of all projects would need to be revised. That does not seem reasonable. Other approaches would apply specific weights specified by the analyst. All bend the general rule that the analyst is to be an impartial observer in the analytic process. Decision makers may not recognize (or accept) the value system assumed by the analyst.

An alternative, the display technique favored by Roland McKean, would supplement general cost and benefit totals with a tabulation of how costs and benefits are divided among the population.[45] Many distributions, such as income, age, race, sex, and geographic area, could be important. By providing such a display, the analyst need not weight the social importance of groups. Decision makers could supply their own weights to each recipient group as desired. The number and type of displays provided would not likely be the same for all projects. If the analyst's goal is to provide information for decision makers and consumers and not to yield conclusive, social-maximizing decisions, such displays seem a prerequisite.

VALUING PROJECTS THAT SAVE LIVES

A sticky problem occurs when public projects seek to reduce the loss of human life, as with transportation safety, cancer research, nutrition education, or fire protection. Life or death can rest on government allocation of resources to particular projects.

---

[43]Burton A. Weisbrod, "Income Redistribution Effects and Benefit-Cost Analysis," in *Problems in Public Expenditure Analysis,* ed. Samuel B. Chase (Washington, D.C.: Brookings Institution, 1968), 177–222.
[44]John V. Krutilla and Otto Eckstein, *Multiple-Purpose River Development* (Baltimore: Johns Hopkins University Press, 1958).
[45]Roland McKean, *Efficiency in Government through Systems Analysis* (New York: Wiley, 1958), 131–33, 208, 242.

Those decisions are distasteful, but they have been and will continue to be made. The real question is whether decision makers know what they are assuming about that value. Any decisions that deny resources to activities that have a lifesaving element have implicitly placed a value on life. They imply that the value is less than the cost of the rejected activity. Is that implicit value—referred to as the "value of a statistical life" in the analysis—reasonable?[46] It isn't valuing any particular person, but it is asking the question, "What does individual behavior observed in market transactions tell us about how much we are willing to pay to reduce the loss of somebody's life?"

A number of methods—none flawless, but some with stronger logical foundation than others—have been proposed to value lifesaving. Historically, the first was average life insurance face-value outstanding, under the logic that this was a value on loss of life that individuals placed on themselves. It is an observable measure, and it emerges from individual market choices. The obvious problems are that individuals buy life insurance for varied motives, including some that have nothing to do with death potential (e.g., forcing themselves to save), and that individual holdings vary substantially by family characteristics. These influences render insurance values generally inappropriate for this use.

A second technique, the human capital or earnings-loss method, views the human as something equivalent to a machine. Thus, the value of a life saved is estimated at the present value of lifetime earnings less subsistence cost through the work career of the individual. This computation equals, it is alleged, the contribution of the individual to the economy—the lost earnings potential of the victim—and is the value of a life saved. There are questions both about what earning pattern to use and whether that narrow production view truly gauges the social worth of an individual. This approach is now seldom used.[47] Most people would be willing to pay more than their lost earnings to avoid death or injury—so governments using such measures probably spend less on life- and injury-saving programs than their public would prefer.

The third technique, willingness to pay, assesses what people would pay for reduced risk to life and then uses that estimate to calculate the value of a whole statistical life. A number of occupations (e.g., logging, offshore drilling) have greater death risks than other occupations requiring similar skills. The wage premiums necessary to recruit workers to high-risk occupations provide an estimate of the value of life in the labor market. Thus, lifesaving values emerge directly from the choices made by individuals. It works like this. Suppose there are two jobs, one a teacher and the other a logger. The logger faces a greater added chance of being killed on the job in any week—a risk higher by 1 in 100,000. Because of the higher risk, loggers have to be paid a bit more—assume market evidence shows that the amount needs to be $50 per week more than teachers. If 100,000 made that choice, each

---

[46]Some discussions use "value of mortality risk" instead of "value of a statistical life." It's a matter of terminology alone.

[47]A close variant is reportedly used in military pilot safety decisions; the value used is the cost of training a replacement. Safety-feature costs are balanced against that value estimate. Should this make military aviators a little nervous? Also, the judicial system uses this approach in wrongful death cases: one element in the awards to families is the estimated net discounted lifetime earnings of the victim.

seeing the extra risk as being acceptable when pay is $50 higher, then collectively loggers are willing to pay no more than $5 million (100,000 × $50) to avoid one expected fatality (100,000 × 1/100,000). There are some logical questions about this method—for one, the values may be artificially low because those jobs apparently appeal to individuals whose attitudes toward risk are different from those of others (they may actually enjoy extreme danger)—but it apparently gives the soundest estimates generally available.[48]

Government decisions do generate implicit values for lifesaving every time one project alternative is accepted and another is rejected.[49] That valuation cannot be avoided. However, being explicit about the numbers can stir up controversy; for instance, there was a firestorm in the media (even making it to *The Colbert Report*) when it was revealed that the Environmental Protection Agency was using a "value of a statistical life" of $6.9 million in 2008, compared to $7.8 million five years earlier. Morally right or wrong? That's a matter beyond the competence of public budgeting, but it does reflect how people are willing to pay for small risk reductions in their individual behaviors. Shouldn't individual choices guide public choices in a democracy? Cost-benefit analysis must ensure that these valuations are conscious and consistent. We can hope for little else. But choices cannot avoid the implicit decisions made as some options are selected and some are rejected, so being explicit is at least appropriate for the objective of public transparency.

Conclusion

Public capital infrastructure contributes to both private and public production. Crumbling roads and bridges, inadequate sewers and outmoded sewage-treatment plants, antiquated schools and public buildings, levees that leak or are too low, low-capacity airports, and so on can have considerable national impact; therefore, governments need to attend to the public capital stock and the capital investment that renews and expands that stock. Leaving future generations with depleted capital assets is just as significant a violation of sustainability as leaving them with a huge debt burden from accumulated operating deficits. Capital budgets, providing a separate review for capital as opposed to current expenditures, establish a process for making choices about the development or replacement of long-life assets such as those just noted. Special concern is warranted because capital investment choices now can influence the quality of life for many years into the future.

---

[48]A pioneering work is W. K. Viscusi, "Wealth Effects and Earnings Premiums for Job Hazards," *Review of Economics and Statistics* 60 (August 1978): 408–16. Estimates can also be developed from contingent valuation surveys asking people what they would be willing to pay for reduced risk of death of injury.

[49]Some government decisions also involve saving human lives in the future. Should there be a discount rate for human life? One study suggests that Maryland households consider six lives saved twenty-five years in the future of equal value to one life saved today (this is about a 7.5 percent discount rate). See Maureen L. Cropper and Paul R. Fortney, "Discounting Human Lives," *Resources* (Summer 1992): 1–4.

Most capital projects involve payments now, when infrastructure is constructed, with a flow of services coming in the future, through the long, useful life of the project. Discounting provides a mechanism for converting these future impacts into their present equivalents. In general, discounting provides a means of converting flows occurring at different times into a standard equivalent and is an important cornerstone of analysis of debt and investments.

Many public projects, including those involving capital investment, involve the use of one sort of resource (concrete to build a highway) to obtain a different return (a saving of travel time with the new highway). Cost-benefit analysis provides a technique for organizing information for the evaluation of public programs when the resources used in the program are dissimilar from the return received from the program. The analysis uses microeconomic market evaluations of the worth of resources and program results.

QUESTIONS AND EXERCISES

1. Roachdale has a population of 32,000, more or less. Several of its important features appear on the following map. The city eagerly awaits the full operation of the Intercontinental Widget plant early in 20X3. Although the plant has few employees now, it will have a workforce of around 900. The plant has caused a shift in city population to the south. Many people are moving to the Wonder Hills subdivision (45 percent developed now), although a good number are located along SR4 outside of town.

   The data presented here, along with department-project proposals, should be used to prepare a capital improvement program for the years 20X0 to 20X4 and a capital budget for 20X0. Financial conditions suggest that the city will be unable to pay more than $900,000 for capital investment in any year, so one part of the exercise requires that priority criteria be established if all requests cannot be included in the budget.

   The city has two special capital asset problems. First, the main sanitary sewer at Westside Elementary School near the Red River has suffered structural failure and must be replaced. Second, the SR4 bridge over the Red River is unsafe. The bridge replacement will take two years. During the first year, traffic will have to be detoured.

   City department heads have proposed the following projects:

   Streets, Roads, and Bridges

   SR4 bridge replacement: 20X0, $350,000; 20X1, $250,000 (costs are totals)

   Street upgrading, Wonder Hills subdivision: 20X0, $600,000; 20X1, $50,000; 20X2, $20,000

   Street sign replacement: 20X0 to 20X9, $18,000 per year (high visibility, breakaway signs)

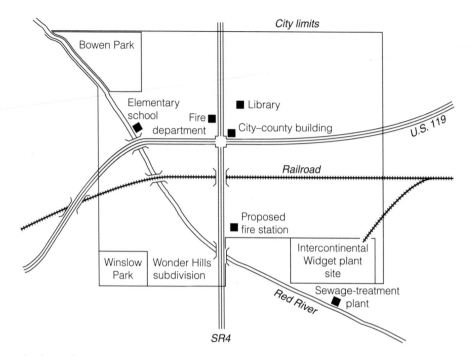

Parks and Recreation

Bowen Park pool: 20×0, $300,000 (construction of new above-ground aluminum pool)

Winslow Park recreation complex: 20×1, $525,000; 20×2, $125,000; 20×3, $300,000; 20×4, $300,000; 20×5, $85,000 (pool, ice skating rink, baseball diamonds)

Libraries

Air-conditioned building: 20×0, $45,000; 20×1, $20,000

Water and Sewer

Water-line upgrading, Wonder Hills: 20×2, $725,000

Storm-sewer installation, Wonder Hills: 20×3, $850,000

Sanitary-sewer replacement (structural failure): 20×0, $150,000

Fire Department

New fire substation: 20×3, $450,000; 20×4, $65,000

Fire equipment: (a) pumper (main station)—20×0, $25,000, (b) pumper, hook and ladder (substation)—20×0, $130,000

2. My son informed me that a comic book I purchased for 10 cents in 1948 is worth $85 today. What has been the average annual compound rate of return on that valuable asset? (See Chapter 2.)

3. Dr. Rubin has $10,000 to invest for three years. Two banks offer a 3 percent interest rate, but bank A compounds quarterly and bank B compounds semiannually. To what value would his money grow in each of the two banks?

4. A time-sharing condominium firm offers prizes to people who visit its project and listen to a marketing presentation. One prize is a $1,000 savings account. Unfortunately, the account would not be available for forty-five years and requires that the winner pay an initial service fee of $55. If one put $55 in an investment account, what annual compound rate of return would cause that sum to reach $1,000 in forty-five years?

5. The Penn Central Railroad has not paid local taxes since 1969, under federal bankruptcy court protection. Some years later the court required Penn Central to offer municipalities a choice of two payment options to clear this liability. (Penn Central had been absorbed by Conrail, so there were no future tax liabilities involved.) The choices were (a) immediate payment of 44 percent of the total liability or (b) immediate payment of 20 percent of the liability, 10 percent paid at the end of each of the next three years, and 50 percent paid at the end of ten years. Which alternative would you recommend to a municipality and why?

6. Two public infrastructure projects have the economic profiles that follow:

	Option A			Option B		
Year	Capital Cost ($)	Operating and Maintenance Cost ($)	Benefits ($)	Capital Cost ($)	Operating and Maintenance Cost ($)	Benefits ($)
1	2,000,000	0	0	2,500,000	0	0
2	1,000,000	10,000	0	500,000	50,000	750,000
3	500,000	70,000	120,000		100,000	750,000
4		90,000	600,000		100,000	750,000
5		90,000	800,000		100,000	750,000
6		90,000	800,000		100,000	750,000
7		90,000	800,000		100,000	750,000
8		90,000	800,000		100,000	750,000
9		100,000	800,000		100,000	750,000
10		100,000	500,000		100,000	300,000

Use these data to compute for each (a) the NPV at discount rates of 10 and 5 percent, (b) the BCR at the same rates, and (c) the internal rate of return for each. Describe the facts about the projects that would dictate which criterion is appropriate, and indicate which project is preferable under each circumstance.

7. The narrow gravel road to Jehnzen Lake is open only for the summer months. At present, the county spends $750 per mile each year to prepare the road for summer traffic and another $150 per mile for maintenance during the period in which it is open. A "permanent" road could be constructed at a cost of $10,000 per mile; the county would have to spend $800 per mile for maintenance (patching, etc.) only every five years through the thirty-year life of the road. Prospects for the area suggest that the road would have to be relocated at the end of that period. If 8 percent is a reasonable discount rate, which option is less costly? What discount rate would cause the two alternatives to have the same cost in present value terms?

8. The irrigation system a farmer uses cost $10,000 eight years ago. It will last another twenty-five years without additional investment. With that system, he produces crops valued at $3,000 per year at a cost of $1,000 per year. A new system would cost $15,000 to install, but would increase production to $7,000 per year. Operating cost would be $2,500 per year. The farmer would have to refurbish the new system twelve years after installation at a cost of $5,000. Assume that investment in the new system occurs at the start of the first year, that revenue and operating cost occur at the end of each year and do not change over the twenty-five years, and that both systems have a salvage value of $1,000 at the end of twenty-five years. Assume a 6-percent discount rate. Should the farmer replace his existing system?

9. What problems involving cost-benefit analysis appear in the following statements?
   a. A public power project uses a discount rate of 8.5 percent, the after-tax rate of return for electric utilities in the area.
   b. Evaluation of a new municipal fire station uses a discount rate equal to the rate at which the city can borrow long-term funds.
   c. Evaluation of a new four-lane highway to replace an older two-lane highway shows saved travel time for truckers and for private vehicles, the value of increased gasoline sales, and increased profits of trucking firms.
   d. A cost-benefit analysis of removal of architectural barriers for people with disabilities from commercial buildings produced the following benefit estimate for a 202,000-square-foot shopping center: economic benefit during fifty-year useful life of center (1975–2024) = $4,537,700, the cumulative gross revenues from leasable area. (This increase in gross revenue per year attributable to new accessibility to people with disabilities is calculated by multiplying gross revenues per year by the ratio of persons with disabilities to nondisabled people in the area. The estimate is based on gross revenue per leasable area experienced nationally in 1969, brought forward to 1975 by the rate of consumer price index increase, and extended through the fifty-year life of the building according to the compounded rate of growth in sales revenue experienced by community shopping centers, 1966–1969. A 7 percent discount rate is employed.)
   e. A benefit-cost study done by the state Department of Environmental Management of an offshore wind power project calculates initial project cost at $811 million, but reduces that estimate by 15 percent to allow for the impact of government incentives expected to be adopted before the project actually starts construction.

10. Highway departments and airports need some substance that will melt ice from roads and runways so that traffic may continue to flow safely when winter storms hit. Here are some options that are available:

    Road salt costs about $30 per ton, and it works fast. More than 10 million tons are spread each year in the United States. It is corrosive to concrete, asphalt, and metal, thus eating roads, bridges, and car bodies. It contaminates drinking water and kills trees and plants. Studies suggest that this damage costs from $600 to $1,000 per ton of salt to correct.

Calcium magnesium acetate, a commercial deicer, is made from limestone and vinegar. It costs about $650 per ton and takes about 15 minutes longer than salt to melt large ice patches. It usually lasts somewhat longer. Scientists think it may actually do some good for soil and plant life, and it is not corrosive.

Contrast financial cost and social cost involved with using these products. Which cost should be used for government decision making? Why?

11. Expansion of London's Heathrow Airport, historically the busiest airport in Europe and behind only Atlanta's Hartsfield Jackson and Beijing's Capitol International airport in passengers served, could require the demolition of the twelfth-century Norman Church of St. Michael's in the village of Stewkley, and doing a benefit-cost analysis of that option requires an estimation of the cost involved with that demolition. The original cost of building the church might have been around 100 British pounds. If property values increased at an annual rate of 5 percent over the 900 years since its construction, its value, to be lost with the construction, would be 1,175,896,676,622,870,000,000 British pounds, and certainly no airport expansion is going to have benefits bigger than that. What do you think about this approach to valuation of a property? What other options might be available?[50]

CASE FOR DISCUSSION

CASE 7–1

Some Rough Cost-Benefit Numbers for a "Bridge to Nowhere"

A widely publicized federal earmark in the 2006 transportation appropriation bill was $223 million for a bridge intended to provide access to Ketchikan, Alaska's airport on lightly populated Gravina Island. The project had the misfortune to become labeled the "Bridge to Nowhere" when the earmark came to light in the 2008 presidential campaign. It is possible to do some rough cost-benefit analysis on the project.

Gravina Island has a population of around 50, so most of the bridge traffic would likely be those using the airport. The island was not inaccessible without the bridge. A ferry serves the island, with ferries leaving every half hour. The primary impact from the bridge would be to reduce travel time on the trips. It has been estimated that the drive to the airport from Ketchikan would take 13 minutes, compared to 27 minutes by ferry. Therefore, the time saving is around 15 minutes per passenger. Ketchikan is a port for cruise ships, which dock on the mainland, so some of the bridge traffic would be ship passengers either joining or leaving the cruise ships. Airline enplanements/deplanements (total passengers coming and going through the

---

[50]Based on "Fight over an Old Church Raises a Tough Question," *Wall Street Journal,* December 9, 1971.

airport) are on the order of 400,000, so that traffic would create 800,000 crossings of the bridge. But let's be generous and round up to 1,000,000 crossings, each saving around one quarter hour by taking the bridge.

How much is the time saving worth? Let's assume that each visitor earns $125,000 in income per year. If the visitor works 50 weeks per year and 40 hours per week, then the work year is 2,000 work hours. Some visitors are children and some are retired—and the earning level assumed here is much higher than the national average—but let's not worry about that. Work it out with different estimates on your own, if you wish. With these numbers, the value of work time equals $62.50 per hour. But this is leisure time for most of the traffic, not work time, so let's adjust the value downward by 50 percent (probably an underadjustment) to get an estimate of the value of leisure time—$31.25. Each passenger saves 15 minutes with the bridge (compared with travel by ferry), so the saving per passenger equals $7.81. Multiply that by 1 million passengers to get $7,810,000.

We will assume that the bridge will last forever and will have no maintenance cost and that 3 percent is a reasonable discount rate (that's lower than the OMB rate of 7 percent, but probably higher than current market interest rates). Divide $7,810,000 by 0.03 (because benefits are perpetual—the value is lower if we use a finite life for the bridge) to get the present value of the services from the bridge of $260.4 million, a large number and, as it turns out, larger than the amount of the appropriation. (If you are uncomfortable with perpetual life, use 100 years and the annuity formula to get a present value of services: $(7.81/0.03)[1 - (1/1.03)^{100}] =$ $246.8 million.)

But that is not the end of the story. In order to make the bridge functional, the state of Alaska has to spend $165 million in addition to the federal government's $233 million. Summing up, the present value of the benefits of the bridge is at most $260.4 million, but its total cost is $398 million.

Consider These Questions

1. Would you consider the bridge to be a worthwhile use of federal resources?

2. Why might the state of Alaska be interested in getting the bridge built, even though the total cost of the bridge exceeds the present value of the benefits from the bridge? From the standpoint of Alaska, what are the relevant costs and benefits?

3. How do the benefit-cost analysis results change if the discount rate is 7 percent? What about 2 percent?

4. The analysis is made with several assumptions about use of the bridge, value of traveler time, and number of visitors. How would the analysis change with alternate assumptions that you believe to be potentially reasonable?

CHAPTER 8

Taxation: Criteria for Evaluating Revenue Options

Discussion about taxation is a sensitive and difficult one because nobody enjoys paying taxes and no politician enjoys levying them. It has been a difficult topic even from the earliest days of the United States. James Madison made that point in 1782, in the exciting early days of the nation: "We have shed our blood in the glorious cause in which we are engaged; we are ready to shed the last drop in its defense. Nothing is above our courage, except only (with shame I speak it) the courage to tax ourselves."[1] If we lack the courage to tax ourselves, financing government services will be a continuous challenge because governments collect most of their revenue by exercising their sovereign power to collect coercive payments—taxes—rather than by selling products or services and reliance on free-will offerings is awfully risky.

These coerced payments differ from prices in that they purchase no specific good or service. Furthermore, businesses and individuals would rather not pay taxes because, by and large, the amount of government services anyone receives is independent of the tax that person or business pays. Paying tax does serve to keep the taxpayer out of trouble with the tax collectors, but, with few exceptions, if the neighbors pay enough to finance a government service, then what the individual pays (or doesn't pay) has no impact on the level of service that person will receive. The taxpayer doesn't get more by paying more or less by paying less. Neither are these payments voluntary contributions offered through some sense of civic duty. They are amounts established in a political process that erects a structure of laws—tax statutes and administrative regulations—to determine how the collective cost of government services will be distributed among elements of the market economy. Some services can, indeed, be sold, and a later chapter discusses the conditions under which such systems (user charges) are feasible. However, governments exist, in large measure, to provide services when the private market has failed or may be

---

[1] William T. Hutchinson and William M. E. Rachal, eds., *The Papers of James Madison* (Chicago: University of Chicago Press, 1965), 4: 330.

expected to fail to provide those services in sufficient quantity or quality, if at all. Attempts to sell public goods would be ineffective, so taxes are the answer.

The disconnection between tax paid and service received creates a tension for the tax administrator and, ultimately, for the public agencies that must live within the revenue raised by the tax system. In a market economy, businesses and individuals are used to the principle of exchange that says, crudely, "You get what you pay for." But that principle does not apply in the tax system financing public services. The tax is the law and the tax collectors enforce the "application of the rules of collection to a tax base,"[2] not the collection of prices charged for services rendered.

The tax may be structured to have quasi-market effects—particularly in regard to distributing the cost to those using a service most heavily and to inducing those consuming or producing a product that inflicts uncompensated costs on others to recognize those impacts in their decisions—but the tax remains an involuntary payment to support collective provision of certain goods and services, not a price for services rendered. Nevertheless, the power to finance by coercion reflects a faith in government that allows government to step in when markets fail and is central to government operations. Once-notorious bank robber Willie "The Actor" Sutton allegedly said, "I rob banks because that's where the money is." The following chapters emphasize taxes because, for most general-purpose governments in the developed world, that's where the money is.

One important point about tax policy should be emphasized before embarking on consideration of standards and, in later chapters, on specific revenue alternatives. This is that tax policy involves two basic, but distinct questions. The first is that of the appropriate *level* of taxation. How high should taxes be? The answer to this question is the result of the expenditure side of the budget process. Whatever the outcome of the spending side turns out to be defines the necessary level that the revenue process must generate. The appropriate level of taxation is not directly a tax issue, but is established by those spending choices. What the budget result is establishes the appropriate tax level—if taxes collected do not cover the expenditures made, there is a sustainability issue; if taxes collected consistently exceed the amount of expenditures made, taxpayers are being overcharged for government services.

The second question is one of tax structure because the level of taxation that is necessary can be generated via many different combinations of taxes designed in many alternate ways. Although the revenue capacities of the various taxes are finite, the size of the revenue task does not define how the revenue is to be raised. A proper design of the structure is important, as Henry George effectively described more than a century ago: "The mode of taxation is, in fact, quite as important as the amount. As a small burden badly placed may distress a horse that could carry with ease a much larger one properly adjusted, so a people may be impoverished and their power of producing wealth destroyed by taxation, which, if levied in any other way, could be borne with ease."[3] Even if you are not familiar with horses, the point that care in

---

[2]John L. Mikesell, "Administration and the Public Revenue System: A View of Tax Administration," *Public Administration Review* 34 (1974): 651.
[3]Henry George, *Progress and Poverty* (1879), Book VIII, Chapter 3. [Online edition: http://www.econlib.org/library/YPDBooks/George/grgPP.html]

structuring the tax is as important as the tax itself in creation of a sensible tax policy should be clear. The structure of the system represents the second issue, one that is independent of the first, and here is where the policy standards for tax structures to be discussed in this chapter come into play.

Taxation in the United States: A Short Overview of the Systems

Governments in the United States collect most of their own-source general revenue from taxes on income, purchases or sales, or property ownership or transfer, as Table 8–1 shows.[4] For all governments, 55.9 percent of total revenue came from taxes, or 73 percent of own-source revenue. Revenue from user charges and from miscellaneous sources (these include lotteries, interest on invested funds, royalties, etc.) play a relatively small role in the finance of general government. Special revenue, shown at the bottom of the table, includes the substantial collections from the payroll tax that funds the federal insurance trust system. This federal payroll tax for Social Security and Medicare is the second largest revenue producer among all sources at all levels; only revenue from the federal individual income tax is greater. But this payroll tax revenue is not directly available for general government.

The table reflects a distinct separation of revenue sources by level of government, although there are no national laws in the United States that assign particular taxes to particular levels of government, in contrast to the practice in many nations. The federal revenue system is not diversified among tax bases. The federal government relies predominantly on income taxes, individual and corporate, for revenue—63 percent of total general revenue from the individual income tax and 9.5 percent from the corporate income tax—and raises about as much from these two taxes as state and local governments raise from all taxes combined. The federal individual income tax is, by a good margin, the most productive of all the taxes; indeed, it produces more money than any tax levied by any other government in the world. Federal dominance in income taxation is even greater because the payroll tax for Social Security amounts to a second federal income tax for individuals receiving only wage and salary income and for the self-employed. Indeed, for lower-income households, payments for this payroll tax far exceed the amounts paid in federal individual income tax.

---

[4]Own-source general revenue excludes (1) revenue from intergovernmental aid and (2) revenue from liquor stores, utility operations, or insurance programs (e.g., Social Security or unemployment compensation). The first exclusion leaves own-source revenue; the second, own-source general revenue. These distinctions do not reflect laws that restrict certain revenues for certain uses (earmarking). For instance, most states earmark motor fuel tax revenue for highway use. The division used here and in census data would consider that revenue to be general and not in the special category.

Table 8-1
Government Revenue by Source and Level, Fiscal 2009 ($ Thousands)

	All	Federal	State	Local	Share of Total Revenue from Source			
					All	Federal	State	Local
Revenue	4,898,946,850	2,341,903,000	1,123,226,058	1,433,817,792				
Total General Revenue	4,354,748,332	1,450,986,000	1,495,730,319	1,408,032,013	100.0%	100.0%	100.0%	100.0%
Intergovernmental revenue	1,027,138,463	-	495,623,675	531,514,788	23.6%		33.1%	37.7%
from federal government	536,760,320	-	475,952,532	60,807,788	12.3%		31.8%	4.3%
from state government	470,706,999	-	-	470,706,999	10.8%			33.4%
from local government	19,671,143	-	19,671,143	-	0.5%		1.3%	
General Revenue Own-Source	3,327,609,869	1,450,986,000	1,000,106,644	876,517,225	76.4%	100.0%	66.9%	62.3%
Taxes	2,433,310,992	1,161,955,000	715,496,219	555,859,773	55.9%	80.1%	47.8%	39.5%
Property	424,014,170	-	12,964,188	411,049,982	9.7%		0.9%	29.2%
Individual income	1,185,825,726	915,308,000	245,880,786	24,636,940	27.2%	63.1%	16.4%	1.7%
Corporate income	184,208,954	138,229,000	39,277,558	6,702,396	4.2%	9.5%	2.6%	0.5%
Customs duties	22,453,000	22,453,000	-	-	0.5%	1.5%		
General sales and gross receipts	291,045,219	-	228,728,864	62,316,355	6.7%		15.3%	4.4%
Selective sales and gross receipts	204,993,796	62,483,000	115,839,127	26,671,669	4.7%	4.3%	7.7%	1.9%
Motor vehicle licensing	21,296,295	-	19,626,624	1,669,671	0.5%		1.3%	0.1%
Estate and gift	28,136,053	23,482,000	4,654,053	-	0.6%	1.6%	0.3%	
Severance	13,391,856	-	13,391,856	-	0.3%		0.9%	
Other taxes	75,991,833	-	53,179,072	22,812,761	1.7%		3.6%	1.6%
Current charges	655,266,090	266,500,000	161,238,746	227,527,344	15.0%	18.4%	10.8%	16.2%
Institutions of higher education	115,641,628	-	89,846,450	25,795,178	2.7%		6.0%	1.8%
Hospitals	103,974,544	-	39,235,615	64,738,929	2.4%		2.6%	4.6%
Postal Service fees	69,000,000	69,000,000	-	-	1.6%	4.8%		
Sewerage	39,453,377	-	506,688	38,946,689	0.9%		0.0%	2.8%
Medicare premiums	57,000,000	57,000,000	-	-	1.3%	3.9%		
Miscellaneous general revenue	268,624,787	52,123,000	123,371,679	93,130,108	6.2%	3.6%	8.2%	6.6%
Total Special Revenue								
Utility revenue	143,803,377	-	16,471,341	127,332,036				
Liquor store revenue	7,456,586	-	6,376,562	1,080,024				
Insurance trust revenue	392,938,555	890,917,000	-395,352,164	-102,626,281				

SOURCE: U.S. Bureau of Census, Governments Division; and Office of Management and Budget, *Budget of the Government of the United States, Fiscal Year 2009, Analytical Perspectives* (Washington, D.C.: U.S. Government Printing Office, 2008).Budget of the U.S. Government, Analytical Perspectives.

Duplicative intergovernmental transactions are excluded.

NOTE: Insurance trust revenue includes old age, survivors, disability, and health insurance contributions; unemployment compensation; employee retirement; worker's compensation; and other insurance trust revenue.

The federal government levies no general sales tax, a rarity among economically developed countries. There is no fundamental "catch" or legal barrier that prevents the federal government from levying such a tax, but taxes on retail sales are a major source for state and local governments. This heavy reliance by states and localities has created political resistance each time the federal government has considered invading that territory, as it did periodically throughout the twentieth century and continues to consider to the present. The federal government does, however, collect sales taxes on selected commodities, like motor fuels and alcoholic beverages, and on certain imported products (customs duties). The amounts collected from these taxes pale in comparison to those from the federal income taxes—just 4.3 percent of federal general revenue.

The federal government collects no property tax. The U.S. Constitution makes the adoption of a federal property tax politically difficult because it requires apportionment of any direct tax (like the property tax): "No capitation, or other direct, Tax shall be laid unless in Proportion to the Census or Enumeration herein before directed to be taken" (Article I, Sec. 9[4]). This provision means that states with one—twentieth of the national population would have to pay one-twentieth of any direct tax. To produce that apportionment, a federal property tax would require high tax rates in poor states and low rates in wealthy states. Any state-by-state difference in federal tax rates would be politically impractical, and to have rates inversely related to state wealth would add an extra degree of difficulty, as the writers of the Constitution surely knew. In his economic analysis of the Constitution, Charles Beard sums up: "Direct taxes may be laid, but resort to this form of taxation is rendered practically impossible, save on extraordinary occasions, by the provision that they must be apportioned according to population—so that numbers cannot transfer the burden to accumulated wealth."[5] The framers of the Constitution, no matter what their many liberal virtues, were generally rich men who appeared not to want to have national taxes placed on their wealth by the masses.

A reasonable question at this point is, What are direct and indirect taxes? Richard Musgrave suggests the possibilities:

> Some have suggested that (1) indirect taxes are taxes which are shifted [i.e., the real burden is borne by someone other than the one paying the tax to the government], and others that (2) they are taxes which are meant to be shifted. Still others hold that (3) they are taxes which are assessed on objects [or privileges] rather than on individuals and therefore not adaptable to the individual's special position and his taxable capacity; or finally (4) that they are simply taxes which are not on income. While (3) is probably the most useful criterion, this is not the place to resolve this terminological matter. It is evident, however, that under most criteria, the classification of certain taxes is far from clear-cut.[6]

Fortunately, the difference has little economic importance, although it can complicate the legal constraints surrounding the tax. For instance, in addition to the constitutional provision previously noted, some states specify certain rate structures or

---

[5]Charles A. Beard, *An Economic Interpretation of the Constitution of the United States* (New York: Macmillan, 1935), 215. As will be noted later, the federal government levied property taxes for short periods in the distant past. The taxes were apportioned.

[6]Richard A. Musgrave, *Fiscal Systems* (New Haven, Conn.: Yale University Press, 1960), 173.

collection processes that differ according to whether the tax is direct or indirect—so there must be determinations about the particular tax in question. If Professor Musgrave is not up to resolving the issue, then there is not likely to be a generally accepted resolution to the question. Indeed, governments who have to enforce the distinction do not all agree. The lack of a definition periodically provides a good income for tax lawyers attacking some tax provision or another according to whether the particular tax in question qualifies as direct or indirect.

In comparison with the federal government, the revenue systems of state and local governments are broadly diversified, as demonstrated in the view of state and local revenue collections in Table 8–1.[7] The three levels of government combined, although forming tax policies independently, manage a tax system split among income, property, and sales taxes. Table 8–2 presents further information on these structures by indicating the number of states that use the major tax bases and contain localities using these bases. State revenue systems tend to have a balance between bases, compared with the income dominance of the federal system or the property dominance of local systems. State governments apply income taxes (41 states levy broad individual income taxes; 44 states tax corporate income), but their aggregate collections do not approach federal government collections. Many states, however, do receive more revenue from income taxes than from any other source. State income taxes often mirror federal taxes. In fact, state tax returns often copy information directly from the federal return in computing state liability, and state tax authorities rely heavily on the efforts of the federal government in enforcing their income taxes. A number of cities levy local income taxes, but in many cases, the taxes are limited to coverage of employee payroll, not taxes on income for all sources. About 3,500 local governments levy local income taxes, but only 900 of these are outside Pennsylvania. Taxes on individual income currently are the largest single source of state revenue, with the retail sales tax close behind.[8] All states receive revenue from sales or gross receipts taxes (general or selective), and only five (Alaska, Delaware, Montana, New Hampshire, and Oregon) do not use a general sales tax. Around 6,400 local governments levy general sales taxes as well, making them second only to property as a local tax source. Although the sales tax shows no sign of eclipsing the property tax in overall local importance, in some large cities it is the major tax revenue producer. Contrary to the local income tax, which is frequently administered locally, local sales taxes are almost always administered by the state government in conjunction ("piggybacked") with the state tax. The U.S. Constitution prohibits states and their subdivisions from levying customs duties, which are taxes levied on imported goods.

The property tax remains the major own-source revenue producer for local government. Despite continued popular attacks on the tax, it remains the predominant

---

[7]Intergovernmental revenue (grants and contracts) is netted out across governments in Table 8–1. Therefore, there are no net grants for all government: one grants, one receives, and net is zero for government as a whole.

[8]In recent years, the individual income tax and the general sales tax have traded off as the largest single source of state tax revenue. From 1947 to 1997, the general sales tax was the largest source, but was replaced by the individual income tax from 1998 to 2002. It returned to its position as largest producer in 2003 and 2004. Sales tax revenue held up somewhat better than did revenue from the individual income tax during the Great Recession, but the income tax held on to the position of largest-yielding state tax.

Table 8–2
Major Tax Sources for States and Localities, July 2012

Tax	States Using the Tax	States with Localities Using the Tax
General Property	Thirty-six states plus D.C. Exceptions: Colorado, Connecticut, Delaware, Hawaii, Idaho, Iowa, New York, North Carolina, Ohio, Oklahoma, South Dakota, Tennessee, Texas, and Utah.	All fifty states.
General Sales	Forty-five states plus D.C. Exceptions: Alaska, Delaware, Montana, New Hampshire, and Oregon. Many Alaskan municipalities and boroughs levy general sales taxes.	Thirty-six states.
Individual Income	Forty-one states plus D.C. Exceptions: Alaska, Florida, Nevada, New Hampshire, South Dakota, Tennessee, Texas, Washington, and Wyoming. New Hampshire and Tennessee levy taxes on dividend and interest income.	Fourteen states.
Corporate Income	Forty-four states plus D.C. Exceptions: Michigan, Nevada, South Dakota, Texas, Washington, and Wyoming. Michigan levies a single business tax (a modified value-added tax) and Texas levies a corporate franchise tax.	Four states.
Motor Fuel	All states plus D.C.	Thirteen states.
Cigarettes	All states plus D.C.	Ten states.
Alcohol Beverages	All states plus D.C.	Eighteen states.

SOURCE: Federation of Tax Administrators; U.S. Bureau of Census, Census of Governments 2007; and CCCH Internet Tax Research Network.

local tax, possibly because it is the only major tax generally within the means of independent local administration and capable of fine statutory-rate differences between geographically small jurisdictions. A number of state governments levy their own general property tax, but its significance in state finances is modest, although it was the dominant state source before the Depression of the 1930s.

How does the tax structure in the United States stack up against that in other industrialized countries? Some comparisons are possible from the data in Table 8–3. Among the countries in the Organization for Economic Cooperation and Development (OECD), the U.S. tax burden as a percentage of gross domestic product (GDP) is toward the bottom—28 percent here against an OECD average of 35.9 percent.[9] Looking at shares of that total by tax source, the United States makes heavier use of taxes on personal income (36.5 percent of the total for the United States compared with a

---

[9]These data include operation of national social insurance systems and aggregate all levels of government.

24.8 percent OECD average); heavier use of other taxes, mostly property (12.3 percent compared with a 9.7 percent OECD average); slightly higher use of taxes on corporate income (11.8 percent compared with a 10.7 percent OECD average); and much lighter use of goods-and-service or sales taxes (16.8 percent compared with a 31.5 percent OECD average). Our Social Security contributions are close to the average.

This point bears repeating. Among the industrialized nations of the world, the United States is a low-tax country. That does not mean that certain economic activities or individuals are not competitively or inequitably disadvantaged by provisions of the American tax systems. But the U.S. tax burden is, on average, low in relation to that of generally comparable countries.[10]

Standards for Tax Policy

Jean-Baptiste Colbert, finance minister in Louis XIV's court before the French Revolution, is alleged to have succinctly summed up the task of financing government: "The art of taxation consists in so plucking the goose as to obtain the largest amount of feathers with the least possible amount of hissing."[11] Taxation based on power alone is an excellent device for inflicting costs on minorities and those with limited political clout, but power so used is inconsistent with leadership and is likely to produce policies that trade long-range damage for quick political gain.

Most people prefer taxes to be paid by someone else because an individual's payment of a tax ordinarily has no influence on whether a public service is available. Former Senator Russell Long (D-LA) elucidated a major principle of tax politics some years ago: "Don't tax you, don't tax me, tax that fellow behind the tree."[12]

That principle, combined with a public that is not familiar with tax structure and tax effects, renders pure public opinion a hazardous standard for revenue choice. Indeed, robbing Peter to pay Paul is an almost certain way to get Paul's vote, a principle that American politicians understand only too well. But attention to opinion may guide approaches through which otherwise desirable changes may be implemented and may identify desirable changes that must await a beneficial political climate.

Economists George Break and Joseph Pechman describe the fundamental principle behind the evaluation of tax policy: "The primary goal of taxation is to transfer control of resources from one group in the society to another and to do so in ways that do not jeopardize, and may even facilitate, the attainment of other economic

---

[10]Compared with the industrialized nations, developing countries tend to have lower tax burdens, greater reliance on consumption as opposed to income taxes, and greater reliance on corporate as opposed to personal income taxes. Vito Tanzi and Howell H. Zee, "Tax Policy for Emerging Markets: Developing Countries," International Monetary Fund Working Paper WP/00/35, Washington, D.C., 2000.

[11]H. L. Mencken, ed., *A New Dictionary of Quotations on Historical Principles from Ancient and Modern Sources* (New York: Knopf, 1942), 1178.

[12]Thomas J. Reese, "The Thoughts of Chairman Long, Part I: The Politics of Taxation," *Tax Notes* 6 (February 27, 1978): 199.

Table 8–3

Tax Revenue as a Percentage of Gross Domestic Product and a Percentage from Major Taxes, 2006, Countries of the Organization for Economic Cooperation and Development (OECD)

		Tax Revenue of Main Taxes as Percentage of Total Taxation				
	Total Taxation as Percentage of GDP	Personal Income	Corporate Income	Social Security Payroll	Goods and Services	Other
Australia	30.6	37.4	21.7	0	27.1	13.7
Austria	41.7	22.3	5.2	30.2	27.7	14.7
Belgium	44.5	29.3	8.3	27.8	25.6	9
Canada	33.3	36.3	11	14.3	24.3	14.1
Czech Republic	36.9	11.5	13	37.3	30.2	8.1
Denmark	49.1	49.8	8.7	2.1	33.2	6.2
Finland	43.5	30.3	7.7	25.8	31.1	5
France	44.2	17.5	6.7	34.3	24.8	16.8
Germany	35.6	24.5	5.9	35.3	28.4	6
Greece	31.3	14.9	8.5	30.2	36	10.5
Hungary	37.1	18.3	6.3	31.7	38.4	5.4
Iceland	41.5	33.7	5.8	n.a.	42.3	18.2
Ireland	31.9	27.8	12	12.7	36.5	11
Italy	42.1	25.6	8.1	25.9	25.6	14.7
Japan	27.9	18.5	17	32.5	18.6	13.4
Korea	26.8	15.2	14.3	21	32.6	16.8
Luxembourg	35.9	21	13.8	24.4	27.9	12.9
Mexico*	20.6	25.1	n.a.	14.9	56.3	3.7
Netherlands	39.3	18.8	8.5	29.1	30.5	13.1
New Zealand	36.7	40.7	15.8	0	32.7	10.9
Norway	43.9	20.7	29.4	18.7	27.3	3.8
Poland	33.5	13.7	7.1	36.3	38.1	4.7
Portugal	35.7	15.4	8.4	30.4	40.6	5.3
Slovak Republic	29.8	8.5	9.9	30.8	38.7	12.1
Spain	36.6	18.9	11.5	29.5	27.2	12.9
Sweden	49.1	31.9	7.5	25.2	26.1	9.2
Switzerland	29.6	35.6	10.1	21.4	23	9.9
Turkey	24.5	15.6	6	18	48.7	11.7
United Kingdom	37.1	29	10.8	17.8	29	13.4
United States	28	36.5	11.8	22.5	16.8	12.3
EU average	39.8	25.1	8.8	25.4	30	10.7
OECD average	35.9	24.8	10.7	23.2	31.5	9.7

SOURCE: Organization for Economic Cooperation and Development, *OECD in Figures*, 2009 ed. (Paris: OECD, 2009).

NOTE: *Mexican corporate and individual income taxes are combined.

goals."[13] Those transfers include (1) shifts of purchasing power among groups in the private sector and (2) shifts of control over purchasing power from the private sector to the public sector. A tax intends to move resources away from private use and will by itself harm the private sector; tax policy seeks to achieve that shift with the least possible economic or social harm. Without this concern for minimizing harm, any revenue would be about as good as any other, and tax policy would not be a significant element in public decisions. In other words, tax policy is about damage control. To summarize, we want a tax system that behaves like a pickpocket and not like a mugger—the government wants the money to finance services, but doesn't want the taxpayer to lie bleeding on the sidewalk.

When public goods are financed, the tax must not be voluntary. Otherwise, rational actions of nonpayers—who could fully enjoy the service provided without financial payment—would keep the system from producing expected revenue. A tax may be distinguished from other ways of raising revenue by its *compulsory* nature. If one possesses the tax base, one pays the tax regardless of whether one uses the services provided by the taxing unit. Absence of voluntarism distinguishes taxes from the user charges—recreation admissions, tolls, college tuition, and so on—that many governments collect. The tax is neither a price for service received nor a voluntary contribution. Furthermore, governments do not rely on "fair share" contributions because fairness is susceptible to widely different individual definitions, particularly what one's own fair share would be.

Criteria for judging taxes and tax systems have been proposed by many observers, but there has been a substantial conformity among those standards. The grandfather of evaluation standards appears in *The Wealth of Nations* (1776), as Adam Smith proposes four classic maxims that should guide taxation in a market-based economy:

> I. The subjects of every state ought to contribute towards the support of the government, as nearly as possible, in proportion to their respective abilities; that is, in proportion to the revenue which they respectively enjoy under the protection of the state.
>
> II. The tax which each individual is bound to pay ought to be certain and not arbitrary. The time of payment, the manner of payment, the quantity to be paid, ought all to be clear and plain to the contributor, and to every other person.
>
> III. Every tax ought to be levied at the time or in the manner in which it is most likely to be convenient for the contributor to pay it.
>
> IV. Every tax ought to be so contrived as both to take out and to keep out of the pockets of the people as little as possible, over and above what it brings into the public treasury of the state.[14]

Although the language of those standards has changed over the years and emphasis has shifted with the development of a more complex economy, modern reform still concerns essentially the same issues. Whether the deliberations involve the 1986 federal tax reform in the Reagan administration, the 1993 Clinton economic plan, design of a tax system for a newly independent nation, the Bush 2001

---

[13]George F. Break and Joseph A. Pechman, *Federal Tax Reform, The Impossible Dream?* (Washington, D.C.: Brookings Institution, 1975), 4.

[14]Adam Smith, *An Inquiry into the Nature and Cause of the Wealth of Nations,* Modern Library ed. (New York: Random House, 1937), 777–79.

tax reductions, the 2005 Bush tax reform panel,[15] or a state tax reform study, attention will be directed to some translation of the basic criteria: equity, economic efficiency effects, and collection cost/simplicity (cost to government and impact on taxpayer), plus revenue consequences. Recent proposals for tax restructuring have brought renewed concern for transparency, the modern translation of the need for taxes to be certain and not arbitrary, with clear political responsibility when they are levied and enough visibility to ensure that the public does not think that government services are free. Even though transparency is an important concern in the new good governance movement, in terms of taxation, it dates back to 1776 Scotland.

Adequacy of Revenue Production

Taxes serve to generate revenue necessary for the provision of government services. Other uses of the revenue system—to direct or encourage certain sorts of economic activity, for instance—are immediately suspect. Hence, the first questions to be answered in an analysis of a tax or system of taxes are in regard to yield. The adequacy question is simple: Does the tax system raise sufficient revenue so that spending on services for the current generation will not place an undue burden on future generations? That is the crucial test for fiscal sustainability because if the system does not raise enough revenue, then future generations will be required to take care of the costs of the past as well as taking care of their own costs. That will negatively impact their standard of living, a clear sustainability violation. If you will recall the discussion about deficits of federal, state, and local governments, you will be able to form your own informed opinion about the current adequacy of these tax systems in the United States. Here is a hint: they aren't doing the job. Attention needs to be focused on tax policies and tax options to get back on the sustainability track.

What about adequacy analysis for a particular tax rather than for a tax system? A tax levied for revenue is worthwhile only if it can generate meaningful revenue at socially acceptable rates.[16] A few taxes may be levied for reasons other than revenue—punitively high rates to stop an undesirable activity or taxes applied simply to keep track of a particular activity—but revenue is the prime objective of most taxes. How much revenue will a tax yield, and how does yield change when a government changes the effective rate applied to a particular tax base? Tax yield (R), or total collections, equals the tax rate (t) times the tax base (B): if the resident income tax rate is 1 percent and resident income equals \$200 million, then tax yield

---

[15]The most recent general federal tax review, the President's Advisory Panel on Federal Tax Reform, was charged with transmitting to the secretary of the treasury revenue-neutral reform options that would "(a) simplify Federal tax laws to reduce the costs and administrative burdens of compliance with such laws; (b) share the burdens and benefits of the Federal tax structure in an appropriately progressive manner while recognizing the importance of homeownership and charity in American society; and (c) promote long-run economic growth and job creation, and better encourage work effort, saving, and investment, so as to strengthen the competitiveness of the United States in the global marketplace." In regard to the last concern, the president might not trust the operation of the free market in terms of growth and job creation, but hoped to use the tax system to intervene in a non-neutral fashion. Executive Order 13369, President's Advisory Panel on Federal Tax Reform, January 7, 2005.

[16]Recall that Adam Smith did not include revenue production among his maxims.

equals $2.0 million. That is the simple accounting relationship for tax revenue. If the tax rate is quadrupled, to 4 percent, the yield quadruples as well, to $8.0 million. The tax revenue equation, $R = t \times B$, is graphed in Figure 8–1 as the straight line from the origin (no revenue is produced when the tax rate is zero). There is a linear relationship between the effective tax rate and the yield from the base. Tax-rate changes produce additional revenue in proportion to the rate change. For example, a 10 percent increase in rate would yield a 10 percent increase in revenue, and so on.

   This accounting relationship, however, ignores the economic response by individuals and businesses that now face a different tax rate, and that response will cause the tax base to differ from what it was at the old rate. In other words, the tax base itself is determined in part by the effective tax rate levied against it: if the resident income tax rate increases to 4 percent, resident income will no longer be $200 million. As Robert Inman explains, "the increase in the tax on residents' income might well cause residents to work less as their incomes are taxed or even cause wealthier families to leave the taxing jurisdiction."[17] Similar economic responses apply for other taxes as well. Furthermore, higher rates provide greater returns from various "fiddles" to illegally remove operations from the tax system. Therefore, the economic relationship between effective rate and revenue yield is not linear, but is one in which the tax rate itself is one of the important determinants of the tax base. In Figure 8–1, the economic response to the higher tax rate causes actual yield to be less than shown from the linear relationship. The economic relationship considers

Figure 8-1
Relationship between Tax Rate and Tax Revenue: The Rate-Revenue Curve

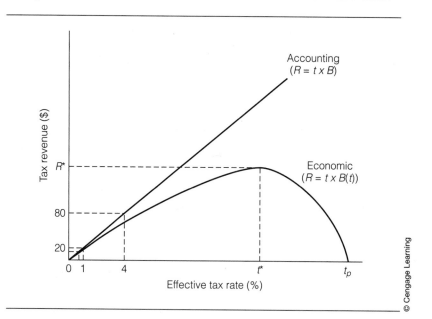

Sidebar 8–1
The Workings of the Rate-Revenue Curve: Accounting versus Economics

The difference between the accounting relationship and the economic relationship in the tax rate/tax revenue relationship can be simply illustrated with an example. On June 1, 2005, Kentucky increased its cigarette tax rate from $0.03 per pack to $0.30 per pack. That is an increase of 900 percent.

Monthly sales went from around 161 million packs at the old rate to around 145 million packs, a decrease in the tax base of around 10 percent. While other factors may also be involved, it is almost certain that one extremely important factor in the sales decline in cigarette sales is the higher tax that is embedded in the price that cigarette purchasers pay. In other words, the size of the tax base is a function of the cigarette tax rate.

What is the impact on cigarette tax revenue? Revenue equals base times rate, so before the tax increase, monthly revenue would have been around $4,830 thousand ($0.03 × 161 million) and after the tax increase, monthly revenue would have been around $43,500 thousand ($0.30 × 145 million)—an increase of 800.6 percent.

The percentage increase in tax collections is considerably less than the percentage increase in the tax rate (800 percent against 900 percent) because the rate increase caused the tax base to be smaller. The base is sensitive to the tax rate, so the accounting relationship does not hold in this case. It may serve as a workable approximation when the tax rate change is small—but not here and maybe not even then. Also notice that, while the rate increase does cause the base to be smaller, it is not the case here that the base reduction causes actual collections to decline. The higher tax rate brings higher tax collections.

So where did the sales go? Some possibilities include sales lost across the Ohio River to Indiana (as well as to other nearby states) as Kentucky retailers lost some of the price advantage they had previously enjoyed, sales lost to Native American smoke shops making sales via the internet without applying tax, and sales lost because people cut back on smoking or quit entirely.

first the negative rate-to-base effect (the base as a function of rate or $B(t)$ of a rate increase and then estimates yield by multiplying this adjusted base by the rate ($t \times B(t)$). That causes the economic relationship to differ from the accounting relationship in revenue yield estimates and in Figure 8–1.[18] Sidebar 8–1 illustrates the workings of the rate-revenue relationship in practice.

Figure 8–1 portrays a maximum yield (R^*). This peak measures the maximum economic yield from that tax base. The peak is neither the optimal nor the ideal. It is simply the highest feasible amount that can be generated from the particular tax base, and there is no reason to believe that this would be the objective of any government. Further tax-rate increases from t^* will cause declining yield as the revenue loss from the tax-induced decline in the base overwhelms the additional yield from the higher rate. Carrying the analysis further, there would be a rate so high (t_p) that

---

[18]One analysis of rate-revenue curves for each tax in a state is Michael L. Walden, "Dynamic Revenue Curves for North Carolina Taxes," *Public Budgeting & Finance* 23 (Winter 2003): 49–64. None of the state taxes had rates that pushed the state beyond the revenue peak.

the taxed activity would cease. The profile of this rate-revenue curve would depend on how responsive the particular tax base is to the effective tax rate. At lower rates and for small relative changes, change impacts may well approximate the accounting relationship. But the economic relationship cannot be ignored for larger changes, and especially when the tax is being applied to a geographically small region or when avenues for avoidance are easy (e.g., close to borders).

Several efforts have been made to estimate what this economic relationship actually looks like for various taxes, and tax policy has sometimes been made on the basis of assertions about its configuration. President Reagan's 1981 tax reductions were based in part on the view, argued most effectively by Arthur Laffer (after whom the rate-revenue curve has popularly been named), that federal personal income tax rates were above t^* and, hence, the rate reduction would help close the budget deficit by increasing tax revenue. Laffer was by no means the first to note the possibility. John Maynard Keynes wrote in 1933: "Nor should the argument seem strange that taxation may be so high as to defeat its object, and that, given sufficient time to gather the fruits, a reduction of taxation will run a better chance, than an increase, of balancing the budget."[19] Careful analysis has shown yields to have been reduced by the Reagan reductions, however.[20] Tests for local taxes usually show actual rates to be below t^*, but not always.[21] Figuring out what might be t^* for the federal individual income tax is not a simple task, given data problems, shifting tax structure, and the like. However, some who have done an exhaustive review suggest that evidence indicates a peak at a top rate of 60 percent or higher, considerably lower than the U.S. levies now.[22]

Yield can be a difficult practical problem—before reaching the limits of economic capacity—when state restrictions limit local fiscal autonomy. For instance, a state may establish a special district to provide services financed only from a single excise tax base or may impose restrictive property-tax-rate ceilings on local governments. These limits can create considerable revenue adequacy problems. In most instances, political constraints to use of tax bases bind well before the maximum economic capacity of the tax.[23]

---

[19]"The Means to Prosperity," reprinted in *Essays in Persuasion: The Collected Works of John Maynard Keynes* (London: Macmillan, St. Martin's Press, 1972), 9: 338.

[20]Donald Fullerton, "On the Possibility of an Inverse Relationship between Tax Rates and Government Revenue," *Journal of Public Economics* 19 (October 1982): 3–22. Influences of changing the top marginal rate—the tax highest-income people pay on additional income—on revenue are far less clear. See Robert J. Barro, "Higher Taxes, Lower Revenues," *Wall Street Journal*, July 9, 1993, A-10.

[21]Studies revealing an actual rate to be below t^* include the following: for city property taxes, Helen Ladd and Katharine Bradbury, "City Taxes and Property Tax Bases," *National Tax Journal* 41 (December 1988): 503–23; for local sales tax, John L. Mikesell and C. Kurt Zorn, "Impact of the Sales Tax Rate on Its Base: Evidence from a Small Town," *Public Finance Quarterly* 14 (July 1986): 329–38; for Long Island school districts, Robert Inman, "Micro-fiscal Planning in the Regional Economy: A General Equilibrium Approach," *Journal of Public Economics* 7 (April 1977): 237–60; and for state sales taxes, Gerald E. Auten and Edward H. Robb, "A General Model for State Tax Revenue Analysis," *National Tax Journal* 29 (December 1976): 422–35. The rate was shown to be above t^* in the following: for New York City business taxes, Ronald Grieson, William Hamovitch, Albert Levenson, and Richard Morgenstern, "The Effect of Business Taxation on the Location of Industry," *Journal of Urban Economics* 4 (April 1977): 170–85; and for Philadelphia city taxes, Inman, "Micro-fiscal Planning."

[22]Emmanuel Saez, Joel Slemrod, and Seth Giertz, "The Elasticity of Taxable Income with Respect to Marginal Tax Rates," *Journal of Economic Literature* 50 (2012): 3–50.

[23]There is no reason for any government to identify and use its maximum revenue capacity. That would mean the government seeks to maximize its budget, and that would almost never be in the public interest. t^* represents the maximum yield, not the optimum yield.

Another capacity problem is that of fiscal disparity. Not all regions of a country or localities within a region have equal tax-base endowments. For instance, some regions contain important commercial centers or valuable natural resources, whereas other regions have no significant revenue base. To the extent that these regions must finance government services from their own revenue sources, the areas with lower fiscal resources are at considerable disadvantage. For instance, Beverly Hills and Temple City are both cities in Los Angeles County, California, and both have populations of around 35,000. However, the taxable sales tax base is $53,870 per capita in Beverly Hills (shopping as a fiscal resource!), but only $3,920 per capita in Temple City.[24] That gives residents of Beverly Hills fiscal opportunities considerably different from those of residents of Temple City. This disparity question is examined in greater depth in a later chapter that discusses intergovernmental horizontal fiscal balance.

Adequacy also includes a dynamic dimension: Is revenue stable in the short run and does it grow in the long run? Efforts to manage the national economy have not eliminated economic fluctuations, as the Great Recession from December 2007 to June 2009 clearly demonstrated. Government functions continue during depressed economic activity and may even grow because of social and economic tensions in these periods. A revenue source with good cyclical adequacy remains reasonably stable during periods of declining economic activity. Such stability is vital for state and local governments because they lack the borrowing flexibility and money-creating powers that can accommodate federal deficits and any rainy-day funds that they may have accumulated are finite. In general, taxes on corporate profits are particularly unstable because of the volatility of that base. Some states historically were reluctant to rely on corporate taxes for that reason, and local governments avoid them as well. Property taxes have considerable stability, except for delinquency problems during deep depressions (including localized economic collapse). Although property tax revenues fell during the recent recession, they continued to be more stable than sales and income taxes. Revenue stability, however, is a problem for government when the economy is growing (and the overall U.S. economy grows more often than it declines, although some regions of the economy are in near-permanent decline). Demand for many government services increases more rapidly than the increase in economic activity. The demand pattern can be examined using the income elasticity of service expenditure, an estimate of the percentage increase in expenditure that will result from each 1 percent increase in income. Those services for which expenditure increases more rapidly than does income have an income elasticity greater than 1, meaning that an increase in income of 1 percent generates an increase in government spending greater than 1 percent. Governments lacking revenue sources with similar growth characteristics face the prospect of increased debt, increased tax rates (or new taxes), or unmet demand for government services. Each of these options is politically unpleasant, so there is a general preference for responsive taxes, taxes whose revenue increases more rapidly than does income (the revenue elasticity or the elasticity of the tax base with respect to income exceeds 1). Table 8–4 reports income elasticities by individual tax bases as found in several

---

[24]Data from statistical reports of the California State Board of Equalization, 2009–2010.

Table 8–4
Compilation of Selected Long-Term Tax-Base Elasticities as Found in Various Tax Studies

	Low	High	Median
Personal income tax (41 states)	0.809	3.983	1.604
Retail sales tax (44 states)	0.339	1.365	0.781
Corporate income tax (9 studies)	0.72	1.44	1.1
General property tax (12 studies)	0.34	1.41	0.87
Motor-fuels tax (50 states)	1.091	0.478	0.739
Tobacco tax (8 studies)	0.00	0.54	0.26

SOURCE: D. Bruce, W. F. Fox, and M. H. Tuttle, "Tax Base Elasticities: A Multi-State Analysis of Long-Run and Short-Run Dynamics," *Southern Economics Journal* 73 (2006): 315–41; Advisory Commission on Intergovernmental Relations, *Significant Features of Fiscal Federalism, 1976–1977,* vol. 2, *Revenue and Debt* (Washington, D.C.: Advisory Commission on Intergovernmental Relations, 1977); and J. H. Bowman and J. L. Mikesell, "Recent Changes in State Gasoline Taxation: An Analysis of Structure and Rates," *National Tax Journal* 36 (June 1983): 163–82.

recent tax studies.[25] Because the exact structure of each tax differs to some degree from government to government and these differences influence performance of the tax, the table provides elasticity ranges as well as the median.

Overall, the individual income tax shows greatest responsiveness (caused by both rate graduation and sensitivity of the base), whereas motor-fuel and tobacco taxes—generally applied on a specific (volume or unit) basis rather than on a value (volume times price) basis—have the least responsiveness. The general sales tax is in an intermediate position. The property tax elasticity estimates are probably artificially high because some studies did not separate the revenue effects of increased property tax rates, so the elasticity result is not purely the outcome of automatic base growth.[26] Because responsive taxes may not be stable, the appropriate choice for adequacy over time depends on whether problems of growth or problems of decline are most likely and whether the government has access to debt markets and the ability to raise rates during periods of economic decline.

So what does income elasticity mean for a state government? Suppose that private economic activity is increasing at a rate of 10 percent annually. If that state has a personal income tax with typical base elasticity (from Table 8–4), personal income tax revenue would generally be increasing at a rate of 16.04 percent annually without any increase in tax rates. If the state happened to rely upon a general property tax, revenue from that tax would generally be increasing at a rate of 8.7 percent annually.

[25]These elasticities are typically computed from a time-series regression of the form $\ln B = a + b \ln Y$, where B is the tax base analyzed, Y is the measure of economic activity, and b is the income elasticity of the tax. Other influences on the base—for instance, statutory-tax-rate changes—may also be included as independent variables. Sometimes analysis is done of *tax buoyancy*. This analysis considers tax yield (base times rate) rather than just the tax base.

[26]A study that extracts both rate changes and general reassessments of property found a property-tax-base elasticity of 0.27 in one state (Indiana). This measurement is more comparable to those reported for sales and income tax bases because it extracts all statutory and administrative sources of base change. See John L. Mikesell, "Property Tax Assessment Practice and Income Elasticities," *Public Finance Quarterly* 6 (January 1978): 61.

This difference in elasticity can significantly influence the fiscal performance of the government. High elasticities can insulate the government in a growing area from having to increase tax rates; low elasticities can bring perpetual fiscal crises.

Equity: Horizontal and Vertical

Given that a government seeks to raise a specific amount of money, how should the revenue burden be distributed? Nobody is going to proclaim that it should be raised unfairly, not politicians, members of the news media, preachers, or even windbags on talk radio. Everybody wants fair and equitable taxes, but what does that really mean? This section will not attempt to answer the fundamental moral question of what *fair* means, but it will outline the concepts that tax analysts use to provide information for those who do make that judgment.

There are two general equity standards: (1) according to taxpayers' benefits from or usage of the public service (*benefits received*) and (2) according to taxpayers' capabilities to bear the burden (*ability to pay*). The approach chosen must finally be partly philosophic and partly pragmatic.

The logic of the benefits-received approach is an appealing complement to the exchange economy for private goods.[27] In this quasi-market arrangement, individuals would pay for a public service if and only if they benefit from the public service, and those who receive more benefits would pay more than those who benefit less. When governments sell services—that is, apply user charges (or public prices)—then only those who benefit must pay, assuming that the service has no considerable external benefit, in which case charge finance is suspect because nonpayers gain. (More is said about this in a later chapter.) Tax structures can be benefit-based as well if there is some tax that will cause tax payments to align closely with benefits received from a government service, even if direct charges are not collected from users of that service. One example might be a motor-fuel tax financing highways: the more a person uses highways, the more motor fuel used, and the more motor-fuel tax is paid on the fuel purchases, so those with heaviest use of the facility make the greatest payment. If the individual benefits, he or she pays a tax (or charge) consistent with that benefit; if not, he or she does not pay. There are neither the wasteful oversupplies of public services that can result when a service's price is artificially low nor the equally wasteful underprovision when prices are too high. A taxpayer receiving 1 percent of the benefits of a public service pays 1 percent of the cost of providing that service; there is no cross-subsidization among taxpayers. The user pays for the service; the nonuser does not bear the burden.

Not only will fiscal cross-subsidization from nonusers to users be prevented, but also revenue production may help guide the allocation of government resources, and the benefit basis may override anti-tax sentiment among the citizenry. People

---

[27]How might benefits be measured? The logically correct measure would be the value of the service to the individual. Failing that, less-satisfactory measures include the cost of rendering the service to the beneficiary, the insurance value of the property protected, or, according to Adam Smith's criteria, the amount of income earned by the individual.

may accept a tax on hunting ammunition, for instance, if proceeds are used for wild-life habitat development. Unfortunately, before tax revenue flow can tell us about the demand for a service, there must be close complementarity between the tax base and the government activity, a situation not often occurring.[28] The link between motor-fuel taxes and use of roads previously noted is a good example of such complementarity. In these instances, the tax becomes a proxy for a price paid for consumption of the government service.[29]

Problems prevent wholesale application of a benefits-received approach. For one thing, pure public goods, by their very nature, provide no divisible exchange in the public-good transaction. Any "purchaser" will buy benefits for others. Furthermore, modern governments typically try to redistribute—providing services directly aimed at transferring affluence from one group to another. In this circumstance, the benefits-received approach fails: the objective of the action is subsidization, not exchange. When circumstances of measurement and redistribution do not prohibit, however, the benefits-received approach has strong logical support.

The benefits-received philosophy implies that for every particular mix of government services provided, there is a different appropriate distribution of the cost of government. The tax structure would identify who benefits and then tax those beneficiaries accordingly. A different mix of services implies that different people should pay. On the other hand, the ability-to-pay approach eschews the market-exchange philosophy and argues that, regardless of services being provided, those most capable of bearing the cost of government should bear the greatest amount of that cost.

The logic of the ability-to-pay principle is that appropriability (and its absence) makes public services and private goods fundamentally different, and only the latter are susceptible to market approaches to payment for services. The decision to provide public services can be considered separately from the choice of financial burden distribution, so the distribution may be set according to concepts of fairness or equity. Unfortunately, scientific tools do not establish what distribution is fair, and your opinion (and that is all that it is) probably differs from mine. If individual satisfaction levels could be measured and compared, tax systems might be designed to yield revenues for public use at the least loss of satisfaction to society. There remains no calibration method, so a scientific distribution of financial burden seems beyond reach. Distribution is a matter of political opinion and political power, within ethical limits that may or may not shape the political process, not a matter of establishing what is scientifically correct.

Application of the ability-to-pay approach has two decision elements: selecting an ability-to-pay measure and choosing the way tax payments should vary with that measure. The appropriateness of alternative ability measures varies with the level

---

[28]Earmarking a portion of a general tax—dedicating a particular share of the state sales tax for support of public education, for instance—provides no evidence of preferences for that service, so the practice cannot be justified on the basis of improving information for public decisions.

[29]This system of highway finance is nearing collapse. Hybrid, all-electric, and some alternative-fuel vehicles break the link between motor-fuel purchase and highway use, thereby rendering the fuel taxes unable to finance highways as before. Fortunately, technology now permits direct highway charges, and states will need to make the switch soon. The state of Oregon is already experimenting with vehicle miles traveled charge systems. [Billy Hamilton, "Oregon Test-Drives Replacement for the Gas Tax," *State Tax Notes*, LXV (July 16, 2012): 209–214.]

of economic development. In an agrarian society—for instance, eighteenth-century America—an effective measure of ability to pay might be property ownership, particularly of land, buildings, carriages, and cattle. Modern economic organizations and systems—the corporate form of business enterprise, the development of complex debt forms, and the importance of intangible values in total wealth—make gross values of property an unreliable measure of ability to pay. Therefore, most public discussion about ability to pay concentrates on current income as the appropriate measure. A more comprehensive measure would encompass net wealth as well (possibly using the annuity formula introduced in Chapter 7 to convert accumulated wealth into an estimated annual flow) because both income and wealth figure into an individual's real affluence. Others argue, as we shall see in a later chapter, that consumption by households is a superior index to income because household consumption measures exactly what the household itself believes that it can afford to buy.[30] Exactly which index should gauge ability to pay is not an entirely settled issue, despite the tendency toward annual income in most popular discussions (and toward household consumption among many tax policy experts).

The second choice—after household ability has been measured—is the appropriate distribution of the tax burden across households. This is a social policy question (with some economic aspects), and it has both horizontal and vertical elements.

Horizontal equity—what might also be called "equal justice"—considers equal treatment of taxpayers who have equal capability to pay taxes. If two taxpayers are equivalent, but one taxpayer pays significantly more tax, the tax structure lacks horizontal equity. Such a condition may emerge when taxes vary by individual taste and preference, as when taxes are levied on commodities that are used by a narrow segment of the population or when some sectors of the economy have extra access to schemes that can reduce their tax liability.[31] It may also occur when tax administration is haphazard or capricious or when the administrative task at hand is particularly challenging. For instance, property tax valuation practices may cause houses of apparently similar market value to bear considerably different tax burdens.

An obvious problem here is defining equivalent taxing units: The behavior that creates the observed horizontal equity—for example, the family's taste for taxed luxury items—may itself be regarded as evidence of elevated taxpaying capability. In sum, the concept of horizontal equity may have problems in application, but the principle is clear. Equal treatment, after all, is a principle implicit in the equal-protection requirements of the U.S. Constitution. In a property tax case, the U.S. Supreme Court explained that "the constitutional requirement is the seasonable attainment of a rough equity in tax treatment of similarly situated property owners,"[32] and that is an exact statement of what horizontal equity entails. The logic extends to other taxes as well. For instance, why should two households with equal income pay significantly different income taxes simply because of differences in the way that income was earned? But, as you will discover in a later chapter, they likely do.

---

[30]For a defense of the consumption view, see Nicholas Kaldor, *The Expenditure Tax* (London: George Allen and Unwin, 1958).

[31]For example, the federal Tax Reform Act of 1986 sought to improve horizontal equity by reducing the availability of tax shelters to the daring, slick, or cagey investor.

[32]*Allegheny Pittsburgh Coal Company* v. *County Commission of Webster County, West Virginia,* 488 U.S. 336 (1989).

Vertical equity concerns the proper relationship between the relative tax burdens paid by individuals with different capabilities to pay taxes. The comparison is among unequals, and the question is, By how much should tax payments differ? No scientific guides indicate what the proper differentiation might be, but most would argue that those with more capacity should pay more tax. This simple observation, however, provides minimal guidance for tax policy. And no major tax in use today does not systematically require larger payments from those with greater economic affluence. What needs to be determined further is whether the tax structure should be proportional, progressive, or regressive; that is, by how much should the tax differ across households of different measured ability?

Table 8–5 illustrates the distributions from three hypothetical tax systems, assuming a simple community with only two taxpayers, one of high income and the other of low income. Each system distributes a tax burden of $10,000 between the taxpayers. The vertical equity concept gauges the relationship between income and effective rates (tax paid divided by the relevant affluence measurement; the examples here use current income). A tax structure is *regressive* if effective rates are lower in high-ability groups than in low (effective rates fall as ability rises), *progressive* if effective rates are higher in high-ability groups than in low (effective rates rise as

Table 8–5
Regressivity, Proportionality, and Progressivity in Tax Systems

Regressive System ($10,000 Total Tax)

Taxpayer Income ($)	Share of Pre-tax Income (%)	Tax Paid ($)	Effective Tax Rate (%)	Share of Post-tax Income (%)
20,000	20	3,000	15	18.9
80,000	80	7,000	8.75	81.1
100,000	100	10,000		100.0

Proportional System ($10,000 Total Tax)

Taxpayer Income ($)	Share of Pre-tax Income (%)	Tax Paid ($)	Effective Tax Rate (%)	Share of Post-tax Income (%)
20,000	20	2,000	10	20
80,000	80	8,000	10	80
100,000	100	10,000		100.0

Progressive System ($10,000 Total Tax)

Taxpayer Income ($)	Share of Pre-tax Income (%)	Tax Paid ($)	Effective Tax Rate (%)	Share of Post-tax Income (%)
20,000	20	1,200	6	20.9
80,000	80	8,800	11	79.1
100,000	100	10,000		100.0

ability rises), and *proportional* if effective rates are the same in all groups (effective rates remain constant as ability rises). Effective-rate behavior distinguishes whether the high-income taxpayer is paying relatively more, relatively less, or the same in relation to income as is the low-income taxpayer. That determines the extent to which the tax structure redistributes affluence in the society. Notice in the table that the proportional structure leaves the shares of post-tax income exactly as the shares were before tax, the regressive structure improves the share of the high-income taxpayer, and the progressive structure improves the share of the low-income taxpayer. These patterns of redistribution reflected in the effective-rate patterns are the essence of vertical equity. What society wants the tax system to do in regard to redistribution establishes whether public policy should seek progressive, proportional, or regressive tax structures, and that is an ethical judgment.

At one time, public finance scholars sought scientific support for the redistribution caused by progressive rate structures through reference to diminishing marginal utility of income: those with more affluence gain less satisfaction from income (increments to affluence) than do those with less affluence. Thus, total utility loss to society to obtain a given amount of revenue would be minimized by applying higher tax rates to those with greater affluence. The diminishing-marginal-utility-of-income argument has not been provable and may be wrong, so progression remains unscientific.[33] There continues, however, a general feeling that tax systems should not place greater relative burden on the less affluent (although, as you will discover in later chapters, several of our important taxes do exactly that).

Table 8–5 also illustrates measurements that do not reliably indicate whether a structure is progressive or regressive. For instance, a comparison of total tax paid by high- and low-income groups does not produce meaningful information about vertical equity. For each structure here, the high-income taxpayer pays more tax, even with the regressive tax. Therefore, simply comparing total taxes paid by income groups does not distinguish the regressivity/progressivity/proportionality of the tax structure. Neither does a comparison of the proportion of total taxes paid by an income group with that group's proportion of total population. In the example, the highest-income taxpayer represents half of community population, and the regressive tax structure causes that taxpayer to pay 70 percent of community taxes, so that comparison is not useful. If the tax base per taxpaying unit is unequal among income groups (as it certainly must be), proportional, regressive, and progressive taxes all cause high-income groups to pay a disproportionately high share of taxes and low-income groups to pay a low share relative to share of the population. Thus, effective-rate comparisons or their logical equivalents are the only reliable guide to vertical equity of a structure.

Equity analysis requires an understanding of what entity actually bears the burden of each tax. The work is complicated because the entity legally required to pay any tax may be able to shift some or all of the real burden elsewhere. In the language of tax analysis, the *impact* or statutory incidence may not coincide with the *economic incidence* of the tax because *shifting* has occurred.

---

[33]See Walter J. Blum and Harry Kalven, Jr., *The Uneasy Case for Progressive Taxation* (Chicago: University of Chicago Press, 1953).

The incidence question most often involves taxes with impact on businesses, like taxes on corporate net income, business property, or employee payroll. As illustrated in Figure 8–2, a business may respond in three ways to a tax:

1. **Forward shifting**. The business increases its prices to reflect the tax.
2. **Backward shifting**. The business reduces the price it pays to owners of the resources it purchases, including the wages paid workers, the prices paid suppliers of raw materials, and so on.
3. **Absorption**. The business may return a lower profit to its owners.

What actually occurs depends on the form of the tax—that is, whether the tax is levied on net profits, sales, or property—and on the market conditions the firm faces, but it can be expected to respond in whatever fashion leaves its owners with the greatest profit after tax.[34] The business will not automatically respond by increasing prices because buyers will respond to the higher prices by purchasing less, and the profit lost from those sales may be greater than the tax recovered from the price increase. No matter how the business responds, however, the business tax reduces the real income of individuals by causing customers to pay higher prices, by causing workers or other resource owners to receive lower income for what they sell to the

Figure 8-2
Tax Impact, Shifting, and Incidence

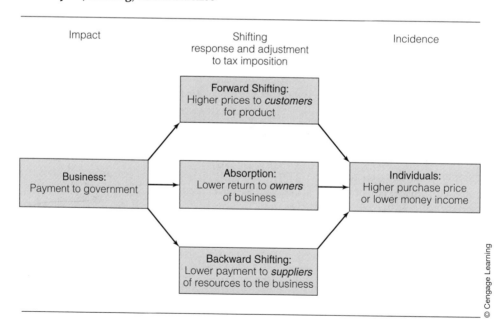

[34]The responses are carefully analyzed in Richard A. Musgrave, *The Theory of Public Finance* (New York: McGraw-Hill, 1959), chap. 13; and in Joseph E. Stiglitz, *Economics of the Public Sector*, 3rd ed. (New York: W. W. Norton, 2000), chaps. 18, 23, and 27. Another good source: Executive Office of the President, Council of Economic Advisers, *Economic Report of the President Transmitted to the Congress February 2004* - (Washington, D.C.: U.S. Government Printing Office, 2004), chap. 4.

firm, or by leaving owners of the firm with lower profits. For example, the payroll tax to finance Social Security has two shares, one paid by the employer and one paid by the employee. Most analysts argue that both components reduce the real income of the employee: The payroll tax paid by the employer represents wages, salaries, and fringe benefits that would have been paid to the employee in the absence of the tax. The employer knows about the payroll tax and adjusts wages downward to cover that tax. Hence, the real burden, or incidence, of this share, along with the employee share, is on the employee. Or another example: The landlord pays property tax on his or her rental units. However, over time, the landlord may adjust the rents upward to accommodate that property tax. If so, the incidence of the tax rests on the renter.

Two important principles about tax incidence are often lost in political discussions. First, laws may define tax impacts (who makes payment to the government), but market forces determine incidence (whose real income gets reduced because of the tax); *to legislate incidence is about as effective as legislating against snowfall*. Second, all taxes are ultimately borne by individuals. Businesses serve as conduits of burdens to people, as buyers, as sellers, or as owners. The shifting process is not easy to sort out, but its determination is necessary to identify the vertical equity of a tax.[35]

In order to illustrate the application of vertical equity analysis, Table 8–6 displays Congressional Budget Office estimates of effective tax rates for federal taxes across families, arrayed by income-group quintiles, to permit some comparability across time and place in selected years from 1980 to 2009. The table is calculated to include all taxes levied by the federal government; more individual attention will be given them in later chapters. The distribution in Table 8–6 makes these incidence assumptions: (1) families who pay the tax bear the burden of the individual income tax (no shifting); (2) the social insurance tax burden is allocated to employee compensation (employer share shifted backward, no shifting of employee share); (3) excise taxes are paid by individual consumers in higher prices (forward shifting); and (4) corporate income tax is paid by families (half shifted back to employees, half shifted to stockholders).[36] Notice that the impact or statutory incidence of these taxes does not always fall on the individuals who bear the final burden or incidence. For instance, product producers usually are responsible for paying the federal excise taxes, but the incidence analysis assumes that the taxes are shifted forward in higher product prices.

The distribution is progressive through the years, with rate differences between the highest quintile and the lowest somewhat greater in 2009 than in 1980. The

---

[35]If businesses serve as conduits of tax burden to individuals, why not forget about taxing businesses and concentrate only on taxing individuals directly? Is it just because of political dynamics? For a good discussion of the logic, see Thomas F. Pogue, "Principles of Business Taxation. How and Why Should Businesses Be Taxed?" in *Handbook on Taxation,* ed. W. Bartley Hildreth and James A. Richardson (New York: Marcel Dekker, 1999), 191–203.

[36]The CBO changed its shifting assumption for 2009. For this year, the corporate income tax is assumed to be borne by capital income. Because capital income is a larger share of income for high income households, the distribution becomes somewhat more progressive. Estimates for earlier years using that assumption are not currently available. The Joint Committee on Taxation and the Department of Treasury use somewhat different shifting assumptions for the corporate income tax in doing burden estimates. They now distribute the corporate income tax 82 percent to capital income and 18 percent to labor income. Julie Anne Cronin, Emily Y. Lin, Laura Power, and Michael Cooper, "Distributing the Corporate Income Tax: Revised U.S. Treasury Methodology," Office of Tax Analysis Technical Paper 5, Washington, D.C., May 2012.

Table 8–6

Federal Tax Distributions and Effective Tax Rates by Income Quintiles for All Families, 1980–2009 (Percentages)

Quintile	1980			1985			1990		
	Income Share	Tax Share	Effective Tax Rate	Income Share	Tax Share	Effective Tax Rate	Income Share	Tax Share	Effective Tax Rate
Lowest	5.7	2.0	7.7	4.8	2.3	9.8	4.6	1.9	8.9
Second	11.0	7.0	14.1	10.1	7.2	14.8	10.0	6.8	14.6
Third	15.7	13.3	18.7	15.2	13.2	18.1	15.1	12.6	17.9
Fourth	22.1	21.3	21.5	21.9	21.3	20.4	21.6	20.7	20.6
Highest	45.8	56.3	27.3	48.6	55.8	24.0	49.5	57.9	25.1
Top 5%	20.7	28.7	30.8	23.4	28.4	25.4	24.3	30.6	27.0
Top 1%	9.1	14.2	34.6	11.5	14.8	27.0	12.1	16.2	28.8

SOURCE: Congressional Budget Office, *Average Federal Taxes by Income Group* (Washington, D.C.: Congressional Budget Office, 2010) and Congressional Budget Office, "The Distribution of Household Income and Federal Taxes, 2008 and 2009" (Washington, D. C.: CBO, 2012).

effective rate paid by the highest-income earners is lower in 2009 than it was in 1980, but the decline is greater for the lowest quintile. The table also shows the share of pre-tax income received and the share of federal tax borne in each quintile; as is characteristic of a progressive distribution, the share of tax is greater than the share of pre-tax income for higher-income groups and the reverse for lower-income groups.[37] These are, of course, average rates for the quintiles, and around that average are considerable differences from family to family. If these differences are large enough, they indicate horizontal inequity.

Analysts occasionally estimate the relative share of taxes paid by businesses and individuals, especially at the state and local levels of government. Business taxes usually include taxes on business property, corporate net income taxes, business gross receipt taxes, corporate franchise taxes, miscellaneous business and occupation taxes, licenses, severance taxes, document and stock transfer taxes, and the like. Taxes on individuals include property taxes on residences and household personal property, individual income taxes, retail sales taxes, and selective excise taxes. Special classification problems arise with taxes on agricultural property (What portion of a farmer's property tax bill is individual, and what portion is business?), unincorporated business income (the business is taxed through the individual income tax system), and sales tax paid on business purchases. Those complexities, however, can usually be resolved by allocations based on a sample of taxpayers.

Of course, the burden of taxes levied on businesses ultimately falls on individuals, even if the tax is collected initially from business. Those engaged in transactions

---

[37]Because individuals face different economic conditions and make different economic choices over their lifetimes, they are not always taxed in the same way and by the same taxes. Some economists have tried to estimate the lifetime incidence profile of a tax system and its elements, moving away from the traditional annual focus. See, for example, Don Fullerton and Diane Lim Rogers, *Who Bears the Lifetime Tax Burden?* (Washington, D.C.: Brookings Institution, 1993). A study that looks at burden over a longer time horizon appears in Congressional Budget Office, *Effective Tax Rates: Comparing Annual and Multiyear Measures* (Washington, D.C.: Congressional Budget Office, 2005).

Table 8–6
(continued)

Quintile	1995			2000			2009		
	Income Share	Tax Share	Effective Tax Rate	Income Share	Tax Share	Effective Tax Rate	Income Share	Tax Share	Effective Tax Rate
Lowest	4.6	1.3	6.3	4.0	1.1	6.4	5.1	0.8	1.0
Second	9.7	5.8	13.4	8.6	4.8	13.0	9.8	4.4	6.8
Third	14.9	11.4	17.3	13.5	9.8	16.6	14.7	9.2	11.1
Fourth	21.3	19.3	20.5	19.6	17.5	20.5	21.1	16.5	15.1
Highest	50.2	61.9	27.8	54.8	66.6	28.0	50.8	68.9	23.2
Top 5%	25.1	35.4	31.8	30.7	41.4	31.0	25.9	39.6	n.a.
Top 1%	12.5	20.1	36.1	17.8	25.5	33.0	13.4	22.3	28.9

with the business as its customers, suppliers, employees, or owners bear the tax. So why tax the business separately from taxing those people directly? Much of the answer is pure politics—lawmakers prefer the fiction that by taxing businesses they are sparing individuals the burden of paying for government services. But there are a couple of reasons that have some logical support. First, there is an economic reason: the business tax may charge the business for costs it generates, but otherwise would not take account of when deciding what, where, and how to produce. In other words, a carefully designed business tax may make the business recognize the cost of otherwise unpriced inputs used in production. The most important costs involved are the cost of services provided by government to the business (public safety, civil court system, and so on) and the cost of environmental damage caused by production of goods and services (air, water, and soil pollution). The business tax can provide signals about resource use to the operators of the business, thus improving the utilization of resources in the economy. Second, it may be more effective and less costly to use the business as a conduit of burden to individuals than to collect directly from the individuals. For example, collection of a retail sales tax indirectly through vendors who add the tax to the price of goods that they sell is much more efficient than trying to collect a comparable tax from individual purchasers after the sale has been made.[38] As far as the owners of a business are concerned, probably more important than the share of taxes paid by business is the amount of those taxes that cannot be readily shifted to suppliers or to customers—the taxes that, under existing market conditions, reduce the return received by owners of the business.

State and local governments are interested in relative business-individual shares, however, for reasons other than equitable burden distribution (or the politically important fact that tax paid by business has a more hidden burden on individuals—politicians are less fervent believers in transparency than are fiscal analysts). In many instances, the individuals ultimately bearing the burden of business taxes, either as owners or as customers of the business, live out of state.[39] A higher business share

---

[38]For a good discussion of the idea of business taxation, see Pogue, "Principles of Business Taxation," 191–203.
[39]Note that certain individual taxes may be substantially exported in special circumstances: for example, residential property taxes in second-home communities and lodging taxes in tourist areas.

thus means that a greater amount of state and local government costs is exported to nonresidents. That exporting is politically attractive, even if the extent of exporting attempted may not always be logically justified. Although those businesses do receive services provided by the host community, the appropriate amount of payment is always subject to dispute between businesses and the government. Furthermore, states must take care that out-of-state businesses are not treated more harshly than are domestic businesses because differential treatment would violate the Commerce Clause of the U.S. Constitution.[40]

The capability to use taxes with the initial impact on business to export the cost of government to nonresidents, however, does have an important limitation. Taxes may adversely affect the competitive position of business in the state. If tax structures designed to export cost to nonresidents place local business at competitive disadvantage relative to out-of-state competitors, the state economy may suffer. Therefore, tax-share data must be tempered with evaluation of the overall tax level in the competitive states (all of a very low total tax burden would have less influence on competitive position than would a moderate share of a very high total tax burden), but the concern with competitive balance does influence the quest for cost exporting. Thus, states frequently trade the desire to export government cost for a competitive balance for local firms.

Economic Effects

Taxes change the way people and businesses behave, often with considerable consequence to economic activity from those distortions. It is important to design tax structures and their administration so that they are not needlessly harmful to the economy. There is a difference of opinion as to whether taxes can be expected to do more than simply produce revenue and cause as little economic harm as possible. Some argue that a tax should be neutral in its effect: market systems can be trusted to function well without intervention, so the most one should expect from a tax is that it disturbs the marketplace as little as possible. The federal Tax Reform Act of 1986, for instance, sought to establish a "level playing field" for types of economic endeavors. In other words, the tax should ordinarily be neutral. Others argue that a tax should have favorable economic effects: the outcome from market operations can be improved by using tax incentives to alter private behavior in some desired fashion. That means that the tax structure should be used to try to improve on the results from the market.[41] Preferences—credits, exemptions, preferential rates, and the like—are designed not to accept the workings of the market, but to try to bend market results in ways that lawmakers prefer. Many people trust market results far more than they trust what a bunch of politicians, even well-meaning ones, would produce.

---

[40]"The Congress shall have Power...to regulate Commerce with foreign nations and among the several States and with the Indian Tribes" (Article I, Sec. 8[3]). Differential treatment by a state involves a power reserved to Congress.

[41]How tax structure may induce (or discourage) development in poor countries is exhaustively reviewed in the excellent survey by Robin Burgess and Nicholas Stern, "Taxation and Development," *Journal of Economic Literature* 31 (June 1993): 762–830.

Regardless of one's view about the appropriateness (or even the possibility) of trying to improve on the results from the market with tax distortions, it is clear that taxes do influence economic behavior and that influences differ among taxes. Taxes can have important effects on economic activity, and tax incentives—good and bad—are part of tax policy discussions. Whenever a tax produces a difference in the return that can be gained between two or more competing economic activities, individuals and businesses can be expected to respond toward the alternative leaving a greater after-tax return. Individuals and businesses change their behavior in response to a tax, but the reaction depends on how the tax is structured, not just its absolute level. Furthermore, the response can come in anticipation of a change in the tax, the response may differ according to whether the tax is believed to be permanent or temporary, and the response increases as individuals and businesses have more time to make adjustments to the tax.

Here are a number of different choices that a tax wedge—the difference between before- and after-tax prices, payments, or rates of return—can create, along with some examples of the effect:

1. **Work versus leisure**. High taxes on extra income earned may induce workers to choose more leisure time instead of working more hours. Working overtime is less attractive if governments tax away a very high percentage of income earned from that overtime, for instance. Suppose that, of each $100 of overtime pay that a worker earned, the government taxed away $80. Do you suppose workers would choose to work as much overtime as they would if the tax amount were only $15?

2. **Business operations**. Firms should not be induced to organize business practices—production techniques, type of business organization, distribution or marketing system, and so forth—on the basis of tax provisions. Thus, a state property tax on business inventory held on a particular date can induce firms to ship inventory out of state on that date for return later. Suppose that Indiana levies a tax of 10 percent of the value of automobiles on the showroom floor on March 1 and that the tax does not apply to automobiles owned by private owners. Do you suppose that auto dealers would have special sales events to reduce their inventory just before the tax day?[42] Taxes can even lead to the creation of new businesses. The high cigarette tax in New York City, combining to $5.85 per pack in late 2011, has led to the establishment of a "roll your own" cigarette shop. The shop sells loose tobacco and cigarette papers and provides machines for customers to use in producing their own cigarettes. The much lower tax on loose tobacco makes the price for these cigarettes much less than that for the regular cigarettes.[43]

---

[42]Historically, newspapers have been published in broadsheet rather than tabloid format because in 1712 Britain introduced a stamp tax on newspapers per sheet of newsprint. Papers responded by increasing the size of their pages to reduce the amount of tax that they would owe. Bigger sheets, fewer pages, lower tax. The traditional size spread globally, and only recently have newspapers started reducing the size of the sheets.

[43]Sam Roberts, "Low-Tax Cigarettes, Made in Store, Draw City Lawsuit," *New York Times*, November 21, 2011. The roll-your-own machines got a major boost when the federal cigarette tax increased in 2009. David Kesmodel, "Roll-Your-Own Cigarette Machines Help Evade Steep Tax," *Wall Street Journal*, August 30, 2010.

3. **Shopping, purchases, and business location**. High tax rates on goods—cigarettes, liquor, or retail sales in general, for instance—in some states induce their residents to purchase those items from nearby states with lower taxes and lower prices. These and other taxes may change where entrepreneurs set up their businesses. Do you suppose that Boston residents, facing a sales tax rate of 6.25 percent, might take the short drive to New Hampshire, where there is no general sales tax, to purchase some appliances and other high-ticket items? In addition, a tax can make things disappear: In 2002, Ireland passed a tax of one-quarter of a euro on plastic bags. If you are in Ireland today, don't even dream of getting your groceries in a plastic bag when you check out because they won't even be available.[44]

4. **Personal management**. Because travel expense to professional conventions can be subtracted from income subject to the federal individual income tax, such conventions may be held in resort locations. Those attending can thus combine vacation and business, while reducing their tax obligation. Also, tax provisions can influence how people prefer to be paid. If, for instance, payments received as fringe benefits are not taxed as income, then employees will prefer more of their compensation in that form rather than in taxable wages and salaries. Suppose your employer can purchase health insurance for you, paying $6,000 per year for that insurance, compensation that is not taxed, or your employer can pay you an extra $6,000 per year, fully taxable, and then you have to purchase your own health insurance. Which option would you prefer?

5. **Productive investment and financial portfolios**. Investment may be expected to be influenced by the after-tax rate of return and by tax-induced rate-of-return differentials between sorts of enterprise. Furthermore, high-income entities may direct investable funds to municipal bonds yielding tax-free interest rather than to other productive investment, the return on which would be taxed. Capital is usually more mobile than is labor, and differences in rates of return can elicit considerable shift in capital investment very quickly.[45]

---

[44]Speaking of Ireland, at the same time that Bono, the Irish rock star and supporter of international good deeds, was pushing the Irish government to contribute more aid to Africa in 2006, he was moving U2's music publishing operation to Amsterdam to dramatically reduce their tax obligations, mostly at the expense of revenue to the government of Ireland. Timothy Noah, "Bono, Tax Avoider," *Slate*, October 31, 2006 [http://www.slate.com/id/2152580/]. Too bad he wasn't willing to pitch in to pay for the good deeds being done by the Irish government.

[45]People do move in response to tax rates, even though the response is small. When New Jersey implemented a millionaire's tax—an income tax rate increase of 2.9 percentage points on its highest-income earners—migration was minimal, mostly among those living on investment income, people working entirely in-state, and retirees. The tax produced revenue, reduced income inequality, and produced no discernible net tax flight by high earners. Cristobal Young and Charles Varner, "Millionaire Migration and State Taxation of Top Incomes: Evidence from a Natural Experiment," *National Tax Journal* 64 (June 2011): 255–84. However, an analysis of the behavior of European football superstars finds a considerable impact of differences in national income tax rates on player movement. Henrik Kleven, Camille Landais, and Emmanuel Saez, "Taxation and International Migration of Superstars: Evidence from the European Football Market," National Bureau of Economic Research Working Paper 1645, Cambridge, Mass., 2010. These are people who earn very high incomes, are young, have short careers, and have little connection to any particular location.

6. **Savings**. Taxes can distort the decision to save by making consumption postponed to the future (savings) more expensive than equivalent consumption in the present. The influence can be on personal decisions to save and on business decisions to retain or distribute earnings to business owners.

Case 8–1 shows how taxes influence a number of basic life decisions. Overall, taxes should not discourage private employment or economic activity more than the minimum needed to extract resources for government operation. Undesirable distortions should be minimized because they cause a waste of productive resources, lower rates of economic growth, and lower national living standards.

Sidebar 8–2 explains excess burden, a measure used in the analysis of distortion. The example in Sidebar 8–2 provides a worst-case scenario because the tax yields no revenue (from Fred), but does create an economic burden (the value lost from the distorted consumer choice). The efficiency objective in tax policy seeks to yield necessary revenue (the tax burden), while keeping economic distortion (the excess burden) as low as possible. Although the illustration is of consumer choice, there is a similar concern with minimizing producer distortions. In general, excess burden can be reduced by (1) keeping tax rates low (a good reason to have broad tax bases); (2) avoiding different tax rates on similar products, similar uses for competing productive resources, or similar ways of earning an income; and (3) avoiding taxes in markets where buyers or sellers react substantially to changes in price.

Collectability

In general, taxes and tax provisions should be designed to keep total tax collection cost as low as possible within the constraint of satisfactory equity and economic impact. Unfortunately, there are frequently trade-offs. For instance, taxes on payrolls represent the income tax format with least collection cost: collection is made by employers (there are far fewer of them to keep track of than there are employees, and the return from one employer will cover many employees), the problem of checking on interest and dividend income is avoided, and special questions about rents and capital gains do not arise. Unfortunately, those with interest, dividend, rental, and capital gain income tend to be more affluent than those receiving only payroll income. Thus, the tax that is simple to administer has equity problems. Narrow-based taxes, particularly selective excises, often simply cannot be collected at low cost and are poor choices for the revenue system.[46] The resources used in their collection can be more profitably used in administration of other taxes.

Efficient collection "avoids complex provisions and regulations; multiple filing and reporting requirements; and numerous deductions, exclusions, and exemptions. The more complicated the tax system, the greater the costs of taxpayer compliance.

---

[46]Some excise taxes function to compensate for social costs associated with use of particular products or services. For example, the federal tax on ozone-depleting chemicals was imposed not for revenue purposes, but rather to cause producers and consumers to recognize the dramatic external cost of use of the chemicals and thus to reduce their use in the economy.

Sidebar 8–2
The Excess Burden of a Tax—Measuring the Value of Economic Distortion

Economists identify two components of the total burden of a tax. These are the *tax burden,* the payment made by the taxpayer to the government, and the *excess burden* (also called the deadweight loss or welfare cost), a measure of the economic distortion caused by the tax. The excess burden is the loss created by changes in producer and consumer decisions that the tax produces. In general, economists expect that free choice by producers and consumers will direct resources to those activities yielding the best return for society and that consumers will use their purchasing power to acquire those goods giving them the greatest satisfaction. Imposing the tax yields revenue to the government—the tax burden—but it also normally causes a reduction in the amount of the subject of the tax (a commodity or an input) sold. That reduction in units sold brings the deadweight loss: those now-unsold units were bringing satisfaction to the purchaser above the price the purchaser was paying and a return to the seller above the price the seller was receiving (otherwise, neither buyer nor seller would have made the exchange). This market loss is above the tax paid to the government. Indeed, we don't worry much about the tax burden—if the government is budgeting wisely, the use of the resources by the government will yield a return above that which could have been earned in the private market.

The idea of excess burden can be illustrated in a simple example. Suppose Fred ordinarily buys three compact discs (CDs) per month at a price of $15 each (spending a total of $45 per month). The government now imposes a new CD tax that adds $3 to the price of each disc. Fred concludes that $18 per disc is simply too much to pay and no longer buys CDs. The government collects no tax revenue from Fred (his tax burden is zero), and he now has $45 per month available to spend on other things.

Does Fred bear any burden from the tax? Certainly, he does, under the assumption that he was making well-informed, free choices before the imposition of the tax. The tax has caused him to move from his preferred use of that $45 to the purchase of something else, a less desirable (to Fred) option. We know it is less desirable to him because he rejected it before, choosing to buy the CDs instead. Fred loses the satisfaction from the CDs and switches to a less preferred use of his money. This loss is called the excess burden by tax analysts.

That governments should avoid excess burden in structuring their tax systems is an application of the general principle that government should avoid doing things that are economically stupid. If the private market is managing its basic role of allocating resources, then the tax system should leave it alone as much as possible.

A less-complicated system of taxation enables understanding of the law and enhances public confidence in the system. From the government's perspective, complexity increases the costs of administration, and frequent changes to tax laws prohibit effective fiscal planning."[47] Complexity is usually the product of well-intentioned efforts to correct some perceived inequity in the tax system or to improve some element of

---

[47]David Brunori, "Principles of Tax Policy and Targeted Incentives," *State and Local Government Review* 29 (Winter 1997): 53.

how the system impacts economic incentives. The complications allow lawmakers to use the tax system for reasons other than raising revenue. There is, indeed, a demand for complexity, and with that complexity come increased costs of compliance and of administration. The quest for tax simplicity is an excellent applause line in political speeches, but members of the public rather like tax complications that reduce their own tax bills. Simplification—and the end to preferences that it would normally entail—should be applicable to somebody else; everyone wants to keep his or her own tax-saving complexities. Naturally, politicians go along with the preference game. Milton Friedman explained: "From the citizen's point of view, the function of tax legislation is to decide who shall pay how much to finance government spending. But from Congress's point of view, tax legislation has an additional and very important function: It is a way to raise campaign funds."[48] In exchange for preferences, lobbyists are quite eager to make contributions to election committees.[49] Therefore, improving collectability in the real world of tax restructuring requires a delicate balancing of tax policy and practical tax politics. The options can be easily summarized: fair or simple, take your pick. And you have the political dynamic working against you.

A complication in examining collectability arises because not all tax collection systems use the same division of responsibilities between taxpayers and the tax administrators in producing revenue. "Taxpayer-passive" systems require tax collectors to do most of the work (and bear most of the cost) of raising revenue. For instance, real property taxes typically require little from the property holder, as government agencies perform all the tax record keeping and calculations. The total cost of tax collection with this system is almost exclusively what the government spends in administering the law. There isn't much compliance cost imposed on the taxpayer, and taxpayers don't see the complexity. Even though the property tax has many complications in its operation, taxpayers don't complain about the complexity—it isn't complicated for them. They complain about almost everything else about the property tax, just not its complexity.

"Taxpayer-active" systems privatize much of the collection effort, that is, impose most of the collection responsibility on the private taxpayer: for instance, the American income tax requires the individual taxpayer to "supply all relevant information, compute the tax base, calculate the tax, and pay the tax, or some installment of it, when he files his return,"[50] while the tax collector distributes forms, verifies taxpayer reports, and manages revenue flows. The tax administrators aim to induce voluntary taxpayer compliance rather than to collect the tax directly with this sort of administrative system.[51] When the system is functioning properly, most revenue comes without direct administrative action, and the bulk of collection cost is the

---

[48]Milton Friedman, "Tax Reform Lets Politicians Look for New Donors," *Wall Street Journal*, July 7, 1986.
[49]One study found that lobbying for a particular tax preference brought participating companies a return of 22,000 percent on their investment. Dan Eggen, "Investments Can Yield More on K Street, Study Indicates," *Washington Post*, April 12, 2009, A8. No wonder firms try to influence tax legislation.
[50]Carl S. Shoup, *Public Finance* (Chicago: Aldine, 1969), 430.
[51]Value-added taxes collected under the credit-invoice structure have sometimes been called taxes that administer themselves. That is not accurate. Tax officials must devote the normal amount of resources to policing divisions between business and personal use, verifying statements of creditable taxes, watching for bogus invoices, controlling delinquency, and so on.

expenses of taxpayer compliance, not government administrative cost. Less than 2 percent of total revenue collected by the Internal Revenue Service (IRS) comes from enforcement actions; the rest comes from voluntary compliance. However, this is not a free-will offering from the taxpayer. While the exact motives behind why taxpayers actually do comply are not fully understood, it is likely that many comply not because they believe they are buying government services, but because they do not want a visit from the tax collector and paying their taxes is a way of keeping this unwelcome visitor away. This system involves modest administrative cost and substantial compliance cost.

Neither collection system is always best, and most taxes could be administered with different mixes of taxpayer and tax collector responsibilities. The approach selected for a particular tax should reflect prevailing economic conditions, compliance environments, and technologies to best meet the tax policy criteria described previously.[52] For example, not all individual income taxes place as much responsibility on the taxpayer as does the U.S. system. In various degrees, income tax agencies in such countries as Great Britain, Germany, and Japan have used information on taxpayer filing status, number of children, and employee compensation to compute tax and handle collections only through withholding, a "return-free" or "pre-populated return" system. Those receiving only that employer-reported compensation and interest or dividends reported by the payer file no tax return.[53] The California Ready Return system provides certain taxpayers (those receiving only wage income who would file a simple return) the option of filing the completed return that has been prepared by the state Franchise Tax Board on the basis of information provided it by the taxpayer's employer or of doing their own return. That system can completely remove the compliance problem for these individuals. Going the other direction, some people argue that a self-assessment system for real property would do no worse than the current taxpayer-passive system.[54]

Because of the difference between taxpayer-active and taxpayer-passive systems, a fair comparison of collectability across taxes must focus on total collection costs, including both the cost incurred by the government in administering the tax and the cost incurred by taxpayers and their agents in complying with the tax's legal requirements (excluding tax actually paid). Because both components of collection cost use resources, neither can be ignored. Although a tax agency may reduce its

---

[52]Technology to integrate sources of information and reduce the compliance work required from taxpayers can significantly reduce compliance cost, sometimes without even altering the structure of the tax. Joseph Bankman, "Using Technology to Simplify Individual Tax Filing," *National Tax Journal* 61 (December 2008): 773–89.

[53]Great Britain now uses a system of self-assessment, a switch referred to as "privatization." General Accounting Office, *Internal Revenue Service: Opportunities to Reduce Taxpayer Burden through Return Free Filing,* GAO/GGD-92-88BR (Washington, D.C.: General Accounting Office, 1992).

[54]Some taxes are collected in advance: cigarette manufacturers purchase tax stamps from states and affix the stamps to packs of cigarettes intended for sale in the particular state. The state gets its money early, and enforcement is easy—just look for the appropriate stamp. In Belgium, residents pay administrative fees—like for a passport or for a change of address—using fiscal stamps that they must purchase from post offices. They buy the stamps at the post office and use them at the administrative office, and the administrative office turns them in to the national government to get the cash. Napoleon created the system a couple of centuries ago because he didn't trust the locals to handle money. John Miller, "As Gregor Samsa Awoke to Less Red Tape . . .," *The Wall Street Journal Europe,* May 17, 2004, A3.

budget problems by shifting greater collection cost to individuals (as with requiring individuals to pick up return forms from revenue agency offices instead of mailing them to everyone on the tax roll), there is no reason to believe that such practices reduce collection cost. In fact, loss of specialization and economies of scale may actually cause total collection cost to increase. The decision focus is properly on collection cost, the combination of administrative and compliance activities.

Combined costs are particularly critical when comparing real property taxes and the major non-property taxes. The non-property taxes are largely taxpayer-administered. For these taxes, the individual or firm maintains records of potential taxable transactions, tabulates the tax base, computes appropriate liability, and makes payments at appropriate times. Government agencies concentrate on partial coverage audits, not direct agency collection, to ensure substantial compliance with the law. The taxpayer bears the bulk of total collection cost. Administration aimed at inducing voluntary compliance would have low administrative cost and higher compliance cost.

The real property tax, on the other hand, ordinarily does not depend on voluntary compliance. A government agent maintains parcel records, values these property parcels for tax distribution, computes the liability for each parcel, and distributes tax bills to parcel owners; the taxpayer is passive. Moreover, when overlapping units of government (city, county, special districts, school district, etc.) levy property taxes, the taxpayer typically receives a single bill for all property taxes. This reduces compliance cost even further. Unless the taxpayer appeals an assessment, payment is the only taxpayer activity. In the normal scheme, the only collection cost is from administration. Thus, comparing the cost of administering a real property tax with the cost of administering a non-property tax is not appropriate.

Table 8–7 presents administrative cost data for a selection of taxes levied by a variety of governments. Because most revenue agencies administer more than one tax and in fact undertake some nonrevenue functions, the joint cost-allocation problem makes completely accurate cost estimates impossible. The data here must thus be viewed as simply estimates prepared through reasonably consistent allocation schemes. None of these taxpayer-active broad-based taxes shows administration costs much above 1 percent of revenue produced, and many show costs substantially lower than that. In comparison, the cost of administering a high-quality property tax system has been estimated at around 1.5 percent of collections, substantially more than the cost estimates presented for other broad-based taxes.[55]

For the major non-property taxes, most revenue comes from taxpayer actions alone (voluntary compliance); relatively little of the total comes from enforcement, audit, or related revenue-department actions. For example, 2 percent of total Michigan collections, 4.5 percent of California sales and use-tax collections, 5 percent of total Arizona revenues, and 1.69 percent of IRS collections come from direct enforcement actions, including audits, penalties and interest, and delinquency collection.[56]

---

[55]Ronald B. Welch, "Characteristics and Feasibility of High Quality Assessment Administration," in *Property Tax Reform,* ed. International Association of Assessing Officers (Chicago: International Association of Assessing Officers, 1973), 50.
[56]These data come from the same sources as the data in Table 8-7.

Table 8–7
Administrative-Cost Estimates for Major Taxes

	Administrative Costs as a Percentage of Revenue
Income Tax	
Colorado (individual and corporate)	0.33
Michigan (individual)	0.64
U.K. individual income, capital gains, and national insurance tax	1.5
U.K. corporate income tax	0.52
General Sale and Use Tax	
California	1.23
Colorado sales	0.22
Colorado use	0.12
Idaho	0.8
Mississippi	1
North Carolina	0.68
North Dakota	0.5
South Dakota	0.41
Washington	0.7
Other Taxes	
Federal luxury excises	0.3
Twelve OECD value-added taxes	0.32–1.09
GAO estimates for 5% broad U.S. value-added tax	1.2–1.8
Taxes administered by IRS	0.53
Arizona taxes	0.61
California alcoholic beverage	0.59
California cigarette tax	3.21
California motor vehicle fuel tax	0.78
Colorado alcoholic beverage	5.27
Colorado cigarette and tobacco	0.1
Colorado gaming tax	5.88
Colorado mileage and fuels	1.44
Colorado death and gift	2.51
Idaho taxes	0.84
U.K. major excises	0.25
U.K. value-added tax	0.60

SOURCES: Colorado Department of Revenue, *Annual Report, 2007* (Denver: Department of Revenue, 2008); Idaho State Tax Commission, *Annual Report, 2007* (Boise: State Tax Commission, 2008); Internal Revenue Service, *Data Book 2011* (Washington, D.C.: Internal Revenue Service, 2012); Sijbren Cnossen, "Administrative and Compliance Costs of the VAT: A Review of the Evidence," *Tax Notes International* 8 (June 20, 1994); Michigan State Treasurer, *Annual Report, 1977–78* (Lansing: State Treasurer, 1980); John F. Due and John L. Mikesell, Sales Taxation (Washington, D.C.: Urban Institute, 1994); General Accounting Office, *Value Added Tax: Costs Vary with Complexity and Number of Businesses,* GAO-GGD-93-78 (Washington, D.C.: General Accounting Office, 1993); Cedric Sanford, Michael Godwin, and Peter J. W. Hardwick, *Administrative and Compliance Costs of Taxation* (Bath, England: Fiscal Publications, 1989); Arizona Department of Revenue, *2004 Annual Report* (Phoenix: Department of Revenue, 2005); California State Board of Equalization, *Annual Report, 2010* (Sacramento: State Board of Equalization, 2011).

Taxpayers—not government agencies—bear the bulk of the total collection costs (record keeping, return preparation, accounting and legal fees, etc.). Those compliance costs vary substantially among taxpayers, and estimates are hazardous. However, for most taxes, compliance cost is several times as large as administrative cost. For instance, Joel Slemrod and Nikki Sorum have estimated that the compliance cost of federal and state income taxes is between 5 and 7 percent of total tax revenue, many times the cost of administering the taxes.[57]

After allowance for the difference between taxpayer-active and taxpayer-passive characteristics, the real property tax does not appear to be an unduly expensive tax to collect. Relative cost of collection—compliance plus administration—does not appear to be a deterrent to better-quality administration. To summarize, a comparison of administrative costs across taxpayer-active and taxpayer-passive tax systems does not provide useful information for public policy consideration. The focus must be on total collection cost. In addition, it must never be forgotten that no taxpayer is thrilled about the prospect of paying his or her taxes. When options are available, taxpayers will make some attempts to reduce their tax liability. Sidebar 8–3 discusses the difference between tax avoidance and tax evasion.

Transparency

The revenue system in a market democracy should be transparent in its adoption, in its administration, in its compliance requirements, and in the amounts that must be paid because democracy requires that the people know who is responsible for public actions, including what goes on with the taxes they must pay. Transparency, shining daylight on operations of the tax system, is critical for good governance in a democracy. However, politicians are seldom keen on transparency. They do not like to admit that taxes are being levied at all, that people bear the burden of taxes, that taxes might need to be increased to keep up with demand for government services, or even that taxes might be necessary to finance the support of government services that people want. A hidden tax is the ideal tax for many American politicians, and maybe for the American public so they can continue with the delusion that the government services they utilize are free.

Tax transparency has several aspects:

1. **Adoption**. Tax laws should be adopted in an open legislative process. The electorate needs to know the origin of tax proposals—who is introducing the legislation and who is voting for it—and their implication for the distribution of the cost of government. There should be a clear and accessible hearing process for receiving public input on legislative proposals. Unfortunately, just as appropriation earmarks slip into spending bills, the same technique gets used by lawmakers to insert tax provisions into tax bills. Special tax deals are probably less likely if legislative changes are openly discussed. A

---

[57]Joel Slemrod and Nikki Sorum, "The Compliance Cost of the U.S. Individual Income Tax System," *National Tax Journal* 39 (December 1984): 461. An extensive catalogue of compliance-cost estimates appears in Francois Vaillancourt, "The Compliance Cost of Taxes on Businesses and Individuals: A Review of the Evidence," *Public Finance/Finances Publiques* 42, no. 3 (1987): 395–430.

Sidebar 8–3
Tax Evasion and Tax Avoidance

Taxpayers attempt to reduce the taxes they would otherwise pay through two mechanisms: tax avoidance and tax evasion. The difference between the two is clear in logic, but can be complicated in actual practice.

Tax avoidance includes efforts by the taxpayer to reduce the amount of taxes that he or she owes by means that are legal. These practices include such activities as investing in debt that pays interest that is not subject to federal income tax, putting money in an Individual Retirement Account, taking advantage of tax credits for purchasing energy-saving windows for one's home, taking a deduction for contributions made to an eligible charitable organization, and so on. By taking these actions, the taxpayer's tax liability is reduced, and the reduction is entirely within the intent of the tax law.

Tax evasion, on the other hand, involves actions by the taxpayer to reduce taxes by illegal means. Evasion includes failing to report income received from work done (payment for installing the water heater at a neighbor's house, for instance), overstating the amount of deductible expenditures (claiming a larger charitable deduction than was actually made), misusing a sales tax exemption (buying a television for home use without paying sales tax by claiming it was for resale), and so on. Evasion generally means understating the taxable base or overstating provisions that subtract from that base.

There are different views about strategizing to reduce what would otherwise be one's tax liability. However, the U.S. Supreme Court is on the side of the tax minimizers. It has ruled the following:

> The legal right of a taxpayer to decrease the amount of what otherwise would be his [or her] taxes, or altogether avoid them, by means which the law permits, cannot be doubted. [*Gregory* v. *Helvering*, 293 U.S. 465 (1935).]

In other words, the money paid to tax lawyers, accountants, and other advisors to help minimize tax liability through legal means is entirely acceptable. Just don't move toward tax evasion—the courts do not approve of that. Concealing income is almost always seen as tax evasion; different interpretations about preferences are treated less severely.

Not all countries are as accepting of tax avoidance as is the United States. For instance, some of the Russian oligarchs being pursued for tax that led to seizure of their businesses in recent years appear to have been guilty mostly of taking advantage of provisions in the tax law as it existed at the time of their actions to reduce their liabilities. They are being treated as felonious tax evaders, if not enemies of the state, rather than as businesspersons who sought to reduce their liabilities by what they believed to be means that were legal at the time. Such violators in the United States would receive a bill for tax plus interest and maybe a penalty, not a ticket to a prison cell. If the actions were legal at the time they were taken, they wouldn't even have tax to pay.

corollary to adoption transparency is that, in order to maintain the security of contracts, tax laws should not be changed retroactively, in the sense of changing the tax treatment of transactions that already have occurred.[58]

2. **Administration**. Tax payments should be based on objective and explicit criteria that should be apparent to all and should appear to be reasonable to all. Taxpayers should have easy access to tax procedures and those who administer them. The tax should not be subject to negotiation on a taxpayer-by-taxpayer basis, and payments should be based on an impersonal and uniform application of the tax law, not the judgments—particularly negotiable judgments—made by a tax bureaucrat. Regulations should be developed in a predictable process, should be reasonably derived from the tax statutes, should operate without special treatment for particular taxpayers, and should be understandable, at least in broad terms, to all taxpayers. Taxpayers must also know the process for appeal and what standards may be used to appeal their tax obligation, must be confident that the appeal will be judged fairly, and must be certain that the authorities will not seek revenge on anyone filing an appeal.

3. **Compliance requirements**. How the tax is to be calculated should not be a mystery. Each taxpayer should understand how the tax he or she is paying is determined, how changes by the taxpayer would change the tax, and what filing responsibilities are. The meaning and effect of different provisions of the tax should be easy to trace and to understand. Everyone should be given full information about all rules and regulations governing economic transactions so all potential competitors can base their decisions on an accurate assessment of potential costs, returns, and market opportunities.

4. **Amount of tax burden**. Each taxpayer should know how much tax he or she is paying (hidden taxes are not likely to allow sound choices to be made about the scope of government) and should know to what government the payment is being made. If taxpayers do not see the tax and believe that the tax is being paid by somebody else, they may believe that the government service has no cost, which is unlikely to produce good fiscal choices. A combined tax bill for several governments (for instance, a property tax bill with a payment that will be divided among a city, a county, and an independent school district) is convenient for collections, but not so good for ensuring that each government's tax actions are clearly understood by taxpayers. However, gauging this standard is not always easy: Is a sales tax (either a retail sales tax or a value-added tax) with a requirement that customers receive receipts separately stating the tax paid and the tax rate on each transaction more transparent in terms of knowing the amount of tax paid than an individual income tax collected through periodic withholding by the employer with a summary filing at the end of the year? The payments and tax rate are obvious through the year for the former, but the taxpayer has almost no idea of what his or her total payment to the government is, whereas with

---

[58]One exception on retroactivity is that when a bill is in preparation, it may establish a particular date upon which the law will be effective for certain transactions, even though the law has not yet passed on that date. That helps reduce the delay of transactions based on a desire to get more favorable treatment (or the acceleration to avoid harsher treatment) from the changed law.

the latter, the taxpayer may have no running idea, but knows precisely the tax paid at the end of the year. The electorate needs to know the cost of government—but which cost is more relevant? What we do know is that making taxpayers believe that taxes paid by businesses somehow involve no tax payment by individuals is fiscally dishonest.

A tax structure that is not transparent, at least in its broad outlines, is likely to be seen as unknown and probably unfair, can hide significant inequities in the treatment of taxpayers in its confused application, is subject to "rigging" to the advantage of those people in power, and opens the tax authority to the presumption—often accurate—that bribes might be taken and deals may be struck.

Some argue that tax structures can create "fiscal illusions" that conceal from the public the actual budgetary cost of government, allowing politicians to behave irresponsibly and probably causing government expenditure to be higher than a fully informed citizenry would prefer. Evidence of this influence, if any, is far from clear—partly because it is difficult to define what a completely transparent tax structure is and then to calibrate how actual systems differ from that ideal and partly because it is difficult to specify how non-transparency might alter fiscal behavior. However, it is difficult to see how tax structures that make it difficult for the public to understand taxes and to identify the cost of public programs can possibly contribute to the objectives of an open, democratic government.

State and Local Taxes and Economic Development

State and local governments are keenly interested in the impact that their taxes might have on economic development, and particularly on jobs. They are cautious about raising rates, they compare their taxes with those of their neighbors, and they make tax concessions to bring businesses into their markets. Competition for industry among the states, within states, and now with the rest of the world is fierce and can serve as a powerful force for keeping these governments efficient and responsive to the service demands of their citizenry. State and local governments really want to manipulate their fiscal systems to influence business location, employment, and physical investment; market-oriented politicians seem perfectly willing to manipulate market forces, thus violating the market process, if it might mean more for their electorates.[59]

---

[59]In *Cuno* v. *Daimler Chrysler,* 386 F.3d 738 (6th Cir. 2004), the U.S. Court of Appeals for the Sixth Circuit ruled that Ohio's corporate investment tax credit for new manufacturing equipment and machinery (in this case, provided for a Jeep assembly plant in Toledo, Ohio) violated the Commerce Clause of the U.S. Constitution because state taxpayers who invested in Ohio received the credit, but state taxpayers who invested outside Ohio did not. That would hinder free trade between states. That is exactly what the state intended, of course—to bias the decision of the corporation toward expansion in Ohio. Although praised by some as the first step in stopping inefficient tax bidding among the states that distorts the operations of the free market, the U.S. Supreme Court reversed the decision on appeal, ruling that the taxpayers lacked standing to challenge the credits because they could not demonstrate injury from them [547 U.S. 332 (2006)].

But do taxes really have much impact? Non-tax influences on business profitability (access to markets, availability of usable business sites, levels of production cost, availability of a good-quality workforce and other resources, access to natural resources, etc.) vary so much between prospective locations that they could swamp the effect of taxes. And workers like amenities, some that can be provided by state or local governments and some that come with nature, and that can help businesses obtain that quality workforce. The question of what governments can do that has an impact has been argued for decades, and it is far from settled now. The evidence does seem to indicate the following in regard to the influence of general tax climate.

First, tax levels have a small effect on interregional location of economic activity. For any particular state, the extent to which its overall tax level differs from the level of states with which it competes matters to a degree, but almost certainly less than publicized. In addition, specific tax provisions can make certain lines of business unattractive in a state or locality. The effect of total tax burden on total economic activity is certainly smaller than the impact of particular tax provisions on particular industries. For example, if a state includes the value of business inventory in its property tax base, that state is not going to be particularly attractive for a retailer's distribution and order fulfillment centers.

Second, taxes have a much larger effect on economic outcomes within a region. In other words, the effect of tax differences on location choice between Louisville and Cincinnati is much greater than between Louisville and Phoenix. Within a region, tax differences are likely to be determining because many other factors—climate, access to resources and markets, and so on—are generally the same.

Of course, the tax influence is only part of the story of government influence on economic development. Taxing governments use the proceeds to finance public services, with some working to enhance the attractiveness of the jurisdiction to business enterprise. Education, highways and transportation, and public safety services seem to be important, but the evidence is substantially less clear than for tax influences.[60]

State and local governments also use various special provisions or narrow tax incentives—targeted abatements that forgive property taxes on new industrial development for specified periods, enterprise zones in which state or local taxes do not apply, deductions or credits for making certain types of capital investment or for hiring certain categories of employees, and so on—that provide exceptional treatment within a general tax to a limited number of taxpayers as an inducement for development. State lawmakers are particularly fond of giving targeted preferences. For instance, a number of states offer special tax preferences to companies making movies in the state. When a movie is made in the state, lawmakers can point with pride to it, suggesting that, without their heroic giveaway of tax dollars, the scenes occurring among the oil rigs might have been made somewhere else—without regard to the fact that the script called for the specific oil rigs of that state and that the preference given the movie company cost state revenue that would need to be made up by taxes levied on other entities within the state if state services aren't to be reduced

---

[60]Ronald C. Fisher, "The Effects of State and Local Public Services on Economic Development," *New England Economic Review* (Federal Reserve Bank of Boston) (March/April 1997): 53–66.

just a bit. Because of the specificness of such preferences, they are even more attractive to politicians than general improvements to the tax climate that might actually improve the economy.

What does considerable resort to tax preferences for economic development tell us about a tax system? When the business climate of a state becomes so problematic that tax laws need to be changed routinely to attract business, the practice may be a symptom of problems with the tax system itself and a signal that systematic tax reform might be a more useful approach. In effect, tax reform treats existing and new firms equally, and responsible reform also systematically accounts for any tax revenue lost due to reform. Sound tax and fiscal policy probably obviates many of the tax perks that businesses seek.[61] Tax analysts are in general agreement that the best tax policy for economic development is a broad-base, low-tax-rate strategy that makes business tax climates more attractive to all firms and less discriminatory among types of business activities.

Getting elected officials to follow a policy of designing a tax structure that is economically attractive to all, as opposed to being laden with special exceptions to entice some particular footloose business or to relieve taxes paid by a particular industry, is a difficult task, however. The problem is that the geeky guy tinkering in his mother's garage is about as likely to come up with what truly transforms the economic prospects of a region as are the bureaucrat-approved scientists working at firms designated by the state as engines of economic growth. That geek could have gotten going even faster if he hadn't been burdened by paying his share of the taxes forgiven from those footloose firms. Attempts at "good discrimination" in taxation have an excellent chance of being as harmful as unintended ordinary discrimination.

Taxes and Externalities

An important exception to the neutrality standard for tax efficiency occurs when private actions create important negative external effects—that is, when production or consumption by one person or firm causes adverse real consequences for some other person or firm. Market forces induce producers and consumers to react to prices that they pay, and they can be expected to economize on the use of goods and services that must be paid for. The impacts on others, the externalities, are outside the market, so producers and consumers watch out for these external interests only out of the goodness of their hearts—a motive often less compelling or reliable than pressures on the pocketbook.

Governments may respond to this problem in many different ways, including but not limited to regulations, subsidies, tradable pollution rights, or taxes.[62] Taxes

---

[61]Michael Wasylenko, "Taxation and Economic Development: The State of the Economic Literature," *New England Economic Review* (Federal Reserve Bank of Boston) (March/April 1997): 49.

[62]For greater detail, see J. B. Opschoor and H. B. Vos, *Economic Instruments for Environmental Protection* (Paris: Organization for Economic Cooperation and Development, 1989).

applied under this argument do not seek neutrality in the ordinary sense of staying clear of pure market outcomes; rather, they intend to change private actions so that external effects directly and predictably enter the decision calculus. The market is then allowed to respond to consumer demand and to obtain production at least cost, but with both buyer and seller economically aware of (not just morally sensing) the external effects of their actions. Indeed, the tax makes the cost now internal (i.e., the external effects get included in the price) to the decisions of both buyers and sellers. These taxes designed to have environment-friendly effects are sometimes called green taxes. Two types of tax instruments can be applied:[63]

1. *Emission taxes.* These instruments, often called Pigovian taxes after a British economist who proposed them long ago,[64] apply a tax per unit of measured pollution output. They require direct measurement if they are to have their desired incentive effect and ordinarily apply to only one emission type at a time. They apply at the last link in the production-distribution chain to those emitting the substance into the environment. Unlike charges, these taxes bring no expectation that the payer receives anything in return, except that he or she is not treated as a lawbreaker.
2. *Indirect taxes on goods or services.* These taxes apply to goods or services, the production or consumption of which causes environmental or other external damage.[65] Taxes on the use of carbon fuels or ozone-depleting chemicals, for example, discourage processes using them and encourage the quest for alternatives. They do not directly tax the discharge with undesirable external effect, but they seek to discourage the discharge indirectly.

Some countries levy what are called "green taxes," and high motor-fuel taxes are one such device. The United States does not levy a high motor-fuel tax (we levy one of the lowest in the developed world), but it could be sensible as a mechanism to make motorists face the full external impact of their fuel purchases. The higher tax would serve partly as an environmental measure designed to discourage emissions of the greenhouse gases associated with internal combustion engines, partly as a measure to reduce highway congestion caused by heavy use of private automobiles, and partly as a measure to reduce use of a product that helps keep the country involved in Middle Eastern politics. But the United States, in addition to failing to use the tax as a Pigouvian tool, adds to the problem by earmarking much of motor-fuel tax revenue for highway maintenance and operation, thus encouraging even further use of motor vehicles.

Governments also identify particular products or services that seem undesirable and use taxes to discourage their production or consumption. Examples include a Canadian federal tax on automobile air conditioners (an extra inducement to convince automobile purchasers to skip an accessory that reduces fuel economy) and the U.S. gas-guzzler tax (a tax applied to vehicles that do not meet prescribed

---

[63]Governments may also provide subsidies through the tax system, as with special credits offered to businesses that purchase certain pollution-control equipment.

[64]A. C. Pigou, *The Economics of Welfare* (London: Macmillan, 1920).

[65]Organization for Economic Cooperation and Development, *Taxation and the Environment: Complementary Policies* (Paris: OECD, 1993).

fuel-economy ratings). Some other examples of green taxes include higher taxes on leaded than on unleaded motor fuel in a number of countries, taxes on batteries in Sweden, a Belgian tax on disposable razors, taxes on plastic bags in Ireland, and taxes on emissions of carbon dioxide in Denmark, Finland, the Netherlands, Norway, and Sweden.[66] The taxes intend to distort ordinary market choices by making polluters face the true (internal plus external) costs of their actions.

Conclusion

The number of handles available to governments seems almost without end. In general, the many possible handles eventually translate into taxes on incomes, taxes on wealth, and taxes on purchase or sales. Taxes require an involuntary payment; they are not collected for services received on a normal exchange basis. Because of separation of service receipt and payment, it is possible to evaluate taxes on the basis of planning criteria. Those criteria are equity (vertical and horizontal), adequacy, collectability, transparency, and economic effects. Design of tax programs for consistency with these criteria involves three steps. First, identify a tax base that is consistent with the logic of either the ability-to-pay or the benefits-received principle for dividing the cost of government. Second, structure the tax so that it is as broad as possible, including as few preferences and exceptions as possible. Third, levy the lowest possible tax rate to the base. That design will produce a broad-base–low-rate tax system that yields revenue with the least possible collateral damage, the fundamental objective of tax policy.

QUESTIONS AND EXERCISES

1. Patterns and structure of revenue for state and local government are important policy concerns because they establish the distribution of the burden of public-service provision. Revenue revision can begin only with a clear understanding of where revenue policy leaves the state and its localities now and what available options have not been selected. Furthermore, it is useful to understand what conditions are like in surrounding areas. Evidence for such discussions can be drawn from sources like the Department of Commerce's Survey of Current Business (monthly); the Census Bureau's Census of Governments (quinquennially), Governmental Finances (annually), and State Tax Collections (annually) and state tax handbooks published annually by Research Institute of America (RIA) and Commerce Clearing House (CCH). From those and similar sources, prepare answers to these questions about the revenue system in your state:

    a. How does the burden of state, local, and state-local taxation in your state compare with that of the nation and region? (Comparisons are often made as

---

[66]"Taxes for a Cleaner Planet," *The Economist* (June 28, 1997): 84.

percentages of state personal income and per capita income. What is the logical difference between the two measures?) Data on state and local tax collections for each state are available at the website of the U.S. Bureau of Census (www.census.gov); look under the section labeled "Government." How does the local share of state and local taxes compare?

b. Prepare an estimate of the relationship between business and individual tax shares for your state. Where are there allocation problems?

c. How rapidly have state and local taxes grown in your state during the past five years? Is that faster or slower than growth in state personal income and the rate of inflation? Have there been tax increases (decreases) affecting that growth?

d. What are the major revenue sources used by governments in your state? How does relative use of those sources compare with the nation and the region? Does your state have any major taxes not common to other states (severance, business and occupation, local income, etc.)? Are some typical taxes not used?

2. The Congressional Budget Office reports that the highest 1 percent of income-earning households paid 38.7 percent of total federal individual income tax collected in calendar year 2009. What does this information indicate about progressivity or regressivity of the federal income tax? Explain.

3. Not-for-profit organizations lack the authority to levy taxes for support of their programs and must finance their operations from a variety of revenue streams. Some are commercial and operate largely from the sale of goods or services (including revenue from service contracts with governments), others are charitable and operate with various sorts of donated support, and others combine revenue from a variety of sources. Select a not-for-profit organization in your area and analyze its revenue resources. The entity should be chosen because you are interested in the service provided by that entity and because the entity will cooperate with your review and assessment.

a. Analyze the revenues received by the entity (taxes, charges, donations, etc.—provide disaggregated data), examine trends and shifts, determine whether sources are sensitive to general economic conditions, explore limits and controls that the entity may face, and review the processes by which revenue decisions are made. You should pay particular attention to the division of revenues from use of endowment, charges for services, and annual donations. To what extent does the entity employ the principle that those using services must pay (an analog to the benefits-received principle in taxation)? In light of the purpose of the entity, to what extent is payment for service appropriate?

b. Examine how the entity manages fund development, that is, money raising. Is it self-administered, or does another entity administer the system, possibly by contract? Are protective controls properly in place? What are the costs associated with this activity?

c. On the basis of your investigation, what do you conclude about revenues available to the entity? Do you have recommendations for reform and restructuring? Be specific. Link your conclusions to the information developed in your analysis.

CASE FOR DISCUSSION

CASE 8–1

Birth, Marriage, Death, and Taxes

Scarlett O'Hara, in *Gone with the Wind*, laid it out for us: "Death, taxes and childbirth! There's never any convenient time for any of them."[67] But timing matters in all things, and it turns out that those events, plus marriage, are related. That's what the empirical evidence shows.

Consider These Questions

1. Do these impacts create social or economic losses for the country?

2. How might these influences conflict with the normal criteria for good tax policy?

3. How could revisions of tax structure reduce these influences on birth, marriage, and death?

A core economic principle is that incentives influence human behavior, and our tax system creates many incentives, some purposeful and some accidental. The incentive results when a change of behavior produces a reduction of tax liability that exceeds any cost associated with that change. (In other words, we expect behavior to change because of gain, not simply because of spiteful behavior against the tax.) We are not surprised to find that tax structures influence where and how people shop, how households and businesses invest, the way businesses structure their operations and organizational framework, and so on.

But what about impacts beyond the scope of economics and finance? Economists believe that incentives shape all behavior, so it is not surprising that they have sought and found a tax influence on some basics of humanity—namely, timing of birth, marriage, and death. Before the non-economists explode in outrage, please understand that the tax impact is on *timing* of events, not the events themselves. The general principle is that wherever there are tax consequences from an action, it is reasonable to anticipate a response to the incentives provided.

The tax impact on births is a product of "all or nothing" provisions in the U.S. Tax Code: if a child is part of a family for one minute of the year, full tax advantages are provided for the year, and these advantages are lost for the old year if the child is born one minute into the next year. There are three tax advantages to families with children: the child tax credit (provided from 1998, the credit directly reduces tax liability for each child in the family), an earned income tax credit (a cash subsidy for working families) that is more generous to families with two or more children, and the personal exemption that reduces the base upon which tax is levied for each member of the family. Whether a child is born in late December or early January can have a significant consequence for total family tax liability over the two years.

---

[67]Margaret Mitchell, *Gone with the Wind* (New York: Macmillan, 1936), vol. 2, pt. 4, chap. 38.

Evidence does indicate a tax-influenced pattern of births. In four of the seven years from 1997 through 2003, the day with more births than any other has fallen between Christmas and New Year's. (The other three were in September, the month of most frequent birth for decades and decades, presumably the result of people spending more time inside the house during the cold and dreary days of winter.)[68] Economists Chaudra and Dickert-Conlin, using a sample of children from the National Longitudinal Study of Youth, find the probability of birth in the last week of December rather than the first week of January is positively correlated with tax benefits from earlier birth (families with more to gain are more likely to have earlier births). They estimate that a higher tax benefit of $500 raises the probability of birth in the last week of December by 26.9 percent.[69] The technologies of caesarian birth and induced labor do seem to be used for tax advantage.

Marriage patterns also appear to be influenced by tax incentives. Although recent years have reduced the likelihood that a married couple would pay higher tax than a similarly situated unmarried couple, for many years the impact could be significant. Sjoquist and Walker found from Census data a significant negative impact on marriages in the early 1990s: fewer couples marry in the last two months of the year relative to marriages in the early months of the year.[70] Alm and Whittington, using data from the Panel Study of Income Dynamics, find a significant impact on marriage probabilities from the last quarter of one year to the first quarter of the next.[71] Interestingly enough, although the incentive ought to work in the opposite direction as well, no impact on divorce rates has been discovered. Maybe noneconomic factors matter more for ending a marriage than for starting one. Or maybe the judicial processes necessary for divorce are more difficult to time.

The impact of deaths may appear when estate tax rates change. Kopczuk and Slemrod examine the timing of deaths around the time of changes in the U.S. estate tax system—increases or decreases—when living a little longer or dying a little sooner would significantly change tax liability. Their analysis of the timing of deaths involving taxable estates around 13 major tax changes from 1917 to 1984 shows a clear impact. In particular, for deaths within two weeks of an estate tax change, $10,000 of tax saving (adjusted to 2000 price levels) increase the probability of dying in the lower tax period by 1.6 percent.[72] And the influence is not limited to the United States. Gans and Leigh analyzed the effect when Australia abolished its estate tax on July 1, 1979. In this case, they found that one-half of those estates that ordinarily would have been taxed in the last week of the tax managed to avoid it.[73]

[68]David Leonhardt, "To-Do List: Wrap Gifts, Have Baby," *New York Times*, December 20, 2006.

[69]Stacy Dickert-Conlin and Amitabh Chandra, "Taxes and the Timing of Births," *Journal of Political Economy* 107 (1999): 161–77.

[70]David Sjoquist and Mary Beth Walker, "The Marriage Tax and the Rate and Timing of Marriage," *National Tax Journal* 48 (1995): 547–58.

[71]James Alm and Leslie Whittington, "Does the Income Tax Affect Marital Decisions?" *National Tax Journal* 48 (1995): 565–72.

[72]Wojciech Kopczuk and Joel Slemrod, "Dying to Save Taxes: Evidence from Estate Tax Returns on the Death Elasticity," *Review of Economics and Statistics* 85 (May 2003): 256–65.

[73]Joshua Gans and Andrew Leigh, "Toying with Death and Taxes: Some Lessons from Down Under," *Economists' Voice* 3 (June 2006): 1–3.

Further, they estimated that one in twenty likely deaths in the last week of June was delayed by enough time to escape the tax. Whether these timing changes involve choices about pulling the plug on granny's respirator, some fudging of death date reporting, or some combination of the two is unknown. This question bears some attention because, unless Congress revises the law, the federal estate tax will briefly disappear and then return with much higher rates in the next few years—and incentives will be huge.

CHAPTER 9

Major Tax Structures: Income Taxes

In this chapter and the following two chapters, we examine the general nature of the three predominant tax bases: income, consumption, and property. Taxes on income and consumption typically apply to current transaction values; property taxes apply to the value of holdings (a stock value), not transactions (a flow value). In many respects, that difference makes property taxes more difficult to administer, although growth of the underground economy—economic activity "off the books," or outside traditional accounting records—has complicated operation of the other two taxes in recent years. It is useful to start with taxes on income. Americans apparently prefer this tax base to other options—we rely considerably more on income taxes than do other developed democracies.

There is one important point to emphasize at the outset. All taxes labeled *income* do not operate in the same fashion, and statements about the yield response, collectability, equity, or economic effects of a particular tax must carefully define what the structure of the tax being examined actually is. (Indeed, an analyst must go behind the label to understand the structure of any tax as a first step in examination of the likely performance of that tax.) Income might generally be defined as the money or other gain received over a period of time by an individual, corporation, or other entity for labor or services rendered or from property, natural resources, investments, operations, and so on. But governments differ in what particular receipts are selected for taxation, how those receipts are manipulated to become the tax base, and what structure of rates applies to that base. Because of those tax-policy options, general statements about burden distribution can be hazardous. For example, the federal individual income tax has a generally progressive burden distribution because statutory rates increase as income is higher and because the tax applies to a broad measure of income that includes some kinds of income that are particularly significant for affluent households; many local income taxes have a generally proportional or slightly regressive burden pattern because they often levy flat rates on a base limited to wages and salaries alone. Not all income taxes have progressive burden distributions; it depends on the structure of the particular tax.

Governments apply taxes to the income of individuals and/or corporations.[1] Unincorporated business (partnership, proprietorship) income is ordinarily taxed through the individual income tax. Wage and salary income (payrolls) and income of the self-employed are taxed both by the regular individual income tax and by separate taxes to finance the social insurance system (Social Security, unemployment compensation, etc.). Individual income tax yield is much greater than that of corporate income taxes, so greater attention is focused on the former. Many of the structural elements of individual taxation apply to the corporate form as well; many other corporate tax questions are too arcane for coverage here. One important issue to which there may be no answer will be considered: How should corporate income taxes be related to the income tax of individual corporate stockholders? Do corporations have tax-bearing ability that is separate from that of the owners of the corporation?

Some Background

Before the Civil War, the federal government relied on excises (sales taxes on tobacco products, distilled spirits, refined sugar, carriages, etc.) and tariffs on imported goods to finance its limited activities. War, however, was too expensive to finance with that revenue alone. The northern states enacted an income tax in 1861 (3 percent on all incomes of more than $800 per year) to help finance their war expenditure, but the law was so unclearly structured that it was not put into effect. An income tax passed in 1862 and was enforced. This tax applied an initial rate of 3 percent and a top rate of 5 percent on incomes of more than $10,000. It expired in 1872, having raised about $376 million (about 20 percent of internal revenues produced during the period).[2] Abraham Lincoln, address the "White House," shows up on the tax list as paying $1,296 on an income of $25,000 for 1864. We know because tax returns were public in that era, and that publicity was the primary device for ensuring that people actually paid the tax they owed.

There remained an important legal question. As Chapter 8 noted, the U.S. Constitution requires federal direct taxes to be apportioned among the states, but it was not clear whether an individual income tax was legally direct or indirect.[3] If the tax was direct, it would have to be divided among the states according to population, and each state's share then raised from its population according to income. A state with lower per capita income would have to apply higher income tax rates

---

[1] A corporation is an entity created by a government (state or federal) and empowered with legal rights, privileges, and liabilities of an individual, separate and distinct from those held by the individuals who own the entity. Owners have liability limited to their investment in the corporation. A growing number of states now allow limited-liability companies, a business form taxed like a partnership (business income is fully distributed to the owners for taxation and is not taxed separately at the business level) and easier to establish than a corporation, but with the liability limits of a corporation.

[2] Harold M. Groves, *Financing Government* (New York: Holt, 1939), 153–55.

[3] Corporate income taxes were never regarded as direct taxes on individuals and thus were never subject to apportionment. The federal corporate tax began some years before the federal individual income tax that is in place now.

than would a state with higher per capita income. The U.S. Supreme Court held in *Springer* v. *United States* (102 U.S. 586 [1880]) that the income tax was, for purposes of the Constitution, indirect and hence valid. By the time of the ruling, the tax was no longer in force, so the ruling had minimal immediate importance.

In 1894, the federal government again enacted an individual income tax, this time in a package with reduced tariffs. The low-rate tax (2 percent of income above $4,000) affected only a small portion of the population, but it was challenged on constitutional grounds. This time the U.S. Supreme Court, in *Pollock* v. *Farmer's Loan and Trust* (157 U.S. 429 [1895] and 158 U.S. 601 [1895]), ruled that the income tax was direct and hence subject to apportionment. Therefore, the tax as levied was unconstitutional and could not be collected. The decision left the federal government with no broad-based revenue source to finance the increased international role the nation was taking in the early part of the twentieth century.[4]

Can you imagine Americans amending the Constitution to explicitly permit an individual income tax now? How did it happen back in the early part of the twentieth century? In 1909, President William Howard Taft agreed to accept an "excise" on corporate net income (which did not require an amendment to enact because the tax was viewed as indirect) if Congress would propose an amendment for a national individual income tax. (A tax business/tax individuals deal!) Both the amendment and the excise quickly passed. Getting approval of the necessary number of states for the amendment to be approved took longer, but when Wyoming became the thirty-sixth state to ratify the Sixteenth Amendment (1913), the revenue problem was resolved: "The Congress shall have power to lay and collect taxes on incomes, from whatever source derived, without apportionment among the several States, and without regard to any census or enumeration." That provided the financial base for defense and, eventually, an expanded federal role in domestic affairs. The 1913 income tax applied a normal rate of 1 percent on incomes in excess of $3,000 ($4,000 for married persons) with a top surtax rate of 6 percent (a combined rate of 7 percent) on incomes above $500,000. Moreover, the tax was not paid by the multitudes. Only about 1 percent of the population had income sufficient to be liable for the tax.[5] There were 357,598 returns filed (so few that the Bureau of Internal Revenue audited them all), with an average tax of $78. Only with the advent of the Second World War did the tax become a tax paid by most of the citizenry as the level of income at which the tax started to apply fell to levels earned by ordinary households.[6] In 1939, 7.6 million returns were filed to yield $1,028.8 million in that fiscal year; by 1945, the number of returns had increased to 49.9 million to yield

---

[4]How desperate was the federal government for revenue at the turn of the twentieth century? So desperate that it even applied a tax to chewing gum.

[5]Richard Good, *The Individual Income Tax*, rev. ed. (Washington, D.C.: Brookings Institution, 1976), 3. There was a problem in the initial law. It applied the tax to "lawful income." Congress soon amended the law to remove the word "lawful," thus clearing up definitional problems and opening up additional enforcement powers. It should be pointed out that gangster Al Capone was sent to prison for tax evasion, not other crimes. The change in the tax law undoubtedly helped stop his villainy. Never forget that it was the Bureau of Internal Revenue, not the Federal Bureau of Investigation, that finally stopped him.

[6]In the early days of World War II, there was serious discussion about financing the war effort with a general sales tax rather than through increased use of the individual income tax. The income tax won out, significantly because that was the preference of President Roosevelt.

$19,034.3 million.[7] Withholding of individual income tax from wages began in 1943, thus dramatically simplifying the collection process and permitting application of the tax to the general population. Until 1944, collections from the corporate income tax had exceeded those from the individual income tax in all years but 1934 and 1937; from 1944 onward, individual income tax collections have always exceeded those from the corporate income tax, now by a great margin.

The third, and newest, portion of the federal income tax structure consists of the payroll taxes for support of the social insurance system. These narrow-base taxes on wage and salary income and certain income from self-employment may legally be imposed on the employer, imposed on the employee, or shared between the employer and employee; most analysts suspect that the economic incidence is on the employee regardless of who is responsible for sending payment to the government. The shifting logic is simple: the employer knows that paying a certain wage to the employee will require an accompanying payroll tax payment to the government. Why wouldn't the employer take account of that payment when deciding how much to offer employees and how many employees to hire? These taxes now support the Social Security system (old age, disability, and survivors income support), Medicare (health insurance for the elderly), and unemployment compensation. The Social Security and unemployment compensation taxes began with the Social Security Act of 1935; the Medicare tax began with amendments to that act in 1965. For many lower-income individuals and families, their social insurance payroll tax liability amounts to more than the amount of individual income tax owed.

The individual and corporate income taxes and the payroll taxes on wages and salaries are the dominant government revenue source in the United States. Table 9–1 reports the pattern for all governments from 1930 to 2010. In 2010, individual income taxes yielded $1,163.3 billion, corporate income taxes yielded $387.4 billion, and receipts for the social insurance system (largely payroll taxes for Social Security, Medicare, and unemployment compensation) produced $992.7 billion, 64.2 percent of the $3,962.8 billion in current receipts to all governments.[8] Revenue from individual and corporate income taxes increased dramatically as a share of gross domestic product (GDP) with the need to finance World War II, but fell modestly when the war ended. The share was from 11.5 to 13.5 percent of GDP until 2000, when it jumped to 14.7 percent. It has now fallen to a post-WWII low of 10.7 percent, although all post-WWII shares are well above pre-WWII levels. The percentage increased a bit in the 1990s, the product of somewhat higher rates and great prosperity of high-income individuals. When social insurance taxes are added in, the share of all government revenue is more than 64 percent and 17.5 percent of GDP. This latter percentage had been generally increasing for 50 years, but has fallen since 2000.

---

[7]U.S. Bureau of the Census, *Historical Statistics of the United States, Colonial Times to 1970: Part 2*, Bicentennial Ed. (Washington, D.C.: U.S. Government Printing Office, 1975), 1107, 1110.
[8]Bureau of Economic Analysis, National Income and Product Accounts [www.bea.gov].

Table 9–1
Individual and Corporate Income Taxes and Social Insurance Contributions in American Government Finance, Selected Calendar Years, 1930–2010

	1930	1935	1940	1945	1950	1955	1960	1965	1970	1975	1980	1985	1990	1995	2000	2005	2010
Individual and Corporate Income Taxes as % of:																	
All government current receipts	19.0%	16.2%	24.1%	57.6%	54.6%	55.6%	49.9%	47.9%	46.8%	43.9%	47.3%	41.5%	42.1%	42.4%	46.9%	43.2%	39.1%
Gross domestic product	2.1%	2.3%	3.9%	13.3%	12.3%	13.0%	12.7%	12.0%	12.9%	11.9%	13.5%	12.0%	12.4%	12.7%	14.7%	12.5%	10.7%
Income Taxes Plus Social Insurance Contributions as % of:																	
All government current receipts	20.0%	17.1%	35.5%	67.9%	62.9%	65.0%	62.1%	61.0%	63.0%	64.2%	68.2%	64.8%	66.2%	66.5%	69.5%	67.1%	64.2%
Gross domestic product	2.2%	2.5%	5.8%	15.7%	14.2%	15.2%	15.9%	15.3%	17.4%	17.3%	19.5%	18.7%	19.5%	19.9%	21.9%	19.5%	17.5%

SOURCE: Bureau of Economic Analysis, *National Income and Product Accounts* "[www.bea.gov]." .

393

The Argument about Taxing Income

For the System of Taxing Income

Many regard an income tax as a fair and reasonable source of revenue because of the nature of the base and the method of its administration—and it certainly is productive and heavily used in the United States. Why do many believe that the income tax is a satisfactory source?[9]

EQUITY—MEASURING ABILITY

Income is an important measure of a taxpayer's capacity to bear the cost of government. Economic well-being is significantly determined by current income. An exception is the person with substantial wealth and minimal current income, so a better measure could include current income and net wealth converted into an income equivalent, but such logic does not appear in income tax codes. Current income remains for most people the most reliable single indicator of relative affluence.

EQUITY—ADJUSTABILITY

The American income tax, which requires annual taxpayer returns, can be made to account for individual taxpayer conditions (family size, infirmities, special economic circumstances, etc.).[10] This offers a unique advantage over taxes not based on that filing. For instance, a package of cigarettes is taxed regardless of the economic status of the purchaser because it would be too costly to do a check of taxpayer circumstances with each transaction. Adjustments when a tax return is filed can allow for circumstances like household income, family size, economic misfortunes during the year, and so on that restrict tax-bearing capacity and might merit adjustment of tax owed. Table 9–2 shows the pattern of the federal taxes on income as they are distributed across quintiles of household income, taking full account of likely shifting of taxes paid by a business to individuals. The pattern is of considerable progressivity of individual and corporate income taxes, even through to the highest-income taxpayers—as household income is higher, the effective tax rate paid is higher as well. Broad-based income taxes can be made progressive, and lawmakers do tend to follow through

---

[9]For many years, the U.S. Advisory Commission on Intergovernmental Relations conducted a nationwide survey to discover what tax Americans viewed as the least fair. The federal income tax or the local property tax was always seen as the least fair. In the last poll (1994), 27 percent viewed the federal income tax as the worst, compared with 28 percent for the local property tax. As in previous surveys, respondents viewed the state income tax as the least unfair (7 percent). This is an interesting finding, given that the state income taxes are virtually all linked copies of the federal income tax, although at lower rates. U.S. Advisory Commission on Intergovernmental Relations, *Changing Public Attitudes on Governments and Taxes 1994* (Washington, D.C.: U.S. Advisory Commission on Intergovernmental Relations, 1995). The Tax Foundation has done similar surveys in recent years, and the federal income tax and the local property taxes continue their status as regarded as least fair [Scott A. Hodge and Andrew Chamberlain,"2006 Annual Survey of U.S. Attitudes on Tax and Wealth," Tax Foundation Special Report 141 (April 5, 2006).]
[10]Not all national income taxes have an annual return, but rather rely on exact withholding of tax by the employer and others paying the individual.

Table 9–2
Distribution of Federal Income Tax Payments and Effective Tax Rates by Income Quintile for All Families, 2009 (Percentages)

Quintile	Individual Income Tax		Corporate Income Tax		Social Insurance Tax	
	Tax Share	Effective Tax Rate	Tax Share	Effective Tax Rate	Tax Share	Effective Tax Rate
Lowest	−6.6	−9.3	1.8	0.5	5.3	8.3
Second	−3.5	−2.6	3.2	0.5	9.7	7.9
Middle	2.7	1.3	5.8	0.6	15.4	8.4
Fourth	13.4	4.6	10.2	0.7	24.0	9.1
Highest	94.1	13.4	77.2	2.3	45.3	7.2
All	100.0	7.2	100.0	1.5	100.0	8.0
Top 1%	38.7	21.0	47.1	5.2	4.2	2.5

SOURCE: Congressional Budget Office, *The Distribution of Household Income and Federal Taxes, 2008 and 2009* (Washington, D.C.: Congressional Budget Office, 2012)

NOTE: Income equals comprehensive household income, which includes all cash income (taxable and exempt), taxes paid by businesses, employee contribution to 401(k) retirement plans, and value of income paid in kind.

on the opportunity. However, the social insurance taxes—Social Security, Medicare, and unemployment compensation—based on payrolls and with flat or even declining rates, no adjustment for economic circumstances, and no coverage of income from capital ownership (particularly dividends, interest, and rent) show a regressive pattern of effective rates at higher income levels. So adjustability to taxpayer conditions can produce a progressive tax pattern and can be difficult for other tax formats.

Income tax burden is concentrated. Table 9–2 shows that almost 40 percent of total individual income tax paid was paid by only 1 percent of the population, the highest-income earners in the nation. This reflects an extreme concentration of income in the United States, a concentration that has increased significantly in the past few years. High-income households have done very well, both absolutely and relative to how middle- and lower-income households have done, and their individual income tax burdens are high as a reflection of that success. In any case, these share patterns indicate that the tax is moving somewhat to its origins as a class tax, not a tax paid by the masses that it became with the shared sacrifice to fight World War II.

YIELD

A broad income base permits significant revenue at socially acceptable rates, and the growth of that base keeps pace with general economic activity. Governments with income taxes need not seek rate increases as often, or apply such high nominal rates, to keep up with growing public demand for services as may governments with narrower bases or bases with lower elasticity to economic growth. The base of both individual and corporate income taxes is, however, subject to considerable cyclical variation. During the Great Recession, collections from both dropped considerably, creating special difficulty for state government finances because those governments must annually balance their budgets.

BASE BREADTH

The resource distortion with the general income tax may be less than with narrower bases.[11] The distortion question, however, is far from clear in the comparison across taxes. Many provisions of existing income taxes do certainly influence the economic behavior of individuals in investment, housing, compensation packages, and so on. It is politically popular to place extremely heavy tax burdens on the affluent, and the data just shown demonstrate that this is exactly what we do in the United States. But there are limits to this because these affluent individuals are exactly the ones most able to take evasive action that distorts the overall production in the economy. To the extent that breadth permits a low rate, there are clearly efficiency and equity advantages.

Against the System of Taxing Income

Many others argue that the income tax system has horrible flaws and that it should be fundamentally changed. Indeed, it is often argued that consumption is a far better base for distributing the cost of government than is income. What are the elements of that anti-income-tax argument?

TRANSPARENCY AND COMPLIANCE

The individual income tax is so complicated that it violates the transparency standard. Taxpayers do not understand the system, its provisions are so arcane as to be beyond the comprehension of all but very few experts, the electorate sees little association between tax paid and the work of government, and some privileged individuals use loopholes (or tax preferences) designed in the backrooms of congressional committees to avoid paying their fair share of the tax. Billions of taxpayer hours are spent on complying with the tax, but, in spite of all the attention, only a tiny fraction understands how the system works, and the withholding process conceals how much individual taxpayers actually pay. In 2005, the individual income tax law contained more than a dozen distinct retirement planning schemes with a confusing array of rules and regulations, at least nine separate preference programs for encouraging education spending, an earned income tax credit (EITC) program for low-income workers so complicated that 72 percent of those claiming the credit paid a tax preparer to complete their returns, and a second tax structure (the Alternative Minimum Income Tax) that penalizes taxpayers for qualifying for certain legal tax preferences.[12] Changes since then have not reduced the complexity. The majority of people have a paid preparer do their taxes (57.3 percent of returns for tax year 2009), so the citizenry really doesn't know much about what goes on in determining their liability.

---

[11]Income taxes may distort work and investment decisions made by individuals and businesses. Thus, the resources-distortion basis for general income taxation is unclear at best. Economists seek an "optimal tax," that is, one minimizing total distortions. See Joel Slemrod, "Optimal Taxation and Optimal Tax Systems," *Journal of Economic Perspectives* 4 (Winter 1990): 157–78.

[12]Testimony of Nina E. Olsen, National Taxpayer Advocate, to the President's Advisory Panel on Federal Tax Reform, March 3, 2005.

For more complicated returns (the regular 1040 return), 92.1 percent of returns were done by a preparer.[13] That is a strong indictment of the perceived complexity of the tax. In terms of seeing the burden, people are more aware of their tax refund at the end of the year than how much their tax liability is. Simplification would make the tax more transparent and would reduce its collection costs. Complexity was one of the most important problems with the existing federal income taxes reported to President George W. Bush's Advisory Panel on Federal Tax Reform in 2005, and no discussion of federal income tax issues is complete without consideration of the complexity problem. Little action emerges, certainly none since the 2005 report, probably because it is often the complications that deliver tax preferences for certain categories of taxpayer, and few want to sacrifice their own tax advantages.

ADMINISTRATION AND COMPLIANCE

The income tax system is expensive to collect. The annual operating cost of the Internal Revenue Service (IRS) exceeds $12 billion, the IRS has more than ninety-five thousand employees, and it deals with more than 140 million individual income tax returns and over 6.5 million corporate income tax returns. The cost that state and local governments incur in collection of their income taxes adds even more to the total. A number of critics maintain that, even with this expenditure, the IRS is poorly administered, is not particularly helpful when taxpayers request assistance, and abuses its powers to inspect individual and business records.

Even though the totals are high, the administrative cost per dollar collected is small—currently reported as less than 50 cents per $100 collected. But this cost is only the tip of the iceberg. The cost to taxpayers of complying with the tax law is at least ten times the cost of administration.[14] The revenues of H & R Block alone exceed $3 billion per year, and all that amounts to taxpayer cost of complying with the tax. Add to that number the revenues of all the other tax preparers, tax accountants, and tax lawyers, and you will understand the concept of high compliance cost. And that is only the dollar cost, with no accounting of the mental pain individuals endure as they struggle to complete their tax returns as the filing deadline approaches each year. Of course, things aren't getting easier. The IRS is required by the Paperwork Reduction Act to estimate the time required to complete each component of the tax return and report those times in its taxpayer instructions. In 1988, completion of a standard return with itemized deductions and reported interest and dividends was estimated to require 15.1 hours for a taxpayer; in 2011, the same forms were estimated to require 22 hours. That is not a victory for simplicity. More complicated returns with more required forms add even more to the time requirement. Even the simplest returns (the 1040EZ) are now estimated to require 7 hours to complete, and far too many people are so flummoxed by the process that even 5.5 percent of these were done by a paid preparer in 2009.

---

[13]Data from Tax Statistics from the Statistics of Income Division of the Internal Revenue Service [www.irs.gov/taxstats].
[14]Marsha Blumenthal and Joel Slemrod, "The Compliance Cost of the U.S. Individual Income Tax System: A Second Look after Tax Reform," *National Tax Journal* 45 (June 1992): 185–202.

ECONOMIC EFFECTS

Critics argue that the income tax has adverse effects on the long-term prosperity of the American economy by discouraging saving and investment and by discouraging earning of income in general. The argument is that income taxation distorts the choices that people make between how much income they consume in a year and how much they save for future spending because the tax applies to interest earned on the savings. By capturing part of the return from "waiting" to consume in the future, the tax distorts the choice between present consumption and future consumption, with the distortion toward present consumption. Accordingly, saving (delayed consumption) is reduced. This matters for economic growth because saving ultimately provides the basis for increased capital stock, which provides a foundation for economic growth. The effect can be even worse under our multiple income tax structure because returns to investment may be taxed once under the corporate income tax and then again under the individual income tax when the shareholder receives those corporate earnings as dividends. A special lower rate for dividend income reduces the discrimination somewhat, but some extra burden remains. Evidence also shows an impact on taxable income from increased marginal tax rates—in essence, higher rates discourage households from earning income. The response is rather small, but higher for higher-income households than for lower-income households.[15] And there is no evidence that increasing tax rates, even for the most affluent, would reduce revenue production at anything close to current rates.

ECONOMIC DISTORTION

Provisions in the tax structure provide varying reliefs and punishments to different sectors of the economy as lawmakers seek to overcome the signals for resource allocation coming from market transactions. Some industries, businesses, and individuals end up facing higher effective tax rates on their capital investment and on their productive labors than do others. That causes economic resources to move because of tax advantages rather than moving according to market forces that reflect consumer demand, resource prices, and production technology. This brings considerable economic loss to the nation and decay in the competitive position of American businesses in the world economy. One element of the economic loss from tax distortions is the effort that taxpayers exert to convert income that would be taxed at a higher tax rate (for instance, income from wages and salaries) into income that would be taxed at a lower rate (for instance, income from gain in value of a capital asset or capital gains).

EQUITY

Many people believe that the income tax distributes the cost of government unfairly. The distribution is, overall, progressive, as the earlier table demonstrated. A good number believe that rates should be about the same for everyone, and many others

---

[15]Emanuel Saez, Joel Slemrod, and Seth Giertz, "The Elasticity of Taxable Income with Respect to Marginal Tax Rates: A Critical Review," *Journal of Economic Literature* 50 (2012): 3–50.

believe that the tax should be more progressive than it is now. But very few believe that people in similar economic circumstances should pay dramatically different effective tax rates simply because of the way they arrange their economic affairs, whether from fortunate accident, clever assistance from tax advisors, or access to special tax preferences or "loopholes" not available to everyone. That appears to be a blatant violation of horizontal equity, and the cost of government avoided by some has to be borne by the rest. Provisions of the federal income tax are such that not all income is treated equally for tax purposes, that certain sorts of economic activity are given favorable tax treatment, and that there can be significant differences in effective tax rates paid by households with similar income. A concern with this horizontal inequity was an important driving force for the 1986 federal tax reform, the last major revision of the federal tax system, but inequities have slipped back into the system.

OVERUSE

The distortions and inequities of any tax become more significant as the tax is heavily used. Problems that are minor irritants when tax rates and burdens are low can become severe when the tax is high. Businesses and individuals find it worthwhile to invest more effort to avoid paying the tax by restructuring their affairs and by hiding operations that would subject them to a tax; at lower rates, such efforts are not worth the expense. Differences in tax between individuals and businesses have little significance when the tax is low, but discrimination becomes a major issue when the tax is high. The economic value of distortions from a tax rises more rapidly than the tax rate and more rapidly than revenue from the tax. Even if the income taxes were otherwise sound in design, their extremely heavy use in the U.S. revenue system could be a reason for seeking tax alternatives. Greater balance among tax sources might relieve pressure created by the dominance of the income tax, especially in the federal tax system.

Individual Income Taxation

The following sections examine the logic of the federal individual income tax and some issues in its design. Because most states link their income tax to the federal tax, understanding the federal structure, its concepts, and its terminology is important for all levels of finance. For instance, some states use federal adjusted gross income (AGI) or taxable income as the initial computation point for their income tax. Only a few local governments tie their income taxes to the federal system, typically indirectly by linking to their state tax; most use independent and much narrower income measures, often payroll. These local structures are usually extremely simple. Figure 9–1 provides a schematic overview of the federal structure (as later sections describe) and captures the structural heart of the federal revenue system. The figure indicates the points at which adjustments, exemptions, deductions, credits, and so on enter into the calculations that implement the structure.

Figure 9–1

Elements of the Federal Individual Income Tax Structure: How the Flow of Calculations Produces the Tax Paid

Total Income*
Minus
Adjustments
Equals
Adjusted Gross Income
Minus
Standard Deduction or Itemized Deduction (Taxpayer's Choice)
And
Personal Exemptions
Equals
Taxable Income
To which apply
Rate Schedule or Tax Table
To calculate
Tax
Minus
Credits
Equals
Total Tax
Minus
Withholding, Estimated Payments, and Other Payments
Equals
Tax Refund or Tax Due**

State income taxes typically use Adjusted Gross Income, Taxable Income, or Tax as the starting point for calculation of state liability, making elements of the federal tax also part of the state tax. The states may also add some unique features, usually deductions or credits, to their taxes. Many local income taxes are narrower than the federal tax, often limiting coverage to payrolls, and lack some complexities of the federal system.

* The Internal Revenue Code does not include as income some flows that would appear to be income under comprehensive definitions of household income. These inclusions may not even be reported on the tax return, although some— like interest received on tax exempt municipal bonds—are reported.

** Some taxpayers will also be required to calculate their tax according to the Alternative Minimum Income Tax scheme and then to pay the higher of the Alternative or regular tax calculation.

Defining Income

Tax statutes do not define income, but list transactions that produce income for tax purposes. Items on the list include wages, salaries, interest, stock dividends, rents, royalties, and so on. There is no general definition for use in cases of doubt. (Instructors usually receive a copy of this book at no charge: Would its value be income for them? Would it depend on whether they sell the book when the semester ends?) Tax lawyers earn healthy incomes in part because of their efforts to structure transactions that give their clients more money to spend, but legally do not cause income as far as the tax laws are concerned. Many analysts favor the Haig-Simons income definition as a standard. The version proposed by Henry Simons defines personal income for tax purposes as "the algebraic sum of (1) the market value of rights exercised in consumption and (2) the change in the value of the store of property rights between the beginning and the end of the period in question."[16] In other words, Haig-Simons income equals the value of consumption plus any increase in net wealth during the year. That is the maximum amount of consumption that would be possible during the year without any reduction of the household's net wealth.

This definition can yield results that differ from application of existing tax law, as three examples illustrate. Suppose Mr. Smith owns shares of a corporate stock that increase in value by $10,000 during the year, but he does not sell the stock during the year. The Haig-Simons concept views that as income: this increase in Smith's net wealth adds to his total potential command over the economy's resources. The existing tax system would not tax that gain; the system taxes such gains only as they are realized—that is, when the higher-value stock is actually sold, not when the return accrues.[17] Second, suppose Ms. Jones lives in a home that she owns. She thus consumes the services provided by that structure. These services (implicit rent) are a part of Jones's consumption and would be part of Haig-Simons income. The current system taxes no such imputed incomes, thus providing a significant incentive for purchase of assets that produce noncash returns to the owner. Third, suppose Mr. White's great aunt gives him $50,000. That clearly increases his net wealth (or permits increased consumption), so it would be part of Haig-Simons income. Because the transaction occurred without any work by White, however, the current system does not regard that payment as part of income. It could be taxable under the gift tax, but White's aunt's economic circumstance, not his, would determine that tax liability. That means the tax on the gift to White (who has an annual income of $5,000) is the same as the tax on the aunt's similar gift to his brother (who has an annual income of $60,000). Same aunt, same gift, same tax—regardless of the recipient's economic status. Defining the tax at the recipient level seems to make more sense than driving it from the owner. Our estate tax system works in this same way, driven by the estate and not the inheritor.

Policy analysts, both inside and outside government, typically use broad affluence measures for distributional analysis and for thinking about how the tax base might be revised. Sidebar 9–1 describes the more comprehensive measures used in analysis done by the Congressional Budget Office, the Treasury Office of Tax Analysis, and the Joint Committee on Taxation to gauge the distribution of the tax burden and in considering changes in the tax structure. All are conceived in the spirit of the Haig-Simons concept, and all escape the legislative definitions of the current tax base.

---

[16]Henry C. Simons, *Personal Income Taxation: The Definition of Income as a Problem of Fiscal Policy* (Chicago: University of Chicago Press, 1938), 50. A similar concept appears in Robert M. Haig, "The Concept of Income–Economic and Legal Aspects," in *The Federal Income Tax*, ed. R. Haig (New York: Columbia University Press, 1921), 7.

[17]Not all national tax systems regard all capital gains as income, and not all American policy analysts agree that the U.S. approach makes sense in terms of equity or economic efficiency. See Bruce Bartlett, "Slaying a Pair of Cap Gains Villains," *Wall Street Journal*, June 10, 1993, A-20. Current law taxes gains as realized, but at a preferential (lower) rate.

Adjusted Gross Income

Adjusted gross income (AGI) is the tax-law measure of aggregate tax-bearing capacity. Because the philosophy of income taxation is that the tax should apply to net income, not gross receipts, the AGI includes, along with the listed salaries, wages, rents, dividends, and interest received by an individual, returns from individual business operation after deducting that business's operating costs.[18] But there are adjustments made to total income before applying elements of the tax structure to calculate liability. First, adjustments are made for alimony payments made (such payments contribute to the recipient's well-being and are taxed as part of that person's income, not that of the one who pays). Second, certain expenses associated with job-related moves and some business expenses are subtracted. It is always difficult to distinguish between relocation associated with earning an income and relocation associated with personal preference; the logic of taxing net income suggests that the former should be subtracted (moving for employment represents a cost of earning that income) and the latter should not (that moving expense is a result of a lifestyle or consumption choice). There is no simple, clear, logical line, so the error is made on the side of encouraging mobility. Third, adjustments are made to encourage certain activities by individuals—the deduction of Individual Retirement Account and other personal retirement plan payments to encourage private retirement saving, the student loan interest deduction to reduce the cost of borrowing to pay for education, and deductions to reduce the cost of private provision of health insurance.[19]

Net proceeds from some transactions simply do not show up in AGI, but appear to be income by both popular and Haig-Simons concepts.[20] Among the exclusions are interest received from certain state and local government bonds, certain transfer payments (e.g., welfare payments, most Social Security benefits, and food stamps), many fringe benefits received by employees from their employers (particularly pension and health plans), income from savings placed in life insurance, and gifts or inheritances. An ordained clergyperson may live in a home owned by his or her religious organization or receive annual payment to allow purchase or rental of a home approved by the congregation—and the number of homes provided the person is unlimited. Again, that appears to be compensation, but outside tax coverage.[21] The value of fringe benefits received from an employer is taxable unless the law explicitly excludes the benefit from the tax, as is the case for many important benefits (services provided at no additional cost to the employer, certain employee discounts, working-condition benefits, etc.). The practical scope of the remaining untaxed

---

[18]Income from businesses organized as a sole proprietorship, partnership, limited liability company, or Subchapter S corporation (small corporation) is taxed on a "pass-through" basis, meaning it is taxed through the individual income tax structure only and not at the business level.

[19]Similar provisions to encourage certain activities may appear in the itemized deductions. However, only taxpayers not opting for the standard deduction receive the benefit of these deductions. The impact of providing relief as an adjustment, rather than as a deduction, is therefore much greater. For instance, changing the preference for charitable contributions from an itemized deduction to an adjustment would significantly increase the number of taxpayers able to take advantage of the preference.

[20]Some federal tax preferences were subjected to an alternative minimum tax (AMT) in the Tax Reform Act of 1979 and continued by the 1986 law, but some exclusions remain.

[21]Laura Saunders, "Tax Relief for Clergy Is Questioned," *Wall Street Journal*, August 2, 2011, C1–C2.

Sidebar 9–1
More Comprehensive Income Measures for Distributional Analysis

The ideal income concept has many possible operational definitions. The tax-code definition of AGI does not meet the needs of being consistent over time, as Congress redefines what the tax system will or will not cover, or of capturing the full scope of taxpayer affluence during the year. It is infected with all manner of preferences and peculiarities and will not do for analysis of tax burden distribution across families of differing affluence. The federal agencies responsible for analysis of the tax system fully recognize the need for using a more comprehensive and stable measure in their work, but they do not agree on what the appropriate measure would be. They all recognize the Haig-Simons concept and work toward a broad concept, although to differing degrees. Here are some examples of these broad measures.

Adjusted Pre-tax Comprehensive Income (Congressional Budget Office)

The Congressional Budget Office uses this measure in analysis, including in the preparation of the effective tax rates that are reported elsewhere in this chapter. This measure includes all cash income (both taxable and tax-exempt received by the household), taxes paid by businesses (they are imputed to individuals according to standard shifting assumptions), employees' contributions to 401(k) retirement plans, and the value of in-kind income (employer-paid health insurance premiums, Medicare and Medicaid benefits, food stamps, etc., including in-kind government transfer payments).

Family Economic Income (Treasury under Clinton)

During the Clinton administration, the Office of Tax Analysis in the Department of the Treasury used family economic income, a measure developed for use before the tax reforms of 1986, for its distributional analysis. The measure attempts to employ a concept of income as consumption plus change in real net worth and is more independent of prevailing tax law than other measures. Family economic income combines income and taxes paid of related family members in a single economic unit. The measure starts with AGI reported on the tax return and then adds:

1. An estimate of unreported income.
2. Deductions for tax-sheltered retirement accounts such as Keogh, 401(k), and Individual Retirement Account programs and taxed employer pension contributions plus interest and dividends from those investments. Included are the employer contributions to accounts.
3. Social Security income that is not already taxed and cash assistance and other welfare investments, including the cash value of food stamps.
4. Employer-provided health benefits and other fringe benefits. The cost of fringe benefits generally amounts to about 35 percent of an employee's salary.
5. Imputed net rent is the estimated amount of money a homeowner would earn if he or she rented the house, minus the money spent on mortgage interest, property taxes, and property upkeep expenses and an allowance for property depreciation.
6. Annually accrued capital gains on stocks, business, land, or a house—for instance, the amount your home increased in value this year.
7. Inflationary losses of lenders are subtracted, and gains of borrowers are added.

(continues)

Sidebar 9–1
(continued)

8. The increase in value of a life insurance policy.
9. Interest on tax-exempt bonds.

Expanded Income (Joint Committee on Taxation)[1]

Congress's Joint Committee on Taxation uses expanded income for its analysis. Expanded income is narrower and follows the existing tax law more closely. The concept starts with AGI and then adds:

1. Tax-exempt interest
2. Workers' compensation
3. Nontaxable Social Security benefits
4. Excluded income of U.S. citizens living abroad
5. Value of Medicare benefits in excess of premiums paid
6. Minimum tax preferences
7. Employer contributions for health plans and life insurance
8. Employer share of payroll taxes
9. Corporate tax payments imputed to individual holders of corporate equity

[1]The administration of President George W. Bush used a cash income concept that closely followed the expanded income concept.

fringe benefits is extensive. The system does not include unrealized capital gains and excludes imputed incomes. Most federal and state-local distributional analysis uses some larger measure of ability (like those in Sidebar 9–1) rather than simple AGI to maintain a consistent measure of economic capacity. The impact of these exclusions can be huge. For instance, the exclusion of employer-provided health insurance is currently the largest single federal health subsidy for the non-elderly. The value of these preferences are called tax expenditures. Their measurement and how they are included in budget presentations will be discussed in Chapter 13.

Several exclusions seem reasonable, particularly those directed to low-income individuals: it is not sensible to assist individuals because of their poverty and then tax away part of that assistance. Some assistance categories, however, are not limited to the poor—that is, they are not need-based, and eligible recipients may have sizable income from other sources. Thus, if one desires to apply tax according to net well-being, there is a case for including retirement pay, Social Security, unemployment compensation, and similar payments not strictly conditioned on current income or wealth. Unemployment compensation is now fully taxable; other related flows may be taxable in certain circumstances.[22]

---

[22]The link between income earned by those receiving Social Security benefits and those benefits within the tax system is troublesome for incentives. Earning income can cause more of Social Security benefits to be taxable and can cause loss of benefits, leaving little, if any, net return from work.

The exclusion of interest received on state and local government debt historically stems from the principle of reciprocal immunity, that the federal government cannot destroy state or local governments (and vice versa). Because "the power to tax involves the power to destroy," the federal government historically did not tax instruments of state and local government.[23] The exclusion represents an important subsidy to state and local governments because it allows these governments to borrow at interest rates below current market rates. To demonstrate the influence of this exclusion, suppose an individual pays 35 percent of any additional income as federal income tax. A tax-exempt municipal bond paying 3.7 percent yields the same after-tax income as would a taxable bond paying about 5.7 percent.[24] Thus, the state or local government borrower automatically receives an interest subsidy through the federal tax system, allowing that government to borrow at artificially low rates. These bonds have been a favorite avenue of tax avoidance for higher-income individuals, and the value of interest subsidization to state and local governments must be balanced against the damage done to tax system equity by the exclusion.

Any suspicion that the nondiscriminatory taxation of interest on state and local bonds might be unconstitutional was eliminated in the 1988 U.S. Supreme Court decision in *South Carolina* v. *Baker:* "The owners of state bonds have no constitutional entitlement not to pay taxes on income they earn from state bonds, and states have no constitutional entitlement to issue bonds paying lower interest rates than other issuers."[25] So the provision remains as a valuable federal subsidy, a subsidy especially important to state and local governments and aggressively defended by them because it is received at their own control. The Tax Reform Act of 1986 dramatically reduced the scope of such borrowing, however, as a later chapter on government debt describes.

Personal Deductions

Personal deductions adjust the measured ability to pay the tax to the circumstances of the individual taxpayer. Personal deductions may improve the tax's horizontal and vertical equity by allowing individuals with such deductions to subtract them from the AGI and hence lower their tax base. Personal deductions may also encourage taxpayers to do things they might not otherwise do because of the tax savings that may result.

---

[23]*McCulloch v. Maryland*, 17 U.S. 316 (1819), is the source of John Marshall's famous "power to tax" quote. The reciprocal immunity doctrine, however, is enunciated in *Collector v. Day*, 78 U.S. 113 (1871).

[24]The taxable bond at 5.7 percent would leave the investor 65 percent (100 percent minus 35 percent) of its yield after tax, and 5.7 percent times 65 percent equals 3.7 percent.

[25]*South Carolina v. Baker, Treasury Secretary of the United States*, 485 U.S. 99 (1988). South Carolina sued because it objected to a Tax Equity and Fiscal Responsibility Act of 1982 provision that requires identification of owners of such bonds. Before that requirement, states could issue "bearer bonds"–whoever presented the bond received the periodic payments, and no questions about ownership were asked. They were popular with tax evaders, for money laundering, and with organized crime. The Court volunteered more answers than the state and local governments would have wished.

There are, logically, three types of spending that the itemized personal deductions identify as reducing the taxpayer's capacity to bear the tax below that of others with similar incomes. First, some expenditures are largely outside the control of the household and reduce ability to share in covering the cost of government. Currently in this category (philosophies and coverage change with tax code revisions) are deductions for medical and dental expenses above 7.5 percent of AGI, losses from casualty or theft above 10 percent of AGI (less $100), and either state and local income or retail sales taxes paid (pick the higher of the two) and property taxes. In each instance, individuals—presumably through little fault of their own—must bear these special expenses that more fortunate individuals do not incur. Thus, an adjustment of measured tax-bearing capacity is permitted.[26]

Second, some expenditures are deductible because the federal government has decided that private spending in those areas should be encouraged by reducing the after-tax cost of those actions. Thus, charitable contributions are directly deductible. This spending is optional (not like state taxes or medical bills), but the federal government seeks to encourage contributions. Interest paid on home mortgages (first and second homes) is similarly deductible as an important encouragement to home ownership, a matter of considerable importance to individuals who have borrowed to purchase homes.[27] Evidence indicates that the mortgage interest deduction has induced Americans to overinvest in owner-occupied housing, has added an incentive to greater urban sprawl, and reduces the progressivity of the tax because higher-affluence households are more likely to pay mortgage interest than are lower-affluence households (45 percent of tax savings goes to the top 10 percent of the income distribution) and that resources could be more productively invested in other capital assets. Indeed, some argue that its main effect is to encourage high-income borrowers to take on more debt. Public opinion puts great store in home ownership, and eliminating the provision has little political traction—although the provision now extends to only two houses per taxpayer.

Finally, some deductions are needed to maintain the principle that the tax apply to net incomes, not gross receipts. In this category are expenses associated with moving to a new job and certain job-related expenses (education expenses needed to maintain or improve skills on the present job, union dues, work uniforms, research expenses for a college professor, occupational taxes, etc.).[28] The latter group,

---

[26]The deduction for the state and local taxes raises some questions. These taxes represent payments for government services and reflect public decisions made to receive higher levels of those services. Why should the federal government be subsidizing (and biasing) these decisions? These payments really are not uncontrollable. The casualty loss deducton raises questions about moral hazard. Are people a little less cautious when the federal government is implicitly picking up some of the consequences of risky behavior?

[27]Other personal interest payments–for credit card, automobile, education, installment, and signature loans–were fully deductible before the 1986 tax act. Furthermore, the 1997 tax reconciliation act made interest paid on certain student loans again deductible (but only for individuals with incomes up to $40,000 and for couples with incomes up to $60,000). Student loan interest now is an adjustment, subtracted in calculating adjusted gross income, even for those not itemizing deductions.

[28]There are disputes about what are legitimate employee business expenses. For instance, Lamar Odom, National Basketball Association player with Los Angeles and Dallas, deducted $190,000 in NBA fines and fitness program fees as business expenses. The IRS disagreed and sent a tax bill for $87,000. Odom appealed and ultimately largely prevailed–the IRS settled for around $7,800. Legitimate business expenses depend on what sort of business you are in.

combined with some miscellaneous deductions (tax-preparation fees, fees associated with earning income from investments, etc.), are deductible only to the extent
they exceed 2 percent of AGI. Gambling losses are fully deductible, but only up to
the amount of winnings.

Each policy choice in designing the tax was made because it seemed to improve the equity or efficiency of the system. Because each provides greater tax relief
to high-income taxpayers (a charitable deduction of $100 has an after-tax cost of
$65 to an individual in the 35 percent bracket and a cost of $85 to someone in the
15 percent bracket), there is a special incentive for such individuals to arrange their
affairs so that their expenses fit into these deductible categories. Thus, professional
meetings are timed to double as vacations, consumer loans are converted to home
equity (mortgage) loans, and so on. As a result, these provisions can reduce the overall progression of the tax system and distort economic behavior. The system works
to reduce this impact by applying a phase-out of several itemized deductions—each
dollar of deduction is reduced by 3 percent for taxpayers whose AGI exceeds a limit;
to add some extra complexity to the system, this phase-out is currently scheduled
itself for phase-out.

Not all taxpayers, however, use the itemized personal deductions. In fact, most
taxpayers do not: for tax year 2010, only 34 percent of individual returns showed
itemized deductions.[29] The rest of the returns took another and potentially simpler
route. Since the early 1940s, an optional standard deduction has permitted individuals to subtract from their AGI base a standard deduction regardless of itemized totals.
This deduction eliminates the need for keeping records of deductible expenses. The
initial idea was to make the tax simpler for the many people who became taxpayers
for the first time during the Second World War (and maybe to give a psychological
boost to people without substantial itemized deductions). The standard deduction
has gradually increased over time and is now indexed to increase with inflation; from
1987 to 2012, for instance, it increased from $2,540 to $5,950 for a single person and
is now double that for joint returns.[30] Unless taxpayers have itemized deductions
totaling more than that amount, they will not itemize; homeownership with the
accompanying mortgage interest payment and local property tax typically creates
the threshold to make itemization pay.[31] For some taxpayers, the optional standard
deduction certainly reduces the complexity of the tax by eliminating the need to
keep records of deductible payments made through the year. But many taxpayers
ultimately using the standard deduction still keep those records, with the intention
of deciding which filing option to take only after comparing the tax advantage of
the two. When all taxpayers have a general deduction, tax rates must be higher to
generate a given amount of tax revenue, diluting the relief for the deserving and the

---

[29] Adrian Dungan and Michael Parisi, "Individual Income Tax Returns, Preliminary Data, 2010" *Statistics of Income Bulletin* 31(Winter 2012): 6–7.
[30] There is an additional standard deduction for taxpayers over the age of 65 and for blind taxpayers. Plus certain real estate taxes are added to the standard deduction, so that taxpayers who do not itemize will get this preference. This special preference doesn't make much sense, but it came from Congress, so we shouldn't be surprised.
[31] For tax years 2008 and 2009, even taxpayers who took the standard deduction were allowed to deduct state and local property taxes that they had paid.

undeserving alike. However, anyone can considerably simplify their federal income tax obligations by electing the standard deduction, no matter what. Those choosing itemization are choosing tax reduction over tax simplification.

The standard deduction/itemized deduction choice is not equally distributed across income groups. As noted earlier, the overall average rate of itemization is only 34 percent. However, among taxpayers with adjusted gross income of more than $200,000, the itemization rate is around 95 percent. That is why some politicians have proposed limits on the use of itemized deduction by higher-income taxpayers, even though that would certainly add to the complexity of the system and to the distortions coming from the system. There are also considerable differences across states in the propensity to itemize, from only 18 percent in West Virginia to 50 percent in Maryland, the result of differing patterns of deductible state and local taxes and home values, two major influences on whether it is to the taxpayer's advantage to itemize or to take the standard deduction.[32]

Personal Exemptions

The tax law allows an exemption for each person in a taxpaying unit—the taxpayer, the taxpayer's spouse, and dependents (certain members of the household who are supported by the taxpayer, usually the taxpayer's children)—plus extra exemptions if the taxpayer or spouse is blind or older than age 65. The exemption is a flat amount for each exemption claimed—$3,700 in 2011 and $3,800 in 2012. (The exemption is adjusted annually for inflation.) The exemption serves to adjust tax payment for size of the taxpaying unit, adds some progressivity to the effective rate pattern, and works to remove many low-income households from the tax system. The structure provides greater tax reduction for those in higher tax brackets (subtracting $3,700 from taxable income reduces tax burden by more for a taxpayer in the 35 percent bracket than it does for someone in the 15 percent bracket), so the system provides that taxpayers above a certain AGI level (it was $239,950 for a married taxpayer filing jointly in 2008) would reduce personal exemptions by 2 percent for each $2,500 or part thereof by which AGI exceeds that threshold. The phase-out provision itself is presently phased out, but may return.

Taxable Income

Taxable income results from subtracting personal deductions, either itemized or standard, and personal exemptions from AGI. It is the base to which the tax-rate structure applies. The elemental identity of taxation is that tax yield equals tax base times tax rate. Therefore, a given tax yield may be generated through

---

[32]Gerald Prante, "Most Americans Don't Itemize on Their Returns," *Tax Foundation Fiscal Fact No. 95* (Washington, D.C.: Tax Foundation, July 23, 2007).

many different base and rate combinations, some involving narrow-based definitions (many deductions, exclusions, and exemptions from the Haig-Simons
or other general income concepts) and high rate structures and some involving
broad-based definitions (few deductions, exclusions, and exemptions) and low
rate structures. The perennial mantra of federal tax reform, reflected in the 1986
Tax Reform Act, but generally eroded in later legislation, has been a movement
toward a broader-based lower-rate option. The idea has been supported by the
beliefs that lower rates at the decision margin do less to discourage investment
and work effort than do higher rates, that broader bases leave fewer protected
pockets that could harbor economic activity profitable only because of tax provisions, and that broad coverage is less likely to engender horizontal inequity. Of
course, lawmakers and taxpayers generally are thinking about broadening the
base to eliminate tax preferences enjoyed by others and not by themselves or
their constitutents. Thus, progress in tax reform is dreadfully slow, in spite of the
conceptual agreement. Broadening the base has much in common with cutting
government spending—it is easier to agree on the principle than it is to identify
what exactly is to be done.

Tax Rates

Federal individual income tax rates increase in steps as income increases. At each
step, the rate applicable to additional income is slightly higher than the rate on
lower income. Figure 9–2 presents recent tax-rate schedules for single and married
taxpayers; Figure 9–3 gives one portion of the tax tables that filers are directed to
use in determining their tax liability. The tax table—which reflects the relevant
rate schedules—does the calculations from the rate schedules in $50 increments
of taxable income, presumably in recognition of the diminished math skills of the
American public. (Higher-income taxpayers must use the rate schedules for calculation of amounts. Either their math skills are better, or they are presumed to be hiring
someone with the skills necessary for the calculations.) The rate schedule is graduated upward with marginal rates (the percentage taxed from each additional dollar
of taxable income) of 15, 25, 28, 33, and 35 percent. A single individual with taxable
income of $85,000 would thus have part of that income taxed at 15 percent, part at
25 percent, and part at 28 percent. Only part of his or her income would face the
28 percent rate, but if he or she earned an extra $100, after tax, only $72 would be
retained. This marginal rate is critical in economic choices. The average tax rate he
or she would pay is substantially less than 28 percent. In a graduated rate schedule,
all taxable income is taxed at the lowest rate, with decreasing portions of the total
base taxed at each increasing rate.[33]

---

[33]In the U.S. system, that isn't exactly accurate because the tax code has a recapture system to remove the
impact of the lowest tax bracket for high-income taxpayers, an extra complication in the system. There
is a similar recapture scheme for the personal exemptions.

Figure 9–2
Federal Rate Schedule for 2011
Married Individuals Filing Jointly

If Taxable Income Is:	Then Tax Is:
$0 – 17,000	10% of the amount over $0
17,000 – 69,000	$1,700 + 15% of the amount over $17,000
69,000 – 139,350	9,500 + 25% of the amount over $69,000
139,350 – 212,300	27,087.50 + 28% of the amount over $139,350
212,300 – 379,150	47,513.50 + 33% of the amount over $212,300
379,150 and over	102,574 + 35% of the amount over $379,150

Single Filers

If Taxable Income Is:	Then Tax Is:
$0 – 8,500	10% of the amount over $0
8,500 – 34,500	$850 + 15% of the amount over $8,500
34,500 – 83,600	4,750 + 25% of the amount over $34,500
83,600 – 174,400	17,025 + 28% of the amount over $83,600
174,400 – 379,150	42,449 + 33% of the amount over $174,400
379,150 and over	110,016.50 + 35% of the amount over $379,150

SOURCE: Internal Revenue Service. 2011 Form 1040 Instructions. Tax Tables.

In comparison with the recent past, the rate structure consists of fewer rate brackets (14 before the 1986 tax reform) and a lower top-rate bracket. Few returns characteristically have been filed by taxpayers paying any tax at the highest marginal rate (although that has changed dramatically in the last decade with the remarkable economic success of high-income taxpayers).

In the years from 1936 through 1981, the highest marginal tax rate was 70 percent or higher (90 percent or higher from 1944 through 1963). Those high rates may harm the national economy without adding much revenue. For example, a person in the 70 percent bracket, a person with considerable income, would face this sort of choice: "I can work a bit more and earn an additional $1,000, of which $700 will be paid to the federal government (and some probably will be paid for state and local income taxes as well) and $300 I can keep for myself. Or I can use that extra time to go to some baseball games or play with my dog. Or I can hire tax advisors to try to structure that additional $1,000 so I won't have to pay so much tax." Two of these alternatives do not contribute much to the national economy, but, given the after-tax return to the individual, many people would select them. That is an important influence behind tax structuring efforts to raise necessary revenue and achieve the desired degree of progressivity without high marginal rates. In designing tax structures, it is useful to think about what tax wedge—the tax-created difference between the total paid by the buyer

Figure 9–3
A Portion of the Federal Tax Table for 2011

If line 43 (taxable income) is—		And you are—			
At least	But less than	Single	Married filing jointly	Married filing separately	Head of a household
		Your tax is—			
83,000					
83,000	83,050	16,881	13,006	17,282	15,524
83,050	83,100	16,894	13,019	17,296	15,536
83,100	83,150	16,906	13,031	17,310	15,549
83,150	83,200	16,919	13,044	17,324	15,561
83,200	83,250	16,931	13,056	17,338	15,574
83,250	83,300	16,944	13,069	17,352	15,586
83,300	83,350	16,956	13,081	17,366	15,599
83,350	83,400	16,969	13,094	17,380	15,611
83,400	83,450	16,981	13,106	17,394	15,624
83,450	83,500	16,994	13,119	17,408	15,636
83,500	83,550	17,006	13,131	17,422	15,649
83,550	83,600	17,019	13,114	17,436	15,661
83,600	83,650	17,032	13,156	17,450	15,674
83,650	83,700	17,046	13,169	17,464	15,686
83,700	83,750	17,060	13,181	17,478	15,699
83,750	83,800	17,074	13,194	17,492	15,711
83,800	83,850	17,088	13,206	17,506	15,724
83,850	83,900	17,102	13,219	17,520	15,736
83,900	83,950	17,116	13,231	17,534	15,749
83,950	84,000	17,130	13,244	17,548	15,761

SOURCE: Internal Revenue Service, Forms and Publications, *Inst 1040 Tax Tables*.

(or employer in labor markets) and the net received by the seller (or worker in labor markets)—has been created. A high wedge on the margin of decision causes distortions and invites strategies (legal and illegal) to keep from paying tax. In the period in which the highest marginal rate was over 90 percent, you can be sure that not much tax was generated in that bracket. Those in danger of confronting such a high tax bite had enough clout with employers to figure out non-taxed ways of getting compensated.

The average rate (tax liability divided by taxable income) always lies below the marginal rate (the increase in tax liability resulting from $1 additional income) in the federal tax structure. With that structure, an individual will never have greater after-tax income by having less income. The percentage of income going to federal tax increases as income rises, but the absolute income left over will not decline.[34]

But the tax rates confronted by taxpayers are more complicated than just the graduated rates shown in Figure 9–2. First, as noted previously, most states (and many localities) levy their own income taxes, applying supplemental rates to federal AGI, taxable income, or the federal tax itself. Each adds another layer to the rate paid, although state returns are filed separately from federal returns. The combined rate cannot be simply found on a single rate schedule; it has to be added up, sometimes with allowances made for differences in statutory coverage between federal and state taxes. Several states do, however, have local governments that piggyback their tax on the state tax, and liability for both state and local taxes is handled in a single return.

A second complication results because not all income is taxed in the same rate structure. Some countries, including the United States, apply multiple rate schedules, in which different sorts of income—wages, interest, or earnings from a business— are taxed at different rates. The federal government taxes income from realized long-term capital gains—increase in value of a capital asset between time of acquisition and time of sale—and dividend income at preferential rates. This income is taxed at 15 percent for taxpayers whose ordinary income is taxed at the 25 percent rate or higher and at 5 percent for those in lower brackets.[35] The idea is to encourage capital investment and to prevent a double taxation of income that is saved, but the scheme creates incentive issues. There is a considerable incentive for taxpayers to attempt to convert ordinary income into flows that would be considered capital gain income—for example, when some investment managers sought to arrange their compensation for managing client money so that it would be taxed as capital gain (at 15 percent) as opposed to being taxed as ordinary compensation (at a 35 percent marginal rate).[36]

Not only does the incentive distort economic resources, but also it requires extra administrative effort to police shelter schemes established to exploit the difference in rates. A difference of 20 percentage points is sufficient to bring tax advisors calling

---

[34]That may not necessarily be the case when effects from government benefit programs are added in, however. For an illustration, see Mary Rowland, "When Working Isn't Worth It," *New York Times,* September 26, 1993, F-15.

[35]Because capital gains are taxed only when they are realized (i.e., when the asset is sold), changes in the capital gains tax rate can have a considerable impact on realization and on revenue; when the rate is known to be increasing, as with the Tax Reform Act of 1986, investors respond by realizing a lot of gains to avoid the higher rate, and capital gains revenues jump. After the higher rate is in place, capital gains realizations go back to roughly their normal level. Congressional Budget Office, "Capital Gains Taxes and Federal Revenues," Revenue and Tax Policy Brief, October 9, 2002.

[36]The controversy was over the taxation of "carried interest," the share of profits that managers of private equity funds, hedge funds, and so on received. Although the managers had no money of their own invested, they sought to have their compensation taxed as capital gains rather than ordinary income. In the 2012 presidential campaign, the fact that Mitt Romney received "carried interest" income from his prior employment at Bain Capital and, as a result, had very high income that was taxed at a very low average tax rate was a point of some contention.

with systems to convert income flows from one class to another. Administrators need to check the transactions carefully.

Taxing different income sources at different rates represents a clear violation of normal principles of tax policy, as it complicates, distorts, and makes the system less certain and transparent. Special treatment of long-term capital gains is supported, however, by concerns about the unfairness of taxing gains that are nominal (inflation) but not real (purchasing power), about the danger of capital being locked in to current holdings (no capital gains tax applies when heirs receive appreciated assets when an estate is settled),[37] and about the possible chilling effect of the tax on saving and investment.

Not all income taxes are levied with graduated rates. At the present time, six states levy flat-rate income taxes, and several countries, particularly several of the newly democratic states of Eastern Europe, also apply such rate structures.[38] The flat-rate tax prevents some of the distortions and disincentives that upwardly graduated rates can produce. If the coverage of the tax is broad enough—in other words, if major preferences have been eliminated—the statutory rate may be low enough to reduce some tax evasion. That may happen if the tax saved at the margin from evasion is not worth the risks associated with being caught. In these flat systems, any progressivity in effective rates is produced by other structural features, particularly large exemptions, not through graduation of the legal rates. Table 9–3 illustrates how a relatively generous exemption by itself can convert a flat statutory rate into progressive effective rates. In essence, the large exemption creates progressive

Table 9–3
Effective Rate Impact of a Flat-Rate Income Tax (10 percent) and a Large Personal Exemption ($10,000) on Selected Families of Three Persons

Family	Before Tax Income ($)	Total Personal Exemptions ($)	Taxable Income	Tax Paid ($)	Effective Tax Rate (%)
A	40,000	30,000	10,000	1,000	2.5
B	100,000	30,000	70,000	7,000	7.0
C	500,000	30,000	470,000	47,000	9.4

[37]This is called "step-up in basis." For eventual capital gains tax purposes, the value of the inherited asset becomes the value at the time of inheritance, not the value at which the asset was purchased. This increase in value from purchase to inheritance therefore escapes the income tax system. Not only is this income not taxed twice when the estate tax applies, but also it wouldn't be taxed at all if not for the estate tax. "Constructive realization," meaning taxing capital gains at the death of the owner, would allow dramatic reduction of estate taxes without substantial revenue loss, while preserving a degree of equity. This was a reform adopted in Canada.

[38]The impact of Russia's implementation of a flat-rate tax, replacing a graduated-rate tax, is analyzed in Clifford G. Gaddy and William G. Gale, "Demythologizing the Russian Flat Tax," *Tax Notes International* 43 (March 14, 2005): 983–88. Some American commentators have erroneously pointed to this experience as evidence that moving from graduated-rate to flat-rate structures boosts economic activity and possibly even tax revenue, but Gaddy and Gale do not find that result in their careful analysis.

effective rates because the exemption provides greater relief *relative to* family income to the lower-income family—$10,000 per person is a much more significant portion of total income for Family A than for Family C (or B). That translates into a much greater impact on the effective rate. This impact on vertical equity works with any rate structure—large personal exemptions make the progressivity of an upward graduated tax structure even greater.

Credits

Tax credits, direct forgiveness of tax owed, are a powerful device for stimulation of private activities. The credit amount reduces tax liability by an amount exactly equal to the credit; it does not reduce the tax base, as is the case for exemptions or deductions, so its tax-reducing impact is not filtered through the rate structure. Therefore, the tax reduction from a given credit is the same for taxpayers in all rate brackets; deductions and exemptions, on the other hand, have greater tax-reducing impact for those in higher tax brackets.[39] But because credits reduce taxes directly, they produce greater revenue loss than do equivalent deductions or exemptions, an important concern for most governments.

Credits have been used over the years to induce political contributions, installation of energy-saving mechanisms, capital investment, and home purchase, to cite some recent federal system examples. Current credits are provided for families with children, for certain college tuitions, for child- and dependent-care expenses, for the elderly and persons with disabilities, and for certain adoption expenses. Furthermore, the federal system provides a credit for low-income workers (the EITC), as described in Sidebar 9–2, a credit defined as a percentage of earned income that substantially relieves taxes for the working poor. State income taxes similarly employ credits to support desirable activities, choosing the power and evenness of support from credits against the substantial revenue loss they produce.

Effective Tax Rates

The statutory, or nominal, rates appearing in the rate schedule, of course, are not the effective rates. Analysis of the income tax system usually is conducted by looking at the relationship between taxes paid and AGI, the federal tax system equivalent of net income, or one of the broader measures in the Haig-Simons tradition. This rate is the average effective rate. The statutory rates are reduced substantially by the tax provisions removing individual income from the base (adjustments, deductions,

---

[39]A number of federal credits and other tax preferences are reduced in stages as income increases; there are about twenty different phase-out ranges and calculation methods. All add complexity and uncertainty to the system, presumably in the name of targeting relief and social engineering. Most members of Congress who voted for these provisions also claim to be supporters of tax simplification.

Sidebar 9–2
The Earned Income Tax Credit

The federal earned income tax credit (EITC) provides needy families with financial assistance, while it gives a positive incentive for work among the lower-paid members of society. It aids these people without the need for a special welfare bureaucracy and appears to reach a higher percentage of those eligible than does any other income support program, possibly because it avoids any stigma associated with programs that more specifically identify the recipients. It also avoids the major work disincentives that some welfare programs have when earning additional income causes countervailing loss of welfare benefits. Quite simply, assistance is provided through the individual income tax system with fully refundable tax credits given to those who qualify. Fully refundable means that if their credit exceeds the amount of federal income tax they would owe, they receive the difference as a refund. Not all credits are fully refundable, so this is a distinct advantage for the EITC.

Here is how the Council of Economic Advisers described the operation of the EITC in the 1994 *Economic Report of the President:*

> The earned income tax credit is often thought of as a type of negative income tax, but in fact it is more complicated than that. The EITC has three ranges: a "credit range" in which it functions like a wage subsidy, a "plateau" in which it has no marginal effect, and a "phaseout" range in which the credit is paid back as earnings rise... .
>
> To illustrate, when the increases enacted in 1993 are fully effective (in 1996), the credit will work as follows for a family with two or more children. (Less generous schedules apply to one-child and childless families.) As earnings rise from zero to $8,425 (all dollar figures are in 1994 dollars), the EITC will provide a 40 percent wage subsidy, so that each $100 of additional earnings will net the family $140. The maximum credit is $3,370, which is therefore reached when earnings hit $8,425. The credit will then be constant as earnings rise from $8,425 to $11,000. Beyond $11,000, however, the family's tax credit is reduced 21 cents for each extra dollar earned. Benefits are thus exhausted when earnings reach $27,000.

Clearly, the EITC provides a marginal work incentive in the credit range (unlike a negative income tax), a marginal work disincentive in the phase-out range, and neither in the plateau. However, to the extent that labor supply decisions involve whether or not to work, rather than how many hours to work, the credit provides a positive work incentive to all recipients.

In fiscal 2011, the EITC provided $55.6 billion in benefits. That compares with $71.8 billion for the Food Stamp program (now SNAP), $49.6 billion for the Supplemental Security Income program, and $21.3 billion for Temporary Assistance for Needy Families (TANF) (what is thought of as America's foundation public welfare program), three of the most important income security programs functioning through the spending side of the fiscal system. More than half of EITC payments go to families below the poverty line. The program has been of particular benefit to families at the bottom of the income ladder and represents a significant component in the economic safety net, even though administered through the tax system and not through the public assistance bureaucracy.

Around half the states have their own earned income tax program, in addition to the federal program.

SOURCES: Executive Office of the President, Council of Economic Advisers, *Economic Report of the President Transmitted to the Congress February 1994* (Washington, D.C.: U.S. Government Printing Office, 1994), 51.

exemptions, and exclusions) and forgiving tax owed (credits). These elements can be regarded as the work of tax loopholes or as the work of tax policy designed to correct inequities or to encourage socially desirable behavior.

One little-observed feature of the federal income tax is the large number of tax filers who pay no federal individual income tax. Refer back to Table 9–2 for the data for 2007. In that year, households in the two lowest income quintiles (actually 46 percent of the population) paid no federal individual income tax; their tax shares and effective tax rates were negative. Indeed, on average, those households received money from the government rather than paying any tax; the workings of deductions, exemptions, and adjustments made their liabilities extremely low, and then the workings of fully refundable credits made their net liabilities negative. Rather than paying income tax to the federal government, the government was paying them. That means that 46 percent of American households are not taxpayers; they are credit receivers. On average, they receive a payment from the federal government rather than facing any income tax liability. About half of them pay no tax because they fall below the basic income level upon which the tax applies, and about half pay no tax because they take advantage of special provisions in the tax code that wipe out tax liabilities and even result in net payments from the government.[40] Is it really the case that more than four in ten Americans have incomes that are so low that they cannot afford to contribute to the general services provided by the federal government? If so, do we conclude that the federal government is just too darn big to be affordable, that America is simply an impoverished country, or that some Americans are getting a free ride from others? When this tally is placed against the concentration of individual income tax payments in the upper categories of the income distribution shown previously in Table 9–2 (61 percent of individual income tax collections come from the top 5 percent of taxpayers and 39.5 percent from the top 1 percent), the extent to which the revenue system depends on a small pool of taxpayers is apparent. Of course, the uppermost income recipients have done extremely well, and that is the primary reason for the concentration of payment—but is it good for sound democratic decision making for the payment for public services to be so concentrated and for so many to have no liability? And are voters likely to be fully responsible when they realize that extra federal spending is likely to have no tax cost for them?

Indexation

When a tax structure has many upward graduated brackets, as the federal structure did until the 1986 tax act, a phenomenon known as bracket creep can occur during high inflation. Suppose a family has an AGI of $28,000, pays a tax of $3,300, and is in the 15 percent marginal tax bracket. In two years, its income has increased to, say,

---

[40]Rachel Johnson, James Nunns, Jeffrey Rohaly, Eric Toder, and Roberton Williams, "Why Some Tax Units Pay No Income Tax," Tax Policy Center, Urban Institute and Brookings Institution, July 2011.

$33,600 (a 20 percent increase), but the cost of living has increased by 20 percent as well, so its real income has not changed. The family would, however, pay tax on that higher income even though its living standard has not really changed, and that income is subject to a higher marginal bracket. Thus, it might now pay $4,300, an increase of tax liability of more than 20 percent, because of the upward rate graduation. Of course, the real value of personal exemptions and standard deductions decreases as well.

This graduation has historically helped stabilize the economy, accelerating tax collections during inflation to provide a macroeconomic brake and slowing tax collections during recession to provide a macroeconomic stimulus without legislative action. During the long economic expansion of the 1980s, governments raised substantial revenue without statutory rate increases simply by letting growth, real and inflated, carry taxpayers into higher-rate categories. Federal and state governments enjoyed growing income tax revenues without the necessity of increasing any statutory tax rates.

After the high inflation rates in the 1980s, governments moved to remedy the problem by indexing significant features of their income taxes to prevent further bracket creep. The adjustment works by formula to annually change personal exemptions, standard deductions, and the starting points of rate brackets to allow for any inflation that has occurred since the prior year. The federal system has done indexing since 1985, and a number of states have followed suit. The idea is to prevent stealth tax increases.

Tax Computation

The nature of income taxation can best be understood by working the mechanics of the tax. Table 9–4 provides an illustration of such a manipulation. It applies the general schematic of the federal income tax to demonstrate deductions and exemptions, as well as the computation of average, marginal, and average effective tax rates. That schematic shows how each provision that shapes tax liability comes into play and how the place in the system at which a preference is installed matters for impact on liability and effective rate. Fully refundable credits have greatest impact, followed by credits, exclusions, exemptions, adjustments, and deductions.

But this computation is not quite everything for certain taxpayers. If their income is above a specified threshold, the taxpayer must calculate an alternative minimum tax (AMT) that might mean extra tax to be paid. AMT, the stealthy federal tax that all political parties and both branches of government love to hate, but can't figure out what to do about, is described in Sidebar 9–3.

This illustrated computation seems reasonably straightforward. Where is the complexity that is claimed to infest the tax system? The requirements for collecting information about deductible expenses and for making sure that all income is reported have already been noted. But that is only the tip of the iceberg. The tax code has a dozen different special preferences to help with educational expenses, with terms of eligibility and benefits differing for each, and the use of one may complicate

Table 9–4
An Example of Income Tax Computation

Mr. and Mrs. Gross have one dependent child. Their total income is $200,000, all from wages and salaries. They also received income from municipal bonds of $7,500, but this money is excluded from the federal individual income tax. They have adjustments of $20,000 from student loan interest, educator expenses, and Individual Retirement Account contributions, so their adjusted gross income equals $180,000 ($200,000 less $20,000). They have itemized deductions of $15,000 (state income tax paid, mortgage interest paid, and charitable contributions). Because this exceeds the amount of the standard deduction for which they would qualify ($11,600), they use the itemized deduction in their filing. Each personal exemption is $3,700, for a total of $11,100. Mrs. Gross's employer has withheld $32,000 of her salary (and paid that amount to the federal government) to cover her tax liability. They file a joint return.

Computing Taxable Income:

Adjusted Gross Income: $180,000
- Less itemized deduction ($15,000)
- Less personal exemptions ($11,100)
- Taxable income = $153,900

Computing Tax Liability:

From Tax Rate Schedule for Married Filing Jointly (Figure 9–2):
- Tax liability for taxable income from $139,350 to $212,300 equals $27,087.50 + 28% of the amount over $139,350 *or* $27,087.50 + .28 ($153,900 − $139,350) = $31,161.50
- Tax owed/tax refund (withholdings less tax liability): $32,000 − $31,161.50 = $838.50 overpayment that can be refunded

Some Important Tax Indicators:

Average tax rate = tax liability/taxable income = $31,161.50/$153,900 = 20.25%
Average effective tax rate = tax liability/(total income plus exclusions) = $31,161.50/ ($200,000 + $7,500) = 15.02%
Marginal tax rate = change in tax liability/change in taxable income = 28% (from rate schedule)

---

the availability of other financial assistance for college. Preferences are subject to phase-out provisions that both complicate tax calculation and alter taxpayer incentives. There are complicated rules for determining what parent can claim a child as dependent that vary according to marital status and parent income. There are special rules for taxation of unearned income received by a child to prevent parents from shifting investment income to their children to take advantage of the child's lower marginal rate (sometimes called the "Kiddy Tax"). There are complicated rules and

Sidebar 9–3
The Alternative Minimum Tax

The United States has two tax systems. The regular system encompasses the standard individual and corporate income taxes, but there is a separate system, the alternative minimum tax (AMT) system, that is designed to ensure that corporations and individuals with substantial income do not exploit tax preferences provided in the tax law to avoid significant tax liability. The AMT system requires the taxpayer to do two distinct calculations of tax liability, one for the regular system and one for the AMT. It has been described as "the best example of pointless complexity in the tax system,"[1] a high distinction indeed.

In 1969, Secretary of Treasury Joe Barr made news when he reported that 155 individuals with incomes over $200,000 in 1967 had paid no federal income tax. Twenty of that number were millionaires. Even though none of these taxpayers had done anything illegal, none was a tax cheat, and none was doing anything other than taking advantage of tax preferences that Congress had adopted to encourage certain economic behavior or to relieve certain perceived inequities in the tax system, a furor erupted. Congress enacted the AMT to ensure that the few high-income individuals who otherwise would pay no tax would pay at least something. The first tax enacted was a minimum tax; the tax was revised in the late 1970s to the current alternative minimum tax.

The AMT process for individual taxpayers is the following.

1. The taxpayer calculates tax liability according to the regular law.
2. The taxpayer calculates AMT liability by adding back most preferences (personal deductions and exemptions) and adjustments to regular taxable income, subtracting the special AMT exemption (the exemption phases out at higher income levels), and computing AMT liability using a simple rate structure (only two rates: 26 and 28 percent).
3. The AMT equals the excess of the alternative calculation over the regular income tax.

By itself, the AMT is simpler than the regular income tax: there are fewer tax preferences to keep track of, and the rate structure has fewer brackets. The added complexity is caused because the taxpayer has to do two tax calculations: the regular income tax and the AMT. In addition, the taxpayer can't easily know ahead of time which income tax he or she will be subject to.

The AMT was intended initially to reach high-income taxpayers, but its net now catches many middle-income taxpayers. The reasons are simple: the regular income tax is generally indexed for inflation and the AMT is not, and recent tax cuts have significantly reduced the regular income tax for many taxpayers. Inflation brings higher income, and the regular income tax adjusts its provisions upward to keep tax burdens from rising simply because of inflated incomes, but the AMT thresholds remain based on price and income levels of the late 1960s. Hence, more and more people find that their income status throws them into the AMT net. These people still are not tax cheats.

What sort of tax avoidance behavior causes people to fall prey to AMT? The people most likely to have AMT liability are those paying high state and local property and income taxes, those with large families, those with high miscellaneous deductions, and those running businesses with large operating losses. It is hard to believe that these people should be hit with an extra

Sidebar 9–3
(continued)

income tax liability, but that's the way the law works. Furthermore, the number of people hit by AMT continues to grow: in 1970, the tax hit 20,000 taxpayers, but applied to almost 8 million taxpayers for tax year 2009.

So why doesn't Congress get rid of the AMT? Quite frankly, it hardly can afford to. AMT revenue in 2009 was $22 billion, and making that sum up when lawmakers are reluctant to pass any provisions that generate extra revenue would be extremely difficult. The amounts coming from the AMT will, unless changed, continue to grow over time. In addition, the AMT works to protect Congress and the president from their own fiscally unsustainable actions: when new tax reductions get passed, the AMT works to bring back some of that lost revenue as liability lost from the reduction is recaptured by the AMT.

Critics point to increased taxpayer compliance burdens, higher IRS administrative cost, redistribution of tax burdens among taxpayers, and denial to taxpayers of entirely legal tax incentives that Congress intended to provide. For a huge number of taxpayers, it requires a second calculation of tax liability with no revenue flowing to the government—the worst sort of tax program. Similar arguments apply to the corporate AMT. The biggest barrier to AMT reform: How could the lost revenue be replaced?

Some observers have suggested a way out. The AMT by itself is simpler than the individual income tax. Why not repeal the regular income tax and change the name of the AMT to the income tax? That would allow taxpayers to make fewer calculations, to keep fewer records, and to reduce their need for costly tax advisors, in exchange for somewhat higher statutory rates. In other words, if you can't slay the dragon, why not convert it into domestic livestock?

[1]Leonard E. Burman, William G. Gale, Gregory Leiserson, and Jeffrey Rohaly, "Options to Fix the AMT," Tax Policy Center, January 19, 2007, 54.

instructions for provisions like the earned income tax credit, a program for low-income taxpayers who may have lower educational attainment. Type of income (e.g., salary and interest versus capital gain and dividend) determines what rate structure is to be used, and there are complicated boundary rules that define the income categorization. It is no surprise that so many Americans throw up their hands at the complexity and hire someone else to fulfill the basis task of tax compliance. All together, it is no surprise that complexity of the system is about as big a complaint as the actual amount of tax being paid. Unfortunately, efforts to simplify run up against the fact that the elements of complication are the source of tax preference—lower taxes—for some taxpayers and those taxpayers accept the complexity in exchange for tax relief.

The Individual Income Tax Gap

There is a federal individual income tax compliance problem. The system relies on voluntary compliance by individual taxpayers to produce revenue, and, for various reasons, not all taxpayers pay the tax that they owe. The IRS struggles to cope with uncollected taxes and does have considerable success, but it estimates that the overall noncompliance rate is around 18 percent. That is money owed and not collected, effectively moving the burden from nonpayers to honest taxpayers.

The IRS works to identify the sources of noncompliance in order to gauge its success and, importantly, to identify where it should allocate its resources in order to do its job as well as it can. Its primary tool is called the National Research Program, a program of research audits that is designed to identify types and size of misreporting, a difficult research task given that those taxpayers who are not paying all the tax they owe are not eager to let the IRS know about it. The results of this research, a summary of which appears in Table 9–5, show how the compliance system is functioning across various types of income.

There are three major conclusions from these data. First, the withholding system is really effective. Only 1 percent of income subject to employer withholding does not get reported. It is easier to enforce the tax obligation against employers than against employees; there are fewer of them to deal with, and they are serving as a conduit between their employees and the government, so they are roughly disinterested third parties in the transaction. Many individuals have their tax overwithheld through the year, probably as a scheme of forced saving, so their filing with the government is a request for refund, not a need for payment of money owed. That is a good incentive for filing.

Second, third-party reporting helps induce compliance. Financial institutions and dividend-paying corporations must report to the IRS their interest and dividend payments made to taxpayers (the 1099 reporting system), so the IRS knows that money has been paid. Under certain circumstances, the payers can be required to also withhold tax, as well as to report payment. As a result, the payment is difficult to hide and provides real encouragement for the taxpayer to report and remit tax owed. Compliance in these income categories is not as high as with wages and salaries, but the misreporting percentage is still quite low.

Finally, pure voluntary compliance doesn't work so well. When income received by a taxpayer is subject neither to withholding nor to third-party reporting, the misreporting percentage skyrockets. That is the case with all forms of business income—farm and nonfarm proprietors and owners of rental properties in particular, but also partnerships, corporations taxed like partnerships, estates, and trusts. This income is known, in the first instance, only to the taxpayer, and whether the taxpayer reports accurately is known only to the taxpayer unless the IRS checks. However, the IRS lacks the resources to do extensive checking. The National Research Program tells the IRS that this sort of income certainly deserves special scrutiny.

Because the income taxes require taxpayers to maintain records, calculate tax owed, and file returns, the IRS does need to verify that taxpayers are being

Table 9–5

Federal Individual Income Tax Underreporting Gap Estimates, Tax Year 2001

Type of Income or Offset	Tax Gap ($Billions)	Net Misreporting Percentage
TOTAL UNDERREPORTING GAP	197	18
UNDERREPORTED INCOME	166	11
NONBUSINESS INCOME	56	4
Wages, salaries, tips	10	1
Interest income	2	4
Dividend income	1	4
State income tax refunds	1	12
Alimony income	7	<0.5
Pensions and annuities	4	4
Unemployment compensation	11	<0.5
Social Security benefits	1	6
Capital gains	11	12
Form 4797 income	3	64
Other income	23	64
BUSINESS INCOME	109	43
Nonfarm proprietor income	68	57
Farm income	6	72
Rents and royalties	6	51
Partnership, S-corp, estate and trust	13	18
OVERREPORTING OFFSETS TO INCOME	15	4
Adjustments	23	2.01
Deductions	14	5
Exemptions	4	5
CREDITS	17	26

SOURCE: Internal Revenue Service National Research Program.

reasonably honest and, indeed, to make tax compliance something that people other than suckers do. Table 9–6 shows the percentage of returns that were examined (audited) by the IRS for returns filed in calendar 2009; overall, fewer than one in one hundred returns was audited. Unless your income was high or you operated a business or received an earned income tax credit, the odds that your return would be audited were awfully small. Even if your return fell into a high audit category, your chances were still rather small. Large corporations were much more likely to get a visit from the IRS, and the largest were absolutely certain to be examined. However, given the modest examination percentages, it is obviously clear that the IRS needs to allocate its examination resources cleverly if it is to adequately police the income tax system.

Table 9–6
Audit Coverage by the Internal Revenue Service by Type of Return (Returns Filed Calendar 2009)

	Returns Filed	Returns Examined	Percentage Covered
United States, total	187,124,450	1,735,083	0.9
Taxable returns:			
Individual income tax returns, total	142,823,105	1,581,394	1.1
Returns with TPI under $200,000:			
Nonbusiness returns without Earned Income Tax Credit:			
Without Schedules C, E, F, or Form 2106	80,254,935	363,424	0.5
With Schedule E or Form 2106	16,052,553	190,746	1.2
Business returns without Earned Income Tax Credit:			
Nonfarm business returns by size of TGR:			
Under $25,000	10,736,434	132,584	1.2
$25,000 under $100,000	3,136,694	79,389	2.5
$100,000 under $200,000	893,707	42,403	4.7
$200,000 or more	705,877	23,569	3.3
Farm returns	1,367,656	4,921	0.4
Business and nonbusiness returns with Earned Income Tax Credit by size of TGR:			
Under $25,000	22,910,578	556,809	2.4
$25,000 or more	1,591,972	28,393	1.8
Returns with TPI of at least $200,000 and under $1,000,000:			
Nonbusiness returns	3,109,116	78,859	2.5
Business returns	1,432,541	41,622	2.9
Returns with TPI of $1,000,000 or more	388,763	32,494	8.4
International returns	242,279	6,181	2.6
Corporation income tax returns, except Form 1120–S, total	2,143,808	29,803	1.4
Returns other than Forms 1120–C and 1120–F:			
Small corporations	2,041,474	19,127	0.9
No balance sheet returns	453,583	2,016	0.4
Balance sheet returns by size of total assets:			
Under $250,000	1,031,229	8,423	0.8
$250,000 under $1,000,000	351,196	4,783	1.4
$1,000,000 under $5,000,000	175,221	3,011	1.7
$5,000,000 under $10,000,000	30,245	894	3.0
Large corporations	61,570	10,207	16.6
Balance sheet returns by size of total assets:			
$10,000,000 under $50,000,000	32,107	4,307	13.4
$50,000,000 under $100,000,000	7,756	1,259	16.2

(continues)

Table 9–6
(continued)

	Returns Filed	Returns Examined	Percentage Covered
$100,000,000 under $250,000,000	8,094	1,191	14.7
$250,000,000 under $500,000,000	4,688	754	16.1
$500,000,000 under $1,000,000,000	3,396	615	18.1
$1,000,000,000 under $5,000,000,000	3,943	1,127	28.6
$5,000,000,000 under $20,000,000,000	1,139	516	45.3
$20,000,000,000 or more	447	438	98.0
Estate tax returns:			
Total	42,366	4,288	10.1
Size of gross estate:			
Under $5,000,000	33,803	2,206	6.5
$5,000,000 under $10,000,000	5,550	1,154	20.8
$10,000,000 or more	3,013	928	30.8
Excise tax returns	783,926	18,249	2.3

SOURCE: Internal Revenue Service, *Data Book 2010* (Washington, D.C.: Internal Revenue Service, 2011).

NOTE: Form 2106 is used to report employee business expenses. TGR, total gross receipts; TPI, taxpayer positive income.

Corporate Income Taxation

The corporation net income tax applies to the net earnings of incorporated businesses, following the theory that the legal person created by incorporation creates an economic entity with tax-bearing capacity separate from the owners (shareholders) of that business.[41] The tax applies to total corporate profit as defined by the accounting system and the tax law, including both earnings retained by the firm and those paid in dividends to the stockholder. Although the tax lacks the personal exemptions and deductions found in the individual tax, it does allow deductions for charitable contributions (to encourage corporate generosity) and for ordinary and necessary costs of operating the business, including recovery of capital expenditure. Because the individual income tax encompasses dividends in its tax base, dividends could be taxed at both the individual and the corporate levels. That means that the U.S. tax system treats corporations and their investors as separate entities and causes an extra tax burden on distributed, as opposed to retained, profits. It puts an extra burden

---

[41]Business income is not the same thing as corporate income. Many businesses, including many that are highly profitable, are not legally organized as corporations. These other businesses, such as sole proprietorships and partnerships, pay tax through the individual income tax structure. Also, certain corporations, because of the manner in which they are organized, are treated by the tax system like partnerships. All these are "pass-through" entities: their income is not taxed at the business level, but is "passed through" to the owners of the business for taxation on their individual returns. As might be expected, these entities are a popular way for organizing businesses.

on income from capital and discriminates against the ordinary corporate form of business organization. This has meant a considerable secular decline in the use of the ordinary corporate form for doing business. Ordinary corporate tax returns constituted 12.5 percent of all business tax returns in 1978 and fell to only 5.4 percent of the total in 2009—the number of regular corporations was virtually unchanged over those years, while the total number of businesses more than doubled. Over that same period, the number of multiple-owner businesses that have income taxed only at the individual level, not at the business level, more than tripled.[42]

The federal corporate income tax rate is 35 percent on income over $18.3 million. There are lower rates (starting at 15 percent) provided as a concession to small enterprises, and there is a "bubble rate" of 38 percent to recover the advantage of the lower bracket rates from more profitable corporations, but most taxable corporate income hits the highest rate. This rate is currently the highest statutory corporate income tax rate in the world—certainly not helpful for U.S. economic development—although the effective tax rate is far less because of many deductions and credits provided our corporations. Reducing special interest preferences, themselves certainly causing economic distortions, would allow a lower statutory tax rate without sacrifice of corporate tax revenue.

The corporate tax base is the profit of the corporation—its revenues received less its costs of doing business. While there are some issues involving operating costs that will be deducted (for instance, is the rental of the skybox at the NFL stadium an ordinary and necessary business expense and hence deducted, or should it be considered a use of the enterprise's profits?), really sticky questions come from the effort to properly deal with the cost of acquiring capital assets, those big-ticket, long-life assets discussed in a previous chapter, but this time being purchased by business and not government. The problem for defining profit in a particular year requires some formula for translating the purchase price of long-life capital equipment and structures, occurring in a lump in one year, into cost for the particular years of the productive life of that asset. The cost of the infrastructure is part of the cost of making the product, but how much of the large cost incurred when the infrastructure is purchased ought to be assigned to (or recovered in) any particular year?

Ideally, the depreciation schedule should provide a "deduction profile over time that mimics the profile of the asset's true economic depreciation."[43] As the asset wears out, a comparable chunk of its purchase price would be subtracted from what would otherwise be profit of the firm. Because there is no administratively feasible way to track actual depreciation for every asset, tax systems adopt arbitrary depreciation rules that define the useful life of broad asset classes and the speed with which the purchase price of the asset can be recovered over that life. Many recovery schemes are possible, but one common rule is *straight-line,* a method under which an equal portion of cost is recovered in each year of the asset's estimated life. Thus, if the asset life is ten years, then 10 percent of asset cost is deductible each year. Other systems

[42]Staff of Joint Committee on Taxation, "Tax Reform: Selected Federal Tax Issues Relating to Small Business and Choice of Entity," Scheduled for a Public Hearing before the Senate Committee on Finance on June 5, 2008 (JCX-48-08); and *Statistics of Income Bulletin.*

[43]Dale Chua, "Depreciation Schedules," in *Tax Policy Handbook,* ed. Parthasarathi Shome (Washington, D.C.: International Monetary Fund, 1995), 136.

allow faster recovery of cost (*accelerated depreciation*), that is, larger deductions in early years of life and smaller deductions in later years. Fastest of all would be to allow expensing, in which all the cost is deducted in the year of purchase. Faster depreciation is often proposed as a means for increasing capital investment and, hence, economic growth. Whatever the system, however, the depreciation rules, along with decisions about what will be considered ordinary and necessary business expense, are critical for determining the profit to be taxed. In order to spur economic activity, most machinery and equipment can be expensed at the time of purchase.

One other complication: Suppose you work for a nonprofit organization. This discussion about corporate income taxation would seem pretty much irrelevant. But wait. It would be unfair and potentially inefficient for entities to have tax advantages over similar service providers simply because of the way in which the entity is organized (i.e., proprietary versus nonprofit). Therefore, we have the Unrelated Business Income Tax, or UBIT, and that tax is discussed in Sidebar 9–4.

Dividing the Profit Base Among Governments

Also critical for taxing the profits of international businesses that have operations in many countries is the price that a part of the business in one country charges for supplies, services, or inventory sold to a part of the business in another. An artificially high price paid for sales to the U.S. operation will cause understated U.S. profit, and,

---

Sidebar 9–4
Unrelated Business Income Tax

Nonprofit organizations enjoy a special relationship with the federal tax system: their income is exempt from tax. They do not pay income tax on flows that would be fully taxable if received by an entity organized otherwise. Most file an information return Form 990 with the Internal Revenue Service.

However, certain income earned by the nonprofit may be subject to the Unrelated Business Income Tax if that income is produced in an activity that is not related to the exempt mission of the organization. The tax, enacted in 1954, seeks to ensure that nonprofit organizations do not gain an unfair competitive advantage over proprietary firms in the same business. It is to create a "level playing field" when both proprietary and nonprofit entities happen to be in the same business. So will the Girl Scouts be subject to income tax on their cookie sales? Will the local Red Cross chapter be taxed on the proceeds of its annual book sale? Will the museum be subject to income tax on profits from sales in the museum shop? Will the nonprofit hospital be subject to income tax on profits from its operations? Will the shelter for battered women be subject to tax on its income from sales of food and lodging? As in many questions of taxation, the answer is "It depends."

Sidebar 9–4
(continued)

As a start, the organization must meet two requirements. First is the "nondistribution" constraint that "no part of the net earnings" of the organization can benefit any private individual or shareholder. Second is the rule that the organization may not engage in prohibited lobbying and political activities. But what about income that such an organization might earn? If it is related to the mission, no problem. But what if the income is unrelated to that mission? If so, then the exemption does not apply.

Income is considered to be unrelated if these three conditions hold:

1. The activity is undertaken as a trade or business, generally meaning that the activity is carried out to produce income by sale of goods or services.
2. The activity is undertaken on a regular basis, meaning the activity is carried out with the frequency and continuity of and in a manner comparable to commercial activities by nonexempt entities. For instance, an ice cream stand operated by the Red Cross at a fall festival would be different from an ice cream shop operated by that entity in the same building as its offices.
3. The activity is not substantially related to the exempt mission of the organization, meaning the activity does not contribute significantly to accomplishing that mission. If the activity is conducted on a scale that is larger than reasonably appropriate to the exempt mission, it is suspect.

The fact that income generated by the commercial activity is used by the organization to support its exempt mission is not relevant.

Even if the three conditions hold, there is an exclusion if the income comes from volunteer labor or consists of dividends, interest, rents, and some capital gains.

Any taxable income would be taxed at ordinary corporate tax rates. Unrelated, profit-making activities are allowed, but if they consume too much of the nonprofit organization's attention, the tax authorities may conclude that the organization has abandoned its exempt purpose and revoke its exempt status. In tax year 2008, the UBIT yielded $336.6 million, with 42,066 returns filed. Individual and corporate income taxes yielded over $1.45 trillion in that year.[1]

State income tax systems typically follow the federal standards. However, there are distinct state systems for determining whether nonprofit organizations are exempt from retail sales or property taxes.

The IRS provides instructions and explanations in IRS Publication 598, *Tax on Unrelated Business Income of Exempt Organizations*. Reporting is on IRS Form 990-T.

[1]Jael Jackson, "Unrelated Business Income Tax Returns, 2008," *SOI Bulletin* 31 (Winter 2012): 131-155 ; and Office of Management and Budget, *Budget of the Government of the United States, Fiscal Year 2013, Historical Tables* (Washington, D.C.: U.S. Government Printing Office, 2012).

therefore, corporate profit tax paid in the United States will be artificially low. The profit will show up in the other country. Multinational firms are frequently accused of establishing internal prices in such a way that high profits appear only in countries with low corporate-profit taxes. Thus, *transfer-pricing rules* (the rules establishing what internal prices are allowed) are critical in establishing corporate liability. If the transfer price is high, profit is increased for the subsidiary where the shipment originates; if the transfer price is low, profit is increased for the subsidiary where the shipment ends up. The profit all ends up with the company owning the subsidiaries, but the total profit tax—part paid to the originating country and part paid to the destination country—differs depending on what the transfer prices are. There is evidence that multinational corporations do manage to report more of their profits where corporate tax rates are lower.[44]

Fairness of profit distribution suggests that the transfer prices should approximate the prices that would be charged in a transaction between unrelated companies, but that is not always simple to establish. An approach that is increasingly popular for multinational companies is the *advance pricing agreement*, in which the tax authority and the company agree on what pricing approach the company will employ in calculating its profits, thereby avoiding the danger that the approach will be disallowed on audit and thus bring fines and other sanctions. Unfortunately, such agreements are time consuming and may make the system a bit overly individualized in its application.

There is a comparable issue among the American states. Only Nevada, Ohio, South Dakota, Texas, Washington, and Wyoming do not currently have corporate income taxes roughly patterned after the federal tax, and the state taxes do create some special tax base distribution problems. The big complication is that corporations conduct business in more than one state (as well as in more than one country). What state gets to tax what profit? Some income may be clearly defined as originating from property or other assets in a single state, but much cannot be so identified. For instance, a particular corporation may have retail outlets in forty-five states, warehouses in nine states, and factories in two states. How much of that firm's profit should be taxable in any one state?

To handle the problem, each state with a corporate income tax has adopted its own income *apportionment* formula to determine how much of the total profit earned by a multistate corporation it will tax. States employ formulas that involve the share of total corporate sales in the state, the share of total corporate property in the state, and the share of total corporate payroll in the state. (Of course, the corporation must be conducting a minimum amount of business in the state in order to be taxable by the state; this contact is referred to as having *nexus* with the state.) One approach is

---

[44]When a U.S. corporation repatriates income from a foreign subsidiary it controls, it must pay a tax equal to the difference between the U.S. corporate tax rate and the rate applicable in the foreign country. For 2005, the American Jobs Creation Act of 2004 created a holiday during which repatriated profits would be taxed only at a rate of 5.25 percent. As would be expected, federal corporate-profit tax collections for 2005 increased dramatically as businesses took advantage of this one-shot window. More evidence that corporations use transfer pricing for tax avoidance: Eric J. Bartelsman and Roel M. W. J. Beetsma, "Why Pay More? Corporate Tax Avoidance through Transfer Pricing in OECD Countries," *Journal of Public Economics* 87 (2003): 2225–52. A higher corporate tax rate caused reported profits to flee the country, but not the corporation's operations.

the three-factor formula, in which the shares are equally weighted. With this formula, if state A has 50 percent of the firm's total property value, 25 percent of the firm's total payroll, and 60 percent of the firm's total sales, that state would apply its corporate tax rate to 45 percent [(50 + 25 + 60)/3] of the firm's total profit.[45] Other states use the same three factors, but give double weighting to the sales factor, whereas yet others use only sales in the formula.[46] States are migrating toward formulas that give greater emphasis to sales rather than to property or payroll in an effort to favor corporations with production facilities in their borders (having production facilities means property and employees, but does not bring an allocation of profit for state taxation if these factors are not in the apportionment formula). In other words, the attempt is to improve the competitive position of the state by shifting factors from those that reflect the origin of economic activity (payroll and property) to those that reflect the destination (sales). States see this change toward heavy weight on the sales share as part of their economic development effort.[47] There is no clearly correct formula for apportionment, of course, but having production facilities in a state certainly requires the state to deliver some services to the business. That is the logic behind having the non-sales factors in the formula. Because many states lack sufficient audit staff to verify the factors computed by all corporate filers, they must accept the calculations done by many corporations. This problem of profit apportionment makes local corporate income taxes extremely difficult in terms of compliance and enforcement.[48]

Integration with the Individual Tax

A major question is whether the structure and operation of the corporate income tax reduce the real income of the stockholders of the corporation, produce higher prices for the corporation's products, or cause the real income of labor and other resources

---

[45]This three-factor formula is frequently called the Massachusetts formula, although Massachusetts no longer uses it.

[46]The U.S. Supreme Court, in a case involving Moorman Manufacturing Company, upheld the Iowa formula that uses only sales. See "New Flexibility on Business Tax Granted State," *Wall Street Journal*, June 16, 1978. The problem was that, when states use a variety of differing apportionment formulas, an unlucky multistate business could find that it paid state corporate income tax on more than 100 percent of its total profits. And more lucky businesses could pay tax on less than 100 percent of their profits. Corporations do face inequitable treatment by states.

[47]Austan Goolsbee and Edward L. Maydew, "Coveting Thy Neighbor's Manufacturing: The Dilemma of State Income Apportionment," *Journal of Public Economics* 75 (2000): 125–43, measures the impact of the apportionment factor on manufacturing employment in a state.

[48]Businesses have another approach to minimizing state income tax. They establish a closely held company in a low-tax or no-tax jurisdiction that owns trademarks used by the business, and that company charges a royalty for the use of those trademarks. The royalty is high enough to capture most or all of the operating profits, eliminating the profit where it would be taxed and realizing it where it is barely taxed. Good deal for the business; not so good for the state. Another example: Wal-Mart stores are on property owned by a separate, but captive Wal-Mart real estate investment trust housed in a state not taxing rental income (like Delaware). Wal-Mart pays rent on the store property, reducing its taxable profit, and the proceeds show up in Delaware and aren't taxed by any state. Jesse Drucker, "Wal-Mart Cuts Taxes by Paying Rent to Itself," *Wall Street Journal*, February 1, 2007, A-1. Other companies do the same, and states fight by claiming that these are sham transactions.

used by the corporation to be lower. Neither theoretical nor empirical evidence is clear.[49] This uncertainty is troublesome because the corporate income tax is the third largest source of federal revenue, and that revenue would be difficult to replace from other sources.[50] Problems with the corporate income tax, however, must be considered. One is the fairness of burden distribution. If corporation stockholders bear the tax, why should dividend income be taxed more heavily than other income to the individual? Wages are taxed only once; why should dividends be taxed twice? Furthermore, because not all households within a particular income category receive dividend income, the special tax on corporate income—as translated through to stockholders—obviously violates the equal-treatment-of-equals rule for appropriate tax-burden distributions. The corporate income tax, however, does fill a gap: without it, the portion of corporate income not distributed would go untaxed.[51] In addition, the corporate income tax probably increases the progressivity of the system because dividend income tends to be more concentrated in higher-income groups. At the state level, the corporate income tax allows the state to extract compensation for benefits that the state provides to corporations whose owners may be largely out of state.

The major problem with the current corporate income tax, however, is its effects on savings and real investment. The corporate income tax probably constitutes a double tax on dividends and thus reduces the rate of savings, with undesirable effects on capital formation. Furthermore, it certainly influences choices by corporate executives between finance by debt (interest payments to bondholders are deductible) and finance by equity (dividend payments to shareholders are not deductible). It definitely has stimulated the creation of business forms that are something like regular corporations (particularly in regard to offering limited liability to their owners), but whose profits are taxable only to the owners and not at the business-entity level (the Subchapter S corporation and the limited liability company, for instance, are such "pass through" enities.). Those businesses have increased from around one-quarter of all American businesses in the mid-1980s to over 70 percent now. Those capital-formation effects add to the productivity problems of the nation, so some change might be appropriate.

Many of the undesirable economic and equity effects would be reduced if individual income and corporate income taxes were integrated either partially or completely to mitigate the extra tax the two systems place on distributed corporate profit. Complete integration would treat the corporation in the same way as partnerships. In other words, the tax would not apply to corporate income at all, but the owners of the corporation would be taxed according to their proportionate shares

---

[49]Most analysts believe the burden is distributed to capital, either generally or to the owners of the corporation, or to employees of the corporation (employees are less mobile than capital and thus are vulnerable to tax shifting). Shifting the burden through prices charged by the firm for its products is viewed as not likely.
[50]Revenue received by state governments from corporate income taxes has been in decline as a share of state taxes for many years. Part of the reason is clever corporate tax avoidance strategies, but part is state fear that having corporations pay for state services they use will cause the firms to move elsewhere.
[51]It may increase the market value of corporate stock and create capital gain income when the stock is sold.

of dividends and retained earnings. If Fred and Jack are partners and their business agreement is that Fred owns 30 percent of the business, then Fred would pay individual income tax on 30 percent of profits, Jack would pay individual income tax on 70 percent of profits, and that would be that. This treatment would eliminate the traditional difficulties with the corporate income tax, but it would create some additional sticky issues.[52]

1. The tax would apply to income not distributed. Individuals would be taxed according to income received as dividends and on income that the corporation retains. There is some question whether this would encourage greater corporate payout of earnings and thus might even lower the rate of real investment.

2. Many holders of corporate stock are tax-exempt entities (e.g., pension funds). Under this integrated structure, those entities would not pay individual income tax on their dividends and retained earnings, and there would be no collection of tax at the corporate level either. How could that revenue loss be replaced?

3. Sizable amounts of U.S. stocks are held by foreign entities. How would that income be treated? What country would be entitled to tax those U.S. dividends and retained earnings? If not the United States, how would that federal revenue loss be made up?

4. Corporations do not have single classes of stock. Corporations frequently have common stock, preferred stock, and possibly other varieties of equity ownership representations. How would corporate income be divided equitably among those various classes of stock?

The alternate approach is partial integration. Partial integration would provide relief only on the share of corporate earnings that are distributed as dividends, either by giving some special credit to dividend recipients to account for the corporate income tax already paid on the flow or by applying the corporate income tax only to undistributed corporate profit. That relief would cut tax collections substantially, and there is the fear that it would appear to be an unwarranted tax break for business. Those two factors have kept interest in such reform low, although there is a revival in connection with the relatively slow growth rate of the U.S. economy and the slow rate of capital formation that has worked to produce that slow growth.[53]

---

[52]R. Glenn Hubbard, "Corporate Tax Integration: A View from the Treasury Department," *Journal of Economic Perspectives* 7 (Winter 1993): 115–32.

[53]Countries of the Organization for Economic Cooperation and Development (OECD) follow several different schemes for mitigating the extra tax. Some eliminate the extra tax at the corporate level by full deduction of dividends paid at the corporate level (Greece and Norway), and some eliminate it at the individual level by giving full credit for tax paid by the corporation (Australia, Finland, Germany [partial], Italy, New Zealand). Others reduce the extra tax by lower rates on distributed profits, partial deduction of dividends paid, or partial credit for corporate tax on dividends received (Germany [partial], Iceland, Spain, Sweden, France, Ireland, United Kingdom, Austria, Denmark, Japan, Portugal). Belgium, Luxembourg, the Netherlands, Switzerland, and the United States do not provide accommodation.

Payroll Taxation

Besides the broad-based individual and corporate income taxes, there are narrow taxes on payrolls or wage and salary income alone, levied on either the employer or the employee.[54] Because they are collected from the employer, they are easier to enforce than are broader taxes based on filings by income recipients. These taxes include those levied by the federal government on employers and employees for the support of the Social Security system and Medicare, those levied by federal and state governments on employers to support the unemployment compensation system, and earned-income taxes levied on employee wages and salaries by some local governments.[55] Most believe the real burden of these taxes, regardless of legal impact, is largely on the employee. When labor markets permit, employers simply adjust their compensation packages to account for the payroll tax for which they know they will be liable. About two-thirds of the American population pay more federal payroll tax than they do federal individual income tax.

The payroll taxes have several peculiarities. First, they are narrow and exclude types of income more likely to be received by higher-income individuals, including interest, dividends, capital gains, and so on. That exclusion increases the likelihood that the tax will treat low-income people more harshly than high-income people. Moreover, people with roughly the same income would pay different amounts of tax according to the kinds of income. Therefore, these are both vertical and horizontal equity questions.

Second, the federal and state payroll taxes for the social insurance system have unusual statutory rate patterns. Taxability begins with the first dollar earned, and, except for the Medicare tax, the tax rate falls to zero on income above some maximum level earned in the year. That means the marginal rate structure is graduated downward, and, for individuals above the maximum, the average rate falls as income rises. Because the tax applies with the first dollar earned, the payroll tax burden is more than that of the individual income tax for many low-income workers. For 2011, the federal tax supporting Social Security applied at a rate of 6.20 percent on the employee and 6.20 percent on the employer, but only the first $106,800 of earnings were taxed. The rate supporting Medicare is 1.45 percent on both employer and employee, and there is no limit on the base. Therefore, the tax paid for a person earning $10,000 would be $1,530 (15.3 percent of total pay), whereas the tax paid by a person earning $150,000 would be $17,593.20 ($13,243.20 for Social Security—12.4 percent of the maximum taxable wage base of $106,800—plus $4,350 for Medicare—the 2.9 percent rate applied to the full $150,000). The average rate on earnings is 11.7 percent for the higher-income person and 15.3 percent for the lower-income person. As earnings increase, the average rate decreases even more.[56]

The payroll tax financing the unemployment compensation system has federal and state components. The federal tax rate is 6.2 percent on earnings to $7,000, paid

---

[54]Payroll taxes are also common in other countries.

[55]A good overview of the social insurance taxes appears in Committee on Ways and Means, U.S. House of Representatives, *Green Book, Background Material and Data on the Programs within the Jurisdiction of the Committee on Ways and Means* (Washington, D.C.: U.S. Government Printing Office). The 2011 version is available on the internet: http://greenbook.waysandmeans.house.gov/.

[56]For economic stimulation purposes in the Great Recession, the payroll tax rate was reduced from its normal level. The tax would return to its normal level at the end of 2012.

by the employer. However, if a state has an approved unemployment compensation system (and all 50 do), then up to 5.4 percent of the state rate is a full credit against the federal liability, leaving a net federal rate of 0.8 percent. States may have a taxable wage base higher than the federal limit (41 do). States also can levy rates on employers that differ from the 5.4 percent standard based on the unemployment experience rating of the firm: those with fewer layoffs pay lower tax than do those with more layoffs.[57] The idea is to encourage employers to stabilize their labor force, while financing the unemployment compensation system.

Finally, the federal and state payroll taxes are all earmarked. That is, their revenues are dedicated to finance only particular social insurance benefits. Because these benefits tend to be more valuable to lower-income individuals, the public generally accepts the unusual features of these taxes that make their burdens regressive. Nevertheless, they do contribute to labor market incentive effects by adding to the wedge between what employers pay and what employees retain. Any surpluses in these funds are invested in U.S. government bonds, thus helping support those markets.

Conclusion

The income tax has been the heart of the federal revenue system from the early years of the twentieth century, providing sizable revenue for global responsibilities and domestic programs. For more than sixty years, the individual income tax has been the dominant source, although the payroll taxes for social insurance have become almost as significant in overall finance. Corporate income taxes now play only a small role in finances. Individual income taxes also make a major contribution to the finances of state governments. While achieving progressivity, the income taxes do have problems of economic inefficiency, horizontal inequity, expensive collection, and failure of transparency. Corporate and payroll taxes raise considerable revenue, but they offer difficult challenges of equity and efficiency. There are enough preferences inserted in the income tax system to raise the belief that lawmakers have lost sight of the fact that the fundamental purpose of the system is to raise money to support government operations.

QUESTIONS AND EXERCISES

1. Identify the important elements of the income tax in your state. Does your state levy individual and corporate income taxes; do local governments levy such income taxes and, if so, are they linked to the state taxes; are the state income taxes linked to the federal income taxes; are the rates graduated; are there preferences in the state taxes that are not also in the federal taxes; and are the state taxes indexed?

---

[57]Rates can range from zero (sixteen states) up to 10 percent (three states). Three states also tax the employee. A number of state unemployment compensation funds ran out of money during the recession that started in December 2007 and were forced to borrow from the federal government to maintain benefit payments.

2. A midwestern state aids its institutions of higher education by giving a credit against its income tax equal to 50 percent of any gift to such institutions (subject to a limit of $50 credit per person). Two residents of that state, Mr. Blue (in the 10 percent federal tax bracket) and Ms. Jones (in the 35 percent federal tax bracket), each contribute $100 to an eligible state university.

   a. How much will the state tax liabilities of each change as a result of their gifts?
   b. State income tax payments and contributions to charitable organizations (such as universities) are both currently deductible from the base used to compute federal tax liability. How much will federal tax liability change for Mr. Blue and Ms. Jones as a result of their contributions?
   c. Considering changes in both federal and state tax liabilities, what is the net after-tax cost of Mr. Blue's and Ms. Jones's gifts? (*Hint:* Subtract the changes in state and federal liabilities from $100.)
   d. Suppose the state program changed from a credit to a deduction. If the state tax rate was a flat 3 percent, how much would state liability for Mr. Blue and Ms. Jones change?
   e. From the previous computations, which approach (credit or deduction) do you suppose universities in the state would favor? Why?

3. Mr. Brown is in the 10 percent federal income tax bracket and wants to invest $10,000 in interest-earning assets. Mr. Black is in the 35 percent bracket and wants to invest $15,000. The current rate on a typical high-quality tax-exempt municipal bond is 3.5 percent and on a high-quality corporate bond is 4 percent. You are the financial advisor to both. Which investment would you recommend to each individual?

4. Ms. Busch has gathered these data about her finances:

Salary	140,000
Taxable interest received	2,500
Municipal bond interest received	15,000
Total itemized deductions	8,000

   The personal exemption is $3,700. The standard deduction for a single filer is $5,800. Use the rate schedule in Figure 9–2 to compute the following:

   a. Her tax
   b. Her average effective tax rate
   c. Her average tax rate
   d. Her marginal tax rate
   e. Her accountant discovers a previously omitted personal deduction of $800. By how much does her federal tax liability fall with that addition?
   f. Amazingly enough, the accountant now discovers a $250 credit omitted from previous calculations (but after discovering the $800 in part e). By how much does her federal tax liability fall because of this credit?

5. A proposed state income tax would require individuals with incomes of $15,000 or less to pay no tax and those with incomes above $15,000 to pay a tax of 10 percent only on the part of their income that exceeds $15,000.

a. Could an individual pay an average tax rate of 7.5 percent under this system?
b. Could an individual pay an average tax rate of 10 percent under this system?
c. What average and marginal tax rates would individuals with these income levels face: $10,000, $20,000, $40,000, and $150,000?

Explain each of your answers and provide examples to justify your conclusions.

6. The Ukrainian tax system in the late 1990s had several components. The personal income tax (calculated and paid on a monthly basis) had these brackets:

Zero	if income was below one NTM
10%	for income from 1 NTM + 1 KBV to 5 NTM
20%	for income from 5 NTM + 1 KBV to 10 NTM, plus the tax on 5 NTM
30%	for income from 10 NTM + 1 KBV to 15 NTM, plus the tax on 10 NTM
40%	for income from 15 NTM + 1 KBV to 25 NTM, plus the tax on 15 NTM
50%	for income above 25 NTM, plus the tax on 25 NTM

KBV, karbovantsi; NTM, non-taxed minimum.

The NTM was 1,400,000 KBV (one U.S. dollar was worth about 180,000 Ukrainian KBV). In September 1995, the average monthly salary was 9 million KBV. Use of the NTM provides an easy way of adjusting the entire tax structure for the impact of inflation.

Employers paid payroll taxes at these rates: 37 percent to the social insurance fund, 12 percent to the Chernobyl fund, and 2 percent to the employment fund. Employees also paid 1 percent to the employment fund.

a. Create a tax rate schedule like that in Figure 9–2 for the Ukraine personal income tax.
b. Create a tax table like that in Figure 9–3 for incomes from 9,100,000 KBV to 9,100,200 KBV.
c. Analysts calculate the tax wedge—defined to be the difference between the amount that the employer must pay to hire an employee and the amount that the employee receives net of all taxes as a percentage of the employee's net—in examining the nature of tax systems. Compute the total tax wedge for a worker at the average monthly salary, at twice the average, and at five times the average.
d. Compute the average effective tax rate and the marginal tax rate for a worker at the three salary levels from part c.
e. Comment on the likely incentive effects of this tax structure.

7. The Bartonia Company manufactures grommets in Georgia and sells them directly to industrial customers in Georgia, Florida, and South Carolina. The company's profit for last year was $20,000,000. The company has its manufacturing plant and headquarters in Georgia, warehouses in South Carolina and Florida, and sales forces in each state. Here are some of its financial statistics:

	Payroll	Property	Sales
Georgia	5,000,000	35,000,000	6,000,000
South Carolina	1,000,000	5,000,000	13,000,000
Florida	500,000	400,000	1,000,000
TOTAL	6,500,000	40,400,000	20,000,000

    a. Suppose each state uses a simple three-factor apportionment formula. What share of company profit would each state tax?

    b. Make that same calculation, but suppose each state double-weights the sales factor.

    c. Make the calculation with each using only the sales factor.

    d. Assume now that Georgia adopts the single sales factor and the other states use double-weighted sales.

    e. Assume now that South Carolina adopts the single sales factor and the other states use double-weighted sales.

    f. Explain why manufacturing firms in some states have pressed for use of the single sales factor. Why have nationwide business organizations not made this switch an issue?

8. Warren Buffett, one of the richest men in the United States and the head of Berkshire Hathaway Corporation, a profitable investment company, complained in 2007 that he was paying a smaller percentage of his income in federal taxes (17.7 percent) than was the receptionist in his office (about 30 percent). Assuming that he was not cheating on his taxes, what factors might account for this situation? Does this information by itself suggest that the federal tax system is regressive?

9. The Georgia state income tax uses adjusted gross income as reported on the federal tax return as the starting point for calculation of its tax liability. The North Carolina tax uses federal taxable income as its starting point. What are the implications of these two different starting points?

CASE FOR DISCUSSION

CASE 9–1

When Marginal Tax Rates Were Really Extreme

Raintree County brought its author fame, fortune, and serious tax liability. The serious novel was 1,066 pages long and full of betrayal, sex, and deviousness and seemed to put its author, Ross Lockridge, Jr., on pace to be the next great American novelist. It was well received by reviewers and was a hit with the public. But the success of the novel brought tax consequences and other problems that sadly brought Lockridge's suicide before he fulfilled his apparent potential. The following article takes you through the tax problems that were endemic in the system of that time.

SOURCE: *Tax Notes*, August 4, 2008, with minor editorial changes. Copyright © 2008 by J. Fred Giertz. Reprinted with permission.

Consider These Questions

1. Use the case to explain why tax analysts worry about marginal rates, not average rates, in looking for incentive effects of taxes.

2. Explain the relevance of this case for discussions about revisions of the federal income tax system.

3. Explain how some changes in the tax system would have made Lockridge's tax problem somewhat less now than in the 1940s.

Taxes in the Shade of the Raintree By J. Fred Giertz

J. Fred Giertz is a professor of economics at the University of Illinois at Urbana-Champaign.
An earlier version of this article appeared in the NTA newsletter *NTA Network*, June 2008.
Copyright 2008 J. Fred Giertz.
All rights reserved.

Some critics assert that the U.S. individual income tax in its current form has never been more intrusive or complex. However, an obscure circumstance that arose 60 years ago suggests otherwise.

In early 1948, Bloomington, Ind., was the focus of the literary world. The book *Sexual Behavior in the Human Male* by Indiana University Prof. Alfred Kinsey was a national sensation, rising to number one on the *New York Times* nonfiction bestseller list. During the same period, the novel *Raintree County* by Bloomington native Ross Lockridge Jr. also reached the top of the *Times* fiction list.

Today *Raintree County* is likely remembered as the flawed 1957 film starring Montgomery Clift and Elizabeth Taylor. The movie was loosely based on the Lockridge novel that tells a complex story of an Indiana native (based on a Lockridge ancestor) from mythical Raintree County (Henry County, Ind.) through flashbacks that occur on a single day on July 4, 1892. It was a serious novel that was also a popular success despite its over 1,000-page length. It has been hailed as a failed but valiant attempt at the illusive "great American novel" and is now considered an important work in environ mental fiction, becoming a staple in American studies courses.

Lockridge was not the stereotypical dissolute, self-indulgent artist. He was handsome and well-liked and an accomplished scholar and athlete who was devoted to his wife and family.[58] After excelling in his junior year at the Sorbonne, he graduated in 1935 with the highest average in the history of Indiana University. He eventually went on to Harvard University to study for a Ph.D. in English. As a graduate student at Harvard and a teacher at Simmons College,

---

[58]Much of the information about Lockridge comes from the biography written by his son Larry Lockridge: *Shade of the Raintree: The Life and Death of Ross Lockridge, Jr., Author of Raintree County.* New York: Viking Penguin, 1994.

a woman's college in Boston, he wrote the monumental *Raintree County* while supporting his wife and four young children.

Unlike many writers, he was also well informed about business and tax matters. After years spent writing the book and enduring a painful editorial process, the book became a literary and financial success. In addition to the normal royalties from the Houghton Mifflin publishing house, the book won an MGM prize of $150,000 (with $125,000 to Lockridge and $25,000 to the publisher) for the screen rights and became a Book of the Month Club choice, generating an additional $25,000. These values can be multiplied by 10 to provide an estimate of their purchasing power in 2008 dollars.

Lockridge went from an unknown, struggling former graduate student and teacher to a rich and famous author almost overnight. By March 1948 *Raintree County* had become the number one fiction bestseller. On March 6 Lockridge completed and mailed his wife's income tax return, wrote a detailed letter to his lawyer dealing with his own tax matters, and being a true Hoosier, made plans to listen to the radio broadcast of a Bloomington High School regional basketball game.

Later that night, he was found dead in his garage from carbon monoxide poisoning—a suicide victim at age 33. It is now known that he was severely depressed and suffered from anxiety. This problem was not well diagnosed 60 years ago and even less well treated. Clearly his suicide was the result of his depression, but in the last year of his life, his distress focused on both artistic and business problems, including taxes.

In the artistic arena, Lockridge found the editing and especially the cutting of his work very painful. The demands of the MGM prize and the Book of the Month Club selection led to the need for cuts of up to 100,000 words in what he thought was the final version. As with most authors, he was also concerned about the reception of his novel, believing that his work was not being reviewed fairly by many critics.

On the business front, Lockridge became unhappy with Houghton Mifflin, where some smaller disputes and misunderstandings eventually soured the overall rela tionship. He operated without a literary agent, so many issues that might have been handled at arm's length became the source of personal bitterness. Within this context, taxes also played a major role.

As a person knowledgeable about business affairs, he was also familiar with taxation issues. In 1947 the U.S. income tax was highly progressive with extremely high marginal rates.[59] There were 24 brackets, with marginal rates ranging from 19 percent to 86.45 percent—the highest rate applying to taxable income over $200,000. Also, there was no income splitting available for families before 1948—one year too late for Lockridge and his wife. All taxpayers had to file single returns. Moreover, there was no explicit forward or backward

---

[59]For more detail, see Joseph Pechman, *Federal Tax Policy*, Washington, D.C.: Brookings Institution, 1987.

averaging. Income averaging made an appearance in the U.S. in come tax laws from 1964 to 1986, but it did not exist in 1947.

Realizing this, Lockridge made an unusual demand when his manuscript was submitted for the MGM prize. He wanted the proceeds of the prize to be paid over several years, not in a lump sum. He believed that this condition had been accepted at the time of submission. When he won the prize, his joy was dampened when he learned that prize was to be paid in one payment in 1947. He was bitterly disappointed about this and felt betrayed by his publisher and MGM.

This was not an inconsequential concern. Arguments for income averaging are usually based on stories similar to Lockridge's situation—a period of long gestation with little or no pay followed by a large lump sum payout. Using the tax tables for 1947, $125,000 of taxable income generated a tax liability of $85,092 for an average tax rate of 68.1 percent and a marginal rate of 84.55 percent.[60] A five-year distribution of $25,000 (or five-year averaging) would have generated a total tax bill (present value considerations aside) of $48,213 with a 38.6 percent average and 56.05 percent marginal rates.

Income splitting with joint returns was introduced in 1948. If full income splitting and a five-year distribution of the $125,000 had been available, the total tax bill would have fallen to $34,343 with a 27.5 percent average and 40.85 percent marginal rate. The overall difference be tween the tax on the lump sum payment and a five-year distribution with income splitting amounts to $50,749, with the lump sum tax 2.5 times the amount of the smaller tax bill.

Lockridge was deeply troubled that taxes had seri ously eroded a payment (well over $1 million in today's dollars) for the best work he might ever produce that could have provided long-term security for him and his family. He spent more than five years working on the book and in 1948 had nothing in the pipe-line for future publication. It should be noted that he and his wife did not object to the welfare state and the resultant high levels of taxation. They were ardent supporters of Franklin Roosevelt and were even against Indiana native Wendell Willkie in the 1940 election. Lockridge was not upset with high taxes in general, but he was unhappy with their impact and perceived unfairness on people in his particular situation.

His problems illustrate the effects of high marginal rates with extreme progressivity.[61] Some of these prob lems were eventually dealt with explicitly through in come splitting and averaging provisions in the tax law and ultimately by lowering marginal rates and reducing the number of brackets.

In addition to attempting to spread his income over a longer period, Lockridge also devised an ad hoc splitting arrangement. Lockridge paid his wife,

---

[60]These tax calculations should be viewed as illustrative in that detailed information about Lockridge's actual situation is not available. In addition to inflation, these results are also not directly comparable to rates today because of differences in the tax base and the availability of avoidance opportunities.
[61]Heavyweight boxing champion Joe Louis was another casualty of this high marginal tax rate era. Bad business advice along with disallowed charitable contributions from the dona tion of fight purses during World War II resulted in a crushing tax bill and interest charges that wrecked his career.

Vernice, $25,000 for her assistance in writing *Raintree County*, which transferred income from his 84.55 marginal rate to her still high 56.05 marginal rate (and a 39 percent average rate). On the day of his death, he was still concerned about how the IRS might view this payment and went to some length to justify the arrangement in a letter to his attorney. He also made deductible charitable contributions to the Indiana University Foundation for an account that would be used by his father, who was active in promoting Indiana history and culture.

No one should conclude that taxes drove Ross Lockridge, Jr. to suicide. However, tax concerns were a source of his distress that was magnified by his depression. This also shows that even with all of its defects and problems, the income tax today could be worse and actually was much worse in the past. Think about how intrusive and disruptive the income tax would be today with marginal rates reaching 50 percent at less than $200,000 in 2008 dollars and over 84 percent at $1 million with brackets not indexed for inflation and without income splitting and tax deferred saving options. We may not live in the best of all tax worlds, but we do not live in the worst either.

CHAPTER 10

Major Tax Structures: Taxes on Goods and Services

Governments in the United States collected more than $539.8 billion from taxes levied on goods and services in 2010.[1] Of that amount, federal excises and customs duties (taxes on imports) yielded $101.5 billion—far behind the collections from individual income, Social Security payroll, and corporate income taxes. State and local sales and excise taxes generated $438.3 billion, in total the most significant base for these governments. As pointed out in an earlier chapter, however, American reliance on goods and services levies (the consumption base) overall is less than that in most industrialized democracies.

Taxes on goods and services have several desirable features as a part of a revenue system. First, they can provide considerable revenue when they apply to a broad base, thus allowing diversification from other tax bases. A range of alternative tax bases can be important because heavy use of any tax is likely to bring out all of its worst efficiency, equity, and collectability problems. Most developed nations have lower reliance on the income base than does the United States because they levy broad-base taxes on consumption. Second, the consumption taxes provide a means for extracting payment from individuals with high economic capacity and low current income, including those who have successfully evaded the income tax or are living off of inherited wealth. If the income tax cheat enjoys an elegant lifestyle with purchases from honest vendors, some tax is collected when purchases are made. This can be particularly important in developing countries. Third, some taxes on goods and services may function as quasi-prices to collect for social costs or to act as surrogates for charges for certain government services. Finally, some argue that consumption taxes can have important desirable production effects because they tax according to what people take from the economy (consumption), not according to what of value they add to the economy (income), and because they encourage saving. Indeed, consumption taxes distribute the cost of government according to the

---

[1]Bureau of Economic Analysis, National Income and Product Accounts [www.bea.gov].

individual's own assessment of what private goods and services he or she can afford to purchase. That's how the cost of producing private goods gets distributed, after all, so why shouldn't the same distribution concept apply to the cost of government services as well?

Goods and services taxes may be general or selective, specific or ad valorem, single stage or multistage, for general or earmarked purposes, and legally applied to the buyer or the seller; all these varieties appear in the slate of goods and services taxes that governments now levy. Before considering the taxes in detail and the special issues each may involve, here is a quick summary of some structural distinctions:

1. **General or selective.** A general sales tax applies to all transactions at a level of economic activity, except for certain listed exemptions (e.g., a sales tax applied to all sales at retail except those of food). A selective sales tax (commonly called an excise tax) applies only to enumerated transactions (e.g., a lodging tax applied to room rentals for thirty days or less).
2. **Specific or ad valorem.** A specific tax (or unit tax) applies only to the number of physical units bought or sold (e.g., a motor-fuel tax might be fifty cents per gallon of fuel). An ad valorem tax applies to the value (number of units times price per unit) of the transaction (e.g., a lodging tax of 10 percent of the hotel bill).
3. **Multistage or single stage.** A tax may apply every time a transaction occurs (multistage tax) or only at one stage in the production-and-distribution process (single-stage tax). The taxed stage may be at the manufacturer level, at the wholesaler or distributor level, or at the retail level. A multistage tax would apply at more than one point of exchange.[2]
4. **General fund or earmarked.** Excise taxes often are earmarked to special funds for expenditure only on specific purposes as opposed to being collected for the general purposes of government. For example, most motor-fuel tax revenue collected by American states goes into special funds for highway-associated expenditure. Unfortunately, such fund earmarking creates rigidity in the budget process, and revenue flows into these funds may not reflect need for public services.[3] Only if revenue going to the fund reflects demand for the

---

[2]Governments have occasionally levied gross receipts (turnover) taxes that apply at a low statutory rate on all business activities, and such taxes are sometimes still proposed. These are particularly obnoxious taxes because they violate several aspects of normal tax policy. They have burden distributions roughly like those of retail sales taxes, but because of their pyramiding nature (discussed later in this chapter), they discriminate across types of businesses and place prospective burden on the least profitable ones, harm the economic competitiveness of the jurisdiction that makes the mistake of levying them, distort the nature of business transactions in the state, violate transparency by hiding and significantly understating their actual effective rate (probably why some states have recently considered them), and are grossly inequitable. Their "charms" are more fully explored in John L. Mikesell, "State Gross Receipts Taxes and the Fundamental Principles of Tax Policy," *State Tax Notes* 43 (March 5, 2007): 615–32; and Charles E. McLure, Jr., "Why Ohio Should Not Introduce a Gross Receipts Tax–Testimony on the Proposed Commercial Activity Tax," *State Tax Notes* 36 (April 18, 2005): 213–15. Ohio ignored his wise advice and passed the tax anyway. Experience with gross receipts taxes in West Virginia and Indiana and in Western Europe before the implementation of value-added taxes amply demonstrates the difficulties associated with these taxes.

[3]The revenues may also simply substitute for other government resources that would have been provided even without the dedicated tax. Because revenues are fungible, it is difficult to ensure that money supports only the dedicated purpose.

service financed by the fund does earmarking make a positive contribution. That can happen when purchase of the taxed item is complementary to use of the government service, that is, when there is a close relationship between purchase of the taxed item and consumption of the government service.

Tables 10–1 and 10–2 present an overview of general and selective goods and services tax collections received by federal, state, and local governments. In the tables, the selective excises are divided into four main groups: (1) sumptuary excises applied "to control the consumption of items that are considered immoral or unhealthy,"[4] (2) transport excises potentially defensible as proxy service charges for transportation facilities, (3) environmental excises levied "to improve efficiency in the use of resources"[5] by causing recognition of damage associated with the taxed product, and (4) miscellaneous excises that have been applied for reasons that include attempting to capture extraordinary taxpaying capacity (the recent federal luxury excises) and the lure of taxing the nonresident (lodging taxes). State yields, combining selective and general taxes, are more than triple the amount of federal excises and almost four times the amount of local general and selective excises. Most of the excise revenue comes from the "traditional" excises on tobacco products, alcoholic beverages, and fuels. In the worldwide context, these are the "big three" excises in terms of revenue production.

Selective excise revenues tend to grow slowly. Because many have specific (or unit) rates, their yields do not pick up the effects of increasing prices, and substantial revenue increases require higher statutory rates. When rates have not increased over time, the share of total revenue from the excise tends to decline. Governments sometimes preserve the administrative ease of specific rates (enforcement officers need only track the items, not their value), while protecting revenue amid inflation by means of automatic adjustment formulas of various types. For instance, some countries of the former Soviet Union defined excise and import duty rates in terms of the euro (the monetary unit of the European Union) rather than their local currency. That protected against both inflation and exchange rate deterioration with no need for regular changes in the tax law. Excise revenue can also be vulnerable to tastes and preferences of the population—for instance, in the United States, cigarette tax revenue has declined dramatically as fewer people smoke. That result can be counted as a success, given that an important reason for cigarette taxes has been to reduce smoking and its damaging external effects.

Almost half of state tax revenue in the United States (and an important amount of major city revenue) comes from taxes on consumption, either from general sales taxes or from selective excise taxes. General sales tax revenue is much greater, producing about one-third of all state tax revenue. Mississippi and West Virginia imposed the first general sales taxes during the early 1930s when existing state revenue sources (predominantly property taxes) were unable to finance state spending of the period. The retail sales taxes (RSTs) got many states through the Great Depression—they could produce revenue even when the property tax failed—and

---

[4]Sijbren Cnossen, *Excise Systems, A Global Study of the Selective Taxation of Goods and Services* (Baltimore: Johns Hopkins University Press, 1977), 8.
[5]Ibid., 9.

Table 10–1
Federal Taxes on Goods and Services, Fiscal Year 2007

	Total ($ Thousands)	Percentage of Federal Receipts (excluding Social Insurance)
Transportation		
Truck, trailer, and semitrailer chassis	1,859,906	0.14%
Tires	356,503	0.03%
Aviation fuels	410,505	0.03%
Motor fuels	35,005,584	2.70%
Fuels used commercially on inland waterways	79,841	0.01%
Transportation of persons by air	7,638,807	0.59%
Use of international air travel facilities	2,401,546	0.19%
Tax on heavy vehicle use	967,081	0.07%
Diesel fuel use by trains	−46,292	0.00%
Transportation of property by air	426,114	0.03%
Passenger transportation by water	31,434	0.00%
Environmental		
Ozone-depleting chemicals	8,953	0.00%
Gas guzzlers	85,226	0.01%
Petroleum (Oil Spill Liability Trust)*	510,277	0.04%
Sumptuary		
Alcoholic beverage	9,496,490	0.73%
Tobacco products	16,614,073	1.28%
Other		
Luxury passenger vehicles**	−25,811	0.00%
Coal	610,068	0.05%
Certain childhood vaccines	328,775	0.03%
Telephone and teletype services	1,123,745	0.09%
Private foundation investment income	258,587	0.02%
Firearms and ammunition	360,814	0.03%
Sport fishing equipment	83,916	0.01%
Tax on policies issued by foreign insurers	463,447	0.04%
Bows, arrows, and arrow shafts	40,091	0.00%
Total Excise Collections	74,730,000	5.76%
Total Customs Duties and Fees	25,298,000	1.95%
Total Excises and Customs	100,028,000	7.71%

*Tax expired January 1, 2003.

**Tax expired January 1, 1995.

SOURCE: *Statistics of Income Bulletin;* and Office of Management and Budget, *Budget of the Government of the United States, Fiscal Year 2012* (Washington, D.C.: U.S. Government Printing Office, 2011).

Table 10–2
State and Local Taxes on Goods and Services, Fiscal Year 2008 ($ Thousands)

	Total ($)	Share of Total Tax Revenue (%)	State ($)	Share of Total Tax Revenue (%)	Local ($)	Share of Total Tax Revenue (%)
Sales and gross receipts	448,688,515	33.7%	358,522,420	45.9%	90,166,095	16.4%
General sales and gross receipts	304,434,833	22.9%	241,007,659	30.8%	63,427,174	11.6%
Selective sales and gross receipts	144,253,682	10.8%	117,514,761	15.0%	26,738,921	4.9%
Sumptuary						
Alcoholic beverage	5,763,336	0.4%	5,292,681	0.7%	470,655	0.1%
Tobacco products	16,575,613	1.2%	16,068,075	2.1%	507,538	0.1%
Pari-mutual	*		218,582		*	
Amusements	*		930,221		*	
Transportation						
Motor fuel	37,901,692	2.8%	36,476,852	4.7%	1,424,840	0.3%
Miscellaneous						
Public utilities	28,130,244	2.1%	14,794,363	1.9%	13,335,881	2.4%
Insurance premiums	*		15,765,657		*	
Other selective sales	55,882,797	4.2%	44,882,790	5.7%	11,000,007	2.0%

*Data for local governments for this tax category are unavailable, but total amounts are small.

SOURCE: U.S. Bureau of Census. Governments Division, *Annual Finances of Governments: State and Local Governments* and *State Governments Tax Collections, 2008.*

the taxes quickly spread to almost half the states before World War II. Their revenue was a significant contributor to the expansion of state government services after the war. These sales taxes were the largest single source of state tax revenue from 1947 until 1998, when their yield was surpassed by that from individual income taxes. Many local governments levy general sales taxes as well, and revenue from these taxes is second only to the property tax in overall significance to local governments. In some cities, the RST yields more revenue than any other tax.

Selective excises are also widespread among state and local governments, but far less productive. All states levy excises, the most common being taxes on motor fuels, tobacco products, alcoholic beverages, public utilities, and insurance premiums. Excise taxes on gaming, part of the amusement excise category in Census reports, are significant in a few states (more than half a billion dollars in Pennsylvania, Indiana, Nevada, Louisiana, and New York), but their effect is minor in aggregate.[6] Many local governments levy selective excises as well, with public utility taxes being most productive.

---

[6] These are revenues from casino excises (taxes on gross receipts, number of gaming devices, or admissions) and are distinct from taxes collected on profits earned by the casinos or on their property and from the profits states receive from lotteries they operate.

Items or services for consumption typically pass through several stages of production, each performed by a separate economic unit, as they go from raw material to the product desired by the user. Figure 10–1 outlines that flow, from the extraction of raw materials to use by that customer. Between each stage there is an exchange transaction, a buyer and a seller, and, at each transaction, a consumption-based tax may apply. Some taxes are designed to apply at more than one level of the flow, as is the case with gross receipts (or turnover) taxes and value-added taxes (VATs). Other taxes apply at only one stage of the flow: manufacture, wholesale, or retail. Unless special allowances have been made in structuring the tax (as is described later in the discussion about VATs) single-stage, retail-level taxes cause the least economic damage associated with the revenue they raise and give the public the clearest idea of what their actual tax burden is.

There are three reasons why single-stage taxes, especially retail, are preferred. First, price increases from tax paid by the customer will likely equal the amount received by the government. Multistage and pre-retail taxes tend to pyramid or cascade. For example, any manufacturer-level tax paid is part of the cost seen by the wholesaler; that is, if the wholesaler buys garden tractors from a manufacturer for $1,500 plus a 10 percent excise, the wholesaler undoubtedly sees its unit cost as $1,650. When selling the tractor to a retailer, the wholesaler adds a markup percentage to that cost—say, 50 percent—for a charge of $2,475 ($1,650 plus 50 percent of the $1,650) to the retailer. The same markup process works for the retailer. When the customer finally purchases the tractor, that 10 percent excise has increased the price of the tractor by more than $150. Therefore, the price of the product increases by more than the tax that the government receives, and the effective tax rate is considerably more than the advertised 10 percent. A single-stage retail tax would not have that impact. Second, multistage taxes strike with each market transaction (purchase and sale). Integrated firms (e.g., those that manufacture, wholesale, and

Figure 10–1
Tax Points in the Flow of Production and Distribution

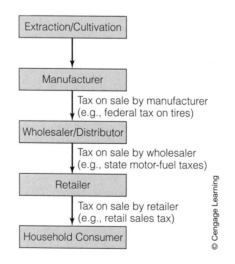

retail) have fewer such transactions and, hence, lower tax embedded in product cost.[7] Single-stage application (particularly at retail) eliminates that effect. Third, retail application causes no incentive for the production process to move to a stage of trade above the point taxed to reduce the base to which the tax applies. In general, the more of total product value produced after the tax is levied, the lower the tax. Retail application leaves no point for escape. The retail application, however, requires some greater administrative effort because there are more retailers than there are manufacturers or wholesalers and, hence, more taxpayers for tax administrators to track. Many selective excises levied by both federal and state governments—on motor fuel, tobacco products, alcoholic beverages, and so on—are collected at the manufacturer or distributor level because of those economies. These taxes are usually applied on a specific basis for ease of enforcement—the amount paid for the product at the point of taxation does not determine how much tax is owed. It is the physical units alone that determine liability. In other words, a tax of $1.00 per pack of cigarettes is the same amount regardless of whether it is levied on the transaction from manufacturer to distributor, on the transaction from distributor to retailer, or on the transaction from retailer to customer. That would not be the case if the tax was defined as 10 percent of the transaction price.

The Equity Question

A difficult policy issue for consumption taxation is that of vertical equity. Evidence from many studies done at many different times and in many different environments shows that consumption spending is higher as a share of household income for lower-income households than it is for higher-income households. This is true for total consumption, and it is also true for most categories of expenditure. This creates an equity problem for taxes on consumption: the effective tax rate (consumption expenditure times the statutory tax rate divided by household income) is higher for low-income households than for higher-income ones. The distribution of the tax burden is regressive. Table 10–3 shows effective rate evidence for federal excises and for the Minnesota retail sales and excise taxes. This pattern is typical for virtually all excises, and it raises a difficult issue in taxation. Consumption expenditure is regarded as a reasonable base for distributing the cost of government, and consumption-based taxes are effective producers of substantial revenue. However, the distribution pattern is regressive. Lawmakers must balance between the revenue productivity of such taxes and the equity issue.

These taxes also raise horizontal equity issues. Consumers have varying tastes and preferences in terms of both overall consumption and consumption of particular items. That variation in consumption patterns within household-income groups

---

[7]Integrated firms move the product through stages of production, but these are bookkeeping transactions within the firm, not sales and purchases, so they are not taxable.

Table 10–3
Effective Tax Rates for Federal Excises and Minnesota Retail Sales and Excise Taxes

| | Federal Excises (2007) (%) | Minnesota State Consumption Taxes (2008) | |
		Retail Sales (%)	State Excises (%)
Lowest quintile	1.60	4.15	1.35
Second quintile	1.00	2.7	0.65
Third quintile	0.80	2.3	0.45
Fourth quintile	0.70	1.85	0.25
Fifth quintile	0.40	1.3	0.1
Top 5%	0.20	1.1	0.1
Top 1%	0.10	—	—

creates variation in effective tax rates borne by households simply based on preferences. Therefore, on top of the vertical equity questions that consumption-based taxes raise, there are horizontal fairness problems as well. The extent to which these issues matter for policy depends on the reason for levying the tax. When revenue is the principal reason, the policy questions are greatest. However, as later sections describe, not all selective excises are levied purely for the revenue they generate. For those nonrevenue excises, the equity issues are somewhat less pressing.

Selective Excise Taxation

Selective excises apply differential tax treatment to particular products or services, causing those purchasing or selling them to bear greater tax burden than general indicators of tax-bearing capacity (income, wealth, or total consumption) would otherwise indicate. Although these excises yield revenue—seldom enough to be a major factor for general government operations—their major attractiveness often lies on other grounds or with other special purposes. Indeed, their intent is often discriminatory: to try to charge people for the social cost of their actions. When that is the plan, selective excises could be judged effective, at least partly, on the basis of nonrevenue effects, not collections.[8] Selective excises, because of their relatively narrow base, require relatively high statutory rates in order to yield significant revenue. That high tax wedge—the difference between the price paid by the consumer (tax included) and the net price received by the seller (tax subtracted)—makes tax evasion a perennial problem as customers and vendors both seek to gain a tax-saving advantage.

---

[8]The best general discussions of selective excises are Cnossen, *Excise Systems*; and Sijbren Cnossen, ed., *Theory and Practice of Excise Taxation: Smoking, Drinking, Gambling, Polluting, and Driving* (Oxford, England: Oxford University Press, 2005).

Luxury Excises

Governments levy luxury excises on goods or services whose purchase is deemed to reflect extraordinary taxpaying ability. They attempt to distribute the cost of government to those best able to pay, so luxury excises may be evaluated on normal revenue policy standards. If the luxury excises raise substantial revenue, they may ease rate pressure on other taxes; seldom does that happen. Recent federal luxury excises have applied to expensive aircraft, automobiles, yachts, furs, and jewelry; all but that on automobiles were repealed in 1993, and the automobile tax ended in 2003.[9]

The objections to luxury excises are several. First, such taxes distort producer and consumer choices: because the tax establishes a difference between the resource-cost ratios in production and the price ratios to which consumers respond, there is unnecessary loss of economic welfare in the economic system.[10] Purchasers and sellers change their behavior because of the tax, and that brings an economic loss to them. (Recall the discussion of excess burden in Sidebar 8–2.) The tax induces them to behave in a different way than they would otherwise prefer. Second, and pragmatically more important, the tax distributes burdens on the basis of personal preferences for the taxed items. The tax imposes higher effective rates on people within an income class who have high taste for the taxed commodities or services. Third, there are administrative problems with these excises. Because retailers would have difficulty separating the sales of the taxed luxury items from other sales, these excises typically apply at the manufacturer or wholesaler level. They thus fall prey to the objections to any levy that applies earlier than retail.[11] However, another administrative problem emerges in the definition of the taxed commodity. For example, a handful of states tax soft drinks, but what is a soft drink?[12] Are powdered drink mixes, imitation orange juice, flavored waters, bottled chocolate drink, and so forth to be taxed? Is low-alcohol beer a soft drink? How is a concentrate, sold to be mixed with water, to be equated for tax purposes with bottled drinks? In each case, a difficult administrative problem in interpreting and applying the tax may well be handled only by separate, brand-name determinations, a process that is time consuming for the tax department's rule makers. Collection costs for narrow excises usually are excessive relative to the modest revenue they produce.

Even though luxury excises can have considerable political appeal, they are not strong elements of a revenue system. Revenue growth for most luxury excises is low, largely because their specific nature does not allow capture of price effects. They do yield some revenue, although at considerable collection cost, and who but industry lobbyists (and the people who make those goods) will stand up for luxury purchases? How important is the revenue? In fiscal 1992, the last year before repeal

---

[9]These taxes applied only to the amount of the transaction above a particular threshold.
[10]John A. Tatom, "The Welfare Cost of an Excise Tax," *Federal Reserve Bank of St. Louis Review* 58 (November 1976): 14–15.
[11]The recent federal luxury excises were at the retail level. They created problems because they applied only on prices above a threshold, an extra complication for compliance record keeping and enforcement.
[12]Is this an example of a luxury excise? Probably so–it doesn't make much sense as anything else and very little sense as a luxury excise, either.

of the federal luxury excises on boats, aircraft, jewelry, and furs, these excises produced $29 million, a year in which the federal individual income tax alone generated more than $475 billion.[13]

As taxes levied for revenue purposes, luxury excises do not measure up.

Sumptuary Excises

Sumptuary excises seek to discourage excess consumption of items considered unhealthy or unsafe, both for the consumer and for the public as a whole. The best examples are taxes on tobacco products and alcoholic beverages: the prices paid to producers do not reflect the social cost of product use and abuse in terms of damage to health, property, and families.[14] More recent examples include the plastic bag taxes levied in Ireland (at one-quarter of a euro each, such bags have largely disappeared in the country) and in Washington, D.C. (at five cents, many fewer bags are used). The tax may charge for these external diseconomies to compensate society in ways not attainable by the market. (The taxes may also have moral overtones and are sometimes labeled "sin taxes"; along with tobacco and alcoholic beverage taxes, special taxes are also applied to gambling activities, and these taxes may be considered sumptuary as well.) Taxes on alcoholic beverages and tobacco products are among the oldest taxes in the United States; indeed, an early test of the new central government was the Whiskey Rebellion (1794)—a violent (and unsuccessful) challenge to a federal excise put down by the military.[15] Would present-day tax protesters want to try to stand up to the 82nd Airborne? It's easier and safer to complain than to take on the troops for real nowadays.

Demand for items subject to these excises is relatively insensitive to price, particularly in the short term, so consumption seldom changes much with imposition of the tax.[16] Legislatures do not propose truly prohibitive tax rates because they want tax revenue—a curious balancing between discouraging harmful activity and maintaining revenue flow from the activity. Moderate increases in sumptuary excise rates

---

[13]"Selected Historical and Other Data," *Statistics of Income Bulletin* 16 (Winter 1996–1997): 167.

[14]One study estimates that a much higher excise on beer would have dramatically reduced the number of young drivers killed in automobile accidents (1,660 lives saved between 1982 and 1988). See Michael Grossman, Frank J. Chaloupka, Henry Saffer, and Adit Laixuthai, "Effects of Alcohol Price Policy on Youth," National Bureau of Economic Research Working Paper 4385, Cambridge, Mass., 1993.

[15]There were serious questions about the tax, among which was the fact that large producers of whiskey (of which President Washington was one) paid a considerably lower tax per gallon than did smaller producers. It also required cash payment, and cash was in short supply in the western United States at the time (which meant western Pennsylvania, the hotbed of the rebellion). Indeed, cash was so scarce on the frontier that whiskey was used for currency, as well as for drinking.

[16]Cigarette tax increases do have an impact on both the number of smokers and the number of cigarettes each smokes in the long term. For instance, the Joint Committee on Taxation estimated "that the increase in the [federal] excise tax on cigarettes from $0.39 per pack to $1.00 per pack will reduce by 1.9 million the number of individuals who choose to smoke in 2017. We further estimate that those smokers will decrease their consumption of cigarettes by 4 percent." Staff of the Joint Committee on Taxation, "Modeling the Federal Revenue Effects of Proposed Changes in Cigarette Excise Taxes," JCX-101-07, Washington, D.C., October 19, 2007.

generally elicit minimal protest from consumers, although sellers complain about illegal (non-taxed) competition. Bootlegging is a continual problem; one enforcement procedure uses stamps applied to units on which tax has been paid at the manufacturer level. The tax is collected early, and enforcement agents need only look for the stamp to verify that tax has been paid. Sizable rate differences among states swamp control structures with evasion.[17] When the tax in a state or locality gets significantly higher than that applied in nearby jurisdictions, a resulting difference in prices charged can induce lots of cross-border shopping, and considerable revenue that was expected from the higher rate gets lost. Tax stamps are effective at making sure that vendor stock has the tax paid; they aren't effective at policing people who cross the border to get their personal supplies.[18]

However, within limits, these excises do raise revenue with minimal public protest. Complaints normally come from producers rather than consumers, and legislators are usually wary of overt support for those interests unless the producers are concentrated in the legislator's home district. The importance of producer politics is demonstrated by the fact that state cigarette taxes have historically been lowest in the states where tobacco production is economically important. Purchasers of the product are likely to bear the burden of the tax on average, but if the tax rate is lower than in other areas, it may give the producers there a competitive advantage in the market.

There are three primary objections to sumptuary excises. First, the demand for the products taxed is often highly price-inelastic, so the tax has little short-term effect on the amount of the product purchased. It may divert consumption from desirable or beneficial activities to pay the tax. (The extreme example sometimes quoted by lobbyists is the alcoholic who fails to buy milk for his children because of the tax he pays on liquor.) Responses to higher taxes increase as producers and consumers have time to adjust, however. Second, the absolute burden of these taxes may be particularly heavy on low-income families and may even involve higher effective tax rates on lower-income families. The tax is applied, after all, on the basis of personal preferences, so the teetotaling millionaire pays less liquor tax than the whiskey-drinking laborer. Third, a problem results from the specific (not ad valorem) nature of these excises. Even though that basis is logical because any social cost involved would be related to the amount of consumption, not its value, it does discriminate against lower-priced brands and those who purchase them. If the tax is $10 per gallon on distilled spirits, the effective rate is much higher on liquor sold for $6 per fifth than on liquor sold for $10 per fifth. This is a special problem if users of the lower-priced brands come from low-income groups. Furthermore, the specific nature of the tax obscures the actual ratio of the tax to the net price, which frequently turns out to be high. It also turns out that how the tax is quoted, specific or ad valorem, has an impact on price competition. Sidebar 10–1 provides an example of that.

---

[17]For a review of the problem, see Advisory Commission on Intergovernmental Relations, *Cigarette Tax Evasion: A Second Look*, Report A-100 (Washington, D.C.: Advisory Commission on Intergovernmental Relations, 1985).

[18]Differences in federal taxation of cigarettes, roll-your-own tobacco, pipe tobacco, small cigars, and large cigars in 2009 created dramatic changes in the market for these substitutes. Government Accountability Office, *Tobacco Taxes: Large Disparities in Rates for Smoking Products Trigger Significant Market Shifts to Avoid Higher Taxes*, GAO-12-475 (Washington, D.C.: Government Accountability Office, April 2012).

Sidebar 10–1
Taxes as Competitive Weapons: Smokeless Tobacco

Moist smokeless tobacco is subject to excise taxation in all states. As of January 2006, 43 states levied a tax based on the wholesale or manufacturer price of the product (ad valorem basis). The others tax according to weight.

One company, UST, has historically had almost the entire market for the product and charged a premium price for it. More recently, competitors have developed lower-priced products, and UST has been losing market share to those products. With this development, the ad valorem tax presents a problem for UST. The company describes the difficulty in its annual report:

> [T]he *ad valorem* method of taxation has the effect of increasing the taxes payable on premium brands to a greater degree than the taxes payable on price-value brands, which further exacerbates the price gap between premium and price-value brands.[1]

As a result, UST initiated efforts in state legislatures to switch taxation from ad valorem to a weight (unit) basis. That would eliminate the tax situation that otherwise put the UST product at an extra price disadvantage. Of course, the low-priced brands lobbied the legislators just as vigorously to retain the ad valorem basis.

The struggle continues.

[1]UST Inc. Annual Form 10-K Report for 2005, p. 9.

SOURCE: Based on Stanley R. Arnold, "Tax Law as a Competitive Weapon," *State Tax Notes* 42 (October 16, 2006): 189–91.

Benefit-Base Excises

Benefit-base excises, primarily transportation-related taxes, operate as a quasi-price for a public good.[19] Highway use normally involves consumption of motor fuel, so a tax on fuel purchase approximates a charge for the use of the highway. These taxes allocate cost to road users and have been less expensive to administer than direct user charges (tolls) for streets, roads, and highways. The motor-fuel tax thus operates as a surrogate for price. It does have difficulties for the truck-to-car relationship because differences in incremental costs of providing highways and of keeping up with highway wear and tear are difficult to calibrate and relate to motor-fuel use, but the system functions to generally distribute the cost of operating the highways to those more heavily using the highways.[20] The motor-fuel tax has provided one of

---

[19]The federal logic of certain excises as user charges is discussed in Chapter 11. In terms of incidence, one study finds that the burden of the federal gasoline tax is evenly split between consumers and gasoline wholesalers and the burden of the state gasoline taxes is on consumers. Hayley Chouinard and Jeffrey M. Perloff, "Incidence of Federal and State Gasoline Taxes," *Economic Letters* 83 (2005): 55–60.
[20]Alternative power sources, such as electricity, create a problem.

the rare instances of strong complementarity between the taxed commodity and the public good being financed.

There are additional questions: whether motor-fuel tax revenues should be segregated for highway construction and maintenance only, whether these funds should be spent for all transportation (mass as well as highway), and whether motor-fuel tax revenue should receive the same budget treatment as other revenue, with no earmarking for transportation. These questions are not yet answered, but if revenues from the gasoline tax do not go to transportation projects, then they are probably subject to the complaints made against luxury excises. They sacrifice their benefit-base logic and must be evaluated on ability-to-pay grounds. On the other hand, if revenue from the gasoline tax goes exclusively to highways, there is a substantial bias for highways in the total transportation system. In most European countries, motor-fuel taxes are high, revenues are not dedicated to use for highways, and the taxes are considered part of an environmental strategy to make travel by automobile less attractive relative to mass transportation, not part of a "user pays" strategy for financing highways. Even though the federal government, all states, and some localities in the United States levy motor-fuel taxes, the combined rates are far lower than those imposed in Europe.

The benefit-base logic of highway or motor-fuel taxes suggests that the tax should be specific because the number of units of motor fuel used is related to the use of the service. At the same time, however, the specific nature of the tax means that, in times of inflation, there are significant pressures placed on the motor-fuel tax fund because of highway operation and construction cost increases. Some states have attempted to avert the need for legislated rate increases by tying the specific tax rate to the prevailing price of gasoline, so that as the price of gasoline is higher, the specific gasoline tax rate is higher.[21] This strategy has not succeeded over the long run because episodes of declining prices brought significant decreases in revenue and price fluctuations brought major revenue instability. Linking the rate to a general inflation index or to road operation and maintenance costs shows greater permanent promise.

The benefit-base motor-fuel tax will not survive. As motor vehicles become more fuel efficient, the typical gallonage rates will not support highway operation and maintenance, and American lawmakers are wary of increasing fuel tax rates.[22] In addition, as hybrids, all-electric vehicles, and exotic-fuel cars become more prevalent, traditional fuel taxes become ever more irrelevant for highway finance. Fortunately, technology now permits direct charging for highway use—monitoring of distance traveled, time of travel, and location of travel is feasible—and some version of that charging must replace the fuel tax if highways are to be financed through payments

---

[21]An extensive review of state gasoline tax problems and of variable-rate structures can be found in John H. Bowman and John L. Mikesell, "Recent Changes in State Gasoline Taxation: An Analysis of Structure and Rates," *National Tax Journal* 36 (June 1983): 163–82.

[22]Increasing the tax rate to accommodate lower quantities of motor fuel being demanded won't automatically fix the problem because the higher rate also impacts fuel purchases. A recent study finds that each cent per gallon increase in gasoline price reduces consumption by 0.2 percent. Antonio M. Bento et al., "Distributional and Efficiency Impacts of Increasing U.S. Gasoline Taxes," *American Economic Review* 99 (June 2009): 667–99. As would be expected, the tax base is a function of the tax rate.

made by users as opposed to general taxpayers.[23] Fuel taxes won't work anymore. More will be discussed about that in the chapter on user charges.[24] Motor-fuel taxes may remain as an environmental levy to discourage use of hydrocarbon fuels (that is how they are used now in Europe), but not as a proxy charge for highways.

Regulatory and Environmental Excises

Excises may be applied to improve resource use efficiency, much like the intent of the sumptuary excises, but without the moral or ethical overtones and without the explicit revenue objectives of the sumptuary taxes. Regulatory excises do such things as tax pollutants (the taxes on ozone-depleting chemicals) and penalize automakers not producing fuel-efficient automobiles (the gas guzzler tax).[25] They reflect the ideas that the polluter must pay and that particular actions should be discouraged or penalized. As described in Chapter 8, they seek to make buyers and sellers cognizant of the full social cost of their actions. The United States is far behind Europe in the use of "green" taxes designed to explicitly make the polluter pay for the cost that pollution imposes on others. Some proponents of environmental excises have argued that there is a "double dividend" from such taxes. First, the imposition of the tax corrects for the external and unpriced damaging impact of the pollutant. Second, the revenue generated by the tax can be used to replace other taxes that distort efficient operations of the economy. Thus, the tax can provide two desirable impacts for the economy, not just one.

The big environmental tax under most serious discussion in the United States today is the carbon tax, a way to induce people and industries to pay attention to carbon emissions that would contribute to global warming. Carbon taxes have been in place in Denmark, Finland, Norway, and Sweden since the 1990s and in British Columbia since 2008, so there is some experience to go on. The carbon excise applies to all fossil fuels in proportion to the carbon dioxide emissions associated with each. The more emissions, the higher the tax rate that applies to that particular fuel. More carbon content per unit of energy means a higher rate—in British Columbia, the rate on gasoline is 2.34 cents per liter and on diesel, 2.69 cents per liter.[26] The idea of the tax is to tax according to carbon emission from the fuel, so each fossil fuel would bear a different statutory rate. The intent is to induce users of fuels to respond to the environmental damage that their consumption entails—at least to pay for the damage and even better to reduce their activities that cause the damage.

---

[23]Some car insurance policies base premiums on monitored miles traveled and time of day traveled, so charging for highway usage on this basis is technologically feasible. As with many reasonable fiscal tools, the barriers are only political.

[24]The Congressional Budget Office reviews some options in *Alternative Approaches to Funding Highways* (Washington, D.C.: Congressional Budget Office, 2011).

[25]The gas guzzler tax applies primarily to very expensive imports. It excludes the major domestic guzzlers–trucks and SUVs–and probably is designed more to give some protection to domestic vehicles than for environmental reasons. The motor-fuel tax probably has more potential for inducing fuel economy than does the guzzler tax.

[26]Brett Borsare, "A Canadian Carbon Tax Blueprint for U.S. States," *State Tax Notes* 52 (June 8, 2009): 817–22.

The big question: How high should the environmental tax rate be? Europeans are more willing to use the market to get corrections made and to collect information from market responses to adjust the tax rates.[27] Americans seem to prefer to use the outmoded command-and-control mechanism of regulations and restraints rather than setting appropriate environmental tax rates and then letting the market function. Of course, we also still have Americans who deny that there might be a climate change problem that merits some attention, so we have two layers of being outmoded that have to be dealt with for progress.

Other Excises

There are some other miscellaneous excises as well. Selective excises on imported items (customs duties) are often levied to raise revenue and to protect local producers during development. Excises may also be narrowly applied to finance research or trade promotion activities, as with agricultural commodity excises functioning through marketing boards or lodging excises used to promote tourism. Particularly narrow excises are often dedicated to a specific purpose, as with the federal vaccine injury compensation fund financed by an excise on certain childhood disease vaccines or the federal excise on fishing equipment that supports sport fish restoration programs. Across all the selective excises, however, the basic criteria for success include "large sales volume, few producers, inelastic demand, ready definability, and no close substitutes unless these can be included in the base."[28] Few selective excises meet all these criteria.

General Taxes on Goods and Services: Retail Sales and Value-Added Taxes

Consumption represents an alternative to income as a general basis for distributing the cost of government among elements of the private economy. Many believe that making a switch from heavy reliance on individual and corporate income taxes would be good public policy. There are two main elements in this argument:

1. **Increase economic growth**. A switch from income to consumption as a tax base "will reduce the difference between the pre- and post-tax return to saving that encourages taxpayers to consume rather than to save, so saving

---

[27]As with other selective excises, a carbon tax could be levied at various points in the production-to-consumption chain: upstream on oil and gas wells, coal mines, and importers; midstream on oil refineries, electric utilities, and natural gas pipelines; or downstream on vehicles, households, commercial buildings, and industries. Jonathan L. Ramseur and Larry Parker, *Carbon Tax and Greenhouse Gas Control: Options and Considerations for Congress*, CRS Report for Congress, Order Code R 40242 (Washington, D.C.: Congressional Research Service, February 23, 2009), 25.

[28]Cnossen, *Excise Systems*, 9.

will be encouraged by the change and the growth path of the economy may subsequently move upward."[29] Future consumption (in other words, saving) is not penalized in comparison with current consumption. The higher saving improves rates of capital formation, labor productivity, and standards of living.

2. **Improve fundamental equity**. Consumption represents a fundamentally more equitable way for assigning shares of the cost of government than does annual income: "each individual [measures tax capacity] for himself when, in the light of all his present circumstances and future prospects, he decides on the scale of his personal living expenses. Thus a tax based on actual spending rates each individual's spending capacity according to the yardstick which he applies to himself."[30] Using the amount the individual believes that he or she can afford in purchases of private goods and services as the standard for distributing a major share of the total cost of government would seem to be appropriate for financing government in a market economy. This equity measure is actual consumption, compared with the Haig-Simons income concept, which equals maximum potential consumption possible without a reduction in wealth.

A general consumption tax may be administered either directly, through administrative systems that follow more or less the same filing and collection structures as the current income tax, or indirectly, through a transaction-based sales tax following either the multistage collection scheme of the VAT or the single-stage collection scheme of the RST. The three administrative systems are economically identical ways of taxing consumption.

A direct consumption tax uses the fact that, by definition, individual income less personal saving equals consumption. Therefore, if a household had income of $75,000 and saved $35,000 in the year, then its consumption was $40,000, and that base can be taxed accordingly.[31] No government currently uses such a system, possibly because of some questions about defining and reporting savings, but, because of the several provisions in the federal income tax system that provide preferences for saving (the many retirement savings programs, provision for medical saving accounts, provisions for tax-preferred saving for education expenses, etc.), the current federal tax has been described as a hybrid income-consumption tax rather than a pure income tax. Some proponents of consumption taxation argue that the easiest and least disruptive way to transform the federal system into a pure consumption tax would be to dramatically broaden the preferences for savings already in the system. In other words, a direct tax would build on existing foundations in a manner that would be impossible for an indirect approach.

---

[29]S. Cnossen and C. Sanford, *Taxing Consumption* (Paris: Organization for Economic Cooperation and Development, 1988), 32.

[30]Nicholas Kaldor, *An Expenditure Tax* (London: Allen and Unwin, 1955), 47.

[31]One careful analysis of such a system: Laurence S. Seidman, *The USA Tax: A Progressive Consumption Tax* (Cambridge, Mass.: MIT Press, 1997). The flat-tax proposals that have emerged periodically over the years often are driven in part by a desire to move toward consumption taxation.

There are two alternative systems for collecting an indirect, transaction-based (i.e., on individual purchases or "over the counter" rather than through individual filing) general tax on consumption. The forms are the RST and the VAT. The RST is the American (United States and Canada) format.[32] The VAT is the format used by virtually all central governments in the industrialized world, including all members of the Organization for Economic Cooperation and Development (OECD) except the United States, all countries of Latin America, all countries of the former Soviet Union, and all countries that are part of or would like to join the European Union (it is a membership requirement).[33] Statutory rates for these taxes may be quoted on either a tax-inclusive or a tax-exclusive basis. Sidebar 10–2 explains the difference and shows how to switch between the two methods of quoting rates.

Both taxes can apply a general, uniform tax on household consumption with minimal distortion of production and consumption choice, but they differ in how each accomplishes that end and, in practice, differ in the extent to which they are general, uniform, and nondistorting. The U.S. RST applies to household consumption by taxing only the last stage of the full production-distribution process. Tax that otherwise would be applied on earlier purchases is suspended through a system of exemption certificates. When a business purchases an input, it provides the suspension certificate, and the vendor does not apply the tax. The VAT applies to each transaction in the full production-distribution process, but, in usual application, every purchaser except the final customer has tax refunded through credits for tax the business has collected on its sales. Thus, when they are functioning properly, both systems relieve tax on all transactions but the last—the one to the final household customer. The difference between the two taxes lies in the administrative mechanism. Both mechanisms are described in detail later because they are at the essence of each tax and are the distinguishing feature between the two taxes.

In contrast to direct taxes, indirect taxes are extremely difficult to tailor to the individual circumstances of the taxpayer. In other words, a direct tax, administered through a periodic filing procedure, can be adjusted for such factors as size of the taxpaying unit and particular events that have befallen the taxpayer during the filing period. An indirect tax collected on a transaction-by-transaction basis is impersonal and cannot easily be adjusted for those sorts of conditions. There may be allowances for the particular transaction (a preferential rate for food, for instance), but that rate will be the same for all purchasers regardless of their circumstances. This inability to target and limit makes preferences provided in an indirect tax less efficient because taxpayers in all sorts of circumstances have access to them.

---

[32]The sales tax is also used in some African countries and local governments in some countries of the former Soviet Union. For a few years, it was an important revenue source for regional governments in the Russian Federation.

[33]British Columbia, Saskatchewan, Quebec, and Manitoba levy provincial retail sales taxes. Alberta and the territories levy no sales tax of their own. The remaining provinces levy a sales tax that is harmonized with the national goods and services tax and is administered by the Canada Customs and Revenue Agency.

Sidebar 10–2
Tax-Exclusive and Tax-Inclusive Pricing

Many Americans traveling in Europe are surprised to find that no sales tax is added to their purchases, just as Europeans visiting the United States are surprised when tax is added to their purchases. Sales taxes are levied on both transactions, but the RST tradition is for tax-exclusive pricing ("separate quotation" or adding the tax at the cash register), whereas the VAT tradition is tax-inclusive pricing (including tax in the sticker price). There are exceptions—for instance, some European hotels and car rental agencies quote prices without the VAT and add the tax on final purchase, and American vending machines usually sell at tax-inclusive prices. Nevertheless, it is normal for American RSTs to be added at the cash register and for VATs to be included in prices. Neither treatment is required by the logic of either tax, although tax laws often make the requirement.[1] They are both sales taxes, and they both can switch between the two approaches. The Canadian VAT—the goods and services tax—is added at purchase, so prices there are quoted without including the VAT, just like with an American RST.

Tax laws may quote rates on either a tax-exclusive or a tax-inclusive basis, but conversion between the two styles is simple. If *TE* is the tax-exclusive rate in percent and *TI* is the tax-inclusive rate in percent, then the relationship is as follows:

$$TI = TE/(100 + TE)$$

and

$$TE = TI/(100 - TI)$$

Therefore, a tax-exclusive VAT rate of 20 percent is equivalent to a tax-inclusive rate of 16.7 percent. A tax-inclusive VAT rate of 15 percent is equivalent to a tax-exclusive rate of 17.6 percent.

Which tax is less transparent? Neither the VAT nor the RST paid on a purchase need be hidden. Cash register receipts in many European stores include a statement of how much VAT was paid on the total purchase, breaking out the tax that was included in the posted price of the items being purchased, just as cash register receipts in the United States include a statement of sales tax paid at the bottom of the receipt. The only difference: the U.S. receipt includes the sales tax as part of the calculation of how much is owed, and the VAT receipt includes VAT paid as a separate display after the total payment. And that VAT total is likely more accurate than the RST total on the receipt: RSTs exclude business inputs less completely from the tax than do VATs, so there undoubtedly is RST paid by those businesses that is embedded in the price and that doesn't show up at all in the statement of RST. That makes the VAT more transparent than the RST.

American politicians and commentators who charge that the VAT is a hidden tax haven't traveled much outside the United States, haven't bothered to look at receipts they have been given

---

**Sidebar 10–2
(continued)**

---

for European or Canadian purchases, or are fibbing. Or maybe someone else is paying their way, so receipts do not matter to them. It is far easier to know how much personal income tax you have paid through the year than to know your total payments of either RST or VAT, however, because you do have to file an income tax return at the end of the year and you can see your total liability quite easily. But, again, to know you have to look.

[1] When the American states were adopting their first RSTs in the depths of the Great Depression of the 1930s, retailer organizations demanded separate quotation laws so that they would not be blamed for the price increases that would come with addition of the taxes. On the other hand, when Russia permitted regional sales taxes in the late 1990s, the national enabling law required that the sales taxes be included in listed prices, following the tradition of their VAT. When the regional sales taxes were abolished a few years later, there was popular concern that the tax would end, but the merchants wouldn't lower their prices accordingly and would pocket what otherwise would have gone to the government.

Retail Sales Taxes

American RSTs share three common features. All are ad valorem taxes "imposed upon the sales, or elements incidental to the sales, such as receipts from them, of all or a wide range of commodities";[34] all have a system for suspending tax on items purchased for resale; and all encourage separate quotation of the tax in each transaction (in other words, the tax is added at purchase rather than being included in the price on the shelf, and tax thus collected is excluded from gross receipts upon which the tax is levied). The taxes—levied by all states but Alaska, Delaware, Montana, New Hampshire, and Oregon and by thousands of local governments, including many in Alaska—yield roughly one-third of the total state tax revenue and rank second to the property tax for local governments, providing something more than 10 percent of tax revenue.[35]

In the middle of 2009, state tax rates ranged from 2.9 percent (Colorado) to 7.25 percent (California). Twenty-three states levied rates of 6 percent or higher.

---

[34]John F. Due, *Sales Taxation* (Urbana: University of Illinois Press, 1957), 3.
[35]The standard reference on general sales taxation is John F. Due and John L. Mikesell, *Sales Taxation, State and Local Structure and Administration*, 2nd ed. (Washington, D.C.: Urban Institute, 1994). Not all state sales taxes have that name in their state laws. For instance, the New Mexico tax is called the Gross Receipts Tax. However, it has the basic features of a retail sales tax, not those of a true gross receipts tax, like the Washington Business and Occupation Tax or the Ohio Commercial Activity Tax. New Mexico suspends business purchases and accommodates adding tax to price; the gross receipts taxes do not.

Piggybacked local rates for city, county, and transit or other special districts add to the total rate in many parts of the country. For instance, in New York City, the rate of 8.875 percent applied on retail purchases combines a 4 percent state rate, a 4.5 percent city rate, and a 0.375 percent Metropolitan Commuter Transportation District rate. In Chicago, state plus local rates equal 10.25 percent (6.25 percent state, 1.75 percent Cook County, 1.25 percent city, and 1 percent regional transit district). Payment to the state is made by the vendor; returns like that in Figure 10–2 from Virginia cover all such transactions for a specified period (quarter, month, year). This state return includes local tax as well because Virginia administers the local taxes.[36] The vendor has, through the reporting period, been collecting tax on each of its many sales; this return accumulates all those transactions for transmission to the government. Reporting on the return begins with total sales of the vendor, and sales that are not taxed are subtracted to obtain taxable sales. The amount of sales tax that is owed comes from reported taxable sales.

Two special evaluation standards apply to sales tax structures: uniformity and neutrality.[37] The first standard holds that the tax should produce a uniform tax on consumer expenditures. Thus, the structure should ease shifting to ultimate consumers, it should apply at a uniform rate to all consumption expenditures unless there is a completely necessary reason otherwise, and it should apply to the transaction amount actually paid by the consumer. Second, to avoid loss of economic efficiency, the tax should not create competitive disturbances among types of distribution channels, methods of doing business, or forms of business organization.

Figure 10–2
The Virginia Retail Sales and Use Tax Return

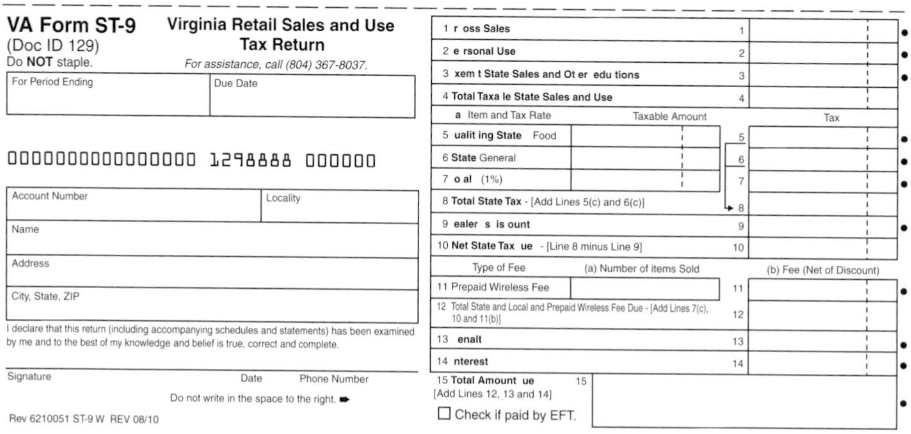
VA Form ST-9 (Doc ID 129) Do **NOT** staple.
Virginia Retail Sales and Use Tax Return
For assistance, call (804) 367-8037.
For Period Ending | Due Date
0000000000000000 1298888 000000
Account Number | Locality
Name
Address
City, State, ZIP
I declare that this return (including accompanying schedules and statements) has been examined by me and to the best of my knowledge and belief is true, correct and complete.
Signature | Date | Phone Number
Do not write in the space to the right.
Rev 6210051 ST-9 W REV 08/10
1 r oss Sales 1
2 e rsonal Use 2
3 xem t State Sales and Ot er edu tions 3
4 Total Taxa le State Sales and Use 4
a Item and Tax Rate | Taxable Amount | Tax
5 ualit ing State Food 5
6 State General 6
7 o al (1%) 7
8 Total State Tax - [Add Lines 5(c) and 6(c)] 8
9 ealer s is ount 9
10 Net State Tax ue - [Line 8 minus Line 9] 10
Type of Fee | (a) Number of items Sold | (b) Fee (Net of Discount)
11 Prepaid Wireless Fee 11
12 Total State and Local and Prepaid Wireless Fee Due - [Add Lines 7(c), 10 and 11(b)] 12
13 enalt 13
14 nterest 14
15 Total Amount ue [Add Lines 12, 13 and 14] 15
☐ Check if paid by EFT.

SOURCE: Virginia Department of Taxation, Sales and Use Tax.

[36]A note for those of you interested in doing tax research: one of the best ways of understanding how a particular tax works is to get a tax return and work through the steps in calculating tax liability. This approach helps clarify when the law, regulations, and instructions become insurmountable.
[37]Due, *Sales Taxation*, 351–52.

Choices should not be distorted because of the tax. Figuring out how to get sales taxes to be uniform and neutral—and as fair, revenue-productive, and collectable as possible—is not a simple task. The next sections on the coverage of nonretail transactions, the problem of equity exemptions, the taxability of services, and the treatment of interstate transactions demonstrate that.

Exclusion of Producers' Goods

Business purchases are a tempting target for taxation. The overall RST base is greater when business purchases are included, so a given statutory tax rate raises more revenue when business purchases are taxed and a large piece of the tax burden is hidden to individual purchasers. These purchases are not consumption, but the lure of revenue without higher statutory rates is attractive: such purchases constitute an estimated average of around 40 percent of state sales tax bases.[38] If businesses must pay tax on inputs to their business operations (raw materials, supplies, utilities, machinery and equipment, structures, etc.), their costs are higher (input price plus tax paid equals cost). Consequently, prices are higher because of those input taxes, but customers are unable to detect the embedded effect of the producer sales tax on prices, a clear violation of the transparency standard, as well as a source of economic distortion. If producers' goods are not excluded, the tax is not a uniform percentage of consumer expenditures (some consumption items require use of more producers' goods than others), the tax affects choices among methods of production (it makes capital more expensive), and it may delay the replacement of old equipment by increasing the after-tax price of new equipment. Furthermore, firms have an incentive to produce goods for their own use rather than purchasing the goods because their internal cost of production is not subject to sales tax. Thus, producers' goods should be excluded from the tax to ensure economic efficiency and equity and to avoid thwarting industrial development.

The American states are stingy in exempting pre-retail purchases. They exempt items purchased for resale, component parts of items for resale (e.g., tires purchased by an automobile manufacturer to install on vehicles being sold), and goods used directly in production (e.g., flour purchased by a bakery). Many producer goods (fuel, fixtures, tools, furniture, machinery, and equipment) often remain in the base, despite the clear logic for excluding them. The business purchasing the item is treated as the final consumer, even though its purchase price, tax included, becomes part of the operating cost of the business that the business will include in the price of what it sells. Taxing these acquisitions makes business investment less attractive, puts American business at a cost disadvantage in international competition, and makes the effective tax rate differ across types of consumption. However, legislatures are

---

[38]Raymond J. Ring, Jr., "Consumers' Share and Producers' Share of the General Sales Tax," *National Tax Journal* 52 (March 1999): 79–90; and Robert Cline, John Mikesell, Tom Neubig, and Andrew Phillips, "Sales Taxation of Business Inputs: Existing Tax Distortions and the Consequences of Extending the Sales Tax to Business Services," *State Tax Notes* 35 (February 14, 2005): 457–70.

reluctant to remove the tax from business—even though the business is almost certain to transmit the cost to its individual customers.

What happens when business purchases are not excluded from the sales tax? Figure 10–3 illustrates how pyramiding works and what its impact is. The figure contrasts a typical state sales tax with an ideal sales tax. The difference between the taxes: the ideal sales tax applies only to sales to the household consumer, and the typical sales tax applies to some business input purchases, as well as to consumer sales. In the ideal case, all input purchases by businesses are exempt from tax; in the typical case, purchases by businesses of inventory for resale and of goods used in the direct manufacturing process are exempt, but other business purchases are taxed. In this example, there are three businesses: a computer manufacturer, an appliance manufacturer, and an appliance retailer. The computer manufacturer sells computers to the retailer and to the appliance manufacturer. Some of the computers sold to the appliance manufacturer are for administrative work, and some of the computers sold to the appliance manufacturer are used in the production process. The state applies a sales tax rate of 5 percent to taxable sales. In the typical case, the flow of business generates $58,000 in sales tax revenue from $1,000,000 of sales to households—the effective tax rate is 5.8 percent, compared with the statutory rate of 5 percent. The higher effective rate results because $160,000 in computer sales to the manufacturer and to the retailer were taxed; the cost of those computers to the businesses is going to be embedded in the final price of their products, so the value of those computers is being taxed twice—once when the businesses purchase them and again when the products of those businesses get sold to the household consumer. This is sales tax pyramiding.

Figure 10–3
Retail Sales Tax Pyramiding: Typical v. Ideal

	Sales by:			Sales Tax (5% statutory rate)	
Sales to:	Computer Manufacturer	Appliance Manufacturer	Appliance Retailer	Typical*	Ideal**
Appliance manufacturer					
Computers used in production line	50,000			—	—
Computers used in administration	150,000			7,500	—
Appliance retailer					
Computers used in administration	10,000			500	—
Appliances		800,000		—	—
Household consumers			1,000,000	50,000	50,000
Total sales tax paid				58,000	50,000
Effective tax rate paid				5.80%	5%

*Typical: Exemption of business purchases of inventory and equipment used in direct production process.
**Ideal: Exemption of business purchases of all inputs.

There are problems with sales tax pyramiding. First, products purchased by households bear differing effective sales tax rates, depending on the way in which products are produced. Those involving more inputs that are subject to tax when businesses purchase them have higher rates than those produced without those kinds of purchases. This distorts consumer and business behavior. Second, businesses have an artificial incentive to vertical integration. In the previous example, a firm that made both computers and appliances would have an economic advantage because its appliance branch could obtain administrative computers without facing any sales tax, while a firm that was not integrated would need to pay sales tax when it purchased computers on the open market. Third, businesses in states that have limited exemptions for business purchases are at distinct disadvantage in interstate and international competition; they face higher costs of production because of the tax paid on their purchases. Finally, the statutory or advertised sales tax rate understates the true sales tax rate. In the example, the advertised rate is 5 percent, but the true rate on household purchases is 5.8 percent. This violates an important transparency standard—taxpayers need to see what tax they are actually paying. In this example, when lawmakers claim that their state sales tax rate is 5 percent, they are not exactly telling the truth. In spite of the attractiveness of hidden taxes to politicians, it is still difficult to see why lawmakers would want to discourage business investment by taxing business inputs.

RSTs remove transactions from the tax system by suspending collection on those transactions. Figure 10–4 illustrates a suspension certificate prepared by the Multistate Tax Commission for use in its several member states (states also provide their own along the same lines). When a business purchases an item or group of items for an exempt purpose, such as buying inventory for resale or acquiring production equipment, it provides the seller with such a certificate. That allows the sale without application of tax. Sales are assumed to be taxable unless a certificate justifies that the tax should not be collected. The accumulation of such sales during a reporting period is reported on the seller's return (see line 3 in Figure 10–2); deducted sales of otherwise taxable items ultimately need to be documented by certificates provided by the purchaser when tax authorities audit the business. States may have a wide variety of such certificates, depending on the range of exempt purchases in the state law. When states exempt purchases by governments or nonprofit organizations, they provide similar certificates for that purpose.

One enforcement problem in sales taxation is fraudulent use of the exemption certificate—for example, if a business owner presents the certificate to suspend sales tax on the purchase of a computer that will be used at home rather than in an exempt business use. It is the responsibility of the vendor to make a good-faith effort to verify that the certificate is properly used before exempting the purchase. If the vendor errs, the revenue is probably lost. This is the weakness of RSTs when the statutory tax rate gets particularly high. Purchasers are eager to avoid the tax when buying an expensive item, and vendors are eager not to lose the sale by denying the misused exemption. Cheating might not be worth it when the tax rate is 5 percent, but it might start looking promising when the rate is 10 percent or more.

Figure 10–4
Suspending Sales Tax Collection by Multistate Tax Commission Certificate

UNIFORM SALES & USE TAX CERTIFICATE—MULTIJURISDICTION

The below-listed states have indicated that this form of certificate is acceptable, subject to the notes on pages 2–4. The issuer and the recipient have the responsibility of determining the proper use of this certificate under applicable laws in each state, as these may change from time to time.

Issued to Seller: _____

Address: _____

I certify that:

Name of Firm (Buyer): _____ is engaged as a registered

Address: _____

□ Wholesaler
□ Retailer
□ Manufacturer
□ Seller (California)
□ Lessor (see notes on pages 2–4)
□ Other (Specify)_____

and is registered with the below listed states and cities within which your firm would deliver purchases to us and that any such purchases are for wholesale, resale, ingredients or components of a new product or service to be resold, leased, or rented in the normal course of business. We are in the business of wholesaling, retailing, manufacturing, leasing (renting) the following:

Description of Business: _____

General description of tangible property or taxable services to be purchased from the seller: _____

State	State Registration, Seller's Permit, or ID Number of Purchaser	State	State Registration, Seller's Permit, or ID Number of Purchaser
AL	_____	MO	_____
AR	_____	NE	_____
AZ	_____	NV	_____
CA	_____	NJ	_____
CO	_____	NM	_____
CT	_____	NC	_____
DC	_____	ND	_____
FL	_____	OH	_____
GA	_____	OK	_____
HI	_____	PA	_____
ID	_____	RI	_____
IL	_____	SC	_____
IA	_____	SD	_____
KS	_____	TN	_____
KY	_____	TX	_____
ME	_____	UT	_____
MD	_____	VT	_____
MI	_____	WA	_____
MN	_____	WI	_____

Figure 10–4
(Continued)

I further certify that if any property or service so purchased tax free is used or consumed by the firm as to make it subject to a Sales or Use Tax we will pay the tax due directly to the proper taxing authority when state law so provides or inform the seller for added tax billing. This certificate shall be a part of each order which we may hereafter give to you, unless otherwise specified, and shall be valid until canceled by us in writing or revoked by the city or state.

Under penalties of perjury, I swear or affirm that the information on this form is true and correct as to every material matter.

Authorized Signature: _____

(Owner, Partner or Corporate Officer)

Title: _____

Date: _____

Taxation of Services

Most state sales taxes, although applying generally to retail purchases of tangible personal property, apply only selectively to purchases of services. States usually tax the lease or rental of tangible personal property (motor vehicles, videotapes, cement mixers, etc.), the rental of transient accommodations, and some utility services. They may also tax other varieties of service purchases made by households; about half the states even tax the repair, installation, or maintenance of the tangible personal property that they tax.[39] However, overall, the omission of services shows a secular vulnerability in the sales tax base. In 1965, 57.4 percent of personal consumption expenditure was of goods; by 2008, that share had fallen to 39.7 percent.[40] A base quite serviceable in a goods economy may be hard-pressed to yield adequate revenue at tolerable statutory rates in a more service-oriented economy.

Taxing services on the same basis as goods can close a horizontal equity gap, allows more revenue at any statutory rate, may improve vertical equity, and may improve secular adequacy of the tax. It would even reduce some compliance problems, as some businesses would no longer need to segregate sales of goods from sales of service in their billing and bookkeeping processes (auto-repair businesses would not need to distinguish between parts and labor, for instance). Why aren't services taxed more widely? The initial objection to taxing services was that the tax on services is a tax on labor income. Of course, labor constitutes much of the production cost of tangible personal property, so the argument lacks merit. And do you think the $75 per hour charge for labor when your car goes in for repair means that the mechanic is being paid $75 per hour? That's a charge by the business for the service, as is

---

[39]John L. Mikesell, "Sales Tax Coverage for Services–Policy for a Changing Economy," *Journal of State Taxation* 9 (Spring 1991): 31–50.
[40]Bureau of Economic Analysis, National Income and Products Accounts [www.bea.gov]. Larger changes appear when business purchases of services are included in the analysis.

the charge for the battery you are buying, and it has a lot of cost items (plus profit for the business) rolled into it. A more meaningful reason for exempting services is the frequent absence of a clear line between the worker-client relationship and the worker-employer relationship (e.g., an accountant doing personal tax returns versus an accountant working for a business firm). The latter, a producer-good relationship, should not be taxed. Furthermore, some services—medical and possibly legal, for instance—possibly should not be taxed as a matter of social policy. Consumers purchasing these services have enough trouble as it is without adding the sales tax to their bill.

Providing different treatment for purchases of services as opposed to treatment of purchases of goods creates interesting patterns of distortion. Consider the following differences: (1) if you buy software to prepare your federal income tax, you will almost certainly pay sales tax on the purchase; if you have an accountant or tax preparation firm do it for you, you will almost certainly not pay sales tax on the bill; (2) if you go to the multiplex to see a movie, you are unlikely to pay sales tax on the ticket; if you rent a video from a local business, you are likely to pay sales tax on the rental; (3) if you arrange for lessons from the tennis pro to improve your game, you will almost certainly not pay sales tax on her charge; if you buy a new racket to improve your game, you will certainly pay sales tax on the purchase; (4) if you go to a dentist for application of tooth whitener, you almost certainly will pay no sales tax on the bill; if you buy a tooth-whitening product from your local pharmacy, you are quite likely to pay sales tax on the purchase; and (5) if you pay a lawyer to write your will, you almost certainly will not pay sales tax on the bill; if you buy a book with blank will forms to fill in, you will certainly pay sales tax. Do these distinctions make any sense at all?

The pragmatic difficulty of taxing services is not surprising, even though the theory is sound and administration generally feasible. Politically, many types of services are sold by businesses with well-developed professional associations (accountants, barbers, lawyers, realtors, etc.), and those associations strive diligently to keep their services outside the sales tax. The problem is not just that these sellers may find adding the sales tax to their bills mathematically challenging. They do understand that adding the tax would have some negative impact on their sales and that dealing with the tax would add to their bookkeeping costs. Only a few states apply broad coverage of consumer services, but the realities of modern society cause extension to many services to be virtually inevitable—and leaving them out of the base of an indirect consumption tax certainly violates the broad-base, low-rate rule for tax policy. The difficult problem is to avoid taxing services sold almost exclusively to businesses; these are politically attractive targets, under the false impression that somehow applying a tax to a business avoids having the cost of government borne by the people.

Commodity Exemptions

RSTs typically exempt some items of tangible property that are clearly household consumption expenditures. The most frequently exempted items are food for at-home consumption (more than half the states) and prescription drugs (all but one state). There is a logical reason for these exemptions based on the standard evaluation criteria for taxes. Purchases of these items constitute a higher percentage of the income of low-income families than of high-income families. Excluding them from the tax base gives low-income families greater relief relative to their incomes than it does for high-income families, so the impact is to make the tax less regressive. The reduction of the effective tax rate on income is greater for low- than for high-income families. Hence, excluding the items improves the vertical equity of the tax. However, their exclusion makes the sales tax more difficult to collect (the state must define what items are exempt, stores selling both food and taxed items must maintain segregated accounting records, and audits are more complex), and the tax rate must be higher to yield a given amount of revenue on the smaller base (food constitutes around one-third of a prospective sales tax base).[41] The food exemption poorly targets relief: consumption studies show that households in the highest-income quintile receive double the tax relief from a food exemption that households in the lowest-income quintile receive (because they spend more in total on food than do low-income households). Given that the neediest families automatically receive a food exemption when they make purchases with food stamps (the federal SNAP program requires that these purchases be sales tax exempt), adding a general state food exemption almost by definition means that assistance gets misdirected. Eight states (Connecticut, Massachusetts, Minnesota, New Jersey, New York, Pennsylvania, Rhode Island, and Vermont) have extended commodity exemption to purchases of clothing under the apparent logic of exempting a necessity from the tax base. Unfortunately, clothing expenditures are less concentrated among low-income groups than in the ordinary sales tax base, so the exemption provides about four-and-one-half times more relief to the highest quintile of families, compared to the lowest quintile; does not improve vertical equity of the tax; causes effective rates within income classes to vary according to relative tastes for clothing; complicates compliance and administration; and causes higher rates for given revenues.[42]

Five states (Idaho, Kansas, Oklahoma, South Dakota, and Wyoming) provide an RST credit or rebate as an alternative to commodity exemption for controlling sales tax regressivity. Rather than providing exemption for all purchasers of selected commodities, the credit systems return a fixed sum to taxpayers at year's end,

---

[41]The distinctions for commodity exemptions can be maddening (as well as expensive to operate and downright silly). These examples illustrate the problem. In Illinois, whether a shave cream is considered a medicine (and some are) determines whether its purchase is taxed at a rate of 1 percent or 6.25 percent. The same rate differences apply between types of bottled water and between juices and juice beverages, according to whether they are considered food. In 2009, Illinois experienced a bit of a crisis when it extended its regular sales tax rate to candy (it had previously been considered food and eligible for taxation at a lower rate)—was Twix a candy or a food? In Pennsylvania, state and U.S. flags are exempt unless sold with a flagpole. In Texas, plain nuts are exempt, while candy-coated nuts are taxed. A number of states distinguish between a single doughnut and a dozen doughnuts in determining taxability. And Iowa decided, a few years ago, that pumpkins were being sold for decorations and not for food and decided to tax them. People could fill out a form to get an exemption if they swore they were going to eat them. That brought out a firestorm of public complaint, plus the national news media, neither of which made the Iowa tax administrators happy. (Tax people do not, as a rule, ever want to show up on the front page of the newspapers or on CNN.) And the administrators changed their decision.

[42]John L. Mikesell, "Exempting Clothing from the Sales Tax: The 'Supply Side Message' from the New York Tax Holiday," *State Tax Notes* (March 17, 1997): 835–38.

usually equal to estimated payment of sales tax on food purchases by individuals in the lowest-income class. If the prevailing sales tax rate is 4 percent and per capita food purchases by individuals in the under-$15,000-annual-income class are about $10,000, the amount returned would be $400. Return of $400 to all individuals—either by rebate application or as a credit on a state income tax return—would effectively eliminate the sales tax on food purchases by very low-income purchasers. The rebate amount would not increase, however, as food consumption increased through the higher-income classes. (High-income people spend more on food than do low-income people; the food exemption works to reduce regressivity because the percentage of income spent on food declines with higher income.) The rebate concentrates assistance where assistance is most needed and eliminates the need for vendors to account for taxed and exempt sales. Overall, the rebate effectively reduces (or even eliminates) regressivity at a lower loss of revenue than commodity exemption. The rebate requires that individuals file returns with the state and that the state make cash payments to individuals, but these would seem small disadvantages relative to the other efficiencies of the device. Canada provides a quarterly payment to low-income individuals and families for the national goods and services tax to accommodate tax that would have been paid on food purchases. There is a similar refund program for provincial sales taxes. The food purchase rebate/credit system allows better targeting of the relief to those in need, thereby getting greater reduction in regressivity per dollar of tax revenue lost and reducing the fiscal impact of the relief provided.

Commodity exemptions (1) narrow the tax base, thereby reducing the case that can be made for the sales tax as a means of general consumption taxation and requiring a higher statutory rate to yield a given amount of revenue; (2) increase the probability that family sales tax burdens will differ according to individual tastes and preferences for consumption items; (3) reduce the stability of the revenue base in the face of a business downturn (household consumption of nondurables tends to be less influenced by recessions than is spending on household durables); and (4) complicate administration and compliance by requiring sorting between taxed and exempt. Nevertheless, legislators find them popular with the electorate; they create the illusion that responsibility for the cost of government is being avoided rather than being distributed to the public in less transparent ways.

Variation in the State Sales Taxes

The states that levy RSTs do not apply the tax to the same transactions. They vary in the exemptions they provide for household consumption expenditure (food, clothing, nonprescription medicines, motor fuels, magazines, etc.), the extent to which they include service purchases in the tax base, and the degree to which they exclude purchase of business inputs from the tax base. The result of these variations is that the breadth of the tax base differs dramatically across the states. A given statutory sales tax rate yields significantly different revenues from one state to another because of these structural differences. In fiscal 2010, the average ratio of sales tax base to state personal income of the five narrowest states (Vermont, Massachusetts,

New Jersey, Maryland, and Rhode Island) equaled 0.247, compared with 0.667 for the five broadest (Hawaii, Wyoming, South Dakota, New Mexico, and South Dakota), the result of the differing choices that lawmakers in the two groups of states have made about including transactions in the tax base and some differences in state economies. That means that one percentage point of sales tax rate would yield almost three times as much revenue in the broad-base states as in the narrow-base ones, a considerable fiscal difference.[43] The structure of the base is critical for revenue yield; the broader the base, the more revenue that can be produced from a given rate, and the evidence is that states with broader bases do tend to levy lower statutory sales tax rates.

It is important to remember that, while there is an American style for sales taxation that states and localities follow, there is no single template for these taxes. The structures are established by state lawmakers, and each state is different in how it chooses to structure its own sales tax. The same principle applies in Canada, the only other country making significant use of the RST, where all provinces but one levy either the RST or the tax harmonized with the federal goods and services tax. With the exception of provinces that have chosen to harmonize with the federal tax , the provinces structure their taxes independently and not according to a national standard.

The Sales Taxes and Internet Commerce: Remote Vendors and Use Taxes

All sales tax states levy use taxes on the storage, use, or consumption of taxable property on which the sales tax has not been paid (in fact, some state laws call them "compensating use taxes" for that reason). The tax may not have been paid because the purchase was made in a jurisdiction without a tax on the item (e.g., hunting boots purchased from an outlet store in New Hampshire for use in Chicago) or because the purchase was made in interstate commerce (e.g., purchase of a computer from an internet vendor). The rules governing interstate commerce (based on the Commerce Clause of the U.S. Constitution) do not allow either the origination or the destination state to levy a sales tax on such interstate business; however, the destination state may impose the use tax on the purchase after it has come to rest.[44] The use tax serves to protect both the state sales tax base and local vendors against sales-tax-free competition. Protection, not direct collections, really is the primary objective; use tax collections seldom constitute as much as 10 percent of combined sales and use tax collections.

The use tax problem is with enforcement. Transaction taxes like the sales tax can best be collected through vendors—in other words, as indirect taxes rather than as direct taxes collected from purchasers. There are far fewer vendors than

---

[43]John L. Mikesell, "State Sales Taxes in Fiscal 2010: Collections Still in Recession," *State Tax Notes* 60 (June 6, 2011): 709–727.

[44]The U.S. Supreme Court, in *Henneford v. Silas Mason Co., Inc.*, 300 U.S. 577 (1937), upheld the Washington State use tax. The tax was on the privilege of use after interstate commerce was complete and did not interfere with interstate commerce itself.

purchasers for tax authorities to track, and vendors have far greater record-keeping and accounting capacity than household purchasers. Trying to administer a tax on individual transactions as a direct tax would be virtually impossible.[45] However, that is how most retail activity subject to the use tax, including internet sales, is expected to be collected—unless the vendor steps in. The key to enforcing any tax applied to individual transactions is getting vendors registered as tax collectors on behalf of the tax administration, and the constitutional standard for requiring vendors to register is "physical presence" in the taxing state, as prescribed by the U.S. Supreme Court in *National Bellas Hess* v. *Department of Revenue,* 386 U.S. 753 (1967), and reaffirmed in *Quill* v. *North Dakota,* 504 U.S. 298 (1992). The Commerce Clause of the U.S. Constitution prohibits states from placing "undue burden" on interstate commerce, and imposing frivolous registration requirements on remote vendors surely would be considered such a burden. For every jurisdiction in which the vendor is registered, it would need to know the rate and base structure in order to collect the tax—and it would need to know that for the thousands of taxing local jurisdictions, not just the forty-five sales tax states plus the District of Columbia. A vendor selling nationwide would need to know them all, and vendors selling via the internet might get an order from anywhere. The Court sought to provide with physical presence a "bright line" standard for firmly establishing when an enterprise would be required to bear the compliance responsibilities of becoming a tax collector. Only vendors with physical presence in a state may be required by that state to register as collectors for its sales and use taxes. If the vendor is physically there, it is not an undue burden for it to learn about the sales and use tax system in place in the jurisdiction.

The situation can be explained by reference to three classes of purchases and how the Commerce Clause of the U.S. Constitution requires that they be handled by state sales and use taxes:

1. **Purchases made from a local storefront.** A local storefront—a store in your local shopping mall—must register with its state as a tax collector and must remit tax from purchases made at that store. Physical presence, registration required. If the purchase is delivered to another state by a common carrier (postal service, package delivery firm, etc.), the sale is in interstate commerce, and the storefront state cannot apply its sales tax. If the storefront uses its own delivery trucks, it has physical presence.

2. **Purchases made from a remote vendor with physical presence in the state.** A remote vendor—internet seller, mail-order firm, telemarketer, home shopping channel, store in another state, and so on—with any physical presence, not necessarily a retail storefront, in the state must register with that state as a tax collector and must remit tax on purchases made for delivery into that state. The presence might be its delivery trucks, a warehouse, or a repair facility. However, physical presence of a subsidiary does not constitute physical presence for a parent company. The tax is a compensating use

---

[45]Most states do try to collect use tax directly from individuals, with varying degrees of rigor. For instance, some states provide use tax reporting on their individual income tax return, but revenues are modest. See John L. Mikesell, "Administering Use Tax as Direct Collection through Income Tax Reports," *State Tax Notes* 13 (May 26, 1997): 1603–6.

tax that the vendor is collecting and remitting on behalf of the purchaser. Physical presence, registration required.

3. **Purchases from a remote vendor without physical presence.** A remote vendor without physical presence may not be required to register as a use tax collector. (Voluntary registration is permitted.) Purchasers owe use tax on their purchases, as in the immediately preceding instance, but they are expected to remit the tax on their purchases directly rather than through the vendor.[46] No physical presence, registration not required.

How does a state collect its use tax? Some out-of-state vendors collect use tax on sales made in the state, either because they have some physical presence in the state (e.g., some catalog vendors also have retail or outlet stores) or because they have voluntarily registered as tax collectors. Some use tax is collected when the purchaser registers the item, as with a motor vehicle or a boat. Some use tax is collected when state auditors check a taxpayer's records and discover major purchases made out-of-state without payment of tax. Finally, some use tax is reported by the purchaser, either on a special return or on a convenience line added to the state's individual income tax return.

States do not presently have any successful mechanism for enforcing use tax on many sales, like those from mail-order catalogs, telemarketing, or the internet, and this is extremely worrisome in terms of fairness of the tax and long-term revenue productivity. States would like to require large firms to register to protect their in-state retailers from tax-free competition and to protect their tax base, but Congress has not yet been convinced of the reasonableness of this effort.

What states have developed is the Streamlined Sales Tax Project (SSTP). Many states are cooperating on the project to simplify and reduce the compliance burden on remote vendors so Congress would allow required registration. States that participate in the project do not adopt a common sales tax base, but they do agree to certain unified sales tax conditions to make it easier for a remote vendor to comply with any sales and use tax responsibilities. In general, the SSTP provisions are these:

1. Any local sales taxes must be state-administered, must apply to the same base as the state tax, and must all use the same tax rate.[47]
2. States must use standard definitions for certain exemptions and exclusions. Important definitions include those for food, drugs, clothing, and tangible personal property. The agreement does not require that the items be exempt, but if they are, the definitions must follow standard lines.

---

[46]The problem is primarily one of purchases made through the internet (or other remote vending format) and delivered through conventional means (postal service, delivery firms, etc.) and not of purchases delivered through the Internet. Only purchases subject to digitization can currently be delivered by electronic means, and that is a small component of the possible tax base. Furthermore, many such purchases are not taxable, even if purchased from a local storefront, because they are not tangible personal property–this is part of the general failure of state sales taxes to keep up with economic change. Some multistate businesses have established internet subsidiaries that are separated from the regular storefront operations of the business. There is an ongoing argument whether presence of a storefront establishes a registration requirement for the internet subsidiary.

[47]Until recently, tax liability had to be based on the destination of the sale (where it was delivered) rather than on the origin (the vendor's shop). This provision is being revised to allow states the choice of the two rules in determining the applicable tax rate and what locality gets the revenue.

3. States must participate in an online sales and use tax registration system that covers registration in all agreement states. A firm needs to register only once to be registered in all participating states.
4. The agreement provides three sales and use tax remittance options: a certified service provider acts as the firm's agent in all sales and use tax functions; the firm uses a certified automated system to handle tax calculation, remittance, record keeping, and reporting; or the firm does compliance itself according to a performance standard acceptable to each agreement state.
5. States adopt a variety of other changes in how taxes are calculated to make compliance easier. For instance, the state must use brackets consistent with major fraction rounding, the state may not limit the amount of tax due on a particular transaction, and the state must require statewide consolidated returns for multiple-location vendors.

States surrender some fiscal autonomy by participating in the agreement. They accept this loss because they hope to induce Congress to revise the physical presence rule and to use required registration as a means of protecting their local vendors and their sales tax base. In the summer of 2012, Congress held hearings on legislation that would provide for registration under certain conditions, but the ultimate outcome is not clear.[48]

Collecting the Retail Sales Tax

The RST has a collection advantage: the vendor who remits the tax to the government is something of a third party in the tax transaction between the purchaser, who most likely bears the burden of the tax, and the government receiving the revenue. This indirect tax relationship approximates that of income tax withholding and greatly simplifies administration and compliance with the tax. Administration is also simplified by the fact that the sales tax base is concentrated in a relatively small number of firms. Looking across states at vendors in the state with annual retail sales exceeding $10 million gives an idea of this concentration: in Colorado, those vendors constitute 1.8 percent of the total number of vendors and made up 65.4 percent of retail sales volume; in Illinois, 0.5 percent of vendors made up 62.5 percent of sales; in Kansas, 2.1 percent of vendors made up 57.9 percent of sales; in Michigan, 0.9 percent of vendors made up 63.8 percent of sales; in Pennsylvania, 0.4 percent of vendors made up 59.2 percent of sales; in Washington, 0.8 percent of vendors made up 56.5 percent of sales; and so it goes.[49] What this means is that state tax departments need only audit and do other enforcement work with a relatively

---

[48]Several large states have not joined the streamline effort, but are attempting other remedies. Some have sought to require registration if the remote vendor has an internet affiliate located within the state. Others have sought registration if the vendor has a subsidiary located within state. Still others have tried to force remote vendors to send customer reports to the tax department. None is particularly successful.
[49]Small Seller Task Force Committee, "Streamlined Sales Tax Governing Board, September 29, 2008, Report" [http://www.streamlinedsalestax.org/Small%20Seller%20Task%20Force%20Committee/Documents/Survey Results.pdf].

small number of firms and still cover an extremely high percentage of the sales tax base. That concentration, combined with the third-party nature of the tax, makes for extremely low noncompliance rates for state sales taxes. The Washington State compliance study, done regularly for a number of years and probably the most comprehensive and careful study of state sales tax noncompliance, estimated sales tax noncompliance at 1.7 percent for 2008.[50] That is in the same range as federal income tax noncompliance for incomes subject to withholding and much lower noncompliance than for the federal tax in total. Noncompliance with the use taxes is much, much greater—unless the vendor is registered with the state, the state has to hope for direct collection from the purchaser and payments from purchasers are rare.

Value-Added Taxes

A value-added tax (VAT) provides an alternate mechanism for taxing consumption.[51] Indeed, the VAT may be regarded as how the world (except the United States) levies a general tax on household consumption. This tax applies to the increment in value at each stage of the production and distribution process rather than applying only at the final (retail) stage. In the United States, the VAT over the years has been proposed as a means of financing the social insurance system in place of or in addition to the payroll tax, as a way to stimulate saving and investment through reducing reliance on income taxation, as an avenue to stimulating exports, as a replacement for the property tax as a means for financing primary and secondary education, as a bridge revenue option until sanity is restored to the federal income taxes, and as a revenue source that might unify state fiscal systems. However, none of the arguments has yet been strong enough for lawmakers to act. Conservative commentators fault the VAT mostly because it is a highly efficient tax, is too effective at raising revenue without doing harm to the economy, and might tempt governments to use it to get bigger. A more disruptive tax might tempt them less. Besides, some argue, the tax is European (German engineered, but first implemented by the French) and, hence, not to be trusted. Nevertheless, Bruce Bartlett, a former domestic policy advisor in the Reagan and first Bush administrations, gives the tax high praise: "From the point of view of efficiency, it is generally considered to be the best tax ever invented."[52] Tax analysts generally regard the value added tax as the most important tax innovation of the last half of the twentieth century, so it merits considerable attention.

---

[50]State of Washington, "Department of Revenue Compliance Study," Research Report No. 2008-5, July 10, 2008 [http://dor.wa.gov/Docs/Reports/Compliance_Study/compliance_study_2008.pdf]. Use tax compliance is considerably lower.
[51]An excellent reference is Alan A. Tait, *Value-Added Tax: International Practice and Problems* (Washington, D.C.: International Monetary Fund, 1988). The tax may also be designed to approximate an income tax, but the consumption variety predominates.
[52]Bruce Bartlett, *The Benefit and the Burden, Tax Reform—Why We Need It and What It Will Take* (New York: Simon & Schuster, 2012): 197.

The value-added tax (or goods and services tax as it is called in, for instance, Canada, New Zealand, and Australia), a simple, but sophisticated way of taxing consumption expenditure, is collected by businesses on their sales of goods and services to their customers.[53] Each business in the flow of production and distribution from manufacturer to retailer charges VAT on its sales and, in remitting payments to the taxing authority, is permitted to subtract from this amount the VAT that it paid on its purchases.[54] Invoices showing VAT paid must be available to support the VAT credits taken on the return, and credit is provided immediately for tax on all business purchases, including capital goods. Businesses of all types must register as VAT collectors in order to get the credits, so there will be more firms registered under a VAT than under an RST, in which only retailers need to register. The result of offsetting tax paid on purchases against tax collected on sales is to impose the tax on value added (sales less purchases) at each stage of production-distribution. The final consumer—the household—is not a business, has no sales through which VAT paid may be reimbursed, and thus bears the tax. It is multistage, but it does not pyramid because the tax applies only to the value added at each transaction, not to the total receipts of the transaction, and businesses are reimbursed for the tax that they have paid on their purchases. Why is the VAT equivalent to an RST? The RST applies to the total value of the product (the purchase price at retail) and is levied at the last stage of the production-distribution process; the VAT applies to the value added at each stage of the process, and the accumulation of these increments equals the total value of the product.[55] Sidebar 10–3 outlines the basic math that shows the economic equivalence of the two taxes.

The logic of a VAT can be demonstrated with a simple illustration. Remember in this example that the business is both a taxpayer (on its purchases) and a tax collector (on its sales). However, the tax that the business pays gets reimbursed (credited or refunded) in the tax that it collects on its sales. Suppose a 10 percent rate applies in a hypothetical production-distribution process that gets a wool sweater to a customer.[56]

---

[53]Although the national value-added taxes follow the same general principles, they do have considerable variation among countries. The taxes in Australia and New Zealand are simpler than those in Europe, with fewer special provisions, exceptions, rate variations, and so on to make compliance complicated. Lawmakers have virtually unlimited capacity to complicate taxes for perceived political advantage.

[54]The tax on the total value of its sales less the tax on the total value of its purchases equals the tax on the value that the business adds. Hence, it is a VAT. A tax on the value of its sales only is a gross receipts or turnover tax. This discussion focuses on the credit-invoice approach to applying the tax, the most frequently used method. Alternatives are examined in Itai Grinberg, "Where Credit Is Due: Advantages of the Credit-Invoice Method for a Partial Replacement VAT," *Tax Law Review LXIII* (Winter 2010): 309–358.

[55]Value added by a firm is also equal to the total amount the firm pays to factors of production (rent to land, wages and salaries to employees, interest to capital, and profit to entrepreneurial activity). The VAT base could thus alternatively be calculated by adding these payments—as is done with the Michigan single business tax and the New Hampshire tax on business enterprise.

[56]This illustrates the credit-invoice method of collection, as used in European-style VATs. The subtraction method, an alternate collection approach, would have businesses subtract purchases from sales and pay tax on the difference, without using invoices and credits. Zero rating, removing certain consumption categories from tax by taxing them at a rate of zero, does not work well, however, with the subtraction method.

1. A farmer sells wool to a textile company for $20, collects $2 in tax ($20 times 10 percent), and sends the $2 to the government. (The farmer's value added equals sales less purchases; that is, 20 minus 0 equals 20.) The textile company receives the wool, for which it has paid $20 plus $2 tax, or $22, and a statement showing that it paid $2 in VAT.

2. The textile company sells the yarn that it spins from the wool to a sweater manufacturer for $50. (Therefore, its value added equals sales minus purchases, or $50 minus $20 equals $30.) The company collects $5 in tax from the manufacturer and sends the government $3 plus the receipt showing $2 already paid when purchasing the wool. The textile company keeps the $2 and is now fully reimbursed for the VAT it paid when it purchased the wool. The sweater manufacturer has the yarn, for which it has paid $50 plus $5 tax, or $55, and a receipt for $5 VAT paid.

3. The sweater manufacturer knits a sweater and sells it to a retailer for $90 (its value added is $90 minus $50, or $40). The manufacturer collects $9 in tax from the retailer and sends the government $4 plus the receipt showing $5 already paid when purchasing the yarn. The retailer has the sweater, for which it has paid $90 plus $9 tax, or $99, and a receipt for $9 VAT paid.

4. The retailer sells the sweater to a final customer for $200 plus $20 VAT (the value added by the retailer, $200 minus $90, equals $110). The retailer sends the government $11 plus the receipt showing $9 already paid when purchasing the sweater from the manufacturer. The customer has the sweater and has paid $200 plus $20 in VAT, or $220. However, in contrast to the businesses in the production-distribution chain, the customer has no avenue to obtain a refund through the next transaction because the customer is the final link in the chain. The customer, not being a business, has no sales upon which the VAT would be applied. The final customer, the household, pays the tax, and the tax paid equals 10 percent of the value of the purchase.

There are, of course, many transactions going on in each of these businesses, but the basic principle of removing the tax from business purchases by refund remains the same. The tax does not pyramid because each business in the chain both pays the tax on its purchases and then receives a refund when it collects tax on its sales. The tax is not embedded in its operating cost. Notice in the example that the value of the sweater at the end ($200) equals the sum of values added at each stage of production ($20 plus $30 plus $40 plus $110 equals $200), that each cash payment to the government equals the tax rate times value added at that stage ($2, $3, $4, and $11), and that the sum of payments equals the VAT rate times the final value of the sweater. The result is thus equivalent to applying a 10 percent RST to the value purchased by the final customer.

VAT accounting can be quite simple for a business. Think about the scheme in this fashion. The business has two boxes. In one box go all the invoices for purchases during the month, with each invoice showing the amount of the purchase and the amount of VAT paid on the purchase. In the other box go all the invoices for sales during the month, with each invoice showing the amount of the sale and

Sidebar 10–3
The Economic Equivalence of RST and VAT[1]

An ideal RST and an ideal VAT are economically the same; they are just administered in a different fashion. Here is an explanation of the logic behind this equivalence. Assume the following economic chain: an extractor who sells to a manufacturer who sells to a wholesaler who sells to a retailer who sells to a final customer. Notice that one entity's sales are another entity's purchases: for example, the product that represents sales by the wholesaler is the product that represents purchases by the retailer.

Let t equal the VAT or RST rate; S equal sales or purchases; the subscripts e, m, w, and r indicate whether the sale is by extractor, manufacturer, wholesaler, or retailer; and R equal total revenue collected in the production and distribution chain.

RST: The ideal RST applies only to the final retail sales to the household customer. All sales between businesses are not taxed via use of the suspension certificate. Therefore, revenue from the RST equals

$$R = t \times S_r$$

VAT: The ideal VAT applies to value added at each transaction in the production and distribution chain. In other words, it applies to the difference between sales made by the business entity to other entities and purchases made by the business entity from other entities. Therefore, revenue from the VAT equals

$$R = t(S_e - 0) + t(S_m - S_e) + t(S_w - S_m) + t(S_r - S_w)$$

or

$$R = tS_e + tS_m - tS_e + tS_w - tS_m + tS_r - tS_w = tS_r$$

This expression reflects two VAT facts: (1) before the final sale to the household consumer, the purchases of one business are the sales of another business, and (2) VAT paid by a business on its purchases will be refunded from the VAT it collects on its sales.

Conclusion: Although the two taxes are administered in significantly different ways, the two taxes apply to the same final base and will yield equal revenue from a common statutory rate. The VAT accumulates through the stages of production and distribution to be a tax on all household consumption.

[1]For a more extensive comparison of the retail sales and value-added taxes, see John L. Mikesell, "Is the Retail Sales Tax Really Inferior to the Value-Added Tax?" in *The Sales Tax in the 21st Century,* ed. W. Fox and M. Murray (Westport, Conn.: Greenwood Press, 1997).

the amount of VAT collected on the sale. When it is time to do the VAT return at the end of the month, the business owner (1) goes to the purchase record box and tallies all purchases made and the tax paid on those purchases, (2) goes to the sales record box and tallies all sales made and the tax collected on those sales,

(3) subtracts total purchases from total sales to get value added during the month, and (4) subtracts total tax paid on purchases from total tax collected on sales to figure the amount of VAT to send to the government. It can get more complicated if the legislature wants to add exemptions or preferential tax rates, but that is how the process works. There are no more records required than for a business income tax, and the calculations from them are less complicated—and the owners of the business are much less likely to bear the burden of the VAT than they are of an income tax.

Figure 10–5 shows a return for the New Zealand goods and service (VAT) tax. Here is the basic structure of the return. The business reports its total sales on line 5, a total that includes VAT that has been collected on these transactions. The business subtracts sales on which it has not collected VAT (in RST terminology, these would be considered exempt sales, but VAT terminology refers to these sales as zero-rated, as in subject to a zero tax rate). The resulting total on line 7 is multiplied by 3 and then divided by 23 to produce the total VAT collected by the business. How does that make any sense? The statutory VAT rate is 15 percent (tax-exclusive). Its tax-inclusive equivalent, from Sidebar 10–2, would equal $TE/(100 + TE)$ or $15/115 = 0.13$. That equals 3 divided by 23, so this calculation yields the amount of VAT collected by the business. The next steps involve total purchases, which include VAT paid on the purchases, and VAT paid equals total purchases multiplied by 3 and divided by 23. Finally, line 15 is the difference between VAT collected and VAT paid—and that difference is paid if collections are higher and is refunded if payments are higher. The return calculation works exactly like the simple system of a box with receipts showing VAT collections and a box with receipts showing VAT payments, with a netting of the two boxes on a periodic basis.

Value-Added Tax Features

VATs are typically levied by national governments, and those governments rely heavily on revenue from these taxes. As a result, statutory VAT rates are usually much higher than typical RST rates. Table 10–4 displays the standard VAT rate for a number of countries around the world. Rates of 20 percent are common, though there are higher rates. Indeed, countries of the European Union are required to levy a minimum rate of 15 percent, and most levy even higher rates. Because the VAT plays such an important role in their revenue systems, high rates are necessary. (Individual income tax reliance is lower as a result.) Many countries also levy special preferential rates on some purchases (food, medicines, etc.) to reduce the regressivity of the tax, and others levy special higher rates on certain luxuries as they attempt to combine excise effects with the general consumption tax. These multirate systems make both compliance and administration more difficult. VAT systems assign a zero rating to goods or services they want to relieve entirely from tax; that relieves the purchaser from tax and allows the seller to have any tax it might have paid to be refunded.

Figure 10–5

New Zealand Value-Added Tax Return (Online Version)

Inland Revenue
Te Tari Taake

Goods and Services Tax Act 1985

Goods and services tax return

You can use the *GST guide (IR 375)* to help you complete this return, which you ll find at www.ird.govt.nz or call us on 0800 377 776.

GST 101A

July 2007

| Registration number | **1** ▶ | |

| Period covered by the return | | |

| from | **2** ▶ to | |

This return and any payment are due

If your correct **postal address** for GST is **not** shown above, print it in Box 3. **3** ▶

If your correct daytime phone number is **not** shown here, print it in Box 4   **4** ▶

Area code   Phone number

Goods and services tax on your sales and income

Total sales and income for the period (including GST and any zero-rated supplies)	**5** ▶ $
Zero-rated supplies included in Box 5	**6** ▶ $
Subtract Box 6 from Box 5 and enter the difference here	**7** ▶ $
Divide the amount in Box 7 by nine (9)	**8** ▶ $
Adjustments from your calculation sheet	**9** ▶ $
Add Box 8 and Box 9. This is your **total GST** collected on sales and income	**10** ▶ $

OFFICE USE ONLY

▶ Operator code   Corresp. indicator

Payment attached   Return cat.

Goods and services tax on your purchases and expenses

Total purchases and expenses (including GST) for which tax invoicing requirements have been met excluding any imported goods	**11** ▶ $
Divide the amount in Box 11 by nine (9)	**12** ▶ $
Credit adjustments from your calculation sheet	**13** ▶ $
Add Box 12 and Box 13. This is your **total GST** credit for purchases and expenses	**14** ▶ $
Print the difference between Box 10 and Box 14 here	**15** ▶ $

Declaration
The information in this return is true and correct and represents my assessment as required under the Tax Administration Act 1994.

Signature

/   /
Date

If Box 14 is larger than Box 10 the difference is your GST refund   (Tick one)
If Box 10 is larger than Box 14 the difference is GST to pay   Refund ○
Has payment been made electronically? Yes ○ No ○   GST to pay ○

Inland Revenue
Te Tari Taake   **Payment slip**

GST 700

| Registration number | |
| Return for the period ending | |

This return and any payment are due

Use the envelope provided to post your return, payment slip and any cheque payment.

Amount of payment $

Copy your total from Box 15 and enter it here. Include any late payment penalties for this period only.

Table 10–4
Standard Value-Added Tax Rates in Selected Countries around the World, March 2012

Members of the OECD	Rate	Selected Other Countries	Rate
Australia	10	Argentina	21
Austria	20	Brazil	17
Belgium	21	China	17
Canada	5	Colombia	16
Chile	19	Egypt	10
Czech Republic	20	India	12.5
Denmark	25	Indonesia	10
Estonia	20	Kenya	16
Finland	23	Latvia	22
France	19.6	Morocco	20
Germany	19	Peru	18
Greece	23	Philippines	12
Hungary	25	Russia	18
Iceland	25.5	South Africa	14
Ireland	21	Thailand	7
Israel	16	Ukraine	20
Italy	20	Venezuela	12
Japan	5	Vietnam	10
Korea (South Korea)	10		
Luxembourg	15		
Mexico	16		
Netherlands	19		
New Zealand	15		
Norway	25		
Poland	23		
Portugal	23		
Slovak Republic	20		
Slovenia	20		
Spain	18		
Sweden	25		
Switzerland	7.8		
Turkey	18		
United Kingdom	20		
U.S.A	no tax		

SOURCE: *Deloitte Touche Tohmatsu, Global Indirect Tax Rates, 2012.*

VAT exemptions do not work in the same way that RST exemptions do. An exemption relieves the seller from collecting the VAT on its sales, but it does not relieve the seller from paying the tax on its purchases. There are no purchase suspension certificates in the VAT. For exempt goods and services, the seller of the service is treated like the consumer of its purchases. In general, with the VAT, businesses do not want their product to be exempt; by being registered vendors of taxed goods or services, they have a mechanism for refund of the VAT that they pay on their purchases. Without that registration, they pay the tax without refund. Unless the business purchases very little from other businesses (certain service providers would be an example), so that very little of its operating cost is covered by the VAT, it will much prefer to be selling a taxed rather than an exempt product.

The typical VAT system does not require small businesses to register as VAT collectors. For example, the registration threshold for 2012 in the United Kingdom was £77,000; any business with annual gross receipts (turnover) below that sum is not required to register as a VAT collector. That relieves them of VAT compliance responsibilities and reduces administration cost for Her Majesty's Customs and Revenue, the United Kingdom's VAT collectors. Of course, that business would not be able to get VAT it paid on business input purchases refunded. Because this threshold is relatively high, the United Kingdom permits businesses to voluntarily register as VAT collectors. Countries have different policies in regard to both size of threshold and voluntary registration, but some threshold is common. The country loses revenue from the value added by these smaller firms, but reduced compliance and administrative costs are seen as making it a worthwhile loss.[57]

Value-Added Tax versus Retail Sales Tax

The VAT is undoubtedly the global choice for general consumption taxation. Why might a VAT be more desirable than an RST?[58] First, the VAT might help if tax evasion and a lack of vendor cooperation are problems. The VAT induces purchasers to require a documented receipt for vendors for taxes paid because the tax payments shown on those receipts are used to pay part of the taxes the purchasers will owe when they make sales. The VAT does not administer itself, but it certainly encourages a good trail of invoices for the audit process. (The reports on those invoices tend to be truthful because the buyer has an incentive to overstate the purchase price while the seller has an incentive to understate the purchase price (to minimize the value-added in the transaction) and the two incentives cancel out to produce the truth.) The tax authorities have to make sure that VAT collections actually end up in the treasury and that VAT payments claimed as credits are not fraudulent. The RST, on the other hand, puts all its collection eggs in one basket—if the retailer cheats, all revenue is lost.[59] Nevertheless, European

---

[57]Charities usually must pay VAT when they make purchases, but seldom have a mechanism for having their payments refunded. One of the few exceptions: Canada does provide a rebate of half the goods and services tax that charities pay.

[58]For a more extensive comparison of the RST and VAT, see John L. Mikesell, "Is the Retail Sales Tax Really Inferior to the Value-Added Tax?" in *The Sales Tax in the 21st Century*, ed. W. Fox and M. Murray (Westport, Conn.: Greenwood Press, 1997), 75–87.

[59]Furthermore, the RST puts the burden of judging whether the tax should be suspended or collected on the vendor. However, the vendor is almost certainly keenly interested in making a sale and could be willing to sacrifice revenue rightfully owed the state, by failing to deny a doubtful suspension certificate, in order to make the sale. The VAT requires payment of tax—which may be recovered by a business making a successful claim to the revenue department.

experience shows that businesses still cheat—for instance, by claiming credit for VAT not actually paid or for running off with the collections—and that businesses are still delinquent in payment, so the tax authorities continue to have a job to do.[60] However, VATs with high statutory rates have been successfully collected in countries with historically bad compliance environments. Most observers agree that traditional RSTs cannot be successfully administered at statutory rates much higher than 10 percent. If a government intends to levy high statutory rates, for instance, in an effort to replace national income taxes, experience teaches that the VAT is the only feasible choice.

Second, countries are able to remove VAT from international trade and international competitiveness considerations. Indeed, this was the primary reason why the European Union selected the VAT as the indirect tax of choice for its members. The chain of tax documentation produced by the VAT makes this extraction simple—the exporter requests a refund of VAT paid at the time inventory is exported and the importer must pay VAT at the time inventory is brought into the country. That levels the tax comparison between foreign and domestic products within the country and removes the VAT from prices of goods the country is selling on world markets. This sort of adjustment is not possible with other general taxes.[61] Under the rules of the World Trade Organization, only an indirect tax like the VAT can be adjusted at borders in this fashion. There is no way to remove RST embedded when pre-retail purchases are taxed from export prices, so there is an international competitive problem. A VAT levied at the subnational level would have issues regarding the administration of cross-border credits or rebates, although they could be handled in one way or another (Brazil illustrates how subnational VATs could function, but their operation does involve border checks that somewhat interfere with free trade.). Subnational RSTs are clearly quite feasible; this may be the best level of government for application of such taxes.

Third, the VAT comes closer to being a general consumption tax than does the RST. The VAT provides more complete exclusion of business purchases than does the RST because the credit-refund device politically seems less like a special break for business than does the exemption certificate, and the VAT achieves more general coverage of services purchased by households. The RST exempts a considerable portion of household consumption expenditure and taxes a considerable portion of business purchases of inputs. Legislatures simply seem unable to accept the idea that exemption of business purchases represents the proper design of the tax base, not an unfair tax advantage to business. Legislatures seem more accepting of the VAT idea of having businesses pay on purchases, but get a refund on their sales, thus permitting the VAT to more closely work as a general consumption tax. Therefore, at higher statutory rates, the VAT is substantially less likely to do damage to economic development prospects and infrastructure investment than is the RST.

---

[60]Henry J. Aaron, ed., *The Value-Added Tax, Lessons from Europe* (Washington, D.C.: Brookings Institution, 1981).
[61]Some suspect that flexible exchange rates may eliminate any impact of the VAT on international trade patterns.

Conclusion

Taxes on goods and services are at the heart of state revenue systems, are an important contributor to local revenue systems, but are relatively unimportant for U.S. federal finance. Though questions of structure persist for each base, there is no doubt concerning the serviceability of these taxes. The case for general sales taxes is much stronger than it is for the selective excises as a general revenue source. The key problem with consumption taxation remains regressivity; no perfect solution exists. VATs and RSTs provide two alternative formats for collecting a tax on general consumption. Although the RST provides an important foundation for state and local revenue systems in the United States, it has significant adverse equity and economic effects. VATs provide an alternative with better economic performance, and these taxes are widely used throughout the world as the mechanism of choice for national general consumption taxation.

QUESTIONS AND EXERCISES

1. Identify the important elements of sales taxation in your state. What governments levy general and selective sales taxes? Identify the following for the RST: What commodity sales are exempt? Are services taxed? What is the nominal rate? What are the brackets? Does your state provide sales tax credits? In regard to selective excises: What selective excises are used? How are their bases defined? What rates apply?

2. It has been proposed that the Foundation for Preservation of the American Badger (*taxidea taxus*) be provided a sales tax exemption for its purchases and for its annual sales of "Badger Booster" cookies. Please analyze according to the general principles of tax policy.

3. The Bureau of Labor Statistics' Consumer Expenditure Survey: 2007 gives the following data:

Income Category of Family	Average Income before Taxes ($)	Alcoholic Beverage Expenditures ($)	Tobacco Products Expenditures ($)
First quintile	10,531	176	259
Second quintile	27,674	272	337
Third quintile	46,213	413	381
Fourth quintile	72,460	506	371
Highest quintile	158,388	917	268

Analyze the likely vertical equity of selective excises on alcoholic beverages and tobacco products.

4. The text worked the logic of a VAT through a production-distribution process from a farmer to the final customer. Work the same process through with a 10 percent turnover or gross receipts tax. Assume that value added at each stage is the same as before, but that no credit for prior tax paid is provided and that

each sales price equals tax-inclusive cost of purchases, plus value added at that stage, plus the 10 percent tax. Compute the final price paid by the consumer and the effective tax rate as a percentage of total value added. Make the same computation, assuming the sweater manufacturer and the retailer merge (i.e., there is no taxable sale in this exchange).

5. Vendors at Municipal Stadium sell their wares at prices that include the city, state, and transit district sales taxes; the total of these taxes is 8.25 percent when added to prices that do not include the sales tax.

   a. Convert this 8.25 percent tax-exclusive sales tax rate into its tax-inclusive equivalent rate. (*Hint:* Use the method outlined for VAT calculations.)
   b. A vendor has receipts (including sales tax) at a game of $15,325. What sales tax must the vendor remit to the tax authorities?

6. Several states have declared sales tax holidays, in which the state does not collect sales tax on certain items for a short period of time. In most instances, the holiday has been for clothing, and the period has been a week or ten days in August, the idea being to give a "back-to-school" discount as families get ready for the new school year. However, states have gotten more adventurous with the idea in recent years and have enacted or proposed holidays for hurricane survival supplies, gasoline, Energy Star appliances, and guns and ammunition. Analyze the idea of such holidays according to yield, equity, administration and compliance, and economic impact.

7. When the Russian Federation allowed its regions to levy a retail sales tax, the national value-added tax rate was 20 percent. Many regions levied a 5 percent tax rate, and the rate applied to purchase prices with the national value-added tax included. What is your view about this approach? (This approach has also been used for some Canadian provincial retail sales taxes.)

CASES FOR DISCUSSION

CASE 10–1

Girl Scout Cookies and the Snack Tax

State sales taxes often exempt food purchased for at-home consumption to help relieve the regressivity of the tax. However, that exemption causes significant loss of revenue. Furthermore, some people question the nutritional value of certain items exempted under the food label and doubt the wisdom of losing revenue in a tax structure to provide relief to such purchases. In difficult fiscal times in the early 1990s, a few states sought additional revenue by narrowing the food exemption, particularly by removing some of these questionable categories from the exempt list. These new laws and their enforcement have produced policy problems testing the resolve of the legislators and tax administrators.

In the 1991 legislative session, Maine passed a package of tax changes designed to increase revenues by $300 million annually. (Total tax collections in fiscal 1990 were $1,560.9 million.) The changes included higher income taxes, an increase in the state sales and use tax rate from 5 to 6 percent, and a revision to remove snack food from the "sales of grocery staples" category, which was then exempt from the state sales and use tax. The new law was estimated to yield $10 million annually.

The new law taxed snack food, as defined by the legislature:

14-C. "Snack food." Snack food means any item that is ordinarily sold for consumption without further preparation or that requires no preparation other than combining the item with a liquid; that may be stored unopened without refrigeration, except that ice cream, ice milk, frozen yogurt and sherbet are snack foods; that is not generally considered a major component of a well-balanced meal; and that is not defined in this section as a grocery staple. "Snack food" includes, but is not limited to, corn chips, potato chips, processed fruit snacks, fruit rolls, fruit bars, popped popcorn, pork rinds, pretzels, cheese sticks and cheese puffs, granola bars, breakfast bars, bread sticks, roasted nuts, doughnuts, cookies, crackers, pastries, toaster pastries, croissants, cakes, pies, ice cream cones, marshmallows, marshmallow creme, artificially flavored powdered or liquid drink mixes or drinks, ice cream sauces including chocolate sauce, ready-to-eat puddings, beef jerky, meat bars and dips. (36 Maine Revised Statutes 1752 [1992].)

The lawmakers soon discovered that the expansion of the sales and use tax base had some unexpected consequences, particularly in regard to the finances of Girl Scouts. Two councils, the Abnaki and Kennebec, served about 19,500 girls in Maine, and 60 to 65 percent of their revenues came from cookie sales. Because neither council was qualified to purchase inventory for resale as a registered retailer, and then charge sales tax on each transaction, the councils now had to pay tax on their cookie purchases. That amounted to around $58,000, or almost 2 percent of cookie revenue (they paid tax on the wholesale price of about 80¢ per box).

The two councils responded differently to the new tax. Abnaki raised its cookie prices from $2.25 to $2.50, but sales fell 7 percent from the prior year. Kennebec lacked sufficient time to react, so it had to absorb about $40,000 in cookie losses. However, neither council thought the new tax was fair. Jo Stevens, executive director of the Abnaki Council, voiced the general view: "We're not selling groceries. We're raising charitable contributions."

The Joint Taxation Committee was generally sympathetic. Its co-chair, Senator Stephen Bost, said, "We had not intended as a committee to include … Girl Scouts in the snack tax." However, proposed legislation to exempt Girl Scouts and related organizations (including the pre-popped popcorn sold by Boy Scouts) would cause a revenue loss of around $175,000 annually—and the state had no clear way to make it up. (Incidentally, candy had been taxed for some time, but candy sales by school groups and parent-teacher organizations are exempt.)

What should Maine do? Here are some options: (1) do nothing—the tax is working as it should; (2) direct the Bureau of Taxation to rewrite the instruction; (3) repeal the snack tax; (4) exempt sales and purchases by the Girl Scouts and similar organizations; (5) require the Girl Scouts to register as retail merchants, buy their cookies using the resale exemption, and collect sales tax on their cookie sales; and (6) exempt sales and/or purchases by all youth or charitable organizations. (You may think of other possibilities.) Use the standards for revenue-policy evaluation (yield, fairness, economic effect, and collectability) to test options and provide a recommendation. Explain which approach is most consistent with the logic of sales taxation. Which parties would have an interest in the eventual outcome of the discussion? What is your overall view of the snack tax, without respect to the Girl Scout issue?[62]

CASE 10–2

Pringles and Preferences from the Value-Added Tax Base?

Legislators put many preferences in tax laws with many different objectives in mind—to alter the distribution of tax burden for reasons of equity and to favor certain producers or consumers to name two. Effects may sometimes be clear-cut, but there may be surprises in their application. There are interesting effects in the conflict between the UK tax authorities and Procter & Gamble UK, the producers of Pringles, as the following describes.

Consider These Questions

1. Explain why Procter & Gamble wanted zero rating and not exemption.

2. Why would the VAT legislation not have explicitly covered Pringles?

3. Tax analysts counsel against tax preferences. How does this case provide support for that position?

4. What are the reasons for the food preference, and what are the reasons for the special treatment of potato crisps? Are there better alternatives for achieving those objectives?

5. Are there lessons for design of a consumption tax in this case?

The VAT and Pringles

"Are Pringles 'similar to potato crisps and made from the potato'? That is the question."[63] Not as weighty as Hamlet's musing, but that is how Lord Justice Jacob (England and Wales Court of Appeal) began his judgment in a case between the Commissioners for Her Majesty's Revenue and Customs and Procter & Gamble UK, the makers of Regular Pringles. And that is what ultimately

---

SOURCE: Data and quotations from "Scouting and Tax Relief," *State Government News* 35 (April 1992): 33.

---

[62]Girl Scout cookies may be a "third rail" for sales tax policy. House Bill 385 in the 2011 Georgia legislature would have, among many other things, applied the state sales tax to Girl Scout cookie sales (along with Boy Scout popcorn sales). The proposal got buried under an avalanche of calls, letters, and lobbying.
[63]*Revenue & Customs v. Procter & Gamble UK* (2009) EWCA Civ 407 (May 20, 2009). In the UK, a "crisp" is what Americans call a "potato chip." A "chip" in the UK is what we call a "french fry."

determined the decision regarding a tax preference in the United Kingdom value-added tax.

Creating a tax preference is always a tricky business because the tax authorities have to draw a line between what gets preference and what doesn't, and, accordingly, some people end up paying relatively more and others pay relatively less because of where the line is drawn. The principles in the law have to be put into practice in a world of brands, product distinctions, and a consistent desire to reduce tax burdens. The trickiness gets more challenging as activities initially on the wrong side of the preference work to get moved to the other side. That is how, after all, that many tax lawyers and accountants justify their pay. Although the maneuvering occurs with every preference, it gets more frantic when the tax wedge is high, when the tax involves excises, and when substitute alternatives for taxed items are easily available.

The UK value-added tax is levied at a standard rate of 17.5 percent. However, as is the case with many VATs as well as retail sales taxes, the law makes special provision for sales of food for at-home consumption in an effort to reduce the regressivity of the tax. In the UK VAT, "Food of a kind used for human consumption" is zero-rated, meaning it is subject to a tax rate of zero.

However, the tax preference is limited and not applicable to everything that humans might eat. An exception is the following:

> Any of the following when packaged for human consumption without further preparation, namely, potato crisps, potato sticks, potato puffs and similar products from the potato, or from potato flour, or from potato starch, and savoury products obtained by the swelling of cereals or cereal products; and salted or roasted nuts other than nuts in shell.

Those products are subject to the standard tax rate of 17.5 percent. Now the question is, What are Pringles? Many people have pondered this question in the United States as well as in the United Kingdom, although not in court, since their arrival on the market in 1968. However, such philosophical questions were not what the Procter & Gamble representatives were concerned about here; it was tax rates. Procter & Gamble argued that Pringles should be taxed at zero rate, not the standard rate, because they really are not potato crisps.[64] Their argument primarily hinged on the fact that the Pringle is only around 40 percent potato and the majority was something else, although no other single ingredient made up as much of the total as potato. Therefore, they argued that it wasn't a *potato* crisp and should be zero rated along with other items for human consumption. Strictly, Pringles were not "made of" potatoes. That would allow consumers of Pringles to pay less and would also allow Pringles a price advantage in the snack food market (although Procter & Gamble did not point that out). It should be noted, however, that there are other vegetable crisps available on the UK market (e.g., turnip crisps) and they were not excluded from the preference.

---

[64]It should be noted that another Procter & Gamble product, Pringles Dippers, had been judged to be zero-rated, apparently because they were to be dipped in salsa or whatever, like tortilla chips, and were not fully prepared for immediate human consumption.

The judge was not impressed: "the VAT legislation uses everyday English words, which ought to be interpreted in a sensible way according to their ordinary and natural meaning. The 'made from' question would probably be answered in a more relevant and sensible way by a child consumer of crisps than by a food scientist or a culinary pedant."[65]

The ruling meant around $155 million in back taxes (which had not been collected from purchasers because of an earlier ruling) and much more to be collected in the future. If it crunches like a potato crisp, looks generally like a potato crisp, and pretty much tastes like a potato crisp, it should be treated like a potato crisp, no matter what the lawyers make their living by arguing. Child consumer trumps food experts.[66]

---

[65]*Revenue & Customs,* op. cit.

[66]An older VAT case involved Jaffa Cakes: if cakes, then food and not taxed; if biscuits (cookies), then subject to the standard rate. The court decided on the basis of what they do when they go stale: cookies go soft and cakes go hard. Jaffa Cakes go hard. (I am not making this up.)

CHAPTER 11

Major Tax Structures: Property Taxes

Annual taxes on property in the United States yield over $400 billion each year for state and local governments. That considerable yield is substantially less than the total from either income or consumption bases, and much less than states collect from those bases, but the tax on real property—roughly 90 percent of the property tax total—is the lifeblood for fiscal independence of local governments. As Glenn Fisher points out: "There are no taxes capable of financing our current system of local governments that can be locally levied and administered, except the property tax."[1] Tax experts argue the case for local property taxes because of their efficiency, equity, facilitation of fiscal decentralization, and transparency, but they are unpopular with the electorate and with enlightened and craven politicians alike. They endure because they produce reliable, stable, independent revenue for the governments closest to the people, and there is no better alternative for providing local fiscal autonomy. Property taxes of various designs are levied throughout the world, although governments in the United States and Canada raise relatively more of their tax revenue from them than is the case elsewhere. Because of their utility for providing a source of revenue subject to local control, they are an important element in fiscal decentralization programs in many countries of Central and Eastern Europe and in China.

Property taxes were once the primary tax for both state and local government finance. Indeed, as recently as 1932, property taxes produced almost three-quarters of all state and local tax revenue and 92.5 percent of local government tax revenue.[2] But in the depths of the Great Depression, much property tax could not

---

[1] Glenn W. Fisher, *The Worst Tax? A History of the Property Tax in America* (Lawrence, Kans.: University Press of Kansas, 1996), 210.

[2] U.S. Bureau of the Census, *Financial Statistics of State and Local Governments: 1932 (Wealth, Public Debt, and Taxation)* (Washington, D.C.: U.S. Government Printing Office, 1935). The federal government has levied property taxes twice, in 1798 and in 1813. The taxes were apportioned among the states, as required for direct taxes by the U.S. Constitution. See Dall W. Forsythe, *Taxation and Political Change in the Young Nation, 1781–1833* (New York: Columbia University Press, 1977).

be collected from farmers, businesses, and individuals who had lost their usual sources of income, and states began to develop transaction-based taxes on goods and services, especially retail sales taxes and motor-fuel excises. These new taxes offered high yield and greater reliability in those difficult times—not to mention their less harsh enforcement mechanisms (enforcement of uncollected property tax on a house or farm, for example, meant seizure and sale of that property)— and state governments especially financed their post–World War II responsibilities with more nonproperty tax revenues. Local governments overall continue a heavy reliance on the property tax, although large cities in some states make significant use of other options. Even during the Great Recession, local property tax revenue held up better than did collections from other broad-based local taxes (retail sales and income, in particular). Those local governments that had not diversified away from the property tax suffered a less severe revenue collapse, and property tax reliance preserved local revenues better than did the more diversified state revenue systems.

Table 11–1 offers an overview of property tax reliance in the United States. Although states obtain only 2 percent of their tax revenue from these levies, local governments collect over 70 percent of their tax revenue from it. Independent school districts rely more heavily on the property tax than does any other type of government, raising over 95 percent of their tax revenue from that source. Because schools receive substantial intergovernmental aid, mostly from their states, the share of all their revenue from the property tax is much lower (around 30 percent), but they still receive more than 40 percent of all property tax collected. Cities and counties both receive more than 20 percent of property taxes, but cities rely somewhat more heavily on nonproperty taxes than do counties. Despite the continuing unpopularity of the property tax, property tax collections have grown at a compound rate of 5.9 percent annually from 1998–1999 to 2008–2009.

Table 11–1
Property Taxes in U.S. Government Finances, 2008–2009

	Total ($ Thousands)	% of General Revenue	% of Tax Revenue	Share of Total Property Tax Revenue	Growth Rate since 1998–1999
State and local governments	424,014,170	17.6	33.3	100.0	5.9
State governments only	12,964,188	0.9	1.8	3.1	1.1
Local governments only	411,049,982	29.2	73.9	96.9	6.1

SOURCE: U.S. Census Bureau, Governments Division, Annual Survey of State and Local Government Finances [www.census.gov].

Property taxes are the closest approximation to annual wealth taxes currently levied in the United States.[3] They are not, however, true net-wealth taxes because they typically exclude some types of wealth (e.g., personal property owned by individuals); they apply to gross, not net, wealth (e.g., the debt against a house or car is seldom completely subtracted from taxable value); and they may apply twice to certain wealth forms (some states tax the value of both corporate stock and properties owned by the corporation). To the extent that the taxes do reach wealth holdings, they may add an element of redistribution from rich to poor otherwise missing from the rest of the tax structure.[4] Because they apply to accumulated wealth, not income, they may also have less effect on work and investment incentives than do income taxes. They are not based, however, on values from current transactions (as is usually the case for income and sales taxes), so the tax requires a value-estimation procedure (assessment). That procedure is the primary weakness of property taxation.[5]

Property taxes cannot be simply summarized. As Richard Almy observes,

> In the United States, "the" property tax is composed of fifty-one separate state level property tax systems, each subject to numerous legal and extralegal local variations and each changing in some fashion over time—through constitutional revision, enactment of statutes and ordinances, changes in administrative procedures, court decisions and changes in the capabilities of tax administration.[6]

Property within the scope of taxation may be either real or personal. *Real property* means real estate, realty, or land and improvements on that land. It encompasses soil and things permanently fixed to it by nature (trees, crops, grass, water, minerals, etc.) or by people (buildings, fences, etc.). Real property may also include air rights, the space above that land, but only when that space is actually used. *Personal property* includes everything that can be owned that is not real property. The category includes machinery and equipment, jewelry, automobiles, inventory, household furnishings, stocks and bonds, and much more. Personal property generally is more easily moved than real property, but there is no general dividing line between the types. Each government develops its own definitions and distinctions, usually resorting to

---

[3]There are federal, state, and local transfer taxes, however. The federal estate tax is the most widely known, although it produces only modest revenue (1.5 percent of total receipts in 2008). In spite of the fact that it is paid by very few estates (fewer than 1.3 percent of estates are covered by the tax because of large exclusions before the tax begins to apply) and is highly progressive in burden, it is extremely unpopular. Because much of the money actually taxed by the estate tax represents unrealized capital gains that have not been taxed by the income tax, the tax fills a gap in the fiscal system and does not represent a double tax on income. Nevertheless, a small group of holders of great inherited wealth stands a good chance of getting the tax entirely abolished. See Michael J. Graetz and Ian Shapiro, *Death by a Thousand Cuts: The Fight over Taxing Inherited Wealth* (Princeton, N.J.: Princeton University Press, 2005), for the drama and for how the wealthy few convinced people who have absolutely no chance, barring a huge lottery win, of ever owing any estate tax that the tax would keep them from passing their wealth, bank accounts, farms, businesses, and collections of baseball cards to their children.

[4]One fact of American society is that wealth is significantly more concentrated than income. The wealthiest 1 percent of the population owns about 30 percent of wealth in the economy, whereas the top 1 percent of income earners receives 20 percent of total income. See Javier Diaz-Gimenez, "Dimensions of Inequality: Facts on the U.S. Distribution of Earnings, Income, and Wealth," *Federal Reserve Bank of Minneapolis Monthly Review* 21 (Spring 1997): 3–21.

[5]The tax may have development and redevelopment disincentives as well, depending on its structure.

[6]Richard Almy, "Rationalizing the Assessment Process," in *Property Tax Reform*, ed. George Peterson (Washington, D.C.: Urban Institute, 1973), 175.

lists of property types to make borderline distinctions.[7] The distinction is crucial because some governments tax personal property more heavily than real property, whereas others exempt certain personal property. The personal property share of the locally taxable property base is small, only around 10 percent on national aggregate, but it is much higher in a handful of states; many states exempt personal property entirely from the property tax base.[8] In most states, real property is assessed by local assessors, subject to state rules and regulations and, to varying degrees, state supervision and evaluation of the work that has been done.

Another distinction is between tangible and intangible personal property. *Tangible personal property* is property held for its own sake, including cars, machinery, inventories of raw materials and finished products, and household items. *Intangible personal property* is property valued because it represents an ownership claim on something of value; intangible properties include stocks, bonds, and other financial assets. Property taxes vary widely in the extent to which they apply to these properties. Many types of tangible personal property are both difficult to locate and, once located, difficult to value (What is the value of a ten-year-old television set or the old sofa where the cat sleeps, after all?); intangible personal property can often be easily valued, but may be difficult to locate. Intangible property is sometimes exempt by law and sometimes exempt by local practice. Seldom is taxation complete.[9]

An alternative to the conventional property tax is the land or site value tax. It has many advantages over the traditional property tax and has been advocated by many reform advocates over the years, particularly those interested in improved land use and urban development, but it has never gained many adoptions in the United States. Sidebar 11–1 describes the logic and advantages of the tax.

Sidebar 11–1
An Alternate Approach: Land or Site Value Taxes

Even more than they like property taxes as a means of financing local governments, tax analysts, particularly economists, like a particular variant of the property tax—the land tax. Noble laureate economist William Vickery summed it up: "The property tax is, economically speaking, a combination of one of the worst taxes—the part that is assessed on real estate improvement... and one of the best taxes—the tax on land or site value.... A tax on land, properly assessed... is virtually free of distortionary effects... while the tax on improvements imposes serious burdens on construction."[1]

---

[7]One interesting problem concerns the treatment of mobile homes: Are they real or personal property? States use rules including permanency of foundation, presence of wheels or axles, highway licensing, and so forth, but there is no general division.

[8]John L. Mikesell, "Patterns of Exclusion of Personal Property from American Property Tax Systems," *Public Finance Quarterly* 20 (October 1992): 528–42.

[9]John H. Bowman, George E. Hoffer, and Michael D. Pratt, "Current Patterns and Trends in State and Local Intangibles Taxation," *National Tax Journal* 43 (December 1990): 439–50.

**Sidebar 11–1
(continued)**

Why is that? The answer lies in the power of taxes to discourage and distort. A property tax on improvements adds to the cost of new development, and that discourages the development activity. Additions to the built infrastructure contribute to the standard of living—so why on earth would it be good policy to tax in a way that discourages development and renewal of that infrastructure? If the property owner upgrades or restores a building or builds a new structure on the site, the owner's property tax bill increases, thereby reducing the return on the activity and, at the margin, reducing the likelihood that development will occur. Does discouraging economic development make sense? That is what a conventional property tax does.

A property tax on land does not have that impact. Land at a particular site is in fixed supply. Applying a tax to the land value does not have an impact on the supply of land, given that it is fixed. Amounts supplied are not increased when return is higher, and amounts supplied are not reduced when return is lower. Indeed, a tax on land value makes sense because the value of that land is determined by the community that surrounds it—the transportation network, the amenities, the utilities, the government services, and so on—and not the efforts of the owner of that land. The tax on land does not impact investment choices in the way that a tax on improvements on that land does and, hence, does not discourage economic development. If the land is taxed according to its market value, its value in the best possible use, then what the landowner actually does with the land has no impact on the tax bill. Letting the land stand idle and generating no income will not reduce the tax bill, so there is no savings from leaving land fallow. (Conventional property taxes that capitalize income flows to estimate value can support keeping productive land idle.) There is no support for engaging in land speculation or delaying the development of land for strategic gain with a site value tax. The pure land tax is the rarest of revenue sources: one that has no adverse economic impact.

A variant of the land tax is the graded tax or split-rate system, in which improvements are taxed, but at a lower rate than land. Some experience with this approach in around eighteen cities in Pennsylvania, including Pittsburgh from 1913 to 2001, and more than two dozen other nations suggests that the system is feasible, can provide adequate revenues for local finance, and can improve the prospects for economic development relative to the conventional property tax. A number of Pennsylvania cities with split-rate systems managed to have less urban decline, and even growth, when comparable "rust-belt" cities were experiencing considerable decay and blight, and observers believe that the tax system was an important contributing influence to the difference.[2] Critics complain that property assessors would have great difficulty separating the value of the land from the value of any improvement to the land. But even a rough separation would have better development impacts than the current system, could produce as much revenue as the current system, and, given the state of many American cities, certainly would seem worth a try.

[1]Quoted in Kenneth Wenzer, *Land Value Taxation* (Armonk, N.Y.: M. E. Sharpe, 1999), 17–18.
[2]An excellent source for more about land taxation: Richard F. Dye and Richard W. England, *Land Value Taxation: Theory, Evidence, and Practice* (Cambridge, Mass.: Lincoln Institute for Land Policy, 2009), includes essays on the logic of land taxation, its administrative practicality, and its impacts on growth and development. Evidence on the development impact of split rates in Pittsburgh appears in Wallace E. Oates and Robert M. Schwab, "The Impact of Urban Land Taxation: The Pittsburgh Experience," *National Tax Journal* 50 (March 1997): 1–21.

Good Tax, Bad Tax?

Academicians and tax analysts like property taxes more than do politicians, the media, and most of the general public. Property tax advocates believe that real property taxation is synonymous with fiscal autonomy for local government. There are no broad-based revenue options that are as well suited for local use as is this tax. If local governments do not have access to a property tax and flexibility to use the tax to cover their service obligations, then they are almost certainly destined to become fiscal wards of their state. There simply is no satisfactory tax option available for local use to replace the lost property tax revenue. Local fiscal autonomy means local property taxation. The specific advantages of the tax for local finance are significant:

1. The base is immobile, so the tax can be administered without fear that it will escape a local jurisdiction before the tax is collected. Even if the owner of the property skips town or declares bankruptcy, the property itself remains, and the tax authorities can take action against (i.e., sell) the property to collect the taxes.

2. Revenue from the property tax is more stable in the face of recession than is revenue from other broad-base taxes (general sales and income in particular). The Great Recession had less impact on localities that remained dependent on the property tax than it did on those who had diversified to other broad-base local taxes or who relied heavily on state aid (states tend to cut aid to local governments as a way of dealing with their own budget problems). Property-tax-dependent localities fared better than did most states.

3. The tax rate can vary within small geographic areas to support even the smallest local governments. The average effective property tax rate on owner-occupied housing is around 1 percent of market value, although there are considerable variations by region and by jurisdiction (city, suburb, rural).

4. The services typically supported by local property taxes provide direct protection to real property (fire and police protection, for instance) or contribute to making real properties valuable (high-quality local schools, for instance). The property tax is a charge for these services.

5. The property tax base associated with industrial development provides a way of compensating those living around the property for the inconvenience (noise, traffic, pollution, etc.) associated with such activity. Property tax revenue is a way of reducing the "Not in My Backyard" (NIMBY) opposition to economic development.

6. Property taxes are visible, and the decisions made about them are close at hand, thus bringing people directly into the fiscal process, as should be the case in a democracy.

7. Many decisions made by local government have a direct impact on the value of real property. A property tax gives the government a direct stake in the quality of those decisions, while leaving property ownership, management, and allocation in private hands.

8. The tax applies to the owners of extremely valuable properties, including owners who have managed to avoid being taxed as their income was received, a particularly important contribution in countries with porous application of

income taxes, either because of poor administration or because of generous tax preferences. It leads to large property tax bills for people with extremely expensive property—but if they can afford the huge house, then they surely can also afford the huge bill for providing government services to that household.

Popular opinion does not hold property taxes in such high regard, and politicians regularly build their campaigns on anti-property-tax platforms. What is wrong with the taxes? There are several main complaints.

1. Property taxes are seen as regressive. Some state studies do generally show that the effective property tax rate does decline as income is higher. The degree is, however, usually not as great as with sales taxes. Nonetheless, the standard view among economists holds that the basic property tax is progressive because ownership of land and capital is concentrated among high-income households.[10] Abnormally high property taxes in a locality may behave like selective excises, but the normal tax likely is progressively distributed. Furthermore, the tax may be simply a charge for services provided the property, in which case the distributional equity is irrelevant. In spite of the evidence, the belief that shapes the political discussion is the regressivity opinion and, as is often the case in modern American life, evidence to the contrary has made little impact.

2. Property taxes are horizontally inequitable. The effective property tax rate varies substantially across properties of similar value, and property taxes borne by families of similar affluence also differ significantly. The former is the result of how property taxes are structured and administered; the latter is the result of differing household preferences for property ownership. There is much evidence of this horizontal disparity problem.[11] Inept assessors working in an inept system are the culprits here.

3. Local property taxes create a scattered pattern of fiscal affluence and fiscal poverty (fiscal disparity or horizontal fiscal imbalance). Some localities have great endowments of property values (those with manufacturing facilities, for instance), and some have minimal property tax values. That creates great disparity in the type and quality of public services that the localities can afford to provide their citizenry. The problem can be particularly acute when elementary and secondary education is driven by the local property tax endowment. These issues are discussed at greater length in a later chapter focused on intergovernmental finances.

---

[10]Wallace E. Oates, "An Overview and Some Reflections," in *Property Taxation and Local Government Finance*, ed. Wallace E. Oates (Cambridge, Mass.: Lincoln Institute for Land Policy, 2001). There are three primary views of property tax incidence: the "traditional view" that the property tax is shifted to consumers in the form of higher housing prices, the "benefit view" that the property tax is simply a charge for services provided by local government, and the "new or capital tax view" that the property tax is a distortionary tax on the use of capital within the local jurisdiction. See George R. Zodrow, "The Property Tax as a Capital Tax: A Room with Three Views," *National Tax Journal* 54 (March 2001): 139–56. Only the traditional view would cause the property tax to be significantly regressive.

[11]There are some systematic problems with the horizontal disparity. For example, Harris finds that majority-minority neighborhoods are assessed at higher effective ratios than are majority-white neighborhoods. Lee Harris, "'Assessing' Discrimination: The Influence of Race in Residential Property Tax Assessments," *Journal of Land Use and Environmental Law* 20 (Fall 2004).

4. Property tax burdens can be shockingly high for people living in areas with increasing property values and can become difficult for people with low incomes. Long-time residents of an area that has suddenly become trendy can experience sudden increases in their property tax bills because of the unexpected increase in value of their properties, and those bills can confront them with difficult choices. Those owning agricultural land on the fringes of rapidly growing urban areas can also suffer the shock of owning unexpectedly valuable land and the higher property tax bills that can result. And sometimes the tax produces results that just don't seem right. If a factory that constitutes a sizable share of the property value in a jurisdiction closes, other property owners in the area will own a higher share of the total property base, their share of the total cost of government increases, and they may receive a higher property tax bill—even though they know that the value of their property hasn't increased. That result stabilizes government finances, but doesn't make the tax popular. The solution—downsizing local government services to reflect the reality of a city without the factory—is not politically easy.

5. A property tax can significantly reduce the prospects for economic development by reducing the after-tax rate of return that can be earned from building productive facilities or refurbishing deteriorated properties. With upgrading come higher values, which cause higher tax bills, thus reducing the return from development. (Refer back to Sidebar 11-1 for the solution.)

The Arithmetic and Application of Rates, Levies, and Assessed Value

Understanding how property taxes operate requires an understanding of the basic property tax rate equation because property taxes can work differently from other major taxes. Most tax rates change only with special legislative action and are not established as part of the annual legislative process—they are the portion of the fiscal system that is most strictly incremental, in the sense of small changes made to a permanent base. That is the case, for example, with state sales taxes and state and federal income taxes. These taxes are adopted and continue in place year after year without further legislative action. Although the property tax rate may be established in a tax code and thus remains in place from one year to the next in the same way as other taxes, local property tax rates in the United States have traditionally been set as a part of the annual budget process, with rate setting as the climax to the process establishing how much will be spent. The rate in most circumstances will be annually readopted at a level sufficient to yield enough revenue to balance the operating budget and to cover current costs of servicing debt obligations (interest to be paid plus any maturing principal).

Property tax rate setting mechanics are conceptually straightforward. Rates are driven by the budget choices that local governments make in regard to the provision of government services within the limits of the tax base and other revenue resources available to them and the controls placed on them by their state governments. The determinations involve both economics and politics and are summarized in the basic statutory property tax rate formula that follows:

$$R_a = (E - T)/[A_a + W_b \times A_b]$$

where

R_a = statutory tax rate applied to the class of property intended to face the lowest statutory rate (often single-family, owner-occupied housing),

E = planned local government expenditure for the budget year,

T = expected nonproperty tax revenue in that year,

A_a = taxable (or net assessed) value of property in the lowest rate class,

A_b = taxable (or net assessed) value of property in a higher rate class, and

W_b = intended multiple of the statutory rate applied to the lowest rate class that this rate class will bear.

There may be several rate classes, each entering into the rate calculation equation as the value in that class multiplied by the multiple of the lowest rate class that that type of property is intended to bear. If all properties are to be taxed at the same statutory rate, then all property weights equal one.

Here is how such a calculation works for a government with three classes of taxable property. Suppose the following information enters the rate calculation process: planned local government expenditure (E) = $8,500,000; estimated revenue from sources other than the property tax (T) = $500,000; taxable value of property in the lowest rate class (A_a) = $60,000,000; taxable value of property in the next lowest rate class (A_b) = $100,000,000; multiple of intended rate in class b to intended rate in class a = 2; taxable value of property in the third lowest rate class (A_c) = $50,000,000; multiple of intended rate in class c to intended rate in class a = 3.

The statutory tax rate for class A_a is calculated as follows:

$$R_a = (8,500,000\text{--}500,000)/[60,000,000 + (2 \times 100,000,000) + (3 \times 50,000,000)]$$
$$= 8,000,000/[60,000,000 + 200,000,000 + 150,000,000]$$
$$= 8,000,000 \div 410,000,000 = 0.0195122 \text{ or } \$ 1.95122 \text{ per } \$ 100 \text{ of assessed valuation}$$

Rates for the other classes are calculated by use of the multiples:

$$R_b = 2 \times R_a = 2 \times 0.0195122 = 0.0390244 \text{ or } \$ 3.90244 \text{ per } \$ 100 \text{ of assessed valuation}$$
$$R_c = 3 \times R_a = 3 \times 0.0195122 = 0.0585366 \text{ or } \$ 5.85366 \text{ per } \$ 100 \text{ of assessed valuation}$$

A classified property tax structure means that all property uses are not the same in terms of fiscal yield. Switching land use from a lower rate category to a higher rate category will improve the revenue potential for that land, allowing other properties the benefit of given services while paying lower taxes or of a higher level of services at the same tax rate. The land use categories that typically bear higher multiples (industrial, commercial, and utility) yield more assessed value per acre than do other uses, so classification adds to the existing revenue bias. Higher rate category land use yields fiscal dividends to other properties in the taxing jurisdiction. And assessors do have an incentive to classify properties in higher rate classes for revenue purposes.

This relationship applies for each government unit levying the property tax. Some units may face limits on levies or may need to raise set sums to cover contractual debt service, others have constrained rates, and others have considerable freedom to establish what rate is necessary to balance their budgets. Regardless of the conditions, however, the formula links those terms and applies to each government using the tax.[12]

This rate-setting process goes on independently for each of the several local governments serving an area (for instance, the county, cities, school districts, special districts, etc.) as if the other jurisdictions do not exist.[13] One conclusion from the rate equation is that, if the assessed values of all properties in a jurisdiction increase by around 10 percent, then unless the planned expenditures increase, the property tax rate will decline by around 10 percent, and property tax bills will not change. If assessed values in a jurisdiction fall, as happened in some areas during the Great Recession, and the taxing jurisdiction does not increase its planned spending, rates will increase to maintain property tax levies needed to finance the spending.

The actual property tax bill received by a property holder is usually like a layer cake of rates imposed by each jurisdiction in which the property is physically located: for instance, $4.58 for the village, $1.22 for the county, and $3.25 for the school district, with a total rate of $9.05 on the net assessed value of the property. Another property located in the same county would face a somewhat different set of rates if it was not in the village (or was in a different village) and in a different school district. The property holder will ordinarily make one payment to cover all the taxes; a single property tax collector (possibly a county treasurer) collects and disburses to each taxing unit. Each of those taxes would have been set in the same way that the village rate was set, but each is done independently.[14]

---

[12]Joseph K. Eckert, ed., *Property Appraisal and Assessment Administration* (Chicago: International Association of Assessing Officers, 1990), 20.

[13]Some states, including California and Indiana, have established overall rate limits within which totals must fall. That then requires some superior body to divide the overall limit among the jurisdictions having taxing authority, an extra complication to the taxing process. At the other extreme, Massachusetts has only one layer of local government so its overall rate limit—established by Proposition 2 ½—can be applied rather simply. And the Massachusetts system is transparent: property owners know exactly what government is responsible for their tax bill without having to do any research.

[14]A government may, of course, see the computed rate, worry about the consequences, and revise the amount of levy it chooses to raise.

There is normally a separation of function in property tax administration. The property assessor is responsible for determining the taxable value of parcels in the jurisdictions, the local governing bodies determine the amounts to be raised for their budgets from the property tax, a clerk or auditor calculates the statutory property tax rate for each jurisdiction, and the treasurer collects the tax owed on each parcel and distributes the collections to the proper governments. The separation of functions, whether the officers are elected or appointed, is consistent with the logic of internal control.

These legal (or advertised) tax rates cannot be directly compared across governments. For instance, suppose that the combined rate in one city is $10.00 per $100 of net assessed value and the rate in another city is $15.00 per $100 of net assessed value. Would it be reasonable to assume that a property worth $100,000 in the second city would face a tax bill that is 50 percent higher than that for a property of equivalent value in the first city? To make the comparison, we must adjust the legal or statutory tax rate for differences in the assessment ratio, the ratio between the value of the property as established in the assessment process and its market value (the price at which a willing buyer and a willing seller would reach agreement on a sale). As we shall see in the next sections, not all property tax systems define the value for tax purposes to be full market value, and not all property tax assessors are equally adept at hitting the legal assessment target. Therefore, to compare property taxes, it is necessary to adjust legal tax rates for differences in assessment ratios to look at effective property tax rates. The effective property tax rate (*ETR*) on a parcel of property equals the property tax (*T*) divided by the market value of the property (*MV*):

$$ETR = T \div MV$$

The property tax equals the legal tax rate (*r*) multiplied by the assessed value of the property (*AV*):

$$T = r \times AV$$

Therefore, the effective tax rate equals the statutory tax rate multiplied by the assessment ratio (the ratio of assessed value to market value):

$$ETR = (r \times AV)/MV = r(AV \div MV)$$

In the previous example, if the assessment ratio was 100 percent in the first city and 50 percent in the second, the effective tax rate would be higher in the first ($10.00 per $100) than in the second ($7.50 per $100), the reverse of the legal rates. Comparisons across jurisdictions—and even across properties in a single jurisdiction—absolutely require consideration of assessment ratios!

Doing Assessments: Standards

The hard part about the practice of property taxation is property assessment. Property taxation requires a basis for distributing the tax burden among property holders.

Because the tax base includes property holdings (accumulated asset values) rather than current flow of property sales during the year, values must be estimated.[15] This estimation—or assessment—determines what the tax value is for each property parcel and, by aggregation, the total tax value of the government; it is the heart of the property tax system. When a reassessment changes property values for tax purposes, some properties pay a higher share of the tax burden and others a lower share, compared with shares before reassessment. This adjustment of tax payments to more closely match perceived capability to pay the tax—as measured by property value—is the objective of assessment.

What is the standard for property appraisal? The most widely used and accepted standard is market value: "Market value is the cash price a property would bring in a competitive and open market."[16] This hypothetical exchange value—the same concept used by banks, insurance companies, and other institutions to determine a property's value for insurance, mortage, and related purposes—assumes that (1) markets have adequate time to function, (2) no undue pressure is exerted on either buyer or seller, (3) both parties are well informed about the parcel at sale, and (4) the transaction is at arm's length.[17] Actual transaction prices—that is, what someone just paid for a property—may provide information about market value, but they are not necessarily that value, both because those conditions may not be met and because the price may include sale of something in addition to the parcel itself.[18] Market value, internationally recognized in both public and private finance, is a standard with the same meaning everywhere, a meaning that is not linked to any particular tax law, legal system, or government structure. Although these value estimates are hypothetical, they can be tested against actual transactions and can be challenged on an objective basis.[19] As is described shortly, a few states in the United States do not use market value as the statutory standard, but it is the assessment basis most widely used.

---

[15]The current value approach to establishing the tax base is used in the United States and Canada, but other approaches are also used. The United Kingdom, for instance, bases tax on the annual rental value of land and buildings ("rates"). Other countries use land or building area as the base. Eckert, *Property Appraisal*, 7.

[16]Ibid., 35.

[17]House appraisals for mortgage lending are increasingly done through automated systems using computer models provided by Fannie Mae (Federal National Mortgage Association) and Freddie Mac (Federal Home Loan Mortgage Corporation) to quickly estimate values for mortgage loans. These appraisals cost much less than traditional in-house appraisals. They are done by mining databases that list selling prices for homes in the neighborhood and comparing those properties with the one being appraised. Freddie Mac and Fannie Mae operate as financial intermediaries by acquiring, packaging, and then securitizing mortgages originated by various entities. The appraisals are done primarily to test the reasonableness of the proposed transaction price for the appraised property—to verify that the property being purchased has sufficient value to protect the lender if the loan goes bad—and are less concerned with great accuracy. However, the principles are consistent with other appraisals, including for property tax purposes. Patrick Barta, "Lenders Tout Home Appraisals by Computer; Human Appraisers Demur," *Wall Street Journal*, July 20, 2001, B1, B3. Both these entities were badly damaged, both financially and in reputation, during the Great Recession. They helped facilitate the bad mortgage loans that were at the heart of the financial collapse.

[18]Such additions may include, for instance, some personal property or some special financing from the seller.

[19]If a property assessed for $75,000 sells for $300,000, we can be reasonably certain that it was assessed at considerably less than current market value. Therefore, current market value estimates are testable and, hence, refutable.

Within market assessment systems, there frequently are special procedures for certain property groups, often agricultural land. An ordinary appraisal assumes that a prospective buyer may put the newly acquired property to a different use—that is, the farmland close to the growing city might be developed into a shopping center, an apartment complex, or a housing subdivision, or a single-family residence near a university might be converted into apartments or offices. That potential for different use might, indeed, be a principal influence on current market value. *Current-use assessment,* however, assumes that the buyer would continue the same use of the parcel. For most parcels, there would be no difference between the market and current-use assessments because there is but trivial chance that a market-driven prospective buyer would change how the property is used—a cornfield in central Illinois far from any city or interstate interchange is unlikely to sprout anything but corn, soybeans, or a comparable agricultural crop when the new buyer takes control. However, the difference can be important where markets are changing with urban or other development and expansion. Generally, the idea is to protect existing property holders from the tax implications of the higher values of the properties and prevent tax-induced conversion away from agriculture and open-space uses.[20] It can also become a good tax dodge: in Florida, land developers rent cows to put on their land so that the property will qualify as farmland and get assessed at a lower rate.

A few states legally require some general assessment standard other than market value.[21] One such alternative standard is the *acquisition value* or assessment-on-sale system required in California by Proposition 13 (1978), required for homestead property in Florida by the 1992 referendum that approved Amendment 10, and introduced in Michigan with the revision of school finances in 1994. In this system, properties are revalued for tax purposes only when they are sold and then at the new transaction price.[22]

---

[20]John H. Bowman and John L. Mikesell, in "Assessment of Agricultural Property for Taxation," *Land Economics* 64 (February 1988): 28–36, find use-value assessment to improve the uniformity of property assessment. However, many studies question the effectiveness of such laws in influencing land use, their primary objective. See, for example, David E. Hansen and S. I. Schwartz, "Landowner Behavior at the Rural-Urban Fringe in Response to Preferential Taxation," *Land Economics* 51 (November 1975): 34–54. A good examination of preferential assessment of farmland, its impacts, and some alternatives is provided in Richard W. England, "Reconsidering Preferential Assessment of Rural Land," *Land Lines* (April 2012): 2–7.

[21]Assessment may also be done with uniform application of an administrative formula, not the standard estimation of a value. It is virtually impossible for a property owner to know whether his or her parcel is over- or underassessed in the system because the owner cannot tell the extent to which the formula has been properly applied to other parcels. If the owner's parcel is properly assessed and other parcels are underassessed, then the owner is overassessed in the system. The only test the owner has is to verify parcel data and application of the formula to his or her parcel. The national property tax imposed by Greece in 2011 (explained in Sidebar 11-2), as an emergency measure to fight against default on government obligations, was assessed according to information that required no valuation process.

[22]Both California and Florida apply across-the-board adjustment increases, but realignments between parcels occur only when parcels exchange hands. Allen Manvel noted the precipitous decline in assessment quality produced by that system. See "Assessment Uniformity—and Proposition 13," *Tax Notes* 24 (August 27, 1984): 893–95. Other states with one form of acquisition value assessment or another include Arkansas, Georgia, Illinois, Maryland, Montana, New Mexico, New York, Oklahoma, South Carolina, and Texas. Terri Sexton, "Proposition 13 and Residential Mobility," *State Tax Notes* 50 (October 6, 2008): 29–36.

This structure of reassessment only on sale disrupts the property market (because prospective buyers would face a different property tax than would the prospective seller), creates a property record substructure of sales without recorded deeds as individuals seek to avoid the property tax adjustments that would accompany a recorded sale, and causes owners of similarly situated properties to pay widely different property taxes. This last problem is especially difficult because it directly conflicts with assessment uniformity, the primary concern of the assessment task. Indeed, in a 1989 case involving the assessment of coal properties in West Virginia, the U.S. Supreme Court unanimously held that valuation of some properties at their recent purchase price when similar parcels are valued on earlier assessments violates the equal-protection clause of the Fourteenth Amendment of the U.S. Constitution. Chief Justice Rehnquist wrote, in a classic statement of the horizontal equity standard for evaluation of tax policy, that "the constitutional requirement is the seasonable attainment of a rough equality in tax treatment of similarly situated property owners."[23] In that case, the plaintiff's property, because more recently purchased, was assessed at values eight to thirty-five times the value of comparable neighboring property, and nothing was bringing the assessments closer together. However, the assessor followed this procedure contrary to the state law. It was, as the Court labeled it, an "aberrational enforcement policy."

A test of acquisition value assessment as the legal state standard came from California in *Nordlinger* v. *Hahn*.[24] Stephanie Nordlinger found that, when she purchased a house in the Baldwin Heights neighborhood of Los Angeles County, the accompanying reassessment on acquisition brought a 36 percent increase in property tax, from $1,247.40 to $1,701 per year. She later discovered she was paying about five times more in taxes than some of her neighbors who owned comparable homes within the same residential development. For example, one block away, a house of identical size on a lot slightly larger than the petitioner's was subject to a general tax levy of only $358.20 (based on an assessed valuation of $35,820, which reflected the home's value in 1975 plus the up-to-2-percent-per-year standard inflation factor). The general tax levied against her modest home was only a few dollars less than that paid by a pre-1976 owner of a $2.1 million Malibu beachfront home.

Nordlinger believed this pattern to be both patently unfair and contrary to constitutional requirements for equal protection. The state, however, disagreed, arguing that the system represented a rational system of classification because there was a legitimate state interest in allowing longer-term owners to pay a lower tax than newer owners of property (1) to avoid taxing property holders on unrealized gains on their properties and possibly taxing people out of their homes, (2) to ensure predictability of tax payments for property owners, and (3) to achieve revenue stability for local governments. The Supreme Court, while showing considerable sympathy for Nordlinger's argument and noting that most of these state objectives could have been better achieved through other means, chose to accept that there was some rational basis for the system—despite its undesirable effects, including dramatic differences in property tax paid by similarly situated individuals. Furthermore, evidence

---

[23]*Allegheny Pittsburgh Coal Co. v. County Commission of Webster County, West Virginia,* 488 U.S. 336 (1989).
[24]*Stephanie Nordlinger, Petitioner v. Kenneth Hahn, in His Capacity as Tax Assessor for Los Angeles County,* 505 U.S. 1 (1992).

indicates that Proposition 13 did induce homeowners and renters to stay put and avoid higher tax rates than they would face when buying new properties: from 1970 to 2000, the average tenure for owners and renters in California increased by slightly more than one year and slightly more than three-quarters of a year, respectively, relative to comparison states.[25] Ordinarily, reduced mobility is regarded as an impediment to economic growth and, hence, regarded as undesirable public policy in market-driven economies. The Court found that there was a rational basis for the assessment scheme and, in contrast to the West Virginia situation, the acquisition value system was constitutional. The system, which also rigidly controlled the property tax rate, strangled the revenue capacity of local governments.

Two other valuation standards are worth noting. These are an area-based assessment, in which the tax is driven exclusively by the size of the property, and a formula-based or cadastral assessment, in which the assessment is driven by the application of a legal formula that uses physical attributes (e.g., size, design, location, soil type, etc.) of each property. The test of a cadastral assessment is not whether it approximates a certain value, but whether the physical attributes have been correctly recorded and whether the formula has been accurately applied to them. These systems are usually applied in situations in which there are few reliable market transactions of the property being taxed, as in developing countries or in countries transitioning from centrally planned to market economies. Sidebar 11-2 illustrates the use of an adjusted area-based system during the recent Greek fiscal crisis.

Local governments in the United Kingdom rely on value-based property taxes to finance their operations. However, they deal with the tricky task of assessment in a fashion that differs from that of the United States and Canada, two other heavy users of property taxes for local finances. The UK system of "banding" is discussed in Sidebar 11–3. This system can be particularly useful when value data are sparse or when values are fluctuating significantly.

Doing Assessments: Cycles

The assessment cycles that governments in the United States use fall into three general categories: *mass cyclical assessment, segmental assessment,* and *annual assessment.* With mass cyclical assessment, all properties in a taxing jurisdiction are valued for tax purposes in a particular year; that value does not change until the next scheduled mass assessment except for new construction, demolition, or change in use of a property. States prescribe mass cyclical assessment at intervals ranging from two to ten years. Examples include Iowa (two years), Maine (four years), Minnesota (four years), Indiana (ten years), and Connecticut (ten years).[26] Some states explicitly

[25]Nada Wasi and Michelle J. White, "Property Tax Limitations and Mobility: The Lock-in Effect of California's Proposition 13," National Bureau of Economic Research Working Paper 11108, Cambridge, Mass., February 2005 [www.nber.org/papers/w11108].

[26]U.S. Bureau of the Census, *1992 Census of Governments, Vol. 2, Taxable Property Values,* No. 1, Assessed Valuation for Local General Property Taxation (Washington, D.C.: U.S. Government Printing Office, 1994), D-1–D-3.

Sidebar 11–2
A Property Tax Alternative: The 2011 Greek Property Tax

Greece was in fiscal crisis in 2011. Many years of substantial government deficits had accumulated into a level of debt that could not be sustained, around 160 percent of gross domestic product at the time. Private lenders were not willing to lend to the government to refinance the existing debt or to support the continuing deficit because they were skeptical of the ability of the government to pay the promised interest or to repay the principal loaned. The government didn't have the capability of covering its obligations by printing more money because it was part of the Eurozone and didn't control its own currency. In order to obtain loans from the International Monetary Fund and European institutions, the Greek government had to devise an austerity program to close its deficit, even though a deep recession continued to haunt the nation.

Part of the government strategy to reduce the deficit was additional revenue from a new national property tax. Official rates for the national income and value-added taxes were already high, thus limiting the capacity to raise revenue by increasing them. Furthermore, tax compliance in Greece has been notoriously low, and raising rates would promise to worsen what was already a low compliance rate. That created the need for a new tax, one that had features appropriate to the operating environment. The tax would need to yield revenue quickly, it had to be generally reliable, and it had to involve as little scope for private noncompliance as possible. It would be considerably outside the current revenue system.

The new Greek property tax has been designed to perform in this difficult environment. The emergency tax applies to all commercial and residential properties in the country. The tax is determined according to the size of the property in square meters. Properties between 0 and 25 years of age are assessed a surcharge of 5 to 25 percent, inversely proportional to age; that is, the surcharge is higher for newer properties. Properties are taxed at a zone rate determined by the physical location of the property, with rates ranging from 0.50 to 16 euros per square meter.

The tax calculation is the number of square meters times the surcharge determined by the age of the property time the zone tax rate. Some parts of the country do not have zones, and properties located there are subject to a rate of three euros per square meter.

The taxes are calculated with data already available to the tax officials (and with data not subject to manipulation or to reporting errors by taxpayers).

The government needed the tax revenue quickly, and there was some reluctance to use the existing tax collection structures. Therefore, property owners received billing through their bills from the government-owned electric company, two installments for the first year of the tax and five installments for the second year of the tax. Initially, payments were made with payment of the electric bill—and those not paying the tax were subject to having their electricity cut off.

Power cuts were instituted in January 2012 for nonpayers, but were halted when harsh winter weather hit. Also, nonpayment of electric bills increased so much that the electric utility faced a cash crunch. The electricity cutoffs for nonpayment of the property tax portion of the bills were eventually found to be unconstitutional, eliminating the government's primary collection tool. Enforcement was changed to garnishment of wages or pensions or seizure of properties.

(continues)

Sidebar 11–2
(continued)

The tax avoided the creation of more disincentives from adding to the income or value-added taxes, eliminated the possibility that taxpayers might cheat on tax returns, could be put into place quickly, and used a collection system that could yield revenues quickly. It was not based on current market values of properties.

SOURCES: Charles Forelle, "At Core of Greek Chaos, a Reviled Tax," *Wall Street Journal,* May 31, 2010, A9; "Greece's New Property Tax," *Living in Greece,* September 19, 2011 [http://livingingreece.gr/2011/09/19/new-property-tax-greece/].

Sidebar 11–3
An Alternative Scheme for Taxing Property to Finance Local Services: Banding

The United Kingdom introduced property value banding when a short-lived poll tax experiment for financing local government services came crashing down.[1] The population rebelled against the poll tax system under which all residents of a jurisdiction paid exactly the same tax amount regardless of income or affluence. While the system—a replacement for a property tax based on property rents—was simple and transparent, it also seemed patently unfair.

The replacement, since 1993, has been the banding system for residential properties (combined with a rental value property tax for nonresidential parcels). With this system, tax payment is determined according to (1) the number of bands into which properties are to be divided, (2) the width of the bands in terms of estimated property value, and (3) the tax rate structure. The system is, in essence, a poll tax, but with some adjustments for differences in property values. In the UK, eight tax bands were established, with one scheme each for England, Scotland, and Wales. The system in England is described here:

Band in England	Property Value Range (UK Pounds)	Ratio to Base Band
A	Under 40,000	6/9
B	40,001–52,000	7/9
C	52,001–68,000	8/9
D (Base Band)	68,001–88,000	9/9
E	88,001–120,000	11/9
F	120,001–160,000	13/9
G	160,001–320,000	15/9
H	320,001 and above	18/9

Sidebar 11–3
(continued)

A tax ratio is established for each band in terms of the identified base band; in other words, each tax band has a set ratio relative to the base. In England, band H tax will be double the base band (and triple that of band A).

Suppose a local jurisdiction has 7,750 dwellings and seeks to raise £1,000,000. The following table presents the distribution of dwellings by band and calculates the base band equivalence in each band.

Band	Dwellings in Band	Ratio to Base	Base Band Equivalent Properties
A	500	6/9	333
B	1,200	7/9	933
C	1,500	8/9	1,333
D	1,000	9/9	1,000
E	2,000	11/9	2,444
F	900	13/9	1,300
G	500	15/9	833
H	150	18/9	300
Totals	7,750		8,476

Therefore, base tax equals 1,000,000 ÷ 8,476 = 118. Band D property pays £118, and other bands pay the appropriate ratio times 118.

Band	Number of Properties	Ratio	Band D Equivalent	Tax Bill per Property (UK Pounds)	Total Tax (UK Pounds)
A	500	6/9	333	79	39,500
B	1,200	7/9	933	92	110,400
C	1,500	8/9	1,333	105	157,500
D	1,000	1	1,000	118	118,000
E	2,000	11/9	2,444	144	288,000
F	900	13/9	1,300	170	153,000
G	500	15/9	833	197	98,500
H	150	18/9	300	236	35,
					1,000,300
					(rounding)

Property tax bills increase as properties are in higher-value bands. However, the effective rate (tax bill divided by average property value in the band) does fall as the band value is higher—the pattern is regressive.

(continues)

**Sidebar 11–3
(continued)**

The advantages of the system are these:

1. Simplicity: The system does not require detailed estimates of the value of properties. There are no complex valuation models required and no detailed data requirements.
2. Stability: The system does not require a short revaluation cycle to keep values up to date. So long as properties do not move from one band to another, there is no reason for a new rebanding exercise.
3. Acceptance: The system is generally accepted and understood by the taxpaying public.
4. Administrative cost: The system is not expensive to implement, the process is quick, and the number of appeals is low.
5. Fiscal transparency: Decisions made about government spending drive the tax bills, and that is completely apparent in the process. Changes in property values do not change the tax bills.

The disadvantages of the system are these:

1. Regressivity: Effective rates fall as property values are higher, and it is not easy to remove that pattern.
2. Applicability: The system is applicable only to residential properties.
3. Complexity: Establishing the number and range of bands and the ratios is a policy challenge.

[1]Peter Smith, "Lessons from the British Poll Tax Disaster," *National Tax Journal* 44 (December 1991): 421–36.

SOURCE: Based on Frances Plimmer, William McCluskey, and Owen Connellan, "Property Tax Banding: A Solution for Developing Countries," *Assessment Journal* 9 (2002): 37–47.

indicate that a physical inspection of real property will be made with the reassessment. Many jurisdictions that operate under a mass cyclical assessment system choose to contract the reassessment with a private appraisal firm so that they do not face great changes in staffing between normal and reassessment years.

Segmental assessment is a procedure by which a specified fraction of real property parcels in a jurisdiction is reassessed each year, moving through the assessing unit in sequence. Thus, if a three-year cycle is used, one-third of the properties in the area are reassessed each year, with all properties reassessed in three years. The last-valued taxpayers can complain about the inflation in their valuations, which is absent from earlier-valued parcels, but administrative convenience and the fact that all parcels take their turn as last valued have preserved the method. Examples include a three-year cycle in both Maryland and Cook County, Illinois.[27] Idaho requires that 20 percent of property in each assessment class be appraised each year.

---

[27]In Cook County, the cycle through reassessment works like this: 2009, reassess City of Chicago; 2010, reassess north suburbs; 2011, reassess south suburbs; 2012, reassess City of Chicago; and so on. See John E. Petersen and Kimberly K. Edwards, "The Impact of Declining Property Values on Local Government Finances," Urban Land Institute Research Working Paper 626, Washington, D.C., March 1993, 49.

The final system is annual assessment, a process that assumes updated values for all real property parcels each year. Computers and modern information technology make frequent reappraisals possible, but a physical inspection and inventory of all parcels, the traditional mark of reassessment, is unlikely at that pace. More often than not, annual valuation employs the physical characteristics of properties as identified in earlier parcel inventories with new value weights applied to those characteristics and a realignment of the significance of neighborhood location to keep up with changing markets. For instance, in earlier years, a fireplace might have added $1,000 to the value of a house; this year it is estimated to add $1,800. Or, after adjusting for other charges, properties in one area may have values altered by 1 percent, whereas in other areas the change may be 2 percent. In that fashion, new value estimates emerge from old physical feature data. Much of the revaluation may be done according to analysis of zones within the jurisdiction, identifying zones in which values seem to be increasing at a particular rate, compared to a different rate in another zone. Of course, annual reassessment can become no reassessment if last year's forms are simply recopied or if all parcels have values increased or decreased by a flat factor of, for example, 3 percent.[28] That process destroys the equity of the property tax because no adjustments are made for properties whose value has either fallen or increased. The fiction that properties are reassessed annually prevents any meaningful realignment of parcel values.

Modern information technology, often involving geographical information systems, makes good-quality annual updates feasible and equitable so long as there is process transparency, careful monitoring of changes in real estate markets, and an appeal process that property owners can navigate without great difficulty. These are conditions infrequently found in local assessing systems in the United States.

Doing Assessments: Approaches

Assessment is a technical process, and each system has distinct peculiarities. There are, however, three general approaches to estimating real property values employed in various mixtures in state and local systems; all are offshoots of private property appraisal techniques used by realtors, banks, and others needing estimates of value. The techniques are (1) the market data or comparable sales approach, (2) the income approach, and (3) the cost or summation approach.[29]

1. **The market data or comparable sales approach** estimates value of a parcel by comparing it with similar properties that have recently been sold.

---

[28]As recent experience certainly demonstrates, up is not the direction that housing values go every year, and, when property values are changing, not all values in a locality move together. In the Boston area, "sales of single-family homes in the upscale town of Wellesley fell 2.2 percent in 1992, with an increase in the median sales price of 8.6 percent. In nearby Malden, a lower-middle-class town, single-family home sales grew 8.3 percent, but median prices fell 2 percent." Christopher J. Mayer, "Taxes, Income Distribution, and the Real Estate Cycle: Why All Houses Do Not Appreciate at the Same Rate," *New England Economic Review* (May/June 1993): 40. Uniform adjustments in assessments cannot substitute for reassessment in improving fairness. The larger the area included, the greater the disparity in changes in value, so standard value adjustments may be feasible in small, but not large, areas.

[29]Eckert, *Property Appraisal*, chs. 6–13.

The approach uses information directly produced by the market about how property owners and prospective owners value properties that are generally like that being assessed. Of course, the approach requires a number of actual transactions in order for meaningful comparisons to be made. It does not work for unique properties because it requires property transactions involving properties similar in economically relevant details.[30] A reasonably good comparison is usually possible for residential property (there are many three-bedroom, split-level houses with about 2,500 square feet of living space in most cities, after all, and some have probably sold recently), but uniqueness can create a virtually impossible problem for most commercial or industrial parcels and some residential parcels.

2. **The income approach** converts the future returns from ownership of a parcel into their present-value equivalent to estimate the amount a willing and knowledgeable investor would pay for the future income flow. Application of the approach requires an estimate of the gross return from holding the parcel, the expenses associated with holding the parcel, and a rate at which the resulting net annual return would be capitalized into a current-value equivalent. In practice, an estimated annual income stream is converted into current value with a capitalization rate derived from market observation that reflects the prevailing relationship between a single year's net operating income and total property value. The approach applies the concept of discounting to convert the flow of future income into its net present value, exactly as discussed in a previous chapter. The approach is most attractive for estimating the value of income-producing properties (apartments, stores and offices, agricultural land, parking lots, etc.). On the market, how many multiples of net annual return are being paid for such properties? That comparison provides the value estimate.

3. **The cost or summation approach** estimates value by adding the depreciated cost of improvements on a parcel to the estimated land value of the parcel. In contrast to the other two approaches, rather than valuing the parcel as a whole (land plus improvements), this approach values each component of the parcel separately. The land value is normally estimated from either sales comparison or income capitalization, the previously noted approaches for general valuation. Often the land valuation uses value zone maps that identify the value per acre (or square foot) from transactions occurring within the zone, with the idea that this information will be used to estimate the value of all land in the zone. In estimating the value of the improvement, the approach typically determines the cost of constructing a standard (average) grade structure like the one being assessed at a particular date (with the labor and materials prices of that time, using the prevailing technology, and in the size and type as the subject property). That cost is adjusted to account for nonstandard construction materials and workmanship of the property being assessed, either higher or lower than standard. To that cost are added extra features not found in the standard unit, such as extra bathroom fixtures,

---

[30]Estimates using forms of regression analysis implicitly use sales comparisons, but the approach is also used without regression equations.

fireplaces, central air conditioning, and so on for residential units; escalators, sprinkler systems, vaults, and so on for commercial units; and cranes, elevators, air handling systems, and so on for industrial units. The "new cost" improvement value is calculated by either of two conceptual methods:

a. *Reproduction cost,* the cost of constructing an exact replica of the building at current prices: the building would have the same materials, construction standards, design, workmanship, and all deficiencies and obsolescence of the subject building.

b. *Replacement cost,* the cost of constructing a building having equivalent utility to the subject building at current prices: the building would be built with modern materials and using current standards and design, but would have the same utility as the existing building. (Replacement cost may ignore the cost of structural elements in the building that provide no utility—e.g., the unused second story of a warehouse could be ignored in costing the building.)

Both the reproduction and the replacement methods should reasonably lead to the same value estimate through logically different adjustments for *accumulated depreciation*. In general, that accumulated depreciation can be from physical wear and tear from elements, and may be curable (primarily from deferred maintenance) or incurable (correction expenses would be enormous and impractical); from functional obsolescence due to lack of utility or desirability in property design (inadequacy or absence of features and superadequacy or presence of nonuseful features); or from economic obsolescence due to changes external to the property (changes in the neighborhood). The depreciation estimate would vary depending on whether "new cost" was estimated using reproduction or replacement concepts.

The three approaches to estimating value are alternatives, but each has special strengths in the assessment process. The income approach is best used for properties bought and sold largely on the basis of income production—office buildings, apartments, motels and hotels, and some types of land. The cost approach, although applicable to most improvements, is especially suitable for special or unique properties that are seldom exchanged on the market (for instance, a purpose-built manufacturing facility) and properties that generate no income (for instance, a public museum). It also, along with the income approach, is vital for use-value assessment. The market data approach applies in any circumstance for which a sufficient number of reliable transactions occur, particularly single-family, owner-occupied housing. The market data and cost approaches are particularly amenable to the requirements of mass reassessment. Each would be tested by the extent to which the value estimate it generated matches the price received in a voluntary, arm's length, knowledgeable exchange of a parcel.[31] When a property owner is appealing an assessment, it is normal for all three approaches to valuation to be applied, even though the assessor likely relied on only one in the initial assessment.

---

[31]Another special case for assessment involves public utility and transportation properties. These properties are usually assessed by the state government rather than by local assessors, and the value of each such property is calculated as an operating unit and divided among local jurisdictions by formula rather than having the value calculated on a property-in-place basis.

Fractional Assessment and Assessment Disparity

The heart of the property tax is assessment, the determination of property value for distributing total tax burden. As previously described, tax law may or may not value property at current market value (what most people understand to be the meaning of "What is its value?" or "What is it worth?"). Even where assessment ties to current market value, prevailing assessment practices may cause substantial difference between market and assessed values. For example, according to the *1982 Census of Governments,* the national median-area assessment rate (assessed value to market value) for single-family, nonfarm houses in 1981 was 36.9 percent (an assessment ratio of 0.369).[32] State median-area rates ranged from a high of 86.8 percent in Idaho to a low of 0.6 percent in Vermont.[33] Much to the chagrin of tax analysts, the *Census of Governments* no longer reports any data having to do with market value, so we cannot tell whether national performance has improved or deteriorated since then. Many states do collect the data as part of their performance evaluation programs, but the information is not comparable across states.[34]

Under normal circumstances, the overall assessment rate has little impact on absolute property tax burdens because assessment levels can be counteracted by differences in the statutory tax rate. For instance, suppose that a municipality seeks $5 million from its property tax and that the market value of taxable property is $80 million. If the assessment rate is 100 percent, a property tax rate of $6.25 per $100 of assessed value will yield the desired revenue. If the assessment rate is 50 percent, a property tax rate of $12.50 per $100 of assessed value will produce the desired levy total. Low assessment rates produce compensating statutory rate adjustments.

Fractional assessment, meaning assessment at less than full market value, creates inequities and other complications, not inadequate revenue.[35] First, low assessment rates increase the likelihood of unfair individual assessments because an individual parcel holder will probably be unaware of any overassessment. Suppose the legal assessment standard is one-third of market value, but the prevailing practice is 20 percent. If a parcel worth about $40,000 is assessed at $10,000, an unwary owner will believe that he or she has a favorable assessment. The tax assessor has valued the property far below the market value and, should the parcel owner know about legal standards, even below the one-third value standard. In fact, the parcel is overassessed—a 25 percent assessment, compared with the prevailing

---

[32]The single-family, nonfarm home is used as a benchmark for assessment evaluation because almost every assessing district contains several parcels of that class and that grouping tends to be more homogeneous than other property types. Furthermore, markets for such properties usually have many transactions in comparison periods.

[33]U.S. Bureau of the Census, *1982 Census of Governments, Vol. 2, Taxable Property Values and Assessment—Sales Price Ratios* (Washington, D.C.: U.S. Government Printing Office, 1984), 50.

[34]There have been studies of individual states, however. For instance, evidence shows that efforts to reform the Indiana property tax assessment system–current market value assessment standard, trend adjustments between reassessments, consolidation of assessment–initially appeared to cause an improvement in assessment quality, but more recently quality has declined substantially. [Olha Krupa, "An Analysis of Indiana Property Tax Reform: Equity and Cost Considerations, *State Tax Notes* (forthcoming, 2012).

[35]Rigid statutory rate ceilings, however, may combine with fractional assessment to create revenue constraints more severe than intended by the law.

20 percent—so the parcel bears an artificially high effective tax rate. Unless the parcel owner has knowledge about the ways of property taxation, he or she will never realize the inequity.[36] As John Shannon observed, "The lower the assessment level, the larger becomes the administrative graveyard in which the assessor can bury his mistakes."[37]

Second, fractional assessment can make state-imposed property tax rate ceilings and debt limits linked to assessed value more restrictive than intended. Many states permit local government debt levels to be no higher than, say, 2 percent of total local assessed value. If assessment rates are artificially low (for instance, assessment at 20 percent of value rather than at 50 percent), that limit becomes artificially restrictive and creates extra incentive to avoid those debt limits. Furthermore, the practice can cause uneven distributions of any state property tax rate across local areas with differing assessment rates. The effective state property tax rate is higher in areas with high assessment rates than in other areas. Finally, state grant assistance, especially aid to local school districts, is frequently distributed in formulas keyed to local assessed value: the lower the assessed value in an area, the greater the amount of state aid. Fractional assessment can obviously distort that distribution, so states typically develop equalization multipliers to get assessed values to a common assessment level for aid purposes. If an area has an assessment rate of 25 percent and the statewide standard is 50 percent, its assessed value would be doubled for aid formula calculations. These equalization multipliers may or may not be applied to individual parcel values for computing tax bills. If rates are flexible and all parcels in a taxing area receive the same multiplier, the process makes no difference.

The major difficulty with fractional assessment occurs, however, when assessment rates of parcels within a taxing area differ. When this occurs, as it does to some extent in all systems, the effective tax rate is no longer uniform, and similarly situated properties bear different property tax burdens because of the assessment system. Thus, if property A is assessed at 30 percent of value and property B is assessed at 20 percent, a property tax of $10 per $100 of assessed value translates into an effective rate of $3 per $100 on property A and $2 per $100 on property B. No tax should be so capricious. Unfortunately, property taxes do show such dispersion in operation. The coefficient of dispersion (CD) measures the extent of dispersion (or the absence of uniformity) in assessment ratios and, hence, the extent to which effective property tax rates vary within a taxing unit. The CD—the average absolute deviation of parcel assessment ratios from the median divided by the median multiplied by 100—equals

$$CD = \left[\frac{\sum_{i=1}^{n} |A_i - M|}{n} \right] \left[\frac{1}{M} \right] \times 100$$

---

[36]There is an extra pitfall in the process. The legal standard is 33 percent; the parcel is valued at 25 percent. Some appeal mechanisms suggest that the appropriate action is an increase in assessed value to the legal standard. That is not, however, the view of the U.S. Supreme Court: see *Sioux City Bridge Co. v. Dakota County*, 260 U.S. 441 (1923).

[37]John Shannon, "Conflict between State Assessment Law and Local Assessment Practice," in *Property Taxation—USA*, ed. Richard W. Lindholm (Madison: University of Wisconsin Press, 1969), 45.

where

A_i = assessment ratio for an individual property parcel,

M = median assessment ratio for all parcels sampled, and

n = number of parcels in the sample.

If assessment ratios of individual properties are clustered closely around the median ratio, the CD is low, and assessments are relatively uniform. If individual ratios vary widely from the median, the CD is high; properties are not uniformly assessed, and the property tax burden is not fairly distributed among taxpayers. Table 11–2 illustrates CD computation. The CD of 17.3 means that the average parcel is assessed 17.3 percent above or below the median assessment ratio. In practical terms, it means that equally situated properties pay substantially different effective tax rates. Referring to Table 11–2, the owner of property D pays an effective tax rate 87.5 percent higher than the rate paid by the owner of property C simply because of lack of uniformity in the assessment process. The higher the CD, the greater the difference of effective rates in the jurisdiction.

Property market fluctuations make it impossible to maintain completely uniform assessment ratios. However, the International Association of Assessing Officers does prescribe clear standards for uniformity as measured by the coefficient of dispersion. For single-family residential properties, "The [CD] for single-family homes and condominiums should be 15.0 or less. In areas of newer or fairly similar residences, it should be 10.0 or less."[38]

Another measure of assessment quality is called the price-related differential (PRD), a measure of assessment regressivity or progressivity. That is, it measures whether there is a tendency for higher-valued properties to be assessed lower (have

Table 11–2

Statistics of Assessment Quality: Assessment Ratio, Coefficient of Dispersion, and Price-Related Differential

Parcel	Assessed Value($)	Market Value($)	Assessment Ratio	Absolute Dispersion
A	15,000	30,000	0.50	0.10
B	20,000	30,000	0.67	0.07
C	8,000	20,000	0.40	0.20
D	30,000	40,000	0.75	0.15
E	15,000	25,000	0.60	0.00
TOTAL	88,000	145,000		0.52

Median Assessment Ratio = 0.60
Sum of Absolute Dispersions = 0.52
Average Absolute Dispersion = 0.52 ÷ 5 = 0.104
Coefficient of Dispersion = [0.104 ÷ 0.60] x 100 = 17.3
Prince-Related Defferential = 0.60 ÷ (88,000 ÷ 145,000) = 1.01

---

[38]"IAAO Standard on Ratio Studies," *Assessment Journal* 6 (September/October 1999): 60.

lower assessment ratios) or higher (have higher assessment ratios) than are lower-valued properties. The PRD is calculated as the mean assessment ratio of all parcels divided by the sum of all assessed values in the sample divided by the sum of all market values in the sample.

PRD = Mean Assessment Ration ÷ (Sum of Assessed Values ÷ Sum of Market Values)

A PRD of 1.0 indicates no assessment bias according to value; a PRD greater than 1.0 suggests that higher-value properties are underassessed relative to lower-value parcels (a sort of regressivity); a PRD less than 1.0 suggests that higher-value properties are overassessed relative to lower-value parcels (a sort of progressivity). In other words, if there are differences in assessment ratios, who is getting the better deal: high-value parcels or low-value parcels? Table 11–2 shows the calculation of the PRD.

Many states conduct annual assessment/sales ratio studies that calculate average assessment ratios, coefficients of dispersion, and price-related differentials for each local assessment district. These studies perform three important functions. First, the state uses these results to equalize assessed values (i.e., to ensure that properties are valued according to the same standard) for use in aid distribution to local governments, for application of a state property tax rate, for equity when local tax rates extend beyond one assessing jurisdiction, and for calculation of local government debt limits. Without such equalization, there is an incentive for competitive underassessment to shift costs to other areas. Second, the studies give property owners a better idea as to whether their property assessment is generally consistent with that of other taxpayers. The property holder knows that an assessment of $36,000 on a house worth about $120,000 is no bargain if the assessment study shows the mean ratio in the community to be 20 percent; without the ratio study, the holder might celebrate good fortune rather than appeal. Finally, the ratio studies are necessary for evaluation of the work done by property tax assessors. A high CD, in particular, means considerable horizontal inequity in the distribution of the tax burden. A coefficient of 25 means that the average property holder pays property tax that is 25 percent lower or higher than it would be if all properties were assessed at the same ratio. Sidebar 11–4 illustrates the meaning of the CD with a practical application. While many states now prepare assessment quality studies for all assessing jurisdictions, Illinois is one state that takes assessment quality particularly seriously. Assessment/sales ratio studies are prepared annually, and assessors qualify for a pay bonus if they meet a standard defined in terms of median assessment ratio and CD.[39]

The property tax rate, defined statutorily as the same for all property overall or within a class, differs substantially as it applies to particular parcels when assessments are not uniform. A high CD means big differences in assessment ratios and big differences in effective rates paid by comparable properties. A number of studies have tried to identify what might improve the uniformity of property tax

---

[39]See Illinois Department of Revenue, *Property Tax Statistics: Assessment Ratios 2010* [http://www.revenue .state.il.us/AboutIdor/TaxStats/PropertyTaxStats/Table-1/2010AssessmentRatios.pdf]

Sidebar 11–4
What the Coefficient of Dispersion Means for Property Tax Bills

---

The CD measures the extent to which assessment ratios (assessed value divided by selling price) of property parcels recently sold differ from uniformity. If all parcels were assessed at the same ratio, then the effective property tax rate—the property tax owed divided by the value of the property—would all be the same (the rate would be uniform) and the CD would be zero. As there are differences in assessment ratios, the CD rises. The implications of this disparity, or lack of uniformity, can be demonstrated in a simple illustration.

During 2007, sales disclosure records gave 502 sales of single-family residential properties in Montgomery County, Indiana, that were valid transactions for analysis (i.e., not foreclosures, not between family members, not including substantial personal property in the transaction, etc.). Analysis of the data showed the median assessment ratio to be 89.3 percent (the state law prescribed 100 percent) and that the coefficient of dispersion was 15.7. That means that the average house was assessed at 15.7 percent above or below 89.3 percent of its market value as measured by comparable transaction prices. In these sales data from disclosures to the Indiana Department of Local Government Finance, the median selling price was $105,000.

What do these data tell us about the property tax bill and the effective property tax rate paid by the typical property?[1] In Montgomery County, 13 properties sold at a price of around $105,000—in other words, from $103,000 to $107,000. Assessment ratios for these parcels ranged from 0.3933 to 1.3495. The statutory property tax rate in Montgomery County varies according to the particular overlaying governments serving a particular location, but in one part of the county seat (Crawfordsville) the rate is around $4.30 per $100 of assessed value. Therefore, for the property with the highest assessment ratio, the annual property tax bill would have been $6,209; for the property with the lowest, the annual bill would have been $1,759. The properties are of essentially the same market value but there is a huge difference in property tax bills, simply because the assessor estimated a different taxable value for the properties—and the CD here is not even in the horrible class. The CD gives a measure of how large, in general, this degree of assessment disparity is, and how large the disparity of tax bills will be. The higher the CD, the greater the variation in effective property tax rates and the greater the horizontal inequity of the tax.

[1]Effective property tax rates are normally calculated relative to market value of the property rather than relative to income of the property holder because the tax is based on the property (in rem) and not on who owns it. Distributional analysis may link owners and their income to properties, but that is a set of questions different from the success of achieving uniform and unbiased assessments of property parcels.

---

assessment. Evidence shows higher uniformity results where assessment ratios are high, reassessments are frequent, assessment personnel are full-time and specifically trained, assessment technology is available (tax maps are current, computer-assisted mass appraisal is used, building permit and deed transfer data are available, etc.), and formal relief mechanisms are available (circuit breakers, use-value assessment, etc.). Size of assessing district, use of contract appraisal firms, and whether assessors are elected or appointed seem not to matter much. Uniformity is greater when property tax rates are higher, presumably because more is at stake. However, much of actual performance depends on local property market and economic conditions.[40]

Property Tax Relief Mechanisms

Governments provide a number of different systems of property tax relief. They may involve reductions in the tax base, preferential tax rates, or direct credit against tax owed. The relief may be provided because of (1) the character of the owner (e.g., exemptions for the elderly), (2) the type of property (e.g., owner-occupied residential property), or (3) how the property is (or is going to be) used (e.g., facilities for pollution abatement).[41] Most programs are established by state legislation for all localities in the state, even though most property tax revenue goes to local government. Some state programs do allow some local choice about granting the relief. Figure 11–1 diagrams the alternative approaches to providing residential property tax relief, all working through the rate calculation equation previously described. Those on the left branch work on the general rate and have an impact on all properties; those on the right branch are focused on particular property groupings, usually residential, although sometimes agricultural. The right-branch reliefs can be more targeted than those on the left, although some can be extremely broad in practice.

Exemptions, Credits, and Abatements

Property tax systems almost always include provisions that subtract a portion of assessed value from the taxable holdings of certain individuals or institutions. Thus, if an individual holding property with assessed value of $8,500 qualifies for a veterans' exemption of $1,500, that person's tax bill would be computed on a net assessed value of $7,000. The exemption reduces the tax base; it is not a direct credit against tax owed. In most instances, the exemptions are additive, so if a parcel holder qualifies for exemption because of age and veteran status, for example, the property tax base would be reduced by the sum of both exemptions. If the relief is granted as a credit, the reduction from the relief is on the tax bill and not on the tax base.

Exemptions may be granted to certain individuals or institutions, or they may be granted to certain types of property. In the first group are exemptions granted conditional on ownership: (1) government property (federal, state, or local, as well

---

[40]John H. Bowman and John L. Mikesell, "Improving Administration of the Property Tax: A Review of Prescriptions and Their Impact," *Public Budgeting and Financial Management* 2 (November 1990): 151–76.
[41]Property tax incentives, i.e., relief mechanisms in the form of exemptions, abatements, credits, etc., for business are examined in detail in Daphne A. Kenyon, Adam H. Langley, and Bethany P. Paquin, *Rethinking Property Tax Incentives for Business* (Cambridge, Mass.: Lincoln Institute of Land Policy, 2012).

Figure 11–1
Forms of Property Tax Relief

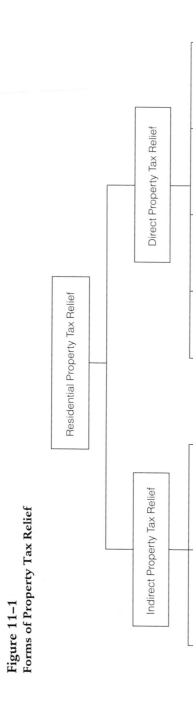

SOURCE: Based on John H. Bowman, Daphne A. Kenyon, Adam Langley, and Bethany P. Paquin, Property Tax Circuit Breakers: Fair and Cost-Effective Relief for Taxpayers. Cambridge, Massachusetts: Lincoln Institute of Land Policy, 2009, p. 5. Reprinted with permission.

as foreign government property not used for commercial purposes); (2) property held by religious, educational, charitable, or nonprofit organizations; and (3) residential property (through homestead, veterans', mortgage, or old-age exemptions). The second group includes preferential incentives intended to induce favored activities without regard for the otherwise taxable nature of the property holder. These include exemptions for economic development (new plants or equipment), pollution control facilities, and land maintained in an undeveloped, natural state. Closely related are abatements, negotiated contracts between a locality and a parcel holder under which some share of assessed value is not taxed for an agreed-upon period of time. The share may vary over time, bringing the parcel gradually into the tax system. The negotiations are normally arranged to induce developers to undertake projects they would not otherwise have done. Whether abatements actually have that effect is not entirely clear. In most environments, to abate the tax on certain properties means that properties without abatement in the taxing unit pay higher tax to support government services; other taxpayers, not the government offering the abatement, bear its cost.[42]

Individuals qualify for many different classes of exemptions. Some of the more important classes used by states (in terms of size of value) are homestead, veterans', and old-age exemptions. Homestead exemptions allow homeowners a given assessed value base before any property tax bill is levied against property. Veterans' and old-age exemptions provide similar partial exemption from the tax. These exemptions can dramatically reduce the base on which the tax can be applied. Nationwide, the partial exemptions reduced gross locally assessed property values by 3.6 percent in 1991. However, the loss of value exceeded 10 percent in several states: Alabama (12.3), Florida (14.1), Hawaii (13.4), Idaho (15.0), Indiana (10.6), and Louisiana (27.5).[43] The redistributions of the cost of government are not trivial.

Such exemption programs are politically popular because of their apparent tax savings and burden redistribution, but they have a number of important problems. First, the programs usually have a statewide purpose, but because property taxes primarily support local government, the revenue consequences are local. They may become a way for state legislatures to win favor with the electorate without losing state revenue. Abatements are locally arranged, but one government (e.g., a city) may contract away a property tax base important to another entity (e.g., a school district). Second, the programs do not focus tax relief on the needy. All people falling into the specific categories (e.g., homeowners or veterans) receive aid, regardless of their specific needs, because there is no income or means test for receipt of the exemption. Despite trials and tribulations, homeowners probably are better off than renters, and not all homeowners are equally well (or poorly) situated. Third, if the exemption program is sufficiently widespread, as in the case of general homestead

---

[42]Abatements are discussed in greater detail in Esteban Dalehite, John L. Mikesell, and C. Kurt Zorn, "Variation in Property Tax Abatement Programs among States," *Economic Development Quarterly* 19 (May 2005): 157–73. Abatements can be thought of as a partial and short-term version of a split rate property tax–a tax reduction for the improvement but not for land.

[43]U.S. Bureau of the Census, *1992 Census of Governments, Vol. 2, Taxable Property Values, No. 1, Assessed Valuation for Local General Property Taxation,* XI. More recent national data are, unfortunately, not available.

exemption programs, the effect may be substantially higher property tax rates to recover lost revenue. For properties not completely exempted from the base, actual relief may be more psychological than real because the owner pays a higher rate on a smaller base, with about the same total tax bill. Fourth, individual exemption programs ordinarily do not apply to rental properties, and renters tend to be considerably less affluent than are property owners. This must be seen as an inherent defect in the structure of exemption programs.

Exemptions also apply to selected types of commercial and industrial property.[44] Cities and counties often seek to encourage economic development within their boundaries through exemptions. Property tax payments made by the benefited facility are reduced; local governments serving that facility either receive less property tax revenue or replace the lost proceeds by adjusting their statutory rates upward on the other taxable properties in their jurisdictions. If all works well, the fiscal impacts of the relief will be bearable because the fruits of economic development, by reducing social expenditure demands and increasing taxable base, will restore the finances of the localities. The exemption may be complete and permanent, or it may abate all or a portion of property tax for a specific period of time. It may also exempt portions of an otherwise taxable parcel, such as pollution-control equipment or solar energy equipment. Some areas also provide special exemptions for rehabilitated property. The idea is to stimulate economic activity of particular types at defined locations. Evidence suggests things other than property taxes—particularly accessibility to markets, resource availability, transportation networks, and environmental amenities—are much more significant in determining the location of commercial and industrial facilities. Thus, the expected return from such exemptions is low. An even greater problem than low return from the exemption, however, may be the effect on existing property in the area if the incentive works. New industries create a demand for public services (police protection, fire protection, planning, etc.), and new people in the area will likely demand more services than can be covered by the residential tax base they bring. With the new industrial property exempt, those costs must be borne by the existing tax base. This system, at best, is discriminatory and, at worst, may eliminate some marginal businesses. Those properties not qualifying for the exemption face artificially high property tax rates because of the assistance provided the new arrivals.

A final exemption group includes properties that are fully exempt because of the religious, government, educational, or charitable nature of the owner. An accurate estimate of the total amount of the potential tax base removed by these exemptions is not available because where the law requires assessment of these properties, officials do not devote much effort on properties that yield no tax revenue. Observers maintain that the taxes forgiven are substantial. The revenue loss is a particular problem because such properties are unequally distributed among localities. Cities, counties, or school districts with major state installations (e.g., universities and state parks) can be particularly affected. They must provide for the peak and special service demands created by users of that facility without the power to include that facility in the tax base. Thus, taxpayers of that locality must subsidize the citizenry of the

---

[44]The best general source of information on these programs is Steven Gold, *Property Tax Relief* (Lexington, Mass.: Heath, 1979). Unfortunately, it is severely out of date.

state. The problem is reduced somewhat when exemptions are conditioned on both ownership and use of the facility (a university classroom building may be exempt, but not a university-owned hotel), but the dual requirement is neither universal nor applied without interpretation problems. The federal government does make in-lieu-of-property-tax payments to state and local units hosting certain federal installations, but states seldom provide similar relief to their local governments. As is discussed in a later chapter, local user charges may well be an attractive option in such instances. In other words, the university may be exempt from the local property tax, but if it wants to have the city pick up its trash, it will have to pay for the service.

Circuit Breakers

Property tax exemptions to individuals fail to target property tax relief to those individuals most in need. That problem can be reduced by conditioning property tax assistance on individual income levels, as is done by property tax circuit breakers. Residential-property circuit breakers, used by thirty-three states and the District of Columbia, pinpoint relief of property tax overload (defined in terms of the ratio of property tax payment to current family income) through integration of the local property tax and the state individual income tax structure.[45] The taxpayer reports, on his or her income tax return, the amount of property tax paid for the year. The property tax paid is compared with the taxpayer's income. If the ratio of property tax to income is excessive as defined in the circuit breaker law (an "overload"), the state returns some portion of that excess to the individual as an addition to his or her income tax refund, a reduction in income tax owed, or a direct cash payment. Thus, the circuit breaker reduces the property tax overload at state expense. In addition, the circuit breaker relief is targeted to those identified as being in need of relief—simply paying high property taxes alone would not be grounds for giving relief.

Critical structural elements for circuit breakers include age restrictions, income definition and limits, renter status, and benefit formulas. Many programs limit overload relief to the elderly, at least partly to reduce program cost. Elderly individuals, however, may be especially susceptible to overload because the property tax bill on property they accumulate during their work careers does not fall as their income falls with retirement. The property tax bill that was reasonable in relation to salary may consume an excessive chunk of the pension. The circuit breaker can reduce the need for forced sale and can ease retirement. Nonelderly low-income homeowners, however, may face similar overloads, particularly in the early years of home ownership or when a family income earner becomes unemployed. Exclusion of these homeowners may not be fair, but it does reduce the cost of the overall program.

Income limitations for the circuit breaker program are another design question. States do not provide circuit breaker formula relief to all, but rather impose income

---

[45] John H. Bowman, Daphne A. Kenyon, Adam Langley, and Bethany P. Paquin, *Property Tax Circuit Breakers: Fair and Cost-Effective Relief for Taxpayers* (Cambridge, Mass.: Lincoln Institute for Land Policy, 2009).

ceilings beyond which the system does not apply. Income definitions are not all the same. The ceilings reduce program cost and concentrate assistance on lower-income people. For these purposes, however, income must be defined more broadly than federal or state taxable income to include nontaxed retirement income sources. If it is not, individuals who are reasonably well off because of pension, Social Security, and other nontaxed incomes would qualify, reducing aid available for the truly unfortunate.

Renters pose a third design issue, under the assumption that they bear a portion of the property tax burden on units they occupy—that is, if the property tax is partially shifted forward. A circuit breaker limited to homeowners would provide renters no assistance, even though many renters are much less affluent than the poorest homeowners. Renter relief, where given, presumes a property tax equivalent as a specified percentage of rent paid. The share is not scientifically determined because analysts have been unable to estimate the extent (if any) to which property tax is shifted to renters. With reasonable income limits, however, the program can be seen as a part of general assistance regardless of property tax conditions.

The final design element is the choice between threshold and sliding-scale relief formulas. The former approach defines a threshold percentage of income as the overload level (somewhat more than half the circuit breaker states use this approach). Property tax payments above that overload level are subject to partial relief. Relief computation follows the formula

$$R = t(PT - kI)$$

where

R = relief to be provided (subject to a lower limit of zero),

t = percentage of the overload that is relieved,

PT = property tax payment,

k = overload threshold percentage, and

I = family income.

Suppose a family has an income of $12,000 and pays property tax of $900. If it lives in a state that defines the overload threshold as 5 percent and grants 60 percent overload relief, the family would receive circuit breaker relief of $180. Some states further reduce their cost by increasing the threshold percentage as income increases (in other words, they have multiple thresholds)—a further effort to economize and focus aid.

The second formula is the sliding-scale approach. In this formula, relief is computed as a percentage of the property tax payment, with the percentage falling as family income increases:

$$R = z \times PT$$

where z is the percentage of property tax relieved for the income class and R and PT are as previously defined. Unless the relief percentage falls to zero at high incomes, all taxpayers receive assistance under this approach, so it is more like general property tax relief than the specific relief of the property tax overload. It does differ, however, from general property tax relief in that (1) there is usually an upper limit to circuit breaker relief available to a parcel holder, (2) taxpayers must file to obtain this relief, (3) only homes occupied by the owner receive the circuit breaker relief (although some states extend the assistance to farm property), and (4) relief is conditioned on income of the property owner.

Circuit breakers are flexible and easily administered in conjunction with the state income tax. Circuit breakers improve property tax equity by targeting relief to those in greatest need and, furthermore, are financed from state, not local, revenue. They provide no incentive, however, for improved property tax administration and may encourage greater use of local property taxes, as some property tax costs are shifted to the state. Choices that states make in setting up their circuit breakers include sliding scale or threshold, elderly only or more general, inclusion of renters or limited to owners, relief by direct payment or by income tax credit, breadth of income inclusion in defining taxpaying capacity, inclusion of homestead property only or other property also, and generosity of relief.

Deferrals

An additional relief device applicable to the special property tax problems of the elderly, persons with disabilities, those with limited income, and farm owners on the fringe of developing areas is tax deferral. With this mechanism, individuals whose property values have risen dramatically through no fault of their own are permitted to pay tax on the basis of old values, with records kept on the difference between that payment and what it would have been at full property value. That difference is deferred to a later time, but not forgiven. In the case of the agricultural property, it is collected when the farmland converts to a different (higher-value) use. In the case of the elderly individual, the deferred tax becomes a claim against that individual's estate.

These recaptures can be complete or partial, and interest may or may not be charged; state approaches vary. The tax deferral relieves special property tax burdens without creating the problems that circuit breakers and special exemptions can often create. Deferrals can relieve without special subsidization—a rare combination in tax policy.

Classification

Nineteen states and the District of Columbia structure their property tax to apply different effective rates to different types of property, making their tax rates classified rather than uniform.[46] Classification assumes that certain property classes have superior taxpaying capability over other classes and should pay higher effective property

---

[46]U.S. Bureau of Census, *1992 Census of Governments, Vol. 2, Taxable Property Values, No. 1, Assessed Valuation for Local General Property Taxation,* IX; and Richard R. Almy, "Property Tax Policies and Administrative Practices in Canada and the United States," *Assessment Journal* (July/August 2000): 41–57. Cook County, Illinois, also uses a classified tax (the rest of the state does not). These taxes still presume uniformity within property classes. The equal-protection clause permits such separation of property into classes and assignment of different tax burdens to each class as long as the divisions are not arbitrary or capricious.

tax rates. Tax-bearing capability, however, varies dramatically within classes, often to a greater extent than variation between classes. In other words, there are afflu-ent and not-so-affluent homeowners, prosperous and poor farmers, and profitable and bankrupt businesses. The classification systems, however, treat each ownership class or property type as if all units in that class were alike. Furthermore, classifica-tion is more likely to be based on political clout or the expected ease of shifting the tax to someone else than on any reasonable justification for allocating appropriate tax burdens. Classification can be accomplished by either variation in assessment ratios or variation in statutory rates. New York City applies rates that differ by type of property, as shown in these rates for 2011–2012: Class 1: includes most residential property of up to three units (family homes and small stores or offices with one or two apartments attached) and most condominiums that are not more than three sto-ries, 18.025%; Class 2: includes all other property that is primarily residential, such as cooperatives and condominiums, 13.433%; Class 3: includes utility property, 12.473%; and Class 4: includes all commercial and industrial property, such as of-fice and factory buildings, 10.152%. Most states employ different assessment ratios. For instance, the Alabama classification by assessment ratios works like this: Class I property (public utility property) is assessed at 30 percent of appraised value; Class II property (real and personal property not falling into any of the other classes) is assessed at 20 percent of appraised value; Class III property (agricultural and forest, historic buildings and sites, and residential property) is assessed at 10 percent of ap-praised value; and Class IV (private automobiles and trucks) is assessed at 15 percent of appraised value. Both systems result in an effective property tax rate—the rate on market value of the property—that differs according to classification of the property.

Each method can produce the same effective-rate pattern, as Table 11–3 dem-onstrates. Classification by statutory rate variation is more straightforward and transparent and interferes less with the assessment process. If classification is to be adopted, that approach is preferable, although it is used only in parts of New York State, Massachusetts, Minnesota, West Virginia, and the District of Columbia.

Table 11–3
Property Classifications by Statutory Rates and Assessment Ratios: An Illustration

Classes of Property	Rate Classification			Ratio Classification		
	Statutory Rate ($)	Assessment Ratio (%)	Effective Rate ($)	Statutory Rate($)	Assessment Ratio (%)	Effective Rate ($)
Owner-Occupied Housing	2.00	50	1.00	4.00	25	1.00
Farms	1.00	50	0.50	4.00	12.5	0.50
Commercial and Industrial	4.00	50	2.00	4.00	50	2.00
Public Utilities	8.00	50	4.00	4.00	100	4.00

Limits and Controls

Extraordinary tax rate limits and controls—beyond the normal process of rate setting—establish a special structure for property tax operation. A categorization of controls appears in Table 11–4. A number of the special controls date from the 1970s, although several have more lengthy heritages. The "tax revolt," especially Proposition 13 in California and related referenda in other states from 1978 through 1980, was partly the product of high and rising effective property tax rates on owner-occupied housing. The rising taxes were created by, among several forces, demands for local public service, limited access to nonproperty tax sources, waste in local government, and special exemptions provided to other property types. A large part of that rebellion, however, surely reflected irritation with government in general and the feeling of powerlessness to do anything about federal or state taxes—those taxes rose without any statutory rate increase for which elected representatives were clearly responsible. The property tax was another matter. The rate would normally vary each year, so it presented an ideal focal point for those concerns. It became the lightning rod for government finance nationwide during the periods of taxpayer discontent.

Property taxes have been subject to extraordinary limitations at least since the Great Depression of the 1930s. Those limits, however, traditionally controlled local statutory tax rates by state law, either in statute or in the constitution. These controls on the tax rate appeared ineffective as assessed values increased dramatically, both in total and for individual property parcels, during the high-inflation 1970s. Governments could adopt statutory property tax rates no higher than those of the prior year and within the statutory limit and still obtain dramatically increased revenue because of the higher assessed values. Property owners whose parcels had been reassessed would face increased property tax bills at the controlled property tax rate. Thus, controls on statutory rates, whether through a statutory rate limit or a rate freeze, seemed powerless as constraints on either local governments or property tax bills.

The approach taken in the 1970s was the levy or expenditure limit, which capped total dollars, not the rate applied to the tax base. That approach does constrain the growth of government activity and prevents increases in assessed value from being automatically translated into higher tax collections and higher tax bills for parcels with increased assessment. With a levy freeze, a general assessed-value increase will require a reduction in tax rates. For example, suppose that a control law permits 5 percent levy growth from one year to the next and that assessed value increases by 8 percent. Rate computations might look like those in Table 11–5. With this control structure, property tax levy ceilings dominate the budget process. Maximum growth in the levy establishes the budget size, and total budget requests must keep within the limit. As soon as assessed value figures are known, property tax rates can be computed because law establishes the total levy. The only unknown is the manner in which the total is appropriated among operating units. In this case, the budget total is not made up of its operating components; rather, the budget total is divided among the operating components, and one extra dollar provided to one agency is truly a dollar not available to any other agency. The total budget cannot expand to accommodate any additions.

Table 11–4

Property Tax Control Structures and Their Impacts

Type of Limit	Example	Impact on Property Tax Rate	Impact on Property Tax Levies	Impact on Expenditures
Legal limit on statutory property tax rate	Cities limited to rate of $5.00/$100 assessed value.	Same ceiling rate statewide.	Levy can increase as assessed value increases or with rate increase for jurisdictions not at legal limit.	Same as levies, plus possible increases from other revenue sources.
Property tax rate freeze	Cities limited to statutory rate applied in 2010.	Ceiling rate varies across state.	Levy can increase only as assessed value increases.	Same as above.
Property levy limit	Cities' 2010 levy cannot exceed 105% of 2009 levy.	Depends on change in assessed value.	Constrained to limit	Depends on access to nonproperty tax revenues.
Expenditure limit	Cities' 2010 appropriations cannot exceed 108% of 2009 appropriations.	Depends on change in assessed value and on change in other revenues.	Depends on access to nonproperty tax revenues.	Constrained to limit.
Assessed value increase limit	Assessed value of any property (or properties) in city may not increase by more than 5% in 2009 regardless of reassessment result.	Depends on regular rate calculation.	Depends on local budget process/race calculation.	Depends on local budget process.
"Truth in taxation"/full disclosure	Cities announce impact of new assessed values on tax levy if rates maintained, what rate reduction would maintain old tax levy and, proposed new tax rate, and call for public input on their decisions.	Depends on regular rate calculation.	Depends on local budget process/ rate calculation.	Depends on local budget process.

SOURCE: Daniel Mullins and Bruce Wallin, "Tax and Expenditure Limitations: Introduction and Overview," *Public Budgeting & Finance* 24 (Winter 2004): 2–15.

Table 11–5
Rate Computations for a Levy Control: Levy Increase Limited to 5 Percent, Assessed Value Grows by 8 Percent

Budget Year	Assessed Value ($)	Levy ($)	Property Tax Rate ($)
1	5,000,000	250,000	5.00 per 100
2	5,400,000	262,500	4.86 per 100

Limits of the 1970s were obviously more stringent than the earlier rate controls.[47] They led local governments to adopt a consistent set of responses. First, governments have reacted by trying to get other governments or nonprofit organizations to take over services the controlled governments has been providing. If the approach succeeds, the services in question are provided, but the controlled government retains the previously committed resources for other activities. Second, governments have sought increased intergovernmental aid (grants, shared taxes, etc.) to continue services without the use of increasingly scarce local resources. This search is particularly intense to finance mandated services, that is, services the government provides largely because it has been required to do so by another government. If that government both restricts taxing powers and mandates new expenditure, the intergovernmental strain is especially intense. The quest for grants is particularly accelerated when spending from such revenue is placed outside any control structure, as is often the case. Finally, governments have searched for charges and nonproperty tax revenues outside the limits. In some instances, the charges are merely disguised property taxes (e.g., fire or police protection fees based on property characteristics), but they can be welcome additions that improve both the efficiency and the equity of service finance. Expanded use of legitimate charges is in fact the most attractive side effect of the new limitation movement.

Another approach limits the growth in assessed value. In this case, when properties are reassessed, the increase in value cannot exceed a particular percentage. Over time, the full increase in valuation is permitted, but it is gradual. It does not otherwise have an impact on the property tax process. It is primarily a control over reassessment shock and the danger that local governments will not adjust their statutory rates when the increase in assessed value hits their financial system.

A final approach to controlling property tax increases, but without the direct constraints previously noted, is the "truth in taxation" or full disclosure requirement, a system in place in several states, including Arizona, Texas, and Michigan. This system requires local governments to call attention to the fact that assessed values have increased and that their property tax levies will increase unless they reduce their statutory property tax rates to allow for the higher assessed values. An illustration of a "truth in taxation" notification appears in Figure 11–2. This notification from the Pima County (Arizona) Community College District warns its citizens that the District intends to increase its property tax levy and that the increase is in addition

---

[47]The exception is for governments experiencing assessed value decline. A levy control for these units permits the accommodating rate increases that rate control does not.

Figure 11–2
Truth in Taxation Notification: Pima County (Arizona) Community College District

TRUTH IN TAXATION HEARING

NOTICE OF TAX INCREASE

In compliance with section 15-1461.01, Arizona Revised Statutes, Pima County Community College District is notifying its property taxpayers of Pima County Community College District's intention to raise its primary property taxes over last year's level. The Pima County Community College District is proposing an increase in primary property taxes of $1,814,406 or 2.0%.

For example, the proposed tax increase will cause Pima County Community College District's primary property taxes on a $100,000 home to increase from $112.59 (total taxes that would be owed without the proposed tax increase) to $114.84 (total proposed taxes including the tax increase).

This proposed increase is exclusive of increased primary property taxes received from new construction. The increase is also exclusive of any changes that may occur from property tax levies for voter approved bonded indebtedness or budget and tax overrides.

All interested citizens are invited to attend the public hearing on the tax increase that is scheduled to be held Wednesday, June 20, 2012 at 6:30 p.m. in the Community/Board Room at the District Office of Pima Community College, 4905 E. Broadway, Tucson, Arizona 85709-1005.

❈ **PimaCommunityCollege**

Pima County Community College 1111
District 1 Dr. Brenda B. Even, *Secretary*
District 2 David Longoria
District 3 Sherryn S. Marshall
District 4 Scott A. Stewart, *Chair*
District 5 Marty Cortez
Dr. Suzanne L. Miles, Interim Chancellor

(520) 206-4500
www.pima.edu

Pima Community College is an equal opportunity, affirmative action employer and educational institution committed to excellence through diversity. Reasonable accommodations, including materials in an alternative format, will be provided for individuals with disabilities when a minimum of five working days' advance notice is given. For the general public, please contact the PCC information line at (520) 206-4500 (TTY 206-4530); for PCC students, contact the appropriate campus Disabled Student Resources office.

SOURCE: http://www.pima.edu/about-pima/reports/finance-reports/docs-budget/FY13-Truth-In-Taxation.pdf. Reprinted with permission.

to any increase that would result from a higher property tax base (the increase from new construction). The District is thus both taking the proceeds of the higher property tax base and adding an increase in the property tax rate to all parcels. The notice announces a public hearing at which the public can express its views about the tax proposal. The idea is to bring more transparency into the rate-setting process and to allow for public response in fiscal decisions. Similar increases in the tax base, of course, occur with taxes on income and consumption, but there are no laws requiring such "truth in taxation" notifications for them.

Tax Increment Financing

Tax increment financing (TIF) offers support for economic development in targeted, usually blighted, areas. A TIF program "largely freezes the assessed valuation of all property parcels in a designated area (the TIF district) for a specific period of years. Property taxes levied in this frozen tax base continue to accrue to local taxing bodies, but taxes derived from the increases in assessed values (the tax increment) resulting from new development are used to pay for infrastructure needs and development expenditures in the TIF district. Thus, TIF serves as a geographically targeted tax, expenditure, and regulatory inducement to a specific location."[48] In logic, the public capital infrastructure needed for a private development project would be self-financed from property taxes from the project. Here is how the scheme could work. Suppose a large manufacturing plant wants to build on a site that lacks certain critical infrastructure normally provided by local government (roads, storm and sanitary sewers, water, etc.). A sponsoring local government could borrow to finance the improvements with payment of debt service (principal and interest) coming from the property tax proceeds from the increased property tax base. Table 11–6 illustrates the general idea of a TIF. If property assessments before development totaled $5 million, taxing units would receive tax proceeds on that

Table 11–6
Tax Increment Financing

	Assessed Value ($)	Tax Rate ($/$100)	Yield to Overlapping Governments ($)	Yield to TIF District ($)
Base (predevelopment)	5,000,000	8.00	400,000	0
Year 1	6,000,000	8.10	405,000	81,000
Year 2	7,000,000	8.15	407,500	163,000
Year 3	8,000,000	8.15	407,500	244,500
Year 4	8,000,000	8.20	410,000	246,000

[48]Joyce Y. Man, "Introduction," in *Tax Increment Financing and Economic Development: Uses, Structures, and Impact*, ed. Craig L. Johnson and Joyce Y. Man (Albany, N.Y.: State University of New York Press, 2001): 1. Some states have included nonproperty taxes in the TIF as well, although this is not common.

base as usual. As assessments rise with development, say, to $8 million, property tax collections on that higher base, regardless of the government levying the tax rate, will be diverted to service the infrastructure debt: property tax on $5 million goes to the overlapping local governments and property tax on $3 million (the increment) goes to service the debt that allowed the infrastructure making the development feasible.

TIFs have proven popular with industry and development officials, but they often irritate other local officials, especially those operating schools, because the transfer of revenue can seriously strain the finances of general government. Also, use of TIF revenues is so uncontrolled in some jurisdictions that they can be returned to developers to recoup costs not related to improving the public infrastructure around the project—something like a tax "kickback."

Conclusion

Almost by default, the property tax is the predominant tax source for local government. Though property taxes represent an opportunity to tax accumulated wealth not offered by levies on other bases, that advantage is overshadowed by haphazard and capricious assessment of the tax base. Because the tax applies to values defined by applying regulations, not values from market transactions, assessment is troublesome and requires special attention. Most problems with the property tax, outside of valuation, can be largely resolved by circuit breakers, deferrals, and the like.

It would be unfortunate if the advantages of the tax were sacrificed solely because of unwillingness to improve administration. The advantages of the property tax for local government finance are several. The base is visible, easily attached in an enforcement action, and physically immobile. The tax can be administered at a leisurely pace, and the rate can be adjusted to a fine degree. Those supporting a considerable degree of fiscal independence for the government closest to the people should consider how important the real property tax is to this independence.

QUESTIONS AND EXERCISES

1. Identify these elements of the property tax in your state: Who assesses property? Are some types assessed locally and some types by the state? What valuation standard is used? When was the latest reassessment of real property? Is personal property taxed? What classification system (if any) is used? What circuit breaker type (if any) is used? Does the circuit breaker extend beyond residential property owned by the elderly?

2. Why is the acquisition value or assessment-on-sale assessment system sometimes called the "Welcome Stranger" assessment system?

3. Knightstown has a property tax base with an appraised value consisting of $150,000,000 of taxable real property and $85,000,000 of taxable personal property. The assessment ratio is 50 percent. Exemptions for the elderly reduce assessed value by $3,000,000. The city has a planned budget of $15,000,000 and expects to receive $800,000 in nonproperty tax revenue.

  a. Compute the statutory property tax rate.
  b. Compute the effective property tax rate.
  c. The Smith family lives in Knightstown. Their property has an appraised value of $42,000. What is their city property tax bill?

4. Central County includes five townships (Nixon, Reagan, Davis, Greasy Creek, and Navaho) and one city (Booneville). It is served by two independent school districts: Seagram United Schools (Davis and Greasy Creek Townships) and Clinton Consolidated Schools (Nixon, Reagan, and Navaho Townships). Each government in the county levies a property tax to finance its activities, although Booneville has also enacted a local earned income tax (it is expected to yield $750,000 in the next year). Property tax rates are applied to assessed value, defined to equal 50 percent of fair cash value. Local unit tax rates fully overlap. The county assessor reports the following fair cash values for units within the county:

Nixon Township	$69,535,000
Reagan Township	$35,000,000
Davis Township	$23,720,000
Greasy Creek Township	$15,922,000
Navaho Township	$27,291,000
Booneville (Davis Township)	$88,450,000
Booneville (Greasy Creek Township)	$75,392,000

The township value data are for the area outside of any city or town that resides in the township. Values within a city must be added to obtain the township total.

The following presents the amounts that each taxing unit has budgeted to spend in the next year:

Central County	$3,428,000
Booneville City	$4,539,000
Nixon Township	$ 99,000
Reagan Township	$ 150,000
Davis Township	$ 250,000
Greasy Creek Township	$ 175,000
Navaho Township	$ 83,000
Seagram United Schools	$6,350,000
Clinton Consolidated Schools	$3,800,000

  a. Set the property tax rate for each taxing unit. Report each rate in dollars per $100 of assessed value.
  b. The Knight family owns property with a fair cash value of $100,000 in the Davis portion of Booneville. Prepare an itemized tax bill for the Knights.

   c. Suppose the current market value of the Knights' property is actually $225,000. What is their actual assessment ratio? What effective total property tax rate do they pay?

   d. There are 1,800 students in Seagram United Schools and 600 students in Clinton Consolidated Schools. How many dollars per pupil would a tax rate of $1 per $100 of assessed value yield in each district? Explain the significance of this comparison.

   e. A factory with an estimated fair cash value of $15 million may be built in Navaho Township. If the factory has no impact on spending by any local government, i.e., levies do not change, and there are no other changes in the county assessed values, what total property tax bill would the factory face?

   f. Suppose that the county undergoes a general reassessment that doubles the assessed values of every taxing unit and that state law forbids any taxing unit from increasing its property tax levy by more than 3 percent. (The factory from part e, sadly enough, ends up in Mexico, so there is no impact from its value.) Assume that the property owned by the Knights (as above) doubles in assessed value and that the city, county, and school districts increase their levies by the maximum allowed, but that there is no increase in levies by any township. What is the Knights' new property tax?

5. The state owns 16,500 acres of state forest land in a county. Forest and untilled open areas (the kind of land largely within the boundaries of the state forest) are valued at $180 per acre on average when in private ownership. Assessed value is one-third of that value. The forest area is in two townships of the county. Sixty percent is in a township with a tax rate of $1.80 per $100, and the remainder is in a township with a rate of $1.64 per $100. According to the aid formula for compensating local governments containing substantial amounts of untaxed state property, the county receives in-lieu-of-property-tax payments of $18,000 per year for division among the affected taxing units of the county. Is the state payment about right in comparison to the equivalent property tax the land would bear? Explain.

6. Mr. and Mrs. Woodward, an elderly couple with no dependents, have taxable source income of $8,000 and Social Security income of $26,000. They own property assessed at $80,000 (current market value of $190,000) and are subject to a property tax rate of $5/$100 of assessed value. They each receive an old-age property tax exemption of $500. They are eligible for the state property tax circuit breaker. The relief threshold is 6 percent of total money income; 25 percent of any overload is returned by the state in an income tax credit. Maximum relief paid is $600 per couple.

   a. What property tax would they pay without circuit breaker relief?

   b. For how much circuit breaker relief are they eligible?

7. There have been complaints about assessment practices in Garfield County. Each of the three townships in the county assesses property independently, using an elected assessor. State law dictates that assessed value equal one-third of market value; the state constitution contains a clause requiring uniform property tax rates. The state agency of which you are an employee judges assessment quality in counties, recommends multipliers to produce overall balance among townships, and can recommend general reassessments where needed.

     You have obtained a random sample of assessed values and selling prices of the residential properties that have sold during the last quarter in the county. All prices are from arm's-length transactions, none involves special financial arrangements, and none involves substantial amounts of personal property. These data are presented below.

   a. Prepare a preliminary opinion of assessment quality in Garfield County. Compute all important statistics.
   b. The Garfield County Board of Equalization wants multipliers to get each township's assessed value/market value (AV/MV) ratio up (or down) to the state-required one-third ratio. What multipliers would you apply in each township? Will the application of these multipliers increase or reduce measured equality of assessment in each township? What would their impact be on measured equality in the county?
   c. Total property tax rates by township are as follows:

Buchanan Township	$6.15 per $100 AV
Arthur Township	$6.00 per $100 AV
Coolidge Township	$5.75 per $100 AV

      What properties pay the highest and lowest nominal tax rates? What properties pay the highest and lowest effective tax rates?

Parcel Number	Assessed Value	Selling Price
Coolidge Township		
1-1	30,190	120,740
1-2	39,060	201,500
1-3	66,690	372,000
1-4	13,830	86,800
1-5	39,720	207,700
1-6	23,550	232,500
1-7	16,650	91,450
1-8	45,870	85,870
1-9	32,910	114,390
1-10	21,060	107,725
1-11	19,740	71,300
1-12	28,620	122,450
1-13	13,920	77,190
1-14	20,370	114,700
1-15	19,290	94,550

Arthur Township

2-1	14,190	71,750
2-2	59,700	54,250
2-3	19,390	52,500
2-4	20,160	134,750
2-5	19,260	100,625
2-6	19,420	94,500
2-7	14,220	77,000
2-8	19,840	54,250
2-9	11,760	68,250
2-10	19,720	64,750
2-11	14,010	61,250
2-12	13,350	94,850
2-13	11,370	87,500
2-14	17,920	44,530
2-15	11,310	91,000
2-16	18,790	54,250
2-17	15,360	99,750

Buchanan Township

3-1	53,440	249,600
3-2	34,880	180,000
3-3	22,720	114,000
3-4	52,320	218,400
3-5	13,600	60,000
3-6	13,840	72,000
3-7	20,160	94,400
3-8	27,400	144,000
3-9	32,720	167,600
3-10	14,320	82,000
3-11	18,360	87,500
3-12	20,200	132,000
3-13	21,880	116,000

8. The following data are for the town of Paragon in the fiscal year starting January 1, 2014.

Budgeted town expenditures	$ 20,000,000
Estimated revenue from grants, fees, and licenses	$ 6,000,000
Assessed value of property	$142,000,000

a. What is the town property tax rate in dollars per $100 of assessed value?

b. The Wooden family has property with a fair cash value of $90,000. The assessment ratio is one-third. The family is entitled to a mortgage exemption of $5,000. That is taken against assessed value. What is their property tax bill from Paragon?

c. Suppose that, for 2015, properties in Paragon are not reassessed, but that new construction increases total assessed values by 5 percent. The state institutes a levy control, allowing 2015 levies to increase by 6 percent over their 2014 level. Nonproperty tax revenue is estimated to be $6.5 million. What is the maximum 2015 property tax rate permitted, what is the maximum town expenditure, and what property tax bill would the Wooden family face?

d. Suppose that, for 2016, properties in Paragon are not reassessed, but that new construction increases total assessed value by 9 percent. The state enacts a new property tax control that allows the 2016 levies to increase only by $1.80 over the 2015 levies. Nonproperty tax revenue is estimated to be $6.75 million. What is the maximum 2016 property tax rate permitted, what is the maximum town expenditure, and what property tax bill would the Wooden family face?

9. The town of Stratford is setting its property tax rate for the upcoming year. Its budget calls for spending of $220,000,000, and it anticipates receiving $700,000 in nonproperty tax revenue. It levies a classified rate structure: nonresidential properties pay a rate that is double that applied to residential property. Its residential assessed value equals $4,000,000,000, and its nonresidential assessed value equals $2,800,000,000. What property tax rates will the town set for residential and nonresidential property?

10. Habitat for Humanity helps low-income families achieve home ownership by using volunteer labor (including that of the prospective new homeowner) and donated money and materials to construct simple and decent houses for the family. Resulting mortgage payments are low, and the revenue flow is used to support even more housing. The organization operates in all states and the District of Columbia, other territories of the United States, and some other countries. A problem has developed for the families. The value of the homes has increased, and with that increase come higher property taxes, often increasing to levels that make the house no longer easily affordable. But if the homeowner sells, any increase in value accrues to Habitat, and the family again becomes homeless. The question: What should be done? Is the problem one for the local governments levying the property tax on the homes (these are the governments providing vital services like elementary and secondary education, police protection, fire protection, and parks to these homeowners)? Is the problem one for Habitat for Humanity (it is the entity putting families into homes that have become unaffordable and that cannot be converted into money to be put into other housing)? Is the problem one for the families (they are the ones benefiting most from the houses)? What policy options are available?

11. *Review Question:* What performance outcome measures would you propose for a revenue department charged with all responsibilities for administration of the real property tax? Would its outcome measures differ from those appropriate for a department administering an individual income tax? Explain.

CASES FOR DISCUSSION

CASE 11–1

Property Taxes and a World-Class House

Consider These Questions

1. What approaches may apply in this assessment question, and what problems do they have?

2. What is your view of the assessment system briefly outlined here?

3. What help does the asking price for the rental property give the assessor?

Ross Perot, Texas billionaire and candidate for president in 1992, owns an 8,264-square-foot house with four fireplaces and five baths on more than twenty-five acres of land in North Dallas. His estate also has a 5,327-square-foot rental house with 2.2 acres he purchased around 1988. This parcel has been for sale for about a year, with an asking price of $1.2 million. In 1992, the Dallas Central Appraisal District assessed the main house and land at $12,279,600 and the rental property at $1,220,340. (Those had been the assessment levels for three years.) For 1993, the values were $11,870,550 and $1,200,000 in recognition of declining residential property values in Texas. The District does use full-market-value assessment in its appraisals, but does often estimate values by area rather than conducting detailed assessments of each parcel.

The District received 65,000 assessment protests in 1993, one of them being from Mr. Perot. He had not protested in earlier years, but comparable sales in the neighborhood led him to conclude that his properties were overassessed. After the initial hearing, his assessment was reduced by $96,100; he filed suit for further reduction in state district court, the normal avenue to continue the appeal. Following routine procedure, assessing officials will inspect and appraise the property; that is the normal approach to beginning negotiations.

SOURCE: This case was assembled from Scott McCartner, "There Is One Thing We Can Be Sure Of: It's a World-Class House," *Wall Street Journal*, September 2, 1993, B-1; Anne Beilli Gesalman, "Perot Sues over Home Appraisal," *Dallas Morning News,* September 1, 1993, 25-A; and Steven R. Reed, "Perot Files Suit to Lower Taxes on His Estate," *Houston Chronicle,* September 2, 1993, 29.

CASE 11–2

Local Finances and Property-Tax-Exempt Organizations

Nonprofit organizations and governments are often exempt from payment of property taxes. The conditions and standards are not the same for all states or even necessarily for all localities within a state, although state law defines the terms for exemption. Furthermore, not all types of nonprofit organizations receive the same exempt treatment. For instance, property owned by governments, churches, educational institutions, and hospitals may be exempt from property taxation, but property owned by other nonprofit organizations may be taxable. The state standards for qualifying as an exempt nonprofit organization are not always the same as those used by the federal government. Local governments that host major exempt organizations (for instance, large private universities or federal or state government facilities) are in a complex situation. On the one hand, there can be considerable benefits in terms of economic impact and prestige associated with hosting the entity (Cambridge, Massachusetts, is proud of being the home of both Harvard University and the Massachusetts Institute of Technology, for instance). On the other hand, the exempt property owned by the institutions provides no tax base for use in providing police and fire protection, education, and other services to the community.

When local governments that rely on their property taxes for the finance of government services face fiscal difficulty, their leaders look toward broadening the tax base as a source of revenue. Getting payments from financially large nonprofit organizations and entities of other governments looks attractive to many. It has been estimated that, nationwide, nonprofit organization exemptions reduced property tax collections by 10 percent, with higher shares in areas with particularly large nonprofit sectors. The discussions become particularly focused when the local government is financially stressed while large tax-exempt organizations it hosts appear prosperous.

The case that follows deals with a dispute between Providence, Rhode Island, and Brown University over the amount that tax-exempt Brown would contribute to the city.

Consider These Questions

1. Why should nonprofit organizations be exempt from payment of local property taxes? Don't they benefit from local services just as much as proprietary businesses? For instance, why should a nonprofit hospital be exempt from the local property tax, while a similar proprietary hospital is taxed? Is the argument for exemption different for a state university compared with a similar private university?

2. If they are to be exempt, what standards would you establish for giving the exemption? Should all nonprofit organizations and government entities be in the same boat? What about state universities, state parks, and the state capitol building?

3. What would be the effect of having a large share of the total potential property tax base in a city owned by tax-exempt organizations? Would it mean lost property tax revenue or higher property taxes paid by taxable entities? Any idea how it might be possible to see whether the impact is higher tax paid by others or lower property tax revenue?

4. In some jurisdictions, there are provisions for exempt entities to make payments in lieu of taxes (PILOTs). Should the PILOT amount be voluntary, or should it

be calculated according to a legislated formula? How should the PILOT be calculated? Should the PILOT approximate the amount of property tax payment on the property? If so, why bother exempting the property? Massachusetts legislators have been considering a proposal to levy a 2.5 percent annual assessment on assets of universities with endowments above $1 billion (the Harvard endowment is $35 billion). Would that be a sensible approach? Does your university make a PILOT to its host local governments? Do other nonprofits in your state make a PILOT payment?

5. State law typically establishes what entities qualify for property tax exemption. That being the case, should the state government provide payments to local governments to compensate them for any lost revenue?

6. Suppose tax-exempt entities are required to start paying taxes—or nonvoluntary PILOTS that approximate taxes. Who do you suppose will bear the burden of those payments? Is this way of distributing the cost of local government services more reasonable than the system currently in place?

7. Would you judge the amount ultimately paid by Brown to be about right? What standard would you apply to decide?

Providence and Brown: Bearing the Cost of Government Services

Providence, Rhode Island, in common with many city governments across the United States, has suffered considerable fiscal stress in the years during and after the Great Recession. Indeed, the Providence mayor, Angel Taveras, warned that the city would run out of money in June 2012 and might need to file for federal bankruptcy protection. Its deficit was around $22.5 million, and that amount could not be managed by the city without devastating cuts in services or huge increases in taxes. Many taxpayers had already seen their taxes increased by 13 percent to get even to that deficit level. The deficit in the previous year was $110 million, so the mayor had made considerable progress. In order to prevent further service cuts or tax increases, he argued that tax-exempt Brown University should make a greater contribution to the support of city services. Indeed, he thought that an extra $5 million per year would be about right.

Rhode Island law exempts private universities, along with many other types of nonprofit organizations, from payment of property taxes. However, Brown—along with many other exempt entities in Providence—had been making voluntary payments to the city, an amount that recently had been around $4 million per year ($1.2 million under a memorandum of understanding between city and university signed in 2003 plus taxes on buildings not used for educational purposes, like the for-profit bookstore; in contrast with many other states, tax does not apply to these noneducational facilities, so that payment was voluntary as well). The mayor believed that the current amount was not enough. City data show that tax-exempt organizations like Brown hold more than half the land in Providence, amounting to 41 percent of assessed value (if those figures can be trusted—assessors throughout the nation do not devote their greatest care to assessing parcels that generate no revenue). Only a significant minority of colleges and universities across the United States make any such voluntary payment, so Brown is already ahead of the norm.

It would be difficult to argue that Brown suffers from grinding fiscal distress. Its endowment had reached $2.5 billion, having grown by 18.5 percent in the previous year. Its budget was $865.2 million (compared to $614 million for the city). Its campus included more than 200 buildings, with a value of more than $1 billion. That property, if taxed at the commercial rate levied by the city, would face a tax bill of roughly $38 million. However, the Brown administration believed that an additional $5 million would be fiscally crippling to the university. Undergraduate tuition for 2011–2012 was $41,328; room, board, and required fees made the total cost $53,136. The university has 8,000 students, employs around 4,500 people (the sixth largest employer in Rhode Island), and spends around $65 million annually with local vendors. It is an economic force in both the city and the state, in addition to being an important educational institution.

After considerable negotiation, Brown finally agreed to pay Providence $31 million more over the next eleven years. At last report, Providence had not filed for federal bankruptcy protection.

SOURCES: Daphne A. Kenyon and Adam H. Langley, *Payments in Lieu of Taxes, Balancing Municipal and Nonprofit Interests* (Cambridge, Mass.: Lincoln Institute of Land Policy, 2010); Michael McDonald, "Harvard's Voluntary Tax Spurs Providence to Press Brown," *Bloomberg,* February 8, 2012 [http://www.bloomberg.com/news/2012-02-08/harvard-s-voluntary-tax-spurs-ailing-providence-to-press-brown.html]; Erika Niedowski, "Brown University Taxes; Providence Takes on School in Town-Gown Money Clash," *Huffington Post,* February 12, 2012 [http://www.huffingtonpost.com/2012/02/13/brown-university-taxes-pr_n_1272785.html]; Stephanie Strom, "Tax Exemptions of Charities Face New Challenges," *New York Times,* May 26, 2008.

CHAPTER 12

Revenue from User Fees, User Charges, and Sales by Public Monopolies

Governments normally collect revenue through their sovereign taxing power to define the payment owed without any connection to the value of any public product or service received by the taxpayer.[1] When public goods are involved, these market processes will fail. However, there are some goods and services that governments sell that potential buyers may or may not purchase, according to their individual tastes, preferences, and affluence. Impacts on others from those purchases are so small that provision is not a public problem. In these instances, revenue to finance these services can be raised without the brute force and compulsion of taxation, but rather through voluntary exchange. There is almost certainly a wide, but not wide-open, territory that governments should explore for such financing, which relieves the general revenue system by requiring specific "customers" to pay for the services they receive. It is good to remember that when government services (parks, cultural events, garbage collection, etc.) are provided without direct charge for their use, those services are not, as they are frequently advertised, "free." Instead, they are "taxpayer paid for," or, more precisely, paid for by someone other than the user. The choice is not between free services and services available through user charge. The choice is between whether the people who actually use the services pay for them or whether the tax system places the cost on somebody who may or may not actually use the service and whose payment bears no necessary relationship to the extent of use. Which alternative distribution of cost seems generally more reasonable to you?

Sales revenue can be tantalizing for governments. By appearing to behave like a private business, government leaders can blunt some critics of tax-and-spend

---

[1]Civil forfeiture, a controversial tool now widely used by law enforcement officials, operates as a tax in that revenue arises from application of the system of laws. Police agencies have no more special right to these proceeds than the Internal Revenue Service (IRS) has a special claim to revenues from the individual income (or other) taxes that it collects.

politics. Although the sums involved may be relatively small in the full scheme of public finance, the revenues do make a contribution, possibly without facing public revulsion to higher taxes. Most important, however, public prices may improve both the efficiency of resource allocation and the equity in distributing the cost of public services. They make the government behave more like a private business and less like an intractable bureaucratic machine.

This chapter discusses three different sorts of "private" government revenue:

1. **User fees** derived from government sale of licenses to engage in otherwise restricted or forbidden activities;
2. **User charges,** or prices charged for voluntarily purchased, publicly provided services that, although benefiting specific individuals or businesses, are closely associated with basic government responsibilities; and
3. **Fiscal monopoly** and utility revenues that the government receives from exclusive sale of a private or toll good or service, including revenue from government-operated utilities, state liquor stores, and state lotteries.[2]

Tables 12–1 and 12–2 present recent sales data for U.S. governments. These receipts are modest in comparison with those from taxation, and that is not surprising. The principal economic reason for governments is, after all, market failure, and that implies that prices will not function properly. Pricing often simply is not feasible and not desirable, and that is what the revenue patterns reflect. If pricing is entirely feasible, then why is a government doing it? Nevertheless, collections from market transactions play an important role in government finance at the margin, and their role is likely to continue to increase for reasons related to both political pragmatism and the quest for improved government—efficiency.

Charges amount to 13.37 percent of own-source revenue states raise, including as own-source the regular own-source revenue, utility revenue, and liquor store revenue.[3] Charges by state institutions of higher education are the single largest source of such revenue. Localities have more opportunity for charge revenue because they provide more individual beneficiary services than do other governments; these services produced 21.92 percent of revenue raised by local governments in 2007–2008. Adding utility revenue increases the percentage to 34.15 percent. Charge revenue from hospitals, sewerage, and water and electric utilities is particularly important to the local revenue totals. Because tax alternatives available to local governments are often tightly controlled by their states, these governments have special incentive for seeking out charge revenues. However, even these governments seldom exhaust possibilities for charging. Among the types of local governments, charges

---

[2]Some countries have operated fiscal monopolies on tobacco products, matches, salt, sugar, caviar, and playing cards. See Sijbren Cnossen, *Excise Systems, A Global Study of the Selective Taxation of Goods and Services* (Baltimore, Md.: Johns Hopkins University Press, 1977), 84–98. They offer an alternative to excise taxation, although there are other issues involved in the choice. Some governments operate a fiscal monopoly to sell the product, but also add an excise to it, doing a fiscal double-dip.

[3]Government sales revenues are not all reported on a consistent basis. For instance, the Governments Division of the Census Bureau reports user charge and utility revenue on a gross basis, without offset for production or acquisition cost. Lottery revenue reported as part of the miscellaneous revenue category is included on a net basis.

Table 12–1

State and Local Government Sales Revenues: User Charges and Miscellaneous Revenues, 2007–2008 ($ Thousands)

	State & Local Total ($)	% Total	State Total ($)	% Total	Local Total ($)	% Total
General revenue from own sources plus utility and liquor store revenues	2,005,527,354	100.00%	1,047,220,179	100.00%	958,307,175	100.00%
Taxes	1,283,262,933	63.99%	757,470,540	72.33%	525,792,393	54.87%
Charges and miscellaneous general revenue	581,508,349	29.00%	267,214,682	25.52%	314,293,667	32.80%
Current charges	350,063,831	17.45%	139,983,603	13.37%	210,080,228	21.92%
Education	102,254,384	5.10%	78,472,814	7.49%	23,781,570	2.48%
Institutions of higher education	86,912,297	4.33%	77,339,948	7.39%	9,572,349	1.00%
School lunch sales (gross)	6,929,238	0.35%	21,762	0.00%	6,907,476	0.72%
Hospitals	91,297,642	4.55%	33,882,113	3.24%	57,415,529	5.99%
Highways	10,645,887	0.53%	6,086,234	0.58%	4,559,653	0.48%
Air transportation (airports)	16,584,133	0.83%	1,216,240	0.12%	15,367,893	1.60%
Parking facilities	1,824,790	0.09%	16,548	0.00%	1,808,242	0.19%
Sea and inland port facilities	3,864,136	0.19%	1,136,790	0.11%	2,727,346	0.28%
Natural resources	3,982,841	0.20%	2,480,294	0.24%	1,502,547	0.16%
Parks and recreation	8,792,334	0.44%	1,495,275	0.14%	7,297,059	0.76%
Housing and community development	5,577,063	0.28%	783,020	0.07%	4,794,043	0.50%
Sewerage	36,081,933	1.80%	31,788	0.00%	36,050,145	3.76%
Solid waste management	14,487,483	0.72%	495,696	0.05%	13,991,787	1.46%
Other charges	54,671,205	2.73%	13,886,791	1.33%	40,784,414	4.26%
Miscellaneous general revenue	231,444,518	11.54%	127,231,079	12.15%	104,213,439	10.87%
Interest earnings	91,977,590	4.59%	47,208,587	4.51%	44,769,003	4.67%
Special assessments	7,684,960	0.38%	520,176	0.05%	7,164,784	0.75%
Sale of property	4,522,253	0.23%	1,089,455	0.10%	3,432,798	0.36%
Other general revenue	127,259,715	6.35%	78,412,861	7.49%	48,846,854	5.10%
Utility revenue	133,932,975	6.68%	16,735,684	1.60%	117,197,291	12.23%
Water supply	43,401,415	2.16%	227,960	0.02%	43,173,455	4.51%
Electric power	70,346,343	3.51%	14,215,666	1.36%	56,130,677	5.86%
Gas supply	8,613,816	0.43%	16,374	0.00%	8,597,442	0.90%
Transit	11,571,401	0.58%	2,275,684	0.22%	9,295,717	0.97%
Liquor store revenue	6,823,097	0.34%	5,799,273	0.55%	1,023,824	0.11%

SOURCE: U.S. Census Bureau, Governments Division, State and Local Government Finances.

Table 12–1
(Continued)

Counties Total ($)	Municipal & Township % Total	Total ($)	Special District % Total	Total ($)	School District % Total	Total ($)	% Total
223,744,494	100.00%	395,104,598	100.00%	129,965,087	100.00%	209,492,996	100.00%
129,915,778	58.06%	204,273,333	51.70%	22,660,978	17.44%	168,942,304	80.64%
88,593,375	39.60%	117,061,644	29.63%	68,087,956	52.39%	40,550,692	19.36%
63,167,749	28.23%	75,087,230	19.00%	52,364,043	40.29%	19,461,206	9.29%
3,282,702	1.47%	1,037,662	0.26%	0	0.00%	19,461,206	9.29%
1,770,834	0.79%	349,797	0.09%	0	0.00%	7,451,718	3.56%
693,170	0.31%	435,391	0.11%	0	0.00%	5,778,915	2.76%
24,348,795	10.88%	8,017,088	2.03%	25,049,646	19.27%	0	0.00%
1,026,371	0.46%	1,899,127	0.48%	1,634,155	1.26%	0	0.00%
2,238,028	1.00%	7,457,287	1.89%	5,672,578	4.36%	0	0.00%
82,314	0.04%	1,645,311	0.42%	80,617	0.06%	0	0.00%
240,206	0.11%	1,227,824	0.31%	1,259,316	0.97%	0	0.00%
179,941	0.08%	171,426	0.04%	1,151,180	0.89%	0	0.00%
1,245,221	0.56%	4,468,022	1.13%	1,583,816	1.22%	0	0.00%
258,288	0.12%	2,088,106	0.53%	2,447,649	1.88%	0	0.00%
4,426,455	1.98%	25,421,368	6.43%	6,202,322	4.77%	0	0.00%
4,921,643	2.20%	8,117,451	2.05%	952,693	0.73%	0	0.00%
20,917,785	9.35%	13,536,558	3.43%	6,330,071	4.87%	0	0.00%
25,425,626	11.36%	41,974,414	10.62%	15,723,913	12.10%	21,089,486	10.07%
10,833,352	4.84%	16,643,058	4.21%	7,901,621	6.08%	9,390,972	4.48%
1,600,098	0.72%	3,330,103	0.84%	2,234,583	1.72%	0	0.00%
568,589	0.25%	1,568,038	0.40%	749,738	0.58%	546,433	0.26%
12,423,587	5.55%	20,433,215	5.17%	4,837,971	3.72%	11,152,081	5.32%
4,694,190	2.10%	73,286,948	18.55%	39,216,153	30.17%	0	0.00%
3,913,905	1.75%	27,963,190	7.08%	11,296,360	8.69%	0	0.00%
223,989	0.10%	35,355,129	8.95%	20,551,559	15.81%	0	0.00%
57,310	0.03%	6,218,964	1.57%	2,321,168	1.79%	0	0.00%
498,986	0.22%	3,749,665	0.95%	5,047,066	3.88%	0	0.00%
541,151	0.24%	482,673	0.12%	0	0.00%	0	0.00%

Table 12–2

Federal User Charge Receipts, Fiscal 2008 ($ Millions)

Corps of Engineers: Harbor maintenance fees	1,467
Department of Commerce: Patent and trademark, fees for weather services, and other fees	1,998
Department of Defense: Commissary and other fees	10,797
Department of Health and Human Services: Food and Drug Administration, Centers for Medicare and Medicaid Services, and other charges	1,743
Department of Homeland Security: Border and Transportation Security and other charges	2,202
Department of State: Passport and other charges	1,807
Department of Treasury: Sale of commemorative coins and other charges	2,588
Department of Veterans Affairs: Medical care and other charges	2,598
Department of Agriculture: Crop insurance and other charges	2,869
Department of Defense: Commissary surcharge and other charges	2,327
Department of Energy: Proceeds from sale of energy, nuclear waste disposal, and other charges	4,303
Department of Health and Human Services: Medicare Part B and Part D insurance premiums	59,435
Department of Homeland Security: Customs, immigration, and other charges	8,609
Department of Interior: Recreation and other charges	6,187
Department of Labor: Insurance premiums to guaranty private pensions and other charges	3,753
Department of Veterans Affairs: Veterans life insurance and other charges	2,358
Office of Personnel Management: Federal employee health and life insurance fees	12,110
Postal Service: Fees for postal services	75,129
Tennessee Valley Authority: Proceeds from sale of energy	10,307
Outer Continental Shelf receipts and other collections	18,285
Department of Energy: Federal Energy Regulation Commission, power marketing and other charges	1,223
Department of Treasury: Bank regulation and other charges	1,170
Federal Deposit Insurance Corporation: Deposit insurance fees and recoveries	2,922
Department of Commerce: Digital Television Transition and Public Safety Fund	1,779
Total User Charges	237,966

SOURCE: Office of Management and Budget, *Budget of the Government of the United States, Fiscal Year 2010, Analytical Perspectives* (Washington, D.C.: U.S. Government Printing Office, 2009).

Note: Only categories exceeding $1,000 million are separately identified.

are most important for counties (hospitals) and special districts (hospitals and electric utilities). For municipalities, water, electric, and sewerage charges are the most important, although overall charge reliance is less than it is for counties and special districts. Special districts survive on charges for services: regular charges and utility revenue combine to create more than 70 percent of their own-source revenue. That is reasonable, in that special districts often exist to provide a particular service to particular customers, the ideal environment for self-financing through charges.

The federal scheme for reporting charge revenue is somewhat convoluted. In federal budgetary accounts, most charge revenues are called *offsetting collections* or *offsetting receipts,* and they do not appear directly in tallies of federal revenue. These are payments for goods and services sold to the public and include such charges as those for postal services, for insurance coverage, for admissions to national parks, for sale of public lands, and for sale of commemorative coins, as well as oil extraction royalties from the Outer Continental Shelf. Table 12–2 identifies some of the more significant revenue producers. The largest sums came from postal services and insurance premiums for optional Medicare coverage. Total collections—$238 billion—represent a modest sum in comparison with the total federal receipts of over $2.5 trillion.

These federal charge revenues are not reported in the way that tax revenues are because they are deducted from gross outlays of a particular agency in the budget process. For offsetting collections, the charges are credited directly to the account from which they will be spent and, usually, may be spent without further legislation. As an example, the postal service may use its charge revenue to finance its operations without annual appropriation. For offsetting receipts, the charges are offset against gross outlays, but are not credited directly to expenditure accounts.[4] Because of this offsetting process, the regular budget displays understate to some degree both total government spending and collections from the public, and the procedures do violate transparency standards. However, the amounts are small in the overall tally of government operations, as is apparent from the data reported in the prior paragraph.

User Fees and Licenses

Governments levy a number of user fees that have some features of public prices, but that reflect the revenue-raising potential of the rule of law rather than voluntary exchange in the private market. (As described in Sidebar 12–1, terminology in the federal budget, rather unhelpfully, broadens the user-charge concept to include narrow-base taxes.) They are not user charges or public prices, even though these fees may share some equity and fiscal advantages of prices.

A license tax is a fee—flat rate, graduated by type of activity, related to business receipts, or whatever—levied as a condition for exercise of a business or nonbusiness privilege. License taxes imposed to regulate specific activities for the benefit of the general public (e.g., massage parlor licenses, hunting licenses, and licenses associated with the ownership or operation of motor vehicles) offer one example. Without the license, one or more governments forbid the activity. The license is a necessary condition for operation, but it does not "purchase" any specific government service. It may thus be distinguished from a user charge, which may be avoided if any individual or firm chooses not to purchase the supplied item or service and the payment of which entitles the individual or firm to a commodity or service, and from fees that are indirectly related to particular privileges. In 2011, licenses yielded more than $51.8 billion to state governments. The largest category was motor vehicle licenses, 42 percent of the total license revenue. Over $10 billion came from state corporate licenses.[5]

The license tax must also be distinguished from the franchise fee. The latter (1) involves contracts detailing rights and responsibilities of both the franchisee and

---

[4]Office of Management and Budget, *Budget of the Government of the United States, Fiscal Year 2010, Analytical Perspectives* (Washington, D.C.: U.S. Government Printing Office, 2009), 282–95. This offsetting process provided a way around the outlay controls of the Budget Enforcement Act of 1990.

[5]U.S. Census Bureau, Governments Division, 2011 State Government Tax Collections [www.census.gov].

Sidebar 12–1
Charging Fees: The Federal System

Most federal revenue comes from taxes that have no relation to any benefits received by the person paying the tax and that are not related to any particular service provided by the government. That is the case with the broad-base taxes on income and payrolls that constitute the great majority of federal revenue. User fees, however, can be appropriate and are feasible when the government can deny use of service to nonpayers or when the government can prohibit activities by nonpayers. Also, as described in Chapter 10, some narrow-base excises can serve to allocate costs to those using certain government services or can cause private entities to recognize the social implications of their actions.

The Congressional Budget Office calls both these fees and narrow taxes user charges and divides them into four classes:

1. User fees are payments for goods or services sold or rented by the government, voluntarily purchased, and not generally shared. They include natural-resource royalties, tolls, insurance premiums, leases and rentals, revenue from sales of resources, fees from use of federal land, admission to federal parks, charges for postal service, and permits or licenses not associated with regulation.
2. Regulatory fees are payments based on government authority to regulate particular businesses or activities that stem from the sovereign powers of the government. They include regulatory and judicial fees; fees from immigration, passport, and consulate services; customs fees; fees for testing, inspecting, and grading; fees for patent, trademark, and copyright services; and licenses through regulatory programs.
3. Beneficiary-based taxes are levied on bases correlated with the use of particular government services (the good or service taxed and the public service are close complements). They include the transportation-related excises (highway, airway, inland waterway, and harbor) and the excises on fuel and equipment associated with boating safety programs.
4. Liability-based taxes are levied for the purpose of abating hazards, discouraging damaging activities, or compensating injuries. They include excises on certain chemicals that are dedicated to the Hazardous Substance Trust Fund, taxes on certain fuels dedicated to the Leaking Underground Storage Tank Trust Fund, taxes on crude oil dedicated to the Oil Spill Liability Trust Fund, taxes on domestically mined coal dedicated to the Black Lung Disability Trust Fund, and taxes on childhood-disease vaccines dedicated to the Vaccine Injury Compensation Trust Fund.

Revenues in the first two groups can be particularly attractive under the Budget Enforcement Act of 1990 control structures because they may be offsetting collections—that is, they are netted against a particular budget outlay. Congressional committees can thus meet outlay ceilings by adding fees rather than cutting programs.

The Government Accountability Office outlines three important questions to consider when developing fees:

1. Who benefits from the program? If a program benefits the general public, then it should be financed by general revenue, not program fees. If the program benefits identifiable users, then it should be financed from fees.

**Sidebar 12–1
(continued)**

---

2. Are there mechanisms for ensuring that fees will cover the intended share of total program costs over time? Costs and other revenues will change as years go by, so a regular approach is needed to make sure that shares continue as intended. Stable fees are not likely a virtue if there is an intended share of cost to be paid by users.
3. Are there mechanisms for determining how much the program costs and for establishing how that cost will be distributed among users? There need to be clear standards for identifying program costs (what activities will be included) and for distributing that cost. There may be different incentives intended for the cost distribution, and these need to be clear.

SOURCES: Congressional Budget Office, *The Growth of Federal User Charges* (Washington, D.C.: U.S. Government Printing Office, 1993); and Government Accountability Office, *Federal User Fees: A Design Guide,* GAO-08-386SP (Washington, D.C.: Government Accountability Office, 2008).

---

the issuing municipality, (2) entails a requirement to service the entire population in the servicing area, and (3) brings a presumption of rate and quality of service regulation. A license simply permits a holder to undertake an activity otherwise forbidden and involves no contractual or property rights.[6] In general, franchises are provided in very limited numbers, whereas licenses are sold to virtually all applicants.

The definitions usually do not differentiate between licenses for revenue and those for regulation. Both varieties are based on the inherent police power of a state. States delegate this power to municipalities by constitution, statute, or city charter grant. Revenue and regulation motives may be hopelessly entangled. Nevertheless, a tentative separation can be suggested. A license ordinance that does not require inspection of the business or articles sold or that fails to regulate the conduct of the business in any manner is a pure revenue license, particularly if license applications are never denied. If controls apply or if licenses are difficult to obtain (not just expensive), the license is regulatory. The distinction may not always be clear. Some states require that license charges be reasonably related to the cost of issuing, policing, or controlling the thing or activity being licensed. When that stipulation applies, it is especially important to review cost and adjust charges frequently.

Both user charges and fees attempt to relieve burdens on the general revenue system by extracting greater contribution from service beneficiaries, but the former more closely resembles private-enterprise pricing.[7] Fees can compensate government

---

[6]Charles S. Rhyne develops this logic further in *Municipal Law* (Washington, D.C.: National Institute of Municipal Law Officers, 1957), 655.

[7]In recent years, many communities have adopted exactions, in-kind or financial payments, on real estate developers as a condition for permits, access to public facilities, and so on. Development for impact fees are one type of exaction. See Alan A. Altshuler and Jose A. Gomez-Ibanez with Arnold M. Howitt, *Regulation for Revenue* (Washington, D.C./Cambridge, Mass.: Brookings Institution/Lincoln Institute for Land Policy, 1993). Such fees have assumed a position of some fiscal significance in developing areas of the western United States.

for extra costs incurred in providing special services to identifiable entities or completing administrative paperwork for individuals. Thus, governments often charge fees for traffic direction or crowd control and for many legal filings. Fees, however, seldom involve the direct sale of a good or service, but rather involve payment for some privilege granted by government. The exercise of that privilege may cause government to incur a cost that the fee seeks to recoup in part or in total.[8]

User Charges

User charges can induce production and consumption efficiency, while gauging citizen preferences and demand for government services. User charges can function only when activities financed have two necessary conditions: benefits separability and chargeability. These are the features absent from pure public goods (see Chapter 1). The further a good or service departs from publicness and the closer it approximates a private good, the more feasible are user charges—and the more one wonders why it isn't being handled by a private firm.[9]

First, user charges are feasible when identifiable individuals or firms, not the community as a whole, benefit from the service. Services to a narrow segment of the community financed by general revenues provide an opportunity for that segment to profit at the expense of others. Those using the service benefit, but pay no more than similarly situated citizens who do not benefit. A user charge prevents that systematic subsidization. If recipients of benefits cannot be identified or if the community in general benefits, a user charge is neither feasible nor desirable. Thus, charges for elementary education would be inappropriate, but charges would be desirable for an adult auto mechanics course. Relying on voluntary provision in the first instance would be foolish. Milton benefits if his neighbor's children receive an elementary education because they help choose his government, they read traffic signs, they go on welfare less often, and so on. In the latter instance, the mechanic does help the community, but that help is for a fee. If Milton's car is repaired, he pays the bill—there are no uncompensated community benefits. However, governments too often lose their resolve to be entrepreneurial adherents to the "user pays" principle when they give away costly services to businesses in the name of economic development.

---

[8]If the licensing system is being operated to generate revenue, it is important to consider whether the charge is an effective revenue producer. If demand for the licenses is elastic, then increasing the charge will have enough impact on licenses being purchased to cause total revenues to decline. If demand is inelastic, then increasing the charge will increase total revenues. However, charges for most licenses (hunting, fishing, etc.) are relatively low, and demand is relatively inelastic. In that case, increasing the charge would produce additional revenues that could be used to improve the services provided by agencies.
[9]Federal policy on and administration of user charges for purchase or use of government resources is described in OMB Circular No. 25 (July 8, 1993).

Second, user charges require an economical method for excluding from service benefits those who do not pay for the service. If exclusion cannot be efficiently accomplished, the charge cannot be collected. Furthermore, resource-allocation gains are greatest if service use can actually be metered, as with water meters, toll booths, and the like, so that heavy users pay more than light users and any user pays more than nonusers. Some discretion is needed here, however, because everything that can be gauged may not be worth gauging. Use of city streets could be metered using the tollgate technology of turnpikes and toll bridges; however, the costs involved, including the time waiting in lines, make that option untenable.[10] Administrative cost—measuring customer service use (metering), calculating charges according to service cost, and billing and collecting computed charges—and compliance cost must not be excessive. Many services can, however, be gauged and controlled by meters, fences, turnstiles, decals, and the like. Others may be indirectly measured—many cities gauge residential sanitary-sewer use by water use, a reasonable proxy for volume down the drain and into the sewerage system. (Industrial use is more difficult to gauge because there is a problem with quality of the discharge in addition to quantity.) Without enforceable charge barriers, user charges are inappropriate.

Charges are particularly appropriate when substantial waste would occur if the individually identifiable service was unpriced. Such would undoubtedly result if, for instance, water was provided through property tax financing. Under that system, efforts to economize on water use would yield the individual consumer no direct return. Payments for water would be determined by property holdings, not the amount of water used. Usage would be much inflated. Investment in supply facilities would have to be abnormally great, and artificially expanded amounts of water would have to be treated. Appropriate user charges could substantially reduce water waste and total water-supply cost.[11]

Advantages of User Charges

User charges have four advantages beyond the naked pragmatism of additional revenue for government functions. These advantages include both the important efficiency effects of appropriately designed charge structures and the improved equity

---

[10]Electronic tags on automobiles are being used for a number of toll facilities to reduce collection costs for frequent users (like the E-ZPass program that is used in fourteen northeastern and midwestern states in the United States). Germany uses a global positioning satellite system for charging truck tolls (16 cents per kilometer for trucks weighing over 12 tons) on its autobahns. Billing goes to a data center, or drivers may pay manually at roadside terminals. A private company (Toll Collect GmbH) operates the collection system for the German government. Microwave sensors are used for collecting tolls in Austria and some other European countries. Technological innovation is reducing the cost of facilities for direct charges for road use. Those systems will become necessary for highway finance in the United States as the motor-fuel tax system for support of highways collapses as high-gas-mileage, electric, and alternative-fuel vehicles break the close relationship between fuel purchases and highway use. The E-ZPass program collected almost $3.9 billion in 2007. Congressional Budget Office, *Using Pricing to Reduce Traffic Congestion* (Washington, D.C.: Congressional Budget Office, 2009), 15.

[11]By charging higher prices during periods when capital facilities, such as highways or airports, are heavily congested, usage may be redistributed, and the need for new construction may be reduced.

from direct pricing. First, user charges can register and record public demand for a service. Suppose a city is considering supporting extensive summer softball leagues for adults. If these leagues are financed by user charges (to either team sponsors or individual participants), the city receives important information on choices about service type, quality, and quantity. Without a user charge, there would be continual—and inconclusive—debate about program advisability and structure. However, as rural philosopher Kin Hubbard observed: "Nothing will dispel enthusiasm like a small admission charge."[12] The charge offers a conclusive test of demand for the service. Furthermore, a program that, through user charges, covers its provision cost is not likely to be eliminated and will not burden other government activities. Not incidentally, citizens who do not want the service do not have to receive it and do not have to pay for it. A user-charge system not only provides a tangible way for citizens to register their preference for particular services, but also provides some funds for providing those services. That's pretty much the same way the private sector works, so user-charge financing represents the ultimate in service privatization, only one step before leaving provision to the private sector.

Those extra funds can be a problem, however, when the charge does not cover all incremental costs of the service. During periods of tight finances, decision makers are tempted to expand revenue-generating activities, often reasoning that any revenue will help with the fiscal problem. Unfortunately, such expansion can actually worsen the overall budget condition. For example, a city may expand its summer tennis instruction program because it generates $25 per person in revenue. If recreation department costs increase by $30 per person enrolled in the program, the expanded revenue produced actually increases any city deficit.[13]

Second, the user charge can dramatically improve financing equity for selected services. If the service is of a chargeable nature, its provision by general tax revenues undoubtedly subsidizes the service recipient group at the expense of the general taxpaying public. User charges can obviously prevent that problem. Less obvious, but equally significant are two related equity problems that user charges can reduce: the problems created by nonresident service recipients and by tax-exempt entities. Many urban services, particularly cultural and recreational, can easily be used by anyone in the region. General revenue financing permits a subsidy to any nonresident consumer; a user charge prevents that subsidy. It is a simple and direct way to reduce burdens placed on one government by citizens of neighboring governments. A user charge also provides a mechanism for obtaining financial support from tax-exempt institutions. Many cities, for example, use property tax revenue to subsidize refuse collection. Charitable, religious, or educational institutions exempt from property tax would contribute nothing to finance refuse collection, even though they receive the service, whose cost must be borne by general taxpayers. If, however, refuse collection was fully financed by user charges, that cost shifting would not occur. Just as these entities must pay for gasoline purchased from a private firm,

---

[12]Quoted in *Forbes*, October 21, 1985, 216.
[13]The program may still be worth expanding, even if the charge does not cover the cost of providing the service. That would depend on the social benefits, if any, that extend beyond the participants paying the direct charge. The point here is that such a program should not be expanded because of *revenue* considerations.

they would pay the refuse collection charge. Tax exemption does not ordinarily exempt institutions from paying for goods or services bought on the open market. For both nonresidents and exempt institutions, the user charge allows governments to extract revenue from entities outside their tax network; if they use, they must pay.

Third, a user-charge program may improve operating efficiency because agency staff must respond to client demand. Agencies usually operate with funds obtained from and justified to a legislative body. That justification elaborates needs as estimated by the agency staff and is defended according to performance criteria established by the agency staff. Those agencies with the best bureaucratic expertise—the ones best able to prepare convincing budget justifications and apply the strategies of the budget process described in previous chapters—are the ones most likely to receive appropriations. In addition, the priorities of the legislators may well differ from those of users of the facilities, as well as the priorities of the facility managers. User-charge finance that allows facilities to retain a considerable share of charge revenue, however, requires a shift to preferences articulated directly by customers. The agency must provide services that are desired by consumers, or it will fail the financial test for survival. It cannot define what clients should want in its budget defense; it must provide the services clients actually will purchase.

Finally, a user charge may correct cost-and-price signals in the private market. Suppose a manufacturing plant places extraordinary demand on traffic control in a neighborhood. That special demand requires additional police officers at a handful of intersections in that area during shift changes at the factory. The way the plant operates thus produces substantial extra costs for the community. If the plant must pay the extra traffic-control costs its operations require, its management has a direct financial incentive to consider whether its current operating pattern (with attendant traffic-control charges) is cost effective. The plant's management may decide that lower peak-flow traffic produced by staggered shifts, van pooling, subsidies for mass-transit use, and so on (and no traffic-control charge) is less expensive. The user charge makes the decision-making unit recognize and respond to the true social cost of its action. In the example cited, without the user charge, the additional traffic control costs the plant nothing; no one can be expected to conserve a resource that appears to be free. The same logic applies in the application of effluent charges to the discharge of environmental pollutants.

In summary, user charges make the public recognize that the services provided are not costless. The public can choose whether it wants the service and, if so, how much to purchase. People may save money by economizing on the service, and receiving the service does not place costs on others. In charge-financed areas, the government has an excellent gauge of what services the public wants and is willing to pay for.

Limitations of User Charges

User charges cannot generally substitute for taxes to finance government services because many public services—in fact, most services provided by most governments—simply do not fit the requirements for user-charge financing. First, activities that have substantial benefits extending beyond the principal recipient are not candidates for user-charge financing. Basic fire protection in an urban area could not, for example, be considered for user-charge financing because fire tends to spread; extinguishing a fire in one building protects surrounding units. Thus, protection financed by one individual automatically protects others; nonpayers are not excludable, so the service cannot be financed by charges. There is a corollary to the external-benefit issue when there are some services for which charges can be collected. The ability to charge for particular services can distort agency decision making. For example, a high school football team may receive magnanimous resources because gate receipts are sizable (even though unlikely to cover even a decent percentage of the program's cost), whereas the girls' volleyball team gets hand-me-downs. The question for resource allocation is contribution to the purposes of the community (or social benefits). The flow of cash is not an unambiguous indicator of what program has the greatest community benefit.

Second, services may intentionally subsidize low-income or otherwise disadvantaged recipients. Charges for these services could be counterproductive.[14] Beneficiaries should not pay if the service has welfare elements. In a related fashion, some have argued that user charges in general are unfair because they often produce a regressive-burden pattern, taking a larger percentage of a low-income consumer's income than of a higher-income consumer's income.[15] That argument is not a convincing attack on user charges for several reasons. For one thing, low-income families not using the service clearly are better off with the user-charge system—no charge to be paid and no tax to be paid to subsidize the service used by others. Furthermore, tax-financing devices may have a more regressive burden than user charges, even if the service is widely used by disadvantaged citizens. Local revenue systems often are very regressive, so it is not unlikely that a shift to user charges could reduce regressivity. Finally, it may be possible to design "payability" tests for the charges because the services are received by identifiable individuals.[16] Suppose a city charges an admission fee to swimming pools. This is a good candidate for financing with charges because benefits are primarily individual (to the swimmer and family), prices can be enforced using fences and turnstiles (public health and safety requires access control regardless of financing technique), and overcrowding may otherwise result when children are dumped at the facility for "free" (or taxpayer-provided) babysitting. Charge opponents argue that free pools are a significant recreation option for low-income families; a charge would harm that redistributive function. Charges, however, can function equitably and efficiently if disadvantaged families receive season passes at no cost or if pools located in low-income areas are free, while charges apply at other pools. In general, protection of the disadvantaged should not be an excuse for subsidizing the well-to-do.

---

[14]There are, of course, more efficient ways of redistributing income in society than providing government services. However, once that method is selected, it should not be thwarted by charges.

[15]Willard Price, "The Case against the Imposition of a Sewer Use Tax," *Governmental Finance* 4 (May 1975): 38–44.

[16]Selma J. Mushkin and Charles L. Vehorn coined the "payability" phrase in "User Fees and Charges," *Governmental Finance* 6 (November 1977): 46.

Third, some charges, though technically feasible, may be expensive to collect. Spending a considerable share of the revenue raised in collecting that revenue is not likely to be a wise use of agency resources. The high cost suggests a degree of publicness that makes the appropriateness of the charge itself questionable.

Fourth, there are important political issues when proposing that a tax-supported service shift to charge financing. The charge may face considerable public resentment based on the view that, having paid taxes, the person is entitled to the public service without any additional payment. Although this argument is roughly the same as arguing that, because you purchased bread, the store should provide meat for the sandwich at no charge, it does often accompany shifts toward charge finance. However, in addition to public opposition, there is frequently bureaucratic resistance. Service providers understand that moving from tax finance to a user charge means that, for the client, the service price is increased from zero (though there are costs of providing the service, those costs are borne by other parts of the fiscal system, with no difference in payment according to use) to some positive amount (the price). This change will ration out some use of the service, a change that goes against the attitudes of public officials. Both service providers and clients tend to offer a unified opposition to user charges in all but fiscally distressed environments. However, the fact that service use may decline when a charge is imposed or raised is not a flaw of the charge, but simply what one expects from downward-sloping demand curves in a market economy—that is, at any given time people will voluntarily purchase more units at a low price than at a higher price.

Finally, there is the ultimate reality in user-charge finance that those who do not pay need to be denied service, and this is often unpopular. If the water bill is not paid, service needs to be shut off for the charge system to be effective, even though the service is necessary. The charge is intended to raise money and to regulate use of the service and, for it to have the intended effects, delinquent accounts cannot be tolerated. If government officials do not have the stomach to pull service from those who are not paying, they should forget about user-charge finance. Unfortunately, enforcement can be painful and inevitably generates stories in the media and from some politicians of the crisis that enforcement causes for some low-income and elderly people. The government adopting an aggressive program of user-charge finance has to understand that enforcing the charges against delinquent customers has the potential for bad publicity and needs to accept that before it adopts the policy.[17] In addition, it needs some sort of safety net or lifeline program to deal with the toughest cases before nonpayment occurs, done in an open and transparent fashion. However, if the delinquents are not successfully pursued, then the cost of providing them service is borne by others—including low-income and elderly customers who do not cheat on their bills. That isn't fair at all.

---

[17]An aggressive program against delinquent water users in Atlanta caused one-quarter of city water customers there to face shutoff. The city had lax enforcement before the new program. Ariel Hart, "Atlanta Shutting Off Water as It Tries to Collect $35 Million Overdue," *New York Times*, November 3, 2004. New York City also has had major problems with water billing, with $430 million in water accounts overdue for over a year. Anthony DePalma, "New York Urged to Get Tough with Its Water Deadbeats," *New York Times*, October 7, 2007. It doesn't do much good to institute a user-charge system and then not have the willingness to enforce the system.

Charge Guidelines

Governments differ in the extent to which they charge for services, partly because of the different services they provide (e.g., national defense, welfare, and highway patrol are hardly priceable) and partly because of political attitudes toward pricing public goods. Outside those constraints, there are some guides for user-charge preparation and manipulation. Any service showing the aforementioned features (individual benefit, susceptibility to excluding nonpayers, and an absence of redistributive elements) is a reasonable candidate for user-charge financing. The short list in Table 12–3 provides some options. Selma Mushkin and Richard Bird nominate for charge (1) household support functions (water, refuse collection, sewerage), (2) industrial development support (airports, parking, special police or fire services, etc.), (3) "amenities" (specialized recreation facilities, cultural facilities, etc.), and (4) services provided to tax-exempt entities.[18] The list and its classifications should give ample direction. Anytime the service is to an identifiable household or business and there are no discernible external impacts of the service, the service belongs on the candidate list.

Table 12–3
Selected Government Services Amenable to Public Pricing

Special police work events	Service for stadium events, alarm servicing
Parking	Garage, meters
Solid-waste management	Collection, disposal (pay-as-you-throw)
Recreation	Golf courses, tennis courts, swimming pools, park admissions, concessions, rescue insurance, instruction, team registration
Health and hospitals	Ambulance charges, inoculations, hospital rates, health insurance premiums
Transportation	Transit fares, bridge and highway tolls, airport landing (departure fees, hangar rentals), lock tolls, congestion charges
Education	Rentals of special books, equipment, or uniforms; college or technical school tuition; facility rentals; special training programs for individual businesses
Resource management	Surveys, extension service inquiries, tree nursery and development stock, livestock-grazing fees, mineral royalties
Sewerage	Treatment, disposal
Utilities	Water, electric, gas, transit
Other	Licensing for use of institution, name, miscellaneous special services provided an individual household or business

SOURCE: Based on Selma J. Mushkin and Richard M. Bird, "Public Prices: An Overview," in *Public Prices for Public Products,* ed. S. J. Mushkin (Washington, D.C.: Urban Institute, 1972): 8–9.

---

[18]Selma J. Mushkin and Richard M. Bird, "Public Prices: An Overview," in *Public Prices for Public Products*, ed. S. J. Mushkin (Washington, D.C.: Urban Institute, 1972), 8–9.

Some governments—often in response to property tax limits, controls, or freezes—have applied general police or fire protection charges based on the value of property protected. These are not true user charges because they are not voluntary; they are simply an escape mechanism around the tax limitations. Assigning service costs in relation to a property's physical characteristics, according to an estimate of how those characteristics produce demand for a service, has greater logical appeal, but should not be considered a true user charge because it cannot be voluntary. Because unchecked fires in urban areas will spread, voluntary decisions about purchasing fire protection are untenable. Protection for one unit protects its neighbors, and an unprotected unit endangers its neighbors. Thus, these financing devices must be structured as taxes (nonvoluntary), but they are taxes based on a concept other than the ability of an economic unit to afford the designated tax burden. The burden of financing that municipal service is allocated among economic units according to the physical attributes of those units that require service cost to be incurred. As such, fire protection fees could have desirable development effects: they could provide owners of structures an extra financial reward for installing private fire-control devices (smoke alarms, sprinklers, fire walls, etc.) in older units and could also cause owners of particularly deteriorated structures to raze them. The fees, of course, would not be related to firm profitability. Some marginal businesses housed in deteriorated, high-fire-risk structures could face substantial fees because of the cost of providing service and the danger that such properties place on surrounding properties. On the whole, however, a rigid structure of fire-risk fees could significantly accelerate the process of structural modernization and, over time, could reduce the total cost of fire protection, even though fire-risk fees are not user charges.

When a government decides that a particular service can be financed by a user charge, the appropriate level of that charge must be determined. That determination is not simple. Frederick Stocker reports: "Evidence suggests that pricing policies used by municipal governments are often fairly unsophisticated, perhaps understandably so in light of the difficulty of determining price elasticities, marginal costs, distribution of benefits and other things that enter into economic models of optimal pricing."[19] The municipality, however, may get some guidance from fairly simple concepts about service costs.[20] In particular, the government should separate its service costs into two categories: (1) costs that change as a result of the service being provided (incremental cost) and (2) costs that do not change with service provision (fixed costs). The latter includes any cost that would continue, regardless of

---

[19]Frederick D. Stocker, "Diversification of the Local Revenue System: Income and Sales Taxes, User Charges, Federal Grants," *National Tax Journal* 29 (September 1976): 320.

[20]Paul Downing maintains that an appropriately designed user charge would have three components: a portion that reflects short-run production costs and varies with output consumed, a portion that reflects plant and equipment costs (possibly allocated as an individual's share of its designed capacity), and a portion based on the cost of delivering the service to a specific customer location. The first portion may vary by the time of day, depending on whether the system is at peak utilization. If so, the charge would be increased. See Downing's "User Charges and Special Districts," in *Management Policies in Local Government Finance*, ed. J. Richard Aronson and Eli Schwartz (Washington, D.C.: International City Management Association, 1981), 191–92.

decisions concerning that service, and thus can be disregarded in the charge analysis. Prices need to be based on market conditions—that is, on demand for the service being sold—and on the offerings of competitive providers of that service. The prospective purchaser is not driven by what it costs the municipality to produce the service, so the municipality is not able to determine what price it should charge from its costs.[21] A knowledge of cost, however, lets the municipality understand to what extent the particular service, after allowance for revenue from the price charged for the service, contributes to or must be subsidized by the remainder of government finances. A price that recovers the incremental cost of providing a particular service means that the provision of that user-charge-financed service does not burden other functions of government.[22] Prices above that level are possible, subject to the demand for the service and the government's desire to use surplus to support other government activities.

How can the government arrive at a reasonable price for the services it has chosen to sell? Setting prices is often an uncomfortable and unfamiliar activity for governments, and the task is made more complicated by a shortage of adequate market information and by political complexities. Sometimes the government may find similar services being sold by private firms and can use this market information as a guide for setting its own prices. Sometimes there may be no similar service being sold, and the government may decide to set its price at some markup of its incremental cost. In either case, the initial price will probably need to be adjusted up or down as customers' responses provide the government with more information about what their preferences really are and as government agencies get better insights into how their operating costs change as the amount of service provided varies. In addition, the government almost certainly will learn from the political response when it moves certain services from tax finance to charge finance. However, decisions are not permanent, and there is no reason why the government cannot experiment with various prices for its services to determine their effect on the amount of service purchased and on net revenue to the government. There is no special economic virtue in maintaining stable prices, although it may be politically more convenient.

A final consideration about user charges concerns their method of application. Alfred Kahn writes, in an analysis of public-utility pricing, "The only economic function of price is to influence behavior.... But of course price can have this effect on the buyer's side only if bills do indeed depend on the volume of purchases. For this

---

[21]A good analysis of government price setting appears in Chapter 8 of David L. Rados, *Marketing for Non-Profit Organizations* (Boston: Auburn House, 1981). Peter F. Drucker *calls cost-driven* pricing one of "The Five Deadly Business Sins" in *Wall Street Journal*, October 21, 1993, A-22. Cost tells the business whether it is making or losing money but customers will tell the business what they believe the product is worth and the price they are willing to pay.

[22]James Johnson has identified six elements in existing municipal sewerage-service charges: water use (a volume proxy), flat charges, number of plumbing fixtures used by the customer, size of water meter or sewer connection, property characteristics (assessed value, square footage, front footage), and sewage strength. Water use is the most frequently encountered user-charge element. See James A. Johnson, "The Distribution of the Burden of Sewer User Charges under Various Charge Formulas," *National Tax Journal* 22 (December 1969): 472–85.

reason, economists … are avid meterers."[23] A similar principle applies to user charges. Buyer behavior will not change unless changes in behavior will influence payments owed. If a refuse-collection customer pays $25 per year for that service, regardless of whether two or fifteen trash cans are collected per week, the customer cannot be expected to change the number of trash cans set out for collection. A charge sensitive to usage, however, does induce behavioral changes by some customers; payment per bag—"pay as you throw"—is more effective than payment per month. To obtain the full benefits of user-charge financing, then, the service must be metered and made usage sensitive. Dividing estimated total costs by the number of entities served and presenting a bill to each entity does not produce the desired effects of public prices.

Public Monopoly Revenue: Utilities, Liquor Stores, and Gambling Enterprises

Government power to own and operate business enterprises, to sell private goods, is extensive, although contrary to the global wave of privatization. Government ownership is the exception, not the rule, in the United States. Whenever a public interest is identified that competitive pressures cannot handle, the normal approach in the United States is for the government to regulate the private firm, not for the government to own and operate the enterprise. A government official seeking long-term public ownership of a private business has not paid sufficient attention to the lessons from the collapse of the Soviet Union.

Government Utilities

Some services are widely provided by municipal utilities, especially in water supply, electric power, intracity transit, and gas supply.[24] The great majority of cities with a population over 5,000 are serviced by municipal water utilities. However, municipal electric-power systems, usually distributors of power produced by others, operate mostly in small communities. Gas supply is predominantly through private ownership. Intracity transit has made something of a resurgence with the failure of private transit systems, but the public systems have been as unprofitable as their private predecessors. Table 12–1 reported the extent to which state and local governments generated utility

---

[23]Alfred E. Kahn, "Can an Economist Find Happiness Setting Public Utility Rates?" *Public Utilities Fortnightly* (January 5, 1978): 15. One of the problems that countries of the former Soviet Union faced as they transitioned to a market economy in the 1990s was the absence of electric, gas, and water meters on the premises of users. "Communal charges" under the old system were flat payments without any metering. To get a sensible system going required the purchase and installation of lots of meters.

[24]Solid-waste management, a candidate for utility finance, is typically managed within general government or by a special district if not provided by a private firm.

revenue in fiscal 2007–2008. In the tradition of census statistics, utilities report gross revenues; they do not net out expenditures made by the utility in producing the service sold to generate that revenue. In fact, expenditures in the utility categories often exceed the revenue taken in by the utility. When that happens, the government may have to subsidize the operation of the utility, or the deficit must be financed.

Why should a municipality choose to operate a utility rather than allowing a private firm to do it? Surely government can better allocate its time to more pressing public concerns than to focus on the mundane questions of utility management. Motivation is, not surprisingly, usually mixed. In some instances, the governing body believes that it can use utility-operation profits to subsidize the operations of the general government. In fact, some decades ago, some cities could boast of being tax-free towns because of profits from electric utility systems. That era has passed, however, and the best that one could hope for is some assistance from the utility to the city, not a fiscal bonanza.[25]

In other instances, the government owner may be more interested in keeping the price of the service as low as possible, perhaps even providing the service at less than cost. That policy requires some subsidization of the utility by the sponsoring government. This practice can be politically appealing—the low-cost service can be an important element in reelection strategy and may be supported by a desire to encourage economic development—but the government decision makers must be certain that other important city services are not shortchanged by subsidizing the utility. Otherwise, the practice can contribute to the city's fiscal decay. However, experience suggests that, compared to private owners, government operation may be less greedy in pricing, but probably not more efficient in producing the service.

Liquor Stores

Seventeen states maintain a radically different sort of monopoly: the operation of liquor stores. In these states, some, if not all, alcoholic beverage sales are made in the state-owned stores.[26] The state establishes a markup over inventory cost sufficient to cover its operating cost, as well as to return a profit for other state operations. In some instances, the state will also add an excise to the price. Table 12–1 reported liquor store revenues, again following the census practice of not netting out cost. In contrast to the utility case, however, liquor stores return a profit to their parent governments. Only in New Hampshire, a state with neither general sales nor individual income taxes, do these profits make more than a negligible contribution to state finances (in 2010, liquor store sales exceeded liquor store expenditures by $82.8 million, compared with total state general revenue of $6,221.9 million).[27]

---

[25]Cities can move costs to the utility operation by charging the utility for services rendered it by city government (charges for the mayor, the city council, use of space in the municipal building, etc.) or by getting free utilities for city operations if direct payments are difficult or legally restrained.

[26]In Canada, all provinces but Alberta run retail liquor monopolies. Such monopolies are also prevalent in the Nordic countries.

[27]U.S. Census Bureau, Governments Division, State and Local Government Finances by Level of Government and by State: 2005–2006 [www.census.gov].

Government Gambling Enterprises: Lotteries and Offtrack Betting

In 2009, the total gross gambling revenue in the United States exceeded $89 billion.[28] Even though that is a small piece of the over $14 trillion U.S. economy, it does offer an attractive revenue opportunity for governments because it is a sector that is politically vulnerable because of the social and moral concerns about evils that gambling might bring. Indeed, that ambivalence appears in how governments respond to gambling. As *The Economist* keenly headlined, "That's So Wicked We'll Do It Ourselves." States restrict its availability, they subject it to high taxes, and they keep the promotion of some forms of it to themselves. Their defense is the same nearly everywhere: gambling is basically a bad thing, so you should have tight rules to ban or restrict it; where it is permitted, it should be discouraged by high taxes; even so, the profits will be huge, so the state should run some gambling itself.[29]

States selectively allow pari-mutuel gambling on certain events (horse racing, greyhound racing, jai alai, and, in Nevada, other sporting events),[30] casinos (either land-based or on riverboats), bingo, card rooms, and lotteries. In addition, Native American reservations may operate gaming operations on tribal lands under regulation of federal laws. State revenue normally flows from taxes on these activities— through the regular income, property, and sales tax structures and, as noted in an earlier chapter, through selective excises or licenses directly on operators or applicants for licenses to operate. The gambling excises may be on the number of admissions (a tax on each person going on a riverboat, for instance), on the total amount wagered in the establishment, or on the number of tables or other gaming devices in the establishment. Casinos offer strong competition for other gambling formats, being identified as an important factor in the demise of some horse and greyhound racetracks and in slower lottery revenue growth—even some decreases—in several states. State revenues from casinos are unstable, driven as they are by private management decisions and competitive forces in the gaming market; are cyclically sensitive to national and regional economies; and are expensive to collect. Furthermore, except possibly for play at destination resorts, casino gambling appears to be distributed regressively.[31]

Seldom do U.S. governments actually operate the gaming facilities, however, preferring to leave the business to private operators who specialize in those activities

[28]U.S. Census Bureau, *Statistical Abstract of the United States*, 2012 (Washington, D.C.: U.S. Government Printing Office, 2011), 774.

[29]"That's So Wicked We'll Do It Ourselves," *Economist* (April 11, 1992): 24.

[30]The pari-mutuel system is one in which those backing the winner divide, in proportion to their wagers, the total pool bet, after a percentage has been removed by those conducting the event. Some lottery games are pari-mutuel as well.

[31]Ranjana G. Madhusudhan, "Betting on Casino Revenues: Lessons from State Experiences," *National Tax Journal* 49 (September 1996): 401–12. Casinos may also reduce state sales tax revenue. See Jim Landers, "The Effect of Casino Gambling on Sales Tax Revenues in States Legalizing Casinos in the 1990s," *State Tax Notes* 38 (December 26, 2005): 1073–83.

and limiting the government's role to regulating and to collecting taxes.[32] There are two exceptions. Offtrack betting may have state (or local, in New York City) government proprietors in some places, and state-operated lotteries have become a standard component of state fiscal systems. Government-operated offtrack betting has seldom been particularly profitable and has not spread beyond the northeast quadrant of the nation, although private operations are common at casinos and race tracks and are permitted as free-standing businesses in some states. Lotteries merit some additional attention because they are state-owned (although sometimes operated under contract with private management firms), have spread throughout the nation, and produce more net revenue for states in aggregate than other gambling activities, although casino excise collections are larger in some individual states.[33] The spread of state lotteries in the 1980s—when they became a standard element in state government fiscal operations—probably paved the way for public acceptance of casinos and pari-mutuel gaming in the 1990s. Indeed, in some states, constitutional amendments in that era to permit lotteries also opened the door to casinos.

In 1964, New Hampshire initiated the first state lottery since the demise of the corrupt Louisiana lottery in 1894. New York followed in 1967, but proceeds in both were disappointing. Greater success came with better merchandising and attention to customer tastes, the approach pioneered by New Jersey in 1970, to generate remarkable revenue totals and substantial public excitement. That approach featured "(a) lower priced tickets; (b) more frequent drawings; (c) more numerous outlets; (d) numbered tickets in lieu of recording purchasers' names and addresses; (e) somewhat better odds; and (f) energetic promotion."[34] By 2010, 43 states and the District of Columbia operated lotteries.[35] Table 12–4 indicates the lottery revenue generated in 2010, a tiny amount in comparison with taxes, but larger than some user-charge categories.

The major lottery formats are these:

1. **Passive.** The customer receives a prenumbered ticket with a winner selected at a periodic drawing. States used this format in early days, but it has been superseded by other games.

---

[32]Casinos operated by Native American tribes, a special type of government, are obviously an exception, although, even here, outside management has been the rule. Tribe members are, however, developing expertise for a more active role. The U.S. Supreme Court, in *California v. Cabazon Band of Mission Indians*, 480 U.S. 202 (1987), effectively removed all existing restrictions on gambling on Native American reservations, thereby transforming a small and isolated activity often limited to bingo halls into a growth industry. The congressional response, the Indian Gaming Regulatory Act of 1988, specifically authorized casino gambling on Indian reservations, established a regulatory framework for this gambling, and created the National Indian Gaming Commission to oversee the industry. Native American casino gaming greatly expanded under this system; the largest casino in the world is a Native American casino. More than half the states host at least one Native American casino.

[33]During the Great Recession era, a number of states considered selling their lotteries to private businesses in order to receive a large lump-sum payment to help with state finances, much as some governments sold public facilities to private operators. However, the Department of Justice issued a memorandum opinion that federal exemptions provided state lotteries would not apply to private operations, thereby killing the possibility of fast cash from a sale [http://www.justice.gov/olc/2008/state-conducted-lotteries101608.pdf]. States may contract with private businesses to operate their lotteries so long as ultimate authority rests with the state. That is the recent format that lottery privatization has taken.

[34]Frederick D. Stocker, "State Sponsored Gambling as a Source of Public Revenue," *National Tax Journal* 25 (September 1972): 437.

[35]Not included is the special state-sanctioned, privately operated statewide lottery for charities in Alaska.

2. **Instant or Scratch Off.** The player buys a ticket and rubs off a substance to reveal whether the ticket is a winner. Some state lotteries offer a video-terminal version of the game that provides instant winners, creating a product much like casino slot machines.
3. **Numbers.** The player selects a three- or four-digit daily number and places a bet on an online computer terminal regarding whether the number will be drawn.
4. **Lotto.** This is a pari-mutuel game in which the player selects a group of numbers out of a larger field of possible selections (e.g., six of a possible forty-four). If no ticket has been sold for the particular group of numbers picked in the weekly drawing, the amount not won rolls over to the next week. Top prize money can grow rapidly, producing multimillion-dollar prizes. Such huge prizes are not produced in the other formats. The lotto games may be offered by a single state or by multistate groups (like those operating the Powerball and MegaMillions games in the United States). Lotto produces more revenue than the other products currently offered.
5. **Keno.** This is a casino-type game in which a player can make a variety of bets, involving long or short odds and large or small prizes, on the selection of numbers from a large field. Play is virtually continuous, with many draws during the day. Play is in sites, often bars, connected to a statewide system.

Lotteries appear to be a painless, voluntary, and enjoyable approach to government finance. What are their limitations? Some answers may be deduced from Table 12–4. First, lottery proceeds, although large in several states, contribute but a small amount to overall state finances. In a few states, the lottery contributes more than 5 percent of state own-source general revenue, but the national share across all lottery states is only 2.06 percent. These amounts are not sufficient to provide either significant tax relief or support for crucial state functions, no matter how politically easy the revenue might be to generate. If a state has important fiscal imbalance, a lottery is unlikely to correct it. Second, lottery revenue is expensive to produce. Both security and advertising are crucial for lottery success; neither is cheap, and the advertising seldom reveals the real chances of winning. If evaluated on roughly the same basis that a tax would be, the ratio of administrative cost to net proceeds to the state, not including commissions of 5 or 6 percent of sales paid directly to lottery vendors, was 22.55 percent. Even though there is no compliance cost to add in for the lottery, advertising, security, and commission costs are much greater than collection cost for taxes. Third, lottery proceeds are subject to considerable change from year to year, making them an unstable base for financing. Lottery sales have an extremely high elasticity to state income. One estimate indicates a 3.9 percent increase in sales for each 1 percent increase in state personal income. That response is tempered by response to the state unemployment rate. Apparently, lower prospects of employment in the economy make the small, but real chance of the lottery jackpot more attractive for households.[36] Fourth, evidence suggests that low-income families spend a higher percentage of their income on lottery tickets than do high-income

---

[36]John L. Mikesell, "State Lottery Sales and Economic Activity," *National Tax Journal* 47 (March 1994): 170.

Table 12–4
State Lottery Performance, Fiscal Year 2010 ($ in Thousands)

State	Year of First Play	Ticket Sales ($)	Net to State ($)	Net as % of Own-Source General Revenue	Net as % of Ticket Sales	Administrative Cost as % of Ticket Sales	Administrative Cost as % of Net Proceeds
Arizona	1981	514,496	141,775	1.03%	27.56%	7.70%	27.94%
Arkansas	2009	362,116	81,239	0.79%	22.43%	9.16%	40.81%
California	1985	2,826,824	1,044,931	0.81%	36.96%	6.03%	16.32%
Colorado	1983	463,050	107,909	0.80%	23.30%	8.94%	38.38%
Connecticut	1972	940,962	294,549	1.88%	31.30%	4.00%	12.78%
Delaware	1975	453,897	331,334	6.37%	73.00%	11.02%	15.10%
Florida	1988	3,727,982	1,252,509	2.73%	33.60%	3.47%	10.32%
Georgia	1993	3,153,145	885,508	4.37%	28.08%	4.39%	15.64%
Idaho	1989	135,796	38,466	0.95%	28.33%	6.67%	23.54%
Illinois	1974	2,191,421	647,385	1.78%	29.54%	10.53%	35.65%
Indiana	1989	689,262	183,465	0.95%	26.62%	7.18%	26.98%
Iowa	1985	240,145	69,663	0.67%	29.01%	8.34%	28.75%
Kansas	1987	221,743	68,526	0.71%	30.90%	9.29%	30.07%
Kentucky	1989	676,090	216,515	1.58%	32.02%	5.57%	17.39%
Louisiana	1991	351,756	131,340	0.93%	37.34%	8.72%	23.35%
Maine	1974	202,998	53,028	1.05%	26.12%	7.46%	28.58%
Maryland	1973	1,593,442	502,627	2.43%	31.54%	3.56%	11.27%
Massachusetts	1972	4,155,916	894,785	3.10%	21.53%	2.08%	9.64%
Michigan	1972	2,156,779	670,410	2.02%	31.08%	3.59%	11.55%
Minnesota	1990	436,706	90,290	0.42%	20.68%	5.68%	27.48%
Missouri	1986	912,015	249,997	1.75%	27.41%	3.72%	13.58%
Montana	1987	44,535	10,758	0.31%	24.16%	17.60%	72.84%
Nebraska	1993	122,470	31,631	0.58%	25.83%	12.91%	49.97%
New Hampshire	1964	221,347	66,396	1.72%	30.00%	7.25%	24.16%
New Jersey	1970	2,460,213	924,160	2.59%	37.56%	2.70%	7.18%
New Mexico	1996	136,942	43,649	0.56%	31.87%	8.68%	27.23%
New York	1967	6,942,886	2,676,574	3.18%	38.55%	4.54%	11.77%
North Carolina	2006	1,321,579	426,606	1.50%	32.28%	4.39%	13.59%
North Dakota	2004	23,247	6,321	0.17%	27.19%	18.42%	67.74%
Ohio	1974	2,336,760	733,307	2.09%	31.38%	3.84%	12.24%
Oklahoma	2005	212,898	94,108	0.82%	44.20%	6.43%	14.56%
Oregon	1985	829,765	541,830	4.46%	65.30%	8.72%	13.35%
Pennsylvania	1972	2,759,355	815,928	1.92%	29.57%	2.77%	9.36%
Rhode Island	1974	494,898	341,235	8.28%	68.95%	1.90%	2.75%
South Carolina	2002	915,995	248,968	1.83%	27.18%	4.22%	15.54%
South Dakota	1987	150,741	118,048	5.41%	78.31%	4.76%	6.08%
Tennessee	2004	1,063,685	325,907	2.30%	30.64%	4.68%	15.29%
Texas	1992	3,542,210	1,057,048	1.81%	29.84%	5.22%	17.50%
Vermont	1978	91,782	20,550	0.60%	22.39%	11.02%	49.21%
Virginia	1988	1,354,728	430,366	1.58%	31.77%	5.29%	16.65%
Washington	1982	460,016	126,075	0.56%	27.41%	9.15%	33.40%
West Virginia	1986	722,442	581,646	8.15%	80.51%	4.54%	5.64%
Wisconsin	1988	480,939	175,411	0.86%	36.47%	6.76%	18.54%
U.S. Total		53,095,974	17,752,773				
U.S. Mean				2.06%	34.88%	6.81%	22.55%

SOURCE: Governments Division, U.S. Bureau of Census, *2010 Survey of State Government Finances* [www.census.gov].

families, thus producing a regressive burden distribution. Although it is a voluntary burden, it does remain a burden that makes distributive correction by other parts of the tax or expenditure system more difficult.[37]

Finally, Charles Clotfelter and Philip Cook raise a fundamental question about state lotteries that is even more important than their fiscal implications: "The lottery business places the state in the position of using advertising that endorses suspect values and offers deceptive impressions instead of information."[38] Should this line of business be something that states operate—regardless of the money it might be able to raise from such an operation?

Lottery proponents note that profits are often dedicated to the support of important and valuable state programs, especially education. The revenue, however, is fungible, leading to the possibility that the lottery profits going to the dedicated program will simply substitute for other budget resources that would have gone to the program anyway. One analysis done of the Illinois lottery's support for education speaks directly to the point: "lotteries which are designated to support education, in all likelihood, do not. Further, there is no reason to believe that other specific programs designated as lottery fund recipients are any more likely to be truly supported by the lottery funds."[39] Money mixes in government operations, and dedication to useful purposes does not ordinarily change the basic points in the case for or against lotteries as an element in government finances.

Conclusion

Public prices can be an attractive alternative to tax financing. Public prices avoid citizen resistance to taxes and can improve both equity in finance and efficiency in service provision. Of the various government levels, cities currently make greatest use of user charges in the United States. User charges have the advantage of voluntarism not found with taxes, but only services with some considerable degree of benefit separability and chargeability are reasonable candidates for user-charge financing. Basic services provided by government usually lack those features. Most governments could increase their user-charge revenues, but seldom can true user charges (not disguised taxes) constitute a major portion of financial support. A similar conclusion is warranted for municipal utilities and state liquor monopolies; it is not clear why, if a government operates such facilities, it would not seek roughly the same objectives as a private owner. Lotteries in recent years have produced, relatively speaking, more public attention and acclaim than revenue.

---

[37]Some have suggested that lotteries can cut into the profits of gambling operated illegally. Unfortunately, lotteries typically offer worse odds than do illegal operations, do not offer regular gambling on credit, and report large winnings to tax authorities, so the competition presented by state systems is not likely to be effective.

[38]Charles T. Clotfelter and Philip J. Cook, *Selling Hope* (Cambridge, Mass.: Harvard University Press, 1989), 249.

[39]Mary O. Borg and Paul M. Mason, "The Budgetary Incidence of a Lottery to Support Education," *National Tax Journal* 41 (March 1988): 83.

QUESTIONS AND EXERCISES

1. The Fernwood Wastewater District—at the gentle insistence of both state and federal agencies—is changing methods of financing the operating and maintenance costs of its system. Presently, all users of the system (residential, commercial, agricultural, industrial, etc.) pay for the system by a property tax; payments to the District are assigned according to individual holdings of property value. If a car wash constitutes 0.0001 of total property in the District, the car wash pays 0.0001 of the operating and maintenance costs of the system. The proposed effluent-charge system would assign cost on the basis of estimated toxic-waste quality and quantity introduced into the system. The structure could easily be applied because a federal agency has data on the amount and type of waste that production and consumption processes generate annually, based on national data. These data would then be used to assign an annual effluent charge to each user, based on the total costs of the District. How do the two systems differ in terms of incentive to reduce wastewater quantity and toxicity?

2. In mid-1985, the U.S. Customs Service proposed a user-charge system for partial support of its services. The system would charge $2 for every passenger arriving on an international flight, $0.25 for every passenger arriving by train from a foreign destination, and $2.50 for every passenger arriving by boat. Fees to inspect airplanes would be $32 and to check passenger and freight carriers, up to $397. The customs system currently was financed by general revenue.
   Does the proposal seem reasonable? Discuss its logic, advantages, and disadvantages.

3. Here is a list of miscellaneous revenue sources received by governments. Categorize them as best you can as (1) user charge, (2) license tax, (3) franchise fee, or (4) fiscal monopoly, using the standards established in the chapter.[40] Explain your logic. What are the incentive impacts of each one of the revenue sources?

   a. A fee for disposal of used tires
   b. A fee to reserve books at the library
   c. A charge for processing the arrest of a convicted drunk driver
   d. A charge for emergency services required when a driver causes an accident through negligence
   e. A charge by the fire department to pump water from basements flooded by a downpour
   f. A fee for the services of a probation officer
   g. A fee for reviewing a developer's plans
   h. A fee for police response to a malfunctioning alarm system
   i. A charge for ball field use by the youth athletic league
   j. Admission to the city zoo
   k. A mandatory fee for municipal garbage collection
   l. A charge for use of the city municipal garbage collection

---

[40]Most of these examples have been taken from Penelope Lemov, "User Fees, Once the Answer to City Budget Prayers, May Have Reached Their Peak," *Governing* (March 1989): 24–30.

m. A charge for yacht owners who dock at the city marina

n. Fees for a summer day camp run by the city parks department

4. Due City has decided to shift municipal garbage-collection financing from the property tax to user charges. Describe some ways in which such a system could be implemented. Make certain that your system is primarily one of user charge, not a disguised tax.

5. The odds against selecting the winning lotto numbers are extreme. The formula

$$N = (c!) \div [r!(c - r)!]$$

provides the number of possible winning numbers (N), where c equals the range of numbers possible and r equals the number from that range to be selected. For example, for the popular 6×44 games, the possible winning numbers could come from

$$N = (44!) \div [6!(44 - 6)!] = 44! \div [6! \times 38!] = 7,059,052$$

different possibilities. Thus, the player's odds of picking the winning series are 1 in 7,059,052. Because the pari-mutuel pool is carried over from game to game until it is won, the lotto jackpot can reach truly remarkable levels, as high as $240 million in recent United States experience. As the jackpot rises, the expected value of the ticket rises as well: Expected value = Probability of winning $\times$ Size of payoff. The rising jackpot brings increased lotto sales to the state as well.

a. Compare the probable effects on the jackpot size and likelihood of having a winner in the first week of play of a 5/36 and a 6/44 lotto game.

b. Discuss the strategic issues, including the revenue flow to the state and the likely player, involved in choosing between those games. Would the strategy differ according to whether the state lottery was old or new? According to what neighboring lotteries were doing?

c. A bumper sticker proclaims the following: "Lotteries are a tax on people who are bad at math." Do you agree that this is true under all circumstances?

CASES FOR DISCUSSION

CASE 12–1

User Charges for Correcting Externalities: London Congestion Charge

Consider These Questions

1. How is this charge system different from simply adding a new annual license charge to all motor vehicles in the London area? Why might this approach be more effective at getting at congestion?

2. Does the logic of the charge depend on how the revenue from the charge is used? Explain.

3. Pick a large city with which you are familiar: Los Angeles, Boston, New York, Beijing, Moscow, or any other. Would a congestion charge system be sensible and feasible there? What are the political, geographic, or economic barriers (or advantages) to applying a congestion charge in the selected city? New York City has sought authority for such charges, but the state legislature has denied that authorization.

4. It has been suggested that congestion charges could be a solution to airport flight delays—in other words, flights would be charged higher takeoff and landing fees at times when the airport was congested and lower fees at off-peak periods—a cheaper response than building more airports or runways. What do you think about this approach?

The London Example

At the beginning of the twenty-first century, traffic in the center of London moved about as quickly as it did in the horse-and-buggy era. The 200,000 or so cars and trucks that entered the city center made their way down narrow and winding streets that were laid out in the Middle Ages. Congestion was so bad that any small mishap brought traffic from its normal slow crawl to a complete stop. Total gridlock hung as an impending threat over the city every day.

The traditional engineering approach—providing more lanes for traffic—was not possible. All the properties in the congested space were occupied by buildings, including many of historic importance. Even if solving the problem with wrecking crews and bulldozers was technically feasible, voters were unlikely to accept the considerable tax burden this approach would involve. Furthermore, the city was reluctant to use a regulation approach—like permitting cars access only on alternate days, based on license plate numbers. The mayor of London, Ken Livingstone, developed a radical approach built on the principles of basic microeconomics: a daily congestion charge for driving in the eight square miles of London. As with many other excellent policy applications of microeconomics, the idea of congestion pricing initially was proposed by Nobel laureate in economics William Vickery—in the 1950s—so the implementation was the new part of the proposal.

A Congressional Budget Office study explains the program.

> The Central London congestion charging zone applies cordon pricing to an approximately 15-square-mile section of the city. The zone first covered an 8-square-mile area in February 2003 and was approximately doubled to its current size in February 2007 by including an area west of the original zone. That western extension is now intended to be removed from operation, but no earlier than 2010 … .
>
> Drivers pay a daily charge of £8 (about $11 at current exchange rates) to drive or park on a street within the zone; the charge was £5 when first implemented in 2005. The congestion charge applies on Monday through Friday, from 7:00 a.m. to 6:00 p.m. Motorbikes, mopeds, taxis, buses, emergency vehicles, and vehicles using alternative fuels are exempt, as are vehicles whose drivers are disabled, and residents of the zone receive a 90 percent discount.

The congestion fee may be paid in advance on a daily, weekly, monthly, or annual basis by phone, mail, or Internet or at retail outlets. If paid on the following day, the charge is £10 (about $14 at current exchange rates).

Entry into the congestion zone is indicated by street signs or pavement markings. The license plates of vehicles moving into or within the zone are recorded by a network of fixed and mobile cameras. Drivers encounter no toll booths, gantries, or barriers on entering the zone, and traffic does not have to stop. License plate numbers are compared with those in a database of vehicles for which the fee has been paid, and a £120 fine (about $166 at current exchange rates) is assessed to the vehicle owner if the fee has not been paid. The fine is reduced to £60 (about $83) if paid within 14 days. Authorities may apply a "boot" to immobilize vehicles with multiple outstanding fines.

Implementation costs for the first two years of the project were £190 million ($348 million at then-current exchange rates), more than twice the amount expected. Approximately £140 million in costs ($258 million at then-current exchange rates) were incurred in extending the zone to the west. Annual operating expenses for the entire tolling system are approximately £130 million ($246 million). [An aside: The U.S. Embassy claims exemption from the charge for its 200 London employees, arguing for diplomatic immunity and citing the 1960 Vienna Convention on Diplomatic Relations. That included a charge for President Obama's armored Cadillac limousine when he visited in 2011. London was not impressed, pointing out that a user charge is not a tax. The unpaid Embassy bill at that time was around $8.5 million. The United States was not alone: diplomatic missions owed a total of $83 million in congestion charges.] The system has covered its capital and operating expenses every year since its inception. In a typical day, the system handles 78,000 payments from nonresidents, 60,000 from residents, and 20,000 from operators of fleets. All together, in the fiscal year ending in June 2008, the congestion fees totaled £268 million ($507 million). All proceeds from the program must be spent on improving transport within Greater London.[41]

Drivers entering the congested area would normally take no account of the fact that their presence had the effect of slowing the progress of other travelers. The congestion charge was intended to make drivers pay attention to the cost they imposed on others—slowed traffic—when they added their vehicles to the mass of metal choking London streets. When drivers must bear this cost, many decide that the trip can be postponed to a less congested time, can be canceled, or can be undertaken on public mass transport (bus or train) rather than by private vehicle because the full cost of the trip is greater than the value of the journey. The hope was that the number of vehicles entering the center would fall by 15 to 20 percent, thus allowing travel at speeds faster than horse-and-buggy. After paying for the cost of the control equipment, all profit was earmarked for transportation system improvements.

---

[41]Congressional Budget Office, *Using Pricing to Reduce Traffic Congestion* (Washington, D.C.: Congressional Budget Office, 2009), 23–24. Footnotes in source are eliminated.

Critics had several complaints in addition to the skeptical view that the system was technologically untested and certain to fail. The criticisms included:

1. The concern that the fee put greater burden on low-income than high-income vehicle owners and was thus inherently unfair;
2. The fear that people would be forced off the roads and onto the bus and train system, creating a crisis there;
3. The complaint that the scheme amounted to charging the public to use public property; and
4. The argument that so many people would be discouraged from entering the charge area that there would be a devastating collapse of economic activity there.

What has been the result of the charges? It is too early to know the long-term effects, but comparisons of traffic measurements in the congestion zone show that traffic congestion in the charge area has fallen by 30 percent (as measured by delay per kilometer traveled), traffic entering the charge zone is down by 18 percent, average driving speed in the zone has increased by 20 percent, and 90 million pounds are being generated yearly from the charges, with the bulk of the revenue going to improve London bus services. There have also been reductions in personal injury accidents and in emissions (carbon dioxide, nitrous oxide, and particulate matter) with the changed traffic. The economic impacts on businesses in the zone are in dispute.

There have been erroneous billings, and a new scam has developed: people locate cars of the same make, model, and color of their own and produce a phony license plate with that car's number so that the owner of the other car receives the bills and fines, based on photographic evidence of that car violating the charge controls. In addition, there have been considerable impacts outside the charge zone as drivers divert around the charge zone, creating congestion where there was none before, and as drivers park at the charge zone border to take public transportation for the rest of their travel. However, the experiment is seen as an overall success: national politicians who opposed the idea before it was implemented have now started to refer to the congestion charges as a transportation success worth replicating elsewhere, and the person who devised the specifics of the system in London resigned to undertake a new career designing similar systems for other cities.

The system has survived a change in mayors, and similar systems have been adopted in Stockholm (voters chose to continue the system after an initial trial there) and Singapore (Singapore started its program in 1975). The state legislature in New York, however, blocked implementation of such a system in New York City.

SOURCES: "Congestion Charging: Ken Livingstone's Gamble," *Economist* (February 15, 2003): 51–53; Glenn Frankel, "Toll Zone Put to Test in Divided London," *Washington Post,* February 17, 2003, A2; and Transport for London, *Central London Congestion Charging, Impacts Monitoring, Fourth Annual Report* (June 2006) [http://www.tfl.gov.uk/assets/ downloads/ FourthAnnualReportFinal.pdf]. For an excellent overview of congestion pricing, see Kiram Bhatt, "Congestion Pricing: An Overview of Experience and Impacts," in *Climate Change and Land Policies, Proceedings of the 2010 Land Policy Conference,* ed. Gregory K. Ingram and Yu-Hung Hong (Cambridge, Mass.: Lincoln Institute of Land Policy, 2011): 247–71.

CASE 12–2

Charging for Firefighting: A Reasonable Financing Option?

Fighting wildfires is expensive. Who should bear that cost? The general taxpayers or the people whose properties the firefighters are working to protect? Global climate change seems to have worsened the conditions for wildfires in the American west and huge fires in California, Arizona, Colorado, and New Mexico have made national headlines in the past several years. The problem seems to worsen with each year because the fire season starts earlier and ends later than it did in the past. The problem promises not to go away and California, along with the other western states, has not developed a good solution to financing the cost of fighting these fires.

Consider These Questions

1. What are the general alternatives that a state would have for financing state services?

2. Would financing this wildfire fighting through some sort of charge make sense? Discuss this alternative as opposed to using general funds. What would be the advantages and disadvantages?

3. If you were to finance by a charge, how would you design the charge, and how would you enforce it? Would your charge include incentives that could lead to reduced fire damages?

4. Is the case for financing CalFire through direct charges different from the case for financing the fire department of, say, San Francisco by charges?

U.S. News: California Ponders Who Should Pay Firefighting Bill; Some Want Owners of Wooded Property to Bear More of Cost

By Peter Sanders

California's fire season has barely begun, but in the past three weeks alone, blazes have burned through 631,000 acres—and at least $112 million in state money. That is stoking a statewide debate: Who should pick up the bill? The state's costs for fighting wildfires over the past 12 months have soared to an estimated $950 million, a 41 percent increase over the same period a year ago. This doesn't include the cost to various local and federal firefighting agencies. The most intense months for wildfires, typically August through October when local vegetation is driest, are still to come, and some officials worry the hefty price tag could further strain an already overstretched state budget. That has prompted several new fund-raising proposals, including one advanced by Gov. Arnold Schwarzenegger.

But some officials are raising the question of whether Californians are paying firefighting costs to protect forests or to protect homeowners who willingly built property in woodlands, which go up in smoke with increasing frequency.

"The fact is the residents of California are simply not paying enough for fire protection," says Christine Kehoe, a Democratic state senator from San Diego. She argues that frenzied building in rural areas increases the burden on state firefighters to defend homes and property and that people who choose to live in those areas should shoulder more of the firefighting costs. "It's a very tough discussion for citizens and politicians to have."

Covering rising firefighting costs is an urgent issue as California battles a budget deficit currently estimated at $17.2 billion. In his proposed 2008–09 budget, Mr. Schwarzenegger has tried to find new firefighting funds with an insurance surcharge on all home and business owners that would raise an estimated $130 million extra annually. Some of that money would help cover the costs of the state's fire department, known as CalFire.

But the state's nonpartisan Legislative Analyst's Office [LAO] doesn't recommend the governor's proposed insurance fee because, it argues, it would unfairly burden taxpayers who aren't threatened by the wildfires. "Because the state provides a service—fire protection—that directly benefits a particular group … it is appropriate that those beneficiaries pay for a portion of the state's cost for fire protection," the LAO wrote in a recent report. It is in favor of a property-tax surcharge on residents who live in areas protected by CalFire.

Ms. Kehoe has introduced a bill in the state legislature similar to what the LAO is proposing, an annual fee paid by residents who live in more rural areas to help offset the costs of firefighting.

Since June 20, more than 20,000 local, state and federal firefighters have fought nearly 1,800 fires. The two biggest—one near the coastal tourist hamlet of Big Sur and another north of Santa Barbara—continue to burn as more hot, dry weather rolled into the state Tuesday.

CalFire has taken the lead in combating more than 1,000 of the fires and as of Tuesday was still fighting nearly 60. The department has 4,700 full-time and 2,200 seasonal firefighters, in addition to thousands of local volunteers and prison inmates it uses to fight wildfires.

CalFire's budget, which last year was about $870 million, comes largely from the state's general fund footed by all California taxpayers. The budget covers such costs as those of buildings and fire trucks as well as of firefighting itself.

When the department needs extra money to fight a big fire, it makes a request for emergency funding to the legislature. For the fiscal year ended June 30, state budget officials had anticipated CalFire would make $82 million in emergency fund requests to fight the year's big fires. The officials are now saying those emergency requests will likely reach about $400 million.

Rampant development in places like San Diego County and Riverside County, which abut wilderness, have brought more fires. But because of the proximity of those fires to populated areas, firefighting costs have grown at an even faster clip.

Typically, the costs are highest when firefighters are trying to protect homes in wooded areas. Using fire engines, helicopters, and airplanes to make a stand is vastly more expensive than using smaller crews to monitor and contain a remote wilderness fire.

"When you are forced to move resources in defense of structures, it means you're often taking resources away from other areas of the fire, or entirely separate fires, which means those fires are harder to contain with less resources," says Timothy Duane, professor of environmental planning and policy at the University of California, Berkeley. "You have to deal with life and property and natural resources, in that order, and when you're dealing with the first two, it increases the extent of the fire and the time period before you can put the fire out."

In 1999, Mr. Duane published a study that noted that between 1970 and 1985 the state's population rose 97 percent, while fires rose 90 percent and acreage burned rose 95 percent. But the cost of fire damage in the same period rose 5,000 percent. CalFire's mission has changed as well. The service is charged with protecting 31 million acres of wildland, including the state's timber stands, watershed and vast agriculture lands. Increasingly, however, the service has to divert resources to protecting the growing number of homes sprinkled throughout the forests.

"CalFire protects land that benefits the public at large," says Brendan McCarthy of the state's LAO. "But there is now an increased burden on the department to do whatever they can to protect neighborhoods ... . It's more expensive ... because it's harder to defend a neighborhood."

Development is approved at the local level, and the local governments then bear little fiscal consequence if the state is responsible for firefighting in the jurisdiction.

Says Ms. Kehoe: "Local land-use approvals for residential development in the backcountry should be tied to the future cost of firefighting. If they want to approve a new development, they should be required to plan for ongoing fire prevention; otherwise, this problem will continue without interruption."

CHAPTER 13

Revenue Forecasts, Revenue Estimates, and Tax Expenditure Budgets

Reliable and trusted revenue predictions provide the foundation for fiscal discipline and for the adoption of an executable public budget. Participants in the budget process need to know how much money the revenue system will yield in the budget period—first as it exists and then with proposed changes. For fiscal transparency, budget participants also need to know the cost of carrying out subsidy programs through tax system preferences rather than through direct expenditures. The predictions are never certain because private economic behavior is not certain, and if the private economy—the source of government revenue in a market economy—is uncertain, so, too, will be revenue yield. Nonetheless, best available predictions are necessary for developing the budget, for preparing long-term fiscal profiles, for understanding the implications of fiscal decisions being considered, and for forecasting short-term cash flow. Financial management without trustworthy revenue predictions is not meaningful.

Three distinct revenue prediction tasks play a prominent role in public financial management: the revenue *forecast* (or baseline), revenue *estimates* (or fiscal notes or scores), and *tax expenditures*. Approaches, methods, and skills required as well as organizational responsibility for their preparation typically differ, although the tax-collecting agency—the tax service, treasury, or revenue department—is the repository of basic data used in each. The tax collection agency (mostly accountants and lawyers) likely does not have the appropriate technical staff (mostly economists and statisticians) to develop the models and procedures necessary for the predictions, but the collectors serve as a conduit of expert data to those preparing the predictions. Official forecasts and estimates may come from executive budget agencies, legislative fiscal staff, or consensus groups representing both the legislature and the executive. Of course, there are many interest groups, lobbyists, consultants, and so on who devise their own forecasts and estimates of varying trustworthiness for their clients and distribute them to whomever in government will pay attention.[1]

Revenue Forecast (or Baseline)[2]

The revenue forecast predicts the revenue baseline, meaning the forecast of what revenue will be collected in the budget period under current law. It is driven by forecasts of economic, demographic, administrative, and other structural conditions in the tax-collecting environment, but it assumes no change in tax policy as represented in the current tax laws. If current law has in place a tax change that will take place during the forecast period, then that change would be part of the revenue baseline. At the federal level, the Office of Tax Analysis in the Department of Treasury prepares revenue forecasts that the Office of Management and Budget (OMB) uses in development of the president's budget, whereas the Congressional Budget Office (CBO) prepares baseline forecasts for the congressional Budget Committees, as well as other fiscal committees.[3] These forecasts drive executive budget development, advise the congressional Budget Committees as they develop the budget resolution, and form the basis for the midsession reviews by the OMB and CBO. States organize their revenue forecasting in many different patterns. Some assign the task to a single executive agency, others develop a consensus forecast from a joint executive-legislative body (often with formal inclusion of independent experts), some contract the forecasting out to a university or private consulting firm, and a few develop separate legislative and executive forecasts.[4] Because revenue forecasts can become political tools, there can be considerable advantage to an open, consensus forecast process. Local revenue forecasts for all but the largest governments tend to be informal, simply done in the budget or finance office. Revenue forecasts are often a controversial part of the state and local budget process. However, they seldom are subject to much dispute at the federal level.

Revenue forecasts are made using several different approaches; seldom will all revenues collected by a government be forecast by exactly the same approach. The more important formal approaches in current use include (1) extrapolation or

---

[1]Many of these consultants started out as government fiscal staff, so their predictions can be of excellent quality. However, many numbers created by interest groups are so tinged with self-interest as to be worthless.

[2]An excellent basic source on general techniques of forecasting is "Chapter 5: Forecasting Techniques," in *The Economist Numbers Guide: The Essentials of Business Numeracy* (London: Profile Books, 1997), 92–119.

[3]Congressional Budget Office, *The Economic Budget Outlook: An Update* (Washington, D.C.: U.S. Government Printing Office, 1994); and Office of Management and Budget, *Mid-Session Review of the 1994 Budget* (Washington, D.C.: U.S. Government Printing Office, 1993), for example.

[4]For an excellent overview of how governments in the United States forecast and estimate, see Marilyn Marks Rubin, J. L. Peters, and Nancy Mantell, "Revenue Forecasting and Estimation," in *Handbook on Taxation*, ed. W. Bartley Hildreth and James A. Richardson (New York: Marcel Dekker, 1999), 769–99.

projection, (2) deterministic models, (3) multiple regression equations, (4) econometric equation systems, and (5) microsimulation from taxpayer data files. All but the first are "cause-and-effect" approaches that try to link economic, demographic, or other influences to revenue sources and then exploit that linkage to forecast revenue. Each method has its appropriate uses in the revenue forecast environment, and all are ultimately time-series estimates because they consider revenue flows across years, quarters, months, or weeks into the future.

Some forecasts are heavily judgmental or nearly subjective, based on the personal experience, intuition, and guesswork of public finance staff from the revenue department, budget or finance agency, or legislative fiscal committees. These intuitive estimates can be devastatingly accurate and immensely useful, particularly in a consensus estimation process in which judgments from multiple "old hands" are condensed into a single forecast and not released separately. These judgmental forecasts are particularly important for use with sources yielding relatively small amounts of revenue that can be subject to major fluctuations caused by institutional or administrative factors; certain intergovernmental transfers and development impact fees offer two examples of sources in which such insights can be especially helpful. If administrative factors can produce major changes in revenue flows, then having the experience from the "old hands," who have seen almost everything play out at least once before, can be crucial to getting those impacts correct in the forecast.

General Guides for Revenue Forecasts[5]

Before discussing each method in some detail, there are several general points about revenue forecasting that need to be highlighted. The first and most fundamental principle is that the forecaster must understand the tax being forecast, how it is administered, and the procedures that generate collection data. That is why this chapter about forecasting comes after the chapters dealing with each of the major taxes—the forecaster needs to understand the structure and administration of the tax before even attempting to do the forecast. It is folly to try to forecast the state insurance tax, for instance, if you do not fully understand the nature (structure and administration) of that tax; having what you believe to be a consistent series of collections data for the tax is not enough. Novice revenue forecasters usually underestimate the problems involved in developing a consistent data series for each tax to be forecast. Messy little transactions (changes in rates or exemptions, failure to properly record receipts for an unspecified period, changes in filing or revenue-processing schedules, loss of revenue reports, inconsistent revenue accounting, etc.) confuse almost every revenue series, causing the revenue estimator to spend many hours to obtain a clean and consistent data series. Sometimes the forecaster may discover that some historical revenue data have been lost forever. Many possible adjustments can remedy problems with independent variables, including the decision to substitute some other variable to drive the forecast, but estimation based on incorrect, misunderstood, or inconsistent

---

[5]A number of forecasting issues, as well as practical illustrations of forecasting applications, are provided in Jinping Sun and Thomas D. Lynch, eds., *Government Budget Forecasting, Theory and Practice* (Boca Raton, Fla.: CRC Press, 2008).

revenue data is nearly hopeless. Furthermore, the forecast is always subject to sabotage, usually accidental, through a repeat of the episodes that messed up the initial data.[6] These problems haunt every revenue forecaster.

Second, the cleaned revenue series to be forecast should be plotted in a simple graph against time. An examination of the graph offers insights into the forecasting task (expansion or decline? large change or small? smooth changes or considerable fluctuations?) and identifies important questions (When were there large increases or decreases in revenue, and what caused the changes? Are the overall patterns consistent with general forces in the regional or national economy?). Additional plots, sometimes against time and sometimes against independent variables ("causes") thought to influence the revenue flow, can be helpful throughout the forecasting process as tests of logic and of strength of relationship.

Third, openness in forecasting is a virtue. Both legislative and executive branches occasionally seek artificially high or low revenue forecasts as a part of a political budget strategy to increase or reduce expenditure. Boosting the revenue forecast is an excellent step toward phantom budget balance. An open and transparent process reduces the opportunity for such manipulation. The general public seldom wins when several different revenue estimates are strategically unveiled during budget sessions. A wrong consensus forecast used by all in crafting a budget leads to more responsible budget development and adoption than does a process with many competing estimates from executive and legislative branches, from each political party, or from factions within parties—even if one of the competitors happens to be absolutely correct. What is really critical is that those preparing and adopting the budget agree to accept the same revenue forecast so that work will be done within a single, hard budget constraint. For that reason, a number of states employ consensus forecasting, an approach that involves both executive and legislative branches in the creation of a single revenue baseline that will be used in all deliberations.[7] Huge forecast errors are most frequent when the business cycle turns (and downturns are difficult to predict accurately) or when politicians intervene to create phantom revenue needed to close a budget gap. An open, consensus forecast prevents the latter problem. State and local government forecasts (and estimates) tend to be more openly prepared than those in the federal government.[8] Historically, political manipulation of revenue forecasts has been more common at the state and local levels than at the federal level.

Fourth, the approach selected often depends on the tasks to be served by the model. If one seeks revenue forecasts for the annual budget process, the multiple regression approach ordinarily yields good results. If one needs to divide annual revenues into amounts expected within the year (quarterly or monthly), univariate analysis may be appropriate. If one seeks the impact of a structural change, in the economy or in the demographic character of the population, microsimulation may be more appropriate.

---

[6]Some revenues are subject to some control by program administrators. For instance, state lotteries can manipulate the introduction of new games, payout rates, or advertising programs and so influence at least the timing of net proceeds to government. Therefore, revenue forecasters must give great deference to what their administrators forecast for their operations–an irritated lottery director can make external forecasters look inept.

[7]Pew Center on the States—Rockefeller Institute, States' Revenue Estimating, Cracks in the Crystal Ball (Washington, D.C., and Philadelphia: Pew Trust, 2011), 32.

[8]Thomas F. Field, "Transparency in Revenue Estimating," *Tax Notes* (January 17, 2005): 329–61.

If estimates are needed for long-range plans, trend extrapolations—sometimes adjusted for guesses about structural changes—are as good as anything. In summary, no single approach is ideally suited for all revenue forecasting tasks.

Fifth, individual revenue sources normally are forecast separately. It would be extremely unusual, for instance, to forecast general fund revenue for a state as a single aggregate instead of adding forecasts of each individual revenue source to obtain the total. Different revenue sources respond to different factors, and they should be separately examined. Furthermore, compensating errors in the separate source forecasts can cause the total forecast—the one upon which the budget is based—to be closer to the actual revenue than any of the individual forecasts.

Finally, revenues need to be monitored carefully and on a regular schedule against the forecast. A single month's variation, though potentially troublesome, can disappear later in the fiscal year, and comparisons between year-to-date actual cumulative and estimated cumulative revenues are more helpful than the comparison for a single month.[9] However, the record needs to be continuously evaluated to maintain control of overall government finances. That performance becomes important information for the development of future revenue forecasts.[10] If you plot the revenue series on a monthly or quarterly basis for the past several years, the seasonal pattern will almost certainly become apparent. You can use that pattern as your guide to how your forecast is doing against actual collections through the year, and you can use that pattern to help develop a cash budget for the year (i.e., to see if there are likely to be points during the year at which the government may not have enough cash on hand to cover its payments). Monitoring through the year usually involves comparisons of revenue collected in months or quarters against shares of annual totals collected in comparable periods in previous years. If 45 percent of total annual retail sales tax revenue has typically been collected by the end of June and this year only 41 percent of the forecasted total has been collected, then the budget agency might want to constrain the pace of spending because the adopted budget may not be able to be executed without unplanned borrowing or reduction of government reserves. At the close of the fiscal year, the success of the forecast needs to be evaluated to permit improvements in future outcomes. Where "cause-and-effect" models are used, variances from the actual need to be divided into (1) the part caused by errors in forecasting the cause(s), (2) the part due to errors in the model, and (3) the part attributed to legislative changes that make the tax for which the forecast was prepared different from the one that produced the revenue.[11]

---

[9]In other words, rather than comparing April actual with April forecast, a better comparison would be the actual for all the fiscal year through April against the forecast for all the fiscal year through April. That gives a better understanding of whether the fiscal year forecast is likely to be on target than looking at a single month.

[10]Useful standards for revenue estimation are presented in National Association of State Budget Officers/Federation of Tax Administrators, *Good Practices in Revenue Estimating* (Washington, D.C.: National Association of State Budget Officers, 1989).

[11]In other words, suppose the retail sales tax (S) was forecast as a function of personal income (I):

$$S = 389.7 + 0.7821I$$

Actual collections could differ from forecast collections because (1) an error was made in the personal income forecast or (2) the forecast relationship between personal income and retail sales did not hold. Legislative changes are a shock from outside the model.

Alternative Methods for Forecasting

The problem in revenue forecasting is not finding a method for doing the forecast because there are many options. It is selecting from among the many methods to produce a satisfactory forecast. Which ones will work best for the current forecast? Unfortunately, you won't know for sure until after the year is over, and that is definitely too late to help with adopting a budget.

UNIVARIATE PROJECTIONS, TRENDS, AUTOCORRELATIONS, AND EXTRAPOLATIONS

Forecasters do projections and extrapolations because they can be quick, inexpensive, done without much data, and accurate enough for some assignments. These forecasts, through complex or simple means, extend past patterns of the revenue into the future. They make no explicit effort to model a cause-effect relationship between some economic or other force and the revenue being forecast. This presents a problem for most tax forecasters: they want to understand causal influences in the revenue system, and so do their legislative and executive agency bosses. The need to understand causes is particularly great when the forecaster must explain a revenue shortfall. Nevertheless, these projections can sometimes be the best choice for the forecaster.[12]

Simple and complex univariate methods share a common feature. Only past revenue data are used to forecast future revenue data (e.g., sales tax collection data for the last fifteen years are used to forecast sales tax collections for the budget year and the out-years). No other economic, demographic, social, or cultural variables are involved.

One method is a simple time-series extrapolation or regression against time. These extrapolations may be by (1) constant increments (collections increased by $5,000 in each of the last five years, so they are estimated to increase by $5,000 this year); (2) constant percentage changes (collections increased by 5 percent in each of the last five years, so they are estimated to increase by 5 percent this year); (3) simple growth models using the average annual compounding formula developed in Chapter 5; or (4) linear or nonlinear time trends in which revenue for the budget year is estimated as an arithmetic function of time ($R = a + bt$) or as a logarithmic function of time ($\ln R = a + bt$), where R equals collections from the revenue source and t equals a time index, choosing between the trends according to which is judged most likely to produce a reasonable estimate. Many local governments use these approaches because they lack the data on the local economy—both historical for identifying the relationships and forecasted for creating the revenue baseline from the relationships—requisite for developing more complex cause-and-effect models. States often use the approach for minor revenue sources when improved estimates have no consequential impact on the overall fiscal pattern. Everybody uses them when there is insufficient data or insufficient time for other methods or when the revenue item is too small to merit much attention.

---

[12]You will recall from an earlier chapter that lots of expenditure proposals in the budget request will be constructed with simple projections of workloads, prices, and so on.

Another simple univariate short-term forecasting approach that can be usable in periods of general stability is the moving average technique. A moving average forecast operates with the following procedure:

$$R_{t+1} = (R_{t1} + R_{t2} + R_{t3} + \ldots + R_{tj}) \div N$$

where

R_{t+1} = revenue for the forecast period,

R_{t1} to R_{tj} = actual revenue for previous periods included in the average, and

N = the number to periods use in calculating the average.

For instance, a forecast of motor vehicle license revenues in 2014 might be prepared during 2013 as the average of actual revenues in 2012 (the most recent year for which actual data are available), 2011, and 2010. The forecaster selects the number of periods according to an expectation about how many will keep the forecast error to a minimum—in general, fewer periods when there have been recent significant fluctuations and more periods when there has been general stability.

Other univariate approaches work with autoregression techniques, more complex moving average approaches (the Box-Jenkins autoregressive integrated moving average model being one example), and various smoothing techniques (spreadsheet programs usually offer several alternatives). The applicability of the more sophisticated techniques is limited by the need for lengthy data series; revenue forecasting seldom has data series that extend for long periods without considerable shocks from change in the fundamental structure of the tax. Again, revenue forecasters do use these techniques for causal variables (like personal income, population, inflation rates, and so on) entering their models.[13]

DETERMINISTIC MODELING

Deterministic models use a preestablished formula (or "rule of thumb") that "ought" to forecast revenue. In other words, there should reasonably be a link between gross domestic product (GDP), personal income, or some other broad economic aggregate and tax revenue; the forecast results from multiplying that aggregate by the formula coefficient for that particular source. For instance, data from several countries show the value-added tax (VAT) to yield, on average, 0.37 percent of GDP for each percentage point of tax rate.[14] The forecaster could use that ratio to develop a rough forecast of VAT yield from a forecast of GDP—possibly developed itself

---

[13]It is wrong to reject these simple models out of hand because they can be remarkably successful in forecasting. For instance, Faust and Wright find that a simple univariate autoregressive forecast of GDP growth is as accurate as substantially more complicated models. Jon Faust and Jonathan Wright, "Comparing Greenbook and Reduced Form Forecasts Using a Large Realtime Dataset," National Bureau of Economic Research Working Paper 13397, Cambridge, Mass., September 2007. In other words, an accurate forecast of GDP growth would result by regressing GDP growth rates against four lagged periods of past GDP growth rates.

[14]Vito Tanzi and Parthasarathi Shome, "A Primer on Tax Evasion," *IMF Staff Papers 40* (December 1993): 823. This is sometimes called "Cnossen's Rule."

by application of a simple guess about annual growth rates. Or there might be an expected elasticity relationship between growth in revenue from a tax and growth in some aggregate measure of economic activity. The forecaster might believe that every 1 percentage point increase in personal income will generate a 1.2 percentage point increase in the income tax, and from that the revenue forecast emerges. Forecasters working in data-scarce environments regularly use such approaches in developing budget numbers. Such conditions may occur, for example, when the revenue source is relatively new and there are insufficient data for meaningful statistical modeling (fitting equations makes little sense when there are only two or three data points), when the national economic environment is too unstable for the results of statistical modeling to be usable with confidence, or when data are of insufficient reliability to make statistical modeling meaningful. For instance, in countries undergoing transition from components of the Soviet Union to independent nations in the early 1990s, there was great economic instability, there were few data points (the nations were formed in 1991), and all the tax sources were new. There was little reason to use sophisticated causal models in that environment.

Another application of such rule-of-thumb forecasting is when one is attempting to provide a perspective on fiscal conditions. For instance, here is a statement by some macroeconomists about state and local fiscal frameworks:

The "Golden Rule of Thumb" for short-run forecasting:

- Expect each 1 percent rise in the state unemployment rate to cut over 5 percent from trend state revenue growth.
- This 5:1 multiplier is the average impact. Governments with a greater reliance on sales and excise taxes or business profits taxes are more vulnerable, and their golden rules would have notably higher multipliers. California, for example, has a multiplier of eight.[15]

A government budget would not ordinarily be built around such a rule-of-thumb forecast, but it could be important in constructing a longer-term fiscal framework for a government. Many longer-term forecasts use such approaches, not because of a shortage of historical data, but because secular change is likely to alter any relationship that formed a model based on those data.

MULTIPLE REGRESSION

The multiple regression model, the most widely encountered forecasting device, forecasts revenue as a function of one or more independent variables determined outside the revenue model. Each equation used to estimate a revenue source is independent of the others. For instance, a state might forecast quarterly retail sales tax collections with an equation like the following one, which was estimated from an ordinary least squares regression program:

$$ST = 5.523 + 0.926PI - 0.034P - 0.773R + 0.022Q_1 + 0.011Q_2 + 0.032Q_3$$

---

[15]Roger E. Brinner, Joyce Brinner, Matt Eckhouse, and Megan Leahey, "Fiscal Realities for State and Local Governments," *Business Economics* 43 (April 2008): 62.

where

ST = retail sales tax collections for the quarter in logarithmic form,

PI = state personal income in logarithmic form, lagged one quarter,

P = the inflation rate measured as a percentage change in the GDP deflator in logarithmic form, lagged one quarter,

R = the statutory sales tax rate applicable in the state, and

Q_1, Q_2, and Q_3 = categorical dummies to indicate the quarter of the year (sales tax revenues being subject to seasonal variation through the year).[16]

The economic data are lagged because allocation processes are such that economic activity in one period generates tax revenue that is received by the government in the next period. In other words, there is a mismatch between when the taxable activity occurs and when the collections from that activity show up in the state treasury. The lagged economic data in the forecasting equation account for that mismatch. Of course, there are several different ways to measure the economic activity that is producing the sales tax revenue, including gross state product, GDP, and national personal income. Each of these measures has some logical attractiveness as a drive force for forecasting state sales tax revenue. The forecaster will almost certainly experiment with each of these possible measures until he or she settles on the one that seems most likely to reliably track the actual path of tax revenue. The forecaster also will experiment with lags of different lengths and with other formats for the relationship.

Forecasts for the independent or causal variables (personal income and the inflation rate in this example) come from analytic and forecasting work outside the tax equations. To use this approach, estimates of the independent variable must be available for the forecast period: an estimating equation for sales tax collections that uses a stock market index, for instance, will not be usable if the necessary index is not available until three-quarters of the way through the budget year because, for budget preparation, the revenue estimate has to be presented well before the start of the budget year. Dummy variables offer an approach to allowing for the influence of unusual qualitative experiences in the past. For instance, a dummy may identify two years in which budget constraints prohibited any out-of-state audits, a tax amnesty, or a period in which the regulations for certain sales tax exemptions differed from those currently in effect.

The equation estimated by multiple regression ordinarily is selected based on the extent to which estimates from the equation coincide with actual revenue collections in prior years. Because many alternative specifications yield similar fit to

---

[16]Because tax collections, personal income, and tax rate are in logarithmic transformation, the coefficients in the equation are interpreted as elasticities. That is, the estimating equation shows that a 10 percent increase in personal income produces a 9.3 percent increase in tax collections and that a 10 percent increase in the statutory tax rate produces only a 7.7 percent increase in tax collections. This evidence is consistent with the idea that the retail sales tax grows more slowly than the economy and that rate increases do have a negative impact on the tax base—but that this tax is not on the downward sloping side of the rate–revenue curve. The forecasting equation is for Indiana with data from third quarter 1977 through first quarter 2005. It is for instruction only and is not the model actually used to prepare the baseline forecast.

historical data (several specifications will be almost indistinguishable in terms of normal tests of goodness of fit and forecast error), trial predictions (simulations or "out of sample forecasts") for earlier years are also prepared: Suppose data are available for 1960–2014 and a forecast is being prepared for the 2016 budget year (the estimate is being prepared during 2015). Possible equations can be developed from 1960 to 2013 and test "predictions" made for 2014. The equation coming closest to the known 2014 result is selected.

Ordinarily, separate equations are prepared for each major revenue category to allow for different responses to changes in independent variables. That is, equations are developed for individual income tax, corporate income tax, retail sales tax, and so on rather than simply for all tax revenue. Careful application of multiple regression models should produce overall predictions within 1 to 3 percent of actual collections, although forecasting success falls off dramatically when the economy turns from expansion to recession or when the economy is in severe recession.[17]

ECONOMETRIC MODELS

Econometric models estimate revenue within a simultaneous system of interdependent equations that express theoretical and empirical relationships between economic and fiscal variables.[18] These models are particularly important when revenue sources are not truly independent (as when the state personal income tax allows a deduction for the state sales tax) and may provide useful insights into the way state economies operate and the way in which they respond to external shocks. Economists generate forecasts from the system of equations by putting current values of key variables into the models and working them through the estimating equations. As a practical matter, however, states have generally found that the revenue predictions from econometric models are seldom more accurate than the estimates that multiple regression models produce, and the regression models are less expensive and have smaller data requirements.[19] The interrelationships that are inherent in these systems also have the impact of causing escalating errors, in that an error in one variable creates errors in others.

MICRODATA MODELS

The Office of Tax Analysis of the U.S. Treasury, the CBO, and some states use microsimulation from sample data files for tax forecasting (and for estimating the effect

---

[17]Accuracy matters much more for governments facing a severe need for low deficits in the executed budget, like states and localities. The federal government, with its deficit-running capacity, is less constrained. The CBO reports that since 1997, its individual income tax forecasts for one year ahead have had an average absolute error of about 11 percent, an error rate that would spell disaster for a state. Congressional Budget Office, "Improving CBO's Methodology for Projecting Individual Income Tax Revenues," Congressional Budget Office Background Paper, Washington, D.C., February 2011.

[18]The independent variables used in the multiple regression approach (possibly state personal income or U.S. GDP) often are the product of larger econometric models of the region of the nation. State and local governments obtain these estimates from numerous sources, including proprietary economic forecasting companies, universities, committees of technical advisors, and government economists.

[19]C. Kurt Zorn, "Issues and Problems in Econometric Forecasting: Guidance for Local Revenue Forecasters," *Public Budgeting & Finance 2* (Autumn 1982): 100–10.

of tax changes as well).[20] Sidebar 13–1 describes the steps in the CBO's forecasting method for its ten-year baseline projection of the federal individual income tax. In general, microdata approaches start with a computer file of tax-return data from a sample of taxpayers. Tax calculator models use this file to forecast how economic activity expected in the budget year tracks into its impact on the taxpayers in the sample. A computer program figures the tax liability for each taxpayer in the sample, the effect within the sample is expanded to the entire population it represents, and the result is the forecast of tax revenue for the new budget year. Full microsimulation models use the same files as the simpler tax calculator models, but they allow the underlying tax return to vary as taxpayers react to changes in tax policy.[21] The approach is particularly valuable in the analysis of policy changes, but it can also be employed in regular forecasting. Much effort is involved in selecting and preparing the microfile, so uses beyond the forecast improve the economic viability of such an effort. As is discussed later, the microfile is extremely helpful in fiscal note preparation, that is, in estimating the revenue consequences of legal changes in the tax structure. However, data in the microfile need to be refreshed as return years go by and modified when new tax provisions are enacted; the sampling must be a continuing process.

Choosing the Method

Revenue forecasts need methods that predict well enough to satisfy the requirements of those developing, adopting, and executing budgets and that can be explained to the satisfaction of executive and legislative tax and budget policy makers. They almost always use a combination of the several forecast approaches to predict the revenue baseline for the executive or legislative budget. In revenue forecasting, the ultimate choice would be whichever produces estimates closest to final yield, but that is something the forecaster finds out after the year is over, too late to be a guide. Among the factors that may enter into the choice of method are the following:

1. **The resources that are available.** The tools of cause-and-effect estimation—computers, software, and data analysts—have come within easy reach of every government with reliable electric supply. The resources that may not be available are sufficient time to perform the tasks necessary to prepare and test more complex estimating formats and the data necessary to employ some

---

[20]A federal approach is described in Howard Nester, "The Corporate Microdata File Employed by the Office of Tax Analysis," *Proceedings of the National Tax Association–Tax Institute of America 70* (1977): 293–306; and James M. Cilke and Roy A. Wyscarver, "The Individual Income Tax Simulation Model," in U.S. Department of Treasury, Office of Tax Analysis, *Compendium of Tax Research 1987* (Washington, D.C.: U.S. Government Printing Office, 1987). The microsimulation model developed for New York State is described in T. N. McCarty and T. H. Marks, "The Use of Microsimulation Models for Policy Analysis: The New York State Personal Income Tax," Proceedings of the *Eighty-Sixth Annual Conference on Taxation of the National Tax Association* (1994): 179–85.

[21]For revenue forecasting, tax calculator and full microsimulation models are not distinguishable in operation because there are no policy changes in the baseline revenue forecast.

Sidebar 13–1
The Congressional Budget Office Approach to Individual Income Tax Forecasting, Fiscal 2001–2011

Note: The CBO prepares forecasts for the fiscal year under way when the forecast is prepared, the budget year, and nine out-years.

Step 1. Begin with a sample of 1998 tax returns. "Age" the sample to match

- Projected demographic changes (such as in population and employment).
- Projected incomes based on the CBO's macroeconomic projections (such as for wages, interest, and dividends), outlay projections (for program benefits), and other projections (such as for capital gains and retirement income).

Result: the projected tax base for 1999 through 2011.

Step 2. Apply the tax calculator (a mathematical formula that represents the calculations required by the tax structure), incorporating

- Tax law parameters.
- CBO's macroeconomic projection of the consumer price index.

Result: projected tax liabilities on individual income tax returns for 1999 through 2011.

Step 3. Adjust projected tax liabilities for consistency with actual collections of owed taxes in 1998 through 2000.

Result: projected collections liabilities for 2001 through 2011.

Step 4. Convert projected liabilities into fiscal year payments by

- Breaking down liabilities by type of payment.
- Applying recent experience in the timing of payments.
- Adjusting for recent legislation not incorporated in step 2.
- Adding fiduciary taxes and back taxes.

Result: projected tax payments for fiscal years 2001 through 2011.

SOURCE: Congressional Budget Office, *Description of CBO's Models and Methods for Projecting Federal Revenues* (Washington, D.C.: Congressional Budget Office, 2001), 8.

---

approaches. For example, microsimulation approaches require complex data files on a sample of taxpaying entities; the approach cannot be contemplated unless the government has devoted the time and money to develop the files. Some governments simply choose to do forecasting on the cheap and do pretty well most of the time. No matter how much money is spent, nobody forecasts downturns very well, and, during the Great Recession, even the best state revenue forecasters got humbled by their inaccuracy.

2. **The materiality of the forecast.** How critical is an error in the forecast being made? If the revenue source constitutes but a small amount of the total, it is a poor use of analytic resources to devote much effort to forecasting it. A huge error in a small revenue source will have vastly smaller importance to budget execution than a small error in a huge source. Forecasting retail sales tax revenue is more important than forecasting the dog tax, so much more attention will be given to forecasting the former than the latter.

3. **The availability of historical revenue data.** Unless a long data series is available to test relationships under a considerable variety of economic and other environments, trying to create a reliable causal model is not likely to be productive. Indeed, an inadequately clean historical series can be a problem for more complex projection models themselves.

4. **The availability and quality of causal data.** A forecasting model with excellent statistical properties does not provide usable forecasts if causal data (the "drivers") needed for the forecast period are not available or if the available forecasts of them are unreliable. For instance, a regression equation may show a strong and reliable relationship between corporate profits and state corporate profits tax collections. Unless there is a good forecast of corporate profits available, this equation is useless for the revenue forecast.

5. **The time period of the forecast.** Long-term forecasts—the years beyond the out-years—will be done with cruder approaches than will budget-year forecasts. Technological, political, and economic forecasts are not terribly reliable in the longer term, and a revenue forecast based on "cause-and-effect" models cannot rise above problems in forecasts of the causes.

6. **The "explainability" of the forecast.** A forecast number is not enough. There must be a story that goes with it for the budget director, the legislative fiscal committees, and the media. "Black boxes" have difficulty surviving the first shaky episode.

These forecasts establish the amount of current revenue that will be available to budget for spending during the fiscal year. For many governments, their presentation is an event of considerable importance because it sets the tone for the deliberations—executive and legislative—that produce appropriations to operating agencies. Although there is no standard template for such presentations, they frequently are organized according to the following format:

1. **A Look Back:** a review of the forecast for the last budget year and why it was wrong;

2. **The Future Environment:** a prognosis of economic conditions for the next year for the nation and, for subnational government forecasts, for the state or local economy that will drive the revenue being forecast;

3. **The Approach:** an explanation of the general approach being used for the forecast; and

4. **The Forecast:** the forecast itself, divided among the major revenue sources.

You don't need to discuss all the approaches you tested before you picked the technique you ultimately used or why you picked the one that you did. It goes without saying that you used every approach available to you and you picked the one that you thought would yield the forecast closest to the actual. Your boss automatically assumes all that, and, if those assumptions aren't accurate, then you aren't long for the job. The presentation normally has charts and tables as appendices accompanying the actual forecast document.

Forecasts for the Long Term

Governments develop longer-term, multiyear revenue (and expenditure) outlooks that extend beyond the annual budget horizon. These prediction tasks vary widely in their sophistication, depending on the term for which they are prepared and on their intended use. They may be prepared, for instance, (1) to guide a city as it prepares an infrastructure development program that fits within likely revenue resources, (2) to show a credit-rating agency what revenue flows might be during the term of a loan to a state or local government, (3) to let planners know the probable financial implications from some major development (a theme park or a truck assembly plant, for instance) in the community, (4) to inform the public or oversight boards what the prospects are when a local government is on the brink of a severe financial emergency, (5) to inform the legislature and the executive what the longer-term implications are of the financial program that the government has in place or might be considering, or (6) as an element in a medium-term economic framework for the development of government policies within available revenues. Indeed, the Governmental Accounting Standards Board has proposed that state and local governments report five-year projections of cash inflows, outflows, and financial obligations as supplemental information in their financial statements. (The proposal is called "Economic Condition Reporting: Financial Projections.") Revenue predictions for the out-years have been particularly important for federal budget resolutions, especially as deficits turned to surpluses and lawmakers began discussion about new spending and tax reduction programs to get rid of the projected surpluses (which they decisively did). Longer-term outlooks can also be used to trace the likely impacts of demographic developments on finances.[22] These outlooks are vital for the development of Social Security and Medicare programs, in which present revenues are expected to finance benefits paid many years in the future.

The longer the outlook is, the less sophisticated the method should be—because of the great imprecision associated with economic, political, demographic, and technological factors that shape underlying forecasts. Available methods are generally the same as those used for budget-year revenue forecasts, although more attention has to be given to estimating the longer-term economic, demographic, and structural trends that themselves will drive the revenue flows, and huge uncertainties cloud the process. In addition, many are prepared using deterministic formulas ("rules of thumb") taken from experience in other jurisdictions. Medium-term forecasts—three, five, or

---

[22]An excellent example of such an outlook study: Congressional Budget Office, *The 2012 Long-Term Budget Outlook* (Washington, D.C.: U.S. Government Printing Office, 2012).

even ten budget out-years—done by the CBO and similar bodies to identify the impact of policy changes, demographic drift, macroeconomic conditions, and so on are done with considerable care to understand links and to identify policy options and are of considerable quality and value. The distant out-year forecasts are important primarily as a part of political drama and advance warning to inform about actions that need to be taken to avoid the forecasted consequences.

Longer forecasts are usually not tested against actuals in the way that budget-year estimates are, and they are replaced by shorter-term forecasts when budget-year choices are being deliberated. Indeed, they often cannot be so tested because they have served their purpose as warning devices and the dangerous practices have been corrected. It must be emphasized that, by their nature, such reports should not be viewed as budget forecasts. The five-year forecast for 2011 for Clearwater, Florida, identifies the role of such analysis: "A financial plan is not a forecast of what is certain to happen, but rather a device to highlight significant issues or problems that must be addressed if goals are to be achieved."[23] Seldom should the predictions be expected to provide great precision; they can, however, assemble information to help with difficult choices and to cause policy changes that keep the projected result from occurring.

The multiyear forecast ordinarily will be prepared with fairly simple, univariate extrapolation methods because forecasts of underlying economic forces in that more distant time horizon are particularly unreliable, because structural relationships between economic factors and the revenue system are not stable for long periods, and because it is quite likely that there will be substantial changes in revenue or expenditure programs over the longer horizon that make forecasts using the baseline conditions wrong. The extrapolations may be adjusted for known future events—if the city is going to host a world's fair in the forecast horizon, for instance—but usually future uncertainty is sufficient that adjustments to the simple projection are not supportable. Multiyear forecasts are not tested according to how close they come to actual outcomes because their purpose is often to warn against outcomes and elicit policy changes that will cause the forecast not to materialize. They are projections of a possible fiscal state based on certain specified assumptions. They cannot have the accuracy expected of financial statements—and accuracy isn't even an appropriate test for them. Longer-term predictions may provide a range of forecast values because of the considerable uncertainty involved; however, forecasts for preparation of the annual budget need to be single numbers.

Wrong Forecasts

There is one sad fact about your baseline forecast: you will be wrong. Expect it and get used to it. You will be wrong when you do your first, and you will be wrong when you have years of experience. The result is that you will seek to constrain your error so that you produce a trusted and reliable baseline. Billy Hamilton, a long-time revenue forecaster for the state of Texas, sums up the situation:

---

[23]City of Clearwater General Fund Five-Year Forecast, October 2011 [http://ebookbrowse.com/a-five-year-financial-forecast-pdf-d295192606].

After you have prepared your forecast, you report the results, and then put the results into some sort of tracking system and wait for collections to prove you wrong—because inevitably you will be. The only thing in question is how far off you are, and that makes a great deal of difference. It's like hitting in baseball. One-in-three hits over a career is a ticket to the Hall of Fame. One-in-five equals a short career and a somewhat less iconic future as an insurance salesperson. My boss demanded accuracy within 2 percent—and 2 percent lower than actual, not higher. Higher is a problem.[24]

In case you haven't gotten the message already: your forecast will be wrong. To test how bad your error is, check the leading newspaper in the capital city when the revenue results for a period (month, quarter, or year) are in. If the forecast results appear on the front page, your error is too big.[25]

Economic forecasts tend to be less accurate when the economy is in recession (the errors during the recession that began in December 2007 were huge in most states), but errors occur in happier times as well.[26] Perfection is not the standard against which any revenue forecasting method should be tested. The appropriate test is the accuracy of other feasible forecasting approaches, and there is evidence that formal forecasting methods are better than simple rules of thumb or pronouncements of politicians.[27] If another forecasting method that can be adopted within available resources can produce more accurate results for the budget, then it should be used. However, it, too, will be wrong eventually. The test can never be perfection, just better than feasible alternatives and not subject to political bias. When revenue forecasters look at their performance over time, they do not check the simple average percentage error because that would cause large over-forecasts to be canceled out by large under-forecasts and that would defeat the examination of accuracy. (Errors of -10% and $+10\%$ would cancel out, giving an average of 0%, which doesn't tell the true story.) They look at average *absolute* errors, so that positive and negative errors will not cancel. (An average of absolute errors of -10% and $+10\%$ would equal 10%, a better gauge of typical error.)

Should the forecast be deliberately pessimistic? That is an open question.[28] However, deliberately optimistic forecasts can be rejected as a violation of the fiscal sustainability principle.

---

[24]Billy Hamilton, "Sympathy for the Bedeviled Revenue Estimators," *State Tax Notes 51* (February 2, 2009): 350.

[25]It could be worse. Shortly after levying a tax on witches and fortune-tellers, the Romanian parliament began consideration of a law that would fine or imprison them if their predictions did not come true. One witch complained that the action should be taken against the cards they use in their procedures, not against the witches themselves. So maybe revenue forecasters could blame their evil computers? "Romania: False-Prophecy Penalty," *New York Times*, February 8, 2011.

[26]Michael W. McCracken, "How Accurate Are Forecasts in a Recession?" *National Economic Trends* (Federal Reserve Bank of St. Louis) (February 2009): 1. Inability to detect turning points and a bias toward optimism are the major problems.

[27]Stephen K. McNees, "An Assessment of 'Official' Economic Forecasts," *New England Economic Review* (July/August 1995): 13–23.

[28]It is an open question in international discussions as well. See Ian Lienert, "Should Budgetary Revenue Projections Be Deliberately Pessimistic?" Public Financial Management Blog (International Monetary Fund), January 14, 2009 [http://blog-pfm.imf.org/pfmblog/2009/01/should-budgetary-revenue-projections-be-deliberately-pessimistic-.html]. One study of thirty-three countries found that forecasts had an overall positive bias (too much money), greater bias in booms, and more bias in the three-year horizon than in shorter horizons. Jeffrey A. Frankel, "Over-Optimism in Forecasts by Official Budget Agencies and Its Implications," National Bureau of Economic Research Working Paper 17239, Cambridge, Mass., July 2011.

Revenue Estimating (or Scoring)

Revenue estimating (called scoring in the federal system, tax costing in the United Kingdom, and preparation of fiscal notes in many states) gives the government a prediction of how revenue will change from the baseline if a new law is passed or administrative processes change. The revenue estimate is the difference between receipts under the current law and receipts under a proposed change in the law. Governments need to know what the fiscal impact will be of legislation that is being deliberated, especially revenue measures being considered. By how much would revenue increase if the personal exemption in the income tax was reduced by $500, or by how much would revenue fall if the capital gains tax rate was reduced by another 10 percentage points? The pay-as-you-go (PAYGO) requirement in the federal budget system demanded these estimates, most states have prepared such fiscal impact notes for many years, and reports from the Senate Finance and House Ways and Means Committees have carried these estimates since the 1974 Congressional Budget and Impoundment Control Act.[29] The Office of Tax Analysis of the Department of Treasury prepares the executive branch revenue estimates.[30] From the legislative side, the Joint Committee on Taxation scores all tax legislation, and the CBO scores tariffs and user charges (along with spending proposals). The CBO incorporates these estimates from any legislation that passes into its ten-year baseline forecast. For states, fiscal notes attached to revenue proposals often come from legislative fiscal staff, although they may also come from the state budget agency or the state tax department.[31]

Revenue estimates often must be rough because existing data sets do not categorize information in the same way that the proposed legislation does. For instance, the revenue loss from a sales tax exemption for grass seed purchases by homeowners in blighted urban areas would be a difficult estimate because neither sales tax collection nor household spending data are tracked to that detail in total, let alone by geographic areas. However, even when developed only as rough approximations, the estimates provide an important discipline for the budget process. They estimate the change in the baseline. Federal estimates normally are for five years; state estimates may be much shorter.

These estimates usually are prepared from a sample of existing returns, supplemented with additional data sources as necessary. In effect, they represent microsimulations, although at widely varying degrees of sophistication—the Office of Tax Analysis uses an extremely complex model created from a large sample of individual tax returns, whereas a state legislative service bureau may use an extremely informal

---

[29]The revenue-impact estimating method used by Congress is described in Joint Committee on Taxation, "Overview of Revenue Estimating Procedures and Methodologies Used by the Staff of the Joint Committee on Taxation," JCX-1-05, Washington, D.C., February 2, 2005.

[30]Emil M. Sunley and Randall D. Weiss, "The Revenue Estimating Process," *Tax Notes 51* (June 10, 1991): 1299–1314.

[31]State scoring practices are described and analyzed in John L. Mikesell, "Revenue Estimation/Scoring by States: An Overview of Experience and Current Practices with Particular Attention to the Role of Dynamic Methods," *Public Budgeting & Finance* 32 (Summer 2012): 1–24.

estimate process. The tax returns give information about transactions currently reported in the tax system and, to the extent the new provision changes those reported lines, can provide a basis for the estimate. However, not all proposed changes will be to transactions on those returns. Therefore, there usually needs to be information taken from outside the tax system.

There is continuing political debate about the protocol to be used in preparation of revenue estimates. Three systems are identifiable.

1. **Completely static estimation/scoring.** This approach assumes that the change in the tax law will have no impact on taxpayer behavior or on the level of economic activity. The estimate assumes that taxpayers will not alter their behavior in the face of the new tax structure. The estimate is based on tax return data, plus supplemental data about taxpayers that may be necessary to estimate the new tax base for each return, and a tax calculator that computes the tax paid on each return under both the baseline law and the proposed changed law. For example, a static estimate of changing the capital gains tax rate would use capital gains reported on each tax return and recalculate the tax at the new rate instead of at the rate under existing law. Adding all returns gives the impact estimate. Revenue estimators usually use this approach only when they have no basis at all for estimating the degree of taxpayer response to a change in the tax law. In the absence of trustworthy data, tax professionals prefer the fiscally conservative approach to their estimates. Neither of the federal estimators—the Joint Committee on Taxation and the Congressional Budget Office—regularly uses a static approach, and neither do most state entities charged with preparing estimates.

2. **Micro-dynamic estimation/scoring.** The approach that revenue estimators normally employ is to recognize that taxpayers do respond when the tax law changes. In other words, estimates or scores are not static. The approach recognizes that taxpayer behavior will shift in response to the incentives added or subtracted by the tax law and, as a result, the tax base with the new law will differ from what it would have been under the old law. The microeconomic behavioral effects may include shifts in the timing of transactions, changes in portfolio holdings, shifts in consumption, use of tax planning and avoidance strategies to reduce liability, changes in work effort, and so on—all impacts that would involve microeconomic behavior. For instance, (1) a higher tax on cigarettes will cause fewer cigarettes to be sold, (2) a lower capital gains tax rate will induce businesses and individuals to realize capital gains that would otherwise have been deferred and to convert ordinary income to formats judged to be capital gains, and (3) a new tax credit for college tuition will induce more students to attend college—so static estimates of revenue from these tax proposals would need to be adjusted for these effects.[32] In these instances, simple use of historical data

---

[32] A CBO analysis of the impact of increasing the cigarette excise tax clearly shows the way in which microeconomic and behavioral responses are integrated into the CBO's work. Congressional Budget Office, *Raising the Excise Tax on Cigarettes: Effects on Health and the Federal Budget* (Washington, D.C.: Congressional Budget Office, 2102).

on cigarette consumption, capital gains, and college tuition would not be entirely sufficient to produce the estimate. The problem is that the effects are difficult to gauge because the data required may be unavailable and the size of taxpayers' response (the demand and supply elasticities) is unknown. Revenue estimates at the federal level and in most states do include these microeconomic impacts when estimating or scoring tax law changes when there is a way to include them. In addition, there is no meaningful debate among professionals that such adjustments are appropriate. The greatest barrier is always the extent to which there is a firm and reliable basis for making the behavioral adjustments.

3. **Macro-dynamic estimation/scoring.** Macroeconomic dynamic scoring adds the impact on revenue from changes in outputs, interest rates, or other macroeconomic elements to the impact from micro-dynamic scoring (the micro-dynamic score is the starting point for the analysis). The microeconomic dynamic estimates work under an assumption of fixed total economic activity (GDP or gross state product). Macroeconomic dynamic scoring seeks to add to the estimate the effect of any change in total economic activity on tax collections. In other words, a tax reduction may have a macroeconomic impact on aggregate economic activity, inflation, interest rates, and so on, and these effects will cause the tax bases to differ from what they would have been without the tax reduction. Any resulting change in tax revenue should be included in the estimate. The static estimate and even the micro-dynamic estimate thus overstate the amount of the revenue cost from the tax reduction. For instance, the reduced capital gains tax rate may increase aggregate economic activity, and that will cause more tax to be collected from several federal taxes, all of which would be included as part of the estimated impact of the tax reduction. Federal estimates traditionally have not included a macroeconomic component, largely because of considerable uncertainty about whether effects exist and the great cost of systematically trying to find out what the effects are, although both the CBO and the Joint Committee on Taxation have developed some macro-dynamic estimates (they do not change the traditional micro-dynamic estimates by very much).[33] Furthermore, there is the added problem of guessing what the Federal Reserve monetary response would be to any fiscal program with considerable macroeconomic impact. The legislatures in a few states do require that estimates include macroeconomic effects, however. Much of the argument about including the macroeconomic component in revenue estimates centers around political efforts to make the official revenue loss estimate of reduced tax rates or enhanced tax preferences lower than it would be with only static and

---

[33]Congressional Budget Office, *Analyzing the Economic and Budgetary Effects of a 10 Percent Cut in Income Tax Rates* (Washington, D.C.: Congressional Budget Office, 2005). Depending on assumptions, as much as one-third of the revenue lost from the reduction might be made up in a decade. The cut would not pay for itself. The Joint Committee on Taxation's experiments are described in "Testimony of the Staff of the Joint Committee on Taxation before the House Committee on Ways and Means Regarding Economic Modeling," JCX-48-11, Washington, D.C., September 21, 2011.

microeconomic components included. Evidence does indicate that use of macro-dynamic scoring makes only a small difference in the estimates. The dream of self-financed tax reductions—that is, tax cuts that pay for themselves with increased tax revenue—is just not supported by the evidence.[34]

Although revenue forecasts are keenly watched and tested against actual revenue collections, revenue estimates are seldom judged for accuracy.[35] Even the federal government, with its great concern and staffing for measuring and evaluating performance, seldom evaluates scoring. A CBO report states: "[I]t is generally not possible to assess the accuracy of past revenue estimates of enacted legislation. Most legislative provisions are part of a large mix of changes, and identifying the revenues associated with a particular provision is impossible. Often, subsequent legislation obscures the effect of previous actions."[36] The estimate matters when the legislation is being considered—particularly when PAYGO requirements are in place or when balanced budget requirements constrain fiscal actions—and then it is typically forgotten and not tested against actual data, particularly when the legislation involves a change in an existing tax rather than the adoption of a new tax. When it is a new tax, it is possible to compare the estimates with the actual. For instance, part of the federal health care program adopted in 2010 was a new 10 percent excise tax on indoor tanning services (the tanning tax), applicable from July 1, 2010. The Joint Committee on Taxation estimated that tax would yield $200 million per year, but through the first nine months of collection, the tax had produced $54.4 million, far less than the expected yield. The estimate anticipated 25,000 businesses would be affected by the tax, but only 10,300 had registered.[37] This illustrates the difficulty with scoring a new tax: Was the analysis wrong, was administration ineffective, or was it a combination of those factors? No one knows, but estimating is tough work when it involves analysis with minimal reliable data to use as the basis. Usually, nobody knows whether the estimates turned out to be right or wrong.[38] Federal battles have usually been about tax estimates, not forecasts.

---

[34]Expenditure proposals have macroeconomic effects that can be at least as large as tax reductions. However, the strongest proponents for dynamic scoring of tax provisions have not made an argument for extending the principles to the spending side of the budget.

[35]Edward D. Kleinbard and Patrick Driessen, "A Revenue Estimate Case Study: The Repatriation Holiday Revisited," *Tax Notes* (September 22, 2008): 1191–202, is an exception. They both review the Joint Committee on Taxation's estimate of the foreign dividend repatriation holiday and explain its estimation process.

[36]Congressional Budget Office, *Projecting Federal Tax Revenues and the Effect of Changes in Tax Law* (Washington, D.C.: Congressional Budget Office, 1998), i.

[37]Treasury Inspector General for Tax Administration, "Affordable Care Act: The Number of Taxpayers Filing Tanning Excise Tax Returns Is Lower than Expected," Reference Number 2011-40-115, Washington, D.C., September 22, 2011.

[38]But sometimes wrong estimates can be exciting. For instance, in 2000, Arizona offered a large tax advantage for propane-burning motor vehicles. The estimate was for lost revenue of $3–$10 million. Part of the way through the first year, lost revenue appeared to be around $420 million: the person doing the estimate did not see an error in writing the legislation that effectively made the program open-ended and miscalculated exactly how attractive the program would be. Jim Carlton, "If You Paid Half Price for That New SUV, You Must Be in Arizona—With Big Rebates to Car Buyers, Clean-Air Law Cleaned Out the State's Coffers Instead," *Wall Street Journal*, October 26, 2000, A-1.

Tax Expenditure Budgets

The Congressional Budget and Impoundment Act of 1974 defines tax expenditures to be "revenue losses attributable to provisions of the federal tax laws which allow a special exclusion, exemption, or deduction from gross income or which provide a special credit, a preferential rate of tax, or a deferral of tax liability." The tax expenditure budget, an accumulation of the estimates of revenue lost through these preferences, thus reflects the dual nature of every tax system—part to generate revenue and part to distribute subsidies—and the conflicting nature of provisions in the system: some provisions are in the tax system to implement traditional tax policy and should be judged according to the criteria of taxation (they raise revenue), whereas others intend to favor certain economic activities or to relieve personal hardships and should be judged according to budget policy criteria. Discussions about broadening the tax base (either to raise additional revenue or to permit lower statutory rates) focus on the tax expenditures. If the base is to be broadened, it will be by elimination of some of these tax preferences.

A tax expenditure is equivalent to having the taxpayer pay the tax that would be owed without the special provision and simultaneously receive a government grant equal to the amount of tax in that provision. A direct expenditure and a tax expenditure are comparable because both provide a benefit to a recipient and reduce public resources available for other uses. However, they look different politically. As Eugene Steuerle points out, tax expenditures "allow politicians to appear to be reducing the size of government (reducing taxes) while actually increasing it (increasing spending)."[39] This represents gross hypocrisy and a clear violation of fiscal transparency. The tax expenditure concept and the tax expenditure budget are both tools for adding transparency because they identify who is receiving these otherwise hidden government subsidies.

The development of a tax expenditure budget is "a classification exercise: dividing the provisions of the tax system into a benchmark or norm and a series of deviations from that norm."[40] But what is normal? The practical problem is deciding what components are part of the *baseline* and what components represent the *deviations* from the norm that constitute a tax preference to be measured by the tax expenditure budget. By classifying most of the tax system as part of the norm, the size of the tax expenditure is reduced. Conversely, by defining the norm narrowly, more provisions in the law become suspect, and the tax expenditure budget is large.

Because there are so many specific translations of tax concepts into tax structures, any tax expenditure budget demands a careful explanation of what the baseline means. The federal budget for 2010 describes two alternative specifications for baseline:

---

[39]Eugene Steuerle, "Summers on Social Tax Expenditures: Where He's Wrong ... or at Least Incomplete," *Tax Notes* 89 (December 18, 2000): 1639.
[40]Organization for Economic Cooperation and Development, *Tax Expenditures: Recent Experiences* (Paris: Organization for Economic Cooperation and Development, 1996), 9.

The normal tax baseline is patterned on a practical variant of a comprehensive income tax, which defines income as the sum of consumption and the change in net wealth in a given period of time. The normal tax baseline allows personal exemptions, a standard deduction, and deduction of expenses incurred in earning income. It is not limited to a particular structure of tax rates, or by a specific definition of the taxpaying unit.

The reference tax law baseline is also patterned on a comprehensive income tax, but it is closer to existing law. Reference law tax expenditures are limited to special exceptions from a generally provided tax rule that serve programmatic functions in a way that is analogous to spending programs. Provisions under the reference law baseline are generally tax expenditures under the normal tax baseline, but the reverse is not always true.[41]

The normal tax defines the ideal or standard tax, the tax that follows the textbook concept of what structure would assign shares of the cost of government in a way consistent with the logic of the tax. It starts with a fundamental principle (notice the track from the Haig-Simons comprehensive definition of *income* here) and allows some appropriate adjustments to define *normal* or *reference*. Differences from that definition constitute tax expenditures. The reference law approach works from a benchmark law, and deviations from that benchmark represent tax expenditures.

Existing federal tax expenditures encourage selected economic activities (investment, housing, municipal borrowing, support of charities, etc.) or reduce taxpayers' liability in special circumstances (deduction of medical expenses, casualty loss deduction, etc.). (Sidebar 13–2 describes an alternate process developed by the Joint Committee on Taxation in 2008.) Estimates by both Congress (the Joint Committee on Taxation) and the president (Department of Treasury) are a regular part of the executive budget and other presentations.[42] Table 13–1 presents estimates of the income tax expenditures with a revenue impact of $20 billion or more, according to the Treasury. Notice that many of these larger tax expenditures are quite popular with the American public and often have organized interest groups that support the preference. That is why serious action on federal income tax broadening is so difficult. Estimates also are prepared on a regular, although not always annual, basis in about forty of the states.[43] Appendix 13–1 describes the criteria and measurement principles that Minnesota uses.

---

[41]Office of Management and Budget, *Budget of the Government of the United States, Fiscal Year 2013, Analytical Perspectives* (Washington, D.C.: U.S. Government Printing Office, 2012), 248.

[42]They may be in revenue or outlay-equivalent terms. The latter estimates the dollar amount of direct spending that would provide taxpayers the net benefits equaling what they receive from the tax expenditure.

[43]An analysis and evaluation of state tax expenditure budgets appears in John L. Mikesell, "Tax Expenditure Budgets, Budget Policy, and Tax Policy: Confusion in the States," *Public Budgeting & Finance*, 22 (Winter 2002): 34–51; and John L. Mikesell, "The Tax Expenditure Concept at the State Level: Conflict between Fiscal Control and Sound Tax Policy," *Proceedings of the Ninety-fourth Annual Conference on Taxation of the National Tax Association* (Washington, D.C.: National Tax Association, 2001). The states in general fail to clearly identify the normal structures upon which their tax expenditure estimates are based. This problem is particularly apparent in the treatment of sales taxes in their tax expenditure budgets: John L. Mikesell, "State Tax Policy and State Sales Taxes: What Tax Expenditure Budgets Tell Us about Sales Taxes," *American Review of Public Administration* 42 (March 2012): 131–51.

Sidebar 13–2
Joint Committee on Taxation Approach to Tax Expenditure Measures

The Joint Committee on Taxation introduced a new approach to tax expenditure measurement in 2008. The reconsideration emerged because the traditional analysis did not coincide with any generally accepted formal definition of *net income* as a starting point, but often appeared to be designed with bias to particular tax reforms. As such, it wasn't the neutral analytic tool or baseline that it pretended to be, but rather was an agenda for restructuring the Internal Revenue Code. The problems hinged around the definition of the "normal" tax. That argument made the resulting tax expenditure measures less useful than they should be. The fight was about what the normal should be, and the discussion did not focus on the tax expenditures. The idea of what tax expenditure analysis was supposed to do had been subverted.

The Joint Committee proposed a new approach, one that generally seeks to avoid defining what the "normal" tax would be, arguing that its alternate approach would be more principled and neutral. The new approach identifies as tax subsidies those provisions in the tax law that are deliberately inconsistent with an identifiable general rule of the present law (no relationship to a hypothetical "normal" law) and cause revenue loss. If the subsidy results in the collection of more revenue than the general rule, the subsidy may be negative. The Joint Committee approach then seeks to determine what constitutes the general rule and what are the exceptions under the Internal Revenue Code. The tax subsidy category is then subdivided into three subcategories: (1) tax transfers, which are payments to persons without regard to their income tax liability (seen as the clearest use of the tax system to substitute for spending programs); (2) social spending, which includes provisions intended to subsidize or induce behavior not related to the generation of business income and subsidy related to the supply of labor; and (3) business synthetic spending, which is related to the production of business or investment income. The approach also adds a category called tax-induced structural distortions to allow for Internal Revenue Code elements that do not represent clear deviations from a general rule, but that do impact economic decisions and impose efficiency loss (mostly including carryovers from the Joint Committee's old tax expenditure system).

In short, the Joint Committee's conception moves toward its identified general rules of the present tax law as the reference baseline and identifies tax subsidies as deviations from that. It moves from the economic measure of "normal" income tax to a reference base that starts from the tax solely defined by Congress. What is clear is that federal tax expenditures have grown over the years, in terms of both number and dollar impact, even as the tax expenditure reports are published and distributed on schedule. Whether this new approach, by attempting to avoid the normative arguments about the definition of a normal structure, will help stem that tide is an open question.

The new approach is described in detail in *A Reconsideration of Tax Expenditure Analysis, Prepared by the Staff of the Joint Committee on Taxation,* JCX-37-08 (Washington, D.C.: Joint Committee on Taxation, May 12, 2008); and in *Estimates of Federal Tax Expenditures for Fiscal Years 2008–2012, Prepared for the House Committee on Ways and Means and the Senate Committee on Finance by the Staff of the Joint Committee on Taxation* (Washington, D.C.: U.S. Government Printing Office, 2008).

Table 13–1

Revenue Effect of Federal Income Tax Expenditures: Provisions with Impact above $20 Billion

Provision	Amount ($ Millions)
Exclusion of employer contributions for medical insurance premiums and medical care	180,580
Deductibility of mortgage interest on owner-occupied homes	100,910
401(k) plans	72,740
Accelerated depreciation of machinery and equipment (normal tax method)	33,180
Exclusion of net imputed rental income	51,080
Capital gains (except agriculture, timber, iron ore, and coal)	62,040
Employer plans	52,330
Deductibility of nonbusiness state and local taxes other than on owner-occupied homes	46,260
Deductibility of charitable contributions, other than education and health	39,770
Exclusion of interest on public purpose state and local bonds	36,210
Deferral of income from controlled foreign corporations (normal tax method)	41,810
Step-up basis of capital gains at death	23,860
Capital gains exclusion on home sales	23,440
Social Security benefits for retired workers	25,620
Exclusion of interest on life insurance savings	25,150
Deductibility of state and local property tax on owner-occupied homes	22,320
Treatment of qualified dividends	21,900

SOURCE: Office of Management and Budget, *Budget of the Government of the United States, Fiscal year 2013, Analytical Perspectives* (Washington, D.C.: U.S. Government Printing Office, 2012).

Tax policy is generally predisposed against tax expenditures—assuming the normal structure is rationally designed—because the differential provisions distort business and household decisions, because their implementation complicates the tax system, because they continue without regular evaluation and legislative approval (they lack the separate authorization/appropriation steps that characterize direct spending in the federal system), because they are open-ended in amount, and because they are not transparent in enactment, in delivery of benefits, or in overall magnitude. It is hard to associate an approach to subsidization that is hidden, permanent, and open-ended with good governance. These same features of tax expenditures make them a great way for special interests to receive subsidies. However, not all tax expenditures are bad because conducting some budget policy through the tax system may be a sensible, quick, inexpensive, and feasible approach in comparison with alternative approaches (e.g., direct expenditure or regulation) to achieving a particular objective. There is no need to establish an administrative structure to operate tax expenditure assistance, and the tax expenditure may reach a wider population of beneficiaries than would a freestanding program that requires special application.

The critical stage in development of a useful tax expenditure budget is that of defining the normal tax, that is, deciding what basic tax policy is. This question is currently under debate at the federal level. Federal budgets presented in the later years of the administration of President George W. Bush, to stress that the current federal income tax is actually a sort of hybrid income-consumption tax, added tax expenditure estimates under a consumption tax base norm. Of course, that causes a different pattern of tax expenditures than under the traditional income tax base norm. In particular, the several tax provisions providing preferences for saving are no longer tax expenditures. The most obvious of these are the several exclusions for contributions for retirement plans shown in Table 13–1. These represent exclusions of savings, so if the normal tax base was consumption, they would become elements that would need to be deducted to produce the normal base (income minus saving equals consumption). This illustrates why a clear consensus on normal tax policy must be reached before the tax expenditure budget can have any practical meaning or utility for policy discussions. If you cannot agree on the basic tax policy, then doing a tax expenditure budget is hardly worth the effort.

A properly drawn definition of a benchmark or normal structure provides a defense *against* arbitrary and capricious tax policy. Most fiscal experts would agree with the Surrey and McDaniel conclusion: "[U]nless attention is paid to tax expenditures, a country does not have its tax policy or its budget policy under full control."[44] The same message applies for American state governments. Without a proper tax expenditure budget, a government has no gauge of the extent to which its revenue system is being used for nonrevenue purposes.[45] According to the Joint Committee on Taxation, from 1972 to 2007, the count of tax expenditures increased from around 60 to 170, and tax expenditures are now 140 percent of federal non-defense discretionary spending.[46] Is that evidence that the process has tax expenditures under control?

Conclusion

Revenue prediction, a portion of administration particularly vital for budget preparation, has three significant divisions: forecasting collections in future fiscal years, estimating the impact of proposed changes in tax law, and calculating revenues currently sacrificed by existing elements of the tax law. The first activity normally produces excellent accuracy (1 to 3 percent error) when it is professionally done and when the forecasts are not politically driven. Errors are usually greater when the country enters a recession. Revenue estimates are important to let policy makers know what the fiscal cost of their policies is likely to be. Tax expenditure budgets tally the revenue effects of provisions in existing tax laws. The practice of revenue prediction, especially forecasting and estimating, has a high degree of art mixed with the quantitative science in its real-world application.

---

[44]Stanley S. Surrey and Paul R. McDaniel, "The Tax Expenditure Concept and the Legislative Process," in *The Economics of Taxation*, ed. Henry J. Aaron and Michael J. Boskin (Washington, D.C.: Brookings Institution, 1980), 124.

[45]Tax expenditure budgets are common in other national fiscal systems as well: Hana Polackova Brixi, Christian Valenduc, and Zhicheng Li Swift, *Tax Expenditures—Shedding Light on Government Spending through the Tax System, Lessons from Developed and Transition Economies* (Washington, D.C.: World Bank, 2004).

[46]Daniel R. Mullins and John L. Mikesell, "Innovations in Budgeting and Financial Management," in *The Oxford Handbook of American Bureaucracy*, ed. Robert F. Durant (New York: Oxford University Press, 2010), 754–55.

QUESTIONS AND EXERCISES

1. A state intangibles tax is levied on the holders of intangible personal property in the state. The tax base is market value of the item of property on the last day of December; for most taxpayers, intangible holdings in December establish tax due by April 15 of the next year (paid with the annual income tax return). Tax rates have been 0.0025 percent, but a phaseout of the tax begins in calendar year 2014. In that year, the rate will be 0.00233 and in the following year, 0.00217.

   Fiscal year (July 1–June 30) collections for the tax from 2006 through 2012 follow, along with estimates previously prepared for fiscal 2013 and 2014 and calendar-year data on state personal income. Both income and collections are in millions.

	Collections ($)	Personal Income ($)
2006	15.6	26,158
2007	17.8	27,776
2008	14.7	26,816
2009	14.1	26,206
2010	16.6	34,132
2011	17.4	36,487
2012	19.2	40,279
2013 (forecast)	19.4	Not available
2014 (forecast)	19.6	Not available

   Estimate revenue from the tax for fiscal years 2014, 2015, and 2016 using any method that is appropriate. (An independent commission has estimated state personal income for the three years to equal $48,660 million in 2014, $52,800 million in 2015, and $57,500 million in 2016.) Describe the method you used and indicate why it is better than other alternatives available.

2. a. Who does revenue forecasts for your state budget? Is it an executive branch or a legislative branch agency or a consensus process?

   b. What entity in your state government prepares revenue estimates for tax legislation? Are the estimates easily available on a state website?

   c. Does your state develop a tax expenditure budget? If so, what are the largest tax expenditure categories for the two taxes that generate the most revenue for the state? Does the tax expenditure budget identify the normal structure for each of those taxes?

3. A state in the southeastern region of the United States operates state liquor stores. Prices at the stores are set in the following fashion: add 41 percent to the wholesale price at which the system acquires the product. To that is added an excise of $8.10 per case. The state sold roughly 36 million cases. The state, however, increases the excise rate to $9.10 per case, and a tentative revenue estimate shows that excise revenue will increase by $36 million. The state economist objects: "The demand for liquor is inelastic, so sales will be relatively insensitive to

a tax increase. Therefore, revenue will increase by more than $36 million." What is your reaction to this objection?

4. Revenue estimates are sometimes at the mercy of the administrative process. Suppose you are developing estimates of corporate income tax collections for a state. In your review of historical data, you find that a large, but quantitatively imprecise amount of collections was moved from one fiscal year to another because overlapping vacation schedules caused the processing system to shut down in the last two weeks of a recent fiscal year. How might you handle this problem in preparing your estimate, both in perfecting the historical data and in delivering your estimate?

5. Your state plans to adopt a tuition tax credit for college students. How would you estimate the revenue impact of this provision? How would the decision to use static, micro-dynamic, or macro-dynamic approaches influence your estimate?

6. When the Soviet bloc broke up in the early 1990s, the Republic of Vardar declared its independence. As the country established a monetary system, democratic processes, and a controlled fiscal system, the early problems of hyperinflation, unemployment, and declining standards of living slowly subsided. In late 1997, the country initiated a personal income tax, heavily dependent on taxes withheld by large employers on wages and salaries, but still broad in coverage. The country has been collecting about 30 percent of its tax revenue from that tax, although a law passed in 2000 is expected to reduce personal income tax collections by 25 percent in the short term. The lower tax rates are expected to stimulate economic activity and to encourage business to move from the shadow to the official (taxpaying) economy, so some of the revenue loss will ultimately be recovered. The Ministry of Finance forecasts collections of 7,789,000.0 thousand markka (MK) for 2001. Data on tax collections are reported below.

a. From this information, would you advise the Ministry to revise its 2001 forecast? Explain.

b. What factors may influence the patterns you see in the data?

c. What other issues would you pursue in addition to the data presented here? Collections are in MK thousand.

	1998	1999	2000	2001
January	668,534.0	625,149.1	559,070.9	714,981.0
February	782,026.6	754,396.9	874,000.0	575,115.0
March	738,856.7	811,506.7	988,047.2	583,592.0
April	826,622.9	880,075.8	916,030.7	586,743.0
May	678,031.1	756,507.9	800,876.8	
June	736,974.5	831,054.5	940,975.1	
July	824,343.7	978,485.6	967,098.4	
August	668,708.8	743,718.4	841,267.5	
September	766,271.3	898,210.0	874,308.1	
October	759,679.8	846,494.2	887,091.4	
November	742,371.5	847,950.2	936,090.7	
December	984,911.2	1,259,467.1	1,204,961.7	

7. These are the collections from a state liquor excise tax for a number of years. There have been no changes in the structure or administration of the tax in that period of time. Collections are in thousands of dollars, and fiscal years end on June 30. Your job is to forecast collections for fiscal years 2016 and 2017.

2006: 144,990

2007: 153,831

2008: 162,083

2009: 170,469

2010: 193,181

2011: 195,179

2012: 212,501

2013: 223,036

2014: 239,494

APPENDIX 13–1

The State of Minnesota Tax Expenditure Budget: Criteria and Measurement

The state of Minnesota prepares a tax expenditure budget on a two-year cycle, delivered on the off-year from the governor's biennial budget. It is notable for the care taken to make it a meaningful document by setting clear standards for identifying the tax expenditures and can serve as a useful model for any jurisdiction considering the development of such a budget. The selection that follows is taken from the 2012–2015 document.[47] Notice the section at the end that discusses the difference between the tax expenditure budget estimates and the numbers that would appear in a revenue estimate for a proposed change in tax law.

The Tax Expenditure Concept

"State governmental policy objectives are sought to be achieved both by direct expenditure of governmental funds and by the granting of special and selective tax relief or tax expenditures." (Minnesota Statutes, Section 270C.11, Subd. 1, in part, reprinted in Appendix A.)

Tax expenditures are statutory provisions which reduce the amount of revenue that would otherwise be generated, including exemptions, deductions, credits, and lower tax rates. These provisions are called "expenditures" because they are similar to direct spending programs. Both tax expenditures and direct expenditures are used for public policy goals, such as funding or encouraging specified activities or providing financial assistance to persons, businesses, or groups in particular situations.

---

[47]Tax Research Division, Minnesota Department of Revenue, *State of Minnesota Tax Expenditure Budget, Fiscal Year 2012–2015* (St. Paul: Minnesota Department of Revenue, 2012).

A tax expenditure is different from a direct spending program in two major respects:

- A direct spending program continues only if funds are appropriated for each budget period, but the continuation of a tax expenditure does not require legislative action. Unless a tax expenditure provision has an expiration date, it continues indefinitely.
- Direct spending programs are itemized on the expenditure side of the budget. Tax expenditures are reflected on the revenue side of the budget and are not itemized. Revenues shown in the state budget are net of tax expenditures.

The Purpose of the Tax Expenditure Budget

The purpose of the tax expenditure budget is to provide information to facilitate a regular, comprehensive legislative review of tax expenditure provisions. Tax expenditure provisions are identified and listed in the report, along with the legal citation, explanation, history, and fiscal impact for each provision.

Minnesota Statutes, Section 270.067, enacted in 1983, required a tax expenditure budget to be submitted as a supplement to the governor's biennial budget. In 1996 the law was changed so that the report is due in each even-numbered year, rather than at the same time as the governor's biennial budget in the odd-numbered years. In 2005 the statute was recodified as Section 270C.11 (reprinted in Appendix A).

Tax Expenditure Criteria

Not every exemption, deduction, credit, or lower tax rate is a tax expenditure. A conceptual framework governs the identification of tax expenditure provisions. Each tax provision is evaluated against a list of criteria. Seven criteria are used to determine if a provision is a tax expenditure. Some of the criteria are taken directly from the authorizing statute; some are based on concepts used in the preparation of federal tax expenditure reports; and others are based on what is believed to be a logical application of the tax expenditure concept. A provision must meet all the criteria in order to be a tax expenditure.

A provision is a tax expenditure if it:

- has an impact on a tax that is applied statewide;
- confers preferential treatment;
- results in reduced tax revenue in the applicable fiscal years;
- is not included as an expenditure item in the state budget;
- is included in the defined tax base for that tax;
- is not subject to an alternative tax; and
- can be amended or repealed by a change in state law.

The first four criteria are based on the statute requiring the tax expenditure budget.

Statewide Tax: The tax expenditure budget is required by statute to include every state tax and any local tax that is applied statewide. A local tax imposed pursuant to a special law is not included in the report. Only taxes that contain tax expenditure provisions are included in the report.

Preferential Treatment: Preferential treatment is a key concept in determining tax expenditures. The first sentence of the authorizing statute, quoted at the beginning of this introduction, uses the words "special and selective." Also, the statutory definition of a tax expenditure uses the word "certain." Minnesota Statutes, Section 270C.11, Subd. 6(1)(emphasis added):

"Tax expenditure" means a tax provision which provides a gross income definition, deduction, exemption, credit, or rate for *certain* persons, types of income, transactions, or property that results in reduced tax revenue.

If a provision is not preferential, it is not a tax expenditure. The personal exemption for the individual income tax is not preferential because the amount of the exemption is the same for each taxpayer, spouse, and dependent. Likewise, the graduated rate structure of the individual income tax is not considered a tax expenditure because each taxpayer with the same amount of tax base pays at the same rate.

Reduction in Revenue: In the statute quoted above, a requirement is that the provision "results in reduced tax revenue." A provision that would otherwise qualify is not considered a tax expenditure if it is not being used or is not likely to be used during fiscal years 2012 through 2015.

The federal law (Congressional Budget Act of 1974, Public Law 93–344) that requires a list of tax expenditures to be included with the federal budget includes in its definition of tax expenditures "provisions of the Federal tax laws which allow . . . a deferral of liability." The Minnesota law does not specifically mention deferral of liability. However, this concept has been adopted in the preparation of the report because a deferral of liability results in reduced tax revenue for a given year.

A deferral of liability involves the time value of money and affects primarily the individual income and corporate franchise taxes. A deferral can result either from postponing the time when income is recognized or from accelerating the deduction of expenses. Taxable income is lower in that year than it would be otherwise, and an adjustment is made in a future year. The deferral of liability is similar to an interest-free loan for the taxpayer.

Not an Expenditure in the State Budget: The tax expenditure budget is intended to supplement the regular state budget and therefore does not include provisions that are itemized as expenditures in the state budget. The state-funded property tax relief provisions are similar to tax expenditures, but they are not included in this report because they are itemized in the state budget as expenditures.

Included in Defined Tax Base: The tax base for each tax must be clearly defined so that exceptions to that base can be identified. Some tax provisions help to define the base; others are exceptions to the base. The tax base for a tax is the working definition used for this report and is not intended to define the ideal tax base. The defined tax base for each tax is explained in the chapter introduction for the tax. Knowing the tax base is important to understanding how tax expenditures are determined for that tax.

Not Subject to an Alternative Tax: In some instances, one tax may be in imposed in place of another tax, and it would not be reasonable for a taxpayer or activity to be subject to both taxes. Therefore, the exemption from one tax is not considered a tax expenditure if the alternative tax is imposed.

The application of the alternative tax concept for this report was limited to these situations:

- The income from taconite and iron mining is subject to the occupation tax in lieu of the corporate franchise tax.
- The purchase of a motor vehicle is subject to the motor vehicle sales tax (Chapter 5) in lieu of the general sales and use tax (Chapter 4).
- Cigarettes are exempt from the general sales and use tax but are subject to a tax in lieu of the sales tax at the wholesale level.
- The solid waste management taxes are imposed in lieu of the general sales tax.
- A number of taxes are imposed in lieu of the general property tax, including the motor vehicle registration tax and the taconite production tax.
- Noncommercial aircraft are taxed under the aircraft registration tax, and commercial airflight property is taxed under the airflight property tax.

Subject to Legislative Authority: The statute requiring the tax expenditure budget specifies that it is to be submitted to the legislature. Therefore, the report contains only state law provisions that the legislature can propose to repeal or amend. Tax provisions that are contained in the Minnesota Constitution, federal law, or the United States Constitution are not included in the tax expenditure budget.

How Tax Expenditures Are Measured

The fiscal impact of a tax expenditure measures the revenue loss from that one provision under current law. Each provision is estimated in isolation, and other provisions in that tax and in other taxes are held constant. The impact of that provision on other tax provisions is not taken into account. Because the estimates measure the impact of the provision as it exists, no change in taxpayer behavior is assumed.

The estimates for provisions that result in the deferral of tax are the net impact for that year. For example, contributions to a traditional individual retirement account (IRA) are deducted in the year that the contribution is made, earnings are not taxed in the year they are earned, and distributions are included in taxable income in the year received. The tax expenditure impact for a given year measures for all traditional IRAs the deduction for contributions made that year plus the exclusion of earnings accrued that year less distributions included in taxable income in that year.

The precision of the estimates varies with the source of the data and with the applicability of the data to the tax expenditure provision. Data from Minnesota tax returns were used whenever possible. Other sources included federal tax expenditure estimates, data from federal tax returns, census data, and numerous other economic and industry sources of data for Minnesota and the nation.

The methodology used to estimate tax expenditures can produce misleading results if the estimates for two or more provisions are totaled. Depending upon the situation, the combined impact of two or more provisions could be more or less than the total of the provisions estimated separately.

When two tax expenditures overlap, generally the overlap is not included in either estimate. For example, the sales tax exemption for Job Opportunity Building Zone (JOBZ) businesses includes purchases that would also qualify under the capital equipment exemption. Neither the JOBZ sales tax exemption nor the capital equipment exemption includes capital equipment purchases by JOBZ businesses. Adding together the two estimates done separately would understate their combined impact.

The graduated rate structure of the individual income tax is another reason that adding together tax expenditure estimates results in misleading information. As income increases, the marginal tax rate increases. The estimate for each exclusion and deduction uses a marginal tax rate appropriate for that provision. If two or more exclusions or deductions were repealed together, the marginal tax rate for the combined impact would be higher than the rate used for each provision. In that case, adding together the estimates done separately would understate their combined impact.

The itemized deductions for the individual income tax illustrate the distortion that can result from adding together tax expenditure estimates. Because other provisions are held constant, the estimate for each itemized deduction compares the total of the remaining itemized deductions to the standard deduction. For taxpayers who would lose the benefit of itemizing by the loss of that one deduction, the tax expenditure estimate measures the incremental benefit over the standard deduction. Adding together the tax expenditure estimates for two or more itemized deductions ignores the fact that the incremental benefit over the standard deduction may be different when estimating them together compared to estimating each one separately.

The report contains six itemized deductions (Items 1.66 through 1.71). If the FY 2013 estimates for the six separate provisions were added together, the total is $766.2 million. However, when the six provisions are estimated together, the combined estimate is $521.1 million. Adding together the six estimates done separately would overstate the combined impact by $245.1 million, or about 47%.

How the Measurement of Tax Expenditures Differs from Revenue Estimates for Proposed Law Changes

The fiscal impact of a tax expenditure provision is not necessarily the same as the revenue that would be gained by repeal of the provision. This distinction is important.

Estimating the repeal of a provision would take into account interactions within a tax or between taxes and may include changes in taxpayer behavior. As explained in the previous section, if two or more provisions were repealed at the same time, the combined impact would be estimated and could be larger or smaller than the sum of the provisions estimated separately.

The chart below summarizes in general how various factors are different for tax expenditures estimates compared to estimates of proposed law changes.

	Tax Expenditures	Proposed
Estimates take into account:		
Changes in taxpayer behavior	No	Yes[1]
Impact on other tax provisions	No	Yes[1]
Combined impact of two or more provisions	No	Yes[1]
Effective date	No[2]	Yes
Other factors, including collectability	No	Yes[1]

[1]As appropriate
[2]Only effective date of changes under current law

CHAPTER 14

Intergovernmental Fiscal Relations: Diversity and Coordination

Federal, state, and local governments provide and finance public services in the United States, sometimes independently, sometimes cooperatively. Governments of each level are selected by their own electorates, and no government level functions as a regional department of another. Even though the localities add up to the state and the states add up to the nation, the balance of choices differs among localities in a state and among states in the nation. Because of that diversity of choice, state and local governments have an important and independent role in providing and financing government services. That includes the power to spend, as well as the responsibility to raise revenue adequate to support that spending.[1]

Completely independent and uncoordinated operation of these levels would, most argue, produce unacceptable results. Such a posture would undoubtedly leave the public without desired and affordable services, inflict severe burdens on some unluckily placed individuals and businesses, and leave some lower-level governments in chronic fiscal crisis. Those problems highlight the importance for regularized fiscal interrelationships among governments.[2]

Subnational governments allow fiscal diversity and choices about which government should provide which services. Although the federal government continues as sole government provider of national defense and postal services, other significant government functions are divided among federal, state, and local governments. State and local governments are dominant for the services of public safety (police, fire, and protective regulation), education (primary, secondary, and higher), recreation and

---

[1]The analysis of the vertical structure of public finance and the practice of government finance across tiers of governmental entities in a nation is called "fiscal federalism."

[2]Not all federations are characterized by the degree of political independence between federal and regional governments that characterizes the United States and Canada. For instance, Russia and India have systems in which regional chief executives are selected in a process that gives considerable control and influence to the national chief executive rather than the free election of state officials that is the practice in the United States and Canada. Also, recall from Chapter 1 that many nations are unitary, not federal. In these countries, the lower tiers of "government" function as subordinates to the central government.

culture, and transportation (highways, air, water, and urban mass transit). They also run elections that select officials for all governments.

States and localities can adjust both levels and types of government services they provide as they respond to the preferences of a heterogeneous population. Maintaining service responsibility at state and local levels almost certainly means great diversity in what services are provided and how they are financed. It may also bring efficiencies in service provision as jurisdictions compete to keep the cost of government service affordable. Centralization would mean greater uniformity and possibly more secure financing. In addition, centralization makes for clear governmental responsibility: with only a single government, there would not have been the competitive finger pointing to identify which government was responsible for mishandling the response to Hurricane Katrina. What establishes the level of government that should have primary responsibility for providing particular services, and how should intergovernmental financing be arranged? To what extent should diverse provision be constrained or coordinated? And to what extent should subnational governments expect to receive revenue from the central government, as opposed to being required to raise the revenue they spend from their own taxing powers?[3]

Correspondence and Subsidiarity

The critical factor in identifying the level of government that should provide (but not necessarily produce) a public service is the range of benefit spillover. A structure of governments "in which the jurisdiction that determines the level of provision of each public good includes precisely the set of individuals who consume the good" satisfies the *correspondence principle* in defining geographic boundaries and government size.[4] Making the spillover area and the decision unit coincide concentrates government attention on the important matters and prevents the problems that occur when beneficiaries do not pay for a service.

To analyze intergovernmental systems, one can define by use of the correspondence principle a hierarchy of public services by the geographic extent of primary spillovers. A completely private good would have no spillovers. In that case, no distortions result from permitting private individuals to decide on the provision of purely private goods. Public goods and services, however, yield external benefits over areas of widely different geographic range. For instance, a neighborhood park benefits a small community of households around it, benefits from basic police and fire protection spill beyond the neighborhood to a broader local community, and interregional mobility causes benefits from elementary and secondary education to extend

---

[3]Among countries of the Organization for Economic Cooperation and Development, Canada and the United States are the leaders in terms of expecting regional and local governments to raise their own revenues. Julia Darby, V. Anton Muscatelli, and Graeme Roy, "Fiscal Consolidation and Decentralization: A Tale of Two Tiers," *Fiscal Studies* 26 (2005): 173.

[4]Wallace E. Oates, *Fiscal Federalism* (New York: Harcourt Brace Jovanovich, 1972), 34.

to whole regions, whereas the benefits of national defense and international relations extend to the entire nation (and beyond). The correspondence rule for assigning responsibilities to governments is that expenditure and service responsibilities (in other words, the size of the government) should align with the benefit areas for each government service. Therefore, services whose benefits do not spill beyond the local community should be locally provided, services that benefit a number of communities should be state (or regionally) provided, and services that benefit the entire county should be nationally provided. Failure to match spillover range and provision range, at least in general terms, can produce substantial misallocations in resources, overspending for some services, underspending for other services, poorly served citizens, badly managed service delivery, and poorly structured revenue systems.

There is a second general principle in assigning responsibility for government services, the principle of *subsidiarity*. The principle is that government responsibility for a function should be at the lowest level of government that can deliver the function efficiently. Jorge Martinez-Vazquez explains why:

> Because subnational governments are closer to the preferences and needs of taxpayers, they are more likely than the central government to deliver services that local residents want. And, to the extent that preferences for public services differ, efficiency will lead to (indeed, will require) diversity among subnational jurisdictions. Reliance (to the extent possible) on locally imposed taxes to finance subnational expenditures internalizes the costs of providing these services and leads residents in turn to demand more accountability from public officials. When the beneficiary pays, there is greater efficiency and responsibility in government decision-making.[5]

Subsidiarity brings devolution, moving government responsibility to lower levels of government. The devolution trend "is largely a reflection of the political evolution toward more democratic and participatory forms of government that seeks to improve the responsiveness and accountability of political leaders to their electorates, and to ensure a closer correspondence between the quantity, composition, and quality of publicly provided goods and services and the preferences of recipients."[6]

Efforts of the U.S. Congress to shed responsibility to the states, of the United Kingdom to give more power to Scotland and Wales, for division of responsibilities between the European Union and its component nations, for making subnational entities more robust in China, and for efficiently rebuilding governments in countries formed from the former Soviet Union have all been driven by the dual principles of subsidiarity and correspondence in deciding which government will do what so that governments serve the people most effectively and efficiently.

A mismatch between spillover range and government jurisdiction can distort the use of public resources. Suppose a city can construct a local sports complex that would cost $1 million with only $50,000 of its own resources, the difference being financed by the federal government. The city would reasonably behave as if the full capital cost of the project is $50,000, even though the project uses $1 million of resources. If the project has minimal beneficial impact beyond the city, there is no significant spillover

[5]Jorge Martinez-Vasquez, "Expenditures and Expenditure Assignment," in *Russia and the Challenge of Fiscal Federalism,* ed. Christine I. Wallich (Washington, D.C.: World Bank, 1994), 99.

[6]Teresa Ter-Minassian, "Decentralizing Government," *Finance and Development* 34 (September 1997): 36.

that federal financing corrects. Thus, the lack of correspondence causes the city to behave as if $1 million of resources have a value of only $50,000. Had the city been required to finance the project itself, it would have been unwilling to pay the $1 million if the project did not return at least $1 million in benefits to the community. When the correspondence principle is not followed, wasted resources are likely.

However, a broader geography for financing can also correct misallocations from spillovers. Consider a situation in which city A's sewage treatment plant dumps partially treated waste into a river. That river flows past city B, which draws river water for the municipal water utility. City A also draws water from the river, but it gets water from a point upstream of the sewage treatment discharge point. The more complete the sewage treatment is by city A, the lower the water-treatment costs are for city B, and the more attractive the river is to the residents of city B. The primary beneficiaries of city A's sewage treatment are residents of city B. Without some intervention by a geographically larger government—assistance designed to relieve city A of treatment plant expense incurred primarily for the benefit of those downstream—socially desirable actions probably would not be undertaken. City A's decision would be made by comparing returns to its residents (only a small portion of total returns) against the full cost of the complex. In this case, federal (or state) financing of a large share of project cost is justified (absent a politically difficult payment from city B to city A to pay for the treatment plant). That financing would allow city A to pay only to the extent its residents receive benefits, whereas federal (or state) taxpayers pay for returns received by outsiders.

Is Bigger Better?

Correspondence and subsidiarity imply relatively small size for providing many government services, subject only to the problems of externalities for some services. However, that ignores the possible unit-cost advantage of larger governments. Economies of scale, in the sense used in government finance, exist if the cost per person served decreases as the size of the service unit increases.[7] In other words, the cost per person of delivering a given level of fire protection would be smaller for a 100,000-person service district than for a 10,000-person service district. The scale advantage may also reflect the non-exhaustion property of public goods. In other words, up to a congestion point, the total cost of providing additional service does not rise as more people are served, so the cost per unit declines with size. If it

---

[7]From microeconomic theory, economies of scale occur in production when doubling all inputs—a double plant size, in other words—more than doubles output: "Because larger scale permits the introduction of different kinds of techniques, because larger productive units are more efficient, and because larger plants permit greater specialization and division of labor, the long-run average cost function declines, up to some point, with increases in output." Edwin Mansfield, *Microeconomics*, 7th ed. (New York: Norton, 1991), 199. In analysis of government services, the focus is commonly on population served and per capita cost rather than on cost per unit of product.

costs $1,000,000 to provide a given level of public service, expanding the population served from 50,000 to 60,000 reduces unit cost from $20 per person to $16.67 per person. If such scale economies exist, then governments can economize by growing and consolidating regardless of the advantages the correspondence principle tells us are available in getting small units to better capture citizen preferences.

There are two problems with the general idea that larger governments operate more economically. First, empirical evidence shows there to be few traditional state and local government services that show economies of scale except at small population sizes. Economies of scale do exist for capital-intensive services such as water supply, wastewater treatment, electricity, and gas distribution; however, for services such as police and fire protection and elementary and secondary education, unit cost seems not to vary much over a wide range of operating scales. That would be expected for most labor-intensive services.[8] In other words, the cost per person of delivering the service is pretty much the same for a small government provider as it is for a large government delivering the same service. Cost economies from bigness do not stand in the way of achieving the advantages of correspondence and subsidiarity from relative smallness.

Second, economies of scale refer to the conditions of production only. Size of government matters only if production and provision of the service are necessarily joined. If production by an external contractor is feasible, then scale economies are of no particular importance for determining size for provision decisions. Just as households need not be large enough to actually build an automobile at low cost in order to buy an inexpensive car, neither do governments need great size to provide service at an attractive price.[9] They may deal with larger governments, form cooperative supply arrangements with other small governments, or contract with private businesses for service provision depending on the circumstances. Therefore, even where there are cost advantages from large size, those advantages are from *producing* the service. Smaller units, designed under the principles of correspondence and subsidiarity, can make the provision decisions and contract with larger units for production, thereby gaining the best of large size for production and small size for purchase. Small local governments can provide a full range of local services without owning any resources for production or having any employees by contracting for service provisions with other governments or private firms.

The bottom line is that bigger might be better, but don't conclude that it is until after you have run the numbers and don't conclude that this would require a big government. Smaller is almost always going to be more responsive to local preferences.

---

[8]Roy W. Bahl and Walter Vogt, *Fiscal Centralization and Tax Burden: State and Regional Financing of City Services* (Cambridge, Mass.: Ballinger, 1975), 13–14.

[9]There may be economies of scope. If that is the case, then a single firm may produce more than one product more cheaply than if each product was produced by a separate firm. For government operations, this would mean that there would be savings to be had from having one government provide a number of government services rather than having a separate government responsible for each distinct service. A merged public safety district would be less expensive than having a fire protection district and a police protection district.

Fiscal Disparity

Another complication in intergovernmental service-delivery questions is disparity between regions. Some parts of a country or state are likely to be more affluent than others. Within the United States, per capita income of states ranges significantly—from an average of $32,176 in Mississippi and $33,326 in Idaho to an average of $56,889 in Connecticut and $53,621 in Massachusetts in 2011.[10] Within each state, some localities have residents with considerably greater affluence than do others. Although resident incomes and affluence do not directly translate into an available tax base, similar differences occur in the tax base available to governments.[11] If fiscal resources differ among governments, otherwise equally situated individuals will have considerably different access to public services because of the relative affluence of their government.

The property tax provides a simple demonstration. Suppose Smith and Jones each own houses assessed at $10,000 for the property tax. Smith lives in a community with a property tax base of $40,000 per pupil in its public schools; Jones lives in a community with a property tax base of $20,000 per pupil. If a quality education uses resources costing $1,500 per pupil, Smith's community need levy only a property tax of $3.75 per $100 of assessed value to meet that cost. Jones's community would require a tax of $7.50 per $100. When both communities spend the same amount per pupil, the Jones's property must pay twice as much as the Smith's property for the same quality education ($750 versus $375). Thus, services rendered from a given tax rate—or level of *tax effort*—are greater where the capacity endowment is greater. Because there often is a mismatch between need for government services and capacity to finance those services, higher governments intervene by providing various fiscal assistance. Higher-level governments can use their tax systems to raise revenue and then distribute that revenue to lower-level governments, using that distribution to even out the disparities in fiscal capacity

---

[10]U.S. Department of Commerce, Bureau of Economic Analysis. Per capita income in the District of Columbia was $73,105. An alternate measure, total taxable resources, prepared by the Office of Economic Policy of the Department of Treasury, more specifically gauges base available for states to tax. Per capita total taxable resources in 2009 ranged from $35,988 in Mississippi and $38,015 in West Virginia to $74,699 in Delaware and $74,021 in Connecticut, again a wide disparity in fiscal capacity. Disparity measured by total taxable resources is discussed in detail in John L. Mikesell, "Changing State Fiscal Capacity and Tax Effort in an Era of Devolving Government, 1981–2003," *Publius: The Journal of Federalism* 37 (2007): 532–50.

[11]An effort to calibrate total fiscal capacity and compare it with actual effort is the Advisory Commission on Intergovernmental Relations' representative tax system: Advisory Commission on Intergovernmental Relations, *1988 Fiscal Capacity and Effort,* M-170 (Washington, D.C.: Advisory Commission on Intergovernmental Relations, 1990). The representative tax system estimates how much revenue a jurisdiction would raise if it applied typical (national average) tax rates to the major tax bases; an index of that representative yield is the capacity estimate. Robert Tannenwald and Nicholas Turner, "Interstate Fiscal Disparity in State Fiscal 1999," Federal Reserve Bank of Boston Public Policy Discussion Paper No. 04-9, Boston, April 2006, estimates per capita tax capacity in Nevada to be 1.74 times as great as that in Mississippi, clearly demonstrating the disparity issue. Canada uses a representative tax system measure of fiscal capacity in its primary financial aid program across provinces and territories.

among those lower-level governments. As is discussed later in this chapter, state governments are particularly concerned with disparity problems as they affect local school finances.[12]

Fiscal disparity can be particularly acute between cities and their suburbs. In any metropolitan area, some parts are considerably more prosperous than others, and the distribution of the local government tax base may not be related well to where the needs for local government services are greatest. Localities with a revenue-rich economic base—for instance, a regional shopping center or an auto-sales mall for local sales tax communities or an electricity generating plant or a major industrial plant for real-property tax communities—can have huge fiscal affluence without much population at all; workers and shoppers generating that revenue base live in many other locations in the metropolitan area, and where they live is where the need for schools, police and fire protection, parks and recreation, and other local services is. A small number of metropolitan areas use *regional tax-base sharing* of the property tax to assist with the disparity problem (as well as to reduce competition among local governments for new base-rich development). In these plans, a portion of commercial and industrial property assessment growth is pooled—the Minnesota Twin Cities program for seven counties captures 40 percent for the pool—to provide revenue for all the localities. A portion of local fiscal independence is surrendered for the common good of the metropolis and to smooth the tax spikes between localities that certain economic activities can produce. However, the sharing concept has critics as well: economic developments that are particularly rich in tax base are often not desirable neighbors, bringing noise, smells, traffic, and so on. That extra tax base—which can be used to enrich local services or to reduce local tax rates—may be a way of compensating the host community for those factors. Fiscal disparity can also be great between urban and rural areas within a state.

The United States differs from many other federations in that the federal government provides no general transfer programs to reduce differences in fiscal capacity among its subnational governments. Equalization grants are important programs in Australia, Canada, Germany, and elsewhere, all designed to reduce significant variation in fiscal resources among the component jurisdictions—regions, states, provinces, and so on. For instance, Section 36 of the Canadian Constitution states that equalization policies will "ensure that provincial governments have sufficient revenues to provide reasonably comparable levels of public service at reasonably comparable levels of taxation."[13] For whatever political, cultural, or economic reasons, such general equalization has not been a component of the U.S. system. There are equalizing elements in some federal grant formulas, but no general program of fiscal equalization among states. Disparity equalization, to the extent it exists, is something that states do among their localities.

---

[12]The disparity issue also applies to other local governments: Katharine Bradbury and Bo Zhao, "Measuring Non-school Fiscal Disparities among Municipalities," *National Tax Journal* 67 (March 2009): 25–56.

[13]Part III, Equalization and Regional Disparities, Section 36, Constitution Act, 1982. Equalization Transfers go to all Territories and Provinces Except Ontario and Alberta. All Provinces Receive Transfers For Support of the Health and Social Systems.

Coordination and Assistance: Tax Systems

Governments can tailor their revenue structures to provide mutually beneficial financial and administrative assistance. Such assistance, although not bringing new resources into a government, may improve access to the existing revenue base and may be arranged with minimal interference to local autonomy. The two general classes of revenue assistance are (1) relief in tax-base use and (2) assistance with revenue administration and compliance.

Revenue relief includes deductions and credits granted the taxes of one unit in tax computations made for another unit. Both are important, but they work differently and have different clout. Deductibility causes the federal government to, in effect, pick up part of the burden of selected taxes paid to state or local government. For example, the federal individual income tax permits deduction of selected state and local taxes (individual income and property in all states and retail sales tax in some states) from the federal income tax base. The power of deduction can be demonstrated with a simple example. Suppose a taxpayer is in the 35 percent federal tax bracket. If his or her state income tax increases by $100, the taxpayer's net tax burden increases by only $65 because deducting that state tax reduces his or her federal liability by $35. The deduction rewards state and local governments that use deductible taxes by making their net cost to taxpayers less.[14] Increasing a deductible tax (like an individual income tax) is cheaper for residents of a state than is increasing nondeductible excise tax or applying a user charge. Of course, the coordination effects are not extraordinarily strong (states continue to use nondeductible taxes), deductibility does not equalize wealth among lower units, and only taxpayers who itemize get the advantage of the deduction. Furthermore, taxpayers in high-tax states are likely to lose the deduction through the operation of the alternative minimum tax.[15]

A stronger device is the tax credit, an arrangement in which the tax levied by one government unit acts as full or partial payment of the liability owed to another government. That was the case for the federal tax on transfer of assets on death. A qualifying state tax would, up to a limit, be a credit against liability for the federal tax, meaning that the state tax would mean no net liability for the estate. That gave an almost overwhelming incentive for states to levy the tax—essentially free money to the state. But a credit does not alter the basic distribution of resources among states or localities. Affluent units remain affluent, and poor units remain poor, leaving one intergovernmental issue untouched. In general, the credit involves substantial implicit control of the lower government unit by the higher government unit.

Deductions and credits create a curious effect for state (or local) tax reductions— the loss of state tax revenue when such a tax cut is greater than the increase in disposable income available to its taxpayers. The other beneficiary of such a state or local tax cut is the federal government. Estimates suggest, for instance, that federal

---

[14]In the pre-1964 tax-reduction period—when marginal rates were as high as 91 percent—deductibility prevented taxpayers from encountering marginal rates above 100 percent.
[15]The tax deductibility issue is discussed in detail in Congressional Budget Office, *The Deductibility of State and Local Taxes* (Washington, D.C.: Congressional Budget Office, 2008).

income tax revenue increased by between $1 billion and $1.7 billion in 1979 as a result of California's Proposition 13 property tax reduction.[16] Every state or local property or income tax reduction program brings more federal tax revenue because of the smaller federal deductions received by taxpayers in the jurisdiction—the state or locality loses revenue, taxpayers in the jurisdiction have increased disposable income, and federal tax collections from taxpayers in the jurisdiction increase.

Deducting and crediting lower-level taxes frees resources for lower-level use and provides incentive for using "approved" tax forms. Both can have considerable coordinating potential. Deductions and credits do not assist lower government levels with administration and do not reduce the burden of complying with multiple government taxes encountered by businesses and individuals.

Another set of revenue tools can assist with that part of the intergovernmental fiscal problem. These devices include source separation, cooperative administration, coordinated tax bases, tax supplements, and centralized administration, arrayed in order of high to low amounts of lower-level government involvement in operations.

Separation of tax sources prevents tax overlapping. Vertical overlapping occurs when governments at different levels (say, federal and state) apply a tax to exactly the same base; horizontal overlapping occurs when more than one government at the same level (say, two different states) applies a tax to the same base. Overlapping not only may produce the nuisance of multiple taxpayer filings, but also may distort economic activity. If each level of government was guaranteed an exclusive use of particular tax bases, the vertical-overlap problem would be effectively eliminated. Table 14–1 presents the record on source separation since 1970. In 1970, local governments dominated the property tax base, collecting 96.8 percent of all property taxes levied; that dominance continued through 2008 However, localities rely somewhat less on the property tax. The property tax constituted 84.9 percent of local tax revenue in 1970, but that share declined to 72.2 percent by 2008. State governments collected 56.1 percent of taxes on sales and gross receipts in 1970. and that share increased to 77.2 percent in 2008. The states' reliance on sales and gross receipts has also declined, from 56.8 percent in 1970 to 46.2 percent in 2008. The federal government continues dominant use of the income taxes, collecting 89.4 percent of that revenue in 1970 and 80.0 percent in 2008. Its reliance on that base has increased, from 84.4 percent in 1970 to 95.3 percent in 2008.

Governments show little taste for source separation as a response to vertical-coordination problems because all want access to the "better" sources regardless of how that may confuse tax administration, compliance, and transparency of the levy. Only sources viewed rightly or wrongly as inferior (like the property tax) are likely to be happily shed by any level of government. Although source separation would be orderly, most governments would prefer expanded revenue options. The exception is, of course, the federal government, which steadfastly sticks with the income base.

Fortunately, there are coordination mechanisms that accommodate more than one level of government using a single tax base. These include (1) cooperative

---

[16]Report to the Comptroller General of the United States, *Will Federal Assistance Be Affected by Proposition 13?* GGD-78-101 (Washington, D.C.: General Accounting Office, 1978). Some state income taxes provide a tax deduction for federal income tax paid. Taxpayers in those states found that the federal income tax rebates of 2001 were taxable under the state income tax because their deduction for federal income tax paid was lower.

Table 14–1

Tax-Source Separation, 1970, 1994, and 2008: Percentage of Revenue from Tax Collected by Level of Government

	Federal			State			Local		
	1970	1994	2008	1970	1994	2008	1970	1994	2008
Reliance of levels of government on tax sources									
Taxes on property	0	0	0	2.3	2.2	1.6	84.9	74.8	72.2
Taxes on individual and corporate income	84.4	91	95.3	26.9	38.3	41.9	4.2	5.7	6.2
Taxes on sales or gross receipts	12.5	4.4	1.0	56.8	49.8	46.2	7.9	15	16.5
Other taxes	3.1	4.7	3.7	14	9.7	10.3	3	4.5	5.1
Distribution of tax sources by level of government									
Taxes on property	0	0	0	3.5	4.3	3.1	96.8	95.7	96.9
Taxes on individual and corporate income	89.4	87.9	80.0	9.4	11	18.1	1.2	1.1	1.9
Taxes on sales or gross receipts	37.6	19.8	3.4	56.1	66.7	77.2	6.3	13.5	19.4
Other taxes	36.6	62.7	34.2	53.9	26.1	48.7	9.4	11.2	17.0

SOURCE: U.S. Bureau of Census, Government Finance Statistics and Executive Office of the President, Office of Management and Budget, *Historical Tables, Budget of the United States Government, Fiscal Year 2012* (Washington, D.C.: U.S. GPO, 2011).

administration, (2) coordinated tax bases, (3) tax supplements, and (4) centralized administration.[17] *Cooperative administration* involves continuous contact and information exchange among taxing units. Sales tax administrators may inform their peers when a firm is found to be violating tax laws in a manner that would generate liability in other states. Income tax administrators may exchange information about audits. The Internal Revenue Service (IRS) may inform a state about audit findings for an individual living in that state. State business tax administrators may exchange information about contractors who should be registered to pay taxes in other states. Coordination is weak, but profitable for the parties because work done by one administration can generate revenue for another with little or no additional work. Bases, rates, and rate structures need not coincide among governments for this cooperation, but all governments can gain from the exchange. Indeed, every state in the United States links its income tax administration closely to the work of the IRS, has information exchange agreements with the IRS, and relies heavily on IRS enforcement for collection of income taxes.[18]

---

[17]George Break, *Financing Government in a Federal System* (Washington, D.C.: Brookings Institution, 1980), 34.
[18]Evidence shows that the federal income tax audit rate does have an impact on state income tax compliance, generally allowing states to do almost no individual income tax audits on their own. [Liucija Birskyte, *The effects of IRS audit rates on state individual income tax compliance*, PhD Dissertation Thesis, Indiana University (2008).]

With *coordinated tax bases,* one government links its tax to some point in the tax structure of another government. For example, several states key their individual income tax to federal adjusted gross income, and a number of localities begin their local sales tax ordinances with definitions taken from their state sales tax. Other elements of the tax may differ from that point—different exemptions, rate patterns, rate levels, and so on—but the higher- and lower-level taxes have important common elements. The links reduce taxpayer compliance problems (one set of records can be used for both taxes, and some of the computations need not be replicated) and simplify administration across governments. However, substantial differences between the taxes reduce the gains in both compliance and administration.

Tax supplements provide more coordination, either through applying a lower-level rate on the base used by the higher level (many state sales taxes have supplements added by localities) or through applying a lower-level rate that is a percentage of tax paid to the higher level. This method dramatically reduces compliance requirements for taxpayers and cuts administration expenses when the supplementing unit refrains from adding extra features. Few government units can refrain from at least a few changes, and each change cuts the savings to taxpayers.

The final coordination system is *central administration* of a "piggyback" tax, a system in which a lower government unit applies its own rate to the tax base used by higher government. Full piggybacking would have the higher unit doing all administrative and enforcement work—the taxpayer reports on a single form to the higher unit, which records for and remits collections to the lower unit. Lower units must adopt the tax to receive revenue (it is not simply a system of tax sharing), but they cannot select a base structured differently from that used by the higher unit. Administrative economies are possible with single-unit administration, and the taxpayer can comply with multiple obligations at one time. Supplemental tax rates, however, do not permit a redistribution of resources among lower units. Most local sales taxes piggyback on their state sales tax—often, the local tax return consists only of some extra lines on the state sales tax return—and local income taxes in Maryland, Indiana, and Iowa are similarly supplements to the state return. Most localities levy income taxes, however, that are not related to either federal or state taxes, often limiting the tax to wages and salaries ("earned" income). States that continue a state property tax apply them to the locally administered base, a rare example of piggybacking from state to local.[19] Piggybacking obviously provides considerable economy in collection, but at the cost of transparency in taxation. Taxpayers seldom know, without considerable checking, which government is levying what portion of the tax that they pay.

---

[19]In Canada, the federal government administers provincial individual and corporate income taxes, and most provincial sales taxes are harmonized with the national goods and services (value-added) tax for federal collection. In Quebec, provincial authorities administer the national goods and service tax along with the provincial retail sales tax.

Coordination and Assistance: Grants

Grants transfer spending power (command over resources) from one government to another. In a multilevel governmental relationship, like that between the federal government and the states or between a state and its localities, grants can compensate governments for benefit spillovers to nonresidents, reduce the problems created by fiscal disparity, encourage programs of special national merit, reduce special problems associated with regional economic decline, and encourage governments to implement management reform by making it a condition for receiving aid.[20] In other words, they can have a purpose in a federal system beyond simply using the supposedly stronger revenue administration capacity of the higher level to raise money for the lower level.

There is a classic conflict between the donor and the recipient in transfer systems, a conflict that can never be entirely resolved. The donor government raises the revenue, bearing whatever political burdens may be associated with the revenue function. The recipient government gets any political benefits associated with service delivery. Because the recipient did not have to raise the money, might it be likely that the funds will be mismanaged or misallocated? To prevent such carelessness (or worse), the donor seeks controls, or "strings," on the use of the funds. The recipient government, of course, views the situation differently. The granting government is less familiar with local conditions, needs, and priorities. Any controls make service delivery more difficult and reduce the ability to provide needed services. The controls that the donor seeks to ensure accountability are viewed by the recipient as barriers to effective response.

A significant amount of the money spent by state and local governments comes from assistance provided by other levels of government. The general pattern of intergovernmental aid between 1971–1972 and 2006–2007 appears in Table 14–2. In 2001–2002, 31.5 percent of state revenue and 40.0 percent of local revenue consisted of assistance in the form of grants from other levels of government. Aid to states was mostly from the federal government and aid to localities was mostly from their states; that continues today. Among local governments, aid is particularly vital to school districts; they received 55.3 percent of their general revenue from aid in 2006–2007, with 96.0 percent of that coming from states. In spite of all the talk from federal politicians about American elementary and secondary education, the finances are mostly state and local. States received a somewhat increased share of revenue from aid in 2006–2007, compared with 1971–1972 (from 28.4 percent to 29.5 percent), and the share to localities has remained about the same (from 37.7 to 37.5 percent). Aid to school districts has increased significantly (from 45.0 to 55.3 percent) for reasons that are discussed later in this chapter.

---

[20]General Accounting Office, *Federal Grants: Design Improvements Could Help Federal Resources Go Further,* GAO/AIMD-97-7 (Washington, D.C.: U.S. Government Printing Office, 1996). A number of local governments instituted external financial audits for the first time because that was a condition to receive federal revenue-sharing funds.

The flows of federal aid to state and local governments have recently increased. As Table 14–3 shows, aid rose through the late 1970s to the mid-1980s to more than 20 percent of total state-local general revenue, but then fell as the environment became what John Shannon called "fend-for-yourself federalism," one in which governments spending money were expected to raise that money.[21] Recently, the share has risen again, driven by what the federal budget classifies as outlays for state and local government aid for payments to individuals, including Medicaid and certain welfare programs, through which state administrative agencies distribute this federal assistance. (It has also increased somewhat with assistance to help states and localities during the Great Recession, although the increase has not been as significant as in other recent recessions.) That category now constitutes almost two-thirds of the total.[22] Aid for regular state and local programs, the "Other" class in Table 14–3, is dramatically less than during the 1970s. A considerable amount of the capital-investment aid comes through trust funds supporting highways and airports. That share is far less now than it once was—and is an important contributor to our crumbling public transportation infrastructure. In terms of government function, virtually all federal aid comes through four categories: health, income security, education, and transportation, as Table 14–3 shows. Growth in Medicaid spending is particularly important for the increase, and it is the largest single federal grant program to state and local governments.

Both federal and state governments operate intergovernmental assistance programs. Many problems and structural features are common to both. The federal grant system has included three types of assistance: (1) categorical grants, (2) block grants, and (3) from 1972 through 1986, general revenue sharing.[23] The last is a type of general fiscal assistance, a more common element of state-to-local grant programs. There is much hybridization of grant styles, making clear classification difficult. However, the great preponderance of federal grant programs—measured in both numbers and outlay totals—are categorical grant programs.[24] A federal website provides the *Catalog of Domestic Federal Assistance* (http://www.cdfa.gov) to guide anyone through the 2,242 federal assistance programs (the count as of 2012).

State aid systems have some elements similar to the federal system, although each state has its own peculiar mix. State grants to general-purpose local governments

---

[21]John Shannon, "The Return to Fend-for-Yourself Federalism: The Reagan Mark," *Intergovernmental Perspective* 13 (Summer–Fall 1987): 34–37. The United States expects subnational governments to raise a considerably greater share of the money spent than do most other nations, including the major federal states (Australia, Canada, and Germany)—it always has, and probably always will.

[22]Medicaid provides medical assistance for low-income people who are aged, blind, disabled, members of families with dependent children, and certain other pregnant women and children. States establish their own coverage rules, scope of benefits offered, and amounts paid for services, all within guidelines established by the federal government. The federal government then pays a portion of the total spent by the state, according to an annually adjusted rate that ranges between 50 and 83 percent; the rate is inversely related to state per capita income. This is a categorical formula grant program.

[23]The federal government also assists state and local governments through credit, either directly via loans and advances or indirectly through loan guarantees.

[24]Advisory Commission on Intergovernmental Relations, *Characteristics of Federal Grant-in-Aid Programs to State and Local Governments: Grants Funded FY 1995,* M-195 (Washington, D.C.: Advisory Commission on Intergovernmental Relations, 1995), 3.

Table 14–2

Source of Intergovernmental Revenue ($ millions)

		Intergovernmental Revenue			
	Total General Revenue	Total	From Federal	From State	From Local
1971–1972					
State	98,632	27,981	26,791	—	1,191
Local	105,243	39,694	4,551	35,143	—
Cities	34,998	11,528	2,538	8,434	556
Counties	23,652	9,956	405	9,252	299
School districts	39,256	17,653	749	16,471	433
1991–1992					
State	608,804	169,928	159,068	—	10,861
Local	579,083	217,996	20,107	197,890	—
Cities	175,116	49,474	8,103	37,380	3,992
Counties	148,367	55,292	3,243	49,663	2,386
School districts	198,320	107,160	1,354	103,084	27,222
1996–1997					
State	815,442	230,859	215,839	—	15,020
Local	747,030	287,003	28,768	258,235	—
Cities	222,190	62,851	11,699	45,932	5,220
Counties	191,271	71,751	4,890	64,007	2,854
School districts	257,342	141,974	1,762	137,246	2,966
2001–2002					
State	1,062,628	33,543	317,583	—	17,851
Local	995,779	398,641	42,964	355,677	—
Cities	286,036	85,290	15,212	62,538	7,539
Counties	257,167	99,122	7,539	86,759	4,823
School districts	350,793	199,544	3,632	191,145	4,767
2006–2007					
State	1,457,803	430,278	410,184	—	20,094
Local	1,344,828	504,407	57,765	446,642	—
Cities	389,170	101,653	20,498	72,811	8,344
Counties	340,979	122,001	11,009	104,639	6,353
School districts	469,181	259,690	4,541	249,373	5,776
Rate of Change, 1971–1972 to 2006–2007%					
State	8.0%	8.1%	8.1%	—	8.4%
Local	7.6%	7.5%	7.5%	7.5%	—
Cities	7.1%	6.4%	6.2%	6.4%	8.0%
Counties	7.9%	7.4%	9.9%	7.2%	9.1%
School districts	7.3%	8.0%	5.3%	8.1%	7.7%

SOURCE: U.S. Bureau of Census, Governments Division, State & Local Government Finances.

Table 14–3
Federal Aid to State and Local Governments

Fiscal Year	Real Federal Outlays for Grants to State-Local Governments (2005 = 100)	Percentage of Grants for			Percentage of Grants by Function				Federal Aid as Percentage of State-Local Revenue
		Individuals	Capital Investment	Other	Transportation General	Education	Health	Income Security	
1960	45.3	35.3	47.3	17.4	42.7	7.5	3.0	37.5	13.7
1965	65.9	34.1	45.7	20.2	37.6	9.6	5.7	32.2	14.9
1970	123.7	36.2	29.3	34.5	19.0	26.7	16.0	24.1	16.7
1975	186.9	33.6	21.9	44.5	11.4	24.4	17.7	18.8	20.6
1980	227.1	35.7	24.7	39.6	14.2	23.9	17.2	20.2	21.7
1985	189.6	47.3	23.5	29.2	16.0	16.1	23.1	26.3	17.8
1990	198.1	57.1	20.1	22.8	14.1	16.1	32.4	27.2	16.1
1995	283.6	64.2	17.6	18.2	11.4	13.7	41.6	25.9	19.2
2000	326.8	63.9	17.0	19.1	11.3	12.8	43.7	24.0	18.5
2005	428.0	64.0	14.2	21.8	10.1	13.4	46.2	21.2	21.1
2010	531.7	63.2	15.3	21.5	10.0	16.0	47.7	18.9	22.2
2011	514.6	63.9	15.9	20.2	10.0	14.7	48.3	18.7	n.a.

SOURCE: Bureau of Census, Governments Division, *State and Local Government Finances: 2011* and Executive Office of the President, Office of Management and Budget, *Historical Tables, Budget of the United States Government Fiscal Year 2013* (Washington, D.C.: USGPO, 2012).
n.a.: Data not available.

(mostly cities and counties) have always been for relatively broad purposes. The grants sometimes distribute earmarked percentages of certain state taxes. In a later section, we examine state aid to schools, a major component of total state aid.

Categorical Grants

Categorical grants finance specific and narrowly defined programs, usually limited to spending for certain activities, such as constructing a wastewater-treatment plant or paying salaries of special education teachers. Such aid seeks to induce the recipient government to behave in a fashion other than the way it would behave without the aid. The grants encourage recipient governments to shift expenditures to particular functions or to guarantee provision of certain recipient government services in a manner consistent with national interest. In these areas, narrow local interest and national interest presumably do not coincide. The grant changes the returns as seen by the recipient to make certain activities more attractive—the federal share makes the aided activity cheaper for the lower-level government—so that recipient actions coincide with national interest.

Categorical grants may be:

1. **Formula,** in which aid is distributed among eligible governments according to a legislatively or administratively determined formula. Formula elements may include population, population in certain demographic categories, per capita income, unemployment, energy use, housing categories, fiscal capacity, program performance, highway lane miles, or other measures. For example, the Dingell-Johnson Sport Fish Restoration Program (Federal Aid in Sport Fish Restoration Act of 1950) distributes funds to state fish and wildlife agencies according to a formula that includes the state share of land and water area, miles of coastline, and paid fishing license holders.[25]

2. **Project,** in which aid is distributed at the discretion of the administrator for particular projects. These grants are usually awarded on a competitive basis from applications made to support a particular proposal from a state or local government (or other entity).

3. **Project/formula,** in which aid is distributed at the discretion of the administrator within constraints set by a formula that limits amounts awarded in a state. For instance, the Recreational Trails program in the Department of Transportation provides formula assistance for development of trails for non-motorized and motorized use with an 80 percent matching requirement.[26]

These grants may have *matching* provisions that require the recipient to spend a specified sum for each dollar spent by the federal government in the grant (the match can often be in-kind contributions to a program, e.g., office space, rather than

---

[25]Find it in the *Catalog of Federal Domestic Assistance* [https://www.cfda.gov/index?s=program&mode=form&tab=step1&id=29bb1c73e764c9635937ebbdd1140393].

[26]Ibid. [https://www.cfda.gov/index?s=program&mode=form&tab=step1&id=97e2194928c0e1bde5aaf7-b62023b196].

cash) or *maintenance of effort* provisions that require the recipient to continue a specified level of spending in a specific area to receive the federal funds and to use the funds to supplement, not supplant, spending.[27]

Project grants—about 70 percent of all categorical grant programs, but considerably less than half of total categorical aid outlay—are the realm of the grants person, the individual assigned by many state and local governments and nonprofit agencies to manage the quest for external assistance. (Formula and reimbursement categories, plus the block and revenue-sharing assistance examined later, do not require competitive application.) This person becomes familiar with the activities of federal agencies and private foundations (state governments tend not to use project grants) and watches available funding announcements published in sources such as the *Federal Register* and the *Catalog of Federal Domestic Assistance* (OMB/General Services Administration). When project requirements and the activities of the government coincide, the manager prepares a project proposal. The funding agency awards go to proposals evaluated as best according to legislative and regulatory constraints. Decisions are based on the extent to which the proposal responds to the requirements presented in the funding advertisement, the extent to which the proposer demonstrates ability to carry out the project, and other factors such as the creativity or novelty of the project approach or the possibility that results may be used elsewhere. Selection criteria and weighting among factors are usually published with program announcements. Skeptics stress the significance of noncompetitive, political factors in some assistance programs, however. These are the earmarked or pork-barrel projects described in an earlier chapter. Sidebar 14–1 outlines basic rules for writing a grant proposal to a government or nongovernment donor.

Sidebar 14–1
Some Basic Guides for Writing Grant Proposals

Most federal assistance to state and local governments is provided on a noncompetitive basis for particular programs, as is virtually all state aid to their local governments. However, some assistance is awarded competitively to particular projects on the basis of grant proposals, as are awards from foundations and other nongovernmental organizations. Although grant writing is more art than science, there are a few simple steps that can assist in grant proposal preparation.

1. Read the materials provided by the granting entity with great care. Often the information comes in the form of a "request for proposals" (RFP), and the instructions included there are to be followed scrupulously. The RFP indicates deadlines for submission (which, for federal

(continues)

---

[27]Evidence indicates that about 60 cents of each federal grant dollar substitutes for state funds that would have been spent anyway. General Accounting Office, *Federal Grants*, GAO/AIMD-97-7 (Washington, D.C.: General Accounting Office), 2.

**SIDEBAR 14–1
(continued)**

agencies and most other donors, are rigidly enforced), instructions for submission, format and style for the submission, and a description of the kind of projects that can be proposed. The proposed project must fit the intent and guidelines of the competition. If it doesn't, then writing the proposal is just a waste of time. If you are not sure whether what you have in mind is the sort of thing that might be competitive, then check with the program officer before devoting much time to the proposal.

2. Write the proposal in the language of the RFP. The proposal should use exactly the same terminology, key phrases, concepts, and so on that the RFP uses. One grantsperson has described this as "writing the RFP back to the agency." This approach is effective in part because the people who wrote the RFP are likely to be evaluating the proposals and seeing their own words coming back is a nice form of flattery. Besides, they are experts in the area being supported, and this degree of consistency is only logical. If you can't use the terminology of the RFP in what you are proposing, then probably this isn't the right grant competition for the project you have in mind.

3. Keep in contact with the granting entity. Unless there are rules that forbid advance contact, you should let the agency know that your proposal will be coming, and you should find out as much about the agency's interests as you can. Part of this work involves studying proposals that have been funded by the agency in the past, if they are available for public inspection, so that you can get hints about what might be sensible in your project and how successful projects have been structured. Even if full proposals are not available, you should be able to obtain brief abstracts, and these can be helpful as you develop your proposal. Many grant competitions have "no contact" periods after the submission deadline. You may not contact the agency about your proposal after that date, and you must take care not to cross the line and have your proposal ruled ineligible by accident.

4. Follow the traditional guidelines for preparing budget requests (review the relevant sections of Chapter 5) in your proposal because, after all, a budget request and a grant proposal are exactly the same in logic. The proposal must describe what is intended in the project, what resources will be necessary, what funds are requested, and what results of the project are expected—just as with a fully developed agency budget request. The RFP frequently specifies a format for the submission, and it usually specifies a particular budget classification structure and certain standards for the budget. These requirements need to be followed to make the proposal eligible for consideration. If the instructions say "double-space," then the proposal absolutely must be double-spaced. No exceptions.

5. Agencies frequently enter into negotiations about the proposal after the first review of competitors. To receive a call for further information or for revisions of your proposal is usually a good sign because it means that your proposal has passed the first set of tests and the chances that your proposal will be funded are very good.

Grant proposals, even for good projects, are not always successful. Following these simple steps can improve the likelihood that a strong project—and some not-so-strong ones—will receive support.

One peculiarity of the categorical grant must be recognized. For the recipient, the grant is most valuable if it supports an activity the recipient was going to undertake even without the assistance. In that case, there is minimal disruption of local interest, and resources are released for use in accord with local priorities. For the donor, the grant is most powerful when it supports activities not ordinarily undertaken at levels consistent with the donor's interest. Thus, there is some divergence of interest between recipient and donor in a well-designed categorical grant.

Critics of the categorical grant system emphasize three particular difficulties. First is the administrative complexity of the categorical grant system. In an effort to ensure that federal policy objectives are met as nearly as possible by the recipients, federal programs establish elaborate control mechanisms to monitor and shape actions taken by the recipient. These mechanisms usually have different planning, application, reporting, and accounting requirements—none of which coincide with those ordinarily used by the recipient government. Not only are these controls an irritation, but also they divert state and local resources to the administrative process.

A second criticism is the program overlap and duplication that has emerged in the federal grant system. Complexity means that some communities do not participate, leaving their residents less well served than would be desirable. Other local governments aggressively seek funds, producing extraordinary assistance for their residents. Governments may even use funds from one program to meet another program's matching requirements, thus thwarting the intention of matching to stimulate local expenditure.

Third, critics complain that categorical grants distort local priorities. Although grant requirements try to reflect national interests, the distortion may exceed the level justified by the traditional spillover-of-local-action argument. Furthermore, the aid may not be reliable. Aid may be eliminated after a few years, leaving state and local governments with program responsibility, but no resources. The combination of these criticisms has been instrumental in movement toward block assistance and calls for a return to general-purpose assistance.

The American Recovery and Reinvestment Act of 2009 (the federal stimulus act) directed about $280 billion of its $787 billion total to spending by state and local governments. The distribution is by existing formulas with major components going to the State Fiscal Stabilization Fund (mostly for education), for Medicaid, and for highway and bridge infrastructure. Most of the money at the beginning is for support of Medicaid programs. In later years of the program, money will be directed to community development, energy, and the environment. Controls and extraordinary reporting requirements imposed by Congress have slowed the pace of this spending. The impact of these grants is not shown in tables presented here because the necessary reports are not yet available.

Block Grants

Block grants are usually distributed to general-purpose governments (categorical grants often go to special-purpose governments or nongovernments) according to a statutory formula to finance activities in a broad functional area. Recipients have considerable discretion in how to spend the money. Among the features of federal block grants are these: "[A]id is authorized for a wide range of activities within a broadly defined functional area; recipients have substantial discretion to identify problems, design programs, and allocate resources; administrative, fiscal reporting, planning, and other federally imposed requirements are limited to those necessary to ensure that national goals are being accomplished; and federal aid is distributed on the basis of statutory formula with few, if any, matching requirements and, historically, spending has been capped."[28] Federal block grants support programs that include health (Community Mental Health Services, Prevention and Treatment of Substance Abuse, Maternal and Child Health Services, Preventive Health and Health Services), crime control (Local Law Enforcement, Juvenile Accountability Incentive), community development (Community Development), social services (Social Services, Child Care and Development, Low-Income Home Energy Assistance, Community Services), aid for the needy (Temporary Assistance for Needy Families), and emergency management (Emergency Management Performance).[29]

The largest single surge of conversion from categorical to block grants in terms of programs involved was in the Omnibus Reconciliation Act of 1981 (P.L. 97–35), when fifty-seven categoricals were consolidated into nine block grants (social services; home-energy assistance; community development; elementary and secondary education; alcohol, drug abuse, and mental health; maternal and child care; community services; primary health care; and preventative health and health services). Federal welfare reform, through the Personal Responsibility and Work Opportunity Reconciliation Act of 1996 (P.L. 104–193), added welfare to the list of block grants to states by replacing Aid to Families with Dependent Children (AFDC), a formula entitlement paid to states for distribution to needy mothers and children, with a multiyear, fixed-appropriation block grant to states for support of the welfare programs. The new program is Temporary Assistance to Needy Families or TANF. The appropriated amount is distributed among states by a formula based on money each state received for programs it replaced—either the higher of fiscal 1994 or fiscal 1995 or the average of fiscal 1992–1994. State programs must be within certain federal standards, and states must achieve certain performance goals to continue to receive the funds.

The Advisory Commission on Intergovernmental Relations maintained that block grants with "well-designed allocation formulas and eligibility provisions" could:

1. Provide aid to those jurisdictions having the greatest programmatic needs and give them a reasonable degree of fiscal certainty.
2. Accord recipients substantial discretion in defining problems, setting priorities, and allocating resources.
3. Simplify program administration and reduce paperwork and overhead.
4. Facilitate interfunctional and intergovernmental coordination and planning.
5. Encourage greater participation on the part of elected and appointed generalist officials in decision making.[30]

---

[28]General Accounting Office, *Block Grants: Issues in Designing Accountability Provisions,* GAO/AIMD-95-226 (Washington, D.C.: General Accounting Office, 1995), 4.
[29]Plus special block grants for Native Americans.
[30]Advisory Commission on Intergovernmental Relations, *Characteristics,* 24.

Block grants should not be expected to stimulate new recipient-government initiatives and should be confined to activities for which a broad consensus already exists. Block grants are not designed to bend local choices in a direction more consistent with national interest or to cause local government units to change their operating methods. They may replace groups of similar categoricals that have already established strong local clienteles. However, critics complain that block grants, especially community development block grants, usually aid affluent as well as poor communities and that some funds get used in ways that would stretch congressional intentions. Donors worry about how the programs can ensure accountability for spending and for outcomes. Federal block grant funding has recently been restrained as one casualty on the path toward expenditure constraint.

Revenue Sharing (General-Purpose Fiscal Assistance)

The third variety of federal grants is revenue sharing, a formula distribution with few or no restrictions on the use of funds provided.[31] The federal revenue-sharing program, started in 1972, used a formula to distribute multiyear appropriations to states and general-purpose local governments. The funding approach—appropriation rather than a share of certain taxes—provided some greater certainty of aid during the appropriation's life (unforeseen changes in federal revenue did not influence distributed shares), but the funds had to be appropriated again when the appropriation period expired. The program was the primary source of the increase in the federal share of state and local general revenue in 1975 and 1980 that was shown in Table 14–3. Each renewal raised questions about the program's continuation; the entire program was excluded from the 1986 budget. Similar (and older) state tax-sharing programs typically dedicate a given share of selected taxes (e.g., 1 percentage point of the state sales tax rate) to a local-aid formula.

Revenue sharing distributed funds according to a formula that combined population, percentage of urban population, tax effort, income tax effort, and per capita income to define the appropriate shares. State governments initially received one-third of revenue-sharing funds, but were gradually removed. The 1980 extension of the program discontinued the share for any state not giving up categorical grants equal to the allocation received, and the state share ended entirely in 1983. Local general-purpose governments (cities, counties, Native American governments, townships, etc.) continued receiving aid through the life of the program. Checks were sent to each eligible government without application and with only minimal restrictions concerning use (there had to be a publicized appropriation process, there could be no discrimination in hiring or compensation, funds could not be used for grant matching, use had to be subject to external financial audit, etc.).[32]

---

[31]Although they are not general, the federal government does have a few shared taxes, levied at the federal level for formula distribution to state government for specific use. The most significant of these support the highway and airport and airway trust funds. These funds do have to be appropriated, however; they are not automatically distributed to states.

[32]Some large American cities had never had an external financial audit before the general revenue sharing era. Inducing them to be audited can be counted as a benefit of the program, over and above any services ultimately delivered by the grant revenue.

Although federal revenue sharing ended at the national level in 1986, such programs continue as an important feature of several state fiscal systems, including those of Michigan, Alaska, Louisiana, Florida, Maine, and Wisconsin. The distributions are sometimes of dedicated shares of particular taxes and sometimes of specific appropriations. The distributions are by formula, and the funds are for general use by the recipient government with few, if any, controls. When these distributions are on a per capita basis, they reduce fiscal disparity to an extent because the per capita amount provides greater relative assistance to lower-capacity areas than to higher-capacity ones. High-capacity areas pay more into the state aid pool than they receive in return.

Programs of revenue or tax sharing can strengthen local spending power and reduce intergovernmental disparities (the great differences in fiscal capacity that exist among governments at the same level across the nation or within a state). Such programs would not shape local priorities to make them more consistent with national interest because of the lack of controls placed on the assistance. They would not be particularly effective as a way to aid disadvantaged groups because advantaged and disadvantaged tend, with few exceptions, to live in the same political jurisdictions. General aid to the jurisdiction can improve capacity to provide services (or reduce taxes with no change in services) for anyone, and probably the advantaged will do better because they usually have greater political clout. Revenue sharing should not be expected to achieve the targeting and revision of public action that categorical programs can produce. Revenue sharing can reduce fiscal disparity among governments and strengthen the expenditure capability of government units with constrained taxing powers.

Tax-sharing programs from central to subnational governments are a common feature of the finances of many countries, including both unitary and federal systems and many countries of the former Soviet Union, but not the United States. In these programs, the central government adopts a tax (for instance, an individual income tax) and establishes what share of collections will be assigned regional or local governments (for instance, 25 percent). In this example, 25 percent of individual income tax collected in each region or locality is distributed to that government. Fiscal choices are made centrally, but a share of the tax accrues to the lower-tier government. Shared revenue may be returned to the region from which it was collected or it may be distributed by formula (for instance, equal per capita shares).

States and School Aid

Elementary and secondary education in the United States has traditionally been a local activity, either of independent school districts or, in some larger cities, of city governments. That arrangement allows local decision making and control so that choices can be made by governments close to the families affected most by the schools. However, state governments have ultimate responsibility for the provision of education; state constitutions contain education clauses that require the state to provide statewide systems of education that are "equitable," "thorough and efficient," "adequate," "general and uniform," and so forth.[33] Local finance seems likely to violate the idea of a "statewide" system because local fiscal capacity (the local tax base) per pupil—and thus access to educational resources—varies widely among districts. Not all local school districts are created equal, so how can the education that they provide be considered equitable across the state? How can this state-provided system of education be accommodated with local control when localities have significant differences in preferences for schooling and in fiscal resources to fund those schools?

There are no simple answers to the dilemma, but one response has been an increased state role in public school finance (Table 14–4). The trend shows an expanding state role in finance, from 30.3 percent of total revenues in 1940 to 48.3 percent in 2009–2010, and a falling local role, 68.0 percent to 43.5 percent in the same period. (The federal role is greater as well, having increased from 1.8 percent to 8.2 percent, but is still small.) However, 2009–2010 state shares do vary widely, from 30.9 percent in South Dakota to 84.4 percent in Vermont.[34] Local school finance remains almost exclusively a matter of property taxation (95.9 percent of school district tax revenue), whereas state finances are usually balanced between sales and income taxes and provide an opportunity for state-aid systems to offset disparities in resources among local districts. In some states, property tax relief has been provided by having the state government assume a greater share of the cost of local schools.

Table 14–4
Public School District Revenues by Source of Funds, Percentage of Total

School Year	Federal	State	Local
1939–1940	1.8	30.3	68.0
1949–1950	2.9	39.8	57.3
1959–1960	4.4	39.1	56.5
1969–1970	8.0	39.9	52.1
1979–1980	9.8	46.8	43.4
1989–1990	6.1	47.1	46.8
1999–2000	7.3	49.5	43.2
2009–2010	8.2	48.3	43.5

SOURCE: U.S. Department of Education Sciences, National Center for Education Statistics, *Digest of Education Statistics: 2010* (Washington, D.C.: 2011).

---

[33]Earlier concerns with equal-protection violations of the U.S. Constitution were resolved in favor of the states in 1973. See *Rodriguez* v. *San Antonio Independent School District,* 411 U.S. 1 (1973). Recent challenges have involved state constitutional requirements. Some of the challenges have brought increased school spending, but some appear to have caused spending to be less than would otherwise have been expected. See Robert L. Manwaring and Steven M. Sheffrin, "Litigation, School Finance Reform, and Aggregate Education Spending," *International Tax and Public Finance* 4 (May 1997): 107–27. Only Delaware, Hawaii, Mississippi, Nevada, and Utah have not had a lawsuit over such school finance issues. Jennifer Carr and Cara Griffith, "School Finance Litigation and Property Tax Reform: Part I, Litigation," *State Tax Notes* (June 27, 2005): 1015.
[34]U.S. Census Bureau, Governments Division, *Public Education Finances Report: 2009–2010* [http://www.census.gov].

There are two big catches with the increased state role in public school finance. First, when the state pays the bills, the state will ultimately want increased control over what goes on in the local schools. The greater the extent of state financing is, the less local officials will have to say about local programs and policies. Second, local school finances become vulnerable to the fiscal condition of state government. A frequent state response to the difficult finances of the recession that started in 2007 has been to reduce the amount of money provided school districts in the state. The state problem gets punted away to the localities. The local districts then get to decide what to do—cut programs, find more revenue, or implement some combination. The choices get even more difficult if the state has placed strict limits on use of the property tax. A local property tax has considerably greater stability than aid from state government.

School-aid systems that states use are remarkable for their complexity as legislators seek to balance local control, state responsibility, and protection for their home districts. It should be no surprise that distribution formulas combine various philosophies, but there are three general systems that have been devised to distribute basic state aid:[35]

1. **Flat grants, general and categorical.** In a few states, every school district receives the same dollar amount per pupil from the state. There is no distinction between high-affluence and low-affluence districts. Some aid may be distributed according to types of students or to finance certain categories of expenditure (such as student transportation on a bus-mile basis).

2. **Foundation grants.** The foundation programs, used in about three-fourths of the states, aid in direct proportion to the number of students and inversely with the local property tax base per pupil. Aid per pupil to a district equals the difference between the per-pupil foundation spending level (the amount of expenditure the state determines to be the minimum acceptable) and the per-pupil revenue the district would collect by applying the statewide target tax rate to the district tax base. States usually require the district to spend at least the foundation amount to receive aid. The aid is designed to fill the gap between the expected foundation spending per pupil and the capacity of the district to finance the spending itself.[36]

3. **Guaranteed tax base (or percentage equalizing).** These formulas provide aid to districts to make up the difference between what the district tax rate raises on the district tax base and what the district tax rate would raise if applied to a guaranteed tax base. Therefore, without regard to actual district affluence per pupil, all districts will raise the same tax per pupil from a given tax rate. Actual aid systems may add other factors, such as adjustments for differences in operating costs among districts, for service to special client populations, or to prevent substantial aid loss from year to year. The

---

[35]Katherine L. Bradbury, "Equity in School Finance: State Aid to Local Schools in New England," *New England Economic Review* (March/April 1993): 25–46.
[36]It is the estimated capacity for self-finance, not actual revenues, to prevent the district from reducing its own taxes to allow more of the cost to be borne by the state.

elements in a state formula may change often, as may the money the state puts into state aid. Many states create hybrids that distribute total aid according to more than one logical system.

States generally are uncomfortable with state school-aid systems. A considerable amount of state revenue has to be raised for school support, and many critics question whether its distribution satisfies the responsibility that states have for seeing to the provision of this service. Local control and state responsibility are real concerns that no system has fully resolved.

Coordination and Assistance: Mandates

A mandate is a constitutional provision, a statute, an administrative regulation, or a judicial ruling that places an expenditure requirement on a government. That requirement comes from outside the government forced to take the action.[37] A state government can mandate local spending, the federal government can mandate either state or local spending, and the judiciary—the branch of government outside the normal budgeting and appropriation flow—can mandate spending at any level. Mandates are like the operating restrictions that governments place on private industry to regulate workplace safety, environmental quality, and so on—or on individuals to purchase health insurance. Indeed, some costly mandates are simply extensions to government of these regulations of the private sector.[38] Much concern about mandates emerges at the local level because these government units typically lack the size needed to respond flexibly to external expenditure shocks (few individual mandates would be sufficiently large, relative to overall expenditure, to significantly disrupt the federal government) and lack the revenue options available to other levels. States also express considerable concern for mandated cost, even as they place such cost on their localities.[39]

---

[37] Advisory Commission on Intergovernmental Relations, *State Mandating of Local Expenditures* (Washington, D.C.: Advisory Commission on Intergovernmental Relations, July 1978), 2. *Gideon* v. *Wainwright*, 372 U.S. 335 (1963), and *Argersinger* v. *Hamlin*, 407 U.S. 25 (1972), illustrate two court mandates.

[38] In *Garcia* v. *San Antonio Metropolitan Transit Authority*, 469 U.S. 70 (1985), the Supreme Court held that the federal Fair Labor Standards Act of 1938, mandating standards for overtime pay and minimum wages, applied to state and local government. The cost implications are substantial. In *Monell* v. *Department of Social Services of the City of New York*, 436 U.S. 658 (1978), the Court eroded the idea of sovereign immunity by extending the right of citizens to sue a government for negligent acts of its employees.

[39] Governments also pick up restrictions as a result of accepting grants from federal or state governments. Grant controls create fewer logistical problems than ordinary mandates because the recipient government accepts obligations as a condition of accepting the funds. There is no compulsion to enter the system. The Advisory Commission on Intergovernmental Relations describes the major federal mandates in *Federal Regulation of State and Local Governments: The Mixed Records of the 1980s* (Washington, D.C.: Advisory Commission on Intergovernmental Relations, 1993).

Mandates seek to cause governments to behave in some manner other than the way they would ordinarily behave. This changed behavior can be directed toward either (1) services and programs or (2) inputs used (normally, personnel). Examples of the former include such things as hours libraries will be open, provision of special education by local schools, jail-condition standards, water temperature in hospitals, provision of legal defense for indigents, and accessibility of facilities to all. Input use mandates encompass required compensation levels, resources acquired, input quality and/or quantity, and the conditions under which the input will be employed. All potentially change the cost of providing any given level of service. Examples include state determination of local welfare-department salaries; required employee training; required funding for pension systems; required participation in unemployment insurance or workers' compensation systems; and regulation of wages, hours, and working conditions. Several of this latter group are simply extensions of requirements applied to private employers.

Beyond the mandates, there are many other state controls on local government action because states establish the "rules of the game" for localities: election frequency, budget and finance structures, permissible forms of government, due process definitions, and so on. Many of these standards cause extra expenditure, but we accept them as reasonable costs of an informed democracy. Rules of the game, however, are often designed to reduce local government costs by limiting competition among local units, restricting direct democracy initiatives and official elections, constraining elected officials' salaries, or defining tax processes on a statewide basis. They are clearly of a different nature than the earlier group of mandates. Other interventions determine tax-burden distribution as the scope of local taxation is defined (e.g., residential electricity may be removed from the local sales tax base). Furthermore, these controls, along with controlling the rules of the game, are best considered with the home-rule issue and the balance between local power and state sovereignty. One of the biggest state mandates on local governments in 2009 was the effort by the state of California to force municipalities to "loan" the state $2 billion in property tax revenue to help the state with its huge fiscal problem. States frequently reduce transfers to their localities when state finances are difficult, but this proposal sets new standards for forceful application of Dillon's Rule.[40]

The case for mandates has two logical elements. First, the benefit of a lower unit's action (or the cost of its inaction) may spill beyond the lower unit's boundaries. For example, an irresponsible action by one government can reduce that unit's expenditures (and the taxes paid by those in that unit), while harming residents of adjacent governments; the state government may mandate service levels to prevent damaging innocent bystanders. Second, the legislature or the judiciary may view statewide uniformity as essential. The state may require equal expenditure per unit for schools, sanitation, and so on to prevent individuals from having low service levels solely because of their residence. Expenditure correction thus is mandated.

---

[40]In another intergovernmental approach to dealing with the state fiscal crisis in 2009, the state proposed to change sentencing guidelines so that inmates sentenced to state prisons could be shifted to local jails. Bobby White, "California Looks to Cut State Prison Population," *Wall Street Journal,* June 13–14, 2009, A3.

Against these arguments for mandates are strong counter-cases. First, many argue that the mandating government unit should be responsible for financing the mandate. The mandate can become a political tool for the higher government unit, while the lower government unit bears the burden of finance—a condition not conducive to careful decision making. Second, mandates can threaten other government programs. If limits constrain a government's ability to raise revenue, mandates for certain expenditures can endanger the provision of other desirable services. Third, mandates are characteristically enacted without cost awareness. Although the mandate's result may be desirable, the cost of its achievement may be excessive, particularly when compared with the return from other uses of government resources. Mandates seldom are imposed in an environment favorable to cost-benefit comparisons. This is particularly true when mandates emerge from the judiciary. More than half the states estimate the cost of state mandates to localities, but there is seldom any effort to identify the cost to the government units that must finance the expenditures. Finally, mandates restrict fiscal autonomy. Mandates are clearly an uneasy companion to home rule.

For decisions about mandates, the appropriate comparison would appear to be whether the resource cost created by the mandate is worth the return generated by the mandate. Inflicting costs on other units may not be a likely way to generate that comparison. Some suggest that mandates without financial assistance sufficient to cover their costs are a violation of intergovernmental fair play. Others point out that governments do not finance mandated activities for private firms or individuals (minimum-wage requirements, safety regulations, etc.); therefore, although mandates may raise questions of appropriate government roles, they do not necessarily require accommodating fiscal transfers.

Concerns about cost imposed on state and local governments induced Congress to pass the Unfunded Mandates Reform Act of 1995 (UMRA; P.L. 104–4) in order "to end the imposition, in the absence of full consideration by Congress, of federal mandates on state, local, and tribal governments without adequate federal funding." Rather than prohibiting mandates or requiring that mandates be financed, the Act requires that the cost of mandates to subnational governments be explicitly identified by Congress before it approves a mandate. The idea is that transparency and accompanying shame might keep Congress from imposing cost on other governments. The Act has three critical elements:[41]

1. **The Act defines** mandates to be "any provision in legislation, statute, or regulation that would impose an *enforceable duty* on state, local, or tribal governments or the private sector, or that would reduce or eliminate the amount of funding authorized to cover the costs of existing mandates." The definition includes direct requirements for state and local spending, provisions that preempt use of certain revenue sources by subnational governments, and reductions in federal aid that defrays subnational government costs of complying with existing federal mandates.

---

[41]Congressional Budget Office, *An Assessment of the Unfunded Mandates Reform Act in 1997* (Washington, D.C.: U.S. Government Printing Office, 1998).

2. **The Act assigns** the Congressional Budget Office the task of informing congressional committees when their bills contain federal mandates. When the total direct costs of government mandates in a bill exceed an inflation-adjusted threshold ($71 million now, initially $50 million) in any of the first five fiscal years in which the mandates are effective, the CBO must estimate those costs (if feasible), and the committees must publish these mandate statements. The CBO statements also assess whether the bill provides funds to cover the costs of any new mandate.

3. **The Act provides** an enforcement mechanism. Neither house of Congress may consider legislation that contains mandates unless the bill has a CBO statement about costs of mandates and provides direct spending authority or authorization for appropriations sufficient to cover the costs. However, the provision is not self-enforcing—a member of Congress must raise a formal objection for the requirements to be applied. A majority of the body can pass the mandate anyway, but the provision guarantees debate on the mandate, should any member so wish.

The UMRA controls exclude certain types of mandates, including those preventing discrimination, establishing conditions of grants, and preempting state and local authority to regulate or provide services that do not carry state or local fiscal implications. The exclusion of grant conditions allows the federal government to continue its influence within the realm of state and local affairs. However, new grant conditions or funding caps for eleven entitlement grant programs, such as Medicaid, are defined as mandates under the Act if state and local governments lack authority to adjust these changes.

From the effective date of the Act in January 1996 through 2011, the CBO reported that only thirteen bills had been enacted that exceeded the mandate threshold established in the Act.[42] Whether this congressional restraint has been a result of the Act is unknown. However, laws with smaller mandates have been passed, and state and local governments note that nothing has been done about the existing mandates.

Conclusion

Multiple levels of government provide public services in the United States and other federal nations. That diversity allows greater individual choice, but service delivery cannot be entirely uncoordinated because of two factors: intergovernmental spillovers and fiscal imbalance. Spillovers occur when an action by one government has an impact (good or bad) on its neighbors. Intergovernmental intervention can induce governments to allow for those external effects. Imbalance emerges because fiscal capacity is unevenly distributed across the nation and within states. Without an

---

[42]Congressional Budget Office, *A Review of CBO's Activities in 2011 under the Unfunded Mandates Reform Act* (Washington, D.C.: U.S. Government Printing Office, 2012). Theresa Gullo, "History and Evaluation of the Unfunded Mandates Reform Act," *National Tax Journal* 57 (September 2004): 559–70, provides a review and evaluation of the operation of the Act.

intergovernmental response, some individuals will be unduly penalized by the public sector simply because of where they live.

Those intergovernmental problems can be reduced by three varieties of coordination: revenue adjustments (relief, administrative assistance, source separation, or coordinated use of a single base), grants (categorical, block, or revenue-sharing), or mandates. The devices together help retain the advantages of multilevel government without some associated problems.

QUESTIONS AND EXERCISES

1. Your state constitution almost certainly contains an education clause. What does the clause say? How might it be used (or how has it already been used) to challenge the system of financing local schools? On what basis does your state distribute assistance to local schools?

2. Mundane County wants to develop an old railroad right-of-way into a hiking and bicycling trail. Information about available federal grant programs appears at the website http://www.grants.gov. Explore that website to determine whether a federal aid program might be available to assist with the program. (This website also is the medium through which federal grant proposals must be submitted, so understanding its features could be useful for your career.) If you do locate an appropriate program, what critical points would need to be in the proposal to improve its chances for success?

3. Which of the government functions listed in the United Nations Classification of Functions of Government (Appendix 6–2) would normally be work for the central government, and which would normally be assigned to subnational governments?

CASES FOR DISCUSSION

CASE 14–1

It Worked Once, But Would It Work Again?

The following selection appeared in the *Wall Street Journal*. No questions about it are necessary.

The Squirrel Memo

Many releases and handouts that cross newspaper desks each day could be offered as prime exhibits for hiking the postal rates on unsolicited mail. But occasionally there's gold in them thar hills, and we offer as evidence a recent item from the news bureau of Washington and Lee University in Lexington, Virginia.

It seems that one Frank Parsons, assistant to the university president, was struggling with a lengthy application for federal funds to be used in building the university's proposed new library. Among other things, HEW wanted to know how the proposed project "may affect energy sources by introducing or deleting electromagnetic wave sources which may alter man-made or natural structures or the physiology, behavior patterns, and/or activities of 10 percent of a human, animal or plant population." The questions go on and on. But you get the idea.

Assistant Parsons plugged away, dutifully answering as best he could. And then he came to the section on animal populations, where he was asked to list the extent to which the proposed library would "create or precipitate an identifiable long-term change in the diversity of species within its natural habitat."

"There are some 10 to 20 squirrels living, or appearing to live, in the site proposed for the new library," he wrote. "Some trees that now provide either homes or exercise areas for the squirrels will be removed, but there appear to be ample other trees to serve either or both of these purposes. No major food source for the squirrels will be affected. It is likely that the squirrels will find no difficulty in adjusting to this intrusion. . . . They have had no apparent difficulty in adjusting to relocations brought on by nonfederally supported projects." To the question of whether the proposal will "create or precipitate an identifiable change in the behavior patterns of an animal population," he assured HEW the squirrels and such would have to make some adjustments but "it will be difficult to tell if they're unhappy about having to find new trees to live in and sport about."

Eventually the application was shipped off to Washington, and lo and behold, before long HEW official Richard R. Holden actually wrote the president of the school. He said: "Perhaps bureaucracy will tremble, but I salute Washington and Lee University. . . . The mountain of paperwork which confronts me daily somehow seemed much smaller the day I read about the squirrels in Lexington. May they and your great university coexist in harmony for many, many years." As copies of the correspondence zipped throughout federal agencies, with all the speed of a confidential memo destined for Jack Anderson, bureaucrats from all over telephoned their congratulations to the "squirrel memo man."

We're still not sure exactly what lesson is to be drawn from all this. Our initial reaction was surprise that anyone actually reads these exhaustive applications, and even now we're undecided whether that's cause for comfort or dismay. Yet while we never doubted that HEW possessed a sense of humor—indeed, we've gotten some of our biggest laughs from proposals emanating from the vicinity of 330 Independence Ave., S.W.—it's nice to know that an occupational devotion to red tape has not completely eroded the agency's ability to laugh at itself.

SOURCE: *The Wall Street Journal by News Corporation; Dow Jones & Co Copyright 1974 Reproduced with permission of DOW JONES & COMPANY, INC. in the formats Republish in a textbook and "other" book via Copyright Clearance Center.*

CASE 14–2

Correspondence, Subsidiarity, and the Tenn-Tom Waterway

You read about the development of the Tenn-Tom Waterway in Case 2–1. Along with political lessons, that case involves dimensions of intergovernmental fiscal relations. In that regard, read the case again.

Consider These Questions

1. According to the principle of subsidiarity, should the Tenn-Tom have been a federal, state, or local project?

2. If principles of subsidiarity and correspondence had been followed, is it likely that the waterway would have been built?

CHAPTER 15

Debt Administration

Federal, state, or local government debt results when that government borrows from an individual or institution. Borrowing changes the pattern of purchasing power between the lender and the borrower. The lender forgoes purchasing power now for the promise of repayment later, and the borrower receives purchasing power now with an obligation for repayment later. The bond representing that debt is a long-term promise by the borrower (bond issuer) to the lender (bondholder) to pay the bond's face amount (or par value or the principal of the loan) at a defined maturity date and to make contractual interest payments until the loan is retired.[1] It is a contract between the borrower and the lender. The borrower is committed to debt service—interest payments as required plus periodic repayment of the principal—through the life of the loan.

Government debt results from (1) covering deficits (annual expenditures greater than annual revenues), (2) financing capital-project construction, and (3) covering short periods within a fiscal year in which bills exceed cash on hand. Not all governments borrow for the same set of reasons. In particular, the causes of the debt of the federal government are not the same as those behind the debt of state and local governments.

---

[1]Some governments, notably the British, have sold obligations with no maturity, but paying interest in perpetuity. Holders of these securities, called consols, may retrieve principal by sale to another investor. Another variation: some debt is sold on a discount basis; the difference between what is paid for the debt instrument by the lender and the amount repaid by the borrower constitutes the interest. Short-term obligations—typically sold on a discount basis—are called bills and notes. Massachusetts Institute of Technology, a nonprofit organization, borrowed $750 million with 100-year bonds in 2011, not exactly a consol, but a close approximation. It locked in an interest rate of 5.62 percent, which it regarded as very attractive. Goldie Blumenstyk, "MIT Borrows for the Long Run with a $750 Million 'Century Bond,'" *Chronicle of Higher Education*, May 12, 2011. The U.S. Treasury plans to start selling floating-rate notes in 2013. On these notes, the rate of interest would be periodically reset to prevailing interest rates as measured by a market index, rather than bearing a fixed interest rate through the life of the obligation, as do other federal debt. [Matt Phillips and Jeffery Sparshott, "Treasury Decides to Offer Floating-Rate Notes," *Wall Street Journal*, August 2, 2012: C4.]

Federal Debt

The federal government's debt is the product of war finance, attempts to stabilize the nation's macroeconomy (i.e., to deal with problems of unemployment and slow growth),[2] and miscellaneous political situations that have caused lawmakers to disregard the relationship between federal revenues and federal expenditures. The amount of debt is the result of federal choices about spending and raising revenue, not a debt objective itself. The level of debt equals the accumulation of all annual deficits since the start of the federal government less all annual surpluses. It is far easier to run a deficit than a surplus, and, when there is a deficit, there will be an addition to total debt. As the General Accounting Office (GAO) explains:

> The federal deficit … is the difference between total federal spending and revenue in a given year. To cover this gap, the government borrows from the public. Each yearly deficit adds to the amount of debt held by the public. In other words, the deficit is the annual amount of government borrowing, while the debt represents the cumulative amount of outstanding borrowing from the public over the nation's history…. [Each year] the federal government pays only the interest costs of its debt. The principal is paid off when bonds come due. The cash to pay the principal comes from additional borrowing; hence the debt is "rolled over" or refinanced. To reduce its debt, the government would need to run a budget surplus and use the surplus funds to pay off the principal of maturing debt securities.[3]

There are two important overall measures of federal debt: *gross debt,* which equals all federal debt outstanding, and *debt held by private investors,* which equals all federal debt except that held by federal accounts and the Federal Reserve System. Figure 15–1 traces both measures of the federal debt since 1940, each as a percentage of gross domestic product (GDP) to accommodate the considerable difference in the size of the economy over those years.[4] Debt rose dramatically—equaling 122 percent of GDP in 1946—as a consequence of financing World War II. (In absolute terms, the federal government has never eliminated the debt issued to finance World War II. The economy grew, and, over time, that debt lost its economic significance without ever actually disappearing. This is an important point: the United States really does not need to eliminate its debt. It does, however, need to

---

[2]Management of the federal debt, including the mechanics of issuing new debt, is intimately connected to decisions about and implementation of national monetary and fiscal policy. A good history of the federal debt and how it has been managed is Donald R. Stabile and Jeffrey A. Cantor, *The Public Debt of the United States: Historical Perspective, 1775–1990* (Westport, Conn.: Praeger, 1991). Most of the federal debt has been issued by the Treasury, but a small amount, less than 1 percent of total federal debt held by the public, has been issued by agencies directly (Tennessee Valley Authority Corporation, Architect of the Capitol, National Archives, Federal Housing Administration, etc.). This agency debt has little practical difference from the rest and is included with federal totals. Office of Management and Budget, *Budget of the Government of the United States, Fiscal Year 2010, Analytical Perspectives* (Washington, D.C.: U.S. Government Printing Office, 2009), 229–32.

[3]General Accounting Office, Federal Debt: Answers to Frequently Asked Questions, GAO/AIMD-97-12 (Washington, D.C.: U.S. Government Printing Office, 1996), 13–16. The exception is the rare years in which there is a federal surplus rather than the persistent deficit.

[4]The federal government started life in debt—the War of Independence was fought with loans from foreign banks—and, with the exception of a brief period in the mid-1830s, has been in debt ever since. We are the best borrowers in the world.

Figure 15–1

Gross and Net Federal Debt as a Percentage of GDP, 1940–2011

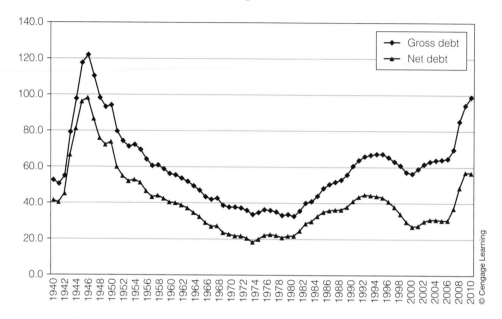

keep it under control relative to the size of the economy, and our elected officials have not done an outstanding job of this in recent years. It hasn't eliminated the debt created from the Civil War or World War I either, but that seems not to have harmed economic progress very much. Refinancing debt as it matured seems to have worked rather well.) From that peak, the percentage fell almost continuously until the mid-1970s—reaching a low of 33 percent in 1981—as economic growth was greater than the rate of increase of the debt; debt in public hands reached a low of 18 percent in 1974. Occasional surpluses sometimes even allowed debt to be retired. Except for a drop in the 1990s, the record has been one of increases in this ratio. It is likely to continue to rise in the foreseeable future. (Recall the rather alarming CBO estimates presented in Chapter 3.)[5]

Details on the federal debt appear in Table 15–1. Debt held by private investors is an impressive number—more than $8 trillion in 2011—but not as large as the gross federal debt—more than $14 trillion. Both have increased dramatically in total and in relation to GDP since the turn of the century. That's what happens when the federal government spends way more than its revenue, and the gap is increasing more rapidly than the economy. The amount of debt in private investor hands depends on accumulated federal deficits (gross public debt), monetary policy

---

[5]See Kenneth D. Garbade, "Why the U.S. Treasury Began Auctioning Treasury Bills in 1929," *Federal Reserve Bank of New York Economic Policy Review* 14 (July 2008): 31–47, for a description of Treasury bill auctions, the most common way the federal government borrows, and the reasons behind creation of the auctions.

Table 15–1
Federal Debt from Fiscal 1940 to 2011

End of Fiscal Year	Gross Debt ($ Millions)	Gross Debt as % GDP	Debt Held by Private Investors ($ Millions)	Debt Held by Private Investors (% GDP)	Average Maturity
1940	50,696	52.4	40,314	41.6	
1945	260,123	117.5	213,390	96.4	
1950	256,853	94.1	200,692	73.5	
1955	274,366	69.3	203,009	51.3	
1960	290,525	56.0	210,317	40.5	
1965	322,318	46.9	221,678	32.2	
1970	380,921	37.6	225,484	22.3	3 yr 8 mo
1975	541,925	34.7	309,707	19.9	2 yr 8 mo
1980	909,041	33.4	591,077	21.7	3 yr 9 mo
1985	1,817,423	43.8	1,337,454	32.3	4 yr 11 mo
1990	3,206,290	55.9	2,177,147	38.0	6 yr 1 mo
1995	4,920,586	67.0	3,230,264	44.0	5 yr 4 mo
2000	5,628,700	57.3	2,898,391	29.5	6 yr 2 mo
2001	5,769,881	56.4	2,785,480	27.2	6 yr 1 mo
2002	6,198,401	58.8	2,936,235	27.8	5 yr 6 mo
2003	6,760,014	61.6	3,257,327	29.7	5 yr 1 mo
2004	7,354,657	62.9	3,595,203	30.8	4 yr 11 mo
2005	7,905,300	63.5	3,855,852	31.0	4 yr 10 mo
2006	8,451,350	63.9	4,060,048	30.7	4 yr 11 mo
2007	8,950,744	64.4	4,255,497	30.6	4 yr 10 mo
2008	9,986,082	69.4	5,311,923	36.9	4 yr 1 mo
2009	11,875,851	84.2	6,775,547	48.1	4 yr 1 mo
2010	13,528,807	93.2	8,207,272	56.6	4 yr 9 mo
2011	14,764,222	98.7	8,463,546	56.6	5yr

SOURCE: Executive Office of the President, Office of Management and Budget, *Budget of the United States Government, Fiscal Year 2012, Historical Tables* (Washington, D.C., OMB, 2011), United States Department of the Treasury, Treasury Bulletin (various issues).

actions by the Federal Reserve that involve purchase and sale of federal debt, and federal trust funds' investable cash balances. Privately held debt excludes federal debt owned by elements of the federal government, leaving debt that represents a net requirement for resource transfer to private holders as the debt is serviced.

Federal agency or trust fund accounts held roughly 30 percent of federal securities in 2012.[6] The Social Security Trust Fund is the largest single holder of federal securities (and, remember from Chapter 3, the value should be even more if the obligations of the fund are to be met). These agencies and accounts acquire the debt in their cash-management programs because such debt is safe and politically neutral—certainly less hazardous in most respects than, say, holding stock in

---

[6]Details on federal debt holdings throughout this chapter come from the quarterly publication of the U.S. Treasury, the *Treasury Bulletin*.

J. P. Morgan Chase or Exxon Mobil or bonds issued by the German government.[7] This debt is not a net claim on federal government resources. The Federal Reserve system conducts monetary policy by sale and purchase of federal debt, so these transactions to change the supply of money in the economy also influence the amount of debt in private hands. Because the Federal Reserve Banks legally must return to the U.S. Treasury sizable portions of interest received and because they are, at least loosely, government agencies, their holdings also—just above 11 percent of the total federal debt in 2012—do not represent an outside claim on the government. For most analytical purposes, it is the debt held by private investors—that debt outside federal agencies, federal trust funds, and Federal Reserve Banks—that is the major concern for federal debt policy. The share of the debt that is privately held—the share that represents a net requirement for resource transfer outside government— declined throughout the 1990s and the first decades of the 2000s, to 58 percent in 2012 from around 68 percent in 1990. The net debt ratio to GDP was 56.6 percent in 2011. That puts the United States somewhat above the median of 42.9 percent for countries of the Organization for Economic Cooperation and Development. Greece (147.8 percent), Italy (109.0 percent), Belgium (96.8 percent), Portugal (88.0 percent), the United Kingdom (85.5 percent), and Iceland (81.3 percent) were at the top in 2010, while Estonia (3.2 percent), Chile (9.2 percent), Australia (11.0 percent), Luxembourg (12.6 percent), Switzerland (20.2 percent), Norway (26.1 percent), and Mexico (27.5 percent) were at the low end.[8]

One notable change in historical pattern is the new importance of foreign and international ownership of the federal debt. Until the mid-1970s, foreign ownership of the federal debt was small, considerably less than 10 percent of the total privately held debt. However, those holdings quickly jumped to around 20 percent in the mid- 1970s and have expanded since then. At the end of 2011, 54.3 percent of privately held federal debt was in foreign and international investor ownership. Repayment of that portion of federal debt cannot be casually dismissed with "we owe it to ourselves." Servicing that debt transfers resources from U.S. taxpayers to foreign bondholders, a condition with substantially different standard-of-living implications for the United States than if the payment of debt service was going mostly to other Americans. As long as foreign entities build up dollar reserves in international trade and world investors regard U.S. government debt as yielding a high return without significant risk of political upheaval, such investment will continue. Bond purchases are made by our major trading partners; those countries are the ones with individuals and institutions having dollars to invest. In December 2011, the major shares of the Treasury securities in international ownership were the following: Mainland China

---

[7]There's even a section of an amendment to the U.S. Constitution giving assurance: Article XIV, Section 4 states: "The validity of the public debt of the United States, authorized by law, including debts incurred for payment of pensions and bounties for services in suppressing insurrection or rebellion, shall not be questioned." So when members of Congress or candidates for president question the value of the assets supporting the Social Security system—those Social Security bonds that sit in a vault in West Virginia— have they committed a treasonable offense? They have questioned the validity of the public debt, which is a constitutional "no-no."

[8]Organization for Economic Cooperation and Development, *Central Government Debt* [http://stats.oecd .org/Index.aspx?DatasetCode=GOV_DEBT].

(23.1 percent), Japan (21.2 percent), Oil exporters (5.2 percent), Brazil (4.5 percent), Caribbean Banking Centers (4.5 percent), Taiwan (3.6 percent), Russia (3 percent), and Luxembourg (3 percent). Other countries held less than 3 percent of the total.[9] Compared to other governments in the world, the U.S. federal government is seen as a safe haven for international funds, and that helps keep the interest rate that the federal government pays on its debt low, even with rising debt levels.

Table 15–1 shows that the federal debt tends to have a short term to maturity, averaging 5 years at the end of fiscal 2011. That is a reflection of the fact that the federal government has historically borrowed to finance its continuing deficits, not to finance long-life capital projects. The maturity has lengthened in recent years, from its low point of 2 years and 8 months at the end of 1975, but it is much shorter than the post–World War II maximum of 10 years and 5 months at the start of 1947.[10] In late 2001, the Treasury stopped selling thirty-year bonds, historically the benchmark bond in many financial markets, with the intention that the longest Treasury bond would have a ten-year maturity. That was in the era in which it was feared that the federal surpluses would wipe out federal debt entirely. However, the return to deficit conditions brought the thirty-year bond back in 2005.[11]

The relatively short maturity combines with the substantial federal debt to create a continued federal presence in debt markets, either refinancing maturing debt or financing new cash needs (i.e., covering the deficit). However, interest rates tend to be lower for short-term than for long-term loans, so maturity shortening can reduce the interest cost of serving the debt.

Although some federal debt is sold directly to the public, most is sold through a small group of primary security dealers who acquire the debt at auction for resale to investors.[12] Yields are normally established at those auctions at fixed nominal levels. Most securities sold by the U.S. Treasury pay a set return, but, as Sidebar 15-1 describes, it also sells some securities that pay inflation-indexed returns to investors.[13]

A reasonable question is why worry about the government debt of the central government? The federal government is an experienced debtor, having been in debt from the instant of its founding to now, except for a brief time in 1835, and has been

[9]Justin Murray and Marc Labonte, "Foreign Holdings of Federal Debt," *Congressional Research Service Report for Congress*, 7-5700 (July 3, 2012).

[10]*Treasury Bulletin* (March 1989), 32.

[11]Most federal debt is in the form of notes or bonds that pay a fixed interest rate through their term to maturity. Another form is the Treasury bill, a short-term maturity instrument with a broad and lively secondary market that allows them to be converted to cash easily. T-bills are sold weekly on an auction basis in which bidders offer less than the face value of the instrument (a discount), with the difference between face value on maturity and the amount paid equaling the return on the investment. The annualized rate of return or yield rate on a discounted bill equals $Y = [(FV - P)/FV] * [360/M]$ where P = the purchase price paid for the bill, FV = the face value of the bill, M = the maturity of the bill, and 360 = the number of days used by banks to determine short-term interest rates. The discount yield for a 182-day T-bill at a price of $9,659.30 for a $10,000 bill would be $Y = [(10,000 - 9,659.30)/ 10,000] *[360/182] = 0.06739$.

[12]The process through which the Treasury borrows is described in Kenneth D. Garbade and Jeffrey F. Ingber, "The Treasury Auction Process: Objectives, Structure, and Recent Adaptations," *Current Issues in Economics and Finance* (Federal Reserve Bank of New York) 11 (February 2005): 1–11.

[13]A good discussion of the U.S. experience with inflation-indexed borrowing is B. Sack and R. Elasser, "Treasury Inflation-Indexed Debt: A Review of the U.S. Experience," *Federal Reserve Bank of New York Economic Policy Review* 10 (May 2004): 47–63.

Sidebar 15–1
Inflation-Indexed Bonds

Conventional bonds repay the bondholder the principal of the loan plus a contracted interest rate; an inflation-indexed bond repays the principal adjusted for inflation plus the contracted interest rate applied to that adjusted principal. That prevents the purchasing power of the investment from being eaten away by unexpected price increases. Price increases in the economy will be matched by higher payments from the indexed bond—so holders of indexed bonds are not hurt by inflation. Their real rate of return is protected.

A number of governments, including those of Israel, the United Kingdom, Australia, Canada, Sweden, Mexico, Argentina, and New Zealand, have sold such bonds. The U.S. Treasury offered its first index bonds in January 1997—$7 billion worth of ten-year bonds with a 3.45 percent coupon rate—with the intent for quarterly auctions of more such bonds. In contrast with conventional bonds, the principal is adjusted before each semiannual payment to reflect any change in the Consumer Price Index since the issue of the bond. By that adjustment, the real return from the bond remains the same for the bondholder—and the U.S. Treasury knows the real, but not the nominal, cost of this debt. These are now referred to by the Treasury as Treasury inflation-protected securities (TIPS).

Jeffrey Wrase of the Federal Reserve Bank of Philadelphia provides a comparison of payments for conventional and indexed bonds:[1]

> Consider a 10-year conventional nominal bond and a 10-year inflation-indexed bond. Each bond is purchased at its face, or principal, value of $1,000. Although Treasury notes and bonds provide semiannual payments, the bonds in this example are assumed to provide annual coupon payments. Each coupon payment on a conventional bond is the coupon rate stated on the bond times the principal. Each coupon payment on an indexed bond is the coupon rate times the indexed principal. The indexed principal is simply the beginning principal of $1,000 scaled up through time at the rate of inflation. We'll assume that the coupon rate on the indexed bond is 3 percent, and that actual inflation over the 10-year horizon turns out to be a steady 2 percent, equal to expected inflation, and that the coupon rate on the conventional bond is 5.06 percent so that its expected real rate of return equals the coupon rate on the indexed bond.

[1]Jeffrey M. Wrase, "Inflation-Indexed Bonds: How Do They Work?" *Federal Reserve Bank of Philadelphia Business Review* (July/August 1997): 5

(continues)

devoid of crises along the way. The deficit is a concern as a violation of fiscal sustainability, but not if the reason for the deficit is the acquisition of productive capital assets (infrastructure) that will yield a return to the future generations that will face the requirement of paying the service on the debt issued to support the deficit.[14] But the debt level relative to the size of the economy can be an economic and financial

[14]It can also be argued that the costs of fighting the Civil War and World War II (and probably World War I) fall into the category of long-life capital expenditures. The consequences of losing those wars would have been extraordinarily bad for the American public, so the return from the huge, one-time expenditure of fighting the war stretched far into the future. That sounds like a classic justification for debt finance within the context of fiscal sustainability.

**Sidebar 15–1
(continued)**

A schedule of nominal and real values of payments on the bonds is given below. The real values give the purchasing power of the nominal payments. For example, suppose a given item today costs $1. With 2 percent inflation, at the end of the year the same item will cost $1.02, and $1 will purchase 0.98 (1/1.02) units of the item. So, $50.60 received at the end of year 1 from the nominal bond will purchase 49.61 units.

As the schedule of payments shows, the nominal value of the conventional bond's principal stays fixed. The real value is eroding through time because of inflation. When received at maturity, the $1,000 principal can purchase 820.35 units of the good. In contrast, when the bond was first purchased, that $1,000 could buy 1,000 units. The payment schedule also shows how the fixed nominal payment of $50.60 per year on the nominal bond has a smaller real value over time because of inflation. Note that for the indexed bond, the real values of the principal and interest payments are preserved for the life of the bond. As the principal gets scaled up, so, too, does the nominal coupon payment to preserve the real return of 3 percent. The indexed bond pays less interest than the nominal bond each year, but that is offset by its larger payment of principal at maturity.

Schedule of Payments

Year	Conventional Bond				Indexed Bond			
	Nominal Value of Principal	Real Value of Principal	Nominal Interest Payment	Real Value of Interest Payment	Nominal Value of Principal	Real Value of Principal	Nominal Interest Payment	Real Value of Interest Payment
1	$1,000	980.39	$50.60	49.61	$1,200.00	1000	$30.60	30
2	$1,000	961.17	$50.60	48.64	$1,040.40	1000	$31.21	30
3	$1,000	942.32	$50.60	47.68	$1,061.21	1000	$31.84	30
4	$1,000	923.85	$50.60	46.75	$1,082.43	1000	$32.47	30
5	$1,000	905.73	$50.60	45.83	$1,104.08	1000	$33.12	30
6	$1,000	887.97	$50.60	44.93	$1,126.16	1000	$33.78	30
7	$1,000	870.56	$50.60	44.05	$1,148.69	1000	$34.46	30
8	$1,000	853.49	$50.60	43.19	$1,171.66	1000	$35.15	30
9	$1,000	836.75	$50.60	42.34	$1,195.09	1000	$35.85	30
10	$1,000	820.35	$50.60	41.51	$1,218.99	1000	$36.60	30

Total Nominal Receipts:	$1,506
Real Value of Principal at Maturity:	$820.35
Total Nominal Receipts:	$1,554.07
Real Value of Indexed Principal at Maturity:	$1,000

concern beyond the worries about the accumulated deficits. First, there is the worry that the debt level will be so large relative to the economy that potential lenders will refuse to lend at all or, if they lend, they will do so only at disastrously high interest rates. Being shut out of the capital market is a major worry because governments need to borrow for capital projects, for bridge financing during the year, and for rollover of maturing debt. In mid-2012, this was the problem that the Greek government faced. Its debt level, around 160 percent of GDP, was so large that lenders were not willing to make loans and international bodies were unwilling to assist without substantial fiscal reforms by the government. The U.S. federal government is not close to this sort of limit, but many believe that some precaution is necessary to prevent that eventuality.

The second concern is important, but possibly without all the draconian implications of the first. As debt levels increase, so must the need for debt service, predominantly interest payments if maturing debt is mostly rolled over into new debt. When interest obligations become large, they crowd out other spending programs from available tax revenue. Legislators face the difficult choice between raising taxes to allow both debt service and public programs and reducing public programs to meet debt service without increasing taxes. Both options create difficult political problems. Those problems can be mitigated by controlling the increase in the debt level, which is easier to do gradually than by waiting until the interest crunch truly hits. The federal government has been insulated from this problem in recent years by the extremely low interest rates during the Great Recession. The concern promises to build, however, as the economy improves and interest rates increase and as debt continues to build. Of course, the way to deal with the debt is actually to deal with the deficit—and that has to do with taxation and expenditure policy, not directly with debt.

The federal government operates under a statutory debt ceiling. The ceiling was first enacted during World War I when Congress got somewhat concerned about the amount of appropriations it was approving for the support of the war and other programs. The ceiling was intended to provide a degree of fiscal control over federal fiscal operations. This approach to control was superseded by the enactment of the federal budget process in the Budget and Accounting Act of 1921—it is far better to control spending before it occurs than to prevent payment for services that have already been provided.[15] Although the original purpose of the debt ceiling had been taken care of by an improved mechanism, no Congress got around to eliminating the ceiling, thus continuing control of paying for bills that had already been incurred rather than controlling the spending itself, a remarkably inefficient constraint concept. The absolute amount of the ceiling got increased by congressional action each time before the actual debt reached the limit. However, in the summer of 2011, Congress balked at enacting the necessary increase (as was discussed in Chapter 3), preferring to return to the World War I logic and threatening default on federal debt service. The nation's creditworthiness was appropriately adjusted downward—the threat of missing a scheduled payment is sufficient to make lenders nervous. A Government Accountability Office study of the episode found that the delay in increasing the ceiling increased Treasury borrowing cost by $1.3 billion and that there will be additional costs in future years.[16] Of course, those extra costs add to the federal debt.

---

[15]As of July 2012, the ceiling was $16,394,000 million. It is anticipated that it will have to be increased in early 2013.
[16]U.S. Government Accountability Office, "Debt Limit: Analysis of 2011—2012 Actions Taken and Effect of Delayed Increase on Borrowing Costs," GAO-12-701, July 2012.

State and Local Government (Municipal) Debt

State and local government debt has similarly grown rapidly since the early 1970s, from $175.2 billion in 1972 to $2,683.7 billion in 2009. In 2007, the most recent year for which debt by type of local government is available, the total was $2,379 billion. This debt, the product of borrowing by states, counties, municipalities, townships, school districts, and special districts as shown in Table 15–2 for 2007, is all called municipal debt, distinguishing it from corporate or federal issues. Total local government debts are larger than are total state government debts, and cities have more debt than any other form of local government. The preponderance of this debt is long-term. That differs radically from the federal debt. Furthermore, municipal debt is typically issued for construction of identifiable long-life assets. Much of the debt is for education, transportation, and public-utility infrastructure. The borrowing occurs to finance an identifiable, specific structure. Such an identification of purposes, of course, would not be possible for federal debt.

State-local debt can be either full-faith-and-credit debt or nonguaranteed (limited-liability) debt. Full-faith-and-credit obligations "have an unlimited claim"[17] on the taxes (and other revenues) of the issuing unit; nonguaranteed debt issues lack that assurance and are sold on the basis of repayment from particular revenue sources only. Because public-debt purchasers (the individuals and institutions lending the money to state-local governments) regard the claim on all tax resources as offering greater likelihood that bond principal and interest payments will be made on time, full-faith-and-credit debt bears a lower interest rate than does equivalent nonguaranteed debt. (Later sections suggest why many governments use nonguaranteed debt, despite its higher cost.)

Most municipal debt is long-term. Long-term state government debt is almost three-quarters nonguaranteed; long-term local government debt is about 45 percent full-faith-and-credit. School districts are major users of full-faith-and-credit—over 95 percent of their debt is of that variety. School districts traditionally have not been operated from user charges (there are strong public policy reasons for providing elementary and secondary education at no direct charge to patrons), so they lack project revenue to support borrowing and must repay from tax and intergovernmental aid revenue. They are the sole sources for repayment, so full-faith-and-credit issues must be the primary mechanism for debt finance for schools. They do establish, however, separate building corporations that issue debt to finance construction with repayment guaranteed by leases charged to a school district, as is discussed later.[18] Other special districts are major users of limited-liability debt—almost 85 percent. Many special districts (waste management, transit, water, etc.) are established on a semi-commercial basis in that they collect charges from their customers and lack a tax

---

[17]Roland I. Robinson, "Debt Administration," in *Management Policies in Local Government Finance,* ed. J. Richard Aronson and Eli Schwartz (Washington, D.C.: International City Management Association, 1975), 23. How "unlimited" that claim actually is is being tested in some municipal bankruptcy cases in 2012.

[18]These building corporations are outside normal fiscal limitations—"off the books" in a manner similar to entities associated with Enron and other private businesses.

Table 15–2
Summary of State and Local Indebtedness 2006–2007 ($ thousands)

Description	State and Local Government Amount	State Government Amount	Local Government Amount	County Government Amount	Municipal and Township Government Amount	Special District Government Amount	School District Government Amount
Debt outstanding	2,411,298,345	936,523,700	1,474,774,645	261,637,207	597,585,042	295,972,455	319,579,941
Short-term	31,939,117	6,576,664	25,362,453	4,284,883	9,716,784	4,023,589	7,337,197
Long-term	2,379,359,228	929,947,036	1,449,412,192	257,352,324	587,868,258	291,948,866	312,242,744

SOURCE: U.S. Census Bureau, Government Division, State & Local Government Finance.

base for guaranteeing their debt. Around two-thirds of city debt is limited-liability. Short-term debt at both levels is almost completely full-faith-and-credit. Nonguaranteed debt is outside the limits frequently placed on municipal government debt by state statute or constitution. Interest on such debt is, however, eligible for the same exclusion from federal taxation received by municipal debt. That creates a logical inconsistency. In order to invoke tax immunity, the agency that issues those bonds must show that they are the obligations of a state or subdivision. However, in order to provide that they are revenue bonds and not subject to the usual debt limitations, the agency must show that they are not the obligations of any such unit.[19]

Creating and defending the appropriate distinctions is the source of substantial income for bond counsel, legal firms that specialize in issuing opinions on the legality of debt issues, the security of pledge for repayment, and the tax-exempt status of issues. The convenience and savings of having the debt interpreted both ways is usually worth the price of the lawyers. Much revenue bond debt is issued by public authorities, entities with public powers that operate outside the normal constraints placed on government. Governments form authorities to build public projects (bridges, power projects, highways, etc.) and pay off bonds used to finance the construction with charges from users; the authorities seldom have taxing authority. An authority may or may not go out of existence when the bonds are retired.[20] (Special entities created for lease-purchase finance are discussed later.)

The municipal bond market is dominated by revenue bond debt, meaning that revenue from a project (e.g., a parking garage, a sewage treatment plant, or a university dormitory) is pledged for debt service rather than the general revenues (or full faith and credit) of the jurisdiction.[21] This nonguaranteed debt was only 38 percent of all state and local long-term debt outstanding in 1960. It now is around 80 percent of the total. The market has continuously shifted toward nonguaranteed debt to allow governments to avoid legal restrictions placed on general obligation debt and to allow revenue-producing projects to float on their own debt. However, the trend is somewhat troubling for older, large cities: "The economic advantage of cities lies in making the marginal maintenance and repair expenditures that can keep the basic elements of their present infrastructure in adequate working order."[22] Nonguaranteed bonds are not easily adapted to generate financing for reconstruction or maintenance, so the shift indicates special problems for those cities. If the infrastructure (streets, water and sewage systems, etc.) is not maintained, the economic advantage

---

[19]B. U. Ratchford, "Revenue Bonds and Tax Immunity," *National Tax Journal* 7 (March 1954): 42.

[20]For a fascinating view of public authority operation, see Robert Caro, *The Power Broker: Robert Moses and the Fall of New York* (New York: Vintage Books, 1975), chap. 28.

[21]Some local governments have added statements about the prospect of using tax revenue if project revenues are not sufficient, in an effort to obtain a lower interest rate. The meaning of such a fuzzy pledge has recently been tested with cities that opted not to come up with the money when project revenues were inadequate and scheduled debt service was not paid (a default). As with most conflicts, the question will be settled in court. Michael Corkery, "The Next Credit Crisis? Munis," *Wall Street Journal*, November 20, 2010, C1. In a Menasha, Wisconsin, case, a settlement was eventually negotiated, with the city using its municipal electric utility in a lease-purchase agreement with a private utility to come up with funds for the settlement, suggesting that the pledge does have some meaning.

[22]George E. Peterson, "Capital Spending and Capital Obsolescence—The Outlook for Cities," in *The Fiscal Outlook for Cities*, ed. Roy Bahl (Syracuse, N.Y.: Syracuse University Press, 1978), 49.

of new cities becomes overwhelming. Debt is not, however, the complete answer to public infrastructure deterioration; much work on maintenance is recurring and should be part of operating financing.

Municipal Bonds and the Tax Reform Act of 1986

The federal income tax adopted in 1913 specified that interest on state and local government bonds would be exempt. The reasoning apparently reflected the doctrine of intergovernmental tax immunity reflected in the 1819 decision in *McCulloch* v. *Maryland* (17 U.S. 316)—in which the Supreme Court stated that "the power to tax is the power to destroy"—and furthered in the 1871 decision in *Collector* v. *Day* (78 U.S. 113)—in which the Court found that the federal government could not tax state judicial officers' salaries. Indeed, the Court's 1895 decision in *Pollock* v. *Farmers Loan & Trust Company* (157 U.S. 492) that the income tax would require apportionment as a direct tax also ruled on a provision that would have included state and local debt interest in the base: "The tax in question is a tax on the power of the states and their instrumentalities to borrow money, and consequently repugnant to the Constitution." Therefore, the constitutional principle appeared clear.

Economic impacts and equity effects, however, soon muddied the issue.[23] Because interest payments on municipal bonds were not subject to tax, municipalities could borrow at artificially low interest rates. That created the possibility of capital-market distortions between taxed and tax-exempt activities and certainly caused lost federal revenue. Furthermore, as marginal tax brackets rose over the years, interest payments that were not subject to federal tax became more attractive to high-income taxpayers as a safe avenue for tax avoidance. That avoidance reduced the progressivity of the federal system, along with reducing federal revenue. After Mississippi (in 1936) introduced industrial development bonds (IDBs), a mechanism whereby a tax-exempt borrower constructed a plant for a private firm and serviced the debt with lease payments from the firm, the distortion problems became especially troubling. Some controls on exempt bonds were inevitable.

Although controls on the bonds started with limits on IDBs in 1968, the most dramatic changes came in the 1986 Tax Reform Act.[24] The law distinguishes between two municipal debt categories: private activity (taxable) and public purpose (tax-exempt). The law and regulations putting the categories into effect are complex; here is a simplified version: (1) Private-activity and taxable bonds pass the private-business-use and private-loan tests.[25] The bond issue is in this category if (a) more

---

[23]For an excellent analysis of the equity and efficiency problems of the municipal bond market, see two articles by Peter Fortune: "The Municipal Bond Market, Part I: Politics, Taxes, and Yields," *New England Economic Review* (September/October 1991): 13–36; and "The Municipal Bond Market, Part II: Problems and Policies," *New England Economic Review* (May/June 1992): 47–64.

[24]The control legislation is chronicled in Robert L. Bland and Li-Khan Chen, "Taxable Municipal Bonds: State and Local Governments Confront the Tax-Exempt Limitation Movement," *Public Administration Review* 50 (January/February 1989): 42–48.

[25]*Bond Buyer 1997 Yearbook* (New York: American Banker, 1997). Such bonds can tap foreign capital markets because of the higher yield that the absence of federal tax advantage requires.

than the greater of 5 percent or $5 million of bond proceeds are used for loans to nongovernment entities (the private-loan test) or (b) more than 10 percent of the bond proceeds are used by a nongovernment entity in a trade or business and more than 10 percent of the debt service is secured by or derived from payments from property used in a trade or business (private-business-use test).[26] (2) Public-purpose and tax-exempt bonds are issued by a state or its political subdivision in registered form and do not pass these tests. Passing these tests would ordinarily not be a good thing for the borrower, in terms of likely interest costs.[27]

Certain private-activity bonds, however, can be tax exempt. Allowable uses include multifamily rental housing; publicly owned airports; publicly owned docks and wharves; publicly owned nonvehicular mass-commuting facilities; hazardous waste disposal facilities; sewage and solid-waste disposal facilities; some student loans; some water, electric, and gas utilities; and some other categories.[28] The annual volume of such bond issues, however, is subject to a state cap of the greater of $50 per capita or $150 million.[29] How states allocate the amounts is their choice. Furthermore, state and local governments may choose to sell their debt in taxable markets; indeed, this accounted for 18.5 percent of outstanding municipal debt at the end of 2011.[30]

The 1986 Act clearly reduced the scope of future tax-exempt borrowing. Furthermore, a 1988 Supreme Court ruling in *South Carolina v.Baker* (485 U.S. 505), a case testing whether state and local governments could be required to issue bonds only in registered form, held that the Constitution does not prevent applying the federal income tax to state and local debt interest.[31] As the federal government seeks

---

[26]Some state and local governments do regularly use these hybrids (taxable municipal securities). Such issues can be attractive to foreign investors.

[27]The new Yankee Stadium, approximately $1.3 billion total cost with $942 million worth of tax-exempt bonds, is owned by New York City. To keep the project from being classed as "private activity," the deal was structured with the city as owner. The Yankees pay no rent and pay no property tax because the city is the owner, keeping away from the private-activity categorization. However, the Yankees make payments in lieu of taxes (PILOTs) that are theoretically equal to the property tax that would have been owed—except the stadium value is inflated for tax purposes to make the payments look like tax and not like rent, allowing the city to say that the city is paying for most of the stadium cost from tax revenue. That all keeps things away from private activity, the bonds are tax exempt and at a lower rate, and the American taxpayers are implicitly subsidizing the Yankees. Joseph Henchman and Travis Greaves, "From the House that Ruth Built to the House the IRS Built," Tax Foundation Fiscal Fact No. 167 (Washington, D.C.: Tax Foundation, April 6, 2009).

[28]The development impact of small-issue IDBs appears doubtful. See General Accounting Office, Industrial Development Bonds: Achievement of Public Benefits Is Unclear, GAO/RCED-93-106 (Washington, D.C.: General Accounting Office, 1993).

[29]Private-activity bonds for airports, docks, wharves, and solid-waste facilities are outside the cap; certain public-purpose bonds (parts earmarked for private activities costing more than $15 million and private portions of advance refunds) are included in the cap.

[30]This includes Build America Bonds, discussed in a later section, as well as other types of taxable issues.

[31]Bonds had been issued as bearer bonds (whoever presents the bonds receives interest and principal owed, no questions asked) or as registered bonds (the owner is explicitly named). There was concern that bearer bonds were being used to launder illicit incomes and to evade gift and estate taxes. The Tax Equity and Fiscal Responsibility Act of 1982 limited tax-exempt status to registered issues alone. The case challenged that provision; the state did not expect the extra comment on tax-exempt status in general. See Bruce F. Davie and Dennis Zimmerman, "Tax-Exempt Bonds after the South Carolina Decision," *Tax Notes* (June 27, 1988): 1573–80.

revenue and reform of its revenue system, municipal bond interest, even for clear public-purpose debt issues, will continue to be one option for base broadening. The preference provided municipal borrowing is a policy choice, not a necessary constitutional requirement.

A New Taxable Municipal Bond Option (Short-Lived)

The American Recovery and Reinvestment Act of 2009 added another layer of complexity to municipal bond markets by creating a new borrowing alternative, the Build America Bonds (BABs) program, an option available for bonds issued in 2009 and 2010. This program allowed state and local governments to issue taxable bonds for capital projects, with the borrower receiving a direct federal subsidy equal to 35 percent of the total coupon payments made to investors. That reduced the total interest cost to the bond issuer and made capital projects less expensive.

The program worked like this. Suppose a state or local government issues a BAB and pays the bondholder $100 interest on the bond. With an "Issuer BAB," the U.S. Treasury then pays the issuing government $35, making the net cost $65 on the bond paying $100 to the bondholder. An alternative format gives the bondholder a nonrefundable tax credit of 35 percent of interest paid each year. The debt might be structured in either format. The program had no volume limitation, so the total amount of subsidy depended on choices made by the states and localities. This program gave financial support for state and local infrastructure programs in amounts controlled by the issuing governments, not by federal granting authorities, just as the traditional tax-exempt bond does, but, in contrast to the traditional format, the tax savings did not vary with the marginal rate of the borrower. The investment could be attractive even for those in low marginal rate brackets. The program converted a tax expenditure to a direct expenditure and made municipal bond purchases more attractive to lower-income taxpayers. Congress did not renew it.

Appropriate Debt Policy

Borrowing provides funds to acquire resources for current public use. The debt from that borrowing must be repaid, with interest, in the future. Therefore, borrowing commits future budgets. Because of the contractual rigidity, debt must be issued with care; unwise use of debt can disrupt the lives of those paying taxes and expecting services in the future (i.e., it may violate the fiscal sustainability standard). Debt-service costs can impair the ability of the borrower to operate normally. The fundamental rule of debt policy is this: do not issue debt for a maturity longer than the financed project's useful life. If the debt life exceeds the useful life, the project's true annual cost has been understated, and people will continue to pay for the project after the project is gone. If the useful life exceeds the debt period, the annual cost has been overstated, and people will receive benefits without payment. The timing-of-payment question is particularly significant across generations and, at the local level, across a citizenry that is frequently changing as people move in and out of the locality.[32]

Long-term borrowing can be appropriate for long-life capital facilities. Economic growth requires expanded public-capital infrastructure, often before any associated expansion of public revenue. A strong case can be made for using debt for these projects when the future revenue stream will be adequate to service debt expansion, to borrow a concept from corporate finance. Some governments, however, have elected to employ pay-as-you-go financing, paying for capital facilities only from current-year operating surpluses. Such a policy can produce both inefficiency and inequity. First, with population mobility, users would not pay an appropriate charge for those facilities. Those in taxing range would pay when the facility is built; they may not be there when the facility for which they have paid is actually providing services. Second, the high single-year ticket price of a major project may discourage construction, even when the project is sound and feasible. Third, pay-as-you-go financing can produce substantial tax-rate instability, with artificially high rates during the construction phase and artificially low rates during operation. Such instability is unlikely to help development of the local economy. Furthermore, debt financing produces annual debt-service charges that are fixed by contract. Therefore, when the area tax base grows, the tax rate required for debt service for a project will decline over time. For large, long-life infrastructure, debt finance can be more sensible and fiscally prudent than pay-as-you-go finance. All this suggests the importance of integrating the capital budgeting principles discussed in Chapter 7 with the principles of debt management discussed here.

Debt commits resources for extended periods and can be misused by public officials who seek to postpone the cost of public actions. Potential for misuse does not preclude debt financing, but it does mean that debt needs to be issued with caution. When properly handled, debt is an appropriate financing medium. In fact, strict pay-as-you-go can be as unsound as careless use of debt. Both financing methods can be appropriate tools in the fiscal arsenal. Appendix 15–1 illustrates a debt policy with the principles of debt management endorsed by the New York state comptroller.[33]

---

[32]Temporary cash needs should be covered by short-term borrowing liquidated within the fiscal year. Carrying short-term cash borrowing across a fiscal year (rolling over) would violate the fundamental principle.

[33]Some municipalities now issue bonds with variable interest rates (variable-rate demand obligations or VRDOs) in an effort to take advantage of the tendency of short-term interest rates to be lower than long-term interest rates. These securities require the borrower to continually reenter the bond market (the floating interest rate resets periodically) and have caused a number of jurisdictions considerable financial difficulty (school districts in Pennsylvania and Jefferson County, Alabama, for instance), but others have successfully escaped the problem. In the early days of the bonds, financial advisors did not adequately explain the risks associated with the issues to borrowers, much to the detriment of the citizenry. Risk to the municipal issuer can be higher than with the traditional bond, which locks in a coupon rate for the life of the issue, but these bonds can tap an additional segment of the credit market.

The Mechanics of Bond Values

Bond sales represent transactions in which a lender exchanges payment to a borrower now for the contractual promise of repayment plus interest at a later date. The bond contract specifies the interest the borrower will pay the lender for using the money, typically with a semiannual interest payment. This stated or nominal return on a bond is its coupon rate, the percentage of par value that will be paid in interest on a regular basis. Thus, a 5 percent coupon rate means that the bond pays $50 interest per $1,000 of face value.[34] The yield on a bond may differ substantially from the coupon rate because the current value of the bond itself may differ from the face value. The bond contract, however, states a coupon rate and face value to be redeemed at maturity.[35] Bond calculations thus employ the time value of money, compounding, and discounting techniques discussed in Chapter 7. Recall that

$$FV_n = PV(1+r)^n$$

and

$$PV = FV_n / (1+r)^n$$

where

FV_n = a value received in the future,

PV = a value received now,

r = the market rate of interest, and

n = the number of years.

The current bond price equals the present value of cash flow to which the bondholder is entitled (return of principal plus interest). Therefore,

$$P = \sum_{i=1}^{m} \frac{F \times c}{(1+r)^i} + \frac{F}{(1+r)^m}$$

---

[34]Municipal bonds are normally issued in denominations of $5,000 face value, even though coupon discussions use the smaller face value. Small denomination bonds ("minibonds") are sometimes sold. Lawrence Pierce describes an issue from Virginia Beach, Virginia, in "Hitting the Beach and Running: Minibonds," *Government Finance Review* 4 (August 1988): 29. Minibonds are not a significant component of the bond market. Some issuers are experimenting with sales through the Internet. Most borrowers need money for large capital projects and cannot work with revenue from bond sales that trickles in via sales to individual investors.

[35]For a bond purchaser, the yield-to-maturity is the total annualized return earned on a bond if it is held to maturity. It includes both the coupon and any difference between the amount paid for the bond and its face received on redemption by the borrower. A bond may be zero coupon, in which case the yield is the difference between the amount paid initially and the amount ultimately received back.

where

P = the market value or current price of the bond,

m = the number of years in the future until maturity of the bond,

F = the face value of the bond,

c = the coupon rate of the bond, and

r = the market interest rate available on bonds of similar risk and maturity.

The first term of the formula requires computing the present value of a constant stream of returns in the future, so the annuity-value formula (Chapter 7) provides a quick valuation method. For a bond with semiannual interest payments, the first term—the value of the coupon flow—would be computed using (2m) instead of m and (r/2) and (c/2) instead of r and c.

To illustrate, suppose a Stinesville Water Utility bond matures in 15 years, pays an 8 percent coupon semiannually, and has a face value of $5,000. The market rate currently available on comparable bonds is 6 percent. The holder receives an interest payment of (F × c)/2, or $200, each six months for 30 periods (2m). At the end of those 30 periods, the holder will receive back the $5,000. The bond price emerges from the formula

$$P = \sum_{i=1}^{30} \frac{(5{,}000 \times 0.08)/2}{\left(1 + \dfrac{0.06}{2}\right)^{i}} + \frac{5{,}000}{(1 + 0.06)^{15}}$$

$$= 3{,}920 + 2{,}086 = 6{,}006$$

It is obvious that the value of a bond can change, causing capital gain or loss for its holder, as market interest rates vary. The value of the Stinesville bond will be higher than computed here if the market rate is less than 6 percent and lower if the market rate is above 6 percent. The change would not cause a cash loss or gain for an individual holding the bond to maturity, but would change the return for anyone selling it early. When market interest rates fall, the value of bonds goes up, and when market interest rates increase, the value of bonds goes down.

Debt Structure and Design

After the decision to borrow has been made, a number of debt-structure decisions remain. They are considered here, along with some institutional detail about municipal bond markets.[36] Characteristics should ideally be designed to ensure least-cost

---

[36]The federal government constantly borrows to accommodate the continuing deficit and refinancing of maturing debt. Decisions about debt maturity are driven not by the life of particular capital projects, but by concerns of economic management. A longer term (Treasury bonds, notes) relieves financial markets of the regular disruptions that occur when maturing debt is refinanced, but may interfere with private long-term capital investment. A shorter term (Treasury bills) usually reduces the average initial interest rate on the debt, but requires more frequent financing, probably will cause higher ultimate interest cost, and may make inflation more difficult to control. These are radically different concerns from those in the municipal market.

marketability of the issue, simplify debt management, and provide appropriate cost signals to fiscal decision makers.

One initial decision involves the type of security and its term to maturity (i.e., the period for which the money will be borrowed). Markets respond differently to full-faith-and-credit bonds than to revenue bonds. The greater security behind full-faith-and-credit debt typically causes a lower interest rate to be paid on that offering. Revenue bonds may be desired, however, because of legal restrictions placed on the full-faith-and-credit debt[37] or because revenue debt provides a good way to allocate costs to the project's users. For instance, a city may enter capital markets to obtain funds for pollution-control equipment for a private electric utility. There is no logic to full-faith-and-credit finance here because charges paid by utility customers should be the sole source of debt service. This isn't the sort of project that the general taxpayers (the basis for full-faith-and-credit finance) ought to be paying for.

Debt maturity should roughly coincide with project life to ensure that the project will be paid for and the debt liquidated before replacement or major repair is required. This maturity-matching principle prevents debt financing for operating expenditures and permits those financing an improvement to receive its benefits. Debt-service costs along the project's life roughly represent a rental (or depreciation) charge. The facility users pay charges or taxes to cover those annual costs. The total charge can thus more accurately reflect the service's annual cost, including both capital and operating costs.

A bond issue—for example, an issue with thirty years' overall maturity—can be either term or serial. A term issue would have all bonds in the issue timed to mature at the end of thirty years. Funds to repay principal would be obtained through the bond issue's life (along with interest charges along the way) and placed into a sinking fund maintained by the bond issuer. At maturity, sinking-fund accumulations would be sufficient to repay the principal. A serial issue contains multiple maturities in a single issue. Thus, some bonds would be for a thirty-year term, some for a twenty-year term, and so on. (Issuers often seek to maintain constant total annual debt service—interest plus retirement of maturing bonds—through the length of an issue by gradually increasing the volume of bonds maturing through the life of the issue.) Portions of the project cost would be paid through the overall term of the issue. The serial issue may improve marketability of many municipal issues. Thin secondary markets (meaning there are not many prospective buyers in the market) for municipal debt cause most purchasers of that debt to hold the bond to maturity.[38] With serial issues, the issuing government can sell its debt to purchasers with funds available for several different periods of time. Either term bonds with sinking funds

---

[37]Full-faith-and-credit debt may be limited to a maximum total amount for the jurisdiction, to a maximum percentage of the jurisdiction's tax base (usually assessed value), or by a requirement that voters approve the debt at a referendum. Revenue bond debt generally escapes all these limits. Limits are reported by state in tables 61–63 of Advisory Commission on Intergovernmental Relations, *Significant Features of Fiscal Federalism, 1976–77, Vol. 2, Revenue and Debt* (Washington, D.C.: Advisory Commission on Intergovernmental Relations, 1977).

[38]Purchasers of corporate bonds are reasonably confident that these bonds can be sold to another person if funds are needed prior to maturity. In other words, a strong secondary market exists. Thus, these bonds are ordinarily not serial.

or serial bonds spread a project's financing over the life of the project and provide financing on a pay-as-you-use basis.

Debt maturity plays an important role in determining what the issue's ultimate interest cost will be because there is a relationship between the debt's term of maturity and the interest rate required. This relationship, the term structure of interest rates, is influenced by economic conditions at the time of borrowing and is often, but not always, upward sloping (the longer the term to maturity, the higher the interest rate required to borrow for that period of time) because borrowers must compensate investors for locking up their resources for a longer period. (The yield curve is called *inverted* when long-term rates are lower than short-term rates.) Expectations about the future of interest rate conditions and the economy, especially expectations about inflation, determine the curve's shape at any time.[39] Figure 15–2 illustrates the term structure of the yield curve for U.S. Treasury securities at the end of December in 2009, 2010, and 2011 (the yield curve here is upward sloping, or ascending). Rates at the short end are extremely low, and longer maturities bear significantly higher rates. The continuing issues from the Great Recession complicate financial markets and contribute to the low rates shown here. A similar yield curve can be constructed for any security, such as municipal bonds of a standard quality. Yields for high-quality municipal and corporate securities tend to move together with market conditions, as shown in Figure 15–3. Municipal debt generally bears lower yields than corporate securities as a result of the lower risk that debt service will not be paid and the exempt nature of interest paid by most municipal bonds.

Figure 15–2
U.S. Treasury Yield Curve

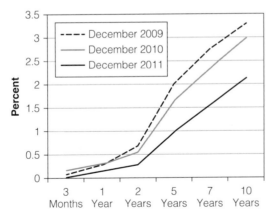

SOURCE: U.S. Treasury Department, *Daily Treasury Yield Curve Rates.*

---

[39]When inflation is expected to be mild, the purchasing power of debt repayments in the distant future will be closer to the same as purchasing power given in the initial loan. Interest rates do not need to compensate for purchasing power loss and hence are lower in money terms. See Peter A. Abken, "Inflation and the Yield Curve," *Economic Review* 78 (May/June 1993): 13–30.

Figure 15–3
Yield of Aaa Municipal and Aaa Corporate Debt, End of Year 1962–2010

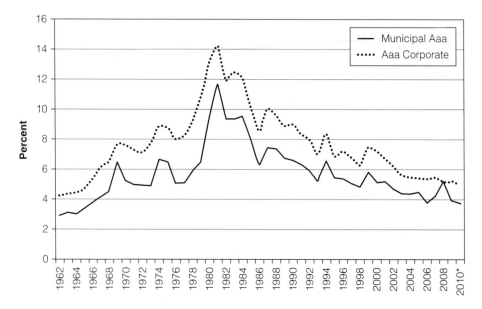

*2010 based on November figure.

SOURCE: Federal Reserve Bank of St. Louis, Economic Research. *Series: AAA, Moody's Seasoned Aaa Corporate Bond Yield* and *Mergent Municipal and Government Manual*.

Municipalities can protect themselves from being locked into high interest rates on long maturity bonds. A *call provision* in a debt issue allows the borrower to repay debt before the normal maturity. The borrower usually refunds the debt, or borrows to cover the repayment, at the lower interest rates prevalent at the time of the refunding. If interest rates fall sufficiently before the first call date, the municipality may use advance refunding—borrowing at the lower interest rate and using the proceeds to cover debt service until the call date allows the initial issue to be entirely replaced.[40] Of course, the possibility of a call reduces an issue's attractiveness to lenders, so issues with such a provision must compensate the investor (with a call premium above face value) to permit marketability of the original issue.

Ratings

When risk (the chance that principal and interest payments will not be made on schedule) is greater, lenders demand a higher return for their loans. Therefore, risk is important to both borrowers and lenders, and, in bond markets, commercial rating firms assess the risk of particular bond issues. Because the assumption of risk must be compensated by higher returns to lenders, this assessment of risk will be critical

---

[40]Proceeds of advanced refunding will be invested. The U.S. Treasury provides special securities for this purpose (since 1972) to prevent violation of arbitrage restrictions (municipalities cannot borrow tax exempt while lending on ordinary markets).

in determining the interest rate paid by the borrowing government. Ratings also allow governments to sell on larger capital markets because they convert bonds issued by a locality into a commodity; all bonds with the same rating carry the same estimated risk. Credit risk is low because defaults in the United States are rare, rarer for municipal bonds than for corporate bonds, although less rare for revenue bonds issued by public authorities than for full-faith-and-credit bonds issued by general-purpose governments. Defaults by the latter are usually linked to major economic recession, flagrant fiscal mismanagement, or unresolved political disputes. Because capital markets have long memories, governments want to avoid "a reputation-based loss of access to future loans."[41] That makes general-purpose governments especially reluctant to miss scheduled debt service. (As described later in this chapter, default is only one way in which government finances can go wrong.)

Three firms—Mergent/Moody's Investors Services, Standard & Poor's (a subsidiary of McGraw-Hill, Inc.), and Fitch Investors Service/ICBA—prepare most creditworthiness opinions in the municipal market.[42] These three are the nationally recognized statistical rating organizations. Mergent/Moody's has been doing municipal ratings since 1919 and Standard & Poor's since 1940; Fitch has only recently undertaken municipal rating, but has been in the market since 1913. (Kroll Ratings was established in 2010, and its share of the market is currently tiny.) These agencies, for a fee paid by the bond issuer, prepare an opinion of the borrower's credit quality (for full-faith-and-credit issues) or of the particular bond issue (for revenue-bond issues). These rating opinions are widely distributed to the investment community and are used nationally to form portfolio strategies. The agencies also prepare sovereign credit ratings, the ratings for central government debt, as international debt markets have grown; U.S. federal government debt has been generally regarded as fully secure and, historically, was the standard against which risk has been calibrated. However, Standard & Poor's downgraded federal debt in the summer of 2011 when Congress threatened the timely payment of debt service in its debates regarding the statutory debt ceiling. There had been debt ceiling incidents in the past, but the position taken by some members of Congress regarding the ceiling and their statements that a default might not be particularly terrible caused the rating agency to warn its clients that federal debt did have some default risk.[43] An issue without a rating seldom sells on national markets, but issues can be unrated if local markets will buy them. Notice in Table 15–3 that a full percentage point or more often separates the highest-grade (Aaa) and lower-grade (Baa) investments. That difference means

---

[41]William B. English, "Understanding the Costs of Sovereign Default: American State Debts in the 1840's," *American Economic Review* 86 (March 1996): 272.

[42]The Securities and Exchange Commission (SEC) identifies these firms as those whose ratings will be used in valuing bond assets of SEC-registered brokers and dealers. A fourth firm, Duff and Phelps Credit Rating Company, specializes in rating financing for water and public power systems, commercial development, toll roads, airports, and education facilities and does sovereign credit ratings, especially in emerging markets. It has a narrower focus than the other three.

[43]Richard Cantor and Frank Packer, "Sovereign Credit Ratings," *Current Issues in Economics and Finance* 1 (June 1995): 1–6. There were similar debt ceiling issues in 1995–1996 and 2002, but they were seen as less serious than the 2011 standoff. Should there actually be a delayed debt-service payment, there would be a ratings impact from all agencies and higher interest payments that would entail considerable extra cost to American taxpayers for many years. While debt-to-GDP ratios are increasing, they do not constitute a threat to ability to service the debt in the near future. Politics does.

Table 15–3
Yield by Moody's Municipal Rating Group, 1940–2012 (End of Year)

	Aaa	Aa	A	Baa	Composite
1940	1.56	1.78	2.11	2.60	2.01
1945	1.11	1.27	1.62	1.91	1.48
1950	1.42	1.60	1.92	2.17	1.78
1955	2.29	2.46	2.81	3.25	2.70
1960	3.12	3.35	3.60	4.03	3.53
1965	3.39	3.47	3.60	3.78	3.56
1970	5.21	5.33	5.60	5.80	5.49
1975	6.50	6.94	7.78	7.96	7.30
1976	5.07	5.50	6.42	6.73	5.93
1977	5.07	5.23	5.46	5.79	5.39
1978	5.91	6.01	6.51	6.76	6.30
1979	6.50	6.69	6.89	7.42	6.88
1980	9.44	9.64	9.80	10.64	9.88
1981	11.70	12.16	12.60	13.30	12.44
1982	9.34	9.85	10.24	10.80	10.06
1983	9.34	9.58	10.08	10.29	9.82
1984	9.54	9.88	10.19	10.45	10.02
1985	7.98	8.31	8.64	9.05	8.50
1986	6.28	6.48	6.84	7.24	6.71
1987	7.45	7.74	7.97	8.42	7.90
1988	7.35	7.44	7.56	7.76	7.53
1989	6.71	6.81	6.86	7.03	6.85
1990	6.63	6.82	6.96	7.10	6.88
1991	6.32	6.43	6.52	6.65	6.48
1992	5.91	6.03	6.14	6.27	6.09
1993	5.18	5.27	5.44	5.69	5.40
1994	6.62	6.59	6.73	7.17	6.78
1995	5.40	5.43	5.53	5.66	5.51
1996	5.38	5.47	5.54	5.68	5.52
1997	5.02	5.06	5.11	5.16	5.09
1998	4.82	4.90	5.04	5.17	4.98
1999	5.83	5.92	6.08	6.25	6.02
2000	5.11	5.18	5.27	5.85	5.35
2001	5.18	5.22	5.39	5.81	5.40
2002	4.70	4.76	4.96	5.57	5.00
2003	4.41	4.54	4.67	4.97	4.65
2004	4.35	4.47	4.61	4.91	4.66
2005	4.46	4.58	4.68	4.92	4.66
2006	3.76	3.99	4.14	4.26	4.04
2007	4.23	4.35	4.58	4.91	4.52
2008	5.17	5.36	6.15	7.06	5.93
2009	3.89	4.10	4.72	5.86	4.64
2010	4.67	4.92	5.57	6.25	5.35
2011	3.72	3.98	4.71	5.49	4.47
2012*	3.43	3.70	4.23	5.12	4.12

*Based on April.
SOURCE: Mergent Moody's Municipal and Governmental Manual (New York: Mergent, 2012).

a lot of money for large debt issues that will mature many years into the future, so municipalities have a considerable financial incentive to preserve a good rating. Grades lower than investment grade (below Baa in the Moody's system) fare less well because many financial institutions are forbidden to hold speculative, lower-rated securities. Table 15–4 relates the ratings definitions of the three major services and suggests the general risk factors associated with each rating.[44]

The rating firms use proprietary schemes for establishing the rating for an issue or a borrower. Statements by the rating firms identify four sorts of factors that are important in their reviews and evaluations of creditworthiness:[45]

1. **The economy.** The economy in which the issuing unit operates is important. A strong and growing economy brings a strong revenue base for servicing the debt. That reduces the credit risk of the issue.

2. **Debt.** The debt history and debt position of the issuing unit are important. A high debt burden and high debt-service requirements in relation to government resources raise questions about the credit risk of the issue. Plans for retiring the debt, the maturity structure in relationship to the project being financed, and any prior defaults are also reviewed. Some ratings agencies now explicitly state that they will also consider the level of unfunded pension obligations, the liability for promised future retirement benefits that is not covered by pension fund accumulations, when they do state government ratings. The view is that these are debt burdens, no different from the formal debt obligations.

3. **The government.** The investigation considers the degree of professionalism shown by the issuing government, the capacity of administrators, the quality of the full budget process (audits, documents, appropriations, controls, etc.), and the quality of government financial reports. Delays in approving budgets are not regarded as a favorable factor.[46]

4. **Financial analysis.** The investigation covers fund balances, trends in revenues and expenditures, adequacy of the revenue base, vulnerability to new liabilities (pension requirements, etc.), adequacy of financial planning, and so on.

---

[44]The rating agencies also rate corporate debt issues. It has been argued that municipal debt has been given lower ratings than comparable corporate issues, thus causing municipalities to pay higher-than-necessary interest rates—municipal defaults are much less frequent than are corporate defaults, and it is argued that the ratings should reflect that difference. Over the 1970–2008 period, the default rate on double-B municipal bonds was 1.74%, compared to a 29.93% rate for comparably rated corporate bonds, so maybe the critics have a point. Liz Rappaport and Karen Richardson, "What If Muni Insurance Disappeared?" *Wall Street Journal*, February 8, 2008.

[45]Standard & Poor's provides an outline of what it is looking for in "U.S. State Ratings Methodology" (January 3, 2011) and "Understanding Ratings: Guide to Credit Ratings Criteria" (2010). They give useful explanations, but do not expect to see how the elements fit together and how one measure is balanced against another to produce the final rating.

[46]The congressional indecision about raising the federal debt ceiling certainly contributed to Standard & Poor's downgrade of the U.S. government. The report on the downgrade from AAA to AA+ stated: "The political brinksmanship of recent months highlights what we see as America's governance and policy-making becoming less stable, less effective, and less predictable than what we previously believed. The statutory debt ceiling and the threat of default have become political bargaining chips in the debate over fiscal policy." Standard & Poor's, "United States of America Long-Term Rating Lowered To 'AA+' on Political Risks and Rising Debt Burden; Outlook Negative," August 2, 2011. Debt burden mattered, but playing games with default mattered as well.

Table 15–4

Credit Ratings by Moody's, Standard & Poor's, and Fitch

Moody's	Symbol
Highest quality; minimal credit risk	Aaa
High quality; subject to very low credit risk	Aa
Upper-medium grade; subject to low credit risk	A
Moderate credit risk; medium grade; possess certain speculative characteristics	Baa
Have speculative elements; subject to substantial credit risk	Ba
Considered speculative; subject to high credit risk	B
Judged to be of poor standing; subject to very high credit risk	Caa
Highly speculative; are likely in, or very near, default; some prospect of recovery of principal and interest	Ca
Lowest rated class and are typically in default, with little prospect for recovery of principal or interest	C

Standard & Poor's	Symbol
Extremely strong capacity to meet financial commitments; highest rating	AAA
Very strong capacity to meet financial commitments	AA
Strong capacity to meet financial commitments; somewhat susceptible to adverse economic conditions and changes in circumstances	A
Adequate capacity to meet financial commitments; more subject to adverse economic conditions; lowest investment security rating	BBB
Less vulnerable in the near term; faces major ongoing uncertainties to adverse business, financial, and economic conditions; highest speculative grade	BB
More vulnerable to adverse business, financial, and economic conditions; currently has the capacity to meet financial commitments	B
Currently vulnerable; dependent on favorable business, financial, and economic conditions to meet financial commitments	CCC
Currently highly vulnerable	CC
Bankruptcy petition has been filed or similar action taken; payments of financial commitments are continued	C
Payments default on financial commitments	D

(continues)

Revenue bond analysis is primarily concerned with the enterprise's revenue potential and the legal protection of bondholders in the bond resolution's covenants. There is little concern with the associated government because there is no precedent requiring bailout of revenue bonds. For instance, in two well-publicized incidents, neither the city of Chicago nor the state of West Virginia prevented default of associated revenue bond issues (the Chicago Skyway and West Virginia Turnpike, respectively).[47] No government intervened to assist the Washington Public Power Supply

---

[47]The finances of the Chicago Skyway have been straightened out, and the city was able to lease the Skyway for 99 years to a private Spanish-Australian consortium for $1.82 billion in 2004.

Table 15–4
(continued)

Fitch	Symbol
Highest credit quality: exceptional strong capacity to pay: unlikely to be affected by foreseeable events	AAA
Very high credit quality: very low default risk, strong capacity for payment Should the highlighted line say "very low default risk"?	AA
High credit quality: low default risk, strong ability but more vulnerable to adverse changes in economic conditions and circumstances	A
Good credit quality: low default risk, adequate capacity for payment	BBB
Speculative: elevated vulnerability to default risk, particularly in the event of adverse changes in business or economic conditions over time	BB
Highly speculative: default risk is present; limited margin of safety remains	B
Substantial credit risk: default is a real possibility	CCC
Very high levels of credit risk: default of some kind appears probable	CC
Exceptionally high levels of credit risk: default is imminent or inevitable	C
Restricted default: experienced an uncured payment default; has not entered into bankruptcy filings, receivership, liquidation, etc.	RD
Default: entered into bankruptcy filings, receivership, liquidation, etc.	D

NOTE: Moody's designates with 1 those bonds with the strongest investment attributes (i.e., Aa1). A plus or a minus attached to an S&P or Fitch rating indicates upper or lower segment of the rating category.

System in its $2.25 billion default in 1983. Thus, revenue bond analysis presumes the project must stand on its financial merits.

The current problem with the traditional ratings agencies is that they made massive misjudgments in the financial collapse of 2007–2008.[48] Indeed, some claim they were instrumental in both creating and deepening that collapse. The rating agencies dramatically understated the risks associated with mortgage-backed securities (moving far away from their traditional work in the municipal bond market), giving stellar ratings to many securities that turned out to be nearly worthless. Some of these issues were novel with no track record regarding performance and so complex that risks were almost impossible to quantify, but the rating agencies swallowed the risk claims of the issuers. This record of failed bonds with high ratings created grave doubts about the credibility of all work done by the agencies, even though the problems were with a relatively modest amount of total rated issues, and not at all with traditional municipal bonds. In addition, conflict of interest issues emerged: the rating agencies are paid by the issuer, and, if a rating is low, that issuer may not continue to be a client of that agency. Skeptics saw in this the possibility that ratings would get skewed from that desire to do business in the future. The problems cast a shadow over all work by the ratings agencies, a cloud from which they only now are beginning to emerge.

[48]The Securities and Exchange Commission examined the problems in *Summary Report of Issues Identified in the Commission Staff's Examinations of Select Credit Rating Agencies* (Washington, D.C.: Securities and Exchange Commission, 2008). In general, it found that the agencies were swamped by the number and complexity of issues being rated—and also may have been influenced by conflicts of interest in relationships with the issuers.

What to do is an unresolved question. The work of the rating agencies provides an important link in financial intermediation, but it needs to be seen as credible. One approach could be a public rating agency financed in a way that eliminates the conflict apparent in the issuer-pays system.[49] Other approaches would involve greater regulation of private rating firms and finance of ratings from the users of ratings rather than from the rated entities. No clear solution has yet emerged, and, in the tradition of the U.S. Congress, nothing substantial has happened.[50] It is difficult to empirically test the work of the agencies rating state or local general obligation debt because actual default on this sort of debt is so rare—testing the accuracy of the ratings would involve checking ratings variations of predicted probability of an event happening, even though the event hasn't happened. Good tests of ratings quality are not simple.

Credit Enhancements

Some municipal bonds have been supported by credit enhancements that may reduce the interest rate that the bond bears by adding a third-party guarantee that service will be paid when due.[51] Such a guarantee would reduce the risk associated with the bond. There have been three sorts of guarantees provided in the bond market: (1) state credit guarantees, (2) bank letters of credit, and (3) municipal bond insurance. Their relevance has changed in recent years.

The state credit guarantees are an "explicit promise by the state to a local unit bondholder that any shortfall in local resources will automatically be assumed by the state. In its strongest form, a state guarantee places the full-faith-and-credit of the state behind the contingent call on state funds."[52] The guarantee may take the form of a state insurance fund into which local issuers make premium payments, the program may guarantee only portions of debt service, the guarantee may not automatically pledge the full faith and credit of the state, or there may be other conditions placed on the backing. About twenty-four states have credit enhancement programs, many for school districts. These often enhance the credit by having a system in place to intercept state aid to the district for debt service, thus dramatically improving the chances that debt service will be paid before any other obligations the district might have. In the final analysis, the guarantee can hardly be stronger than the state's finances. That fact, plus the many different shades of the guarantee, makes generalizations about this form of third-party credit strengthening particularly hazardous.[53]

---

[49]M. Ahmed Diomande, James Heintz, and Robert Pollin, "Why U.S. Financial Markets Need a Public Credit Rating Agency," *The Economists' Voice* 6 (June 2009): 1–4.

[50]The Dodd-Frank Act requires the Securities and Exchange Commission to adopt additional rules regarding the nationally recognized rating agencies and the Commission has required some additional disclosures. In characteristic American political fashion, opinions range from the view that this is too aggressive to not nearly aggressive enough.

[51]Rating agencies may give municipal issues two ratings, a credit-enhanced rating and an unenhanced rating.

[52]Ronald W. Forbes and John E. Petersen, "State Credit Assistance to Local Governments," in *Creative Capital Financing for State and Local Governments,* ed. John E. Petersen and Wesley C. Hough (Chicago: Municipal Finance Officers Association, 1983), 226.

[53]There is considerable doubt about the wisdom of such guarantees because they reduce the incentive for fiscal responsibility by the borrower. In no case should the guarantees be open-ended.

A second form of guarantee is the bank letter of credit (LOC). The LOC is a commercial bank guarantee of payment of principal and interest on a bond if the issuer cannot do so.[54] The bank LOC, always a relatively small element of the municipal market, has significantly fallen in significance because major money-center banks—the ones most likely to be able to offer LOC enhancement—have lost their high credit ratings. Without the high credit rating, the LOC isn't worth the annual fee charged for the coverage.

The third bond guarantee, municipal bond insurance, has historically been the most widely used since its inception in 1971. This insurance, purchased by the bond issuer, guarantees timely payment of principal and interest on that issue and thus allows a low-rated issue with insurance to sell at roughly the same interest rate as a higher-quality issue. The insurance premium is paid when the bond is initially issued. The recent problem is that insurance is only as good as the insurance company that sells it, and insurance company quality has plummeted.

The first insurance was sold in the early 1970s, and 3 percent of issues were insured in 1980. Insurance coverage became common, and in 2007, approximately 60 percent of issues were insured. In 2007, these bond insurers enjoyed triple-A ratings from the ratings agencies: AMBAC Assurance, Assured Guaranty Corporation (AGC), CIFG Assurance North America, Financial Guaranty Insurance Company, Financial Security Assurance, MBIA, and Syncora Guarantee (XL Capital Assurance).[55] Purchasing insurance meant that security from the finances of the highly ranked insurance company was added to the finances of the bond issuer. However, the insurance companies expanded their markets from the sure profits of insuring municipal bonds, which were extremely unlikely to default, to insuring complex debt obligations tied to the subprime mortgage market. Part of the problem was associated with the fact that the ratings agencies had the ratings wrong for these obligations and, accordingly, the insurance companies had bad data for setting their premiums for covering this debt. But it is also true that the insurance companies did not fully understand the instruments that they were insuring and, when the claims on defaulted obligations came in, the insurers were not prepared. The claims and the exposure to more claims in the future threatened the capacity of the insurance companies to meet their obligations, and, by late 2008, none of the bond insurers enjoyed triple-A ratings from all ratings agencies. What a change even from 2007. By 2012, only about 5 percent of municipal bonds had insurance.[56] That represents a dramatic change in the municipal market as issuers find no added value from insurance and prefer to sell based on their own financial prospects (recall that municipal defaults are extremely rare). While there is likely a market for the insurance and it is

---

[54]Entities may also obtain a line of credit, with annual renewal, but this access can be terribly expensive.

[55]Congress established the for-profit firm, the College Construction Loan Insurance Association, with federal seed money in 1986 to insure low-rated issues (S&P's BBB or lower) from higher education institutions. "Connie Lee" covered less than 1 percent of all insured issues in 1996—a poor fifth place among insurers. Some have argued for an extension of its role. Private insurers are not amused.

[56] An additional company, Berkshire Hathaway Assurance, was briefly in the market in 2008. It withdrew quickly as Warren Buffett, its founder, found the risks to be excessive relative to the premiums that could be charged. Assured Guaranty remains in the market. A new firm, Build America Mutual Assurance, entered the market in 2012. It is a mutual company, thus owned by the entities it insures, and has a Standard & Poor AA rating. It wisely intends to limits its insurance to municipal issues.

likely to return, finances of the insurance companies must be significantly better if they are to provide value to borrowers. In the meantime, default rates on municipal bonds remain low, and the market has adjusted to bonds without insurance.

The market has changed. In 2005, the peak year, 63 percent of municipal issues by principal issued were sold with credit enhancement of one type or another. By 2009, only 17 percent had credit enhancement, a percentage that continued for 2010 and 2011.[57]

Underwriting, Interest Rates, and Ownership

Bond issues are usually too large to be bought by a single investor, and the issuer cannot effectively market the issue to large numbers of individual investors. Thus, bonds are typically sold to an underwriter, a firm that purchases the entire issue. The borrower receives the entire issue's proceeds quickly, without worrying about marketing. The underwriter hopes to resell the issue at a profit to investors. The gross profit (or underwriting spread) equals the difference between the price the firm pays for the bonds and the price the firm receives from their sale to investors. From that spread, the firm will pay all costs of distribution involved in the transaction. An increase in market interest rates can cause bond values to fall, so underwriters typically want to sell the bonds quickly.

Underwriting firms are selected either by negotiation or by competitive bid. In the former case, the underwriter is selected as the bond issue is being designed. An interest rate is negotiated between the borrowing unit and the underwriting firm. The underwriter engages in presale marketing and assists the borrower with such organizational services as preparing official statements, structuring the bond issue, and securing credit ratings. Negotiated bond sales dominate the revenue bond market (three-quarters of the issues by dollar volume), and competitive sales dominate the general obligation market (three-quarters of the issues by dollar volume). Unfortunately, noncompetitive selection opens the door for possible favoritism and bribes and eliminates market forces that reduce the spread.[58] Fifteen states have bond banks that underwrite and provide other services for municipal offerings; these sales are also negotiated.[59]

---

[57]U. S. Securities and Exchange Commission, *Report on the Municipal Secutities Market* (July 31, 2012), p. 50.

[58]The Public Securities Association recommended in 1993 a moratorium on political campaign contributions to candidates in states where public finance firms do bond business. This represents a major change in prior practice. Some scandals involving the selection of underwriters in that year produced that recommendation, but similarly piqued the interest of the federal SEC. The SEC has historically provided little supervision of municipal securities, but, to prevent market abuses, it proposed in 1994 to pursue securities-fraud charges against state and local government officials if they (1) fail to disclose conflicts of interest, including the acceptance of political contributions from underwriters or financial advisors; (2) fail to issue annual financial statements and inform investors of significant financial developments; (3) fail to disclose terms and risks of bonds; or (4) make inaccurate statements of the finances of the jurisdiction. The idea, if fully implemented, would make municipal-security information requirements more consistent with those placed on private issuers.

[59]Bond banks reduce interest costs to local borrowers. See Martin T. Katzman, "Municipal Bond Banking: The Diffusion of a Public-Finance Innovation," *National Tax Journal* 33 (June 1980): 149–60; and David S. Kidwell and Robert J. Rogowski, "Bond Banks: A State Assistance Program That Helps Reduce New Issue Borrowing Costs," *Public Administration Review* 42 (March/April 1983): 108–12.

Two important documents must be prepared during the sale of bonds: the official statement and the legal opinion. The *official statement,* a requirement when the underwriter will be selected by competitive bid, contains two sections providing information prospective underwriters and investors need before committing funds to the borrower. One section provides information about the borrower's ability to repay its debt: a description of the community and its industries, its major taxpayers, debt currently outstanding, a record of tax collections and bond repayments in the past five years, and future borrowing plans. The other section describes the proposed bond issue: purpose, amount, and type of issue: its maturity structure and interest payment schedule: all provisions: date and place of bidding: whether a bond rating has been applied for: the name of the counsel preparing the legal opinion (described later): and where bonds will be delivered. The official statement also indicates any maximum interest rate and discount. Most official statements include a disclaimer indicating a right to refuse any and all bids, even though that right will seldom be used by units intending to maintain good relations with underwriters.[60]

The second document is the *legal opinion* prepared by a bond counsel, a certification that the bond issuer has complied with all federal, state, and local legal requirements governing municipal debt. Seldom will local law firms do this work; underwriters and large private investors require opinions from specialist law firms. The bond counsel ensures that the issuer has legal authority to borrow, that the revenue source for repayment is legal and irrevocable, and that the community is legally bound by provisions of the bond. The bond counsel also indicates whether interest paid on the debt will, in its opinion, be exempt from federal and state income tax. The bond counsel offers no judgment about the borrower's capacity to repay the debt; the bond counsel's concern is with how tightly the contract to repay binds the borrower. Without a satisfactory opinion, the bond issue is virtually worthless on the tax-exempt market.

A competitive bid is the typical method of selecting underwriters for full-faith-and-credit bonds and for many revenue issues. In this method, the issuer selects the amount of principal to mature at various years through the issue's life, and underwriters bid on the interest rate the issuer would have to pay. The rates, of course, need not be the same for different maturities, but would be the same for all bonds in a single maturity. The issuer chooses the underwriter bidding the lowest interest rate for the total issue. The winning underwriter bid determines what the interest cost will be to the issuer.

Two methods are used to compute interest cost when determining the lowest underwriter bid: net interest cost (*NIC*) and true interest cost (*TIC*). Both represent averages of the several coupon rates in the serial issue. The *NIC* method computes cost according to the formula

$$NIC = \left(\frac{\text{Total interest less premium or plus discount}}{\text{Bond dollar years}} \right)$$

---

[60]SEC rules effective in 1990 have placed extra controls on municipal disclosure in the official statement. Although the rules are directed at underwriters, the statements to which they apply are those produced by municipal borrowers. See John E. Petersen, "The New SEC Rule on Municipal Disclosure: Implications for Issuers of Municipal Securities," *Government Finance Review* 4 (October 1988): 17–20.

It produces an average annual debt cost as a percentage of the outstanding principal of the debt. First, compute N, the total dollar cost of coupon payments over the life of the bond:

$$N = \sum_{i=1}^{n} (C_i \times A_i \times Y_i) + D$$

where

N = net dollar interest costs;

n = number of different maturities in issue;

C = coupon rate on each maturity;

A = par amount, or face value, in each maturity;

Y = number of years to maturity; and

D = bid discount (bid premium is a negative discount).

N equals the total interest paid through the life of the bond issue. The bond dollar years (BDY) formula is

$$N = \sum_{i=1}^{n} (C_i \times A_i \times Y_i) + D$$

BDY represents the amount borrowed and the time for which it is borrowed: $1 borrowed for two years equals two bond dollar years, $2 borrowed for five years equals ten bond dollar years, and so on. Thus,

$$NIC = \frac{N}{BDY}$$

The *TIC,* or the Canadian interest cost, method is more complicated because it takes into account the time profile of interest-payment flows, but it is the norm in competitive bidding. If two bids have the same net interest cost, but one bid involves higher interest payments in the early maturities of the issue and lower interest payments in the later maturities (frontloading), then that bid would be less attractive because it requires the issuer to surrender resources earlier and thus to lose the return that could have been received from use of those resources. The second bid is, in present value terms, lower than the first. True interest cost is the interest rate that equates the amount of dollars received by the bond issuer with the present value of the flow of principal and interest payments over the issue's life. The *TIC* formula is

$$B = \sum_{i=1}^{m} \frac{A_i}{(1 + TIC)^i} + \sum_{i=1}^{m} \frac{I_i}{(1 + TIC)^i}$$

where

B = aggregate dollar amount received by the issuer (the amount borrowed less discount or plus premium),

i = number of years until a cash payment occurs,

m = number of years to final maturity,

A_i = annual principal in dollars repaid in period i,

TIC = true interest cost, and

I_i = aggregate interest payment in period i (assuming one interest payment per year).

In a *TIC* computation for a municipal bond sale, the bid price or amount to be paid by the underwriter to the issuer (B) and the stream of debt-service payments (I_i) are specified by the bidder. The issuer defines the number of years to future payments (the maturities). The implied interest rate (*TIC*) is solved by iteration for successive approximations until the left and right sides of the equation balance.[61] Larger offerings require computer assistance for *TIC* calculation, but smaller issues can be handled using standard methods for approximating the internal rate of return. Table 15–5 illustrates *TIC* and *NIC* computation.

The successful underwriting firm or syndicate (a group of firms) then sells the bonds to investors. Underwriters cover their costs and make any profit from the difference between the price the underwriters pay the issuer and the price the underwriters receive from purchasers (the spread).[62] As the previously discussed bond market mechanics demonstrated, an increase in market interest rates causes bond values to decline. If increases in market rates cause a substantial decline in the issue's value before the firm has sold the bonds, that spread can be negative.

Table 15–6 reports the types of entities holding municipal bonds. Ownership in any class is concentrated among units in higher tax brackets—those are the purchasers to whom the tax-exempt status of municipal bond interest is especially attractive. Household holdings are a smaller share than twenty years ago, although they still account for roughly one-third of the total. They would own more indirectly through money market and mutual funds. The role of commercial-bank purchases has declined. Banks lost the ability to deduct from income for federal tax purposes the interest they paid on deposits used to purchase tax-exempt bonds in tax reforms in the 1980s; that caused a considerable reduction in their market share. Commercial banks have recently started direct loan programs to municipalities, avoiding the traditional bond market, as a generally safe use of their funds. The loans generate tax-exempt interest (within limits), and most lending expenses are deductible. They replace in part the letter-of-credit line of business the banks once had. The loans, however, have some extra risk for the borrowers because there could be a

---

[61]The internal-rate-of-return function on spreadsheet programs quickly performs the calculations.

[62]In 2007, the average gross spread was $5.27 per $1,000 face value of bonds, averaging $5.40 for negotiated issues and $4.09 for competitive issues. The competitive spread typically is less than the negotiated spread, however. For comparison, the average spread was $8.10 in 1995. *The Bond Buyer/Thomson Financial 2008 Yearbook* (New York: Source Media, 2008), 61.

Table 15–5
A *TIC* and *NIC* Computation Worksheet

Bonds Sold July 1, 2011, and Interest Payable on July 1 Thereafter. Bid Amount = $39,920

Maturity Date	Amount ($)	Bid Interest Rate (coupon) (%)	Annual Paid ($)	Bond Interest	Bond Dollar Years
July 1, 2015	5,000	6	300	4	20,000
July 1, 2016	5,000	6.5	325	5	25,000
July 1, 2017	5,000	7	350	6	30,000
July 1, 2018	5,000	8	400	7	35,000
July 1, 2019	10,000	9	900	8	80,000
July 1, 2020	10,000	10	1,000	9	90,000
TOTAL	40,000				280,000

Schedule of Payments by Dates Paid

Payment Date	Interest ($)	Principal ($)	Total ($)
July 1, 2012	3,275	-	3,275
July 1, 2013	3,275	-	3,275
July 1, 2014	3,275	-	3,275
July 1, 2015	3,275	5,000	8,275
July 1, 2016	2,975	5,000	7,975
July 1, 2017	2,650	5,000	7,650
July 1, 2018	2,300	5,000	7,300
July 1, 2019	1,900	10,000	11,900
July 1, 2020	1,000	10,000	11,000
TOTAL	23,925	40,000	63,925

Solving for *NIC*:

$$NIC = \frac{23,925 + 80}{280,000} = 8.573\%$$

Solving for *TIC*:

$$\$39,920 = \frac{3,275}{1+TIC} + \frac{3,275}{(1+TIC)^2} + \frac{3,275}{(1+TIC)^3} + \frac{8,275}{(1+TIC)^4} + \frac{7,975}{(1+TIC)^5}$$
$$+ \frac{7,650}{(1+TIC)^6} + \frac{7,300}{(1+TIC)^7} + \frac{11,900}{(1+TIC)^8} + \frac{11,000}{(1+TIC)^9}$$
$$TIC = 8.503\%$$

call for early repayment that would not be part of a regular bond issue.[63] Other bond-holding entities' shares have been rather stable and rather small except for the development of mutual and money market funds as an important financial intermediary. These holdings might properly be added to household holdings.

---

[63]Michael Corkery, "In Shift, Municipalities Turn to Banks for Loans," *Wall Street Journal*, July 14, 2011.

Table 15–6
Distribution of Municipal Debt by Holding Entity (End of Year)

	1985	1990	1995	2000	2005	2010
Total outstanding	100%	100%	100%	100%	100%	100%
Households	46.0	55.0	42.1	35.9	36.9	33.7
Money market funds	4.2	7.1	10.1	16.4	15.1	18.5
Mutual funds	4.1	9.6	16.6	15.6	14.0	14.5
Other insurance companies	10.3	11.6	12.7	12.4	14.1	14.2
Commercial banks	27.0	10.0	7.4	7.7	7.1	8.0
Closed-end funds	0.1	1.2	4.6	4.6	4.0	2.9
Government-sponsored enterprises	0.2	0.3	0.6	2.0	1.8	1.2
Nonfinancial corporate businesses	3.0	2.1	2.9	2.2	1.4	1.0
Brokers and dealers	2.3	0.7	1.0	0.8	1.9	1.4
Life insurance companies	1.1	1.0	0.9	1.3	1.5	1.8
Savings institutions	0.4	0.3	0.2	0.2	0.4	0.3
State and local governments	1.1	1.0	0.4	0.2	0.2	0.2
State and local retirement funds	0.1	0.0	0.1	0.1	0.1	0.1
Nonfarm noncorporate business	0.0	*	0.2	0.2	0.2	0.2
Rest of the world	0.1	0.2	0.3	0.5	1.3	1.9

*Indicates that category makes up less than 0.1% of total.
SOURCE: Board of Governors of the Federal Reserve System, *Flow of Funds Accounts of the United States* (Z1 Release).

Lease-Purchase Finance and Certificates of Participation

Leases and certificates of participation provide governments a backdoor method for obtaining capital assets. Governments utilize two types of leases: operating leases and capital leases. Although there may be other reasons driving some of these transactions, capital leases are often used to avoid legal and procedural constraints on issuing debt to construct capital projects. From an accounting perspective, operating leases are treated like rentals. At the end of an operating lease, the leased equipment is returned to the lessor. If any one of the following conditions is met, then the lease is not an operating lease but instead is considered a financing arrangement or capital lease:

- There is a bargain purchase option.
- The lease transfers the title of the property to the lessee.
- The term of the lease equals or exceeds the full life of the property.
- The lease payments plus interest exceed the fair value of the property.

Capital leases, or lease-purchase financing, resemble an installment purchase. A lessee—in this case, a government—buys a property from the lessor through installment payments made over a given period of time. The capital lease is treated as debt instead of an expense in the government's accounts. Unlike an operating lease, the government carries the equipment on its books as the owner.[64] From an accounting perspective, interest paid on a capital lease may be treated as debt; from a legal perspective, it can be exempt from debt ceilings through the use of a nonappropriation clause, which means that lease payments have to be appropriated annually. Often nonappropriation clauses contain restrictions to protect the lessor from the replacement of equipment should the lease not be appropriated. For instance, a leased telecommunications system might have a covenant restricting the purchase or lease of a new system should the lease be terminated.[65]

On larger transactions, investors buy certificates of participation (COPs), which give them a share of lease payments made on that property; for smaller purchases, a bank or other financial intermediary may handle the entire transaction. The interest portion of these lease payments can also be exempt from federal taxation if the standards for issuer and purpose are met: if certain state-specific conditions are met, the financial obligation is not subject to constitutional or other limits in regard to voter approval, capacity ceilings, and so on because they are not strictly debt obligations. More issues have been raised in California than in any other state because of high infrastructure demand and strict controls on traditional finance there, but Arizona, Colorado, Florida, Georgia, Illinois, New Jersey, New York, North Carolina, South Carolina, and Washington each issue high volumes.[66]

Figure 15–4 illustrates the flow of transactions in a COP arrangement. Suppose a government wants to acquire a new jail. It would arrange for the establishment of a nonprofit building corporation from which it would lease the new jail. The building corporation would borrow from private investors enough to build the jail, using the promised lease payments as the basis for prepayment of the loan.[67] A trustee, usually a bank, handles the distribution of lease payments, as they come from the government, to individual COP holders and manages any legal proceedings if lease payments do not arrive. The COP provides lenders less security than bonds because funds normally must be appropriated on a year-to-year basis and politics may intervene. This flow has been a problem in the Great Recession era, as revenues supporting the leases have faltered and leaseholders have limited capacity, at best, to sue localities associated with the leased facility.[68] However, the requirement for annual appropriations, a nonappropriation clause, is legally critical to distinguish these transactions from debt subject to referenda, ceilings, and the like.

---

[64]Federal lease-purchases generally are recognized as borrowing from the public in budget documents. See Office of Management and Budget, *Budget of the Government of the United States, Fiscal Year 2006, Analytical Perspectives* (Washington, D.C.: U.S. Government Printing Office, 2005), 251.

[65]Richard Baker, "Public Policy Implications of Tax Exempt Leasing in the United States," *International Journal of Public Policy* 1(2005): 148.

[66]Craig Johnson and John L. Mikesell, "Certificates of Participation and Capital Markets: Lessons from Brevard County and Richmond Unified School District," *Public Budgeting & Finance* 14 (Fall 1994): 42.

[67]There is another variety used to patch deficits. In this approach, a government sells an existing facility to a holding corporation, uses the cash for government operations, and then leases the facility back from the corporation. For a particularly unfortunate example, see Craig Johnson and John L. Mikesell, "The Richmond School District Default: COPs, Bankruptcy, Default, and State Intervention," in *Case Studies in Public Budgeting and Financial Management*, ed. A. Khan and B. Hildreth (Dubuque, Iowa: Kendall/Hunt, 1994).

[68]Mike Cherney, "Cities' Rentals Hurt Bonds," *Wall Street Journal*, May 11, 2012, C1.

Figure 15–4
A Certificate-of-Participation Arrangement

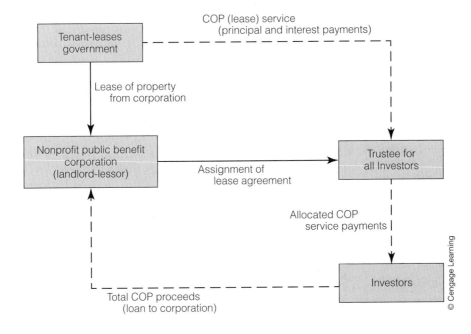

When Government Finances Go Horribly Wrong

Government finances have gone bad in recent years in national, state, and local governments. The revenues available have been insufficient to cover expenditure obligations, the capacity to cover the fiscal gap has been inadequate, and government leaders have had to take severe actions with adverse consequences for everyone associated with the government (citizens, employees, suppliers, etc.). The problems go beyond economic scarcity. In the real world, resources are not and have never been sufficient to cover all human wants. Hence, choices must be made from among the many different ways that those scarce resources could be used. The problem is logically the same for families, businesses, or governments. Having to cut, stretch, and fiddle with finances can be trying and irritating, but it is a normal consequence of human existence in this world and does not constitute fiscal crisis. Economic and fiscal choice cannot be avoided. In the realm of government, those choices may involve higher taxes or reduced services, neither of which is necessarily a marker of something particularly wrong with the government. Indeed, the government may function with an operating deficit for the year—which will mean using prior accumulated surpluses or borrowing on the basis of prospects for the future. That is not ordinarily a recommended strategy, but it happens—as we know from operations of the U.S. federal government. In recent years, along with the economic problems associated with the Great Recession, local governments have been pressed by the cost of programs for retirees (public employees' pensions and health insurance—early retirement and lucrative defined benefit programs with inadequate funding) and wages for current employees (personnel costs are the predominant part of total operating cost for most local governments). Accordingly, one objective in several of the options discussed below is to get these employee benefits reduced—if not by voluntary agreements between the government and its employees, then by court or receiver decree.

The process of fiscal choice can go badly wrong, sometimes through economic or social misfortune, sometimes through incompetence or malevolence, sometimes through a stubborn unwillingness to make tough choices, sometimes through political deals, and often through a combination of causes. At the worst, governments may face or consider default, repudiation, receivership, or bankruptcy as an outcome of fiscal crises that cannot be managed by tough manipulation of finances to reduce spending or to increase revenue. The terms are often carelessly used in public discussion; they do have different meanings and different consequences. All are, for American general-purpose governments, extremely rare.

Default

A government defaults when it does not meet a scheduled payment of principal or interest on a debt issue. It is believed that the first municipal bond default was by Mobile, Alabama, in 1839. They are notorious because they represent a clear violation of the public trust and, probably more importantly, because they are extremely rare in normal economic environments. While there were many defaults during the Great Depression of the 1930s, there have been few during the recent Great Recession. Widely publicized defaults in the municipal securities market over the past few decades include New York City and Cleveland in the 1970s and the Washington Public Power Supply System in the 1980s. In the New York case, the issuer defined the episode to be a "technical default" because it unilaterally announced a slower-than-contracted payment schedule. Bondholders may not have appreciated the distinction. Most defaults are of small issues by special-purpose districts, often involving industrial development projects. The 1978 Cleveland default was the first general obligation bond default since the Great Depression (Arkansas and Louisiana). Some defaults are permanent, as with that of the Washington Public Power Supply System bonds; some defaults are only temporary, as with those of the New York City and Cleveland bonds. Bondholders may be protected from the economic consequences of default by bond insurance purchased by the issuer.

Municipal bond defaults are exceedingly rare, rarer than are corporate bond defaults. Over the 1970–2011 period, there were seventy-one municipal bond defaults in total among bonds rated by Moody's, only five of them being general obligation bonds. Between 2009 and 2011, there was only one general obligation bond default—that of Harrisburg, Pennsylvania in 2010. That is a very low rate: Moody's had ratings established for roughly 9,700 issues at the end of 2011. The ultimate recovery rate on municipal defaults, in other words, the amount of debt service that gets paid, was 65 percent over the 1970–2011 period, considerably higher than the 49 percent rate for corporate issues.[69]

The default may occur without any discernible impact, at least in the short term, for those receiving services from the defaulting government, but the impact is felt when the government proposes to borrow again and faces higher interest rates because of the market reaction to the earlier default. A number of states defaulted in the 1840s (Arkansas, Florida, Illinois, Indiana, Louisiana, Maryland, Michigan, Mississippi, and Pennsylvania) and a few more in the 1870s (Alabama, Florida, Georgia, Missouri, North Carolina, South Carolina, Tennessee, Virginia, and West Virginia). Most eventually made good on their obligations. National governments also default on their debt issues. Hatchondo and colleagues tally fifty-six separate sovereign defaults in the period from 1976 to 2003, for instance.[70]

Receivership

About twenty states have provisions for state assistance and control for municipalities in fiscal distress. In many respects, the receivership is a state-controlled approach that avoids the federal bankruptcy program. A government enters receivership when an appointed third-party manager takes control of operations of the government. The receiver, appointed by a superior government or by a court, has the responsibility to protect the assets of the unit and to meet legitimate demands made by those owed money by the government. The receiver usually has authority to change employment contracts and benefit programs for retirees, as well as to fire employees without the normal termination procedures. In many cases, the receiver completely replaces all elected officials of the jurisdiction. States often appoint receivers or trustees to manage the finances of local governments in great jeopardy; for instance, Massachusetts appointed a receiver to take over the management of the city of Chelsea in the face of major financial irregularities, including alleged theft of city funds and properties, discovered there. School districts in California have also been placed in receiverships by the state. State control boards—in which states take over financial operations of particular localities (usually cities)—behave something like receiverships. Examples include the Pennsylvania Intergovernmental Cooperation Authority (for Philadelphia in 1991, Pittsburgh in 2004, and several smaller jurisdictions since the state created the oversight law called Act 47 in 1987), the Miami Financial Emergency Oversight Board (1996), the Buffalo Fiscal Stability Authority (2003), and the New York State Financial Control Board (for New York City in 1975). There are also emergency procedures for municipalities in Ohio. The Michigan Local Government and School District Fiscal Accountability Act (Public

---

[69]Moody's Investment Service, *Special Comment: U.S. Municipal Bond Defaults and Recoveries, 1970–2011* (New York: Moody's Investment Service, 2012).

[70]Juan Carlos Hatchondo, Leonardo Martinez, and Horacio Sapriza, "The Economics of Sovereign Defaults," *Economics Quarterly* 93 (Spring 2007): 163–87.

Act 4, 2011) gives emergency managers installed by the state powers to void collective bargaining agreements, fire elected officials, and privatize or sell government assets. In mid-2012, four cities (Benton Harbor, Pontiac, Ecorse, and Flint) plus two school districts had managers in place. Washington, D.C., lost most of its fiscal independence to a congressionally appointed board in 1997, for similar reasons.

Courts may also appoint receivers for public entities, although less frequently than for private firms or nonprofit organizations. In 1986, the Wayne County Circuit Court appointed a receiver to operate the city of Ecorse, Michigan, after suits by Detroit Edison, the Detroit Water and Sewerage Department, and others for nonpayment of bills. The city emerged from this receivership, but later fell into the emergency manager system. Receivers may well dramatically change the services supplied by the government and possibly the taxes it levies, so the population almost certainly will see a difference from the experience.

Bankruptcy

Governments enter bankruptcy by a formal filing with a federal court under Chapter 9 of the federal bankruptcy code (a chapter created during the Great Depression of the 1930s). After the filing has been accepted, the court protects the government from financial claims while the government develops a plan under which it can pay a large share, but usually not all, of its financial obligations. Only municipalities fall under the bankruptcy process because the Tenth Amendment to the United States Contitution provides for the sovereignty of states, thus forbidding Congress from imposing an involuntary debt restructuring plan on the states. Seldom does the bankruptcy result from an excessive amount of bonded indebtedness because debt service normally is only a small portion of total spending. It does often result from poor decisions made by public managers and elected officials about investments, public projects, and compensation to employees. The precise rules for municipal bankruptcy are less well defined than the rules for corporate bankruptcy because municipal bankruptcies are so rare (fewer than 600 since the 1930s, mostly involving special districts rather than cities or counties, out of a current count of over 80,000 jurisdictions). However, it is clear that in order to receive bankruptcy protection, the municipality must be insolvent, meaning that the municipality is not able to pay its bills when they come due. The strong prospect that the municipality will not be able to pay its bills at some point in the near future is not enough.

The bankruptcy aims to ensure that the government can continue to provide services to its citizenry and retain its assets. The bankruptcy court cannot in practice force the jurisdiction to either raise taxes or reduce spending. In contrast to corporate bankruptcies, liquidation of the bankrupt municipality is not permitted. Also in contrast to individual or corporate bankruptcies, governmental bankruptcies can only be voluntary. That is, they cannot be forced into bankruptcy by creditors. In many respects, bankruptcy is more lenient than state receivership programs. After the 1991 effort by Bridgeport, Connecticut, to declare bankruptcy, Congress changed the bankruptcy code to require specific state authorization before a municipality may file for bankruptcy. Historically, bondholders have been superior creditors, so debt service ordinarily flows on schedule (besides, the government wants continued access to municipal capital markets), but other contractual obligations may not be met.[71] For instance, wages and salaries may be reduced from the previously agreed-to levels. In some recent bankruptcies, the jurisdiction has defaulted on debt service to reduce the need for other cutbacks.[72] In order for the municipality to enter into bankruptcy, it must be insolvent—in other words, unable to pay its obligations when they come due—a stronger requirement than for corporate bankruptcy filing. The municipality may or may not have bonded debt outstanding when filing for bankruptcy protection. Only slightly more than half the states permit their local governments to declare bankruptcy, and bankruptcy protection is usually not an option for state governments. Recent bankruptcy filings of city or county governments include Vallejo, California (population 117,000) in 2008; Stockton, California (population 291,000) in 2012; Jefferson County, Alabama (population 659,000) in 2011;[73] Orange County, California (population 3 million) in 1994; Boise County, Idaho (population 7,500) in 2011; San Bernardino, California (population, 213,000) in 2012; Westfall, Pennsylvania (population 2,300) in 2009; Moffett, Oklahoma (population 127) in 2007; and Central Falls, Rhode Island (population 9,000; there had been a state receivership before the bankruptcy filing) in 2011.[74] The bankruptcy court rejected the Boise County filing.

In spite of the fiscal problems created by the Great Recession, there has been no dramatic run to bankruptcy protection for local governments. The big question

---

[71]The private-sector bankruptcies of Chrysler and GM in 2009 did not follow the principle of bondholders as superior creditors. It is not clear whether this would be generalizable to municipal bankruptcies in the future. The 2012 Stockton bankruptcy filing identified bondholders and city employees as the groups most likely to be impacted by the bankruptcy.

[72]Moody's reports that median debt service as a percentage of expenditures for state and local governments is in the 5 to 8 percent range. Moody's Investors Service, "Municipal Market Investor Confidence: Linkages to Credit Quality," January 6, 2011. Unless the government has debt service considerably above the typical level, trimming debt service is not going to be as important as reducing a cost category that is more significant in the total budget—hence, the particular attention to labor costs, current and past, in bankruptcy discussions.

[73]The several mistaken choices that led to the Jefferson County bankruptcy are analyzed in Michael E. Howell-Moroney and Jeremy L. Hall, "Waste in the Sewer: The Collapse of Accountability and Transparency in Public Finance in Jefferson County, Alabama," *Public Administration Review* 71 (March/April 2011): 232–42.

[74]It has been presumed that revenue bond service would be immune from bankruptcy filings of a government. These bonds do not pledge the resources of the government, but only project revenues. In the Jefferson County, Alabama, filing, the county sought to reduce payments to holders of sewer project revenue bonds to protect other operations of the county from cuts and even to repair the sewer system itself. Municipal bankruptcy filings are so infrequent that the law is not clear on how bondholders, either general obligation or revenue, are to be treated, although it was presumed that they were superior claimants. It is no longer clear. Presumably, Jefferson County plans never again to try to borrow at normal rates. Kelly Nolan, "Muni Market Sounds Alert," *Wall Street Journal*, November 29, 2011, C4; and Michael Corkery and Katy Stech, "County Bond Fight Begins New Round," *Wall Street Journal*, April 17, 2012, C1. Rhode Island passed a law in 2011 that places bondholders ahead of all other creditors in a municipal bankruptcy in an effort to make sure that Rhode Island jurisdictions would not face an interest rate penalty because of the Central Falls problem. The Moffett, Oklahoma bankruptcy is curious. The tiny town was an infamous speed trap and when state action ended its ability to get traffic ticket revenue, its finances collapsed.

in bankruptcy is whether bondholders, current employees, or retirees are going to get stiffed because that is what the bankruptcy involves. In contrast to private businesses, governments seem to regard breaking contracts freely arrived at as something more weighty than just getting a fresh start. One problem with a bankruptcy is the reputational impact on neighboring jurisdictions. As Birmingham, Alabama, was preparing for a bond issue in 2012, the city took great pains to distinguish itself from the bankrupt county (Jefferson) in which it is located. Although it had substantial cash reserves and a AA rating on its general obligation debt, it seemed likely that a bond issue for capital projects would have to pay a slight premium because of the negative bankruptcy halo.[75]

While there has been no avalanche of municipal bankruptcies in the aftermath of the Great Recession, there is some concern that municipalities may start viewing them as viable strategy. That has not historically been the case: "Municipalities traditionally have believed that using bankruptcy as a tool to put their finances in order wasn't worth the risk of alienating creditors and being closed out of the $3.7 billion municipal bond market."[76] Because of their rarity, it is not clear what the ramifications would be when a general purpose government—a city or a county—emerges from bankruptcy. Vallejo, California emerged from three years under bankruptcy protection in 2011 with a much smaller government, many facilities that formerly provided government services closed forever, renegotiated employee contracts and fewer municipal employees, a continuing obligation to repay a large amount of the debt that had been incurred before the bankruptcy, a participatory budget system in place, a higher city sales tax rate, and substantial legal bills—plus, almost certainly a renewed appreciation for the importance of the rules for fiscal sustainability.

Repudiation

Repudiation occurs when the borrower announces that it will make no more principal or interest payments on debt, that it will no longer recognize that debt as a liability. This action is rare because bond markets have long memories and a government that has repudiated debt will have difficulty borrowing again. As Spiotto observes, "Repudiation of validly issued public debt destroys the credit rating for the issuer and makes any subsequent return to the public-debt markets problematic at best."[77] Some American states repudiated debt issued in the first half of the nineteenth century to finance canals, roads, railroads, and other internal improvements and some others in the South did so after the Civil War. Some of the projects were absolutely scandalous, and money almost certainly was stolen by both government and private thieves. However, these repudiating governments faced premium interest rates on their borrowing well into the twentieth century because the capital markets

---

[75]Michael Corkery, "Birmingham Angles for Extra Credit," *Wall Street Journal*, June 26, 2012, C1.
[76]Michael Corkery, "Muni Blues Worry Investors," *Wall Stree Journal*, July 26, 2012, C1.
[77]James E. Spiotto, "Financial Emergencies: Default and Bankruptcy," in Robert D. Ebel and John E. Petersen, eds., *The Oxford Handbook of State and Local Government Finance* (New York: Oxford University Press, 2012): 759.

remembered that experience. The bond market affects even cross radical changes in government. For instance, questions about payments on Russian tsarist debt issued in France from 1822 to 1914 complicated Russia's entry into international bond markets in 1996. A French bondholders' association (Association Francaise des Porteurs d'Emprunts Russes) kept rating agencies informed and warned prospective investors. Eventually, the governments of Russia and France reached an agreement for at least partial payment of that old debt, and the new Russian government was able to enter the market. Bond markets collectively have long memories and repudiation is a distinctly poor option for dealing with difficult debt obligations.

Conclusion

Government debt exists because expenditure has exceeded revenue. Federal debt represents the accumulated effects of annual deficits, while state and local government debt largely represents the outcome of capital-project financing. State and local government debt costs can be managed through care to maintain good creditworthiness (ratings), careful tailoring of maturities and timing of debt issues, use of the recently narrowed ability to issue federal tax-exempt debt, and use of available debt guarantees. Debt itself is not necessarily evidence of poor fiscal management.

QUESTIONS AND EXERCISES

1. What restrictions are placed on state and local government debt in your state? What methods are used to avoid those limits? Is there a state bond bank? Does your state have any program for credit enhancement for local debt?

2. Investigate the debt and debt-rating history for a large city of your selection. Have debt issues been full-faith-and-credit or limited-liability? Have issues been insured?

3. Indicate which bond in the following pairs of bonds is likely to bear the higher interest rate (yield) and state why. If there is no general reason for a difference, indicate that they would be the same.

   a. A corporate bond rated Aaa or a municipal bond rated Aaa
   b. A municipal bond rated Baa or a municipal bond rated Aa
   c. A general obligation bond issued by a city or a revenue bond issued by a city
   d. A general obligation bond rated Aa issued by a city or a general obligation bond rated Aa issued by a county
   e. A municipal bond (term) with maturity in five years or a municipal bond (term) with maturity in twenty years

4. A city advertised for bids for the purchase of $2 million principal amount of Sewage Works Revenue Bonds. Bonds will be delivered on April 1, 2007, and interest will be paid on April 1 of the following years. The bonds mature as follows:

Maturity Date	Amount ($)
April 1, 2012	50,000
April 1, 2013	50,000
April 1, 2014	50,000
April 1, 2015	100,000
April 1, 2016	100,000
April 1, 2017	100,000
April 1, 2018	150,000
April 1, 2019	150,000
April 1, 2020	150,000
April 1, 2021	550,000
April 1, 2022	550,000

Two bids were received:

From Five Points Securities: Pay $2 million
The interest rates for each maturity:
2012 through 2020, 5.50 percent
2021 through 2022, 6.25 percent

From Wellington-Nelson: Pay $2 million
The interest rates for each maturity:
2012 through 2014, 4.19 percent
2015 through 2020, 5.75 percent
2021 through 2022, 6.50 percent

For each bid, compute the net interest cost (NIC) and the true interest cost (TIC). Which bid is more advantageous to the city?

5. From tables in the *Wall Street Journal* or other papers that carry quotations on U.S. Treasury bonds, notes, and bills, determine the general shape of the term structure of interest rates. Trace the difference between short-term and long-term interest rates over the past year.

6. An Eminence Water Utility Revenue Bond matures in fifteen years, pays a 5.5 percent coupon rate semiannually, and has a face value of $5,000. The market interest rate for similar risk and maturity municipal bonds is 4 percent. What is the current price of the bond? What would be its price if the market rate was 6 percent?

7. Solomon Keith, a bank janitor, won a large prize in the New York lottery in 1987. Unfortunately, Mr. Keith died before he could collect all of the twenty annual payments of $240,245 each to which he was entitled. To pay taxes and legal fees (as well as to distribute some of this estate to heirs), an auction was held in early July 1992 for rights to the sixteen annual payments remaining in the prize (the first to be paid on July 15, 1992). Presidential Life Insurance Company was the winning bidder, paying $2.1 million for the prize. Suppose other comparable investments of Presidential's funds could have earned about 5 percent annual interest. What do you think of the wisdom of its investment?

8. Does your state permit its localities to file for bankruptcy protection? Is there some sort of state receivership or similar program for fiscally distressed localities? Are there any localities in your state in such a program? Are there municipal bond issues in your state that are in default?

APPENDIX 15–1

General Principles of State Debt Management

The following principles outline the debt management policies endorsed by the Comptroller of the State of New York. They are consistent with the concept of fiscal sustainability and could serve as a reasonable model for any state or local government for guiding its use of debt.

1. Do not use refinancing to extend debt maturity.
2. Ensure present value and cash flow savings in every year.
3. Maximize the economic benefits of debt refunding.
4. Integrate the capital and financial planning process.
5. Update both plans quarterly and provide realistic four-year projections.
6. Maximize the use of PAYGO financing.
7. Target projects with low periods of probable usefulness.
8. Maximize the use of surplus revenues to retire older and expensive debt.
9. Use nonrecurring revenues for capital spending/debt reduction.
10. Issue long-term debt for capital purposes only.
11. Issue no debt for operating expenses.
12. Issue debt for capitalized interest only in extraordinary circumstances, such as a pending construction of a revenue-producing facility.
13. Keep debt to an affordable level.
14. Limit outstanding debt and debt issuance.
15. Minimize the costs of debt issuance.
16. Limit the term of debt to maximize intergenerational equity.
17. Issue no debt beyond the period of probable usefulness.
18. Provide comprehensive and clear debt reporting.
19. Continually strive toward superior disclosure practices.
20. Use competitive sales rather than negotiated sales.

SOURCE: *New York State's Debt Policy, A Need for Reform* (Albany, N.Y.: Office of New York State Comptroller Alan G. Hevesi, February 2005), 101.

Index

Note: Page numbers followed by letters indicate the following: f indicates figures, n indicates notes, s indicates sidebars, and t indicates tables.